Principles of
Economics

Principles of Economics

WELDON WELFLING

Professor of Economics and
Chairman, Banking and Finance Department
Case Western Reserve University
Cleveland, Ohio

McGRAW-HILL BOOK COMPANY

New York   St. Louis   Dallas   San Francisco

Düsseldorf   Johannesburg   Kuala Lumpur   London   Mexico   Montreal

New Delhi   Panama   Rio de Janeiro   Singapore   Sydney   Toronto

This book was set in Helvetica type and printed by Quinn &
Boden Company, Inc. The designer was Richard Stalzer; the
part opening drawings were done by Joseph Papin. The editor
was Joseph G. Bonnice. Cathy L. Dilworth edited the manuscript.
Elizabeth Huffman supervised the editing. S. Steven Canaris
supervised the production.

Principles of Economics

123456789   QBQB   0987654321

ISBN 07-069185-1

Preface

1577545

Recognition of the importance of economic education has spread extensively in recent years. Once a subject studied only by a minority of college students, economics is now widely introduced in high schools and included in many types of college curricula. Study of economics has been stimulated by the realization that many young people have little or no grasp of basic economic principles or even of the fact that these principles exist. Yet each person is inevitably faced with a wide variety of problems that are basically economic. As a consumer, employer, employee, lender, borrower, saver, investor, and citizen each of us is constantly called upon to make economic decisions.

This text has been written in the belief that economics is an interesting field for the beginning student and that the basic principles can be usefully applied early in the student's progress. Indeed, the principles are more obvious if they are related to current problems. Consequently, in each chapter the relevant principles are worked out in terms of examples, and each chapter ends with a case selected or designed to illustrate the application of these principles.

ORGANIZATION OF THE TEXT

The general plan of the book is to progress from the more obvious materials already somewhat familiar to the student to the less familiar. The first two chapters explain why some form of economic organization is essential, how different types of economies may come about, and how an economy relying largely on competitive markets arose in the United States. These chapters provide a broad view of the principal economic institutions and tie them together.

The four chapters in Part 2 build on the introduction of the market economy by developing the basic principles of market pricing. Here are developed the basic ideas of supply and demand, the relationships of costs and prices, and the usefulness of marginal analysis. Differences of real-world markets from ideal pure competition are examined and illustrated by examples of agriculture and other industries. The last chapter in Part 2 emphasizes the applicability of much of the preceding material through an elementary discussion of managerial economics.

Part 3 bridges the traditional gap between micro- and macro-economics by combining the two chapters on the distribution of functional income with the two chapters on the national income and its determination. Integrating the discussion of these topics suggests that they are basically aspects of the same underlying problem—the size of the national output and how it is shared.

In Part 4 the role of money and the operation of the monetary system are taken up. This discussion describes the relevant institutions and provides the concepts needed to understand monetary and fiscal policies. Included is a chapter devoted to savings institutions for several reasons: their

v

practical importance to most individual citizens and their role in transforming the monetary savings of the public into real capital by acting as financial intermediaries, among others. This is also an appropriate place to discuss the influence of public finance on the economy.

Parts 5 through 7 take up types of economic issues. Part 5 consists of two chapters on fluctuations and growth, one analyzing the causes of business fluctuations and growth, the other describing and explaining monetary and fiscal policies. Part 6 explains the government's role in regulating business, especially in regard to antitrust problems, labor relations, and the attack on poverty. Part 7 deals with international economic problems and the operation of the planned economies.

The final chapter attempts to place economics in perspective as a social science, to clarify the limitations and potentials of the science, and to "wrap up" the insights it is hoped the student has gained. It contains material often presented in introductory chapters but which, it is hoped, should be much more meaningful at the end.

Besides the cases provided as discussion topics for each chapter, there are also questions for review and questions to analyze. As these terms imply, the former are designed to remind the student of what he has read and to help clarify them; the latter are designed to allow him to apply what he has learned and to push forward his grasp of the material. The cases are, in general, based on real problems or situations in which application of basic principles clarifies the issues. As is usually true of cases, they have no completely right or wrong answers.

SUPPLEMENTARY AIDS

A study guide correlated closely to the text is available. It provides an outline summary of each chapter to integrate the material of that chapter and to supply a handy review. A matching problem using important terms introduced in the chapter tests the student's grasp of these terms. Multiple-choice questions check his comprehension of the material. Several exercises or problems require application of the principles explained in the chapter and bring out their significance.

An instructor's manual and key is also available. It contains suggestions about coverage and omission of material, sources of new or additional information, and related matters. In addition, it provides comment on the study guide and the cases.

ACKNOWLEDGMENTS

I am especially grateful to the American Institute of Banking for permitting me to draw freely on the organization and content of the AIB text *Economics* written by Professor K. Laurence Chang and myself. Although the present volume differs in several major respects, many ideas worked out for that text have been useful in the preparation of this one. Chapter 23, especially, is a direct descendant of a chapter in the AIB text.

Several of my colleagues have made helpful suggestions on various points. Professor Gerhard Rosegger kindly reviewed several chapters and gave me the benefit of his comments. I am also indebted to Wylie A. Walthall, Dean, College of Alameda, Alameda, California, who read an early draft of the manuscript and made many useful suggestions for improvement.

Weldon Welfling

Contents

Part 1
Organization
of the Economy

1
Economics and Economic Systems

The study of economics rests on a simple fact of life: Nature does not freely provide satisfactions for all man's wants and desires. The production of goods and services requires the expenditure of time and effort. Production thus entails costs. But beyond the fact of production costs, economic life involves the basic problem of choice. Since man, or an economic society, is unable to meet all man's wants, society must choose which desires to satisfy and which to leave unsatisfied. Economics is the study of how society makes these choices.

Measured by world standards, the United States has made such rapid progress in increasing output per person that it is often said that we live in an age of affluence, not an age of scarcity. But affluence and scarcity are relative. It is true that many more wants are currently satisfied than were satisfied in the past, but it also remains true that "we can't have everything." Nearly every family recognizes that its income must be allocated to the things the family wants most, either in the present or in the future. As a nation we are aware that foreign aid, space exploration, slum clearance, highway construction, education, and a host of other desirable objectives make competing demands on our available resources.

ECONOMICS AND THE PROBLEM OF CHOICE

The economic choices open to a primitive or undeveloped country are much more restricted than those open to an advanced nation. Material goods and services are scarce, and there is little choice except to produce as much food, clothing, and shelter as possible in the limited ways known. An economically advanced country is one that has learned techniques of production that make possible much greater output per person and therefore a wider choice among the things that will be produced.

Economics deals largely with the production and use of material goods. But man has many wants and desires that are not material, and these often motivate economic actions. For example, a father's desire to provide his children with advanced education may lead him to work harder, to risk his capital, and to save. People generally want friends, a sense of achievement and responsibility, freedom, and a family life in addition to necessities and certain comforts. Material goods are more highly valued by some people than by others, and a person's preference tends to change from time to time. But regardless of their relative importance, material goods are desired by virtually everyone. As the English economist P. H. Wicksteed once said, "A man can be neither a saint, nor a lover, nor a poet, unless he has comparatively recently had something to eat."

Economics is not based on the assumption that material goods are more important than anything else—any more than aeronautics is based on the assumption that flying is—it simply carves out an important segment of man's knowledge about himself and the world and attempts to build upon this knowledge. It is a study of man's behavior with respect to goods and services. More specifically, it deals with how man produces, exchanges, and consumes goods and services and with the growth, development, and stability of the economy. It is thus a behavioral science and a social science.

If nature were so generous as to provide us with goods and services free of costs of production, there would be no need for economic study. By present world standards, production and levels of living are high in the United States. Americans are often accused of being wasteful and spendthrift. Yet, although production of meat in the United States is relatively very great, the output amounts to only a fraction of a pound per person per day and many citizens have very little. The United States produces as many automobiles as does all the rest of the world combined—in the neighborhood of 10 million each year—but this number provides a new car for only one in six families. Thus there is a scarcity of automobiles in the sense that more people want them than can get them, and they do not get them because they choose to allocate their limited incomes to other more urgent wants.

There are very few *free goods*, those that do not involve costs of production, and it seems that these are becoming even scarcer. Not long ago clean water and clean air were virtually without cost. Now, because air and water are becoming polluted in the process of producing other things, even these goods entail costs. Goods that must be produced and are sufficiently in demand to be sold or exchanged for other goods are called *economic goods*. Economic goods may be plentiful in the United States in comparison with other economies, but they are scarce in comparison to people's wants.

Decisions can be made to reduce the scarcity of some goods, but such decisions generally involve increasing the scarcity of something else. At a given moment of time, the production of an economic good can be increased, but the increase must be at the expense of production of other goods. For example, in the absence of idle plant, machinery, and labor, the production of automobiles could be increased only by reducing the production of trucks, tractors, trailers, and other goods that use the same *resources*. Over a period of time resources can be shifted from other uses and more automobiles could be produced at the expense of television sets, farm crops, and other goods. The land on which a factory is built cannot be used to raise corn, and the labor on the assembly line can make only one product at a time. As time passes and knowledge and technology improve, more of virtually everything can be produced but we never produce as much as we want. The real scarcity is not, therefore, in the products—the automobiles, the television sets, the drugs and medicines—so much as in the resources available for their production. At any one time there is a limited amount of usable land and raw materials (*natural resources*); plant, equipment, and tools (*capital*); and workmen, typists, engineers, managers, and others (*labor*).

Factors of Production

Virtually all goods and services result from combining natural resources, capital, and labor, which are called factors of production. Even services require capital and natural resources. The lawyer needs office space in a building, books and periodicals, and other things such as furniture, paper, typewriters, communications equipment, light, and heat. He cannot just sit outside on a log and dispense legal advice. Medical services require buildings, X-ray and other diagnostic equipment, medicines and drugs, and so on.

Most goods pass through several or many intermediate steps in the process of production. The body and chassis of an automobile started as iron ore and other minerals that were turned into iron and steel. The tires were once natural rubber or synthetic rubber manufactured from natural chemicals. The upholstery was once natural cotton or wool, or coal and petroleum products that were turned into synthetic fibers. The glass windows, electric wiring, paint, and other parts of the car are the result of combining natural resources with capital equipment operated by labor.

Capital goods consist of products which are used in the *process of production* (rather than in satisfying consumers' wants directly). Machines, trucks, computers, desks, offices, materials-handling equipment, furnaces, and countless other goods are all of this type. They are managed and operated by a labor force consisting of skilled and unskilled labor, engineers, lawyers, secretaries, mathematicians, executives, salesmen, and so on.

Natural resources, capital, and labor are called factors of production because they are required for the production of goods and services that are used for immediate enjoyment (consumer goods) or for production (capital goods). One who combines the three factors is called an *entrepreneur*, from a French verb that means "to undertake or to be enterprising." Since an entrepreneur is a human being or perhaps a corporation run by human beings, it might appear that entrepreneurs are part of the labor force, but a distinction is made because the entrepreneur functions in pursuit of profit while he obtains labor at market prices. Entrepreneurship, or management, is therefore considered a fourth factor of production.

Although a country may have large absolute amounts of all four factors of production, the factors are limited and capable of only slow increase. The United States has a large expanse of land, yet there are few large estates in comparison to small city lots because of the economies of living close together. Natural resources are lacking for the production of many goods in the quantities demanded; we produce other goods and exchange them in international trade for bananas, coffee, tea, tin, copper, newsprint, and crude oil. Although the labor force numbers nearly 90 million, there are often shortages of particular skills, such as those of airline pilots, secretaries, college professors, doctors, and scientists. It is estimated that 90 percent of all the scientists who ever lived are alive today, but in many specialized fields more scientists are sought. In the United States the average investment in capital goods is about $20,000 per worker—a ratio that is much higher than anywhere else in the world. Yet more investment constantly is being made because new technology brings new methods of increasing output per worker. Annual additions to the stock of accumulated capital goods are relatively slow because these goods are not free and must compete with all other goods for the available factors of production.

Although output per person has risen greatly in the advanced countries since the Industrial Revolution in the late eighteenth century, there are still unsatisfied wants. The typical resident of India, Egypt, or Indonesia, not to mention the primitive countries, would consider the standard of living of the average American the height of luxury. But most Americans do not consider themselves very well off; they are aware of too many things they cannot afford. The battle against scarcity will probably never end because man's wants increase as the means of satisfying them increase. Many things that we want today were not even known a generation ago. As more people are able to satisfy their basic wants to a greater degree, the factors of production are shifted into industries producing such goods as jet aircraft, television sets, computers, outboard motors, snow-mobiles, snowthrowers, and new medicines and cosmetics, while also producing more expensive forms of food, clothing, and housing.

Relative Scarcity

It follows from these comments that scarcity is always relative. There is less scarcity in the United States than there once was and less than in most areas of the world. Scarcity is also relative in the sense that some things are more scarce than others. Limousines are more scarce than loaves of bread. The factors of production required to produce a limousine are much greater than those required to produce a loaf of bread; on an equivalent dollar basis, the same total amount of resources could produce one limousine or thousands of loaves of bread. Basically, this is why a limousine costs more than a loaf of bread; if society wants limousines, it must do without that much bread or the equivalent in other goods.

Some economic societies have had greater success than others in reducing the degree of scarcity. While availability of natural resources is often important, cultural characteristics, such as attitudes toward engaging in business and the organization of the economy, are also important because they influence the extent to which capital is accumulated and the effectiveness with which labor is used. In some countries commerce is not considered a dignified occupation. Economics is partly a study of the reasons for the success or failure of different economic systems—why some economies provide steady annual increases in average personal income and why others hover on the edge of actual starvation. Economics attempts to formulate policies that lead to economic growth and development.

Limitations of Economics

Economic problems do not exist in a vacuum or in a laboratory; they exist in the real world and are usually intertwined with other problems of politics, international relations, and social relations. The perfect economy has not been invented, although we are sure that some are better than others, and the perfect way of managing our economy has not been discovered. Some of the limitations of economics should be pointed out at the outset of this study:

1. Economists do not know all there is to know about human motivation. Psychologists are still learning why people fail to cooperate harmoniously in the process of production (labor disputes, low productivity, absenteeism, and the like) and why consumers buy what they do. Do people buy something because it is relatively cheap or something else because of the "snob appeal" of a higher price? How do people balance their desire for income and their desire for leisure?

It is recognized that these are not purely economic problems. For example, people work not only for economic gain but also for prestige, for job satisfaction, for altruistic reasons and service to the community, and out of habit. In analyzing a given problem, the economist must make various assumptions about people's behavior. If these assumptions are incorrect, the solutions are likely to be incorrect. For example, in 1968 personal income taxes were raised 10 percent in order to reduce consumer spending. In determining whether 10 percent was the proper increase in the tax rate, estimates of how much consumer spending would be reduced had to be based on assumptions about how people in general would react with respect to their consumption and saving. If they reduced their saving by the full amount of the tax increase, consumption would not be affected.

2. Since economics is essentially a matter of choice, the choices have to be made on the basis of some scale of values. Economists are not automatically experts in ethics or political philosophy. The economist can point out some of the effects of financing a government program by one form of taxation or another or by government borrowing, but he is not necessarily a better judge than anyone else of whether the program should be adopted. The economist can describe measures that would provide an annual growth rate for the economy of 7 percent, but these measures might be unpleasant for the many persons who might have to change jobs or relocate their homes. Whether to seek an annual growth rate of 4 percent or 7 percent tends to become a problem in politics. One rate is not necessarily better than the other for all people or at all times.

Value judgments often have to be made collectively, by the members of a group or by the nation. Some people believe that the government should collect more taxes and spend the money for better highways; others think that the government should encourage the development of new mass public transportation systems, subsidize commuter railroads, reduce traffic congestion and air pollution, and prevent the construction of highways through residential areas and open country. The economist can estimate the relative costs, but the decision tends to be made on the basis of the kind of urban and suburban living people prefer. As a private citizen, of course, the economist may have a strong preference.

The study of economics emphasizes the fact that, when choices are made, there are costs and benefits. Not all the costs and benefits can be fitted with dollar signs; some must be measured by other standards. But weighing costs against benefits is at the heart of the study of economics.

3. Economists study what appear on the surface to be everyday occurrences. Economic problems are so pervasive that everyone thinks he knows a good deal of economics simply because he is familiar with such phenomena as prices, wages, taxes, money, selling, and the rest. We are prone to the error called the *fallacy of composition*, or the belief that what is good for a part of the economy is good for the whole economy. Each worker knows that he is better off if he gets a wage increase, but it may be difficult for him to see that if everyone gets a bigger money income, no one is better off unless there are more goods to be purchased with these incomes. A single business firm may be afraid to raise prices because it might lose many customers, but if all firms raise prices, each may lose very few. What would be an unwise policy for a single firm might not be unwise for the whole industry. To take the example further, the higher prices may not be beneficial for the economy as a whole although they would be for the industry involved. One state might reduce taxes in order to attract companies, but if all states do the same, none gains any advantage. Everyone tends to jump to the conclusion that what benefits him would be beneficial to society. In the study of economics the difficulty of detaching oneself from self-interest in order to see the whole problem often hinders the development and general acceptance of correct policies.

Some Economic Problems

To illustrate some of the problems to be studied in subsequent chapters, we shall list a few that are receiving considerable attention at the present time. Most economies have experienced disruptions during which the economic process fails to work as well as expected. A principal objective of all economic systems is to avoid such periods of disruption.

1. Inflation and Deflation. Rapid changes in the price level—whether up or down—disrupt normal economic activities. Profits are created when sellers' prices rise rapidly and losses sustained when these prices fall. Production is affected correspondingly, but the industries that are led to expand production most rapidly may not be those that would benefit from normal consumer preferences. Inflation and deflation create many inequities. When the price level rises rapidly, people on relatively fixed incomes, such as the elderly living on pensions and savings, and teachers, policemen, and social workers, whose wages and salaries do not respond quickly, are unable to buy as much as formerly. Deflation makes it more difficult to pay debts, as more work or output is required to earn a given number of dollars. In recent decades inflation has been a greater problem than deflation because governmental efforts to promote full employment have been more successful in preventing deflation than inflation.

2. Unemployment. The mass unemployment that characterized the depression of the 1930s has not returned. In that unusually severe depression, some 15 million people, or 25 percent of the labor force, were unable to find jobs. Many people lost mortgaged houses, and many businesses and farmers went bankrupt. Young people were unable to go to college, some could not start businesses, capital goods were produced to only a very limited extent, and hardly anyone escaped some economic loss. The production lost during those years of unemployment was lost forever; a man or machine that does not work this week cannot work two weeks next week. We presumably know enough at present to prevent such an economic catastrophe from recurring, but since World War II there have been levels of unemployment that were higher than generally acceptable. In the recessions of 1958 and 1960, unemployment exceeded 6 percent of the labor force, and it remained above 5 percent for the whole period from 1958 to 1964.

The recovery beginning in 1961 proved to be one of the longest on record. Indeed, the record of economic fluctuations since World War II suggests that economists and government officials are better able to prevent significant swings in employment than before. However, the economy does not seem to be able to stay at full employment by itself; some conscious manipulation of tax rates, government expenditures, and other measures seems to be required.

Although mass unemployment does not pose the threat it did in the prewar economy, other problems of unemployment remain. There is concentrated unemployment in such geographic areas as Appalachia because industries have died out and have not been replaced by new ones. There is also the problem of high unemployment rates among the untrained, the young, and racial minority groups.

3. Growth and Change. Continuing growth of the economy is necessary if an increasing population is to enjoy a rising standard of living. Total output must rise by about $40 billion per year, equivalent to over a million jobs, just to provide employment for the average increase in the labor force. Economic growth is also necessary to provide higher incomes for those people who earn only a poverty-level income, estimated now to be less than a tenth of the labor force. A growing output is also necessary to pay for many desirable public programs, such as rebuilding cities, extending the highway system, providing recreational areas, and cleaning lakes and streams.

The problems of economic growth are not simple ones. As technology advances, industries move because local resources are exhausted or because they find more profitable locations. As a result, some workers find it very difficult to obtain gainful employment. Those lacking education and modern skills may find themselves unemployed indefinitely and unable to share in a general improvement of living standards, unless public or private aid is extended through training and relocation programs.

In an economy as wealthy as ours, some economic growth is almost inevitable. A considerable amount of personal and corporate income is saved; these savings are then spent for additional capital goods. Research and development carried on by business and government lead to improvements in the quantity and quality of output. But change often means disruption for some; progress is seldom completely painless. The accelerating speed of industrial automation is basically no more than a continuation of the technological progress that has been taking place for many decades, but the impact is now being felt by more people and in a shorter period of time.

Many other economic problems will be examined in later chapters. An intelligent approach to all these problems requires a knowledge of basic economic principles. For example, in order to understand the international balance of payments problem that has plagued the United States for some time, one must be familiar with the elementary theory of pricing. Before a physician can diagnose the illnesses of patients, he must learn a good deal about physiology—how the body is structured and functions. Similarly, before he can understand specific economic problems, the economist must learn how the entire economy is structured and functions.

To continue the analogy, all people are different, but they share many characteristics in common. The same is true of economic systems. The

American economy is different from any other, but all economies have many features in common, stemming from the basic fact of scarcity. Our next step is to examine the organization and some of the principal institutions of the American economy.

ECONOMIC INSTITUTIONS

The basic questions of choice—what shall be produced, by what methods, by whom, and to whom it shall go—may be answered in many ways. As familiar and commonplace as the American economic system seems to us, it appears unusual and different to most of the world. Throughout our history, the American economy has been influenced by many aspects of our political, social, and scientific development.

The fundamental aspect of the American economy is that it is primarily market-oriented. Most of the goods and services produced are sold in competitive _markets._ Generally the markets are impersonal and anonymous. The producers of cigarettes, toothpaste, automobiles, wheat, corn, and shoes do not know who will buy their output. They do know within reasonable limits, however, what quantities they can sell at given prices. Most employees make products they will never see again once the products leave the factory, and they spend their incomes on products made by thousands of workers who are complete strangers. Everyone depends upon the continued working of the system for his own income and for his share of the goods and services produced by others.

Production for Profit

A market economy implies that production is carried on for profit. In his pioneer treatise, _The Wealth of Nations,_ written in 1776, Adam Smith noted that we rely not upon the kindness and benevolence of producers but upon their self-interest. Production is undertaken by entrepreneurs when it appears that people will pay a price that is greater than costs of production. When this is the case, the public will pay more for the commodity than the manufacturer paid for the factors of production. The difference between this price and these costs is _profit_. The costs exist because the factors of production could be used to produce something else—the underlying problem of scarcity. Entrepreneurs who wish to use land and other natural resources, labor, and capital for the production of some economic good must be able to bid these factors of production away from those who would use them to produce alternative goods. The total cost of producing one good, then, tends to measure the value of its factors of production in terms of alternative outputs. Our economy today does not use many resources for the production of clipper ships, whale-oil lamps, or buggies and buggy whips, but there was a time when these things were highly desirable and commanded prices sufficient to cover the costs of their factors of production.

Production for profit in a market economy tends to allocate resources in such a way that the public's preferences determine what shall be produced. The public is able to buy those goods for which prices cover costs and allow a profit; it is unable to buy those goods for which prices do not cover costs and return a profit. The public gets the quantity of a given good for which price will cover costs of production. Businessmen are thus led to increase or decrease production of specific items in response to the relative profitability or unprofitability of all the products they are capable of making.

Capital and Private Property

The American economy makes extensive use of plant and equipment. As noted earlier, the average investment in capital goods per worker exceeds $20,000. The figure is much higher in industries where sophisticated equipment has been developed; it exceeds $100,000 in petroleum extraction, refining, and transmission. In the textile industry, on the other hand, it is only about $10,000, and it is even less in the leather and leather products industries and in the furniture and fixtures industries. The investment per worker is much higher today than it was a century ago, and no doubt it will be much higher in future years.

Investment in capital goods has to take place in anticipation of sale of the product in the future. Anticipations may not be accurate, so there is some risk that the product will not be as profitable as anticipated. In that case the capital goods may not be able to earn the expected profit, and some or all of the investment can be lost because the capital goods lose value and become worth some smaller amount related to what they can earn. Where there is production for profit, the risk of loss accompanies the chance for gain. The advances in technology that bring about new opportunities for gain are likely to cause the decline of older industries. A few obvious examples of this are the effect of airplanes on railroad travel, of television sets on the motion picture industry, of automobiles on livery stables, and of synthetic fibers on natural fibers.

The American economy is characterized not only by the extensive use of capital but also by the fact that most capital invested in plant and equipment is privately owned. Statist (state-controlled) economies may also use large amounts of capital—after all, the countries of Eastern Europe have factories, railroads, and airlines—but in the American economy these investments are made by private persons in response to the profit motive. In countries where production is determined by a central plan, it is obviously necessary for the government to decide what investments to make and to own the means of production, or to allow ownership only by those who will follow the government's plan.

The freedom to own *private property* is one of the rights of American citizens. The economy is based on the premise that citizens are generally free to produce whatever promises to make a profit, by being worth more to the public than the factors of production necessary to produce it. A person is free to learn to be a barber and to sell haircuts or to be a contractor and to sell houses; an automobile company can decide whether to expand its output of small cars. It is true that government, at one level or another, may require the barber to demonstrate his competence and to maintain a sanitary shop, the contractor to follow building codes, and the automobile company to install safety equipment, but within these rules each is free to make his decisions.

Another facet of the right to own property is that income earned in the production process may be spent for whatever goods and services the recipient chooses. He may consume his income promptly or delay consumption in order to acquire personal property in the form of housing, clothing, appliances, or whatever he prefers.

In the modern American economy, a large part of the capital equipment is owned by *corporations* rather than by individuals. But individuals own the corporations. The corporation is a creature of law and has many of the rights of natural persons, such as the right to own property. The corporate form of organization has made practical much greater aggregations of capital than would otherwise be possible under private enterprise, because a corporation can combine the savings of individuals and its own retained earnings to acquire vast quantities of plant, equipment, and other capital. It is obvious that such accumulations of capital are advantageous in industries such as steel, automobiles, mining, and paper. The corporate form also facilitates the organization of many small businesses. Many big corporations were once small, and today thousands of small business enterprises operate as corporations because of various legal advantages of that form.

Freedom of Choice

The way in which economic activity is organized in a market economy implies a good deal of individual freedom of choice. The freedom of producers to choose what to produce and in what quantities is part of a broader spectrum of freedoms. The freedom of producers is balanced by the freedom of consumers to choose what commodities, and in what quantities, they will consume. These freedoms are not unlimited; no one can ignore income taxes in allocating his income, nor can he choose to buy alcoholic beverages in some localities or certain drugs without prescriptions. Within the broad limits imposed by the democratic process, however, one may decide to buy an expensive automobile rather than send his child to college, to buy corporate securities rather than sports equipment, or to live in an apartment instead of a house. Because of the basic problem of economic scarcity, one's income may not cover both the automobile and the college education, the securities and the sports equipment, or two houses. But the higher the value placed by the market on the services of one's labor and capital, the wider are the choices open in the disposition of income.

A major aspect of freedom of choice is freedom to select an occupation. It is true that an untrained high school dropout cannot make a choice between engineering, computer programming, and medicine; but for that matter an engineer or any other professional person cannot always have the position he wants. However, within the limits of being able to afford education and training, people are free to compete in the areas of their choice. Freedom to compete does not carry with it the right to succeed, only the right to try to succeed. A basic social problem is how to improve the opportunities for all people and to broaden their choices of occupation through wider education and training, so that the decision is dictated less by the availability of income to cover these expenses.

Competition

The foregoing discussion implies that a market economy is also characterized by competition, which assures the operation of some of the other institutions of a market economy. If only one producer is able to decide to produce a small automobile and he thus obtains a monopoly, he is able to evade the *discipline of the market.* In other words, in a free market a producer must sell his product at a price that attracts customers from similar products, and at the same time he must pay prices for factors of production that other users of these factors are willing to pay. Without competition, the producer can probably charge a higher price for his product and perhaps pay lower prices for factors of production, and thus distort the allocation of resources between competing uses. There is less consumer satisfaction at higher cost. One of the tasks of government in a market economy, therefore, is maintaining competition and preventing monopoly or, in some appropriate instances such as the public utilities, regulating monopoly.

THE ROLE OF GOVERNMENT

No economy has ever been a completely free market economy. The freedoms discussed in the preceding section are matters of degree. In the American economy these freedoms are relatively unrestricted, but in some economies they are virtually nonexistent. Economic activity is not carried out solely by private enterprise; some is carried out by government. Government is also charged with enforcing the "rules of the game" under which entrepreneurs operate. To complete the basic description of the American economy, the various roles of government are listed below. Further discussion of governmental activities will be presented in later chapters.

Governmental Services

The extent to which it is appropriate for government to provide goods and services directly and to regulate or influence production by the private sector of the economy is a matter of considerable political disagreement. It is widely agreed, however, that some basic governmental functions are appropriate. Providing for the national defense and for internal order have long been considered proper functions of government, although particular measures may lead to great disagreement. Government is expected to set certain standards for the monetary system and the system of weights and measures. Government dispenses justice through the courts, assures safety through traffic control and building codes, and provides a variety of communal services in the form of highways, schools, sanitation systems, penal institutions, fire protection, recreational facilities, and so forth. Education constitutes one of the largest categories of governmental expenditure; welfare expenditures for mental health, aid to the poor, and similar costs are also large.

Some of the total output of society is produced by governmental officials and employees. They teach school, legislate, sit on courts, protect fish and game, and so on. In total, about a fifth of all output is channeled through the government at different levels. It is significant, however, that government does not attempt to produce this fraction of total output by itself. To a large extent, government purchases output from the private sector with funds raised through taxation or borrowing from the private sector. Government pays private enterprise for the construction of roads and bridges, for military equipment, for government buildings, and for the supplies used by governmental employees.

Fiscal and Monetary Policies

Since a fifth or more of total output is produced in response to governmental purchases, government must have a significant influence on what and how much is produced. There is considerable political agreement, therefore, that government — especially the federal government — should use its expenditures and its fund-raising activities in ways that will contribute to, rather than deter, full employment, stability of the price level, and economic growth. Such measures are called *fiscal policy.* Neither major political party advocates that the federal budget be balanced each year but, rather, that the federal government increase expenditures or decrease taxes when total output is below a full-employment level and decrease expenditures or raise taxes when inflation is a threat.

The central bank of the United States, the Federal Reserve System, similarly uses its powers to influence the growth of the stock of money and the availability and cost of credit, which in turn influence business conditions. Monetary policy attempts to be expansionary when the economy needs additional expenditures and to be restrictive when aggregate expenditures should be restrained. From time to time the federal government, where it is a principal customer, attempts to influence the course of specific prices or wages through its ability to make or withhold purchases.

Regulating Markets

Besides its ability to influence the economy in general, government has several powers it can use to regulate the way in which the private economy operates. Some of these powers are broad, others are more specific. Many of them relate to specific markets, such as for meat, drugs, and securities; some of these will be discussed later in connection with the description of markets. The government's powers may also be classified as those aimed at maintaining competition, regulating competition, or regulating monopoly. For example, the antitrust laws attempt to prevent monopoly "in any line of commerce." In the markets for meat, other foods, and drugs, there are specific standards of sanitation and quality. Labor markets are subject to considerable regulation by all levels of government, covering such items as limitations on the work of women and children, maximum hours, minimum wages, safety conditions, and collective bargaining.

GROSS NATIONAL PRODUCT

A broad overall view of the economy is presented through the data on gross national product. Gross national product is a measure of the total output of goods and services for a period of time, and the principal categories are the purchases of the main sectors of the economy. The data in Table 1-1 give the relevant figures for the predepression year 1929, the depression year of 1933, the year 1950 (after the depression and World War II), and the year 1969. The growth of the economy from 1929 to 1969 — about a generation — is apparent in the increases in the totals and

various subtotals in the categories. Some of this increase, however, reflects price increases rather than growth of real output. The last line of
the table shows the growth in real output by measuring it each year in
terms of prices prevailing in 1958.

Discounting the influence of price increases, gross national product
rose from about $200 billion in 1929 to over $700 billion in 1969 (both
taken at 1958 prices). Personal consumption expenditures rose from $77
billion to $576 billion in actual prices. Expenditures on durable goods
—furniture, appliances, automobiles, and the like—which fell to about
$3 billion in 1933, approximated $90 billion in 1969. As a wealthy nation, we use machines to provide services in the home as well as in the
factory.

There are interesting and significant variations in the size of expenditures on investment goods—plant and equipment. These shifts receive
considerable attention in later chapters. It may be noted that output of
producers' durable equipment fell from $5.6 billion to $1.5 billion between
1929 and 1933, a decline of nearly 75 percent, but was over $65 billion in
1969. Similarly, residential construction fell to $.6 billion, or over 85 per-
cent during the great depression, but exceeded $32 billion in 1969.
It is interesting that expenditures on business plant and on producers'
durable equipment were virtually the same in 1929, that by 1950 equipment cost about twice as much as plant, and that in 1969 the latter pro-

Table 1-1
Gross National Product, Selected Years
(Billions of Dollars)

	1929	1933	1950	1969
Gross national product	$103.1	$ 55.6	$284.8	$932.1
Personal consumption expenditures	77.2	45.8	191.0	576.0
Durable goods	9.2	3.5	30.5	89.8
Nondurable goods	37.7	22.3	98.1	243.6
Services	30.3	20.1	62.4	242.6
Gross private domestic investment	16.2	1.4	54.1	139.4
Fixed investment	14.5	3.0	47.3	131.4
Nonresidential	10.6	2.4	27.9	99.2
Structures	5.0	.9	9.2	33.4
Equipment	5.6	1.5	18.7	65.8
Residential structures	4.0	.6	19.4	32.2
Change in business inventories	1.7	−1.6	6.8	8.0
Net exports	1.1	.4	1.8	2.1
Government purchases	8.5	8.0	37.9	214.6
Federal	1.3	2.0	18.4	101.9
National defense	....	....	14.1	79.2
Other	....	....	4.3	22.7
State and local	7.2	6.0	19.5	112.7
GNP in constant (1958) dollars	203.6	141.5	355.3	727.5

Source: *Federal Reserve Bulletin*, May, 1970, p. A-68.

portion held true. These figures indicate that equipment has become much more sophisticated and complicated—and therefore more expensive—as well as much more extensively used since 1929.

The government component of total purchases suggests that many widely held notions are inaccurate. In 1950 state and local expenditures slightly exceeded federal expenditures and have usually done so since. Clearly, the bulk of federal purchases is for national defense purposes. This fact, of course, provides the basis for political disagreement between those who would prefer to see less spent in this manner and more spent to solve domestic problems and those who consider problems of defense more pressing. It should be noted that the data in this table refer only to purchases of current output; thus the figures for federal purchases are considerably less than the government's total budget expenditures. The budget includes expenditures classified as *transfer payments,* which do not purchase output directly. Payments such as those for social security benefits and interest on the government debt do not buy output directly, but the recipients of these payments make purchases, mostly as personal consumption expenditures. Also, some of the expenditures of state and local governments are made with funds received as transfer payments from the federal government.

THE PERFORMANCE OF THE ECONOMY

Gross national product provides a measure of the performance of an economy. Personal incomes are closely related to the value of total output, because it is this output that is shared through the disposition of incomes. Per capita output or per capita income figures are better than aggregates, however, for measuring the welfare of the members of an economy. If our gross national product were twice that of another country but our population three times as large, income per person would obviously be less. In terms of material output per person (a reflection of *productivity*), the American economy is outstanding, and this is also true of the growth of the economy.

International Comparisons

Per capita incomes in different countries cannot be compared with a high degree of accuracy, because it is difficult to translate monetary differences into real differences and because of variations in statistical methods. The gap in living standards between the advanced nations and the developing nations is so great, however, that general conclusions are obvious. The majority of the world's people live in poverty unknown to most Americans. Millions of people in the underdeveloped nations own nothing more than the few clothes they wear, a few cooking utensils, and perhaps enough food for a day or two. Their lives are characterized by high birth and death rates, malnutrition and actual hunger, disease, illiteracy, and low productivity. These conditions exist even in countries where there are also wealthy people, handsome estates, and beautiful buildings.

At the top of the income heap is the United States, which has a per capita income in excess of $3,500. This is not to say that there are no poor people in the United States for, if the average income exceeds $3,500, there are many people below that average, just as there are others above it. Switzerland, Sweden, and Canada are also in the top group, although their per capita incomes are closer to $1,500. These countries are joined by the United Kingdom, Denmark, Australia, New Zealand, and a few others to constitute the advanced nations with the highest incomes. A middle group consists of Belgium, France, West Germany, and Norway with about $1,000 per capita, the Netherlands and Soviet Russia with about $800, and Italy and Ireland with about $600. Others, such as several South American nations, have about $400. The bottom group, where per capita incomes do not exceed $100, includes Indonesia, India, Thailand, and Pakistan in Asia and the Orient, and nations such as Kenya, Nigeria, and the Congo in Africa.

Economic Growth and Development

Comparisons of economic growth rates are equally imprecise because of differences in the outputs compared and dates chosen for comparison. In the 1950s comparisons of economic growth in Communist and Western nations received much public attention, but to some extent the rapid rates attributed to the former resulted from their emphasis on physical goods in contrast to services.

Economic growth does not consist simply of producing more and more of the same things. An important element of growth is change in the composition of output. We do not today produce more of everything produced in 1800 or 1900; we actually produce less of many things that were needed in those days. New products, industries, and occupations characterize the developing economy. An economy continuing to produce more of the same goods and services would be like a baby growing uniformly in all directions—it would grow but not develop.

The Industrial Revolution enabled the countries of the Western World that participated in it to shake off the stagnation of the past and to begin to increase per capita output significantly. As output increased, social institutions made possible a relatively greater increase in capital goods. Life for the wage earners was admittedly not ideal, and employers were able to collect large profits, which they reinvested in additional factories and machines. The economic history of the early 1800s reveals much poverty, misery, and exploitation, but the foundations were laid for ever-growing output, which eventually was shared more and more generally. Some other countries, of which Japan is an outstanding example, joined the expanding economies later by adopting foreign methods of production.

A vicious circle still exists in those countries that have not gone through the early stages of development, in which it is necessary to get incomes up to a level where voluntary saving provides for growth in accumulated capital. In these countries per capita income is so low that it all has to be devoted to consumption, and there is almost no personal saving with which to buy capital goods for future production. People cannot save because they are poor, and they are poor because they have not saved. In recent decades many domestic and international programs of these countries have demonstrated that it is not easy to break out of this vicious circle.

The average annual rate of growth, as measured by gross national

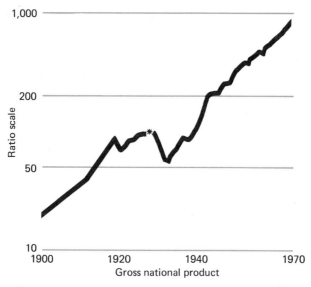

* New series

Figure 1-1. Gross national product in current dollars, 1900–1969.   Source: *Federal Reserve Historical Chart Book,* 1969, p. 66; *Federal Reserve Monthly Chart Book,* April, 1970, p. 51.

product, has been about 3.5 percent in the United States. In some periods it has been somewhat higher, and in others lower. This figure may seem like a slow rate, but it must be remembered that it is a compound rate— the increase each year is based on the preceding year. At 3.5 percent compound interest a sum doubles in about twenty years. An economy that doubles its total output every twenty years cannot be said to be growing slowly. Considering the increase in population, the growth in per capita output during the life of this nation has averaged about 1.6 percent. At this rate average income doubles during the normal working span of a human life, or in about forty years. Such an increase is illustrated by a comparison of living conditions in the 1970s with those in the 1920s. By the time a person is fifty years old, average per capita income is 2.3 times what it was when he was born.

Figure 1-1 shows the long-run rise in gross national product. This chart is plotted on a ratio scale, which shows the rate of growth rather than the amount of growth. At any point on the chart, a doubling— whether it is from $10 billion to $20 billion or from $100 billion to $200 billion—is shown by equal steepness. If absolute amounts were used as the scale, the curve would rise very steeply because the amounts in recent years are much larger than those of earlier years—the principle of compound growth rates.

Performance Since 1880

The typical young person of about 20 years of age has parents who were born around 1920 and grandparents who were born in the 1880s. While the grandparents were growing up, the typical workweek was about 63 hours per week. The normal factory workweek was 6 days of 10 hours each, but in many other jobs, including farming, people worked longer hours. A person who worked in a retail store or bank probably walked to work or traveled by horsecar. When he arrived at work early in the morning, he brought in coal or wood for the stove, swept out the premises, and met the day's first customers around eight o'clock. There were few women employees, records and communications were written in longhand, and most goods were sold in bulk rather than in packages. The telephone was a newfangled invention, and urgent long-distance messages were sent by telegraph.

Measured in terms of prices prevailing in the late 1950s, family income in the 1880s was about $2,200 — family income, not per capita income — and, of course, in dollars current then, it was much lower. Families then were generally larger than they are now, and disposable income per person was the equivalent of about $530 today. People born in the 1880s had a life expectancy of about 50 years, while today's 20-year-old has an average life expectancy of about 70 years. Children spent an average of only 81 days a year in school, and only 10 million were in school. Many children worked, not many finished high school, and very few went to college.

By 1915 more and more people were living in cities. City living was stimulated by the development of indoor plumbing, telephones, gas lights, and rapid interurban transit systems. Many people maintained a carriage and a horse or two and could visit relatives who lived a few miles out in the country. Conservationists were beginning to point out that, at the rate the economy was using them up, natural resources could not last forever. Population was pushing toward 100 million; it was only 50 million in 1880, so it was obvious that the population per square mile nearly doubled between 1880 and 1915. Women were beginning to break out of their limited occupations — domestic service, nursing, and teaching — and to invade offices as clerks, secretaries, and typists. More children could afford to stay in school and a larger proportion finished high school.

In 1920, after World War I, the average factory workweek had fallen to 46 hours. The average factory worker's earnings bought about half as much as they do today. Children born in 1920 had an average life expectancy of 55 years. The 1920s was the period in which the automobile changed the nature of American life. Factory sales of cars, which had been only 4,000 in 1900, had risen to 181,000 by 1920. At that time a few million cars were registered, but 10 years later 23 million cars, as well as 3.7 million trucks and buses, were registered. The automobile started as a plaything of the wealthy but soon became an object of general desire, and then a necessity. The problem of building highways as fast as required by the increasing number of automobiles began, and the business of extracting and refining petroleum and getting it to the consumer grew by leaps and bounds. The growth of suburbs was stimulated, railroad passenger traffic declined, and motels, filling stations, garages, and repair shops were built by the thousands.

In the boom year of 1929, gross national product exceeded $100 billion for the first time. People paid $2.6 billion in personal taxes and had $83.2 billion of disposable income left, from which they spent $79.1 billion for personal outlays. The number of young people in school reached 30 million, including 5 million in high school and a million in college.

The father of today's young adult probably had a difficult time during the 1930s. The depression, which lasted almost the entire decade, was severe as well as long. Personal income did not reach the 1929 level again until 1941, when business was stimulated by preparations for World War II; by then, population was also larger. In the depths of the depression, unemployment reached a point at which one in every three or four workers was out of a job. Many businessmen and farmers became bankrupt when markets for their wares faded away and they could not pay their bills. Banks and insurance companies had to foreclose many properties for which they had no ready market. The necessity for relief caused government transfer payments to rise from $1 billion in 1930 to $3 billion in 1936; in the same period, government purchases of goods and services rose from $4 billion to $12.2 billion. The principal topic of political debate was this expansion of the sphere of government in the economy.

With the coming of World War II, economic conditions were reversed in the 1940s. Instead of widespread unemployment, there was a scarcity of labor; instead of deflation, inflation; instead of attempting to put floors under prices and wages, the government imposed ceilings on them. Federal purchases of goods and services reached $165.4 billion in 1944 — nearly half the gross national product of $361.3 billion. As many women joined and older people remained in the labor force, it increased from 56.2 million in 1940 to 65.3 million in 1945. Vice President Wallace had been considered a dreamer when he wrote a book in the late 1930s called *Sixty Million Jobs,* in which he looked forward to greatly expanded employment. Under the forces of wartime purchasing and inflation, however, unemployment dropped below 2 percent of the labor force and these jobs became a reality. The elimination of unemployment and the increase in the total labor force (including the armed forces) showed that the economy was capable of producing all the goods and services required by the most destructive war in history and also maintaining essentially the same standard of living as in 1940.

The economy has grown consistently, although not at a steady rate, since World War II. There have been four recessions, minor by prewar standards, although the one in 1957–1958 was sharp, if brief. Retarded by two of these recessions, the growth rate in the 1950s was slower than after the recession of 1960–1961. Under present circumstances of population growth and age distribution, output must grow approximately 4 percent a year to absorb the growth in the labor force; when there is unemployment, output must grow more rapidly in order to absorb the unemployed.

This review points out how the slow changes in the economy from year to year accumulate in a few generations into a revolutionary change. The present size of the economy is so much greater than it used to be that, by past standards, the average annual increase is an enormous absolute amount. The annual increase in the American gross national product alone is greater than the entire gross national product of most countries and even greater than a large fraction of the output of the other most advanced countries.

A simple review of the statistics cannot fully convey the change in economic life in recent generations. Output per person is more than four times what it was in the 1880s, and this output results from many fewer hours of work. This growth of output has been accompanied by significant shifts in the relative distribution of income and in the relative amount of output provided through governmental channels. The hours of work per capita required to produce the gross national product have fallen by over 50 percent. Technology, greatly increased use of capital, and managerial science have brought gains in productivity. Increased output per person combined with a larger labor force has greatly increased total output. A much larger proportion of the population is now in school. This trend has been accentuated in recent years because the population contains un-usually large numbers of young people. Nevertheless, the labor force has grown, mainly because of the entry of about 20 million women since 1880. Although the labor force is reduced in numbers because of those in school, it becomes more productive because of their education and train-ing. Each hour of work today results in five times as much output as in 1880. Each worker today uses ten times as much horsepower, or mechani-cal help, than in 1880.

These statistical measures still fail to describe the change in economic life in terms of leisure and recreation, books produced and enjoyed, spread of information and entertainment through radio and television, travel at home and abroad, higher levels of education, improvements in medicines and health care, speed of travel and communication, and so forth. But there is another side to the coin. With the growth of population and increasing industrialization, many trout and salmon streams have be-come polluted and dead, fresh water is scarce in many places, large areas in the major cities have turned into slums where crime and ill health abound, and much of what statistically contributes to gross national product is actually the production of sanitation agencies, traffic control agencies, and social work agencies required by these developments. Presumably few people would willingly return to life as it was in 1900, even though distance lends enchantment and many aspects of life then seem attractive now. Few people would make the sacrifice in order to turn back the clock, once they counted all the things that they would be required to give up to make the change. That is why these things are called prog-ress.

SUMMARY

By comparison with the rest of the world and with the past, the American economy is highly productive; it has about 6 percent of the world's people and about 7 percent of the land area, but pro-duces about a third of the world's output. These figures translate into a high income per person. Many aspects of our economic sys-tem apparently contribute to this productivity, some of which we have surveyed in this introductory chapter. The American economic organization seems to be highly successful through stimulus to in-centive, utilization of capital, and access—either directly or through relatively free trade—to natural resources.

Economic Terms for Review

free goods	entrepreneur	profit
economic goods	relative scarcity	private property
resources	value judgments	corporations
natural resources	fallacy of	competition
capital	composition	gross national product
labor	inflation	productivity
factors of	deflation	economic development
production	markets	

Questions for Review

1. What distinguishes economic goods from free goods?
2. What is a factor of production? a capital good? an entrepreneur?
3. What is meant by the statement that economics is largely a study of costs and benefits?
4. Who is harmed when the price level rises rapidly? Does anyone benefit?
5. What is the fallacy of composition? Give an example.
6. In the national income accounts, what are the principal sectors of the economy?
7. What is the average income per person in the United States? How does this figure compare with the same figures for the rest of the world?

Questions for Analysis

1. Can you think of any explanations for the persistence of poverty, even in a rich country like the United States?
2. What is a market economy? Does a *command* economy like that in the Soviet Union have markets? How do the two economies differ?
3. What is the function of profit in a market economy?
4. What are some of the risks of owning and operating a business?
5. In what ways does government affect the operation of the economy?
6. What are some of the major changes in American economic life during the last fifty years? Can you visualize those likely to come in the next fifty years?

Case for Decision

When Ivan Stepovich arrived at his Kremlin office one morning in 1971, he realized that during the day he would have to come to a decision on his recommendation for the number of passenger cars to be produced in Russia the following year. Ivan was a member of the central economic planning body of the government (the Gosplan), which was putting together production plans.

Ivan knew that there was one automobile for every 235 Russians and that the current production of 280,000 cars provided one for every 839 persons. He also knew that in the United States there was one car for every 2.4 persons and that the annual output provided one for every 22 persons.

In preliminary discussions by the planning body, two points of view had clearly taken shape. Some members pointed to the disparity between the Russian and American statistics and demanded that Russian production catch up more rapidly. Others claimed that the automobile was not as suitable for Russia as for America; rail and airplane travel were more suitable for great distances, and modern forms of public transportation—subways and buses—were more economical for local transportation.

In order to estimate what level of automobile production might be possible, Ivan had asked his staff to prepare several sets of figures. He had asked for data on the additional productive facilities needed to produce 400,000, 750,000, and 1,000,000 cars and for data on what uses other planners were hoping to devote these resources to. He included requests for data on the number of foundry workers, mechanics, and engineers and the number being trained, sources of rubber tires, and components that might be imported more cheaply than manufactured inside Russia. He also requested estimates of how many Russians might buy a car similar to an American compact car (1) at prices set to barely cover costs of production and (2) at considerably higher prices. He also checked on potential production and imports of petroleum products and on other demands for them.

Putting yourself in Ivan's place, decide how you would go about considering the following problems:

1. What would be the effects on other industries of a doubling of automobile production? (Some goods are *substitute* goods and some are *complementary* goods.)
2. What would be the effects on Russia's foreign trade?
3. How should a price on the car be set? (What do you want the price to accomplish?)
4. What kind of car should be considered—size, power, style, economy of operation?
5. What should be done if many more Russians want the car at the price chosen than there are cars?

Knowing that you can only make a recommendation and not the final decision, how would you go about deciding on a recommendation?

The Market Economy

There is a fable about several blind men attempting to describe an elephant. One of the blind men felt the trunk and thought that the elephant resembled a snake. Another felt a leg and decided that the elephant resembled a tree; the other blind men found different comparisons. How one describes the American economy depends largely upon the characteristics that one considers important. And an evaluation of the economy depends very much on what characteristics one emphasizes. One person may be impressed by the fact that our economy has provided the highest standard of living of any country in the world; another may point to the fact that about 20 million persons are considered below the poverty line and that these people constitute about 7 percent of all white families and about 30 percent of all nonwhite families. The economy has many critics and many defenders.

THE STRUCTURE OF THE ECONOMY

The economy of the United States is based primarily on the existence of markets in which there is more individual freedom than in most countries to purchase materials, components, and services and to sell the resulting products. An economy of this type differs in many respects from those which do not use free markets to allocate resources.

Roots of the American Economy

The structure of the American economy has developed largely from beginnings rooted in the *Industrial Revolution* of the late eighteenth century in England. After 1775 England changed from an agricultural nation to the leading industrial nation because of the invention and spread of new techniques of production. As a result of growing production and wealth, England was the leading political and economic power until World War I. The process by which England developed is still taking place in many other parts of the world.

The Industrial Revolution brought about the widespread use of machinery in place of manual labor, the development of factories where laborers congregated instead of working at home, and the rise of industrial cities. Other related developments were the separation of capitalists and laborers, the subjection of laborers to the discipline of the factory, the beginnings of labor organizations, the development of huge impersonal markets to absorb the output of factories, and the need for large accumulations of capital. The new class of capitalists, or owners, chafed under the old governmental restrictions on all aspects of production and trade and demanded reduction of these rules. As capitalists gained political power and as the ideas and philosophies of freedom spread more widely among all classes of people, England was led to adopt free trade with other nations and a minimum of internal regulation.

For a variety of reasons, businessmen were more free in England than elsewhere to invest in new enterprises and adopt new machine methods. The old craft guild system had largely broken down. Serfdom had also disappeared. Employers were free to offer jobs, and labor was free to accept. England had cities and towns where labor was available as new plants were built. Trade barriers between towns had come down. Religious persecution on the Continent had led skilled artisans to move to England. Englishmen who had prospered in shipping were willing to invest in factory ventures. And the English had markets in colonies abroad as well as at home.

Beginnings in America

The early American colonists brought personal freedoms with them; in fact, many came principally to seek additional freedom. Shortly after the establishment of the new nation, the restrictions on foreign trade stemming from the Napoleonic Wars and the War of 1812 led to the domestic manufacture of many goods that had been imported from England. Once these industries started, they received government protection from the competition of imports. But the United States remained largely an agricultural country until after the Civil War, because of the abundance of land to the west of the early settlements. At that time industrialization was greatly stimulated by the development of various metal and metal-using industries. Workers in the United States were spared much of the misery and poverty to which the English workers had been subjected, because the frontier provided a sort of safety valve; if life in the East became too hard, workers could scrape together a small grubstake and become pioneers.

The climate and availability of water power in New England led to the early establishment of textile mills. These mills imitated the English mills in using power looms and other machines invented in England. Some small furnaces were established to make iron, out of which pots and pans and other small articles were fashioned. During the American Revolution firearms had to be handmade one by one. The new government set up armories at Harpers Ferry, West Virginia, and at Springfield, Massachusetts, and contracted with various persons for further production. Eli Whitney, who invented the cotton gin but was unable to collect royalties for its use, was one of those contracting to make firearms. He developed a system at his factory in Connecticut whereby workmen could make identical, _interchangeable parts_ for assembly into rifles. This method greatly speeded up production but required trained workmen and special machinery for casting or forging parts. Other producers of firearms and also producers of items such as clocks adopted this method. The use of interchangeable parts became the foundation for _mass production_ in later industries, such as automobile manufacturing.

The American continent provided a favorable environment for the exercise of ambition and free enterprise. Discoveries of iron ore, limestone, and coal provided the materials for a great steel industry. Petroleum, first found in western Pennsylvania, opened up other great opportunities. Forests provided wood for housing, raw materials, and fuel. Vast areas of free land offered opportunities in agriculture. Social and cultural characteristics quite different from those in Europe also favored the development of industry. The early settlers expected to work hard, and there was no nobility to exercise political power. Unlike other countries, engaging in trade, banking, or industry was not considered beneath one, and the prospects of one's children improving their economic and social status encouraged people to work, to save, and to invest in business.

As different industries developed, they tended to follow a variety of patterns. Between the Civil War and the beginning of the twentieth century, mass production became commonplace. A large output of many items could now be produced at low cost. This result was possible because of an increase in the technical knowledge of how to produce, the existence of a large domestic market where goods could be sold freely, the availability of capital funds (often from abroad) for investment, and the ability of management to supervise large enterprises. One development in industrial technology led to another—higher-quality metals, new cutting and drilling tools, better fuels, more complicated machinery, sophisticated measuring devices, and new transportation methods.

Capital

One of the important factors making possible the development of industry was the accumulation of funds for investment in factories, machines, railroads, canals, and other capital goods. In the early days of the country such investments were not large; a clipper ship was a major investment, as was a small factory. By 1850 the investment per worker was still less than $1,000.

Many industries today have relatively small plants with fewer than a hundred workers. Even in such plants, however, the workers tend to use expensive machinery and tools which are operated by electric power. Such plants often specialize in producing a few items that are sold to larger companies to be used in other products. In some other lines of production, such as automobile assembly, there are great advantages in bringing together thousands of workers and great accumulations of capital equipment under a single management. Many of the industries in which the United States outpaces the world are those in which it has been possible to increase greatly the size of the producing unit. When one company manages several great factories, it is indeed a large operation. The output of General Motors Corporation alone exceeds in value the entire output of some countries. A visit to a large manufacturing establishment quickly reveals the extent to which the output results from the use of interchangeable parts produced by automatic machinery run by nonhuman sources of power.

Division of Labor

The American economy illustrates to a high degree the division of labor into specialized tasks. The efficiency of the modern factory stems largely from the fact that jobs are broken down into tasks and subtasks, many of which can be done automatically; generally, what labor does is the repetition of a single operation.

Division of labor began as people started to specialize in broad trades —that is, when one man spent all his working hours making shoes and another farming. Today it has gone far beyond this point and, except for a few artisans, the trade of making shoes no longer exists; in shoe factories some workers cut out the soles, other workers cut out the uppers, others sew parts of the shoes, others dye them, and so on. The importance of division of labor in increasing efficiency was noted by Adam Smith, who in 1775 wrote what is generally considered the first comprehensive treatise on economics and whom we will have occasion to quote from time to time because of the pertinence of his early observations. Smith noted that one man working by himself could produce about 20 pins a day, as he had to cut the wire, sharpen it at one end, and place a head on the other. But if the process were split into 18 operations and divided among 10 men, over 48,000 pins a day could be produced. The gains from specialization are often magnified by assigning some of the processes to machinery.

As Adam Smith also noted, there are several reasons for the gain in efficiency. Since each worker performs only one or two simplified operations and does them repetitively, he develops a higher degree of skill and speed. Division of labor eliminates the waste of time that arises when a worker puts away one set of tools and takes up another task; it takes time to get going in the new job. There is a further waste if each worker has tools he uses only part of the time while his other tools are idle. The more that jobs are subdivided, the more likely it is that machines can be invented or adapted to do them.

The social criticisms of the high degree of division of labor today are familiar. It is claimed, and often rightly, that factory labor is monotonous and that, because it is carried on at a pace set by the machinery, it can be very tiring. As a result of rising output per worker, on the other hand, the number of hours in the standard workday and workweek has declined drastically. A hundred years ago workers in factories may have had more varied work, but it is doubtful that the work was easier. Furthermore, they usually worked twelve hours a day and six days a week. Today most factory laborers work about forty hours each week. Going back even further, it is also doubtful that the work on the medieval manor, the southern plantation, or the New England farm was not monotonous in its own way. Today there is much more time for leisure and amusement—whether it is used wisely or not can, of course, be debated. Society has accepted the development of modern mass-production methods; apparently people think that the greater output justifies these methods.

Markets

An economy in which there is highly developed division of labor, such as in the United States, must also have highly developed markets. Everyone produces a great quantity of one or a few things which he does not need for himself and which he must sell in order to buy the products of other specialists. Much of this exchange of goods is accomplished indirectly and through the use of money. That is, the worker sells his labor to an employer, the employer sells the product, the worker buys goods with his wages, and the employer buys goods with his profits. It does not pay to carry division of labor very far unless there is a sufficiently great market for the product.

Mass production is obviously impossible unless the product is one for which there is a market of many buyers. It would not make sense to invest billions of dollars in facilities to make a product which would have very few sales. In the United States the advantage of having a market as wide as the continent has been very important in justifying the investment of large sums to develop highly efficient industries.

Since the ability of workers to sell labor and of producers to sell the products of labor depends on the ability of others to buy, the economy represents a vast cooperative effort. The cooperation is unconscious and often unrecognized, but essentially the market economy is the way in which the entire population cooperates to produce the goods and services it wants. Each person is dependent on others for most of the things he consumes. Similarly, producers are dependent on other producers for their purchases of materials, power, supplies, and transportation.

Thus, in contrast to the early American, the American of today is typically not a person living in a rural area, in a house that he and his neighbors built, wearing clothes made out of cloth produced at home, and being therefore largely self-sufficient—but poor. Today he is more likely to be a city dweller, working for eight hours or less a day in a factory or office building, and consuming articles his grandfather never heard of. Modern man has many frictions and worries; he is not consoled by the fact that he has an income five or ten times that of his grandfather but instead frets over the monthly payments on his automobile and color television set, wonders where to spend his next vacation, considers whether to add to his savings bank account or to buy common stock, and complains about the government's expenditures for space exploration. Economic progress may never lead to Utopia, but it is doubtful that many people would want to return to the economy of a few decades ago. Even when the subway stops because of a strike, the lights go out because of a power failure, the garbage piles up because of another strike, or the automobile cannot be repaired for a week because of the backlog of work at the garage, few people decide to emigrate to countries where these problems may not exist.

Types of Industries

The broad categories of goods produced by a country reflect the stage of its economic development. Being a highly developed country by world standards, the United States produces goods and services that reflect this advanced stage of development. The emerging nations tend to specialize in *primary commodities*—those produced directly from the land, such as tea, coffee, rubber, and minerals. Nations whose level of living is at or near subsistence produce mainly basic commodities through fishing, agriculture, and forestry. Processing industries become important only when the need for secondary goods, those used in the production of other goods, arises. These goods include the various metals, glass, and simple chemicals. In mature economies, third-level industries arise, including such service industries as banking, insurance, and advertising and the professions of law, medicine, and teaching. Any country is likely to have some of each type of industry; it is the degree of importance of each type that characterizes a country as emerging or mature. For example, in the United States, employment in manufacturing no longer constitutes half of total employment; it is overshadowed by employment in trade, services, and government. Some of the less developed nations of the world are attempting to manage their economies so that they can skip quickly to the stage where they have many advanced industries. Japan is an example of a country that borrowed techniques and methods from the other advanced nations for its economic advancement.

THE ROLE OF GOVERNMENT

Government is important in the economic life of every nation. Although the American economy is often called one of free enterprise, it is also called a *mixed* economy because it contains elements of both free enterprise and government participation. It is probably fair to say that the basic orientation in the United States is toward free enterprise but that modern urban life produces many problems requiring greater participation by government (federal, state, or local). The roots of the preference for free enterprise go back to the reactions that arose against mercantilism during and after the Industrial Revolution and which were so well expressed in Adam Smith's *The Wealth of Nations. Laissez-faire* became the general philosophy of government during the nineteenth century.[1]

The belief in laissez-faire did not rest solely on considerations of economics but also on other philosophical and social ideas that were becoming widespread. These ideas emphasized the importance of the interests of the individual as against those of the nation or special groups. They asserted that the greatest good for all was represented by the greatest good for each; that if each person could seek his own well-being without governmental restriction or guidance, the general level of well-being would be maximized. Each person could seek out his own best occupation and, in the process, best serve the whole of society, even if for selfish reasons.

Basic Rights in the Economy

Broadly speaking, three principles underlie the general organization of the American economy: individual freedom, private property, and individual initiative. Together these principles describe a free economy, as opposed to a command, or controlled, economy.

Americans take a high degree of personal liberty for granted and often fail to relate their political freedoms to their economic well-being. Until modern times personal liberty was not something that people automatically had. Many of the ancient Greeks were slaves, and throughout the Middle Ages most Europeans were serfs bound to the land on which they were born and to the lord of the manor. Even after greater personal liberty became common, economic activities were still severely limited, as one could not freely enter any occupation, engage in any trade, or produce goods to his own standards.

Private property is also a modern institution. Much of the property in ancient times was owned communally or by the king or chief. During the Middle Ages the king and the nobility owned most of the land. It has since become a common right for any citizen not only to own property and to enjoy its benefits but to bequeath it to his heirs.

[1] *Laissez-faire,* a French term, means literally "let alone" and has come to imply noninterference by government in business affairs.

As the mercantilistic restrictions on production and trade gave way, more room was created for the exercise of individual initiative in starting and managing business ventures. Under the former rules of the artisans' guilds and governments, how much could be produced and in what manner, where goods could be sold and at what prices, and how much apprentices should be paid were all spelled out in detail. Today there are broad rules of behavior and many examples of detailed regulation in some lines of commerce, but the general rule is that businessmen produce what they consider profitable and seek ways of producing goods at lower cost.

The three basic principles of personal freedom, private property, and individual initiative imply certain other freedoms. It would be an overstatement to say that anyone can go into any business he chooses, produce whatever he wants, sell at whatever prices he can get from buyers, and buy from suppliers at any agreed-upon prices. Many laws and regulations stand in exception to such a statement—minimum-wage laws, regulations for quality standards in foods and drugs, resale-price-maintenance laws, and regulations covering transactions in stocks and bonds, for example. Practitioners in many fields where standards of ability and cleanliness are important to the general welfare must be licensed. But with these exceptions, such freedoms do exist; they are the general rule and not the exception. Although barbershops, dairies, and restaurants must be licensed, anyone is free to enter these businesses if he qualifies.

As a result of these freedoms, a free market can exist. It cannot exist where the government decides what shall be produced, by whom, for whom, and at what prices.

Personal freedom extends to the disposition of income earned in business or as wages. The government does not intervene, except to impose taxes for the maintenance of government services. People are assumed capable of spending their incomes in the manner that provides them with the greatest satisfaction and of earning these incomes where there is the greatest net advantage. Thus another characteristic of the market economy is *competition*—the freedom to compete for occupations and to compete for sales in the search for income. It has been assumed that if producers are free to compete and if consumers can buy what they want and refuse other things, the result will be maximum production of the most-wanted goods and services. In the American political system it is a function of government to protect these individual rights, not to restrict them.

Control of Competition

One of the important roles of government in the economy stems from the fact that competition may not always work in a beneficial manner. On the one hand, it is sometimes necessary to maintain competition because otherwise monopolies would arise and, on the other hand, it is sometimes necessary to regulate competition so that it does not have undesirable results. When a group of businessmen, laborers, or perhaps professional persons is able to interfere with the allocation of resources and incomes by preventing the free movement of prices, a demand for governmental intervention usually arises.

The ideal of a free society rests on the belief that freedoms lead to a high degree of cooperation, even if the cooperation is unconscious and unplanned. The maintenance of free and open competition is looked upon as the way in which to assure opportunity and fairness for all. But competition may be thwarted by the rise of monopoly and, when competition is free, it may work hardships on some who are unable to compete effectively. In either case, social objectives may not be attained without governmental interference in the operation of the economy.

The basic law intended to maintain competition is the Sherman Act of 1890, often called the Sherman Antitrust Act. This act was passed to combat various combinations of businesses and railroad companies, which often used the legal device of depositing voting stock of previously competing companies with a trustee in order to accomplish the combination. This law declared illegal "every contract, combination . . . or conspiracy in restraint of foreign or domestic commerce" and provided for damages to injured parties. Difficulties of interpretation and application led to additional legislation, the Clayton Act and the Federal Trade Commission Act, in 1914. The Clayton Act made certain practices illegal if their effect was to lessen competition, such as a seller's requiring a distributor or dealer to carry a full line of his products as a condition of carrying any of his products. The Federal Trade Commission was established to police industry practices such as this and to prevent so-called unfair methods of competition.

These laws and their application are examined in Chapter 17. It may be said here that in recent years much of the legal action brought against companies has dealt with collusion over prices and with mergers. A few years ago several prominent firms in the electrical machinery industry were fined and some executives given jail sentences for conspiring to fix prices. Many mergers have been prevented or later broken up as a result of suits brought by the Department of Justice. In the area of defining unfair methods of competition may be mentioned the famous 1911 case involving the old Standard Oil Company, in which rebates (kickbacks) to large buyers were condemned, and more recent cases which limit the discounts that suppliers may grant chain stores. The Food and Drug Act, passed in 1906, sets up standards for foods sold in interstate commerce and requires that drugs be adequately tested and their quality controlled before they can be marketed.

Often advances brought about by new technologies require government to be the referee in matters of competition. The development of railroad transportation brought problems of regulating rates, which were deemed too low where roads competed with each other and too high where they had local monopolies. Air routes must be allocated among the various airlines. When radio and television were invented, there had to be some means of distributing the available wavelengths and channels. Who can provide microwave facilities is another problem for regulation. Regulation has also arisen where competition alone could not prevent exploitation. After the 1930s most states regulated the business of making small loans to consumers, and in 1968 a federal law began to require more complete disclosure of loan terms. Minimum-wage and other fair employment practice legislation reflects the decision that completely free competition in labor markets is undesirable.

It should be noted that a substantial number of the members of an industry often want government regulation to protect them from the unethical practices of competitors. Legislation requiring honest labeling is a common example. The honest manufacturer of all-wool sweaters, as well as the public, is handicapped if competitors can label part-wool sweaters as all-wool. Laws against murder do not come about because all or most people are murderers, and the same is true of laws regulating business practice.

Regulation of Monopoly

Monopoly, in which a single company controls the entire supply of a commodity, is rare, but often one company controls enough of the total supply to be able to affect the price. Thus, legal regulation of monopoly usually takes the form of preventing or regulating competitive practices that distort the operation of a free market for a good or service, as has been noted previously. In some industries the technology of production and the size of the market make a monopoly more efficient than numerous smaller producers. When these industries produce a commodity generally considered an essential one, they may be given the status of public utilities.

The characteristics of a *public utility* are that the product is essential, competition among several producers would inconvenience the public, and large amounts of fixed investment are necessary for economical production. To be economical, the investment in plant and equipment may require large sales, and if the market were divided among several producers, none of them could attain an economical level of output. For these reasons, such industries are also called *natural monopolies.* For example, telephone service, electric light and power, and gas are considered highly essential. Great inconvenience could be caused if several competing companies had to tear up streets in order to lay cables or mains or if they each erected poles to carry wires. In a given local market, a single firm can probably supply the service more economically than could several. Much of the equipment would be duplicative if more than one firm supplied it. In addition to the industries mentioned, water companies, bus and rapid-transit services, and other forms of local transportation share these characteristics.

If there were several competitors in such an industry as one of those just named, each would be led to cut its rates in order to expand its market. Investment in some of the companies would tend to become worthless, and surviving companies would find themselves in a monopolistic position. Thus, competition could be destructive and inconvenient to the customers and perhaps lead to monopoly anyway. Consequently, public utilities are granted a monopoly to begin with, but government sets up standards of service and performance and oversees the rates charged.

The objectives of granting a monopoly to a public utility are that the single supplier will operate with reasonable efficiency, that the service will be available to all, that different users will pay rates that are not discriminatory, and that the monopoly will be able to earn a fair return on the investment. Each of these criteria leads to difficulties of interpretation and application. For example, the general rule that the utility should

earn a fair return cannot imply that it may do so even if operated ineffi-
ciently. The availability of the service to all means that a bus company
must operate some buses on routes at times when the individual run
is unprofitable and that a telephone company must extend its lines into
sparsely populated areas. Establishment of a rate of return that can be
defended as fair is difficult and complicated. However, a general rule
has arisen that a rate which allows the utility to attract needed investment
funds is adequate. Measuring the investment base on which the return
is allowed is also controversial, as a case can be made for using prudent
original cost, cost to reproduce the plant today, cost to replace the plant,
original cost less depreciation, or others.

Distribution of Income

The federal government has long had some concern with the way in
which income and wealth are distributed. For example, the distribution
of free land in the West, minimum-wage laws, support for land-grant
colleges, programs to support farm prices, and many other measures
have been concerned at least partly with this objective. The personal
income tax is, of course, an important determinant of *disposable income.*
In recent years, however, the interest in establishing a minimum income,
reflecting social standards of equity, has become much greater. Several
large federal programs aimed at improving earning ability, education,
housing, and opportunities for the poor have been adopted. There is
considerable public debate, not so much about whether any measures
should be taken, as about which measures may be the most effective.
For example, there are supporters of family income allowances, while
others propose a *negative income tax* under which the government would
pay those whose earned income fell below certain standards. Some of
these proposals are examined in Chapter 19, which deals with poverty
and economic welfare.

The question of what is a satisfactory distribution of income cannot be
settled by economic principles alone. Economics, sociology, political
science, and history all contribute to the standards that become generally
accepted. It seems clear that there is very little support for trying to make
all incomes equal, and at the same time there is general support for the
idea that free markets do not distribute incomes equitably, perhaps
mainly because all people do not start out with equal opportunity. One
of the principal considerations is the extent to which inequality of income
provides incentives for those who are capable of earning high incomes
to do so and, in the process, for them to benefit society through their
greater productivity.

THE INDUSTRIAL STRUCTURE

American industries differ in structure from each other in several
characteristic ways. Some of the ways in which one industry differs from
another are in the typical legal organization of its firms (whether they are
individual proprietorships, partnerships, or corporations), the extent of
concentration of output in a few large companies, and the arrangements
made for marketing products. An important characteristic, because it
influences the market behavior of the industry, is the degree of concentration of total output in a few companies. Measuring the degree of concen-

Table 2-1
Number and Size of Farms, 1964

Size in Acres	Number	Percent	Farmland (Percent)	Cropland (Percent)
Under 10	183,000	5.8	0.1	0.1
10 to 49	637,000	20.2	1.6	2.1
50 to 99	542,000	17.2	3.6	4.6
100 to 179	633,000	20.0	7.8	12.0
180 to 259	355,000	11.2	6.9	11.8
260 to 499	451,000	14.3	14.4	25.1
500 to 999	210,000	6.6	13.0	19.9
1,000 and over	145,000	4.6	52.6	24.3

Source: U.S. Bureau of the Census, *Statistical Abstract of the United States*, 1969, p. 592.

tration is not as easy as might be supposed because an industry, and even the product, may be defined in different ways. During World War II, the Office of Price Administration found that it was impossible to write price regulations for industries because many companies could be classified in any one of several industries. An important product for one company might be a minor product for another. General Electric, for example, can be classified as being in the electrical machinery industry, the consumer appliance industry, or several others. Even selecting the product of an industry can be complicated: a given industry might be considered those companies producing cornflakes, processed foods, cereals, or cold cereals, for example.

Concentration of Output

Industries have been classified in various groups and subgroups by the United States Department of Commerce. Data have been collected which show the extent to which a few companies in an industry share total assets, invested capital, sales, or profits. Using any of these criteria, one finds that the American economy is characterized by having relatively few very large firms and literally thousands of smaller ones. About 1 percent of the 1.5 million corporations in the United States control about 75 percent of all the assets. The degree to which concentration exists varies widely from industry to industry.

Agriculture is a standard example of small-scale business operations, yet farmland is increasingly concentrated in larger and fewer farms. The number of farms declined by more than 50 percent between 1940 and 1968, from over 6 million to about 3 million. Not all the decline represented a shift to more concentrated farm ownership because farms also disappear when land is used for urban expansion and highways. The distribution of farms by size in 1964 is shown in Table 2-1.[2] It may be noted that farms of 1,000 acres or more, although only 4.6 percent of the farms, contained over half of all farmland. Farms smaller than 100 acres consti-

---

[2] These kinds of data become available with some delay, and the 1964 figures are the latest released.

tuted 43 percent of all farms. Sales from farms naturally show similar relationships. Only about 5 percent of total sales came from farms with annual sales of $2,500 to $4,999, but 85 percent came from farms with sales in excess of $10,000. Roughly half of the latter figure came from farms with sales in excess of $40,000. Farming has become big business for some operators, as is indicated by the fact that 2 percent of the farms owned 25 percent of the value of all farmland and buildings. Each of these farms was worth $200,000 or more, and the average value was about $500,000. The disparity is shown by the average value of all farms, about $50,000, and the average value of $7,000 for the smallest 40 percent of all farms.

The amount of land devoted to farming has remained relatively constant since 1935, but the average size of farms has risen from 155 acres to 369 acres. Between 1935 and the present, the population on farms has declined from 32.2 million to about 10.8 million. About a third as many people are producing a larger volume of farm products because of the development of new methods and the greater use of capital. Total assets of farms have approached $300 billion in value.

These assets are rather small, however, in relation to those of some of the giants of the industrial world. Each year *Fortune* magazine publishes lists of the largest companies in manufacturing, merchandising, transportation, other utilities, banking, and insurance.[3] The tabulation shows the sales, assets, net worth, net income, and number of employees of the largest companies. In 1969 the 10 largest industrial companies were:

	Sales	Assets
	(Millions of Dollars)	
General Motors	$24,295	$14,820
Standard Oil (New Jersey)	14,930	17,538
Ford	14,756	9,199
General Electric	8,448	6,007
International Business Machines	7,197	7,390
Chrysler	7,052	4,688
Mobil Oil	6,621	7,163
Texaco	5,868	9,282
International Tel. and Tel.	5,475	5,193
Gulf Oil	4,953	8,105

The importance of automobiles and petroleum products in the American economy is highlighted by the names of these companies. Seven of the largest companies produce either automobiles or petroleum products; another, General Electric, counts both of these industries as major customers.

A clue to the nature of different industries is suggested by the relationship of sales to assets. It may be seen that each of the three largest automobile manufacturers needs less than a dollar's worth of assets to produce a dollar of sales, while each of the four petroleum companies needs more than a dollar's worth of assets for each dollar of sales, as does IBM. These companies, although the largest, are not necessarily the

[3] *Fortune,* May 15, 1970, p. 182 ff.

most profitable in terms of return on invested capital; often a company that has succeeded in carving out a rather special market wins this honor. In 1969, Skyline Corporation (mobile homes) earned the highest rate on invested capital, 40.9 percent, and Avon Products earned 35.8 percent.

The importance of invested capital in increasing the productivity of employees is suggested by additional figures relative to the largest 500 companies. The assets per employee ranged from $98,400 typical in petroleum refining to $10,200 in apparel and averaged $21,545. In other words, for each job in these companies, on the average, someone had invested over $21,500. There is a similar variation in the amount of sales per employee—from $82,555 in petroleum refining to $15,799 in apparel. Obviously, the amount of sales per employee allows for covering far more costs of capital equipment in petroleum refining than in the apparel industries. In 1969, the 500 largest companies made about two-thirds of all industrial sales and about three-fourths of all industrial profits. One hundred fifteen companies each had sales greater than a billion dollars, and the 500 companies combined had sales of $444.7 billion.

In merchandising, the largest company is Sears, Roebuck and Co., with sales in 1969 of $8.9 billion; the Great Atlantic & Pacific Tea Company had $5.7 billion. The next three include two other grocery chains, Safeway Stores and Kroger, and a general retail chain, J. C. Penney. The largest transportation company is the Penn Central Railroad, with operating revenues of $2.2 billion; United Air Lines was second with $1.5 billion of operating revenues. Next were Southern Pacific, Trans World Airlines, and Pan American World Airways. But the largest of all companies is American Telephone and Telegraph, which had assets of about $43.9 billion at the end of 1969 and annual operating revenues of about a third as much. Other large utilities are Consolidated Edison (New York) and Pacific Gas and Electric (San Francisco).

The American economy is also served by several large financial institutions. The largest life insurance companies are Prudential Life Insurance Company and Metropolitan Life Insurance Company, both with more than $25 billion in assets. Their size is indicated by the fact that the fiftieth largest insurance company had assets of $451 million in 1969. The fifty largest companies had nearly $1 trillion of life insurance in force, and about half of this total was held by the five largest companies. Commercial banking is also characterized by a few very large banks, a few hundred medium-sized banks, and several thousand small banks. The largest bank, the Bank of America (San Francisco), has over $25 billion in assets. Four of the five largest banks are located in New York City. The five largest banks hold about 16 percent of all commercial bank assets and the fifty largest hold about 40 percent.

Degrees of Concentration

It is natural that, in industries containing very large companies, there are only a few of them. A typical pattern in American manufacturing is that a relatively few companies produce the bulk of the output. Sometimes, a rather large number share the remainder. In the manufacture of such products as automobiles, tin cans, cigarettes, electrical machinery, and many others, advantages in production or marketing or both have led to the growth of large firms. Sometimes the growth has been internal, and sometimes it has resulted from merger. In some other industries, good examples of which are the ladies' garment industry, contract construction, and service industries such as the laundry industry, either the advantages of size are not so great or small firms have offsetting advantages. In these fields many small firms are the typical pattern.

The degree to which concentration is deemed to exist depends much on how the product is defined. One Senate investigation found that four companies produced 98 percent of the "passenger cars" in 1954, but a similar study made by the Bureau of the Census found that four companies produced 75 percent of the "motor vehicles and parts." Characteristics of the product and of the industry often affect the degree of concentration. The necessity of being near both supplies and customers keeps printing companies and the manufacturers of paperboard boxes, for example, from concentrating production in a few plants. Advantages in advertising and marketing cigarettes and detergents, however, lead to large plants and few companies. In the steel, petroleum, and automobile industries, the large capital investment required before a company can compete effectively makes it virtually impossible for small companies to get started. In fact, some of the "small" automobile companies, which have had difficulty competing with the three largest companies, would be considered large in many other industries.

THE BUSINESS FIRM

In an economy that relies on market forces to allocate resources, some sort of organization must exist for the purpose of bringing together the factors of production that produce the goods and then selling them. The business firm is such an organization. It is the means by which an entrepreneur collects capital, labor, and land, utilizes their services, and produces goods or services. His intent is to make a profit by producing something the public will value more highly than the resources he uses — something that will sell for more than it costs.

The process of renting or buying land, hiring labor, and investing one's own or borrowed capital funds involves entering into contracts and agreements. Incentives or rewards must be offered to attract each factor of production to the enterprise. Some may be offered fixed returns, such as a stated amount of rent offered to the owner of land. Others may be offered a share in the prospective profits. Thus arises a group of property rights in the enterprise. How the risks, control, and income of a business are to be shared must be understood by the participants. As a result, different legal forms of business enterprise have been developed.

Individual Proprietorship

In most states an individual may choose to enter a business without any legal formalities. While there may be qualifications to be met, these are not limitations on the type of legal organization of the business. In other words, the individual can be the business firm simply by setting himself up in business. Many housepainting businesses, repair shops, small retail stores, and other businesses are owned, controlled, and managed by individuals. Such a business is an individual, or sole, _proprietorship_. The individual is solely responsible for the debts incurred by the business enterprise, as he is for his personal debts, and he is the sole recipient of the net profits of the enterprise after meeting all its current costs.

The sole proprietor can make his own decisions and has no associates with whom agreements must be reached. While he assumes all the risks, he also assumes all the control and receives all the net income.[4] The sole proprietorship has disadvantages, however, as a business enterprise of any large size. One person may be unable to raise as much capital as is warranted by the business unless he takes in additional investors, not as creditors but as joint owners. Even if he is able to provide sufficient funds, the risk may become excessive. The individual proprietor has *unlimited liability* in that he is responsible for the business debts. His liability is not limited to the assets used in the business but extends to all his property.

Partnership

The partnership arrangement alleviates one of the problems of the individual proprietorship by permitting a larger aggregation of capital. A partnership is a voluntary association of two or more persons. Thus it involves questions of the relationships among the partners and of the relationships of the partners to the public. The partners must decide how much each invests, what functions each performs, how profits are to be shared, and whether any of them assume any unusual risks. These agreements, along with those relating to the purpose of the association, how long it shall last, and how it may be dissolved, are part of the partnership contract or agreement. Such a contract should obviously be in writing, but it is usually binding even if it is not.

To some, the legal fact that each partner is an agent of the partnership in dealing with the public can be a disadvantage. Unless the partners have confidence in each other, there is a risk that one partner can commit the group to an action they would not approve. Each partner is a *general agent* of the business firm.[5]

A partnership does not avoid the difficulty of unlimited liability. Each partner is responsible for all the debts of the partnership. The partnership agreement may fix this responsibility among the partners, but it is not binding on the public. For example, suppose that Mr. Abbott, Mr. Brown, and Mr. Chase operate as a partnership. If Mr. Dunne, a creditor, cannot collect the debt from the partnership, he may take legal action against any one of the three partners, say Mr. Abbott. If the partners' agreement calls for sharing losses equally, Mr. Abbott may in turn try to collect from his partners.

Corporation

The advantages of the corporate form of business enterprise in raising large amounts of capital and in making possible participation in huge business ventures without the assumption of unlimited risks have made it

---

[4] The sole proprietor may enter into agreements that limit his control and disposition of business income in order to limit the risks of others, such as lenders of funds. For example, in order to obtain a business loan, he may agree not to take more than a stated income from the business and to invest the remainder, or he may agree to refrain from obtaining additional loans without the approval of the lender.

[5] It is possible for a partnership agreement to include *limited partners,* who invest in the enterprise for a return but are strictly barred from participating otherwise.

the most important type of business organization. In some lines of business, such as finance, mining, and public utilities, it is virtually the only type in existence.

The corporation differs from the other forms of organization already described by having a legal existence of its own. The sole proprietorship and the partnership exist only as their owners do. If a partner dies, the partnership automatically ends and must be re-formed if the remaining partners wish, with or without a new partner.[6] The corporation is said to be an artificial being or legal person and to exist "only in contemplation of law." In the eyes of the law, then, a corporation is a person and can, therefore, enter into contracts, buy, sell, sue and be sued, and do other things that a human person can legally do in business. Its existence does not depend on that of its owners; it is brought into existence by being granted a charter by the state. The owners may transfer their ownership to others without affecting the life of the corporation.

An important difference for the individual investor is that the owners of a corporation have no additional personal liability, beyond their investment, for the corporation's debts. If the original *shares of stock* issued by the corporation are fully paid for, the original owner may lose his entire investment if the corporation fails, but he is not liable for additional loss. Subsequent owners are in the same position. The liability of the corporation for its own debts is, of course, unlimited.

Another advantage of the corporate form, especially with respect to very large businesses, is that management may be delegated to hired managers. The president of a corporation is one of its employees; he may or may not be a significant owner. In many small enterprises the stockholders elect themselves as directors who, in turn, select management, which may be themselves. But in the giant corporations, representing investments of billions of dollars, top management seldom owns more than a tiny percentage of the total stock outstanding.

Since the corporation is a separate entity, it is subject to the income tax—the corporate income tax. This may be an advantage or a disadvantage under differing circumstances. Partnership income, for example, is taxed to the individual partners as part of their personal income, but it is not subject first to a "partnership income tax." By meeting certain tests, some small business corporations may elect to be taxed as partnerships; that is, they can avoid the corporate tax by considering all the corporate income taxable to the owners, whether they leave it in the business or take it as current income.

Extent of Corporate Form

Except in farming, contract construction, some services, and the professions, the corporation is the dominant form of business enterprise and is used by large firms in these occupations as well. In recent years, Treasury estimates based on tax returns place the number of sole proprietorships at about 9 million, with business receipts of over $250 billion. Partnerships are a little less than 1 million, with receipts of about $100 billion. There are about 1.5 million corporations, with receipts of over $1

---

[6] The reason for this choice is that a person is considered to have the right *not* to be a partner of someone else; a new partner cannot therefore simply buy the interest of an existing partner without the consent of all partners.

trillion. It is clear from this huge number of companies that it would be a mistake to equate corporations with big business; there are many thousands of small businesses organized as corporations. A study made by the New York Stock Exchange in 1965 found that only 6,724 corporations were *publicly held,* defined as having shares of stock traded on a national exchange or otherwise available to the public and held by at least 300 stockholders of record. A Treasury study found that in the early 1960s 40 percent of American corporations were controlled by individual persons each of whom owned more than 50 percent of his company's stock.[7]

About two-thirds of the publicly held companies have shares which are traded *over-the-counter* rather than on organized exchanges, but larger companies' shares are usually listed on the New York, the American, or a regional exchange. The proportion of the population owning corporate stock has been rising steadily, but most people still are not stockholders. The New York Stock Exchange estimated that in 1965, 20 million persons, in 13 million families, owned stock in publicly held corporations. The number of stockholders was only about 7 million in 1952. Women stockholders outnumber men by a small margin. Shareholders' average annual household income in 1965 was $9,500, and their total holdings exceeded $400 billion.

THE LABOR FORCE

A visitor to Earth from another planet would undoubtedly be interested in how people earn their living. A survey of the composition and organization of the labor force provides much information about the American economy. The labor force is considered those persons aged sixteen or older who are able and willing to work and are either employed or seeking employment.

Employment in Major Industries

The total population of the United States approximated 203 million at the beginning of 1970. About 139 million of those not living in institutions were sixteen years old or older. The total labor force consisted of almost 85 million persons, including 3.4 million in the Armed Forces.[8] Of the 81.4 million persons in the civilian labor force, 75.8 million were employed in nonagricultural occupations and 3.0 million in agriculture, leaving 2.6 million unemployed, or about 3.2 percent of the total. As other occupations have grown in relative importance, agricultural employment has declined from nearly 20 percent of the total in 1930 to less than 5 percent.

Figure 2-1 shows broad trends in the major categories of employment over the last several decades. Employment in nonindustrial categories has become larger than that in manufacturing, where employment has been fairly stable since about 1950. Employment has risen in retail and wholesale trade, finance, services, and government. Output in agriculture and manufacturing has continued to rise because of greater productivity per worker.

Over a longer span of time, as the American economy has developed, the labor force has shifted considerably among occupations. During the

[7] *Wall Street Journal,* Sept. 11, 1968, p. 1.

[8] *Economic Report of the President,* February, 1970, p. 202.

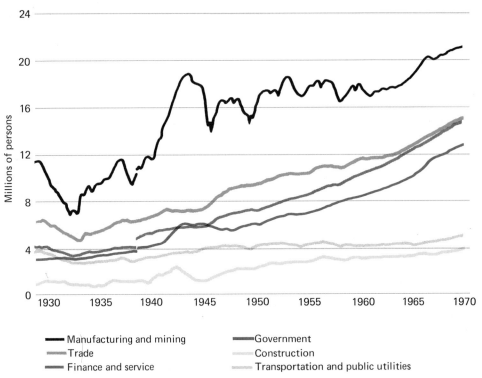

Figure 2-1. Components of nonagricultural employment, 1929–1970.   Source: *Federal Reserve Historical Chart Book,* 1969, p. 81; *Federal Reserve Monthly Chart Book,* April, 1970, p. 56.

twentieth century the number of workers in agriculture has declined by about 60 percent and in mining by about 15 percent. In construction, services, manufacturing, and trade, employment has tripled, quadrupled, or more. Employment in government has increased about tenfold since 1899. These shifts reflect the development of the economy in new directions as investment, new products and services, and employment have followed suit.

Composition of the Labor Force

The labor force can be described in many ways, including its distribution by sex and age, the income of its members, and whether it is unionized. Incomes are discussed in later chapters. In 1967, approximately 23 percent of the civilian labor force was unionized—about 19 million workers—and these constituted nearly 30 percent of nonagricultural employment. The composition of the labor force by sex and age is shown in Table 2-2.

Most people find it necessary to work for a living, being either employed by others or self-employed. The proportion of the male population in the labor force is nearly 80 percent and is as high as 95 percent for those from 25 to 54. The proportion drops off sharply at age 65, after which less than a third are in the labor force. The highest proportions of women in the labor force occur at age 18 or 19, when it is 50 percent, and from 45

Table 2-2
Age and Sex of the Labor Force, 1968
(Millions)

Age in Years	Males	Females	Total
16 and 17	1.7	1.1	2.8
18 and 19	2.5	1.8	4.3
20 to 24	6.7	4.3	11.0
25 to 34	11.4	5.1	16.5
35 to 44	11.1	5.9	17.0
45 to 54	10.4	6.1	16.5
55 to 64	7.0	3.9	10.9
65 and over	2.2	1.0	3.2

Source: U.S. Department of Labor, *Handbook of Labor Statistics*, 1969, p. 25.

to 54, when it is 52 percent. About two-fifths of the women in the population are in the labor force, and a bit more than half of these are single. It is estimated that about 1 worker in 20 holds a second job.

Table 2-3 presents broad occupational categories and illustrates the widely known fact that men and women are not equally at home in all occupations. The percentage of employed women in some occupations is considerably higher than that of men, and in others much less.

Table 2-3
Occupational Groupings of the Labor Force, 1968

Occupation	Percentage of Males	Percentage of Females	Percentage of Total
Professional, technical, and kindred workers	13.2	13.6	13.3
Farmers and farm managers	3.7	.3	2.5
Managers and proprietors	13.3	4.4	10.0
Clerical and kindred workers	7.1	33.3	16.8
Salespeople	5.6	6.9	6.1
Craftsmen and foremen	20.1	1.2	13.1
Operatives	20.3	15.8	18.6
Private household workers	.1	6.1	2.3
Service workers	6.9	15.9	10.2
Farm laborers	2.2	1.8	2.1
Other laborers	7.5	.5	4.9
Total	100.0	100.0	100.0

Source: U.S. Department of Labor, *Handbook of Labor Statistics*, 1969, p. 33.

SUMMARY

This chapter has described a variety of important characteristics of the American economy. Together, these characteristics make the economy one of free enterprise, modified by many governmental activities and regulations. Many of these characteristics can be traced to their origins in the Industrial Revolution, especially in Great Britain. But they have been modified by American conditions and preferences, and in the process the American economy has become considerably more productive than the older ones of Europe.

The broad outlines of the industrial structure have been sketched, including the extensive use of capital and the predominance of the corporation. The roles of the government in promoting competition and regulating monopoly, in protecting consumers and wage earners from some results of free competition, and in other activities have been noted. Brief attention has been given to the distribution of incomes, to characteristics of the labor force, and to occupational groupings of the population. All these points merit greater consideration and are discussed further in following chapters.

Economic Terms for Review

Industrial Revolution	public utility
interchangeable parts	concentration
mass production	proprietorship
division of labor	partnership
primary commodities	corporation
laissez-faire	shares of stock
monopoly	labor force

Questions for Review

1. What did Eli Whitney contribute to the development of industry? How is this development important?
2. What are some of the gains from division of labor?
3. What public benefits are supposed to flow from free competition? Why is competition sometimes restricted by government?
4. Show how the manner in which a market economy allocates resources to production of various goods is illustrated by the decline in the number of farmers. Is the output of farm products less than it was in 1920?
5. Compare the liability for debts of a (a) sole proprietor, (b) corporation, and (c) stockholder of a corporation.
6. What is a laissez-faire policy?
7. Why are many small businesses corporations?

Questions for Analysis

1. How did the Industrial Revolution change (a) methods of production, (b) markets, (c) the position of labor, and (d) attitudes toward government?

2. Do you think that the right to hold private property implies the right to bequeath property to others at death? the right to inherit property? Can you think of any reasons why these rights arose? (Consider agricultural societies.)

3. What are the characteristics that make an industry a public utility? Why are milk production and banking not public utilities?

4. What would be some of the difficulties if all incomes were made equal? if they were left to depend completely on market forces?

5. Why are most manufacturing companies corporations and most farms not?

6. Can you think of reasons why large steel companies usually control their sources of iron ore but large milling companies do not control farms? (How do production and marketing of ore and wheat differ?)

Case for Decision

John Adams is a young man who, until two years ago, was employed by an electronics firm. During this employment he spent much of his spare time developing a new type of connector for wires used in electronic equipment. His employer was not interested in producing this component, but he did express interest in using it if it were on the market. He encouraged Adams to set up a small shop for himself.

Adams had about $10,000 that he and his wife had saved. His father agreed to lend him $10,000 for a long period. Several of Adams' friends at the electronics company were willing to lend him a total of $10,000 more. Thus Adams could command $30,000 of capital. Of this amount, $24,000 was needed for the purchase of equipment, material, and supplies. At relatively small expense, his garage could be converted to a shop.

Adams was more fortunate than many owners of new businesses because in a few months he was selling enough conductors to be able to produce them profitably. However, he was unable to withdraw much income from the business because he found that as the business grew he had to invest more in accounts receivable and inventories of materials and finished connectors. Accounts receivable rose because it is customary in this line of business to grant purchasers thirty days in which to pay for their orders. In any month, therefore, Adams was collecting cash for the previous month's sales, which were less than the current month's sales. His expenses each month were for that month's sales and for connectors to go into inventory for future sales. As his sales increased, he needed larger inventories, too. Even though each month's sales produced a profit, most of this profit had to be invested in these larger accounts receivable and inventories.

In view of the fact that $30,000 was invested in the business by Adams and his long-term creditors, the local commercial bank agreed to lend him the funds he needed for materials as production rose. The maximum the bank would lend at any one time was $30,000.

At the present time Adams faces several problems. He knows of several additional accounts he could get if he had additional manufacturing capacity. This would require more space, equipment, and employees to operate the equipment. The space and equipment would require investment of funds in advance of any sales, and the employees would have to be paid before Adams would begin collecting for the additional sales. He would also have to buy materials for them to use. His financial condition at present is shown by his balance sheet:

Adams Connector Company

John Adams, Owner

Assets		Liabilities	
Cash	$ 16,000	Note payable to bank	$ 30,000
Accounts receivable	24,000	Accounts payable to suppliers	26,000
Inventories	20,000	Accruals °	6,000
Equipment	36,000	Long-term loans	20,000
Other assets	4,000	*Owner's Equity*	
Total	$100,000	John Adams, capital	18,000
		Total	$100,000

° Accruals are obligations that accumulate (accrue) over time and will become payable on future dates. For example, wages accrue each day until paid and the property tax on plant and equipment accrues similarly.

This balance sheet shows the assets that have been accumulated in the business as of the present time and also the debts, or liabilities. The assets exceed the liabilities by $18,000, which is Adams' *equity*, or value of his ownership of the business. Since he originally invested $10,000, the books show that he has "plowed back" $8,000 of profits since the business began.

Adams has been discussing the formation of a partnership with two friends and his father-in-law. All three are willing to join on the following basis: Bill Brown, now working at the electronics company, would contribute a recently inherited plot of land, on which a shop could be built. The property is worth approximately $30,000. Charles Cox, in the building materials business, would contribute $10,000 in cash and $20,000 worth of building materials for the new shop. Profits of the partnership would be figured after a salary of $12,000 for Adams and one of $10,000 for Brown, who would leave his present job. These three men agree to share profits and losses equally and to provide a share one-third as large to the father-in-law in return for his changing his loan to a partnership contribution; he would not be active in the business but a silent partner.

The prospective partners have discussed thoroughly the fairness of this split. In effect, the profits (or losses) after the two salaries are paid would be split into tenths, with each major partner having three tenths and the silent partner one tenth. Brown and Cox are making the largest capital contributions, but Adams founded the company and has valuable contacts and know-how.

Should Adams proceed with forming the partnership? What are the risks and prospective gains for each of the four partners? What would be the advantages and disadvantages of forming a corporation, with each prospective partner buying stock instead of making a capital contribution? Would you expect the commercial bank to be willing to lend larger amounts to finance current production if the partnership is formed?

Part 2
Markets and Prices

3
Market Prices

There is probably no more basic or central problem in all of economics than that of explaining the different values of things. Philosophers have been intrigued by the fact that an unnecessary good, such as a diamond, may have a very high price while a necessary one, such as a loaf of bread, may be rather cheap. The economic value of the diamond is many times that of the loaf of bread, yet this fact seems to conflict with other standards of value applied to diamonds and bread. To call the diamond a luxury and the bread a necessity seems to imply that the former should be less valuable.

ECONOMIC VALUE

When the word *value* is used in economics, it means simply the amount of some other good for which a good would exchange in a free market. Value is related to exchange; it is not inherent. If a ton of coal would exchange for a pair of shoes, the value of a ton of coal is a pair of shoes or, in more precise language, the ton of coal and the pair of shoes have the same value. If the ton of coal would also exchange for a coat, it would follow that a ton of coal, a pair of shoes, and a coat are all of equal value.

Prices

It is not customary in modern society for goods to be traded for other goods. Usually, goods are sold for money and money is used to purchase goods. Purchase and sale, however, are simply a convenient means by which goods and services are exchanged for each other. The farmer sells his wheat or his hogs and buys numerous other things; the worker sells his labor for wages and also buys whatever he chooses with his money. The farmer is interested in obtaining as high a price as possible for his wheat and in paying as low prices as possible for what he buys. This is the same as saying that he wants to obtain as many other goods as he can in exchange for his wheat.

When one sells his output or his labor for money, he uses money in two ways. In the first place, it is the *medium of exchange* by which he disposes of what he sells and purchases what he buys. In the second place, money is a standard, or *measure of values,* which permits him to compare the values of many items.[1] The farmer does not need to bear in mind all the possible ratios of value that might interest him—he does not need to recall the value of a bushel of wheat in terms of neckties, bread, gasoline, newspaper subscriptions, college tuition, aspirin, television

---

[1] The functions of money are described more fully in Chapter 11.

sets, and so on without limit, because it is much easier to compare the *price* of a bushel of wheat with the prices of things he may want to buy.

Price is therefore merely the value of something in terms of the monetary unit, the dollar in the United States. If the price of wheat is $3 per bushel and the price of a pair of shoes is $15, the value of the shoes happens to be equal to the value of five bushels of wheat.[2] If the value of wheat were to rise while the value of the shoes remained the same, this change would be reflected in changes in their prices. The price of wheat might rise to $5, in which case a bushel of wheat is worth a third of a pair of shoes rather than a fifth, or the price of the shoes might fall. The relative values of wheat and shoes might stay the same while the value of money itself changes. If the two prices, $3 and $15, both double, money itself would be worth half as much, as it would take $6 to buy a bushel of wheat and $30 to buy a pair of shoes.

Noneconomic Values

There are other meanings of the word value than the economic meaning. We speak of ethical, moral, educational, and many other kinds of value. There is this similarity: If we say that one college course has a greater educational value than another, we imply that in some sense it is better; likewise, if we say that a diamond has a greater value than a loaf of bread, we imply that it is somehow better or that one would normally rather have it.

It is often necessary to estimate values; these estimates are better called *valuations.* For example, accountants must estimate the values of the plant and equipment of a company in order to draw up its financial statements, and public utility commissions must *evaluate* the fixed assets of a utility company in order to measure whether its earnings are adequate. Tax assessors must estimate the values of houses in order to have a base on which to levy the tax rate. The homeowner wants this "value" to be lower than the price at which he could sell the house—its true value—in order to minimize his tax.

DEMAND

The paradox of the diamond and the loaf of bread is solved by the economist's law of supply and demand, with which this chapter is chiefly concerned. The confusion arises from thinking of bread in general, rather than of a loaf of bread. If society had to give up either bread or diamonds, it might well choose to get along without diamonds. But the real choice is always between more bread and more diamonds. Any given loaf of bread is not very important to society because many loaves are produced. To those who are interested in owning diamonds, a diamond is very scarce and, consequently, it is worth to them many loaves of bread.

Demand and Supply

All the forces that affect the value of anything can be cataloged into two groups, the demand for the article and the supply of it. The greater the demand, the more it tends to be worth; the greater the supply, the less

---

[2] Note that when stating either values or prices, it is necessary to state, or at least have in mind, the unit in which goods are traded. It would be meaningless to say that the price of wheat is $3 unless the unit—whether it be a pound, bushel, ton, or something else—is known.

each unit of it tends to be worth. The demand may be thought of as the amounts of other things people are willing to give up for given quantities of the article. The demand is therefore a sort of measure of how much people want the article. The supply may be thought of as the quantities that would be offered for sale at different prices. The supply is therefore largely determined, in the case of most articles, by costs of production. If not many units of something can be produced at a certain price, the supply of that article is less than would be the case if costs were lower. In order to understand why the price of something is low or high, then, it is necessary to understand why the demand is small or great and whether this demand meets a large or a small supply. If people generally want an article very much and that article is expensive to produce, there is a large demand and a small supply and only those who are willing to pay a high price can obtain the article in a free market. We shall analyze the factors that determine the demand for any given article first and then the factors that determine supply.

Law of Demand

It may be seen intuitively that, as a general rule, the more units of some-thing one already has, the less of other things he is willing to sacrifice to have more of it. If a housewife has at home a dozen oranges, she might purchase another dozen on her weekly shopping trip if the price is 75 cents, but if the price is $1 she might prefer to spend that dollar on other goods. However, if she had no oranges at home, she might buy a dozen at $1 because otherwise the family would have no oranges.

To state the situation a little differently, a man would pay, if it were necessary, a very high price for a suit of clothes if it were to be his only suit. If he finds that suits cost $100, he might buy only one. If, however, suits cost $75, he might buy two because a second suit would be worth as much to him, in terms of satisfaction, as would any other goods he could obtain for $75. A second suit would not be as important to him as would the other things he could obtain for $100. And if suits cost $50, he might buy three on the same line of reasoning—a third suit would give him at least as much satisfaction as would other things he could get for $50.[3]

A preliminary statement of the law of demand thus follows: The lower the price, the more units that can be sold.

Marginal Utility

Why does this general rule, that more of something can be sold at a lower price than at a higher price, hold true? People respond to price in this way primarily because of two characteristics. For one, they have psy-chological reactions to goods; they "want" them to varying degrees. A man virtually must have one suit if he is to work where it is customary to wear suits. He would say that he not only wants the suit but "needs" it. He probably wants a second suit very much so that he can appear in a different suit, have a fresh suit for social occasions, and for other reasons. Any person may also "want" suits particularly; he may obtain great

---

[3] We are here ignoring the possibility that there are different kinds of suits available at different prices. This possibility does not change the basic point being made; it merely opens up more options.

pleasure from appearing neat (or flashy, or whatever appeals to him) and simply from having several suits hanging in his closet. Another person may try to own as few suits as possible, in order to spend his income on other things. But in the aggregate, there are all these individual desires for suits—or oranges, shoes, gasoline, or any other example.

The second characteristic that affects people's buying behavior is the fact that incomes are limited. Virtually everyone could dispose of a larger income than he has, but in the long run he can spend only his income. One can consume more than his income in the short run by borrowing, but when he repays the borrowed money, he must curtail his consumption. So consumer behavior is determined partly by the fact that people have to spread their incomes over a limited amount of purchases. Presumably, they will attempt to maximize the satisfactions available from these purchases. This does not mean that everyone acts in a perfectly rational and calculating manner, figuring out the best way to spend his last penny, but it does mean that he avoids what he would consider foolish expenditures and he buys those things that would give him more, rather than less, pleasure or satisfaction.

This situation can be illustrated by the man deciding whether to have one, two, or three suits. It is clear that he would obtain more satisfaction from two suits than from one and more from three than from two. The total utility of two suits is greater than the total utility of one suit. The difference is the marginal utility of the second suit. Similarly the difference between the total utility of three suits and of two is the marginal utility of a third suit. Note that either of the two suits is the "second" suit; we are not saying that he already has one suit and then buys a second. We are saying that he is deciding between buying one or two suits, or between two or three. If he buys three, any one of them may be called the third or "last" suit. The point is, however, that three suits provide more satisfaction than do two, and this extra satisfaction is provided by having a third suit.

Unfortunately, there is no objective standard by which satisfactions can be measured. We can draw a hypothetical curve, as in Figure 3-1, to illustrate the point. On this graph, we indicate the satisfaction added by having one suit, by having two rather than one, and by having three rather

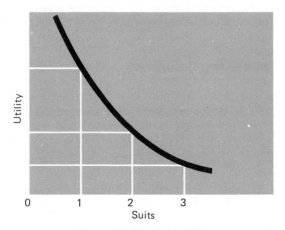

Figure 3-1. Marginal utility.

than two. All we can show is that one suit adds a great deal of satisfaction, a second adds somewhat less, and a third adds even less. Conceivably, some large number of suits would begin to add negative utility if the extra suits would be more of a nuisance and expense to store than they would add in terms of satisfaction.

Although it is impossible to measure satisfaction because it is inherent to the individual and, for all we know, differs greatly among people, the concept of marginal utility is useful in explaining consumer behavior. If we start from the assumption that people are going to try, at least in a rough way, to maximize the satisfactions from their limited incomes, the idea of marginal utility helps explain how they will select their purchases. Suppose that there are only two goods available in the market, food and clothing. Any consumer will attempt to buy as much of each as will make the marginal utilities of a dollar's worth equal. For example, if he has some of each, his next purchase will be that article which would add the most satisfaction — the one with the higher marginal utility. When he has enough food so that clothing would add more utility, he buys clothing; if he pushes the marginal utility of clothing below that of food, he next buys food. When he has disposed of all his income (or that part he has decided not to save), the marginal utilities of food and clothing should be equal. If the utility of another dollar's worth of food would add more than a dollar's worth of clothing he actually bought, he could have gained more total utility by buying that food rather than the clothing. The example may be expanded to any number of goods: The total satisfaction must be greatest if the marginal utilities are equal. Otherwise, the consumer would be able to buy more of one good that has a high marginal utility instead of another good that has a lower marginal utility.

Of course, this does not mean that the consumer buys equal quantities of all goods. The marginal utility of one good may be low if he has only a few units, while he must have many units of another to bring its marginal utility equally low.

Similarly, this does not mean that he spends equal amounts of money on all goods. The comparison each time is between the marginal utility and the price. It may be that clothing costs twice as much as food. In that case, a unit of clothing should provide at least twice the marginal utility of a unit of food or it would not be bought. If the consumer succeeds in maximizing the satisfactions available from his limited income (in the light of his own psychological preferences), he equates the marginal utilities of a dollar's worth of each good.

It should be clear that this explanation also helps explain the general rule with which we started. In the process of maximizing his satisfactions, the consumer is limited in his purchase of each good by its price. If its price were lower, it would pay to buy it when its marginal utility is less and, therefore, it would pay to buy a larger quantity. But if its price is higher, it must have a higher marginal utility to justify its purchase, and fewer can be purchased in competition with other goods on which the dollar could be spent.

The Indifference Curve

Because the concept of marginal utility is a useful one as a beginning explanation of the nature of demand and because it does have the disadvantage of not being measurable, economists have developed an alternative method of explaining why the general rule of demand holds good. In this method various combinations of goods that might be purchased are compared and put together in combinations that are equally good for the individual consumer. Since these are all equally satisfactory, the consumer is said to be *indifferent* as to which he has. This approach is best illustrated by an example that assumes there are only two alternative commodities, some unit of food and some unit of clothing.

From the discussion of marginal utility, it is probably apparent that a combination of a great deal of food and a small amount of clothing might be equal in total satisfaction with another combination of little food and much clothing. If we start with much food, we could add a great deal of satisfaction by adding a relatively small amount of clothing. To sacrifice this much satisfaction from food would require giving up a good deal of food. Thus we might have the following tabulation of combinations that would provide equal satisfactions:

Food	Clothing
20	1
13	2
9	3
7	4
6	5

This tabulation shows that the consumer who has 20 units of food and 1 unit of clothing would be equally well off if he gives up 7 units of food in order to add 1 more unit of clothing. To add still another unit of clothing, however, he would be willing to give up less food because he is starting from only 13 units; similarly, if he had 9 units of food and 3 of clothing, he would give up only 2 units of food to get another unit of clothing. To read the table in reverse, if he had 6 food units and 5 clothing units, he would give up a unit of clothing to get only 2 more food units, but if he had only 2 clothing units, he would not give up 1 for less than 7 food units.

The application of this idea of indifference combinations is that it explains consumer behavior in light of market prices, assuming limited income. Let us examine two possibilities: In one, food costs $1 and clothing $5, and in the other food costs $1 and clothing $3. The situation is illustrated in Table 3-1.

Table 3-1
Indifference Combinations

Units of Food	Units of Clothing	Food at $1	Clothing at $5	Total Cost	Food at $1	Clothing at $3	Total Cost
20	1	$20	$ 5	$25	$20	$ 3	$23
13	2	13	10	23	13	6	19
9	3	9	15	24	9	9	18
7	4	7	20	27	7	12	19
6	5	6	25	31	6	15	21

It is clear that when prices are introduced, it is no longer a matter of indifference which combination is selected. It is still true that any combination provides equal satisfaction, but the costs are different. If prices are $1 and $5, an equal satisfaction can be purchased for $23 as for various higher total costs, if 13 food units and 2 clothing units are selected. If prices are $1 and $3, an equal satisfaction can be purchased for $18 as for various higher costs, by purchasing 9 units of food and 3 of clothing. The significant point here is that with clothing relatively cheaper, more clothing is purchased. When a unit of clothing costs three times as much as a unit of food, the consumer selects 9 units of food and 3 of clothing, but when it is five times as expensive, he selects 13 units of food and 2 of clothing.

This relationship further illustrates that the consumer tries to equate the marginal utilities of each dollar of expenditure. It also illustrates the law of demand, as more clothing is bought at $3 than at $5. The law of demand is also illustrated by the drop in food sales, as food is now more expensive than it was in relation to clothing.

Figure 3-2 illustrates the indifference curve that results from plotting the figures in Table 3-1. Food is measured in units on the vertical axis, and clothing on the horizontal. Since each point on the curve yields equal satisfaction, there remains the question of how the consumer makes a choice of combinations of food and clothing. As we have just seen, he would normally choose the cheapest combination since they are all of equal satisfaction. If his income is exactly $23, there is only one combination that he can afford to buy when prices are $1 and $3, and if his income is larger, he can afford a little more of both—in other words he could move to a new indifference curve that lies to the right of the old curve.

If his income does happen to be $23, he can buy a variety of combinations. If he spends all his money on food, he can buy 23 units, but of course no clothing. Each unit of clothing he buys reduces his funds left for food by $5, or by 5 units. For example, if he buys 1 unit of clothing, he has $18 left for 18 units of food. Thus we can add a straight line to Figure 3-2, called the *consumption possibility curve*. This line shows the combinations the consumer can afford to buy. These combinations are com-

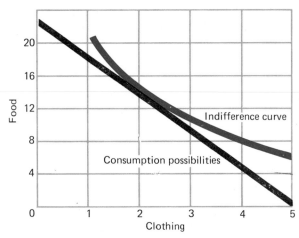

Figure 3-2. Indifference curve and consumption possibility curve.

Table 3-2
Indifference and Consumption Possibility Combinations

		Indifference Combinations			Consumption Possibilities	
Food in Units	Clothing in Units	Food at $1	Clothing at $5	Total Cost	Food at $1	Clothing at $5
					23	0
20	1	$20	$ 5	$25	18	1
13	2	13	10	23	13	2
9	3	9	15	24	8	3
7	4	7	20	27	3	4
6	5	6	25	31	0	5

pared with the indifference combinations in Table 3-2. Both the curve and the table show that there is only one indifference combination that the consumer can afford, 13 units of food and 2 units of clothing. The consumption possibilities show that if he spends his income in any other fashion, he will have fewer units of food than are necessary to provide as much satisfaction, with the given amount of clothing, as do 13 units of food and 2 units of clothing. Accordingly, the curve of consumption possibilities lies below the indifference curve except at this one combination.

Effects of Changes in Price

We have already seen, in Table 3-1, that a change in the price of clothing to $3 makes it possible for the consumer to purchase 9 units of food and 3 units of clothing — a combination as good as any other one listed — for $18 and that this total cost is less than the cost of any other combination. The drop in price is equivalent to an increase in income for the consumer. For the same $23 of income, he could have the same 13 food units and 2 clothing units as before, with $4 left over (since this combination now costs $19). But an equal satisfaction is now available for $18, so he adjusts his consumption to 9 food units and 3 clothing units. In this case, he has $5 left over, and he may increase his consumption of food, clothing, or both.

The effects of the change in price are therefore twofold. The _substitution effect_ takes place when the consumer substitutes an added unit of clothing for 4 units of food. How he spends the extra $5 constitutes the _income effect_. He may decide to enjoy somewhat more than 9 units of food with part of his money, but it is probable that he will still use less than 13 units. (Four more units would cost $4 and leave only $1 for additional clothing.) Usually the substitution effect results in some reduction in sales of the product that becomes relatively more expensive, in spite of the income effect.

Demand Schedules

The concepts of marginal utility, indifference combinations, and consumption possibilities with a limited income all provide logical reasons for what can be generally observed — the law of demand. All other things held unchanged, a lower price leads to increased amounts purchased and a higher price leads to decreased amounts purchased. As we have noted, a housewife might purchase oranges if the price is 75 cents a dozen, but not if it is $1. The addition of all these individual reactions to price provides a schedule of prices and quantities called a demand schedule. Such a schedule is shown in Table 3-3.

As the title of the table implies, it is necessary to know what market is being studied, whether the shopping area of a town, the whole United States, or the world. The quantities that buyers would take are obviously related to the extent of the market. Similarly, they are related to the period of time covered; the figures in the table would be larger at each price if the period were a month or a year.

The whole schedule represents, or is, the demand for oranges in this market. The demand cannot be described by a single quantity; one cannot say, "The demand is 1,000 dozen." The *quantity demanded at 70 cents* is 1,000 dozen. The reason for insisting on careful language when discussing supply and demand will become clear in the following discussion, but it should be noted that it is difficult to think accurately about changes in demand unless the right words are used. The demand is no greater at 60 cents than at 70 cents although one is tempted to say so through carelessness. The reason for greater purchases at 60 cents is the lower price, not a greater demand. Thus the word *demand* embraces all the possible pairs of prices and quantities that might exist with a given demand.

At a given moment of time, only one of the pairs can exist. The price might be 90 cents, in which case purchases that week would be 600 dozen. Purchases could not be 800 dozen because the demand is not great enough. But another week—the demand not having changed—price might be 80 cents, and in that week purchases would be 800 dozen.

Demand Curves

One of the most useful tools of the economist is the demand curve, along with the supply curve. It is a shorthand way of expressing the demand schedule. The demand curve for oranges described by the demand schedule in Table 3-3 is shown in Figure 3-3. It is customary to

Table 3-3
**Demand Schedule for Oranges in a
Given Market for a One-Week Period**

Price per Dozen	Quantity Demanded (Dozens)
$1.00	500
.90	600
.80	800
.70	1,000
.60	1,300
.50	1,700

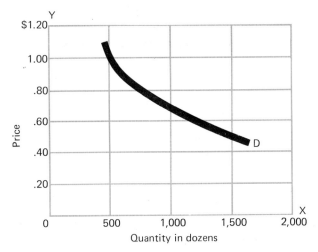

Figure 3-3. Demand curve for oranges.

measure price on the vertical, or *Y*, axis and quantity on the horizontal, or *X*, axis. The six price-quantity combinations in Table 3-3 are plotted and connected to form the demand curve in Figure 3-3.[4]

Like every graph of this type relating two variables to each other, this graph has a curve with two important characteristics. One is its position on the graph; the other is its steepness, or slope. If the position of the curve changes, it shows a different demand. If the curve falls off steeply, it shows that the quantity demanded does not increase much at lower prices. These two characteristics of demands for various goods and services merit further investigation.

Changes in Demand

The demand for oranges may change for a variety of reasons. Table 3-4 reproduces the demand already shown and a larger and a smaller demand. The demand may change from that shown in column D_1 to that in column D_2 because more people come to like oranges, because other fruits have become more expensive, or because incomes have risen and more people can afford to buy more oranges.[5] People's tastes change as they become acquainted with a wider variety of goods. Sometimes tastes change with customs. For example, many years ago few people wanted to eat calf and beef liver until they were discovered to be highly nutritious; then more and more people were willing to buy them at the very low prices that prevailed and the prices were forced up.

The demand for a given commodity may change because the general level of incomes has changed. If incomes rise, people are willing to buy more oranges, beef, vacation trips, and many other things, as was implied

[4] Sometimes people have to be reminded that such a graph is a snapshot and not a moving picture. That is, it shows all the combinations, any one of which might exist. The graph does *not* show the path these combinations have taken over time but represents the relationship between two variables at a moment of time.

[5] Note that we do not include the possibility that oranges have become cheaper and more plentiful. This cannot be a reason for an increase in demand. It can be a reason for an increase in the amount demanded at the same old demand.

Table 3-4
Changes in Demand for Oranges

Price per Dozen	D_1 (Dozens)	D_2 (Dozens)	D_3 (Dozens)
$1.00	500	700	400
.90	600	800	500
..80	800	1,050	700
.70	1,000	1,300	900
.60	1,300	1,600	1,100
.50	1,700	2,100	1,500

in the discussion of consumption possibilities. When incomes decline, some purchases have to be curtailed. A change in incomes affects the demands for some goods much more than others. Consumer durable goods are likely to be demanded in greater quantity when incomes are high, as are sporting goods, jewelry, restaurant meals, and things generally considered luxuries. On the other hand, one does not materially increase his consumption of salt and pepper when his income is higher. The demand for a good in the former group is said to be *income-elastic;* it increases and decreases with income. Families with very low incomes buy few of these items. The demands for salt, pepper, light bulbs, bread, milk, and the like are *income-inelastic.* Although nearly all of us want some of these things, we do not want considerably more when our incomes are higher.

Changes in the population may bring changes in demands for various goods. More people to feed, more youth to educate, and more young families to house all tend to raise the demand for food, schools, and apartment buildings. Shifts in the availability of some good may lead to changes in demand for another good. If beef becomes expensive, more

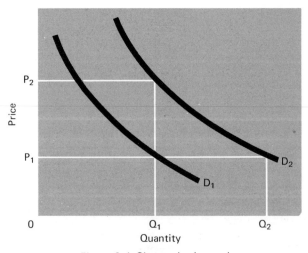

Figure 3-4. Change in demand.

people demand pork; as automobiles became available, fewer people demanded buggies. All these reasons for change in demand—changes in taste, custom, population, and prices of other goods—result in people being either more or less willing to buy a certain quantity of a product (or a service) at a certain price. Thus a change in demand tends to bring about a new price.

A change in demand is shown graphically by a new demand curve. In Figure 3-4, the curve D_1 is the demand before an increase and the curve D_2 is the increased demand at a later time. Or, of course, the situation could be reversed, in which case D_1 would represent a later and smaller demand. Note that D_2 is a larger demand in two respects. If the quantity purchased with D_1 is Q_1, the price is P_1, but with the increased demand, D_2, people would pay P_2 for this quantity. Or, if the price is held at P_1, people would be willing to buy the quantity Q_2 at the greater demand.

Price Elasticity of Demand

We have seen that there is an inverse relationship between price and the quantity demanded. Other things being given, people will buy more of a good at a low price than at a high price. But how much more? It is often important for a seller to know whether he can sell a great deal more as a result of reducing price, or only a little more. The change in sales is likely to be quite different for different products. We may find this sort of situation:

Price	Product X	Product Y
$1.00	100	100
.80	115	150

If the price of X were $1, people would buy 100 units, but if the price were 80 cents, they would buy 115; if the price of Y were $1, people would buy 100 units, but if the price were 80 cents, they would buy 150. The demand for Y is much more *elastic* than the demand for X. The response of a change in quantity to a given change in price is greater.

In this example, the demand for X is *inelastic* because the increase in quantity is proportionately less than the decrease in price. If the price were 20 percent lower, sales would be only 15 percent higher. As a result, the total revenue would be smaller at 80 cents. The total revenue at $1 is $100, and at 80 cents it is $92; the lower price has more effect than does the increased quantity. The demand for Y is elastic because the increase in quantity is relatively greater than the decrease in price (50 percent as against 20 percent). In the other direction, an increase in price from 80 cents to $1 (a change of 25 percent) is relatively less than the decrease in quantity (33.3 percent). Accordingly, the total revenue is larger at the 80-cent price, where it is $120.

Index of Elasticity

A simple test of whether the demand for a commodity is elastic or inelastic—at least between two specific prices—is thus to see whether the total revenue would be larger or smaller at the lower price. A more precise measure is provided by the index of elasticity:

$$\text{Coefficient of elasticity} = \frac{q_2 - q_1}{q_1 + q_2} \div \frac{p_1 - p_2}{p_1 + p_2}$$

where q_1 = original quantity and q_2 = new quantity
p_1 = original price and p_2 = new price

This formula shows the *elasticity of demand* for product X between $1 and 80 cents to be:

$$\frac{115 - 100}{100 + 115} \div \frac{1.00 - .80}{1.00 + .80} = \frac{27}{43} = .63$$

and the elasticity of demand for Y between $1 and 80 cents to be:

$$\frac{150 - 100}{100 + 150} \div \frac{1.00 - .80}{1.00 + .80} = \frac{9}{5} = 1.8$$

The demand for a product is said to be elastic if the coefficient, or index, is greater than 1 and inelastic if the index is less than 1. In this example, the demand for Y is elastic and the demand for X is inelastic. If the index were exactly 1, the demand would be neither elastic nor inelastic but would have *elasticity of unity*.

Reasons for Different Elasticities

The basic reasoning that explains why the demand curve slopes downward also explains why different demands have different elasticities. The steeper the slope, the less elastic the demand curve; the flatter the curve, the more elastic. Curve D_1 in Figure 3-5 is much less elastic than curve D_2.[6] If the price were P_1 instead of P_2, the quantity bought would be larger by the distance AB. On curve D_2, the quantity bought would be larger by the distance CE.

We have seen that a smaller quantity of a good is bought at a higher price because more income is spent on substitute products. The other products need not be substitutes in the usual sense (remember the example of food and clothing used earlier), but if there are *close substitutes* available, people can readily shift their expenditures to them. When the price of a commodity rises, people can shift their expenditures to close substitutes and reduce their purchases of the good in question. If there are numerous close substitutes for the good, the quantity demanded is senstive to changes in price and the demand is elastic. If there is no good or close substitute, it is not easy to reduce purchases of the higher-priced commodity and its demand is inelastic.

A commodity on which total expenditures are small tends to have an inelastic demand because even a large percentage change in price does not affect much of the consumer's income. Commodities like salt and sugar have inelastic demands because there are no close substitutes (closer for sugar than for salt) and because they take only a small fraction of the consumer's income. It is sometimes said that essential goods, or necessities, have inelastic demands, but this is merely a way of saying that such goods have no satisfactory substitutes. Goods for which there are close substitutes and which require more substantial outlays have

[6] Whether D_1 is actually elastic or inelastic depends on the figures represented by the letters on the graph. The different scales on the two axes could result in either answer, but in either case D_1 is more inelastic than D_2.

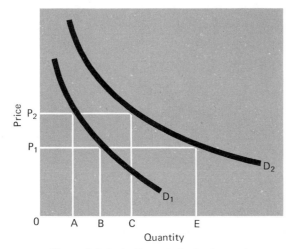

Figure 3-5. Inelastic and elastic demand.

more elastic demands. Examples are extra pairs of eyeglasses, expensive cuts of meat, books, cameras, and long-playing records.

The importance of elasticity will become clear as the study of market price proceeds. The behavior of the business firm depends a great deal on the nature of the demand for its product. If a firm can increase its output sufficiently by charging a lower price, it follows that course. What is a sufficient increase in output depends, in turn, on how the firm's total costs would be affected. The elasticity of demand is also important in considering the effect of a tax levied on a commodity or its sale. If the demand is highly elastic, the increased price required by the tax can reduce sales significantly and thus the potential tax revenue.

SUPPLY

Just as the demand for a commodity is a schedule of the quantities that would be purchased at different prices, the supply is a schedule of the quantities that would be offered for sale at different prices. The law of supply states that larger quantities would be offered at high prices than at low prices. Thus quantity is positively related to price, rather than negatively.

The reason for the upward slope of a supply curve, or *supply schedule,* such as that shown in Figure 3-6, is simply that price functions to bring out supply by covering costs. The higher the price of a commodity, the greater the quantity that can be produced because only the cheapest levels of output can be afforded when price is low. Table 3-5 shows a hypothetical supply schedule for oranges. This schedule reflects the fact that when the market price of oranges is low, growers can divert some factors of production—land, labor, or capital equipment—from the production of oranges, perhaps to increase output of other types of fruit. They can even switch some resources to other types of products or, if price is low enough, they can produce very little, even allowing fruit to remain unpicked. When the market price of oranges is high, however, growers can shift their resources to the production of oranges or they

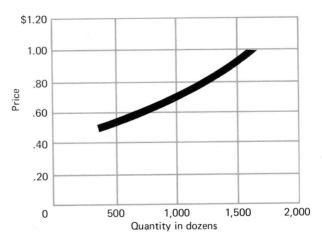

Figure 3-6. Supply of oranges.

can divert the supply of oranges to the markets where the price is most attractive. These shifts may not be great in the short run, as pictured in Table 3-5, but over a period of time they can be substantial. Table 3-5 and Figure 3-6 picture a supply situation in which growers have certain groves, equipment, and available labor and, under these circumstances, would offer the quantities shown at the prices listed.

Changes in Supply

This supply situation may change over a period of time. For example, at a later date, orange growers may have larger groves, which required time to grow, more and better equipment, better availability of transportation, and other facilities to permit the growers to produce profitably a larger quantity of oranges at any given price. Thus there would be a greater supply than existed before. At any price, more oranges would be offered for sale. Opposite developments would bring about a reduced supply. Under these conditions, growers would offer for sale fewer oranges at each price than the quantities in Table 3-5.

On a graph, a greater supply is shown by a curve that lies to the right of the old supply curve. Thus it indicates that, at any particular price, the

Table 3-5
Supply of Oranges

Price per Dozen	Quantity Offered (Dozens)
$1.00	1,700
.90	1,500
.80	1,300
.70	1,000
.60	700
.50	400

quantity offered for sale would be larger. By the same token, it indicates that a given quantity would be offered at a lower price than before.

Elasticity of Supply

Since a supply curve has a slope, it describes whether the supply is elastic or inelastic. If the curve rises steeply, it shows that a considerable change in price is required to bring forth a given increase in quantity; if it rises slowly, it shows that a given change in price is associated with a large change in quantity.

SUPPLY, DEMAND, AND PRICE

Supply and demand are the two determinants of price. Every imaginable influence on the price of a commodity can be classified as a supply factor or a demand factor. That is, the only way a price can be influenced is through a change in the demand for the product or a change in its supply—or both.

Market Price

How market price is determined by supply and demand can be illustrated by putting together the schedules of supply and demand for oranges. This is done in Table 3-6. These figures indicate that the quantities demanded and supplied are not equal except at one price, 70 cents. If these two quantities are not equal, the forces of competition tend to cause buyers or sellers, or both, to change the price until quantities are equal.

Suppose that the market price happens to be 90 cents. This is not an _equilibrium price_ because sellers are willing to sell 1,500 dozen in this market but buyers are willing to take only 600 dozen. If suppliers put 1,500 dozen on the market, there will be a considerable surplus of unsold oranges. Some sellers will take a lower price than 90 cents rather than sell none of the 900-dozen surplus, so they offer their oranges at some lower price. Other sellers, however, are no longer willing to supply oranges at the lower price, but buyers are willing to take more than 600 dozen. At 80 cents, for example, buyers take 800 dozen but there is still a surplus supply and still sellers who would rather take a lower price than fail to sell their oranges. These sellers thus cut the price further. Each cut takes

---

Table 3-6
Supply, Demand, and Price of Oranges

Price	Supply (Dozens)	Demand (Dozens)
$1.00	1,700	500
.90	1,500	600
.80	1,300	800
.70	1,000	1,000
.60	700	1,300
.50	400	1,700

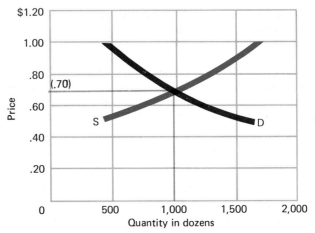

Figure 3-7. Supply, demand, and equilibrium price for oranges.

some sellers out of the market and brings more buyers in or, what amounts to the same thing, some sellers offer fewer oranges in this market and some buyers purchase larger quantities. This process stops when price reaches 70 cents because there are no longer unsatisfied sellers or buyers. An unsatisfied seller is one who would rather reduce his price than hold unsold oranges; an unsatisfied buyer is one who would rather pay a higher price than go without oranges.[7]

The same line of reasoning applies to a price below the equilibrium price. If price is 60 cents, some buyers find all the oranges sold when they get to market, as people want 1,300 dozen and only 700 dozen are offered. Some sellers find that they can charge a higher price. This higher price brings in some additional quantities—some buyers refuse to pay the higher price but others do pay it. When the price reaches 70 cents, there are no more upward pressures on it.

This discussion is pictured graphically in Figure 3-7, where the demand for and supply of oranges are shown together. The two curves meet at the combination of 70 cents and 1,000 dozen. Above this price, the demand curve shows fewer would be demanded and the supply curve shows more would be offered. Below this price, the demand curve shows more would be demanded and the supply curve shows fewer would be supplied.

Effects of a Change in Demand

As we have seen, supply or demand conditions may change over time. If the demand for a product increases, buyers are willing to pay a higher price for the existing quantity rather than do without and they are willing to take a larger quantity at the existing price. The extent to which the in-

[7] Both buyer and seller may be unsatisfied in the popular sense of the word. Buyers may complain that the price of 70 cents is high, and sellers may complain that it is low. Although each may be unhappy, enough buyers will take oranges at 70 cents to balance the quantity offered by sellers at 70 cents, and this is untrue of any other combination of price and quantity.

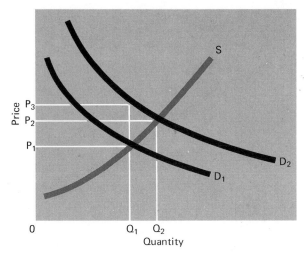

Figure 3-8. Change in demand and price.

crease in demand is reflected in a higher price or in a larger quantity of sales depends on the elasticity of the supply. This fact is illustrated in Figure 3-8.

Suppose the demand increases from D_1 to D_2. As buyers try to obtain a quantity larger than Q_1, they bid up the price. Supply conditions are such that at the higher price, which might rise temporarily as high as P_3, additional quantities are offered for sale. These additional quantities keep the price from rising as much as it otherwise would. The new equilibrium comes at P_2 and Q_2, with both a higher price and a larger quantity. This is always the result of an increase in demand with no change in supply conditions.

Figure 3-8 illustrates that if the supply curve were steeper—more inelastic—price would rise more and quantity would increase less. Such a situation would reflect cost conditions in the industry in question. It would suggest that large new supplies cannot be produced unless rather high costs of these units are covered. If the opposite situation prevailed, the supply curve would be flatter and much less of an increase in price would bring forth greater quantities for sale. The increased demand would be met to a large extent by increased quantity and to a small extent by increased price.

D_2 may be considered the original demand and D_1 a new and smaller demand. In this case, Figure 3-8 represents the decline in price and reduction in quantity that accompany a decline in demand. Both must fall when demand falls, and the extent of each depends again on the elasticity of the supply.

Effects of a Change in Supply

A change in supply is pictured in Figure 3-9. When supply increases over a period of time, the supply curve shifts to the right to indicate that larger quantities would be offered at any given price. The curve S_2 repre-

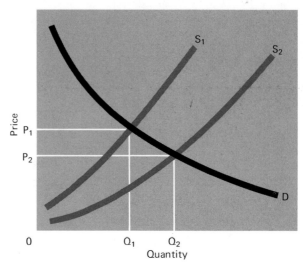

Figure 3-9. Increase in supply.

sents a larger supply than S_1. Sellers' costs must be lower than in the case of S_1. Formerly, with the given demand, price was at P_1 and the quantity Q_1 was sold in the given time period. With the greater supply, price falls to P_2 and quantity increases to Q_2.

When supply increases, price must fall and quantity sold must increase. The extent to which the change is reflected in price or in quantity depends on the elasticity of demand. If demand is highly elastic, buyers will take considerably more units with only a small reduction in price.

Conversely, S_2 might be called the original supply conditions and S_1 would then represent a smaller supply. S_1 indicates that higher cost conditions prevail in the industry. At P_2 not so many sellers are willing to offer as much output as before and the withdrawal of their supplies creates a scarcity at the old price. Some buyers are willing to pay more rather than do without and the price rises. When it settles at P_1, the amounts offered and taken are equal, but smaller than before.

The cause of the increased costs might be the imposition of a tax. If a tax of 10 cents per unit is levied on the production or sale of this commodity, the supply curve shifts upward by 10 cents at each quantity. Unless the demand curve is completely inelastic—straight up and down— the price will rise but by less than 10 cents. If there is any elasticity, people will not buy as many as before the tax. After paying the tax, sellers will have smaller proceeds out of the higher price than they could keep formerly. To them, the result is the same as a fall in price, so they produce less by cutting out their highest-cost units of production. The smaller quantity permits a higher price, but the elasticity of demand keeps the price from rising by as much as the tax. Thus such taxes are generally levied on commodities thought to have inelastic demands, so that the quantity of the commodity on which the tax is collected will not be greatly reduced by the tax.

SUMMARY

In a monetary market economy, values are expressed in terms of prices. If one commodity has a price twice that of another commodity, its value is twice as great. Values are explained by supply and demand. The demand for a commodity is based on the utilities it has for potential purchasers. Different combinations of commodities may be thought of as having equal total utilities, or satisfactions, for individual buyers. Thus the buyer attempts to find the combination that has the lowest cost.

With a limited income, each consumer has many consumption possibilities. He shifts his purchases in order to obtain the combination that gives him the greatest possible satisfaction available with his limited income. In general, he shifts away from high-priced goods to lower-priced goods and, in the process, helps to determine the total demand for each good.

The general law of demand is that purchases are greater at a low price than at a high price. Demand curves slope downward to the right, illustrating this relationship between price and quantity. In some cases they slope downward steeply, indicating inelastic demand; in others, slowly, indicating elastic demand. When changes in incomes, tastes, total population, or similar influences occur, demand changes. A change in demand is shown by moving the demand curve.

A supply schedule, or supply curve, shows the quantities that sellers would be willing to offer at a variety of possible prices. Such a curve slopes upward to the right because sellers generally cannot offer larger quantities unless they incur higher costs. The behavior of costs and the nature of supply schedules are examined further in Chapter 4. When there is a change in *cost rates,* such as wage rates, prices of materials, or excise taxes, the supply situation is affected accordingly. An increase in the level of costs for any given quantity of output shifts the supply curve to the left and upward.

Market price is determined by the interaction of supply and demand. In a free market, the quantity offered for sale tends to equal the quantity demanded. When these two quantities are not in equilibrium, either sellers lower the price in order to sell more or buyers bid up the price in order to get more. The market price is in equilibrium when all those who are willing to sell at that price can do so and when all those who are willing to buy at that price can do so.

Economic Terms for Review

economic value	demand schedule
medium of exchange	elasticity of demand
marginal utility	supply schedule
indifference curve	elasticity of supply
substitution effect	market price
income effect	equilibrium price

Questions for Review

1. Why is a diamond more valuable than a loaf of bread?
2. Why is it inaccurate and misleading to say, "If the price drops from $1 to 90 cents, demand increases from 500 to 600 dozen"? How should the sentence be changed?
3. Part of the demand curve for an article shows the following:

Price	Quantity
$2.00	1,000
1.75	1,100
1.50	1,300

Is the demand elastic between $2 and $1.75? between $1.75 and $1.50? What does your answer suggest regarding the availability and prices of close substitutes?

4. What are some of the factors that have presumably increased the demand for gasoline in the last twenty-five years? Would you expect the demand for gasoline to be relatively elastic or inelastic? Are sales taxes levied on gasoline?
5. What is meant by the expression that there are no unsatisfied buyers or sellers at the equilibrium market price? In this sense of "unsatisfied," can either buyers or sellers be unhappy?
6. If the demand for an article increases while supply remains the same, what happens to price? to quantity sold? Suppose that the quantity offered for sale cannot be increased—then what happens?

Questions for Analysis

1. Explain: "Value is related to exchange; it is not inherent." To illustrate, think of some good that is much less valuable now than in the past. Why did it lose value?
2. Explain why a consumer tends to equate the marginal utilities of a dollar's worth of each good purchased.
3. Suppose a consumer is indifferent about which of the combinations of two articles listed in Table 3-1 he may have. If food costs $1.50 and clothing $4, which is the cheapest combination? What happens if the price of clothing goes to $7?
4. By calculating the amounts of food the consumer in Question 3 could buy along with the amounts of clothing listed, show that all combinations except one are inferior to the combinations on his indifference curve. Assume that his income is $25.50 when clothing costs $4. (Carry your answers to one decimal place.)
5. How does the behavior of the consumer in Questions 3 and 4 help explain the demand for clothing? for food?
6. Draw an imaginary supply and demand curve for sirloin steaks and another pair for pork roasts. Show an increase in supply of sirloin steaks and the effect on price and quantity. Show how this effect alters the price and quantity of pork roasts.
7. A supply curve for steel ingots would reflect the capacity in the steel industry, which is greater than it was twenty years ago. Suppose, nevertheless, that the supply curve shows a smaller supply.

What would you conclude about the change in costs of operating a steel mill from twenty years ago?

8. Suppose that a new process is invented whereby great quantities of table salt can be refined from seawater very cheaply. What would happen to the price of salt? the quantity consumed? How would current sources of supply be affected?

Case for Decision

The city council of Central City is considering ways and means of raising additional revenue. The council does not have legal authority to levy an income tax in Central City, and most of the councilmen believe that property taxes should not be higher.

Three proposals have been made, one for a tax of 1 percent on all retail sales in the city, one for a tax of 2 cents per gallon on all gasoline sold in the city, and one for a tax of 2 cents on each package of cigarettes. Since the first would presumably raise more revenue (total retail sales being much more than twice those of gasoline or cigarettes), its proponent, Councilman Abel, also proposes to reduce the tax on real estate. Councilman Baird argues that people would not particularly mind paying another 2 cents per gallon for gasoline and that part of the revenue would be collected from tourists and travelers who stopped for gasoline. Councilman Crofts argues that cigarette smoking should be discouraged anyway and that people who can afford to waste money on tobacco can afford to pay more in taxes.

Representatives of the Retail Merchants Association argue that the average margin of profit in many stores is only about 1 percent and that they could not afford the proposed sales tax; that if they could charge 1 percent more, they would already be doing so. Gasoline-station operators argue that people would go out of town to buy gasoline for 2 cents a gallon less. Cigarette sellers argue that cigarettes are already heavily taxed by the federal and state governments, more than half of their retail price representing taxes.

As a member of the council, how do you evaluate the arguments for and against the three proposals? To what extent would you expect each tax to affect the sales on which it is based? Which tax would probably be least effective in raising revenue?

4
Costs and Prices

In Chapter 3 it was noted that the supply side of the supply and demand equation is determined largely by the costs of production of the commodity in question, but little attention was paid to the nature and behavior of these costs. How much a thing costs to produce generally varies with how many units are produced; cost is not the same regardless of the level of output. There are several different kinds of costs, and these are related to the level of output in different ways. Consequently, in order to understand better why a business firm produces a given quantity of output rather than some other quantity, it is necessary to examine costs of production.

TYPES OF COSTS

An entrepreneur has to consider two kinds of problems in determining how much his goods cost to produce. One kind deals with the prices he must pay—the wage rate for a day's labor of a certain kind, the prices of alternative materials, competing shipping rates, and so on. The more the various factors of production cost, the higher the individual firm's costs. But the cost *per unit of output* depends on a second problem, the efficiency with which the factors of production are used. This efficiency tends to vary considerably according to whether the plant is operated to produce the volume for which it was designed or a much greater or much smaller volume.

Outlay and Allocation Costs

Some production costs are quite obvious. Such expenses as wages, power, heat, light, and materials require *outlays* of money. As a rule, these costs are current expenses. That is, they are expenses for things used or used up currently and paid for more or less as they are used.

There are other costs, usually related to the fixed investment in capital goods, that do not involve current outlays. Suppose a firm has a machine that cost $10,000 and is expected to last ten years, after which it will be virtually worthless. It would clearly distort the costs of production to include the $10,000 in the costs for the year in which the expenditure is made and then to ignore it for the next nine years. Production costs would appear to be very high for one year and comparatively low for the next nine years. Consequently, the firm might include $1,000 each year as a cost of depreciation in order to recover the investment of $10,000 over the life of the machine. Or it might decide at the beginning that, since the machine would produce about 100,000 units over its lifetime, each unit should bear a cost of 10 cents to pay for the machine, whenever that unit is produced. Accountants endeavor to devise methods of *allocating* costs such as depreciation and obsolescence so that these costs are applied to the time period or to the output they consider most appropriate.

As we shall see, one significant difference between outlay costs and allocation costs is that it may pay a firm to produce for a while even if the market price does not cover the allocation costs. The outlay costs must be covered in the short run or the firm will quickly run out of money. In the long run, price must cover both kinds of cost or, again, the firm will run out of money. This would happen when the capital goods need to be replaced but the investment in them has not been recovered out of sales revenues.

Implicit Costs

Entrepreneurs should recognize a different category of costs if they are to have a true picture of the profitability of their operations. When a businessman invests his own funds or uses his own plot of land in his business, he gives up the interest he could have obtained by lending the funds to others or the rent he could have received by having a tenant on his property. The business enterprise should earn enough to compensate him for such *implicit costs,* after covering the outlay and allocation costs, or he has not made the best use of his resources. Implicit costs are also called opportunity costs, to imply that the cost of using the resources is the foregone opportunity. This is an important concept in economics because opportunity costs influence people's behavior in accepting jobs, making investments, and making other decisions.

If a man has a choice of three jobs paying $12,000, $13,000, and $14,000, he has to give up the opportunity of earning $13,000 in order to accept the $14,000 job. If extra work required, additional responsibility, or a less promising future makes the $14,000 job less than $1,000 better to him, he will accept the $13,000 job. In this sense, the second job constitutes a cost that the first job must cover if he is to be attracted to it. By the same reasoning, a man who can invest $10,000 in government bonds and receive $600 a year in interest should be aware of this fact when he chooses to invest in his own business or make any alternative investment.

Because the economic facts of life require people to make choices, there is usually some alternative to virtually any decision. A college student foregoes the income he might earn if he were to take a job instead of going to college. The cost of a year of education is actually more than the outlay costs involved for tuition and other expenses because of this amount of foregone earnings. But the economic value of the education is presumably great enough in terms of future earnings to justify both the outlay and opportunity costs.

The existence of implicit costs needs to be noted because they are not included as costs in the usual accounting procedures. The accountant is interested in measuring the performance of the firm and considers its overall earnings. If these earnings include interest on the owner's own investment, the accountant does not allocate some of the profit to such a category. The same is true of a large corporation; earnings after the outlay and allocation costs are called profit. If we think of costs as those that must be covered by price in order to bring forth output, however, it follows that implicit costs must be covered or funds would not be invested.

Fixed and Variable Costs

Costs may be classified by whether they increase as output is increased or whether they stay the same. In general, outlay costs do vary with output. In order to produce 20 percent more output, a firm would have to use roughly 20 percent more labor, power, and materials. However, some outlay costs would not vary with output. Presumably, about the same amount of heat and light would be required at either level of output. Allocation costs are likely not to vary with output. For example, if the depreciation of a building is 4 percent per year, it stays at that figure—one twenty-fifth of the original price of the building—regardless of whether the plant operates at capacity or less. Implicit costs also may not vary with output. If a sole proprietor could earn $12,000 working for someone else, this fact remains true whether he produces a large or a small volume of output.

The important distinction in this regard, however, is not whether the cost is outlay, allocation, or implicit but only whether the cost is increased if output is increased. Since some costs do not increase with a larger output, the total cost of the larger output may not be proportionately larger. It is important for the businessman to know whether his costs would rise by 10, 20, or 30 percent if he were to increase output by 20 percent.

Whether a given cost is considered fixed or variable depends very much on the length of time one is considering. Suppose a businessman is considering expanding output by 20 percent. If he has plenty of time, he can order new machines and construct an addition for them, but it may be two years before the machines are installed and ready to operate. If he is thinking of expanding in a shorter period of time, he must consider hiring more labor or having labor work overtime at higher wages and operating the existing machines more hours per day. If a contractor is deciding whether to build more houses in a year, he has to consider using more carpenters and other craftsmen on each house in order to complete it more rapidly and move on to the next one.

In the short run, then, some facilities and some costs are fixed. Depreciation and obsolescence go on whether a machine is worked six or ten hours a day. Interest on funds borrowed in the past remains the same. The property tax on the plant and equipment is the same whether they are used at full capacity or at half capacity. Some of the expense of the clerical staff, watchmen, and utilities is independent of the level of output.

Expenses for factors of production that can be dispensed with if output is reduced are naturally the variable costs. If output is reduced, there can be less expense for labor, materials, power, transportation, and perhaps salesmen and maintenance.

LAW OF DIMINISHING RETURNS

At any moment, each plant, each company, and each industry has a given capacity. That capacity is the result of many decisions made in the past. In the past, decisions were made to build new plants, adopt new methods and types of machines and develop new products. Or decisions were made not to replace worn-out equipment and to let capacity decline. If the demand for the product has been sufficient so that larger quantities are sold at existing prices or if higher prices have been anticipated, the capacity of an industry has probably been rising. Entrepreneurs have probably channeled their own and other investors' funds into this industry because the investments promised to be profitable.

Industries producing automobiles, computers, television sets, aluminum, and many other items have generally added to their fixed investment in plant and equipment over the years. A supply curve for television sets would be different at one time than at a previous time, as it would show more sets offered for sale at a given price.

Costs in the Short Run

When we consider a change in the quantity of an article supplied, it is therefore important to know whether the change results from a shift in the supply schedule or from a shift in the price. In the short run, entrepreneurs must decide how much to produce with their fixed factors of production. They must decide how much of the variable factors to combine with the fixed factors. By definition, the short run is a period of time too short to allow material change in the fixed factors. In other words, if a greater quantity is supplied, it must result from a higher price because the supply curve cannot be shifted.

With a given plant and its equipment, a businessman can combine a larger amount of labor, materials, supplies, and other variable factors, up to the limits of capacity. The same is true of a farm. A farmer has—for the time being—a fixed extent of land and a fixed supply of buildings and heavy equipment. He can vary the amount of seed, fertilizer, workers, and tools.

Combinations of Factors

Not all combinations of variable factors with the fixed factors are equally productive. The differences in productivity are governed by the *law of diminishing returns,* or the *law of variable proportions.* This law states that if all the factors of production are held constant except one, as that one factor is increased, output also increases but, after some point, by less and less. At some point, in other words, the increases in output are not proportionate to the increases in the variable factor.

This relationship is called a law because its operation is a fact of life and unavoidable. If it were not true, all the automobiles bought in the United States could be produced by a single small factory, which would simply add workers until output was sufficient. Or a single farmer could add workers or fertilizer until his farm could feed the entire population. Since the law does exist, it implies that pushing output beyond a certain point makes that output very expensive.

Table 4-1 gives a hypothetical illustration of diminishing returns. Here we assume that the amounts of land, seed, tools, and fertilizer are held constant and ask what output of, say, wheat would be with differing numbers of farm workers. With no workers, there would be, of course, no output. If there were one worker, he could produce 200 bushels in a year, but two workers could produce 500 bushels. The difference in the output of one worker versus two workers is 300 bushels; this is the *marginal output* of a marginal worker.[1] Similarly, if three workers were used instead of two,

---

[1] Just as we pointed out in Chapter 3 that if a man chooses to buy three suits rather than two, any one of the three suits can be considered the marginal one, so here either man can be called the marginal worker. Both men are considered equal in productivity. The difference is that two men are more productive than one.

Table 4-1
Diminishing Returns in Agriculture

Land, Seed, Tools, Fertilizer	Number of Farm Workers	Total Output (Bushels)	Marginal Output (Bushels)
Constant	0	0	0
Constant	1	200	200
Constant	2	500	300
Constant	3	720	220
Constant	4	880	160

output would be 720 bushels and the marginal output with this number of workers 220 bushels. The table illustrates that the marginal output drops as more workers are considered although the total output, of course, rises. Having five workers rather than four would add only 100 bushels to the output.

These figures illustrate that two workers make a better combination with the given amount of land and other fixed factors than does one worker. The average output per worker is 250 bushels, as against the 200 that one can produce. Average output for three workers is 240 bushels, also better than for one but not as good as for two. As the marginal output declines, it naturally brings down the average output at that level of employment.

The reason for the decline in the marginal and average output is simply that there is less of the fixed factors for each worker to use. If more than two workers are used, the change in the proportions of factors used makes for a less efficient combination of factors. If there are a great many workers, there must be, by the same token, a scarcity of land or other fixed factors. If one is relatively abundant, that simply means that other factors are relatively scarce. When some factors of production are excessively abundant, the resulting combination of factors must be relatively unproductive.

Average or Unit Costs

It is probably clear from the figures in Table 4-1 that the farmer might employ more than two workers if the price of wheat made the extra, or marginal, output worthwhile, and it is also clear that the cost per bushel would be higher if four or five workers were used than if only two were used.[2] A more complete illustration of this relationship is shown in Table 4-2, which is applicable to a manufacturing plant. In manufacturing we would expect costs to rise, if output was already at a reasonably efficient level, because of such reasons as overtime pay, machine breakdowns, use of more distant or more expensive sources for materials, crowded conditions in the plant, more units of defective work, and so on.

[2] Notice that to increase output from 500 bushels to 980 — not quite 100 percent — the farmer would need to increase the number of workers from two to five, or by 150 percent.

Table 4-2
Short-Run Costs in Manufacturing

Units of Output	Total Fixed Cost	Total Variable Cost	Total Cost	Average Fixed Cost	Average Variable Cost	Average Total Cost	Marginal Cost
(1)	*(2)*	*(3)*	*(4)*	*(5)*	*(6)*	*(7)*	*(8)*
0	$100	$ 0	$100	....	....	....	....
10	100	50	150	$10.00	$5.00	$15.00	$ 5.00
20	100	90	190	5.00	4.50	9.50	4.00
30	100	120	220	3.33	4.00	7.33	3.00
40	100	160	260	2.50	4.00	6.50	4.00
50	100	210	310	2.00	4.20	6.20	5.00
60	100	280	380	1.666	4.666	6.333	7.00
70	100	370	470	1.43	5.29	6.71	9.00
80	100	480	580	1.25	6.00	7.25	11.00
90	100	620	720	1.11	6.89	8.00	14.00
100	100	780	880	1.00	7.80	8.80	17.00

In this table Column 1 lists possible levels of output, from no units to 100 units; these figures refer, of course, to a period of time, such as a day. A given plant and its equipment are assumed to exist and are used at different levels of capacity for the different outputs. Thus the fixed costs remain at $100 throughout the whole range of output. Column 3 shows the amounts of variable costs that would have to be expended for variable factors at different levels of output. Column 4 combines the fixed and total costs. Column 5 shows the fixed cost per unit of output—the $100 of fixed costs divided by the output. Column 6 shows the variable costs per unit of output. These two may also be called the average fixed cost and average variable cost. Column 7 shows the average cost per unit. It may be obtained by dividing the total cost (Column 4) by the output or by adding together the average fixed cost and the average variable cost. The *marginal cost* is the cost required to produce an additional unit. It is therefore the amount by which the variable costs rise. For example, to produce 20 units rather than 10 requires an increase in variable costs of $40, from $50 to $90. The extra 10 units each add $4 to variable (and total) costs.

Behavior of Costs

Table 4-2 illustrates the different behavior of the fixed, variable, and total costs per unit. Since the fixed costs remain fixed in total regardless of the level of output, the higher the output, the less of these fixed costs each unit has to bear. If only 10 units are produced, the $100 can be spread over these units and amount to $10 per unit. If 100 units are produced, the fixed costs can be spread over them and amount to $1 per unit. If all the costs were fixed, the businessman would obviously like to produce as much as physically possible.

The variable costs rise slowly from very low levels of output and then more rapidly. This is because very low levels of output are inefficient and much less than the plant was designed to produce. People cannot work together effectively if only 10 or 20 units per day are produced. Perhaps they have to carry parts to other areas, cannot use an automatic machine, or are not constantly busy. Thus, adding $50 worth of variable factors would allow production of 10 units; adding $40 more would permit production of 20 units; adding $30 more would permit producing 30 units. From that point on, the amount of variable costs required for 10 more units rises. This is not necessarily because the plant is becoming less efficient; it is more likely that it cannot become more efficient. The average variable cost remains at $4 at the output of 40, after which it is forced up somewhat as the variable cost per unit rises.

It can be seen that $4 is the lowest unit cost that can be reached as far as the variable costs are concerned. But we must not overlook the fixed costs per unit, which decline as long as output is increased. They decline more and more slowly, however, for a simple reason of arithmetic. When output is changed from 10 to 20 units, it is doubled and cuts the fixed cost per unit in half. When it goes from 40 to 50 units, it increases by a fourth, so the fixed cost per unit is reduced by much less. The decline in the average fixed cost from $2.50 to $2, however, happens to be greater than the rise in the average variable cost at this point—$4 to $4.20. Consequently, the combined effect is to reduce the average cost per unit by 30 cents. In fact, the average cost does decline from $6.50 to $6.20.

This cost is the lowest average cost that can be achieved. If 60 units are produced, the average fixed cost falls only by 33.3 cents while the average variable cost rises by 46.6 cents. Thus the average cost rises 13.3 cents. It may be seen that the combined effect on the average cost is to raise it from $6.20 to $6.333.

Marginal cost reflects the same factors that affect variable cost but only with respect to the marginal units rather than all the units. It shows how much additional units of output cost at each level of output. One could say that the reason why the average variable cost drops from $4.50 to $4

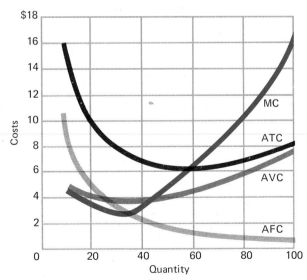

Figure 4-1. Short-run costs.

when 30 rather than 20 units are produced is that the additional 10 units each add $3 to costs. There are 20 units with an average variable cost of $4.50 and 10 additional units with an additional cost of $3. Thus 30 units in all have an average variable cost of $4. When the marginal cost is less than the average variable cost or the average total cost, it brings them down. When it becomes higher, it begins to bring them up.

These relationships are shown in Figure 4-1, which is based on Table 4-2. It may be seen that the average fixed cost (AFC) declines, but more and more slowly. The average variable cost declines at first and then rises. The average total cost is the sum of the average fixed and average variable costs. In this example, therefore, it declines beyond the point of the lowest average variable cost, but then it rises as variable costs raise it more than fixed costs lower it. The marginal cost is less for small outputs than the already-existing average variable cost, reaching a low point of $3 as output increases from 20 to 30. The marginal cost cuts through both the AVC and the ATC at their lowest points because when it is higher, the production of the extra high-cost units raises the AVC and the ATC.

COSTS AND OUTPUT

This behavior of costs explains how the individual firm decides how much to produce. One might suppose that the firm described in Table 4-2 would want to produce 50 units a day because that is the cheapest level of output, where the unit cost is $6.20. Whether this is the most profitable level of output, however, is another story. Clearly, the firm cannot earn any profit unless price is above $6.20. Any lower price is below the lowest cost the firm can achieve. If the price is sufficiently above $6.20, it may pay the firm to produce at a level higher than 50 units.

Marginal Revenue

The quickest way to discover how many units it pays to produce is simply to compare the marginal cost with the marginal revenue. The marginal revenue is the revenue added by an extra unit of output. If the firm can sell a larger volume without lowering its price, its marginal revenue is the same thing as the market price. In other words, if the going market price is $5, the firm can add $5 to its revenues by producing and selling another unit; and if the price is $10, it can add $10 to its revenues by producing and selling another unit.

Under conditions of what economists call *pure competition,* each firm in an industry is too small to affect the price by increasing or decreasing its output. Price is determined by total supply and demand, as described in Chapter 3. If, for example, there are 100 firms each producing about 1,000 units per day, the amount supplied is 100,000 units. Even if a firm should double its output, the total amount coming on the market would rise only to 101,000. While this change of 1 percent would have some effect on the market price, it would be small and probably negligible. Of course, if all firms increase their output considerably, there is a substantial effect on the price. However, from the point of view of the individual firm, price is something that is outside its own power to change.

In industries that conform rather closely to this model of pure competition, the entrepreneur cannot decide how much to charge for his product

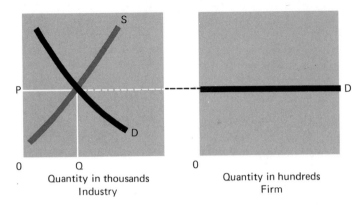

Figure 4-2. Demand for output of industry and firm.

because that is set by the market price. But he can – and must – decide how much to produce at that price. The standard example of pure competition is agriculture. There are thousands of farmers and, if a farmer decides to destroy his entire crop rather than sell it, he cannot materially affect the price. And even if he could affect the price, he could not profit by doing so because he would have destroyed his crop. Other examples of pure competition exist where the product is fairly uniform – each seller is offering about the same article – and there are numerous sellers.

From the point of view of the individual firm, therefore, the demand curve *for its own output* appears to be a horizontal line. The horizontal line shows that the firm can sell any quantity within its powers to produce at the going market price. This situation is illustrated in Figure 4-2. In the left panel are shown the supply and demand curves for the entire industry, with the resulting market price. In the right panel is shown how this price appears to the individual firm – the same for any output it selects.

Producing at a Loss

Simply by comparing marginal cost with marginal revenue, the firm can tell what would be the best, or *optimum, output*. If the marginal cost exceeds the marginal revenue, the extra units obviously should not be produced. Suppose that the price is only $5.50. The firm can see that it could produce 10 units by adding variable costs of $50, or $5 apiece, to its costs; it could add another 10 units at an extra cost of $4 apiece, another 10 units at an extra cost of $3 apiece, and so on. It could produce 50 units rather than 40 by adding $5 apiece to its costs, but in order to produce 10 more, a total of 60, it would have to add $7 apiece to its costs. Should the firm produce any additional units?

It should produce that quantity beyond which marginal cost would exceed marginal revenue (price, in this instance). If it produces 50 units, it can sell them for $5.50 each, or a total revenue of $275. If it produces none, the fixed costs continue at $100 per day. The $275 more than covers the variable costs necessary – $210 – and leaves $65 for fixed costs. The firm loses $35 per day but that is better than losing $100. If the price never rises above $6.20, the firm will continue to lose money and be unable to cover its allocation costs; eventually it will have to go out of business. But in the short run, it loses less by producing at a loss than by closing down.

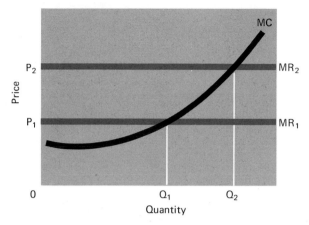

Figure 4-3. Optimum output.

The reason why production of 50 units is desirable is simply that, up to this output, the price of each unit adds more to revenues than it does to costs. The marginal cost consists only of variable costs, so this is the same as saying that the price more than covers the variable costs. If it covers variable costs by enough to cover the fixed costs also, the firm can make a profit.

When the firm considers producing 60 units, it notices that the additional 10 units would add $7 apiece to costs because variable costs would rise by $70. Since these extra units would sell for $5.50, they should not be produced. They would increase the loss by $1.50 each. This is proven by reference to total revenue and total cost. The 60 units would produce a total revenue of $330 and have a total cost of $380. The loss would be $50, $15 more than with 50 units.

The comparison of marginal cost with marginal revenue tells only what level of output produces the least loss or the largest profit, as we shall note in a moment. To find the amount of profit or loss, one must refer to the total revenues and total costs. This may also be done, of course, by comparing the price to the total unit cost. For example, at 60 units, each unit costs $6.333 and thus causes a loss of 83.3 cents ($6.333 minus $5.50), or $50 in total.

Determining the optimum output by comparing marginal cost with marginal revenue is illustrated in Figure 4-3. Two demand, or price, lines are drawn in order to show how a higher price makes additional output worthwhile. The graph helps to make clear that it pays to produce just up to the point where marginal cost equals marginal revenue. Each unit of output up to that level adds more to revenues than to costs; beyond that level, each unit adds more to costs than to revenues. The output yielding the greatest profit or least loss must, therefore, be at that level where *MC* equals *MR*. If it is possible to adjust output by single units, the unit at which *MC* equals *MR* neither adds to nor subtracts from profit.

Producing at a Profit

If price is above $6.20, all costs are covered and a profit can be earned. If price is $9, it exceeds marginal cost for outputs up to 70 units. Beyond 60 units, 10 more would add $9 each to costs and $9 each to revenues.

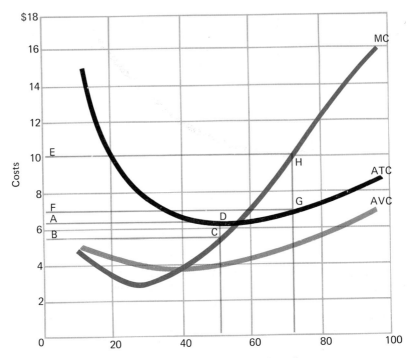

Figure 4-4. Optimum output and profit.

These 10 units are marginal; it barely pays to produce them. Profit is the same—$160—at both 60 units and 70 units. Any price above $9 would make production of 70 units worthwhile. At $10, each of the extra 10 units would add $1 more to revenues than to costs and thus increase profits by $10. The profit on 60 units is total revenue of $600 minus total costs of $380, or $220; the profit on 70 units is $700 minus $470, or $230. Although 70 units have an average total cost of $6.71, they are more profitable than 60 units costing $6.33.

Figure 4-4 illustrates the profit or loss existing at the optimum output. A price line is drawn from the price of $5.50 to where it intersects *MC* and shows the optimum output to be 50 units. Since the average cost per unit at this output is $6.20, a loss of 70 cents per unit occurs. Seventy cents is the distance between the price line and *ATC* at 50 units of output, or *CD*. The area of the rectangle *ABCD* is therefore 70 cents times 50 units, or $35, which is the loss incurred.

When the price is $10, the price line meets *MC* at 70 units. The average cost of 70 units is $6.71, so there is a profit per unit of $3.29, represented by the line *GH*. The profit on 70 units is shown by the rectangle *EFGH*.

Marginal Cost and the Supply Curve

It is now possible to explain supply schedules and supply curves much more precisely than it was in Chapter 3. It is fairly obvious that a firm would not produce at any point where its *MC* curve is falling. By adding more units of output it could lower its costs. The significant part of the *MC* curve is where it is rising. When it reaches the market price or marginal revenue, it shows the optimum output. The higher the price, the larger the output it pays to produce. Thus the *MC* curve becomes the supply curve of the individual firm. Once it rises above the *AVC* curve, additional units of output can be produced only at higher variable costs. These additional costs will be incurred only if the price is high enough to meet the marginal costs. The *MC* curve therefore shows how many units the individual firm will produce at higher and higher prices. When all the individual firms' supply curves are added together, they show the supply curve for the industry. Thus is explained the upward slope of the typical industry supply curve.

LONG-RUN EQUILIBRIUM

The foregoing discussion shows that the cheapest level of output is not necessarily the most profitable level for the firm to select in the short run. The firm is willing to produce either a larger output at a higher average cost, if price is high enough, or a smaller output at a higher average cost, if that is the way to minimize losses. But this willingness to produce in either direction at costs higher than might be attained should not suggest that the entrepreneur is not trying to minimize his costs. Earlier in the chapter it was noted that the businessman is concerned both with the prices he must pay and with the efficiency with which resources can be used at different levels of output. The businessman is always seeking a cheaper source of materials or machinery, a cheaper way of packaging his product, or some other economy. In other words, he attempts to keep his whole *AVC* and *ATC* curves as low as possible. Along the curves, however, he selects the most profitable, not the cheapest, level of output.

Shifts in Supply

All the preceding discussion has dealt with the businessman's choice of a level of output in the short run when he is deciding how much to produce with his fixed factors of production. In the long run the profitability of an industry determines how much is invested in the fixed factors. If the demand for a commodity increases and thus sets a higher price in the market, the individual firms benefit because they can expand output according to their marginal costs. Selling a larger volume at a higher price increases their profits. Society benefits also in being able to buy the additional output at prices the public is willing to pay. But if the demand remains high, or is expected to, the high prices need not be permanent. Existing firms expand their plants or build new ones, and new firms may enter the industry. Although it is worthwhile to produce beyond the point of lowest *ATC*, it would be even more profitable to have a greater capacity and be able to produce the present volume at the lowest *ATC* on a larger curve.

As time goes on, additional plants are built by either existing or new firms. As these plants come into production, a new supply curve arises. Now each firm, and therefore the industry, offers a larger output at each possible market price. But the effect of the shift of the supply curve is to lower the market price. The long-run effect, therefore, is for a larger output to enter the market but at lower prices. The price may eventually settle near where it was before the original increase in demand.

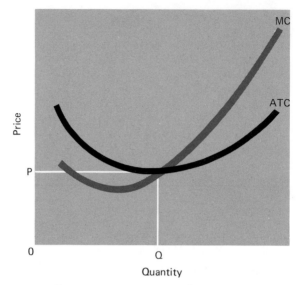

Figure 4-5. Firm in long-run equilibrium.

This process can be visualized graphically as a succession of lower price lines drawn across the graph in Figure 4-4. Each time the market price comes down, the firm restricts its output and moves closer to the output that has the lowest *ATC*. Total output in the industry is larger than it was originally, however, because there are more plants. The process continues until the incentive is removed, and the incentive is the profit made possible when price brings out production beyond the lowest *ATC* point. If there were no further changes in demand and no changes in the technology of production, the industry would tend to respond to profit by expanding and by adjusting each plant closer and closer to its lowest *ATC*. Eventually each plant and each firm would be earning the minimum profit necessary to keep it in business and the public would be obtaining the commodity at the lowest possible average cost. Technically, marginal cost, marginal revenue, price, and average cost would all be equal.[3] This is shown in Figure 4-5.

This tendency for a competitive economy to adjust its industries so that they are producing at the lowest possible costs is one of the bases for the philosophical approval of a free-enterprise system and for the instinctive resistance to monopoly. Dynamic changes in the economy prevent this long-run *equilibrium output* from ever being fully attained, but an understanding of it helps in understanding the short-run changes that take place constantly in the economy. At any one moment of time, firms are producing at a profit or a loss, but as they do so they are making long-run adjustments to the situation. Industries that are no longer profitable tend to shrink while profitable industries tend to grow. As the profitable industries grow, they produce more of what the public wants, and the in-

---

[3] Remember that each firm tries to produce where *MC* = *MR* and that, in pure competition, *MR* = price. *MC* cuts through the *ATC* curve at the latter's lowest point, so when the firm is producing at that point, all four are equal.

creased supply keeps the price from being as high as it would otherwise be.

Constant and Increasing Costs

If new firms are free to enter an industry and if the raw materials, supplies, and skills needed in the industry are not restricted, the industry can grow and continue to produce at about the same unit costs. In many industries these conditions exist — such as those industries that produce clothing and textiles, chemicals, entertainment, furniture, and a host of manufactured articles. Even if there are no technological advances that reduce costs, more and more plants can be built, each with costs similar to those already in existence.

In some other industries considerable expansion in the long run can take place only if the price remains higher than before the expansion. This tends to be true where the industry uses raw materials that have to be sought and extracted at greater expense and where persons with the necessary skills can be attracted only by offering great inducements. These industries are called *increasing-cost industries.* Their prices must rise even to keep output at the old levels. The silver industry is a good example; medical services may be another although the illustration is complicated by rapidly changing technology. In fact, technological advances may keep costs in an increasing-cost industry from actually rising but they have less chance of reducing average unit costs than they do in other industries. Inventions and more productive types of capital equipment are constantly lowering costs in most industries.

TYPES OF COMPETITION

It is probably obvious that not all industries fit the model of pure competition that has been the framework of this chapter. In fact, it was pointed out in Chapter 2 that, typically, an industry consists of only a few large producers, with a varying number of additional firms. The amendments that need to be made to the analysis developed here are not great, however, and how firms adapt their output and price policies where they do have some control over price is discussed in Chapter 5. This chapter concludes with some additional descriptions of types of competition.

Pure Competition

The most complete response of the economy to changes in demand is likely to occur in industries characterized by pure competition. We have already noted that pure competition implies an industry of numerous sellers of a standardized product; it also implies numerous buyers.

There is little opportunity for collusion among sellers if they are numerous. It is difficult for them to agree, either explicitly or tacitly, to maintain or raise prices or to restrict production in order to hold prices up. The best way open to them to increase profits is to operate efficiently and to reduce costs. Buyers also are unable to have collusive agreements to hold prices down and must therefore pay whatever costs efficient producers incur. The natural tendency of these conditions is for efficient plants of the best size to develop.

These conditions are most likely to exist when the product is a standardized one, familiar to buyers, such as a 1-inch wood screw or a tenpenny nail. Standardized items such as these do not permit convincing claims that one product is superior to or distinct from another, and thus there is little expenditure on advertising and other means of urging consumers to purchase one product rather than another. Competition among producers is confined primarily to cost and price; and advertising, although it may be worthwhile, consists mostly of information about the availability of the product, its price, and so on.

Situations of true pure competition are relatively rare because it is difficult to find industries in which a standardized commodity is produced and in which both buyers and sellers are numerous. The staple agricultural products would be examples except for the existence of programs of governmental aid to agriculture. The production of gray cloth seems to fit the model, but few other products do. This is not to imply that other industries depart greatly from the ideal model but that many do so to some degree. Some have only a few producers, some have a limited number of buyers, and in others each seller's product is differentiated in some way from those of his competitors.

Oligopoly

There are no examples in the United States of pure monopoly, in which a single producer controls the entire supply. Some years ago the Aluminum Company of America was the sole producer of aluminum, but now there are several. There are many examples of local monopoly, where there is only one seller in a local market. For example, a small town may have only one physician or dentist, one building contractor, or one automobile dealer. However, modern transportation makes it possible for patients or customers to deal with other sellers in most instances. There are also instances of monopolies regulated as public utilities.

There are numerous examples of industries in which there are only a few producers. As we have noted earlier, there are three major producers of automobiles and a limited number of major producers of soaps, detergents, cigarettes, steel, copper, tin cans, beer, and many other things. Such industries are called *oligopolies,* meaning "industries of the few." Because the individual company in an oligopoly does have some discretion over the price it charges as well as the volume of its output, it will be examined further in the next chapter.

Monopolistic Competition

This contradictory-sounding term refers to a situation in which there are many sellers but each has control over some differentiated product that is a close substitute for the others'. In effect, each seller has a monopoly on his own branded or otherwise differentiated product, but the products are such close substitutes for each other that the monopoly has little value. For example, many firms make dinnerware, but each attempts to differentiate its own by designs, patterns, and advertising. There are several producers of ballpoint pens, including many small local firms. Some of the producers attempt to differentiate their pens by establishing some difference in appearance or marketing, such as providing an extra cartridge. A minor difference in dishes or pens may attract some buyers to a particular seller's product.

Sometimes the differentiation is achieved by providing some auxiliary service or benefit, such as home delivery of groceries, parking facilities at a store or bank, especially friendly salespersons, air conditioning, generous credit terms, and so on.

There is some public benefit in monopolistic competition in that different tastes and preferences are served. (Critics would add that sometimes they are created in order to be served.) The numerous and close substitutes create a high degree of competition, even though the competition is not confined to cost and price. But the price cannot be much higher than if the product were standardized in most instances, and where it is, consumers often have a choice between the higher-priced article and the lower-priced article. For example, the consumer can purchase an appliance or article of clothing in a quiet, pleasant shop with the aid of a helpful salesperson, or a similar or identical product at a lower price in a plain, possibly noisy and crowded discount store. Many service businesses, such as barbershops, dry cleaners, beauty parlors, and bowling alleys, attempt to attract customers on some basis other than price, but at the same time most of them cannot get much "out of line" in price without losing customers to competitors.

SUMMARY

How much an individual firm is willing to produce and sell depends crucially on the price it can get in the market. This is because the costs of goods are not fixed but depend partly on the volume of output.

The average or unit cost of a commodity varies with output because some costs are fixed in that they do not vary with the level of output. Other (variable) costs do change with output but not necessarily in proportion, because of the law of diminishing returns. Consequently, two opposing forces are at work on the unit cost of production. The fixed costs can be spread more and more thinly over larger and larger outputs, but beyond the point of diminishing returns in a factory, in a store, or on a farm, the variable costs per unit tend to rise.

There is some point, or perhaps band, of output that has the lowest average cost, but this output may not be the most profitable output for the individual firm. The firm tends to expand output until additional units would add more to cost than to revenue. The general rule is that the output where $MC = MR$ is the most profitable output, or the one with least loss, in the short run. In pure competition, marginal revenue and the unit price are the same thing.

In the long run, short-run profits lead industries to expand and the increased supplies tend to restrict the rise in price that created the profits. There is a tendency for competitive industries to adjust their productive facilities so that they produce at the lowest possible costs, but in the short run they tend to reap profits or incur losses.

Firms behave somewhat differently according to whether their industries are purely competitive or depart from that model. Monopolistic competition differs from pure competition in that, in the former situation, many sellers are able to differentiate their products

from those of competitors. Except for emphasizing nonprice considerations such as service, credit, or pleasant surroundings,
however, sellers in monopolistic competition behave much like
those in pure competition.

Economic Terms for Review

outlay costs	marginal cost
allocation costs	marginal revenue
opportunity costs	pure competition
fixed costs	optimum output
variable costs	equilibrium output
diminishing returns	increasing-cost industries
marginal output	oligopoly
average costs	monopolistic competition

Questions for Review

1. Why do such costs as depreciation and the salary of the president of a corporation have to be allocated?
2. What are some of the implicit costs incurred by the owner of a small store?
3. In what sense are fixed costs fixed? Do they ever change in amount? Is a property tax a fixed cost when the tax rate is changed? (Yes; why?)
4. Give an example of an industry that is said to operate in pure competition; in oligopoly; in monopolistic competition.
5. Give a clear definition of marginal cost.
6. Why is optimum output that at which $MC = MR$?
7. Describe the long-run equilibrium position to which business firms constantly tend.

Questions for Analysis

1. With the following possible levels of input and output, at what level do diminishing returns begin?

Variable Input	Output
0	0
1	100
2	300
3	500
4	600
5	700

How is this level indicated by relative rates of increase in input and output? by the average output? by the marginal output?

2. Assume the following short-run costs in a manufacturing plant:

Daily Output	Fixed Costs	Variable Costs	Total Costs
0	$50	$ 0	$ 50
10		25	75
20		45	95
30		60	110
40		80	130
50		105	155
60		140	190
70		185	235
80		240	290
90		310	360
100		390	440

By reference to the total costs, calculate the marginal costs for each additional 10 units. Do you get the same marginal costs by referring to variable costs only? (You should.) If the article has a market price of $2, how many is it worth producing? (The answer is not 20 units; keep going.) If the unit price is $5, how many should be produced?
3. What is the overall profit or loss if price is $2? $5?
4. What is the lowest price at which any production is worthwhile? What is the profit or loss at this price?

Case for Decision

John Adams, president of a small company producing connectors used in electronics plants, is pondering whether to expand his equipment (see the case at the end of Chapter 2) in order to increase sales of a particularly successful connector, which are running at 1,000 dozen per week. Adams considers this item highly profitable because he estimates the fixed costs attributable to its production ($200) at 20 cents per unit and the variable costs at 40 cents, while the price is $1. Adams thus estimates the weekly profit on this item at $400.

Adams is convinced that in the near future he could boost sales to between 1,500 dozen and 2,000 dozen with some additional sales effort and expense. He also believes that in a year or two sales could be well over 2,000.

In arriving at a decision, Adams must consider costs and methods of production. If he expands production with his present equipment, he knows that he will have to have a man work overtime or on a night shift because the machine that forms this connector is busy all day as it is. Furthermore, since the price of the connector includes delivery and any new customers will be somewhat farther away, increased sales will entail slightly higher delivery charges. Adams believes that his fixed costs would not be affected by boosting output to the 1,500–2,000 dozen range, but he estimates that his variable costs per unit would be as follows:

Weekly Output (Dozen)	Average Variable Cost
1,000	$.40
1,500	.50
1,600	.55
1,700	.60
1,800	.65
1,900	.70
2,000	.75

A salesman from a machinery manufacturer recently called on Adams and offered to develop a machine to form these connectors that would be more efficient than the homemade machine Adams is now using. Adams figures that using the new machine would double the fixed costs (to $400) but would considerably reduce labor hours and the number of rejected pieces. He estimates that the variable costs, using the new machine, would be:

Weekly Output (Dozen)	Average Variable Cost
1,500	$.40
1,600	.41
1,700	.42
1,800	.43
1,900	.44
2,000	.45

Should Adams increase sales to 2,000 dozen per week, using his present equipment? Should he purchase the new machine? What other things should he consider in purchasing the new machine besides its effects on the unit cost?

5

Types of Product Markets

A purely competitive market is often considered ideal because competitive pressures, among both sellers and buyers, promote efficiency and bring about market prices closely related to the lowest possible average costs. But there is another side to the story. If there are many individual firms, each must be considerably smaller than if there were only a few firms. The capital of each firm may be too limited to permit the acquisition of costly equipment. Modern technology is often reflected in equipment and machinery that operate at low cost per unit of output but have high purchase and installation costs. Automated machinery and electronic computers are examples of this type. Although they increase productivity and efficiency, they may not be available to the small firm because of their initial high cost.

SIZE OF FIRMS

Small firms tend to merge into larger ones in order to be able to take advantage of such investments as expensive machinery. The technology of some industries may be such that many firms can exist and be large enough to be efficient. A bank, for example, need not be huge in order to afford a computer. Even banks too small to be able to operate one much of the time can share one through a service company. The economies of large-scale operations do not go on forever in every branch of industry. But in some industries there are great advantages in using assembly-line techniques and other methods of mass production, and great advantages in marketing on the side of the large business unit. The large automobile companies operate many plants, as a huge single plant would not be efficient, but the advantages of marketing the product of several plants under a single name make it difficult for a smaller company to compete.

Other cost advantages may be closed to the small company. In recent years research and development have become extremely important in industry. These costs are not only large but risky, in the sense that they may or may not show adequate returns. A small firm is unlikely to be able to support a scientific or engineering laboratory in which to develop new products or new methods of production.

Whether a firm is large or small is relative to its industry. In the "industries" represented by the many barbers, dry cleaners, building contractors, and physicians, the advantages of large size do not usually overcome the advantages of small size. Even in these occupations, however, larger units can be more efficient, such as when a group of physicians offers cooperative health services at one location. Although the automobile industry is huge, the advantages of large size have brought about a situation in which most of the production comes from only three companies.

Occasionally there are spectacular exceptions, but as a rule new products and improved methods come from relatively large companies. The output of many large companies consists largely of products they did not make ten or twenty years earlier. It may be that the traditional preference for pure competition stems from a more static period in history when dynamic changes, inventions, and improvements came much more slowly. Progress and growth may require a reassessment of the desirability of pure competition but, as they do so, they raise new questions concerning market power and control over the corporate giants. Many people who watched the astronauts on their trips to the moon in late 1968 and 1969 could remember when there was no television, when even radio was a newfangled gadget, and when Colonel Lindbergh's flight across the Atlantic was a spectacular achievement.

AGRICULTURE

Agriculture is often cited as an example of pure competition. Farms are numerous — although each does not produce the same products — and farm products are largely standardized. One grade of wheat is the same on any farm.

American agriculture is highly productive by world standards. American farmers are probably better educated and at least as hard-working and healthy as those anywhere. But to a large extent, the productivity of American farms does not stem from the farmers themselves nor from the fact that there are millions of them. The principal advances in farm technology, such as the development of new strains of corn and new breeds of hogs and turkeys, have come mainly from research performed by universities and government agencies. The chemical industry, not the farmers, develops new kinds of fertilizers and manufactures them, and the farm-equipment industry develops new kinds of tractors and other types of farm equipment. Sales representatives of these companies and county agents of the United States Department of Agriculture visit and advise farmers on new methods of production. The chemical and farm-equipment industries both fit better the model of oligopoly than that of pure competition.

Problems of Agriculture

Some farms are very prosperous but, as an industry, agriculture has seldom fared as well as most others in the economy. Rural incomes have typically been below urban incomes, averaging about $1,000 per person below in recent years. In the great depression of the 1930s many farms were bankrupt and in the decade before that, while there was a general prosperity, farmers suffered from low prices. The persistence and severity of the economic problems of farmers have brought a variety of programs of assistance from the federal government.

The mere fact that agriculture is a purely competitive industry does not explain the problems that plague it. The facts of competition are interwoven with other characteristics peculiar to agriculture. These characteristics relate to the natural environment and to the demands for farm products.

1. Weather Conditions. Manufacturing is carried on almost entirely indoors under conditions controlled by man. Agriculture is carried on under whatever conditions the weather brings. Nature may be benevolent or cruel; she may cooperate by bringing favorable weather or she may bring droughts, floods, or untimely freezes. If a crop is ruined by bad weather, the farmer's efforts, perhaps those of a whole year, are worthless.

2. Price Inelasticity of Demand. The demands for most agricultural products are inelastic. Large increases in output cannot be sold except at considerably reduced prices. If good weather, advanced technology, and hard work bring forth a large crop of wheat or corn, the price may be depressed severely. It is possible for the price to fall sufficiently to produce a smaller total revenue for a big crop than for a small crop. A bumper crop is not necessarily a blessing. Figure 5-1 illustrates that a bumper crop of 60 million bushels of wheat might have to sell for $1.50 while a crop of 50 million would have sold for $2 a bushel. As a result, the total revenue is $90 million rather than $100 million.

Since most agricultural products are staple products, most people do not change their consumption of them much because of a change in price. When wheat and, consequently, bread rise in price, most people do not reduce their consumption substantially and, by the same token, when wheat and bread go down in price, they do not eat much more. Only a substantial change in price brings about much change in consumption.

3. Income Inelasticity of Demand. The elasticity of demand with respect to income is similar to that with respect to price. As people's incomes rise they do not consume a correspondingly larger amount of farm output. They may shift to more expensive cuts of meat or otherwise spend more but, as they shift, they consume less of something else. Over the years total expenditures on farm products have risen but not as fast as in-

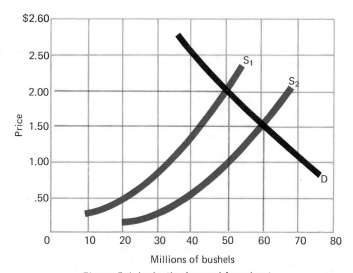

Figure 5-1. Inelastic demand for wheat.

comes have risen. An increase in income is more likely to be spent on less essential goods—automobiles, appliances, furniture, education, recreation, and the like—than on more bread, cereal, and beef.

As the population increases, there also tends to be a larger demand for food and fibers, but the increase in population is no more rapid than the advance of farm technology. Based on the annual output in 1957–1959 as 100, crop production per man-hour was at an index of 28 in 1929 and at 173 in 1967. In other words, output per man-hour was six times as great. Livestock production per man-hour rose from 48 to 176, or by more than three times. Total farm output for human consumption rose by 17 percent from 1957–1959 to 1967. Food grains increased by 34 percent, meat animals by 18 percent, and poultry and eggs by 139 percent.

4. Inability to Control Output. When the demand for the output of an automobile manufacturer or furniture manufacturer declines, he can reduce his output accordingly. The manufacturer can lay off workers, reduce his outlays for materials, and otherwise adjust to the smaller demand. On most farms, however, the work force is the farmer and his family, and thus the farmer cannot reduce his outlays for labor by laying off his workers. Like the manufacturer, the farmer has fixed, or overhead, costs in the form of interest and property taxes. If he could cut his variable costs drastically by producing less, he would do so, but since he cannot he attempts to cover as much of his fixed costs as possible. Farmers may produce as much in the face of declining demand and prices as they would if prices were rising. Consequently, the decline in price may be all the more severe because it is not limited by reduced output.

5. Immobility of Productive Factors. It is relatively easy for a farmer to shift from growing one crop to another, but it is more difficult for him to shift completely out of farming. Unless the farmer can dispose of his land for some urban use, there is little or no alternative use for the land other than farming. Unless the land is farmed, it becomes worthless or, at least, unproductive.

The farmer himself may find it difficult to change from farming to another occupation. Abandoning the farm for a city job usually involves a move of some distance and a completely different kind of life from the one he is used to. Many farmers continue even though they do not expect their lot to improve much. Over a period of time, migration takes place more because farm children leave the farm. When jobs are plentiful in the cities, migration takes place more rapidly than in periods of recession when times may be hard on the farm but few jobs are available in the cities. Thus the number of farms changes rather slowly although, as we noted in an earlier chapter, there is a definite trend toward fewer but larger farms and toward a smaller farm population.

Although many farmers are well-to-do, there is farm poverty or relative poverty when these five characteristics combine to make earning a living difficult for some farmers. The difficulties have been augmented since 1915 by two world wars and the great depression. During World War I, agricultural production in Europe was limited and American farmers expanded their farms and equipment, largely by borrowing the necessary funds. After the war their output was excessive, especially when European production recovered. Agriculture continued to be in a depression throughout the decade of the 1920s and farm incomes, after payments on debt, were low. Unemployment and low incomes in the cities brought further depression to farming during the 1930s. Prosperity returned with the greatly increased demands for farm products during and after World War II but was not long-lasting.

Prices of farmland rose sharply during World War II as farmers tried to expand their farms. These high prices represented high costs after the war. Agriculture has experienced wide swings in demand, and such swings require equally great adjustments in supply. To a great extent, the difficulties of agriculture can be attributed to the fact that agriculture is not well suited to making large shifts in supply.

Government Programs

If farms were much less numerous — if they were combined into fewer and larger units — each might be stronger financially. Even so, the other characteristics of farming would probably make it difficult for farmers to adjust output to changes in demand. The federal government has developed programs that are designed to speed this type of adjustment and to minimize the effects of disparities between supply and demand.

The principal legislation to achieve these ends is the Agricultural Adjustment Act, which was passed first during the New Deal days of the 1930s and which has been amended frequently. There were earlier legislative attempts to raise or stabilize farm prices, but they provided for government purchase of farm products without limitation of output. Consequently, there was little incentive for farmers to restrict output and the government found itself buying and storing surplus production.

Current farm programs provide for price supports and restriction of production through allotment of acreage for various crops. Production of wheat and corn is limited chiefly through acreage allotment; marketing quotas exist also for wheat, rice, cotton, and tobacco. The *support price* is maintained by a device whereby the farmer can sell his crop to a government agency, the Commodity Credit Corporation, when the market price is below the support price. Often the arrangement is that the farmer can borrow the value of his crop at the support price from the CCC. If the market price rises above the support price, he can reclaim the crop used for security and sell it on the market; if the market price is below, he can forfeit the crop rather than repay the loan.

The support price is related to the *parity price,* which is the market price that bears the same relationship to other prices as existed in a base period when it is assumed the relationship was "normal." Selling at the parity price would enable farmers to purchase other goods with the same ability as was provided by a bushel of output in the base period. The original base period chosen was 1910–1914, as it was thought that the relationship between farm prices and other prices could be considered normal at that time. Amendments to the Agricultural Adjustment Act have adopted later base periods for some purposes. In general, the Secretary of Agriculture is empowered to set the percentage, such as 70 percent or 80 percent, of the parity price that will be the current year's support price.

In its simplest form, the idea of parity price is that if other prices have doubled since the base period, the price of wheat or corn should also be doubled because then a bushel of output would still exchange for the same amount of manufactured goods. This simple approach, however, overlooks changes in productivity and costs. It might be, for example, that the cost of producing a bushel of corn has not doubled, because of rising output per man-hour or per acre, so that a doubled price would bring greater profits than in the base period. The relationship between prices paid by farmers and prices received by farmers between 1940 and 1970 is shown in Figure 5-2.

Elementary economic analysis tells us that if the government is willing to pay a higher price than would be set by supply and demand in a free market, producers will want to produce more than they would at the free market price. At the same time, if the price is kept above the equilibrium level, buyers will take somewhat less of the commodity. Thus a surplus tends to arise because producers are willing to offer for sale more units than buyers will take at the support price. In Figure 5-3 this surplus is the quantity AB. The equilibrium price in a free market is P_e, and the equilibrium quantity taken is Q_e. If the government supports the price P_s, buyers take the quantity OA but sellers offer OB; consequently, the government must purchase the quantity AB in order to prevent the price from falling.

For this reason, some program of crop restriction is necessary with a program of price support. Unless the government is willing to purchase and hold the surplus output in hopes that future crop failures will make the stored commodities salable, it must either let the price fall to where it will clear the market or prevent output from exceeding the quantity OA. In different instances, the government has allowed only those farmers who agree to restrict acreage to borrow, has penalized farmers who produce more than assigned quotas, or has made acreage restriction mandatory. A contradiction is inherent in any program of price support for farm products. Although such a program is designed to improve the incomes

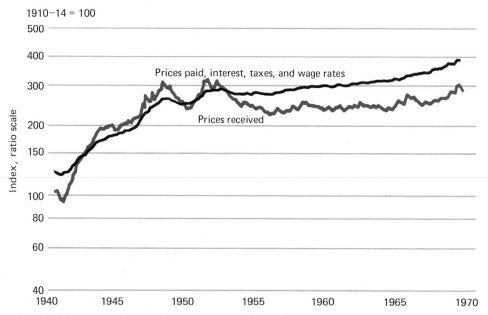

Figure 5-2. Prices paid and received by farmers, 1940–1970.   Source: *Federal Reserve Historical Chart Book,* 1969, pp. 102–103; *Federal Reserve Monthly Chart Book,* April, 1970, p. 80.

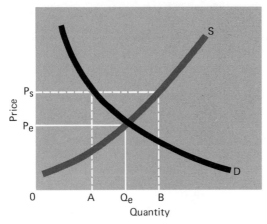

Figure 5-3. Farm support price.

of the farm sector of the economy, higher incomes tend to delay the shift of resources out of agriculture. And this shift would, in turn, limit supply and raise farm prices. Another contradiction in the farm programs is that when payments are made to farmers who hold acreage out of production, the farms having the largest acreage get the largest payments. Yet the farm programs are intended to ease the lot of the small farmer, who may receive only a small sum for holding a few acres out of production while the owner of a giant farm may be paid several hundred thousand dollars. A ceiling on the amount that may be received by any one farm has often been proposed. In addition, it is uneconomic to keep some of the acres of the largest, most efficient farms out of production.

The government has expended huge sums on price-support programs, and in many years large surpluses have accumulated. These surpluses "overhang" the market and tend to hold down prices because of the threat that they may be sold. Individual farmers have seen their own advantage to be in a policy of producing all they can within the rules. They naturally tend to produce more intensively on their allotted acres. Technological advances such as hybrid seeds, more efficient fertilizers, and pest controls have tended to offset the reduction of acreage. Since acres not used to produce controlled crops may be used to raise other crops, the prices of these crops have tended to fall. As a result, programs have had to be added whereby farmers are paid for keeping land completely idle. Programs have also been devised whereby farmers are encouraged to devote land to nonagricultural use, such as camping and recreation.

Although farm surpluses tended to accumulate in government hands up to 1965 and to cost large sums for storage, after that time the problem of surpluses tended to ease. Some of the surpluses were used as shipments to needy countries; India received large shipments in 1965 and 1966 because of hunger and starvation in that country. Within this country, farm surpluses have been used to provide free lunches for needy school children.[1] Prices of some commodities climbed for a while to or above parity in 1966 but drifted down over the next two years. The support price of

---

[1] A major criticism of this program is that the foods provided are those that happen to be in surplus supply rather than those that might otherwise be selected for this purpose.

wheat was $1.25 in 1966 while the market price reached $2, but in 1968 the market price again approximated $1.25.

In one sense the farm programs have been successful: They have maintained farm prices at levels above what they would have been otherwise. At the same time, the persistent trend toward fewer farmers and larger farms has continued. The conflicting objectives contained in the programs, combined with the peculiarities of agriculture as an industry of pure competition, have continued to make the problem of adjusting supply to demand a complicated one.

The problems of agriculture are political as well as economic. Agriculture tends to have a strong voice in the Congress. Each state, whether largely urban and highly populated or mostly agricultural and sparsely populated, has two senators. Many Congressmen, even from urban states, come from rural agricultural areas. Once begun, subsidies are difficult to reduce or eliminate because many become dependent on them. The various programs designed to limit output and raise prices made considerable sense in the depression of the 1930s but now require revision.

MONOPOLY PRICES

In the study of the determination of market prices, monopoly markets are at the opposite extreme from markets characterized by pure competition. Like pure competition, monopoly is rare, but the principles of how price is set under monopolistic conditions are reasonably simple. A monopolist is the sole producer or seller of a commodity for which there are no close substitutes. Thus the monopolist controls the entire industry, and the demand for the product is the demand for his output. Within the limits set by the conditions of demand, the monopolist is free to find the most profitable price. The social and economic disadvantages of monopoly, therefore, are that (1) the monopolist tends to restrict output in order to raise the price, (2) he gains a monopoly profit that does not lead to expanded output, and (3) he may be under little or no pressure to innovate as he would be if he had competitors.

Marginal Revenue in Monopoly

Since the monopoly is the entire industry, the monopolist visualizes the demand for his output as the demand curve for the product and not as a horizontal line, as it would be in the case of pure competition. Suppose the demand is as shown in Table 5-1. Clearly the monopolist would not

Table 5-1
Demand for Monopolist's Product

Price	Quantity	Revenue
$10	100	$1,000
9	150	1,350
8	200	1,600
7	250	1,750
6	300	1,800
5	350	1,750

Table 5-2
Demand and Costs for a Monopolist

Price	Quan-tity	Reve-nue	Mar-ginal Revenue	Total Cost	Average Cost	Marginal Cost	Profit
(1)	(2)	(3)	(4)	(5)	(6)	(7)	(8)
$10	100	$1,000	...	$ 800	$8.00	....	$200
9	150	1,350	$7	1,100	7.33	$6.00	250
8	200	1,600	5	1,320	6.60	4.40	280
7	250	1,750	3	1,450	5.80	2.60	300
6	300	1,800	1	1,600	5.33	3.00	200
5	350	1,750	−1	1,775	5.07	3.50	−25

want to sell 350 units because the total revenue would be less than for 300 units, and it would certainly cost more to produce 350 units. Ignoring costs, he might select 300 as the output to produce because that output, which he can sell at a price of $6, creates the largest total revenue. But when he considers his costs, he may find that an even smaller output is more profitable. Suppose that his costs of production are as tabulated, along with these demand figures, in Table 5-2.

It can be seen in the profit column (8) that the largest profit occurs if 250 units are sold at a price of $7. The total revenue is $1,750, total cost $1,450, and profit $300. As in the case of pure competition, this optimum level of output can be found by comparing marginal cost with marginal revenue. The table shows marginal cost per unit, the additional cost at each step divided by the additional 50 units. But since the monopolist, facing the demand curve for the product, must reduce price if he wishes to increase quantity sold, the marginal revenue is no longer the same thing as the price. If he sells 100 units at $10, his total revenue is $1,000, but if he wants to sell 150 units he must charge $9. The total revenue is therefore $1,350, and selling 50 more units adds $350 to total revenue. This is because he must reduce the price for the whole 150 units, not only for the marginal 50, and so the 100 units he could sell for $1,000 bring only $900. The 50 extra units bring $450, for the total of $1,350. Thus selling 50 more units adds $9 apiece to $900, not to $1,000, and the gain in revenue is $350, or $7 apiece, which is less than the price being charged.

At larger volumes, marginal revenue is even less because price must be reduced on a larger quantity if additional units are to be sold. To sell 300 units instead of 250, the price has to be reduced from $7 to $6. The extra 50 units add $300 to revenues, but the price reduction on the other 250 lowers revenues by $250, leaving a net gain, or marginal revenue, of only $50, or $1 apiece.

When the monopolist compares these marginal revenues with his marginal costs, he finds that additional units of output add less to costs than to revenues up to an output of 250 units, where marginal cost is $2.60 and marginal revenue is $3.00. Each of the 50 units above 200 adds 40 cents to profit, a total of $20 (and we can see in Column 8 that profit is $300 rather than $280). The maximum profit ($300) comes at an output of 250 units because additional output would have marginal cost greater than marginal revenue.

Under conditions of pure competition, price would tend to be lower than $7. The average unit cost is smaller for outputs larger than 250 units. If there were many producers with costs similar to the monopolist's, each would expand production at the price of $7 because his marginal cost is less than $7.

Figure 5-4 illustrates the determination of price under monopolistic conditions. In fact, the curves show that if the monopolist can adjust his output by increments smaller than 50 units, he can maximize profit by selling just over 250 units at a price just below $7. The optimum output for the monopolist is shown by the intersection of the *MC* and *MR* curves. The closest output to this point in Table 5-2 is 250 units, but the curves intersect at a slightly larger output. Directly above this point is the point on the *AC* curve showing the average cost at this output, and directly above that the demand curve (*D*) shows what price could be charged for this output. The rectangle made by lines drawn back to the vertical axis shows the monopoly profit ($300 in Table 5-2).

Pure competition and pure monopoly are the two extreme conditions of competition under which price is determined by market forces. We have seen that pure competition is ideal in some respects but that it has real-world disadvantages, as in the case of agriculture. There is nothing ideal about monopoly. The monopolist tends to restrict output and to charge a monopoly price that yields a monopoly profit. In the process, goods may not be produced at as low a cost as would be brought about in more competitive markets.

Whether the monopolist has considerable discretion over the price-quantity combination to select or whether his monopoly power is weak

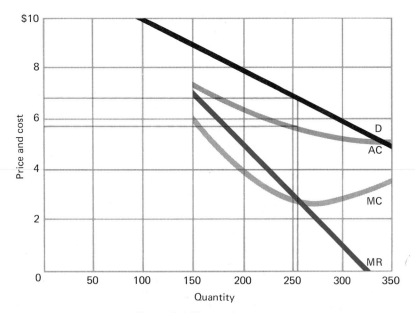

Figure 5-4. Monopoly price.

depends on the elasticity of demand for his product. Although there is no close substitute, there is some substitute for virtually everything. The slope of the monopolist's demand curve reflects the fact that buyers can turn to something else when the price is high enough — or they may simply do without.

Many firms have some degree of monopoly power, as we shall examine in the next section. This power tends to be rather limited, partly by the existence of competitors' products and partly by fear of government regulation if the monopoly becomes too great or is abused. Government action in the field of monopoly has already been referred to and is discussed more thoroughly in Chapter 17. The very large firms can afford modern equipment, expenses for research and development, and many other advantages of specialization. Even though their prices may include some monopoly profit, they may be lower than they would be without these advantages. Fortunately, the economies of large size are usually not so great that they lead to the existence of a single firm in an industry, especially in an economy as great as that of the United States. In some industries it appears to be true that the largest companies are not the most efficient, and this suggests that they run into diseconomies as well as economies. Often the second-, third-, or fourth-largest company seems to be the most efficient and progressive and to earn the largest profit on invested capital.

There is more likely to be improvement and innovation in industries that have at least several large firms. Each has a considerable incentive to lower its costs and to be able to seize a larger share of the total market. There is not only a purely economic motivation but a spirit of rivalry among a few firms that does not exist when one competitor has thousands of rivals. When there is only one firm, however, there is a greater possibility that the lack of competition can lead to complacent attitudes and a policy of leaving well enough alone. This kind of attitude seems to exist more commonly in some European countries than in the United States. The giant American Telephone and Telegraph Company, which controls the largest fraction of the telephone business and is also regulated by state commissions and the Federal Communications Commission, maintains a position of leadership in research in the communications sciences. Its management realizes that the telephone is not the only means of modern electronic communication and that rival methods are sure to be developed, if not by AT&T then by others.

OLIGOPOLY

An industry is called an oligopoly when it consists of only a few firms or when only a few produce most of the output. The firms are then called oligopolists. This type of industrial structure is common in the United States, as we have had occasion to note. Three companies produce most of the automobiles although a few smaller companies produce a small percentage and foreign companies also command a small share of the market. In the tin can industry, there are two major producers and several smaller ones. The steel industry is considered an oligopoly although there are about 200 firms producing and processing steel, because the ten largest firms produce about 80 percent of the total, as measured by steel ingot production. They employ the bulk of the workers in the industry. In most of the important American manufacturing industries, two-thirds or more of the output comes from four or fewer companies. Besides the oligopolistic industries just mentioned, there are those producing rubber tires, tractors, computers, liquor, transformers, cigarettes, man-made fibers, phonograph records and record players, aluminum, soap, light bulbs, typewriters, locomotives, and other items.

Characteristics of Oligopolies

Some oligopolistic industries produce standardized articles, like steel and aluminum, while others produce differentiated products like type-writers, cigarettes, and phonograph records. Sometimes the former industries are called pure oligopolies, as any control or discretion over the prices they charge stems solely from the fact that they are few. With the latter group, however, control of trademarks and other differentiating characteristics may add to their discretion in selecting prices.

There are said to be few companies in an industry if a company controls enough of the output that the others cannot ignore changes it may make in its prices or quantities sold and, by the same token, it cannot ignore changes made by its major competitors. Pricing policies are determined largely in the light of anticipated reactions on the part of competitors. For example, United States Steel might raise its prices on some articles in response to an increase in demand or an increase in costs if its executives believe that other major producers would follow suit. But it would probably refrain from raising its prices if it believed that the other firms, perhaps because of excess capacity, would not "go along." In that case, the company that raised prices would lose sales to the others and it would have to restore the old price. Similarly, in setting list prices, Ford, General Motors, and Chrysler must each consider what the other two are likely to do.

A common arrangement in the oligopolistic industries is for one company to act as a _price leader_. This company announces from time to time its list prices, and generally the other companies then announce identical or similar price lists. The price leader is not necessarily always the same company. In banking, for example, a large bank may announce a change in its prime rate, which is the rate available to the largest and most credit-worthy corporate customers. Generally, other major banks promptly announce the same rate. Occasionally, however, bank manage-ments disagree in their assessments of coming credit conditions and other banks refuse to follow. In that case, the first bank usually has to go back to the preceding rate. If it has raised its rate, it will lose business and, if it has lowered its rate, it may get more than it can handle. Or it may turn out that the first bank is correct in its forecast and so the other banks fall in line after a delay. The next time the rate changes, it may be announced first by a different bank.

There are thus several contrasts between oligopoly and pure competi-tion. The pure competitor has no price policy because all he can do is to accept or refuse the going market price. If he produces a nonperishable article, he can hold production off the market, hoping for a higher price, and if enough producers do so, the price may rise. Or he may reduce his output. But he has no opportunity to decide that he will sell a certain quantity and charge a certain price; he must take the going or anticipated price as given and decide how many it would pay to sell. In pure competition the price is impersonal. No one sets it; it just comes about in the markets for wheat, hogs, and other such products. And of course the seller in pure competition has no list prices. The hog farmer does not publish a list of prices at which he is willing to sell hogs; he reads in the morning paper or hears on the radio what hogs are selling for and decides whether to send any hogs to market that day.

Another distinction related to these is that in oligopolies prices tend to stay the same for some period of time. Steel companies announce a price for a given type of steel for a quarter of the year. Sometimes, however, when demand turns out to be less than anticipated, salesmen have to "shave" prices in order to make sales. When this practice becomes widespread, it usually leads to the announcement of new list prices more closely in line with actual prices.

Although oligopoly is a typical kind of industrial structure, different industries have reached this condition through different routes. Sometimes the three or four major companies have attained that status by superior efficiencies in production or marketing. Other companies have gone out of business or perhaps merged into the more successful ones. General Motors Corporation is the successor company to several preceding ones which have become divisions of the successful company. Ford Motor Company, on the other hand, is the result primarily of internal growth. It is estimated that between 1903 and 1926, over 180 companies entered the business of producing automobiles.[2]

In some instances, possession of important sources of raw materials assures the position of some companies in an industry. Before World War II the Aluminum Company of America was the sole producer of aluminum because it owned the major sources of bauxite, the basic ore. Some of the steel companies reached major status because of their ownership of iron ore in Minnesota, Wisconsin, or Michigan. In other cases, the development of inventions and holding of patents protect a major producer's position. General Electric, Westinghouse, and RCA are innovators and thus holders of patents. In other instances a head start has been important. This can almost be said to be true of nearly all leading companies, but it is particularly true of those that were early entrants into such fields as broadcasting and computers.

A great merger in 1901 combined three groups of steel companies, themselves the result of previous mergers, into United States Steel. This company brought together the three combinations that had already been formed by the leading steelmakers, Morgan, Carnegie, and Moore.

It is characteristic of these industries that great aggregations of capital are required to attain an economical size. Some of these companies have grown to this size but, now that they have, it is difficult for new companies to enter the industry because of the amount of investment required. Finally, the existence of well-known brand names is also an advantage for the older firm and a disadvantage for the new. Such trade names as Chevrolet, Ford, Plymouth, Firestone, Goodyear, Budweiser, General Electric, and Westinghouse have real value to their possessors.

[2] D. A. Moore, "The Automobile Industry," in Walter Adams (ed.), *The Structure of American Industry,* The Macmillan Company, New York, 1954, pp. 278–279.

Oligopolistic Pricing

Since the oligopolist produces a substantial share of the total supply, he is keenly aware of the nature of the demand for the product. He must be alert to shifts in the demand and familiar with the elasticity of demand. He tends to select the output that produces the largest profit, but what this output is depends on the policies of his major competitors and how their output affects the price.

Figure 5-5 illustrates how price is set by the oligopolist. The situation is essentially similar to that of the monopolist, except that the demand curve is assumed to be more elastic because buyers have the choice of buying from other sellers if they do not like the oligopolist's prices. Given the willingness of the other oligopolists to accept the price P, the oligopolist will choose this price, at which he can sell an output Q, because it provides the maximum profit. At smaller outputs he could increase output and MC would be less than MR, but beyond the output Q, MC would exceed MR.

If the oligopolist's major competitors do not want to have the price at P, they may establish other prices. If, for example, they want to try to expand sales and consequently lower the price, the demand curve for this oligopolist shifts to the left because he can no longer sell as many units at such high prices as before. The MR curve shifts correspondingly to the left and intersects the MC curve at a smaller output. The oligopolist's profit is reduced, but it would be reduced even more if he refused to cut his price at all.

It follows that if there is considerable ease of entry into the industry and existing firms wish to expand their market shares, there may be virtually as much competition as in the model of pure competition. The profit shown in Figure 5-5 may be gradually reduced by the entry of new

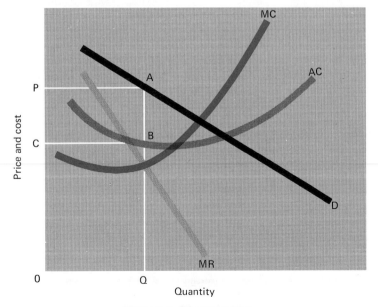

Figure 5-5. Oligopoly price.

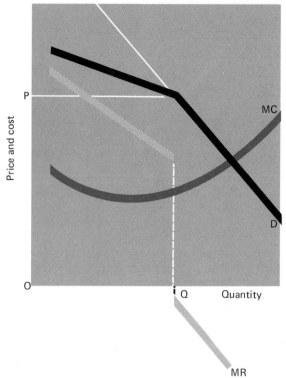

Figure 5-6. A kinked demand curve.

firms, reducing the share of the market that is dominated by any one firm. Realizing this fact, oligopolists have to bear in mind what other firms will do if one of them changes the price he charges.

A price leader in an oligopolistic industry is likely to reason that if he raises his price, other firms may not because in that way they can attract customers from him. This might well be the situation if capacity is not fully used and each firm can lower its average unit cost by producing a larger quantity (note that in Figure 5-5 the firm is not producing at its lowest average cost). On the other hand, the oligopolist might also figure that if he lowered price in order to expand sales, the other firms would have to lower their prices also to avoid losing sales to him. When this situation prevails, the demand curve appears to the oligopolist to have a "kink" in it at the present going market price. This situation may be termed one of *kinked demand*.

This type of reasoning is shown in Figure 5-6. The demand curve, *D*, is very elastic to the left of the point of intersection with the going market price, *P*. This means that if the oligopolist raised his price, he would be able to sell only a considerably reduced quantity, on the assumption that his competitors would not also raise theirs. If he should assume that they would also raise their prices, however, the demand curve for his output would not have this kink but would rise along the upward extension of the demand curve, which is shown by a white line in Figure 5-6.

The oligopolist also figures that if he reduced price, he would not gain sales from his competitors, on the assumption that they also would reduce their prices. The only gain in sales would result from the elasticity of demand; all competitors might sell a bit more at a lower price. Since the oligopolist does not anticipate any substantial gain in sales from a lower price, there can be no addition to total revenues as a result of the lower price. If the demand curve is at all inelastic below the point of the kink, the marginal revenue becomes negative at that point. Graphically, there is a gap in the *MR* curve. As long as the demand curve is elastic—down to the point of the kink—some revenue could be added by selling more units and lowering the price. At the point of the kink, the demand curve turns inelastic and *MR* suddenly becomes negative.

In Figure 5-6 the *MC* curve is drawn so that it goes through the gap in the *MR* curve. This is to show that there is no intersection that would clearly define the most profitable output. The oligopolist tends to prefer to let well enough alone and to go along with the going market price unless there is a considerable change in demand or in his costs. If his costs were raised substantially, he would find the *MC* curve intersecting the *MR* curve at a smaller output and he would be motivated to raise his price but, unless this happens, he is better off not raising the price. Similarly, there is nothing to gain by lowering the price.

Partly because of the oligopolist's uncertainty over the most profitable price, competition among oligopolists often takes nonprice forms. The oligopolist may decide that he is better off competing by increasing his advertising expenditures, improving his product, bringing out a new model, and the like. But even then he cannot be certain how competitors will react to these forms of competition. Thus a kind of game theory applies to the decisions reached. For example, an executive may set up a matrix in which he assesses the likelihood and the results of four possibilities:

	We advertise	*We do not advertise*
Rivals advertise		
Rivals do not advertise		

While the curves in Figure 5-5 show that the oligopolist attempts to extract some *oligopoly profit* from his position in the market and that this action leads to restriction of output more or less as in the case of monopoly, what is unknown is whether the public actually pays a higher price for a given volume of output than would be true under more purely competitive conditions. The oligopolist may not produce at the lowest point on his average cost curve, but he may have a lower curve than would a smaller competitor. Present knowledge does not give us complete answers to such questions.

It is probable that business firms do not need to become as large as some have in order to benefit from the *economies of size*. Professor Joe S. Bain has studied several industries and concluded that firms need not be as large as the largest three or four in many industries in order to achieve the economies of present technology. He estimates that a steel company large enough to produce 2 percent of the total supply is large enough to attain these economies. The percentage of industry output is also about 2 percent in automobile tires and petroleum refining, about 4 percent in rayon, and about 10 percent in typewriters.[3]

When the oligopolistic industry produces differentiated products, such as toothpaste and cigarettes, the competition among producers tends to emphasize advertising and marketing techniques rather than price itself. When the product is differentiated by a brand name and other distinguishing characteristics, each producer has, in a sense, a little monopoly because only he can sell that particular brand of product. However, the products are so easily substitutable that no producer can exploit his monopoly position very much—the demand for his particular product is too elastic. This form of competition may be generally beneficial or it may be of little public benefit. For example, it seems unlikely that the differences among cigarettes, so emphatically advertised, matter greatly to most smokers, but improvements in the safety of automobiles, the durability of tires, the fidelity of record players, and the efficiency of household appliances do benefit buyers. There seems to be a correlation between the difficulty of creating really differentiating characteristics and advertising expenditures. Where the products are essentially similar, producers advertise their real or supposed differences all the more extensively.

It should be emphasized that the concern of the oligopolist with the pricing and output policies of his competitors need not lead to collusion. Throughout the history of American business there have been numerous examples, however, in which the fewness of competitors has led to agreements among them on pricing, market sharing, and the like. As is detailed in Chapter 17, such agreements are contrary to the antitrust laws.

SUMMARY

In this chapter three types of product markets in which goods are sold have been examined. A fourth type, monopolistic competition, was noted in Chapter 4, along with its basic similarity to pure competition. At one extreme is pure competition, in which there are numerous buyers and sellers of a standard product. In this case, no seller can influence the price because he controls too small a share of the supply. Price is set wholly by impersonal market forces, and each seller adjusts his output to that price. At the other extreme is monopoly, in which there is but one seller. Since he controls the entire supply, he can pick that combination of output and price that provides the highest profit. Even the monopolist, however, is subject to the competition of substitute products— his demand curve has some degree of elasticity—and he is also subject to potential competition from new entrants into the industry

[3] Joe S. Bain, *Barriers to New Competition,* Harvard University Press, Cambridge, Mass., 1956, pp. 80–86.

unless he possesses some unique control, such as over raw materials.

A typical structure in American industry has come to be called oligopoly. Here the bulk of the output, and perhaps all, is produced by a few firms. Each has some discretion in selecting the price to charge and correspondingly the output to produce. Each is limited by the nature of demand; if it selects a certain output, it must accept the price at which that output can be sold, and if it selects a certain price, it is limited by that price in selecting its output. Since the amount sold by other major competitors is a principal determinant of how much the oligopolist can charge and produce, each oligopolist tends to alter the going price only if he is convinced that he will not be harmed by the reactions of his competitors.

Economic Terms for Review

price inelasticity	monopoly profit
income inelasticity	price leader
support price	kinked demand
parity price	oligopoly profit
subsidies	economies of size

Questions for Review

1. What are some of the economies enjoyed by large firms?
2. What characteristics of agriculture make adjustments of supply to demand difficult?
3. Why are factors of production in agriculture immobile?
4. Why do crop-price-support programs include restriction of output?
5. How are parity prices related to support prices?
6. How does the demand facing a monopolist differ from that facing someone in pure competition?
7. Why do MC and MR meet at a smaller output in a monopoly than in pure competition?
8. What does an oligopolist have to consider, in setting his selling price, that a pure competitor does not?
9. Why is an oligopolist likely to be uncertain what price would produce maximum profit?

Questions for Analysis

1. Why is a farmer likely to find that his best course is to produce as much as possible rather than to restrict output?
2. Why are so many farms small and unprofitable?
3. What would be some of the results of a program under which the government offered to buy at some price above the unsupported price any part of a crop offered?
4. Suppose that a monopoly has the following cost and price structure:

Price	Quantity	Total Cost	Average Cost	Marginal Cost	Marginal Revenue	Profit
$17	50	$ 600		.....	.....	
16	75	950				
15	100	1,200				
14	125	1,400				
13	150	1,650				
12	175	1,950				
11	200	2,300				

(a) At what output does *MC* begin to exceed *MR*? (b) What is the monopolist's profit?

5. If the firm in Question 4 were one of many similar firms: (a) What would it do if the market price was $14? (b) What would the price tend to be in this competitive industry?

6. Suppose that price is at the kink in the demand curve in Figure 5-6. Why does the oligopolist not raise the price?

Case for Decision

Three leading producers of fishing lures produce about 75 percent of all lures sold in this country. Their shares of the present market are 30, 25, and 20 percent. The John Milton Company, the largest, has designed a model of a lure it thinks would sell well, the Dingbat.[4] Mr. Milton, president and sales manager, is weighing the pros and cons of putting the lure into production.

Some of the questions Mr. Milton has been asking himself are:

1. Do fishermen tend to spend a fixed amount for lures so that the Dingbat would reduce sales of other lures?
2. If so, how much would Milton's sales be decreased?
3. How many lures are bought by nonfishermen to be given away?
4. The second largest company has a comparable lure already on the market, the Little Daisy. What steps would that company take to maintain sales?
5. If the Dingbat is produced, should it be priced the same as other Milton lures, the same as the Little Daisy, or higher or lower than the Little Daisy?[5]
6. Should the Dingbat be added to the line of lures quietly or with considerable advertising?

Mr. Milton thinks he knows the market well from years of experience. He estimates:

1. The Dingbat would reduce sales of other Milton lures slightly because it is not closely similar to any other.
2. The Dingbat would appeal to nonfishermen who might buy a lure to give away.

[4] It is often suspected that lures are designed at least as much to catch fishermen as to catch fish.

[5] The price of the Little Daisy is well above direct costs of production of the Dingbat.

3. If the producer of the Little Daisy does nothing beyond present efforts, the Dingbat sales should be about 200,000 in each of the first two years, with a 40-cent profit on each, if it is introduced quietly. Expenditure of about $30,000 on advertising might make the sales about 300,000.

4. Rival sales efforts would probably not keep sales of the Dingbat below 100,000 with no advertising or below 150,000 with advertising.

5. The producer of the Little Daisy would probably match the price of the Dingbat if that of the Dingbat is lower.

From the information given, what should Mr. Milton decide? What additional information would be useful?

Managerial Economics

The principles discussed in the preceding chapters on prices and costs are directly applicable to day-to-day business problems. These concepts have been worked out by generations of economists principally to explain the operation of the whole economy, but the business manager who understands them can also see more clearly how his own operations may be made more efficient and profitable.

MARGINALISM

Sometimes students are skeptical that business managers actually try to equate marginal cost with marginal revenue or even know what the words mean. To this skepticism there are several responses. Many businessmen are very much aware of the need to keep the additional cost of some proposed project or increase in output below the anticipated additional revenue. Whether they use the terms *marginal cost* and *marginal revenue* is not very important, as long as they understand them and act accordingly. But it is also true that many businessmen seem to focus their attention more on average costs than on marginal costs. When this is the case, their attempts to maximize earnings may lead them to behave much as they would if they were concentrating on marginal units and marginal profits. In some instances, however, they fail to operate as efficiently as they might. In this section we will look first at an example of the conscious use of marginal analysis and then at some other types of business practice that appear to ignore this type of analysis.

Marginal Airline Flights

A few years ago *Business Week* reported on the manner in which Continental Air Lines, Inc., was making decisions about scheduling flights.[1] The report pointed out that during the previous year only half the available seats on its Boeing 707 flights had been filled. The average use for the nation's airlines was 65 percent; Continental's 707s often carried only 30 passengers although their capacity was 120. By eliminating only 5 percent of its flights, Continental could have raised its utilization rate considerably.

If Continental had figured in all the overhead costs for each flight and tried to eliminate the flights that did not cover all costs, fixed as well as variable, it would have flown fewer flights. But it would also have had lower net earnings. The line deliberately ran flights if they could be expected to return more in revenues than the out-of-pocket expenses in-

[1] "Airline Takes the Marginal Route," *Business Week,* Apr. 20, 1963, pp. 111–114.

curred by the flights. The flights thus were expected to add more to revenues than to expenses and to contribute to fixed costs and profit.

As an example, the *Business Week* report showed that on a given flight the full costs were $4,500. This figure includes not only the variable costs of the particular flight—wages for the crew, fuel, terminal costs, and so on—but the flight's share of the fixed costs. Fares taken in as a result of this flight were $3,100. Does this mean that the flight would lose $1,400 for the company and should, therefore, not be undertaken? The out-of-pocket costs of the flight were $2,000. Consequently, the company was $1,100 better off by having the flight.

This example illustrates that once the fixed and overhead costs have been established, they are no longer relevant in the short run in making decisions about the level of output. These costs, which amount to $2,500 in this case, would go on whether the flight was run or not. Therefore, the only relevant consideration is the extra variable costs that would be incurred—the marginal cost of the flight—in comparison with the marginal revenue. This comparison shows that the flight should be scheduled.

It should be pointed out that in estimating the $3,100 of revenue, the company would have to be sure that this revenue could not be obtained on other scheduled runs. If the passengers on this flight might have filled more completely another flight of the same company, the income would not really be additional revenue for the company.

This type of analysis does not deny that, in the aggregate, all the flights must cover all the costs. Obviously, if the flights cover only the variable costs and some of the fixed costs, the remaining fixed costs represent a financial loss for the period. Even so, the loss is less than if the fixed costs were not covered at all. Given the fact that some flights more than cover their fixed costs and their variable costs, the problem then is whether to schedule any flights that fail to cover all costs completely. This type of analysis shows that the profit will be enlarged if the flights that are scheduled contribute more to revenue than to cost.

In principle, it is simple to determine just what the marginal costs are; in actuality, it is sometimes a complex matter. Marginal costs are any costs that would not occur if the work were not undertaken. In the case of the airline, all costs should be considered, of course, when planning the schedule and the rates to charge. Once it appears that all costs can be covered, the question may be asked whether some additonal flights might add to profit, even though they do not bear their full costs. In the case of Continental Air Lines, an effort was made to discover what additional costs would be entailed if a proposed flight were added. For example, if a ground crew would be available anyway and could service the plane, none of their wages and other expenses would be included. Some costs, such as the need for a crew to roll the plane to a hangar if it did not fly on to another stop, might even be avoided by making the flight. Although one flight sometimes had very few passengers, it was worth making to avoid overnight rental of a hangar. Sometimes a flight would be scheduled, even at an out-of-pocket loss, if it would bring passengers to a connecting flight whose overall profitability could more than absorb the loss on the feeder flight. The need to consider the overall situation is also illustrated by the company's scheduling two flights with different origins that arrived at Kansas City at the same time. Because of the need for an extra ground crew and fueling equipment, an additional cost of $1,800 a month was involved. However, shifting schedules around so that the planes would arrive at different times threatened a loss of $10,000 a month in fares of passengers who would probably use other airlines.

The Break-Even Point

Some companies use a variation of marginal analysis by figuring the volume of output at which they would break even at some assumed price. This analysis also recognizes that fixed costs are *sunk* and that nothing can be done about them in the short run. Figure 6-1 is an example of this approach. The height *OF* is the amount of the fixed costs, which are the same for any amount of output. Total cost is found by adding the variable costs to this level of fixed costs. The usual behavior of the variable costs is to rise less rapidly along the normal range of output than at small and very large outputs. If the firm can sell any reasonable volume at the same price, the total revenue curve is a straight line—the more that is sold, the greater is the revenue. Where total cost and total revenue are equal is the break-even point, at the output *B*. At larger outputs, profit arises because revenue goes up faster than variable costs and fixed costs are covered. If the volume is too large, the variable costs, and thus the total costs, would rise sharply and reduce the profit. The similarity of this approach to the analysis in Chapter 4 should be apparent.

Interest in the break-even point grew during the inflationary period after World War II. In industries that could not raise prices as fast as costs were going up, rapidly rising wages and other costs tended to reduce profit margins on sales. Companies were also interested in the effect on

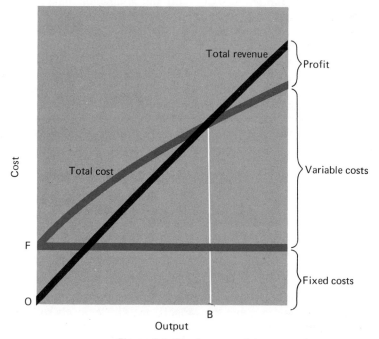

Figure 6-1. Break-even point.

profits of a decline in volume as wage rates and some other costs became more rigid and less easily reduced in periods of slack demand. In other words, with a smaller profit per unit of sales, what volume of sales is needed to reach profitability? And, if sales decline by some percentage, how much will profit decline? Thus the interest in the break-even volume. This volume might be measured in units of output or expressed as a percentage of capacity. For example, point B in Figure 6-1 might be a certain number of units of output or it might be a percentage of capacity.

The effect on profit of a shrinkage of sales depends very much on the extent to which fixed costs make up total costs. The more the total costs consist of fixed costs, the more vulnerable the firm is to a decline in sales. Compare two possible cases. In one, net sales are $10 million per year. Fixed costs are $8 million and variable costs are $1 million, so operating income is $1 million, or 10 percent of sales. In the other case, sales are also $10 million but the costs are reversed—$1 million of fixed costs and $8 million of variable costs. Profit again is $1 million, or 10 percent of sales. Now suppose sales decline by 10 percent. In the first case, sales are $9 million, fixed costs $8 million, and variable costs (which are assumed to decline equally with sales) $900,000. Thus operating income is $100,000 and only 1.1 percent of sales. In the other case, sales are $9 million, fixed costs $1 million, and variable costs $7.2 million (down by 10 percent). Operating income is $800,000, or 8.9 percent of sales.

The process also works in reverse. If sales were to rise from $9 million to $10 million, the first company would have a rapid rise in profit because most of its costs are fixed, and the second company would have a small growth in profit because its large variable costs would rise with volume.

This example illustrates the business risk involved in heavy fixed investment in plant and equipment. Plant and equipment must be utilized sufficiently to recover the fixed costs of property taxes, interest, and depreciation. Many corollaries stem from this fact. It can be observed that typically the oligopolies are industries that have heavy fixed investments. The control that each company attempts to gain over the prices it charges is related to the need to avoid the risk of loss that would follow a considerable decline in price. Industries that do not require much investment in fixed capital are easier to enter and generally come closer to the model of pure competition.

The break-even point may also be visualized arithmetically. Suppose a company is earning 15 percent on sales because of the following relationships:

Sales	$10,000,000	(100 percent)
Fixed costs	6,000,000	(60 percent)
Variable costs	2,500,000	(25 percent)
Total costs	8,500,000	(85 percent)
Operating income	1,500,000	(15 percent)

Clearly the company is operating at a point above its break-even point, since it is more than covering its costs. If it is assumed that the fixed costs are completely fixed and that the variable costs vary closely with output, the variable costs would remain at 25 percent of total sales, or revenue, at any level of output. Thus the fixed costs would be 75 percent of revenue at the point where total costs equal revenues and profit is zero. In other words, fixed costs become a larger proportion of revenue as profit becomes a smaller proportion. If the fixed costs remain at $6 million, but become 75 percent of revenue, revenue must be $8 million at the break-even point. If sales fall to $8 million, variable costs fall to $2 million (if they fall proportionately), and with $6 million of fixed costs, constitute $8 million of total costs, so profit is zero.

These dollar figures could be proportions instead. We could call the $10 million of sales *capacity* or perhaps desired capacity, and in that case the break-even point would be at 80 percent of capacity.

These examples are a bit simplified because variable costs are assumed to vary in strict proportion to output. As was explained in Chapter 4, this is not necessarily the case. However, the variation is likely to be reasonably proportionate except for very small and very large outputs. It is also simplified in that some fixed costs can be eliminated in fairly short periods. For instance, unnecessary clerks, whose salaries are overhead expenses, can be eliminated if sales fall sufficiently. In other words, many expenses are fixed within a normal range of operations but can be changed as a result of extreme fluctuations up or down.

OTHER PRICING POLICIES

The objectives of many business firms are so diverse and yet so interrelated that it is probably an oversimplification in the analysis of business behavior to assume that profit maximization is always the chief goal. Business managers have many motivations, and in the complicated world of the big business corporation, maximizing profit in the short run may not be uppermost in the mind of management. Many studies have been made in an attempt to check economic theory against actual business behavior. It has been found that firms that do not operate in pure competition — and we have seen that most do not — may have goals other than short-run profit maximization. For example, the management of a large company may be primarily interested in maintaining or increasing the company's share of the market. A particular management group may be more eager to increase earnings per share of stock year after year than to do so well in one year that they cannot match those earnings again for a period of years. Some other business practices with respect to pricing are examined briefly in this section. It must be emphasized that, although some of these policies seem to ignore profit or at least profit maximization, some concept of adequate earnings is very important in each.

Cost-Plus Pricing

The general impression of how a businessman determines what price to charge is that he calculates his costs, adds a profit, and arrives at a price. This view is too naïve to be accurate. It implies that whatever his costs — efficient or inefficient — the businessman can sell the volume he wants to sell. It also leaves unanswered the question of how he selects a profit margin to add to his costs. However, many businesses do use such an approach in order to arrive at the price they would *like to* charge. If demand is inadequate or competitors' products are cheaper, they must decide whether to charge a lower price or to forego production; if they find they can get a higher price, they are likely to charge it.

Industries that use this approach, such as iron and steel foundries, have accounting methods that permit them to calculate *standard costs*. That is, if an order is received for a certain casting, the foundryman estimates the number of hours of direct and indirect labor and the amount of materials that will be required, and then adds a percentage to cover overhead costs and a margin for profit. The percentage for overhead must be arbitrary because it is based on a standard volume of production. For example, if a million pounds of iron are cast in a year, each pound costs a certain amount in terms of the overhead expenses.

How the margin of profit is arrived at is difficult to explain. Often it is one that has been in use in the industry for many years. What is its significance? Typically, the businessman figures his costs as above, or in a similar fashion, adds his customary 10 or 20 percent profit, and quotes a price to the customer. If the customer accepts the price, the businessman then says that this is the way he sets prices. If the customer buys from someone else and the businessman does not fill the order, he may still feel that the quoted price is his price for that article. But if he knows that competitors have idle capacity and that prices in the industry are soft, he may add less than his usual profit margin when he makes his next quotation. If he loses several such orders, he may devise a more efficient way of making the article. He may even develop a particular skill in making a specific type of the article cheaply and be able to add more than the customary profit margin. In any event, it would be erroneous to think of price setting as a one-way street leading from cost to price. The demand conditions are ever-present, and in one way or another price must conform to demand. Rarely can an electric refrigerator be sold to an Eskimo.

Stable Prices

It has already been noted that stability of price is important to businesses that have large fixed investments in capital equipment. In oligopolistic industries, companies with such investments are inclined to keep the going market price rather than to cut it, and they may also be slow to raise the price under certain conditions. For example, companies in the steel industry are usually producing to meet orders on hand, and these orders have been accepted at certain prices. In addition, the steel companies are generally able to expand output if demand rises without much, if any, increase in cost per ton. In other words, the supply of steel is likely to be elastic at most times. When demand changes and supply is elastic, the price should not be expected to change much, if at all. The fact that price stability is a goal of the seller is not a complete explanation of the fact that he can attain this goal.

In some industries supply is less elastic, and companies in these industries are less capable of attaining price stability. In contrast to steel, meat is highly perishable. Once the hogs and cattle are purchased by the big meat-packing firms, the meat must be processed and sold promptly. A similar situation holds true for animals in the hands of farmers. Once raised, the animals must be sold. A change in demand tends to bring a quick change in price—the quantity to be sold is fixed in the short run and supply is inelastic. A commonly heard expression in the meat-packing industry is, "You sell it or you smell it." Prices of fresh beef, pork, and lamb may vary rapidly over a period of time and the usual small margin of profit on sales may change considerably. This is one reason why some of the larger companies have diversified and begun to manufacture less perishable products—such as canned dog food, fertilizers, soaps, chemicals, and other products.

Target Return on Investment

Some large companies set targets for return on investment and try to set prices that will provide these returns.[2] The fact that these large companies do not, in general, come close to these targets suggests that either they do not follow the target closely or that market conditions are more important than their own efforts. General Motors, for example, has generally exceeded its stated target objective (15 to 20 percent) while some other companies have never attained their stated objectives.

Price Leadership

A variety of pricing arrangements, such as pricing to meet competition and administered prices, are examples of price leadership. As was noted in the discussion of oligopolies, when there are only a few major producers, each posts a price list and follows it until some major competitor announces a new list, at which time all the competitors tend to follow suit. This has often been the situation with iron ore, steel, brass, petroleum, tin cans, and other basically standardized commodities. Prices in such industries are said to be administered prices.

Generally the price leader commands the respect of the industry for its ability to assess market conditions. If it raises the price, the competitors know that it has not only considered its own costs and profits but has also thought about whether the rest of the industry would welcome a price rise or whether some companies would be tempted to try to expand their market shares by holding the old price. Similarly, if the leader lowers the price, competitors realize that in its opinion current prices are too high for an adequate volume for the industry.

It often appears, also, that the company that is the price leader holds its position because of dominant size. If a competitor, supplying perhaps 2 percent of the market, is convinced that it should raise its price, it obviously cannot do so without losing many customers. A small competitor may also hesitate to refrain from following a price rise initiated by the leader or to initiate a price cut, because the larger firm could set a still lower price if it wanted to enforce discipline on the industry.

While many methods of setting prices that reflect the institutions of particular industries have been worked out, none of these methods present any strong evidence that demand is less important in the process of determining price than was suggested in the preceding chapters. Rather, they are alternative ways in which sellers adjust their price and output policies to market conditions.

Even when a business appears to be following goals other than maximizing profits, in the short run the principle of marginalism can maximize

[2] A. D. H. Kaplan et al., *Pricing in Big Business,* The Brookings Institution, Washington, 1958, pp. 127–164.

the profit available within the constraint of the other objectives. For example, suppose that the management of a steel company has come to the reluctant conclusion that the future of the steel industry is not bright and that the company should try to expand into some other products. For a period of five or ten years, management may divert funds from replacement and modernization of steel facilities into building up their new capacities. Annual profits will suffer, for two reasons: first, the company is not producing steel as efficiently as possible; and second, the company has not reached an efficient level of operations in the new ventures. During this period, however, it remains true that comparisons of marginal costs with marginal revenues will indicate how the profit being earned can be improved. For example, whether to maintain an inventory of steel in one place or in another, whether to close one plant or another first, and similar questions can be answered by reference to the related costs and benefits.

MEASUREMENT OF DEMAND

The importance of demand to the individual business is illustrated by the efforts of many firms to forecast sales for future periods. Most large firms make some effort to estimate sales because many other decisions hinge on this figure. Financial management must have some idea of the revenues that will flow in from sales and of the funds that will flow out as a result of the costs of production. Cash budgets are, therefore, prepared on the basis of sales forecasts. Once future sales are estimated, it becomes possible to estimate future cash inflows and outflows and to make plans for borrowing funds when they are needed for investing in equipment or inventory, for estimating profit and taxes, and for other uses.

Elasticity and Position of Demand Curve

A demand curve has two characteristics, its elasticity, or slope, and its position. As a result, a difficulty arises, in both logic and statistics, in ascertaining just what a demand curve looks like for a specific product. Consider the demand curve D_2 in Figure 6-2. If at three different times the market price has been at P_1, P_2, and P_3, one cannot assume that shifts in supply brought about these prices along the demand curve D_2. It is equally possible that the demand was originally D_1 and that, while price moved from P_1 to P_3, the demand shifted to its position at D_3. Statisticians have attempted to isolate the effects of shifts in demand from the effects of elasticity. In forecasting sales, a company must bear in mind the price at which it expects to make the sales.

Figure 6-2 represents a company selling the quantity Q_1 at price P_1. Its production staff notes that the quantity Q_2 could be produced at a lower average unit cost. Before determining whether to produce the larger quantity, it is important to decide whether the price would fall to P_2, which it would if the demand is relatively elastic, as in the case of D_2, or whether the price would fall to P_3, which it would if demand is more inelastic, as in the case of D_1.

There are two ways of estimating whether the demand curve looks like D_1 or D_2. One is to use time-series analysis, which relates past prices and past quantities. As previously noted, factors other than price can cause

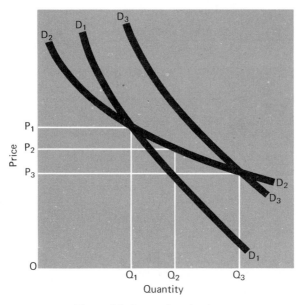

Figure 6-2. Demand and sales.

changes in the quantity demanded. Demand may shift because of changes in incomes or for other reasons. But if there is a fairly clear pattern of price-quantity relationships and if there is no reason to believe that other factors have shifted the demand curve, time-series analysis offers a strong clue to the nature of the demand for the product. Figure 6-3 shows such an approach. Each square is the price-quantity relationship during a given month or year; an estimated demand curve is drawn, either freehand or by mathematical formula, to fit the squares.

The other method is cross-section analysis, whereby a study is made of the characteristics of the purchasers of the article. If it is found that purchases of the article are closely related to income, it may follow that a

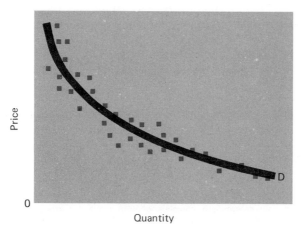

Figure 6-3. Estimated demand curve.

lower price would attract more buyers whose incomes are somewhat below those of current buyers.

Because it is difficult to separate the different factors that affect the shape of the demand curve or its position, attention is usually concentrated on estimating the volume of sales that will result from all the factors affecting quantity demanded. An attempt is made to list all the factors that influence sales, whether through price or through the position of the demand curve.

Determinants of Sales

A company producing a household appliance, such as a refrigerator or a record player, might conclude that its volume of sales depends on the price it charges, consumer incomes, the prices of competing appliances, the extent of its own advertising, and other less important factors. Another company might discover that the availability of consumer credit is a significant factor, while still another might find a close correlation between its sales and the average age and scrappage of existing appliances. Still another company might find that consumers' expectations of future incomes and future prices are important considerations.

Often, total sales of a product like meat, automobiles, or appliances are closely related to consumer income. Then the individual company has to estimate the share of the market it can command. An appliance company, as just noted, might express the demand for its product in an equation such as $Q = f(P, Y, S, A, \ldots, E)$. This equation states that its quantity of sales (expressed in units or in dollar volume) is a function of the price charged, the level of consumer income, prices of substitute brands, its expenditures on advertising, other unspecified factors, and consumer expectations. By statistical methods, the company would then attempt to correlate each of these variables with sales volume, by measuring how much sales have changed in relation to each in the past if the others are held constant.

In the case of automobiles, studies by the Department of Commerce have found that sales are closely related to family income, number of households, prices of automobiles, and average age of cars.[3] These studies found, for the period covered, that a change of 1 percent in real disposable income per household was associated with a change of 2.5 percent in new-car sales.[4] The ratio of real disposable income to that of the preceding year was also important; an increase of 1 percent was associated with an increase in sales of 2.3 percent. Sales were reduced when automobile prices rose faster than average prices.

Advertising

Firms operating in pure competition have no reason to advertise because they can sell all that is justified by the market price and because advertising would not permit them to charge a higher price. Buyers consider the product of one producer as good as that of another, and the only basis for choice is price. Sellers in most markets, however, have

---

[3] The statistical measurement of these determinants is found by correlation. A study in 1952 found that these four determinants "explained" 96 percent of passenger-car registrations. The methodology is explained in *Survey of Current Business,* April and May, 1952.

[4] Real disposable income is disposable income corrected for changes in the price level.

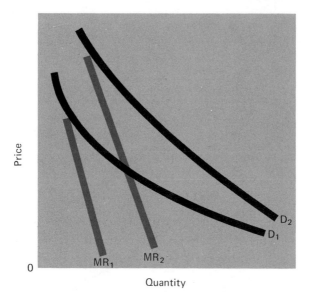

Figure 6-4. Advertising and demand.

some ability to expand sales by advertising, or at least to prevent loss of sales that would otherwise result from competitors' advertising.

The object of advertising is to shift the demand curve to the right and upward, as in Figure 6-4. Since advertising is not relevant to pure competition, D_1 is a sloping curve with an associated MR curve.[5] Successful advertising would affect buyers' preferences so that the demand curve shifts to D_2 and perhaps becomes more inelastic.

An illustration of how advertising might improve the profits of an oligopolistic seller is shown in Figure 6-5. The old (MR_1) and new (MR_2) marginal revenue curves are shown, along with the firm's average cost curve before advertising (AC_1) and with the advertising expenditure (AC_2). Since advertising is a fixed, or overhead, cost, it does not affect the MC curve, which reflects only additions to variable cost. Without advertising, the firm can make a maximum profit by producing Q_1 units at a price of P_1 (this is where $MC = MR$). With the addition of advertising expense, average cost is higher but demand is shifted upward and produces a new MR_2. It now pays to expand production and to charge a higher price. The profit per unit is a little greater, and more units are sold.

The managerial problem of deciding how much to spend for advertising and how to spend it is considerably more complicated than these graphs might suggest. Advertising is one of the determinants of the shape and position of the demand curve; how important it is in relation to other factors is not easy to measure. How much an increase of 1 percent in advertising expenditures increases sales volume, through quantity or price, is important to management. In principle, advertising expenditures should be pushed to the point where they no longer add as much to revenue as to cost, but this point is very difficult to discover.

[5] It might pay the entire industry to advertise cooperatively. Some agricultural products, such as apples and milk, are promoted in this fashion.

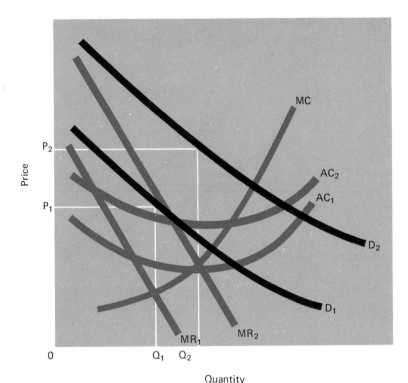

Figure 6-5. Advertising and profit.

Various checks on the efficiency of advertising have been developed. One method is to test-market a product. When a company has a new product, such as a new dog food, a new type of canned soup, or a new brand of household cleanser, it might advertise it and make it available in one or two test areas. If the product sells well, the company has a basis for marketing the product more broadly; if the product does not sell, the experiment was much less expensive than a national one. Of course, the company (or its advertising agency) should be sure that the *test market* is a reasonably good sample of the larger market. In the case of a consumer good, it should be marketed where the households are reasonably similar to others in respect to age, income, and cultural characteristics. Cleveland, Ohio, is sometimes selected as a test market because the population of the metropolitan area is just about 1 percent of that of the nation.

The relationship between the degree of *product differentiation* and the amount of advertising of the product is apparent. If one company's product is essentially the same as another's and if sales are made to professional buyers who purchase according to specifications, advertising can have little impact. Cigarettes, liquors, automobiles, quality fountain pens, and typewriters are highly differentiated.[6] These products, as well as petroleum products, automobile tires, and expensive shoes, are advertised heavily. Such products as copper, cement, and tin cans are advertised much less and only to select groups of potential buyers.

[6] Joe S. Bain, *Industrial Organization,* John Wiley & Sons, Inc., New York, 1959, pp. 222–223.

LINEAR PROGRAMMING

The foregoing examples show some of the ways in which businesses react to their cost and demand conditions in determining levels of output, prices, and expenditures designed to influence demand. Many choices to be made among possible alternatives can be selected by the use of various mathematical solutions. The use of a variety of techniques is called *operations research;* the technique illustrated here is called *linear programming.*

Operations research was greatly stimulated by World War II, when the American and British armed forces called on scientists from several fields to help solve problems of economizing on resources. For example, the armed forces wanted to know how to get maximum coverage of an ocean mine field with the minimum number of mines, the best number and location of air-raid warning devices, where to stockpile ammunition for maximum efficiency, and answers to many similar problems. These problems were often attacked by teams of specialists, each member contributing some special knowledge. After the war such teams were increasingly used to solve similar problems in business.

Determining a Product Mix

Often a problem, especially when it involves choosing between only two alternatives, lends itself to linear programming. A simple example of linear programming is shown in Figure 6-6. A manufacturing plant has 50 shaping machines and 40 drilling machines. It can produce one article (*A*), which requires two hours of work on a shaping machine and one hour on a drilling machine, or another article (*B*), which requires the opposite—one hour of shaping and two hours of drilling.

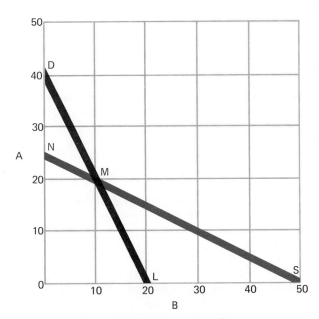

Figure 6-6. Linear programming.

Line *NS* in Figure 6-6 shows the *production possibilities* for the two products with 50 shaping machines. Since each unit of output of *A* requires two hours on a shaping machine, maximum output of *A* is 25 units per hour on 50 machines. If output of *A* is 25, no machines are available to produce *B*. Two units of *B* can be produced instead of one unit of *A*, up to a maximum of 50 units of *B*. On the shaping machines available, any combination of *A* and *B* lying on line *NS* can be produced — for example, 10 of *A* and 30 of *B*. No combination to the right of line *NS* is possible. For example, 15 *A* and 30 *B* would require 60 shaping machines.

Production is constrained not only by the number of shaping machines available but also by the number of drilling machines. Line *DL* shows the production possibilities under this *constraint*. Forty units of product *A* can be produced per hour, each requiring one hour, with no output of *B*. At the other extreme, 20 units of *B* can be produced. With respect to drilling machines, any combination on line *DL* is possible; 30 of *A* and 5 of *B* are such a combination. No combination to the right of line *DL* is possible. For instance, 30 of *A* and 10 of *B* would require 50 drilling machines.

When both production possibility lines are considered, it is apparent that the line *DM* is irrelevant because it lies outside the possibilities along *NM*. In other words, some combination like 30 *A* and 5 *B* is possible with the 40 drilling machines, but the 50 shaping machines cannot produce this combination. (The required machine time is $[2 \times 30] + 5 = 65$.) Similarly, the line *MS* becomes irrelevant because the drilling machines cannot handle any combination on it. (For example, 10 *A* and 30 *B* would require $[2 \times 10] + 30 = 50$, and only 40 are available.)

Consequently, the maximum production possibilities that exist under *both* constraints lie along the line *NML*. Smaller combinations are, of course, possible if some machines are not used. Any combination of *A* and *B* under the line *NML* is possible, such as 15 *A* and 10 *B* per hour. (This would require forty hours of shaping machine time and thirty-five of drilling.)

As a further simplification, assume that *A* and *B* are equally profitable. Point *M* indicates the maximum profit combination of *A* and *B* because it is the point of maximum output. Geometrically, the area *OLMN* is the largest that can be drawn under the two constraining lines *NM* and *ML*. The best combination to produce is 20 *A* and 10 *B* per hour. If the profit were not the same on *A* and *B*, the *X* (units of *B*) and *Y* (units of *A*) axes could be marked off in units of profit rather than units of output, which would change the slope of the two lines and make them intersect at a different combination. If, for example, *B* were more profitable, line *DL* would move over to the right and would indicate a larger output of *B* and a lower output of *A*.

The same answer can be obtained algebraically by maximizing *A* and *B*. This can be done by the equations:

$$2A + 1B = 50 \text{ (constraint of shaping machines)}$$

$$1A + 2B = 40 \text{ (constraint of drilling machines)}$$

It can be seen that $A = 20$ and $B = 10$ fits both equations, as shown by the graph.

Other Uses of Linear Programming

Often there are many more than two alternatives and the use of linear programming requires pairing off each two for comparison. However, this complication is not great when a computer can be used. Linear programming has been used to solve many kinds of problems; for example, finding the cheapest combination of ingredients to produce a given set of nutrient values for animal food, locating warehouses to minimize shipping of goods to local outlets, finding the most efficient sources of materials or supplies, and determining the best amounts of different goods to be kept in inventory.

Numerous other devices have been developed to help management make choices more precisely than has been possible in the past. Many problems can be solved by queuing theory, which is concerned with flows of customers or traffic. In a bank, for instance, it is desirable to have enough tellers so that customers do not have to wait long in line. On the other hand, if there are enough tellers for peak loads, some of them are idle at other times. The same situation exists at airports, where the flow of travelers is not uniform throughout the day, and it is related to such problems as how many taxis should operate in a given area, how many waitresses should serve in a restaurant, and so on. The economic rule in such problems is simple: Each variable factor should be used up to the point where it begins to add more to cost than to revenue. But applying this rule is often difficult and complicated. Consequently, modern management has sought help from new statistical and accounting tools.

SUMMARY

This chapter is not designed to describe all the problems and techniques of business management but rather to illustrate how the basic principles of economics are applicable to the explanation of the behavior of business firms. In the operation of a typical business firm, management must make decisions in many areas that are not discussed here. In the area of finance, efficient management must determine how much investment is justified in fixed capital and how to minimize investment in inventories, accounts receivable, and cash. In the area of marketing, management must determine the most effective and profitable ways of distributing the product and getting it to customers. Labor relations is another basic area of management, and executives dealing with labor require expertise in several related fields. Each of these broad areas, and others, constitute a body of knowledge and principles applicable to appropriate problems.

Examples have been presented in this chapter to illustrate that the principle of marginalism is directly applicable to business output policies and pricing policies. The more a firm is interested in current profits, the more important equating marginal cost and marginal revenue becomes. If a firm seems to have objectives other than maximizing current profits, frequently it is simply taking a longer-run view of the profits to be maximized. That is, it might incur costs for the purpose of expanding its market and taking a larger share of the total market, but these costs are expected to pay off in the future.

Much of the skepticism about the relevance of economic theory to the actual behavior of businessmen stems from the fact that businessmen must operate in a world of uncertainty. They must make investments in fixed capital on the basis of forecasts of many variables, such as future demand, sales, prices, costs, taxes, competition, interest rates, and so on. And what appears to be a reasonable forecast to one businessman may seem overconfident or too conservative to another because men assess or react to uncertainty in different ways. Hence they make different decisions.

Economic Terms for Review

break-even point	measurement of demand
cost-plus pricing	test market
standard costs	product differentiation
target return on investment	linear programming
administered prices	production possibilities

Questions for Review

1. Show that a company will decide on the same price and output whether it considers *MC* and *MR* or average costs and price.
2. Why did Continental Air Lines schedule flights they knew would be only 25 to 50 percent filled?
3. How is a break-even point found?
4. If you expected demand for your product to rise, would you want your costs to be predominantly fixed or variable?
5. The sales of a corner grocer are declining, so he decides to raise prices enough to maintain overall profit. Is he wise?
6. Why do heavy industries prefer stable selling prices?
7. Why is it difficult to picture a real demand curve?
8. What factors determine overall sales of automobiles? of Fords?
9. Why is it difficult to determine how much advertising is best for a company?

Questions for Analysis

1. A printing shop can get an order if its bid is lower than its full-cost formula shows is the total cost of the order. Under what circumstances might it make the bid?
2. A company has monthly fixed costs of $100,000 and variable costs of 50 percent of sales revenue at normal volumes. What is its break-even point?
3. In the home-building business there are speculative builders who construct houses and then sell them and contractors who bid to build houses for customers. Compare how the speculative builder prices his houses with how the contractor sets his bids.
4. You are the second largest producer of tin cans, with 30 percent of the market. The largest, with 40 percent, has just raised its prices 5 percent. You have been losing sales to nonmetal containers. Do you have a problem?
5. How would you go about estimating the elasticity of demand for a popular brand of chocolates produced and sold locally?

6. You are manager of a variety store in a city of 35,000 people. Make a list of conditions under which you would tend to spend rather heavily on advertising.

7. You can produce Product A by using Machine 1 two hours and Machine 2 one hour, or Product B by using Machine 1 one hour and Machine 2 two hours. What is the maximum output possible if you have 75 of Machine 1 and 60 of Machine 2?

Case for Decision

In the early days of the iron and steel industry, cost factors made it important to minimize the cost of materials. Pittsburgh became a steel center because of its location between the iron ore and limestone of the Great Lakes region and the coking coal of central Pennsylvania. Later, economies in the manufacturing process and in transportation and the decline in relative importance of the Great Lakes region as a source of ore made this kind of location less important, and steel mills began to be located nearer major customers and consuming areas. As a result, Chicago became a major producer. The trend of locating near customers appears to be growing.

The American Iron and Steel Company owns and operates a relatively modern plant in the Midwest that is oriented primarily to a surrounding consuming area. This area is growing in population, and industrialization and consumption of steel are expected to increase. American has the only mill within the consuming area. Its sales, which are near capacity, are about $10 million this year and the profit on these sales is about $1 million.

The manager, John Miller, is considering requesting the headquarters office to authorize an expansion of capacity to $15 million of sales. Because an expanded plant would operate with much the same managerial and sales costs, Miller believes the profit from sales of $15 million would be $1,600,000. In other words, the return would be $600,000 on the additional investment. He is bothered, however, by the possibility that a competing company may be planning to construct a new steel mill not far away.

If the rival plant is built and has a capacity, with modern equipment, of $10 million of sales and American's expansion is built, the two together would have a combined capacity of $25 million. Miller believes that sales of this volume can be achieved within a decade, but in five years he thinks $20 million would be the maximum. He has jotted down these figures as estimates of the situation if both investments are made:

	American	Competitor	Combined
Capacity	$15,000,000	$10,000,000	$25,000,000
Sales	12,000,000	8,000,000	20,000,000
Profit	900,000	800,000	1,700,000

He has also thought about what would happen if American does not expand, in which case the competitor would almost certainly move in. In that case, he estimates:

	American	Competitor	Combined
Capacity	$10,000,000	$10,000,000	$20,000,000
Sales	9,000,000	9,000,000	18,000,000
Profit	850,000	900,000	1,750,000

He estimates sales a bit lower in this second case because American's cost per ton would be higher without the expanded capacity, and he thinks both companies would be a bit less aggressive in trying to sell at considerable distance from the mills.

Miller is trying to evaluate the probabilities of the possible developments: (1) that American builds and the rival decides not to, (2) that both build, (3) that American does not and the rival does, and (4) that neither builds. He is trying to estimate the effect his actions may have on the rival and the costs and benefits to American according to what the competitor does.

What do you think Miller should recommend to headquarters? What are the principal reasons?

Part 3
The Nation's Income

7
Income Distribution: Wages

The preceding chapters dealing with market prices are concerned primarily with product markets. Factors of production, or their services, are also bought and sold in markets. The returns to the factors of production are prices, and as such they can be explained within the same framework as can prices of goods. Thus wages are the price commanded by labor, rent is the price commanded for the use of land, and interest is the price commanded for the use of capital. These three incomes, along with profit, constitute the functional distribution of income. Functional distribution explains the division of shares of the national output according to the functions of the factors of production that contribute to that output.

CATEGORIES OF FUNCTIONAL INCOME

The study of functional distribution begins with an examination of how each factor of production is evaluated in the market. Any income earned in the process of production can be classified as the wages of labor, the rent of the landlord, the interest of the capitalist, or the profit of the entrepreneur.

Many people are owners of more than one factor of production. The farmer who owns his farm, buildings, and equipment and who also works on the farm is landlord, capitalist, and laborer, and also entrepreneur. Some laborers own stock in the companies for which they work. In these and similar examples, persons receive more than one form of *functional income*. There are other personal incomes that are not earned in the process of production; these are ways of sharing the national product among those who do not currently contribute to it. A simple example is a child's allowance from his parents; more important examples are pensions, subsidies, and welfare payments.

National Income Groups

Since functional incomes are forms of market prices, their determination is explained by the forces of supply and demand in their respective markets. Each type of market has peculiarities of supply and demand that make the explanation somewhat different in each case. In the short run the supply of land is generally limited, leading to a peculiarity of supply. The determinants of the number of workers available for employment are obviously different from the determinants of the volume of loan funds in capital markets.

The distribution of income is a normal and continuing function of the process of production. The wage earner is paid regularly for supplying his labor. The landlord is paid by an entrepreneur who rents his land.

Loan contracts between borrower and lender determine payments of interest. Profit is a residual income, being that portion of the receipts of a business retained after payment or allocation of the other three market rates.

Any business makes many payments that are directly incomes for others, such as wages. It also has such expenses as materials, power, and transportation. These payments become gross incomes of some other business units, and they in turn pay them out either directly as incomes or as other payments to businesses (and governments).

Because there are so many instances of people earning incomes through a combination of their labor, land, and capital, there are no direct statistical measures of the amount of the earnings of each factor. The national income accounts of the Department of Commerce have to be set up on a different, although related, basis. The distribution of national income for 1969 is shown in Table 7-1. Compensation of employees includes not only wages and salaries but commissions, bonuses, and gratuities, as well as fringe benefits such as employer-provided housing and contributions to retirement and health insurance plans. Compensation of employees includes salaries of corporation presidents and other executives as well as wages of the labor force. Table 7-1 indicates that this total compensation is by far the largest fraction of national income. Defined broadly, labor's share of the total has been between 60 and 70 percent in most years since these statistics became available in 1929. This share divided among the number in the labor force (about 80 million) provides roughly $6,000 per worker.

The supplements to wages and salaries (mostly fringe benefits of various kinds) have become much more important since 1929, when they amounted to about 1.4 percent of the total compensation. Currently, these forms of postponed income (which are current costs to employers) constitute about 10 percent of the total.

Corporate profits are the second largest component. In the past they have fluctuated considerably along with the business cycle. Every year some business firms experience losses rather than profits, but in the depression years of 1932–1933 there were net losses, on balance, for all corporations combined. The corporate profits listed in Table 7-1 are the

Table 7-1
National Income in 1969

	Amount (Billions of Dollars)	Percentage
Compensation of employees	$564.3	73.2
Proprietors' income	66.3	8.6
Rental income of persons	21.6	2.8
Corporate profits	88.2	11.4
Net interest	30.6	4.0
National income	$771.0	100.0

Source: *Federal Reserve Bulletin*, June, 1970, p. A-68.

profits before income tax and include a small adjustment for inventory change. Corporate profits are about the same percentage of the total as in 1929 although the percentage has fluctuated.

Rent and interest received by persons (excluding corporations) are small percentages of total income. Rent and interest received by corporations are included in their gross incomes and contribute to corporate profits.

The income of unincorporated businesses and professions and the income of farm proprietors are lumped together as proprietors' income. This income is generally a composite of functional incomes, consisting of salaries and wages that proprietors earn for themselves (called wages of management), implicit rent and interest on land and capital used by proprietors in their own businesses, and economic profit. In the aggregate, the noncorporate segment of the economy receives incomes far below those of corporations.

The national income accounts thus do not measure what the economist calls wages, rent, interest, and profits. Wages of management are not included under compensation of employees because they are earned by the self-employed and reported as profits. Rent and interest are understated since they appear as profits of corporations or of unincorporated businesses unless they are received by persons.

High and Low Incomes

The factors of production and the ownership of property rights in them are unequally distributed, in both quantity and quality. Consequently, incomes are unequally distributed. Inequality of income among individuals and families has always existed; even modern Communist countries do not distribute incomes equally.

The distribution of income among the approximately 50 million multiperson families in 1968 is shown in Table 7-2. These figures show that about a sixth (16.4 percent) of these families received less than $4,000; fewer than half received less than $8,000.[1] About one family in seven received more than $15,000, and only 2.6 percent received more than $25,000. In interpreting these figures, one's standards of comparison are very important. Although these figures suggest that there are many poor people in the United States, by world standards most of these poor are well off. Helping those in the low-income brackets improve their economic lot is one of the most pressing problems of the present time.

The disparity in incomes shown in Table 7-2 stems largely from the disparity in ability to earn with one's own labor or property. A person's income depends primarily on his productive resources and the rates of pay the resources command. The ownership of productive resources depends upon many factors; it depends upon legal factors such as the treatment of inheritance and taxation, on sociological factors such as family organization, and on political factors such as the degree of government intervention in the distribution of income. How a person owning the rights to a plot of ground needed for a shopping center or municipal stadium come into possession of the property explains the level of income for that person. How fortunes were accumulated in the early days of the

---

[1] The median income was $8,630 in 1968 and $9,433 in 1969; half got more and half got less.

Table 7-2
Families by Income Brackets, 1968

Income Group	Percentage	
	In Group	Cumulative
Under $1,000	1.8	1.8
$1,000 to $1,999	3.4	5.2
$2,000 to $2,999	5.1	10.3
$3,000 to $3,999	6.1	16.4
$4,000 to $4,999	6.0	22.4
$5,000 to $5,999	6.9	29.3
$6,000 to $6,999	7.6	36.9
$7,000 to $7,999	8.2	45.1
$8,000 to $9,999	15.2	60.3
$10,000 to $14,999	25.0	85.3
$15,000 to $24,999	12.1	97.4
$25,000 and over	2.6	100.0

Source: U.S. Bureau of the Census, *Current Population Reports*, Series
P-60, No. 63, Sept. 8, 1969, p. 2.

iron ore industry, the fur trade, and other pursuits explains incomes for others today. How physicians, lawyers, and physicists completed their education and training explains their incomes. In other words, the ownership of productive factors, including possession of talent, intelligence, or skill, is not solely a problem in economics. The other determinant, the rates of pay set in competitive markets, is more closely related to economic analysis.

DETERMINATION OF WAGES

The markets for productive factors have some things in common. Such problems as determining the wage of a clerk, the salary of a company president, the rent of a given plot of land, and the interest to be paid for a given loan raise the question of how prices of factors of production are brought about in their respective markets.

Demand in Factor Markets

Supply and demand determine prices in markets for land, labor, and capital in much the same way as they do in markets for goods and services. In product markets, buyers are households and sellers are businesses; in factor markets, buyers are businesses and sellers are households. This distinction is blurred by the fact that businesses buy products from each other before selling them or their services to households, and businesses also sell or rent productive factors to other businesses. But basically businesses obtain the productive services of land, labor, and capital from households, directly or indirectly, and sell the products to households, again directly or indirectly. In a simple illustration, a business firm hires labor and pays out a cost in the form of wages. The household of the laborer purchases products from business, using the wage payments as income. These two transactions constitute a circular flow of income, from businesses to households and back to businesses, which is basic to the later study of national income.

In a market economy business firms do not want to incur costs for factors of production that cannot be recovered in the prices of the products. Their demands for labor, land, and capital are said to be _derived demands_ — that is, arising from the _final demand_ for the products. The only reason for the existence of a demand for labor in an automobile plant is that the demand for the automobile provides a market price that covers the costs, at least in the long run.

How much a business firm is willing to pay for a factor of production and how much of that factor it wants to employ depend, therefore, on how much the factor of production contributes to output. We may assume that the entrepreneur attempts to combine the factors of production in such proportions and in such quantities as to maximize his profit. The resulting demands of each entrepreneur can be combined into the market demand for each factor. As in product markets, we can expect the demand curve to slope downward to the right, to reflect the fact that the more expensive a factor becomes in the market, the less of it each entrepreneur tends to use.

Development of Wage Theories

The question of what determines labor's share of the national output has been an intriguing one from early times. Philosophers and the early economists became interested in this question because of the obvious relationships between the level of wages and the extent of welfare. There are also questions of equity and fairness in the way incomes are distributed in a market economy. One criterion of fairness is that the reward earned by labor be related in some way to the individual laborer's contribution to society in the form of output. Any acceptable theory of wages has to explain why a talented athlete may earn $50,000 a year or more while a policeman may earn only $7,000. The early theories relied more on philosophical arguments than on economic analysis. Their conclusions reflected the organization of earlier economies. The principal economic institutions of the Middle Ages or of the Industrial Revolution naturally suggested explanations for the level of wages and the share of labor.

Many of the early theories of wages resembled the medieval thinking about prices — that there is a just or fair wage that employers should pay. Application of supply and demand analysis, and especially the emphasis on marginal demand and marginal supply, did not become important in economic thought until about a hundred years ago. In early societies the emphasis was largely upon the ethical and legal obligations of employers to employees. Rules came into existence to regulate the payment of wages, to enforce the duties of workmen and the obligations of employers, and to prevent oppression.

In the Middle Ages the concepts of fairness and justice were important because most workers were bound to the manor under the feudal system, and they were not free to bargain over wages in a free market. Output was shared according to arrangements between the serfs and villeins on the one side and the lord of the manor on the other. The resulting codes of ethics and law set up the customary sharing that appeared fair and equitable in the existing society.

As the manorial system gave way to the mercantilist period and eventually to the Industrial Revolution, workers were no longer tied to the manor but depended more on finding employment with a merchant or manufacturer. Production on a larger scale required movement of workers into factories and payment of money wages. The worker became more insulated from the eventual buyer of the product while the employer became the go-between who employed factors of production at money costs and sold the product for money prices. Before the Industrial Revolution, the master artisan employed apprentices and journeymen. How long an apprenticeship lasted and how much the workers were to be paid were determined primarily by tradition and custom as expressed in guild regulations and royal edicts.

The transition to a market economy brought much poverty and distress to the workers. In general, the supply of labor exceeded the demand, and the new class of employers was able to employ the workers coming from farms and villages at very low wages. Often an entire family, including young children, found it necessary to work in a mine or textile mill in order to earn a family living. The hours of work were generally from sunrise to sunset, and no one had heard of lunch hours or coffee breaks. Observers rather naturally concluded that the "natural" wage was one just sufficient to keep body and soul together.

Early Economic Approaches to Wages

Adam Smith was the first person to write a comprehensive analysis of the economy, the *Wealth of Nations*. Writing in 1775, he was interested in the way in which the mercantilist restrictions still in effect hampered the development of a free economic system. As was noted earlier, he recognized the potential benefits of division of labor and specialization, which in turn depended upon the ability of entrepreneurs to sell the resulting output in wide markets. Smith accepted the general idea of *subsistence wages*—that wages tend to fluctuate near the level of subsistence—because he believed that employers were able to pay as low wages as workmen could live on. Wages could not for long be below the level of subsistence, however, because such a situation would lead to a scarcity of workers. Smith noted that in an expanding country the demand for labor could raise wages above the subsistence level, but he also had an early concept of an equilibrium situation in which expansion had gone as far as possible and all prices and wages had become adjusted. In this situation, a wage above subsistence would lead to a growth of population, a surplus of labor, and a fall of wages to the subsistence level. This explanation became known as the *iron law of wages* and was one of the reasons for economics being called at that time the dismal science.

Later writers who built on Smith and his contemporaries attempted to give more thought to the demand side of the wage bargain. John Stuart Mill, who wrote in the middle of the nineteenth century, emphasized the importance of saving by employers so that they could hire labor. Since labor works on goods to be sold in the future, there must be output for them to consume while they work and which they can buy with their wages. Mill visualized a *wages fund,* amassed by employers out of past income from which they paid wages currently.

One of the best-known writers among the early economists was the Reverend Thomas Malthus, who wrote after Smith and before Mill. He added precision to the idea of subsistence wages by developing the thought that population tends to outrun production. He postulated that although population could double with each generation, say every twenty-five years, the capacity of a society to produce could not increase by any similar geometric ratio. In other words, according to the *Malthusian theory,* population, if unchecked, would increase geometrically in the manner of 1, 2, 4, 8, 16, 32, . . . while productive capacity would increase arithmetically in the manner of 1, 2, 3, 4, 5, ... Thus Malthus concluded that the supply of labor would always tend to press on the ability of society to support the population and that employers would always face a labor supply permitting them to pay only subsistence wages.

The conclusions of the early economists were used by Karl Marx as part of the basis for his writings. Marx was a contemporary of Mill but, of course, had an entirely different viewpoint. Marx borrowed from Adam Smith (and others) the idea that the value of an article is determined by the amount of labor required for its production, whether that labor was employed directly on the article or on earlier production of capital goods. Capital goods themselves received relative values in this way and were thought of as *congealed labor.* Marx combined this idea with that of the subsistence wage. A worker was supposed to be able to produce enough to provide his subsistence in part of a day, but he was required by market conditions to work a whole day for the subsistence wage. Thus according to Marx, the employer could exploit the workers by keeping the output in excess of the subsistence wage. On the basis of this theory of exploitation, Marx was able to draw other conclusions about the inevitability of business cycles, the increasing misery of the working class, and an eventual revolution in which workers would take over the capital equipment and divide the output among themselves.

Clearly, in countries where free-market economies developed in the hundred years after Marx, standards of living rose and wage levels climbed far above subsistence for most workers. The concept of subsistence no doubt changes as living standards rise, and a distressingly large fraction of even the American population lives close to subsistence by today's standards. But subsistence living today is not the same misery that it was in the early nineteenth century. Output has risen faster than population in developed countries, and the operation of product and factor markets has distributed this output much more broadly than the early economists and the socialist critics could have imagined. Instead of the rich getting richer and richer while the poor got poorer and poorer, as Marx predicted, the rich have been getting richer, but the poor have been getting rich faster. There is less inequality between the high and low incomes and more concentration of incomes around the middle brackets today than in the recent past.

This brief survey of some of the earlier thinking about wages is included to illustrate that even those who were unconvinced by Marx's analysis had to recognize that Marx had taken the classical economic explanation and turned it into a compelling criticism of the economy. Consequently, much additional thinking about wages, in particular, and the distribution of the national output, in general, was stimulated. Economic theory became concerned with the demand side of the price equation, in both product and factor markets. In time, a theory of distribution based on the *marginal productivity* of each factor of production developed. This is still the basic explanation of the returns to labor and other factors.[2] The basis of this theory will now be examined.

DIMINISHING RETURNS AND EARNINGS

The relationship of the law of diminishing returns to the behavior of costs of production was noted in Chapter 4. There it was observed that when some factors of production are held fixed and a variable factor of production is added to the combination, the proportions of the factors of production change. Some combinations are more efficient in terms of the output of the variable factor than are others. Up to a point, a percentage addition of the variable factor may increase output by a greater percentage, but at some point the additions to output slow down. As each unit of the variable factor has less of the fixed factors to work with, it is able to add less to output. Because of the effect on costs, this law is also applicable to the amount of the variable factor that the entrepreneur wants to employ. As we shall see, the entrepreneur does not want more marginal units of a variable factor than the number of units that adds as much to output and sales revenue as it does to cost.

Combinations of Factors

It was also brought out in Chapter 4 that whether the entrepreneur's factors of production are fixed or variable depends on the length of the time period being considered. Given enough time, all the factors can be changed; in the short run, only the variable factors can be changed because the fixed factors take time to be altered.

In planning an enterprise, the businessman naturally takes into account how he will produce. At the beginning he has a free hand. If, for example, he is considering the production of shoes, he will calculate the cost per pair resulting from different methods of production. The average cost depends upon the market prices of the different factors that he might use. If he is in a country where capital is scarce and labor is relatively plentiful, he is likely to find that shoe machinery has a high cost and that he would have to pay a high rate of interest for funds with which to buy it. Even though he could combine cheap labor with the capital equipment, the fixed costs of this combination would result in a high average cost per pair of shoes, even at the lowest-cost output. He is likely to find that

---

[2] There were many contributors to the development of the marginal productivity theory. In Austria several economists of the late nineteenth century were concerned with the analysis of demand, and they applied their thinking to factors of production as well as to products. In this country John Bates Clark was a notable contributor to this line of thinking and, in the early twentieth century, Alfred Marshall in England combined much contemporary thinking in his famous *Principles of Economics,* which was one of the first comprehensive books to use the term *economics* rather than *political economy.* This shift reflected the development of economics as a separate body of thought less concerned with the development of government policies in economic matters.

using labor to perform some of the operations that the machines might do will result in a lower combination of fixed and variable costs.

In a country where capital is plentiful and labor therefore relatively scarce, the businessman's calculations are likely to dictate a different combination of factors of production. The businessman must pay the going market rates for labor which are determined by the wages labor can earn in competing occupations. Since capital goods are plentiful, they have less scarcity value than in the first country and, since capital funds are plentiful, interest rates are lower. Thus the entrepreneur finds that investing heavily in machinery will result in a lower average cost per pair of shoes at the lowest-cost output than would result if labor were used for some of the machine operations.

In both cases the resulting cost figures depend on technical or engineering relationships as well as on market prices for machines, labor, and loan funds. If machines were even more productive in the first country, the entrepreneur would be able to get a higher output per machine hour and thus a lower cost. Given the technology of the moment, however, the important determinant is the relationship of market prices of the different factors that might be used. Thus it happens that in some areas of the world, goods can be produced cheaply by using little machinery and other capital goods and much labor, while in other areas of the world, it pays to substitute capital goods for human labor. Because of technological factors, however, even in the same country, some commodities are produced largely by hand and others almost completely by automatic machines.

The combination of factors to be used, then, is determined by the cost of the product over the long run, as forecast when the combination is put together. Once it is put together, however, some of the factors are relatively fixed for some period of time. Then the entrepreneur must decide how many units of the variable factor (such as labor) to use in the short run. As was noted in Chapter 4, the entrepreneur tends to use that quantity and to produce that amount of output that maximize his profit.

In order to provide a specific example of how diminishing returns is related to the demand for a factor of production, Table 7-3 shows the

Table 7-3
Diminishing Returns in Wheat Production

Fixed Factors (Land, Seed, Fertilizer, Tools, Machinery)	Variable Factor (Number of Workers)	Percentage Increase in Variable Factor	Total Output (Bushels)	Percentage Increase in Total Output	Marginal Output (Bushels)
Constant	0	.....	0	.....	0
Constant	1	.....	200	.....	200
Constant	2	100	500	150	300
Constant	3	50	720	44	220
Constant	4	33+	880	22+	160
Constant	5	25	980	11+	100

operation of diminishing returns to labor in the case of wheat production. All the other factors—land, capital in the form of seed, fertilizer, tools and machinery—are assumed to be fixed. The basic information is the same as in Table 4-1.

Naturally, total output is zero if no workers are employed. If one worker is employed, output is 200 bushels. If two men are employed, an increase of 100 percent, output is 500 bushels, or 150 percent more. Employment of two men rather than one represents increasing returns. But employment of three men rather than two (an increase of 50 percent) brings an increase in output of 220 bushels, or 44 percent. Diminishing returns begins with the employment of three men, since the output expands less rapidly than the input of the variable factor. Throughout the table, output can always be increased by the addition of another worker, but each addition to output is less.

All the workers who might be employed are assumed equal in competence. The reason for the decline in *marginal output* with larger numbers of workers is that each worker has less land, tools, and other fixed factors to work with. Five workers make a less efficient combination of productive factors with this set of fixed factors than do three workers—in terms of output per worker. (Output per acre or other unit of fixed factors is higher with five workers than with three. Output per worker is the crucial figure, however, because we are interested in the demand the entrepreneur has for laborers.)

In deciding what level of output to produce, the entrepreneur also decides how many units of the variable factor to employ. If he considers 720 bushels the optimum output in light of market prices, he automatically decides to employ three workers; if 880 bushels is more profitable (in spite of a higher average cost for labor), he employs four workers.

Marginal Productivity

The outlines of the marginal productivity theory of wages are most easily traced if it is assumed that all workers are alike (labor is homogeneous) and that there is pure competition. Once the outlines are seen, it is easy to allow for different wages for different types of labor and for different types of competitive conditions.

The marginal product is the key to the entrepreneur's demand for labor or any other variable factor, in much the same manner as his marginal cost is the key to the supply of his product. Because of the law of diminishing returns, the employer cannot add labor indefinitely to his fixed factors without running into higher marginal costs. At any market rate of wages, the employer tends to add labor up to the point at which another worker's addition to output would not pay for his wages. This is the crucial level of output and employment, because higher levels cost more than they are worth. If all employers fail to employ all the available workers at the going wage, the excess of workers seeking employment tends to lower the wage rate. At the equilibrium wage rate, all workers are employed.

Physical and Revenue Products

In order to know whether a slightly larger labor force would be more profitable than a slightly smaller one, the employer must translate the marginal product into dollar terms. The additional output must be multi-

Table 7-4

Physical and Revenue Product

Number of Workers	Total Physical Product (Bushels)	Average Physical Product (Bushels)	Marginal Physical Product (Bushels)	Average Value Product	Total Revenue	Marginal Value Product
0	0	0	0	0	0	0
1	200	200	200	$320	$ 320	$320
2	500	250	300	400	800	480
3	720	240	220	384	1,152	352
4	880	220	160	352	1,408	256
5	980	196	100	313+	1,568	160

plied by the price in order to find the additional revenue. Table 7-4 uses the data from Table 7-3 and applies a price of $1.60 per bushel.

The average physical product is the average product per worker—the total product divided by the number of workers. The average value product is the value of the average physical product. At a price of $1.60, for example, the 500 bushels produced by two workers are worth $800, or $400 per worker. The *marginal value product* is similarly the value of the marginal physical product; the extra 300 bushels resulting from the employment of two workers rather than one have a market value of $480. Total revenue, of course, is the market value of the total physical product. The difference between total revenues at two stages of production also shows the marginal revenue product.

The entrepreneur will not hire workers in excess of the number at which marginal value product just covers the extra wage cost. For example, five workers will not be used if the wage is more than $160.[3] If the entrepreneur hires five workers instead of four, total revenue rises by $160. If wages exceeded this amount, the entrepreneur would not add a fifth worker, but it would pay to do so if wages were anything less than $160. He would not hire four workers if the market wage were in excess of $256, because that is the amount by which the total revenue of the product of four workers exceeds that of three workers.

Since the workers are assumed equal in all respects, each gets the same wage. If three workers are available and the employer hires them because the market rate is not above $352, this is the wage for each. The employer would rather bid the wage up to this point than do without any of the three workers. The total wage cost is thus $1,056. Since the total value product is $1,152, there is a difference of $96 for other costs and profit at this stage of production. In other words, it would be erroneous to read Table 7-4 as if one worker is paid $320, another $480, and a third $352. Any one of the workers is marginal in the sense that it is a matter of indifference to the employer which one he would discharge if he employed only two—as he would do if the wage exceeded $352.

[3] This is the wage for the period of time in which the output in Table 7-4 is produced. Since the example happens to be one in agriculture, the period covered by the table is presumably one year.

It follows that the marginal value product determines the individual entrepreneur's demand for labor. In Figure 7-1 the average value product (*AVP*) and the marginal value product (*MVP*) from Table 7-4 are plotted. The segment of the *MVP* curve below the *AVP* curve becomes the firm's demand curve for labor. It shows the number of workers that would be hired by this firm at different wage rates. It is a typical demand curve in that it slopes downward to the right. The part of the *MVP* curve above the *AVP* curve is not applicable because the entrepreneur would not hire two workers at a wage of $480. The total wages would be $960, which is more than the value of the product of two workers ($800). Below point *a*, however, the firm would employ three workers at a wage up to $352, four workers at a wage up to $256, or five workers at a wage up to $160.

The reasoning is similar to that whereby we found that the part of the firm's marginal revenue curve that is rising constitutes its supply curve. Here, the part of the marginal-value-product curve that is falling constitutes its demand curve for the variable factor under consideration.

Demand and Types of Competition

In developing the marginal productivity analysis, it has been assumed that workers are homogeneous and that the business firms operate in pure competition. Now we shall drop these simplifying assumptions. First, the effect of different kinds of competition will be noted.

If the entrepreneur operates in pure competition, he can sell whatever output he finds most profitable at the going market price. His average revenue is the market price, and his marginal revenue is the same because each additional unit adds to revenue by the amount of the price. If the entrepreneur is not operating in pure competition, however, his output is important enough to influence the price. Since he can sell larger outputs only at lower prices, the marginal revenue is less than the price or average revenue. It becomes clear that the entrepreneur's demand for labor is related to the demand for his product. If the latter is highly inelastic, so that he must cut his price sharply if he intends to sell an increased output,

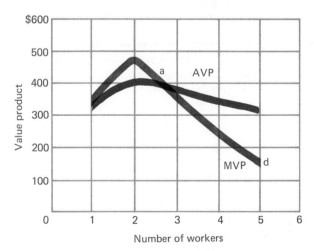

Figure 7-1. Average value product and marginal value product.

the marginal revenue will be small. Consequently, he does not demand additional labor unless the wage is correspondingly low.

Where the seller has a horizontal or perfectly elastic demand curve, as in pure competition, the marginal value product is simply the marginal physical product times the price, as in Table 7-4. If the market price is $2 and a marginal worker adds 6 units to output, he would be hired at any wage up to $12; if an additional worker then would add 4 units, he would be hired only if the wage does not exceed $8.

Where the demand curve slopes downward, as in other types of competition, the situation facing the employer is different. Suppose the demand curve for his product indicates that he can sell 100 units at $2 or 110 units at $1.95. The increase in revenue from selling 10 more units is only $14.50 ($214.50 for 110 units minus $200 for 100 units). An additional employee capable of increasing output by 10 units would be worth any wage up to $14.50 since he could add that amount to the employer's revenues. In this case, the value of the marginal product is not the marginal revenue product, as it is in pure competition. The marginal product is 10 units, each worth $1.95, and the total value of the marginal product is $19.50. But the marginal value product is only $14.50. The decline in price of 5 cents on the 100 units that could otherwise be sold for $200 accounts for the $5 difference. This is another way of noting that the monopolist or producer in other forms of nonpure competition may have an incentive to restrict production.

The Market Rate of Wages

Most of the discussion has been in terms of the demand for labor of the individual entrepreneur. Adding together the individual demands provides the total demand curve for labor. Since labor is not in fact homogeneous, it is necessary to examine the demand for and supply of different types of labor. Before turning to the supply side, however, we may note that marginal productivity analysis explains how the demand for labor is derived from the demands for the products of labor, when labor is combined with other factors of production.

With a given supply of labor the market rate of wages reflects the relative availability or scarcity of labor. Where there is much productive land and available capital, the fixed factors are plentiful and the marginal productivity of labor is high. Labor can be highly productive in many industries, and the individual entrepreneur can have a high demand for labor. If labor is more plentiful, the marginal product is less and the total supply of labor can be employed only at a lower wage rate. Thus the wage rate measures the marginal contribution of labor to the total output or national income. The total wage bill is the wage rate set by marginal productivity times the number employed. If marginal productivity is low, the total wage bill is a smaller fraction of the total value of output and a larger fraction remains for the other factors. Thus the scarcity and greater value of the other factors are reflected in the higher returns going to them.

This relationship may be illustrated by the data in Table 7-4. If three workers are employed at the marginal-productivity wage of $352, the total wage bill is $1,056. Since the value of the total product is $1,152, $96 is left for the other factors and profit. If four workers are employed at $256, the total wage bill is $1,024, and $384 is left from the value of the product,

$1,408. If five workers are employed at $160, the total wage bill is $800, the value of the total product is $1,568, and the remainder for the other factors and profit is $768.

The concept of marginal productivity helps explain the role of labor unions in the markets for labor. The underlying purpose of a union is to ensure that the workers obtain wages equal to marginal value product. Bargaining conditions may be such that a single employer or a small group can obtain labor for less than the marginal value product. If there is free and active competition among employers, it would be assumed that each employer would expand employment to the point where marginal value product equals the wage. If such competition does not prevail, a union can provide a kind of monopoly position for workers to match that of employers.

In addition, a union may be able to raise the marginal product of its members by restricting the supply of labor in a particular segment of the labor market. If workers with a particular skill are kept scarce through union restrictions, apprenticeship rules, and the like, the marginal product of each is raised. Employers find it worthwhile to pay a higher wage rate to share in the restricted supply. This kind of restriction is comparable to that employed by the monopolist and is subject to the same kind of criticism. Not only is the cost of the particular product raised and resources inadequately attracted to its production but workers who are barred from this employment go into others, where they tend to lower wage rates.

SUPPLY OF LABOR

If labor were a purely economic commodity, changes in demand would bring about long-run changes in the supply of labor—the amounts of labor offered at different wage rates. In effect, this is what the old iron law of wages stated; it looked upon the supply of labor as responsive to the price of labor. If wages went up, they covered the "cost of production" of more labor and population would rise; then the increase in supply would drive wages back to the cost of subsistence of the larger population.

Overall Supply

The amount of labor available is controlled principally by the size of the population and the proportion in the labor force. The amount can be increased by bringing more people into the labor force—the young, the old, women, and immigrants—in response to higher wages. Clearly, the supply of labor is considerably inelastic as it would require large increases in wage rates to effect significant changes in the labor force.

In the long run, the supply of labor would be elastic if it were true that higher incomes lead to larger populations. In the advanced economies of the modern world, this does not seem to be the case. Many factors other than income affect the formation of families and the birth rate. While high incomes may encourage earlier marriages, the attainment of satisfactory levels of income may also lead to restriction of the size of families. Families may be planned with the consideration of such restraints as the cost of higher education for the children. Social factors are more important, apparently, than changes in income levels alone. Urban families tend to have higher incomes than do rural families, but they also tend to have fewer children. Wars seem to stimulate marriages, and after each war there tends to be a baby boom.

Social and cultural constraints also rigidify the proportion of the population in the labor force. In our society the very young cannot enter the labor force and there are many pressures for those more than sixty-five years old to leave it. Retirement incomes, the appeal of leisure, and business practices all lead people to retire, although increasingly more people could remain active longer.

Women constitute about a third of the labor force. The social conventions that deterred women from working have been relaxed so that many women now work, both before and during marriage. The entry of women into the labor force was stimulated by World War II. Since then, many occupations have become more available to women. Greater demands for labor in many occupations have led to this breaking down of barriers. Not only have young women entered many occupations that were virtually closed to them in the past, but demands for school teachers, social workers, librarians, and nurses have called older women back after their children are grown.

The presence of women in the labor force not only increases the supply of labor available at any given level of wage rates but also presumably makes the supply somewhat more elastic, because some women who are enticed back to work by higher wages would stop working if wages were lower. The supply curve may be visualized as something like curve S_1 in Figure 7-2. Such a curve is relatively inelastic but not perfectly so. It reflects what we assume to be the case, that because of the need for income, not many workers leave the work force when wages are lower and not many enter the work force when wages are higher, because of all the other influences on the proportion in the labor force. Therefore, only some workers can enter or leave. Another element of elasticity is that some workers can take extra jobs or work overtime.

Adding together many individual demand curves for labor (such as from Figure 7-1) to obtain the total demand and superimposing this demand curve on curve S_1 in Figure 7-2 enables us to find the intersection

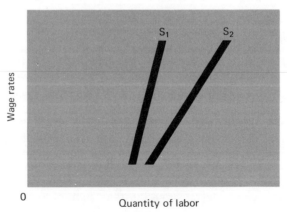

Figure 7-2. Supply of labor.

determining the market rate of wages. Assuming labor to be homogeneous, this market rate would determine the equilibrium quantity of labor
employed, given the demand and supply. If labor were all alike, there
would presumably be only one wage rate and labor would be equally productive in all occupations. Since this is obviously not the case, it is still
necessary to allow for wage differentials.

Wage Differentials

Labor is the services of human beings, and it exhibits all the variations
of human beings. Some labor is skilled, other labor is unskilled. People
have different abilities, talents, and aptitudes; some people are driven by
ambition, others are not; some have cultural and social advantages,
others disadvantages. It is not, therefore, a matter of indifference to
an employer which human being he employs. Some people can teach
atomic physics, but others cannot compete with them for such teaching
positions; some people can pilot airplanes, but others cannot compete
with them for such available jobs.

But individual differences are not so great that people cannot be
grouped together and considered at least roughly equivalent for particular tasks. Although no two molders in a foundry are identical, what is
important to the employer is that each molder can produce about the
same number of molds in a day.

Although molders may have similar productivities and be sufficiently
similar to compete among themselves, they are not airplane pilots and
airplane pilots are not molders. Each group competes for jobs in a different market, and a different group of employers competes for each
group of workers. The wage of a molder does not become the same as
that of a pilot because neither can transfer to the other market to take
advantage of a higher wage. However, in the long run more people may
train to be pilots if their wage is higher; in this way the labor resource is
attracted into occupations where its productivity is high.

All labor markets are interconnected in this way, although very loosely
in the short run. Policemen and firemen have been known to study law
at night and eventually become lawyers. In the longer run, the sons of
policemen and firemen may take legal training. Thus occupations are not
completely blocked out as in a caste system but are entered and left as
people compare the relative rewards to be earned and costs of entering
one occupation against another. Many people select an occupation for
a number of personal reasons or perhaps only because there is an opening. The marginal shifts, as in other economic problems, occur because
of the financial differences and, in turn, limit and determine what these
differences are.

Consequently, the supply curve in each separate labor market has some
elasticity because of the possibility that some people can shift into a
given occupation if the rewards increase. The greater the difficulty in
terms of the human capabilities required and the greater the costs in
terms of training, the more inelastic the supply is expected to be. Figure
7-3 shows two supply and two demand curves, illustrating the supply and
demand situations in a market for highly skilled labor and in a market for
unskilled labor. D_1 is the demand for highly skilled labor and, although
it is a smaller demand than that for unskilled labor (D_2), the resulting

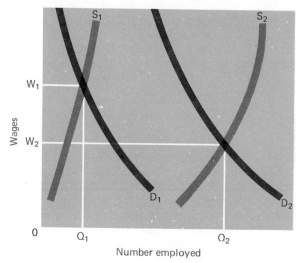

Figure 7-3. Determination of wage differentials.

wage is considerably higher because the demand is being met by a very small supply. Although there is a large demand for unskilled labor, the supply is large, and the result is a lower wage than for highly skilled labor. Similar illustrations could be prepared for any of the great variety of labor markets—for pilots, mechanics, physicists, college presidents, and so on.

Over a period of time the demands for different types of labor change because technological advances require people with new kinds of knowledge and skills. In recent decades the salaries of natural scientists, social scientists, statisticians, and specialists in public health have risen significantly, as more potential employers have realized the contributions that these specialists can make. A well-educated person of a generation or two ago might not be considered well-educated today. In virtually every occupation the participants have had to continue to learn or else become less productive and valuable. In contrast to the wages of many specialists, those of the unskilled have probably changed little in real terms (corrected for price changes), except as the general standard of living has risen. The widening *wage differentials* serve to channel young people into occupations where their labor is most productive. At first, the longer period of time spent in educational institutions tends to reduce the overall supply of labor, but later the supply in particular fields is augmented.

SUMMARY

The standard supply and demand analysis that explains the relative prices of commodities also explains the prices of the different factors of production and thus the shares of output going to land, labor, and capital. In the case of labor, the demand is determined by the marginal productivity of the labor factor. The more labor there is, the more there is available to be combined with the other factors and, beyond the point of diminishing returns, the lower is its marginal productivity. The demand for a factor of production is not based directly on the utility that factor provides for consumers, but it is indirectly because the demand for a factor is derived from the demand for the product.

In the case of reproducible goods, supply and demand analysis shows that costs tend to come into line with demand. Under the prodding of profits or losses, supply adjusts to demand so that the average unit cost of an article tends towards the market price while the market price also moves towards the average cost. In markets for factors of production, however, supply may not be based on costs of production. Early theories of the determination of wages explained wages in terms of labor's cost of production, and it was assumed that population would expand with the means of subsistence and keep wages at this bare minimum. Since changes in population in developed countries depend on many factors other than income alone, it is no longer assumed that the overall supply of labor adjusts itself to changes in the level of wages and, in effect, keeps labor's marginal productivity at a very low point. Rather, in developed countries the overall supply tends to expand more slowly than the ability to produce. As a result, market rates of wages allow labor to obtain a stable or even growing share of an expanding national output.

The general level of wages conceals many differentials in the wages of different labor groups. Individual laborers are not interchangeable over the whole spectrum of occupations. Consequently, there are many markets, more or less insulated from each other, for different types and kinds of labor. However, the markets are linked because, in the short run, some people can move from one occupation to another in response to wage incentives and, in the long run, new entrants into the labor force can select the occupations that have the most attraction. Obstacles to entry into some occupations that require special talent, aptitude, or training maintain favorable differentials in these occupations.

Economic Terms for Review

functional income	marginal productivity
derived demands	marginal value product
subsistence wages	in pure competition
Malthusian theory	in other markets
marginal output	wage differentials

Questions for Review

1. Why are statistics on the amount of rent, interest, and profit lacking?
2. What is the approximate share of compensation of employees in the total national income?
3. What was the median family income in 1969 (half of the families got more and half got less)? Get the latest figure for GNP and for the U.S. population. What is the GNP per person?
4. What is the reasoning whereby it used to be believed that wages tended to be barely sufficient to cover subsistence? How did economic conditions during the Industrial Revolution lead to

this belief? How has the relationship between supply and demand in labor markets changed since then?

5. Are there any limits to the ability of unions to raise wages?

Questions for Analysis

1. Suppose that a physician has a reputation of being very successful in treating some particular disease and that he earns $60,000
a year. Is he exploiting his patients? What would happen if he
charged half as much? Does a famous baseball or football player
who is paid $80,000 per year exploit his employer or the public?
Would the price of admission tickets be any lower if he voluntarily
accepted $30,000? (Probably not; reason it out with the aid of
supply and demand.) Who would benefit?

2. In establishing a new plant, how does an entrepreneur decide
whether to install a good deal of machinery or to have many
functions performed by hand labor?

3. Wages are presumably paid to overcome the disutility of labor.
It is also common observation that, in general, the highest-
paying jobs are those that seem to be the least unpleasant. How
does wage theory resolve this paradox?

4. An argument for the free-price system is that it permits people
to earn what they are worth. To what extent do you think the
system works in this respect? How is this worth measured?

Problem for Solution

This problem illustrates the theory of wage determination. Assume that there is pure competition in product and factor markets
and, in order to simplify the problem, assume that there are only
three employers. These employers have production situations in
which workers would have marginal value products as tabulated
below:

Number of Workers	Employer 1		Employer 2		Employer 3	
	MVP	Total Revenue	MVP	Total Revenue	MVP	Total Revenue
1	$10	$10	$15	$15	$20	$20
2	15	25	16	31	22	42
3	14	39	17	48	20	62
4	13	52	16	64	18	80
5	12	64	15	79	16	96
6	11	75	14	93	14	110

If there are 12 workers, each willing to take whatever market wage
arises, what will the wage per time period become in this society?
(If you need a hint or a check on your method, read the footnote at
the bottom of the page.)[4] From the data in the tabulation, draw a

[4] Perhaps the easiest approach is to see which employer would take a single worker, which
would take two, and so on. If there were only one worker, Employer 3 would outbid the other
employers because he can pay up to $20 (MVP of one worker). In fact, at $20 Employer 3 would
take three workers. He would also take four if the wage does not exceed $18 and neither of the
other employers can pay $18. However, Employer 2 would take three workers at $17. Thus
seven of the twelve workers are accounted for. You can probably allocate the other five by the
same process.

demand curve for labor. Draw a supply curve on the assumption that all the workers will accept any wage not below $16 but no one will accept a lower wage. (Refer to Figure 7-1. Both curves will be a bit unusual.)

What would be the society's gross national product in this problem? Of this GNP, how much would go to labor?

8
Rent, Interest, and Profit

In economic analysis, rent is the price the use of land commands in the market and interest is the price commanded by capital. Profit is the return to entrepreneurial activity, and it differs from wages, rent, and interest in that it is a residual. The entrepreneur assembles labor, land, and capital with which he produces and markets a product. To the extent that the value of the product differs from the value of the productive factors used — his cost — he makes a profit or a loss.

Essentially, the explanation of rent and interest is comparable to the explanation of wages. The more productive that land is when combined with labor and capital, the greater the demand for land is and the higher the rent the landlord can charge. The more productive that capital is when combined with the available land and labor, the greater the demand for capital is and the greater the return commanded by the owners of capital. As in the case of labor, the supplies of both land and capital have their own characteristics, which are important in determining market value. Since the marginal-productivity analysis of demand was stressed in the explanation of wages in Chapter 7, these peculiarities of supply are given more attention in this chapter.

ECONOMIC RENT

Land differs from other factors of production in that its total supply is fixed by the extent of the earth's surface. This fact is so obvious that it was noted by the earliest thinkers about the distribution of society's output. Adam Smith, David Ricardo, and others foresaw a situation in which land would become more and more scarce, and thus more and more valuable, in relation to the supply of labor and capital. The fact that the supply of land cannot be expanded (except for minor additions such as filling in shore lines and the like) has led to putting land into a special category in the theory of distribution. Rent is the return to this special factor of production.

It is common to speak of the rents of buildings and other durable goods, but in economics rent has a different meaning. These rents are prices for the use of such goods that are reproducible at some cost of production. These rents are, therefore, the way in which the costs of production are recovered and a return earned by those who devoted income to this type of production. In other words, the rent of a building recovers the cost of the building over its life. But the rent of land is different. Land has no original cost of production. Further, as it becomes more valuable, no more can be produced to keep its market price down.[1]

[1] Minor exceptions such as land fills have already been noted, but these are more like capital goods than land because they have been produced at a cost, with the expectation of recovering this cost through the use of the extended land.

Adam Smith called rent "the price paid for the use of land," and since that time this has been the role of rent in distribution theory. To Smith, in settled countries rent was a monopolistic price because the landlords owned all the land there was or could be. Thus demand alone set the level of rents that could be charged. He considered rent a payment for the fertility or other characteristics of a plot of ground that made it superior to another plot.

Ricardian Rent Theory

Ricardo was able to be somewhat more precise about rent than Smith, and much of Ricardo's thinking is still basic to rent theory. He defined rent as "that portion of the produce of the earth which is paid to the land-lord for the use of the original and indestructible powers of the soil." [2] Rent is not paid, however, because nature is bountiful and productive; just the opposite: rent is paid because nature is niggardly. Highly productive land, whether because of fertility or location, is scarce and the owner can command a high rent. Thus rent is a payment for the use of better-quality land instead of land that is barely worth using under current conditions of population and technology. Such marginal land is no-rent land because there is insufficient demand to create a rent for it.

The Ricardian explanation rests, consequently, on two peculiarities of land: (1) it is limited in quantity and (2) different plots differ in productivity. In a new country where there is plenty of land for a small population, landlords cannot charge rent because people can simply move to other plots. As the population grows, however, land becomes scarce and the best land begins to have value. Suppose, for example, that on the best land a man can grow 100 bushels of corn and that corn is the best crop for this land. Suppose that on the next-best land, a man can grow 90 bushels. When all the best land is in use, people have a choice of moving to. the second-best land or paying the landlords rent to be able to stay on the best land. Competition drives this rent payment up to 10 bushels. Thus the rent is a measure of the superior productivity of the best land. When it becomes necessary to bring third-grade land into use, on which a man can raise 80 bushels of corn, the choice becomes threefold: use the worst land in use and pay no rent, use the second-best land and pay 10 bushels, or use the best land and pay 20 bushels.

Of course, the owner of the land and the cultivator of it need not be different people. If the owner of a plot of the best land cultivates it himself, his income is 100 bushels; if the owner of a second-grade plot cultivates it, his income is 90 bushels, and so on. But if the demand for corn is sufficient to support a man on third-grade land where the output is 80 bushels, the owners of second-grade and first-grade land get larger incomes than does the owner-cultivator of third-grade land. This extra income — 10 bushels for one and 20 bushels for the other — is attributable not to their own efforts but to the characteristics of their land. They can rent the land to others for this extra income because the alternative others have is to earn what they can on marginal land.

Ricardo believed, therefore, that rent would become a larger and larger fraction of total output. As population grew, the *margin of cultivation* would be pushed out to the point where land on which a living could

[2] L. D. Abbott (ed.), *Masterworks of Economics,* Doubleday & Company, Garden City, N.Y., 1946, p. 301.

barely be made was in use. The margin of cultivation could not be pushed beyond this point because a greater population could not be supported. Output would become more and more expensive, and landlords could command more and more units of this output.

Rent as Surplus

According to this explanation of the nature of rent, rent is not one of the costs of production. It is a surplus over and above the costs of production necessary to bring forth the supply. The cost of corn, in the example just used, is its cost on the marginal plots where 80 bushels can be produced. This is the marginal cost and the one that determines the value of corn. Corn must sell for a price that covers this marginal cost or it cannot be produced on third-grade land. The cost of producing corn is even lower on second- and first-grade land. Thus the rent that accrues on the better land is not a part of the cost of producing corn there but is the differential that exists between the price of the corn and its cost on the better land. If the rent were included in the cost, the cost would be the same on all grades of land.

This point is clear in the case of the owner-cultivator, but if a tenant pays the owner of first-grade land 20 bushels (or their market value) in order to use that land, it seems to him that the rent is one of his costs. From his point of view he is correct, but there is nevertheless an important distinction. The market price is not high because the rent is paid on good land. The rent on good land is paid because production is pushed to marginal land where the marginal cost is high, and the price is high because this marginal cost is high. Thus the rent is a result of the market price and not a cause of it. It is a surplus above the output on no-rent land. If the demand for corn were less, so that production took place only on the first two grades of land, rent would disappear on second-grade land and fall on the best land.

There are many everyday examples of this relationship. A store building in a central location commands a higher rent than would an identical building on a less desirable site. If many potential customers pass a store located in the center of the city, many retailers will want to locate there. But only one store can occupy a given site. The high volume of sales and the high level of profits create a demand for that plot of ground. The rent that can be charged tends to become the difference between what a retailer could earn there as against what he could earn in the poorest location in use. In the financial district of New York City there are great advantages in a large bank's being located where many of the nation's financial transactions take place. The market demands of these large banks, securities dealers, and other financial institutions make land located within the financial district very valuable. One of the nation's leading banks is unlikely at present to relocate miles away in a suburb, but it is conceivable that, in the future, with the extension of modern electronic communications, data transmission, and transfer of funds, it may not be worth so much to be physically located in the center of the financial district.

Diminishing Returns and Rent

The idea of diminishing returns from more extensive use of land is clearly implied in the Ricardian doctrine. Another view of the situation appears if we consider not only the possibility of a single worker employed on each plot but the more realistic possibility of several workers employed on each. In that case, workers would be added to the first-grade land until marginal productivity fell to the point where additional workers would be more productive on second-grade land. Then workers would be added to both first- and second-grade land until it became worthwhile to begin using third-grade land, and so on. In other words, the marginal product of labor (or by the same token, capital) would be the same on all grades of land. However, the value of the output in excess of the wage bill would be greatest on the best land, and so on down.[3]

Because land has no cost of production and is virtually fixed in amount, historically the explanation of rent has followed Ricardo's explanation. That is, land has been thought of as the fixed factor, and additions of variable factors (labor or capital) have been viewed as creating the surplus that becomes rent. This surplus arises because of diminishing returns. The additional variable factors become worth less and less (because of marginal productivity) and leave more and more for the rent factor.

In order for this explanation to be consistent with that of wages in Chapter 7, however, the other factors can be thought of as fixed in the short run and land can be thought of as the variable factor. That is, more or less land can be employed along with the fixed factors. As additional acres are added to a fixed quantity of labor and capital, output would tend to rise but at a decreasing rate, according to the principle of diminishing returns. The available land would tend to be used, up to the point where the marginal output would not be worthwhile. This is basically the same conclusion that is reached with the Ricardian approach. However, in this line of reasoning land constitutes a variable cost.

The demand curve for land would reflect the ease or difficulty of substituting other factors for land. If other factors could be substituted with little decline in output, the demand for land would be more elastic, as more land would be used only if it were cheaper. If substituting other factors would greatly reduce output or if many other factor units were necessary to maintain the same output, the demand for land would be highly inelastic. Land would be used even if it were considerably more expensive.

The demand curve meets a perfectly inelastic — vertical — supply curve, which shows that the quantity of land is the same at any price or rent, at least in the short run. This is why more capital is combined with land in areas where land is scarce or highly productive. Investment in a multistory office building or high-rise apartment is a substitute for investment in additional land on which smaller buildings might be constructed.

The supply and demand situation is represented in Figure 8-1. Since there are many grades and types of land, varying according to fertility, location, and other characteristics, this graph actually represents the determination of the rent of a particular kind of land.

Urban Rents

The rent on land used for urban housing, businesses, and related purposes is determined similarly to rent on land used for agriculture. Agricultural land is valuable according to its fertility and location in respect to markets; urban land is affected more by location alone. Characteristics that make factory sites desirable are nearness to lines of transportation and to markets, proximity to supplies of labor and materials or power, and

---

[3] A numerical example appears in the problem at the end of the chapter.

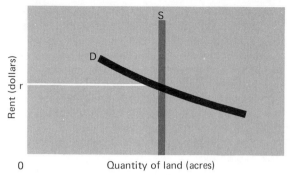

Figure 8-1. Supply and demand for land.

similar features. Other characteristics are important if the land is used for retailing, wholesaling, financial business, or certain other purposes. Each plot of land tends eventually to be used in that business in which it is most productive in value terms. The adjustment process may be slow when heavy investments have been made in a building that no longer represents the best use of the particular plot but which is still too valuable to tear down.

Just as there is a margin of cultivation on an agricultural plot, capital is combined with the urban plot up to the margin of profitability. As already mentioned, a site in the financial district of a large city is in great demand and becomes used by some business that can justify a great investment in an appropriate building. No one grows corn or cattle on Wall Street in New York City. There is also an extensive margin, in that there is always the choice of competing with other uses for a central location or moving farther out where the returns may be less but the costs are less also. The individual firm chooses between a greater investment, or higher rent, at a superior location and a lower rent at an inferior location. At the margin, it is no longer worthwhile extending the operations of the enterprise.

Private Ownership

The Ricardian explanation of rent suggests that the landlord has a stranglehold on society. Since land is naturally here and no one created it—it is God-given—many reformers have believed that land should be owned communally rather than privately. As a matter of fact, it is not generally realized how much of the land area of the United States is not privately owned. For example, in 1966 the federal government owned 33.7 percent of the land area of the country. Over 710 million acres remained from the original public domain, and about 54 million acres had been acquired by other methods. In 1964, land owned by individuals, partnerships, and corporations constituted 58.7 percent of the total and Indian lands, 2.2 percent. Besides the federal land (33.8 percent) there was state land amounting to 4.5 percent and municipal and county land amounting to 0.8 percent.[4]

Ricardo and the other early classical economists had a gloomy view of the future of economic society because they postulated that wages tended

[4] U.S. Bureau of the Census, *Statistical Abstract of the United States,* 1968, pp. 194–195.

towards subsistence, which was mainly the cost of food. The cost of food was set at the margin of cultivation; any additional output at the margin in excess of subsistence became profit, and all the other output of land superior to the margin—the *surplus product*—became rent. "In the natural advance of society, the wages of labor will have a tendency to fall, as far as they are regulated by supply and demand; for the supply of labourers will continue to increase at the same rate, whilst the demand for them will increase at a slower rate." [5] If this were to be the course followed by the economy, the thought would naturally occur that the output commanded by rent should be shared in some fashion by all.

The Single-Tax Proposal

Some have proposed that land be nationalized and others that a special tax be levied to recover rents for the benefit of all. One of the best-known proposals is that of Henry George, who published a widely read book, *Progress and Poverty,* in 1880. Henry George had a large following, and was nearly elected mayor of New York City in 1886. His proposal was for a *single tax* on land rent, as he believed that no other taxes would then be necessary.

George was essentially a follower of Ricardo; he held that price covers not only the wages, interest, and profit necessary to call forth production but also rent, which is unnecessary. If rent were not paid or if it were confiscated, production would continue because the land would remain.

In spite of George's persuasiveness, the single-tax movement did not remain an important political influence. The proposal raises many questions. In the light of present governmental expenditures, it is unlikely that such a tax would actually be sufficient to raise the entire revenue. In 1969, rental income of persons was only about $20 billion, as against governmental expenditures (at all levels) of more than $200 billion. Of course, the imputed rent on land owned by corporations was probably much more than $20 billion. However, the main point is not whether a single tax would be adequate but whether a tax on land rent as such is equitable. There would be many practical difficulties as well.

It is extremely difficult to estimate how much of the income of a business enterprise consists of a return to land. Corporate income, and much individual income, is a conglomerate of returns to factors of production. If the economic rent were overestimated, a tax would impinge on wages, interest, or profit. Reported rents are likely to diverge considerably from the economist's concept of economic rent. The rental of a building includes the payment for the building itself, which is a capital good, as well as the payment for the land site. Such a rental also includes compensation for services of elevators and maintenance, and perhaps for utilities. The farmer gets some return from his grading, draining, and fencing, as well as from the "original and indestructible powers of the soil." Pure economic rent may not be an enormous sum when these other payments are deducted.

The equity of the proposal for this type of tax is affected by the fact that the original settlers on land are usually no longer the owners, nor are their heirs. A plot of land may have been sold and resold many times.

[5] David Ricardo, *Principles of Political Economy and Taxation,* Everyman's Library, London (no date), p. 57.

The present owner has paid the past one for his property rights; it would be unjust to allow the past owner to invest the proceeds and avoid the tax while the tax prevents the new owner from benefiting from his investment. The past owner is benefiting from the rents in the sense that he was paid the present value of the future rents when he sold the land.

While fortunes have been made by some who were fortunate or astute enough to acquire land that later became very valuable, these people may also have performed a service in the process. The development of new lands and territories often has depended upon the willingness of pioneers to invest time and money in starting enterprises where none existed before.[6] If there were no prospect of profit in the form of rising land values, a stimulant to development would be lost. Of course, development goes on today and did not end with the passing of the frontier.

Capitalization of Rent

Several references have been made to the price of land as well as to the rent paid for the use of land. Obviously, the two must be related. In principle, the present price of a plot of land is the capitalized value of the future rentals, as closely as these can be estimated. When a person buys a plot of ground, the future rentals are to be the return on his investment. Thus investment in land is competitive with investment in various forms of securities or in capital goods.

The annual rentals provide some percentage return on the price of the land. The price and the rent are related through this rate of return. If market rates on comparable investments are 6 percent and the annual rent is expected to be $600, the current value or price of the land is $10,000. The annual rent is 6 percent of this value. If one person estimates future rentals to be higher than does the present owner—rightly or wrongly— he is probably willing to pay a price that the owner is willing to accept.

Quasi-Rent

The English economist Alfred Marshall introduced a useful concept in his *Principles of Political Economy* when he observed that there are numerous instances of supply being fixed comparably to the supply of land. Sometimes this fixity is permanent, as in the case of a mineral spring whose waters are supposed to be highly beneficial. No more springs can be created, so the owner can charge whatever the traffic will bear. Of course, this example is actually one of land, broadly defined to include all the characteristics of land.

Sometimes the fixity or scarcity is one of talent. The question of why a famous athlete can earn $50,000 or more was raised in the discussion of wages. The answer can be phrased in terms of the supply of and demand for his peculiar labor—there is a great derived demand for his services because his employer can sell a great many tickets to customers. The answer can also be phrased in terms of rent. Suppose the athlete's unique ability enables him to hit 40 home runs a year as a baseball player. If he did not play baseball, he might be able to earn $15,000 a year in some other occupation. In baseball he might earn $65,000 a year. This differ-

---

[6] One of the many books relating to the development of virgin lands in this country is Lew Dietz, *The Allagash*, Holt, Rinehart and Winston, Inc., New York, 1968. This book describes how the wilderness of Maine passed into private ownership.

ential of $50,000 is similar to rent—a quasi-rent like that of the mineral spring—which the athlete is able to command because there is no close substitute player who is willing to work for less than $65,000. If there were a choice of playing baseball for $40,000 or earning $15,000 in another job, he still might be glad to play baseball, but since there is no close substitute to whom the employer can turn and pay $40,000, the employer agrees to the $65,000 salary.

Sometimes the scarcity is temporary. When the Suez Canal was blocked in 1967, there was a great increase in the demand for shipping since ships had to take longer routes and shippers of petroleum and many other products needed more ships. Shipowners could raise rates and serve only those who could afford them. Shipping thus became temporarily much more profitable. Shippers can be said to have paid a quasi-rent, in the sense that the ships would have sailed at lower rates but market conditions (demand) brought about higher ones.

Summary: Rent

Because the factors of production are land or natural resources, labor, and capital, each earns a return in the process of production. This return is the price entrepreneurs find it worthwhile to pay for the services of land, labor, and capital, in the light of market prices for products.

The peculiarity of the supply of land is that it is a natural gift and not reproducible to any great extent by man. As a factor of production it therefore has no original cost of production, but it is necessary and, in a system of private property, must be paid for. The explanation of the market price for the use of land—rent—is similar to the explanation of wages. That is, if other factors are held constant and the entrepreneur considers the results of using different quantities of land, diminishing returns apply to land and each entrepreneur has some best quantity of land to use. Thus there is an aggregate demand curve for land, which places a value on the fixed quantity of land.

The return to land can also be explained, as it has traditionally been done in economics, by considering land as a fixed factor to which other factors can be added. In this explanation, the diminishing returns applicable to additional increments of other factors make land more and more valuable. Rent arises at the margin of utilization; the least productive land in use earns no rent while better grades (in terms of natural fertility or location) can command higher rents. In this view, payment for the use of land is not necessary to maintain production, since land exists whether the landlord is able to collect rent or not. This view is similar to the reasoning we noted earlier whereby a price need not cover the fixed costs to make it worthwhile for the entrepreneur to produce in the short run. It differs, however, in that fixed costs must be covered in the long run or capital goods cannot be replaced and production ceases. The land need not—in fact, cannot—be replaced and has no cost of production in that sense.

INTEREST

Interest is the return to capital. Analysis of the determination of the market *rate of interest* requires first a definition of capital. Capital may be thought of as the dollar amount spent for capital goods, or it may be thought of as the capital goods themselves. Interest is commonly thought of in monetary terms, such as $5 of interest for a one-year loan of $100. However, it can also be viewed as the return earned by capital goods. As in the case of wages or rent, it is necessary to consider the demand for capital and its supply.

Supply of Capital

In real terms the capital existing in society at a particular time is the stock of nonconsumption goods, or goods that have been produced for the purpose of further production. Buildings, machines, railroads, trucks, computers, and a host of other things exist not for use in consumption but for use in the process of production.

By using capital goods, man engages in indirect, or *roundabout* production. For example, instead of catching fish with his bare hands, primitive man devises a net which enables him to catch more fish. He must forego catching some fish while he manufactures the net, but his incentive is greater consumption in the future. While he devotes some of his resources (labor) to obtaining the materials and weaving the net, he must reduce his consumption. His total output, which is also his real income, consists partly of consumer goods and partly of capital goods. Thus he is said to save, by devoting some of his income to the production of capital. In an advanced society the process is much more complicated, but the basic fact remains true that capital goods are produced because there is a demand for them. Someone therefore must divert demand from consumer goods to capital or producer goods, and saving remains an essential part of the process. In a modern monetary society people who wish to save often do not wish to purchase machines, trucks, or other capital goods, but they do want to share in the earnings of these goods. Chapter 13 describes how the savings of individuals and corporations are channeled through savings institutions to the purchase of capital goods by business firms.

If the primitive man expects to catch the same amount of fish whether he uses his bare hands or whether he spends part of his time making a net, there is no incentive for him to use capital. The incentive to postpone current consumption is the prospect of having greater consumption or income later. Given a choice between a certain amount of income or consumption today and that same income or consumption in the future, people generally choose the present. There is a *time preference* for consumption now rather than in the future. If someone were to offer you a gift of $100 now or next year, you would probably prefer to have it now. If an employer were to offer a raise now or next year, the employee would probably take it now. As a result, people are not motivated to save a given sum now if they expect to get back only that sum at some future date.

No doubt, some people would save even if they expected no reward or interest. As in every market, some people would react at a lower price. A person much interested in having funds for retirement might set aside some income for future consumption, even if he expects the funds to buy no more then than they do now. Some people might save even if they had to pay to do so; they might save $100 today in order to be sure of having $90 at some future time. At the other extreme, some people might be so profligate—have such a high rate of time preference—that they could not be enticed to save even at very high rates of interest. But, at given levels of income, people, in the aggregate, are attracted to saving (postponing consumption) by a greater reward.[7]

Capital goods will therefore not be produced unless they promise to create enough additional income to overcome this reluctance to save. I might, in a primitive society, produce a plow rather than goods for immediate consumption, but only if I thought it would increase my future output sufficiently to overcome the present sacrifice. Or I might rent the plow to others, demanding in return some of the extra output that they would obtain. Correspondingly, in a money economy, I might spend some of my money income for a plow or I might lend the money to someone else who wants to buy a plow. In that case, I would demand the future return of the money plus interest in money.

Loan Funds

In a modern society, saving takes the form of diverting money income from consumption. The saved funds may be spent directly for capital goods, as is the case when corporations save and spend the funds for plant, equipment, or inventory or when a farmer buys a tractor or fencing materials. Often, however, the saved funds are lent to a borrower. The borrower wants the loan funds either to expand his own consumption or to expand his stock of capital goods.

The interest rate that appears in a modern monetary economy is consequently the monetary rate, or the ratio between the number of dollars paid for a loan and the number of dollars lent. Real rates are called *implicit* rates, as for example, the increase in the quantity of fish caught with a net over that caught without the net, compared with the investment in the net. Loans are here defined very broadly and include all transactions in which the use of money is transferred, whether through loans, purchases of bonds, or deposits to savings accounts, and so forth. The problem becomes one of analyzing the supply of loan funds and the demand for loan funds.

Supply of Loan Funds

Each sector of society may not use all its collective income currently and be willing to supply funds to other sectors. (The sectors of society are households, businesses, and governments.) Foreign supplies or demands may also be considered, and in the problem of analyzing the supply of and demand for funds, the commercial banking system must be included.

Personal saving is an important component of total saving. In recent years personal saving has ranged between 5 percent and over 7 percent of personal income after taxes. A principal determinant of the amount of income diverted from personal consumption is the level of income itself. A family with an income of $20,000 a year tends to save considerably more than a family with an income of $10,000. In terms of the analysis of demand in Chapter 3, the $20,000 of income can be spread over many purchases because the marginal utilities of the things purchased can be lower. As the desires for current consumption are met, other purchases become as attractive as additional consumer goods. Thus the family

---

[7] The qualification *at given levels of income* is important, as will be clarified later in the discussion.

with a high income devotes some of its income to such assets as bonds, savings accounts, and other assets that return an income over the future.

As average incomes rise from year to year, households in the aggregate tend to save more. The proportion of income saved may not rise, but even a stable proportion of a growing income provides a larger amount of income to be saved. From year to year, however, the proportion tends to fluctuate within certain limits. When there are great uncertainties about future prices, tax rates, or incomes, people tend to save more. When there is generally a high degree of confidence in price stability, in rising incomes, and in political stability, people tend to consume more freely and to save a smaller percentage of their incomes.

Each year households supply billions of dollars to loan markets, either directly by purchasing securities issued by business and government or indirectly by turning funds over to financial intermediaries like savings and loan associations or savings banks. In turn, these institutions make loans to businesses, governments, or home builders and home buyers who purchase current output not being purchased by the savers.

Business saving is equally important. Corporations normally do not pay out to stockholders all their corporate income but, on the average, they pay in the neighborhood of one-half. Retained earnings are often about the same volume as household savings—in recent years around $30 billion. In the aggregate, however, business corporations spend all their retained earnings for additional capital goods and inventories and add additional funds borrowed from households. The business sector saves and borrows at the same time. But within the aggregate there is a considerable amount of lending by some businesses to others, through the various markets for different kinds of loans.

Governments save when their incomes exceed their expenditures, and the surplus is used to retire existing debt. This process returns funds to other savers (investors), who generally then seek other ways of lending their funds. In recent decades, federal, state, and local governments have in most years added to, rather than reduced, their debts.[8] Since World War II, state and local governments have had more expenditures for roads and highways, hospitals, educational buildings, and other capital additions than have been paid for by current tax revenues. The federal government has borrowed in more years than it has reduced debt.

In addition to current income diverted from consumption, an important source of new funds in loan markets is additions to the supply of money brought about by the operation of the central banking system and the commercial banks. The extent to which the money supply is allowed to grow is governed by the policies of the Federal Reserve System. This is a topic of sufficient importance to be discussed further (Chapters 11 and 12), but it may be noted here that the money supply is generally expanded when the monetary authorities wish to make funds more available in loan and other credit markets. In times when business is slack and unemployment is rising, the monetary authorities attempt to make it easy for businesses to get loans, and at lower interest rates.

The behavior of saving in the principal sectors of the economy throws light on the relationship between the amount of income currently being saved and the level of interest rates—elasticity of supply of loan funds.

[8] Chapter 14 discusses government finance.

From the foregoing summary, it appears that there is some elasticity of saving with respect to interest rates, but not a great deal. If time preference were the only factor to consider, the supply of saving would presumably respond considerably to higher interest rates. It is doubtful, however, that households respond any more, if as much, to changes in interest rates than to other determinants of saving. All other things kept constant, households no doubt save somewhat more at high rates than at low rates, but the change is apparently inelastic.

Similarly, business saving depends considerably on the level of corporate income, just as household saving depends on the level of personal income. When corporate profits are rising, corporate saving tends to increase because corporations continue to pay the same proportion of profits in dividends, or even allow the proportion to fall. When corporate profits fail to rise, or actually fall, corporations in the aggregate continue to pay about the same total amount of dividends, and thus retain less.

Government saving also rises when government income rises, or at least government borrowing tends to decline. Additions to the money supply, created by the banking system, are not made in response to the level of interest rates but are made in the light of the Federal Reserve System's assessment of business conditions. Actually, interest rates are likely to be high after a period of business expansion and low unemployment, so the Federal Reserve is likely to restrict the growth of the money supply at such times. Thus it must be concluded that the supply of loan funds is relatively inelastic.

Demand for Loan Funds

Each sector of the economy also has demands for loan funds. Some loan funds are demanded for increasing consumption, others for spending on capital goods. The spending on capital goods is business investment plus households' expenditures for housing. Although governments purchase a great deal of what might be considered capital goods — dams, highways, buildings, and so on — these are not generally classified as investment because they are not acquired for the purpose of producing income. Instead they are lumped into general expenditures.

The role of marginal productivity in the determination of interest rates comes in in the business demand for loan funds. Businesses borrow in order to acquire additional capital goods that promise to be productive by increasing output and revenues. The demand for physical capital goods can be explained in the same manner as were the demands for labor and land. With labor and land held as constant factors, additions of capital in a business enterprise add to total revenues but at a declining rate after the point of diminishing returns. A $5,000 machine adds something to output; a $5,000 truck adds something more; $5,000 spent for air-conditioning equipment adds something more; and so on. Additional expenditures cannot be made indefinitely without finding that still more would not add as much to revenue as to cost. The firm will not spend its own funds and will not borrow additional funds, then, unless the interest rate it can get by lending or must pay to borrow becomes lower. The investment demand curve for loan funds slopes downward in the usual fashion.

It should be noticed that the productivity of capital can be measured only as the capital goods are capable of replacing their own cost. A capital good adds nothing to the value of output unless that value increases by enough to replace the good at the end of its life and bring in additional revenues. The replacement must be accomplished by deductions for depreciation and obsolescence from total revenue. If a machine costs $10,000, it must earn more than $10,000 over its life in order to recover its own cost and produce a return. It may confuse the issue to some extent to recall that, in actuality, it may not be possible to add capital equipment without adding other factors. For example, it may be impracticable to add another truck without hiring another driver. However, the net productivity of the truck can be calculated by deducting all the extra costs that are incurred if it is purchased, including not only the wages of a driver but also costs for fuel, maintenance, repairs, taxes, and so on.

Explanations other than marginal productivity are required to understand the demands for loan funds from nonbusiness sectors. In the modern economy consumers borrow vast sums in order to purchase appliances, boats, snow vehicles, and many other goods. These durable goods can be considered investments, in the sense that they provide income in the form of consumer services and thus maintain some value over a long period, even though they do not provide a monetary income by producing goods for sale.[9] Many families can afford these items if they pay for them in installments, adding the cost of interest on the borrowed funds to the cost of the items.

Consumer borrowing may be viewed either as a reduction in consumer saving or as an increase in the demand for loan funds or credit. In the consumer sector as a whole, if one family saves $1,000 and another borrows $1,000 for additional consumption, consumption is the same as if there were neither the saving nor the extra consumption. But consumer borrowing has become very sizable and an important factor in loan markets, so it has come to be treated as a demand for loan funds.

Some consumer borrowing is probably related to interest rates, but this relationship does not make this part of the demand for loan funds very elastic. Like other forms of consumer spending, that for goods bought on installment responds to levels of income and opinions about future prices, incomes, and tax rates. In fact, expenditure on such goods depends even more on such factors than does expenditure for staple articles.

Borrowing for the purchase of housing has been thought to be responsive to interest rates. In the past, it has been stimulated by drops in the interest rate, as in the recessions of 1954, 1958, and 1960. The behavior of the mortgage markets in 1966 and 1968 creates some doubt about the elasticity of mortgage borrowing with respect to interest costs. In 1966 and 1969 home building declined sharply as interest rates rose steeply. But the declines may have been due as much to inability to find lenders with available funds as to the higher rates. In 1968, when mortgage rates were also high, housing starts were numerous.

Governments' demands for loan funds are also inelastic to interest rates in most cases. Some state and local projects tend to be postponed

---

[9] However, it may be argued that some such goods provide monetary income in the sense of saving on cash outlays. A washing machine may save on laundry bills; a television set may reduce expenditures for movie tickets, and so on.

when interest rates are high, partly because officials believe it wise to wait for lower rates and partly because some state constitutions or other legal restrictions make it impossible to pay the high rates. The federal government is not controlled to any great extent by the level of interest rates. That is to say, other considerations are much more important in determining whether the federal government covers all its expenditures with tax revenue or not. All in all, there is a weak relationship between the interest rate and the amount of funds demanded by governments.

A fourth type of demand for funds needs to be mentioned although discussion of it is more appropriate later. This is the demand for cash as a particular asset that is attractive to own. Everyone and every business needs some sort of a cash balance out of which to make payments when payments do not coincide perfectly with receipts and as a liquid asset. The perfect liquidity or spendability of money makes it more desirable, up to a point, than other assets. Holding money, however, means that the holder can have neither the goods nor the interest-bearing assets the money would buy. Thus this demand for funds is thought to be closely related to the level of interest rates. If rates on other money-market instruments are low, the opportunity cost of holding cash is not great, but if interest rates are high, a larger income is foregone if cash is held.

The Equilibrium Rate

Early economists derived a theory of the determination of the interest rate by concentrating almost entirely on the business demand for capital funds with which to buy capital goods and on the supply from personal savings. The resulting theory stated essentially that the demand for capital rests on the marginal productivity of capital goods and the supply is determined by time preference. Thus the typical demand and supply curves could be postulated, showing the interest rate and the equilibrium volume of saving.

Such an explanation is valid up to a point, but it fails to take into account a paradox of modern monetary economies. A high demand for capital may bring about a high interest rate but, if the supply of savings is also stimulated, there will be less spending for consumption and incomes will tend to fall. This fall in incomes will, in turn, reduce the volume of savings because saving depends crucially on the level of income. This paradox will be explored further in the chapters dealing with the national income. It is noted here because it turned attention to the monetary factors that are important in setting interest rates in markets for loan funds.

In the resulting theory there are four types of demands making up the total demand for loan funds—demands for investment, for consumption, for government spending, and for cash balances. Taken in conjunction with the total supply of loan funds, this total demand provides a market rate of interest that clears the market. The total supply comes from the same sectors that provide demands and from the creation of new money through the banking system. An important factor on the supply side is the level of income of each sector and its influence on the amount of funds each sector saves.

The central banking authorities can bring about a lower market level of interest rates by providing the banks with additional reserves, with which the banks make more loans and investments. As the additional money supply comes into the hands of those who spend it for current output of capital and consumer goods, incomes rise throughout the economy. As incomes rise, saving rises and permits the continuance of the lower interest rates. All this, however, assumes that the process starts with a certain amount of unemployment and slack in the economy, so that the additional expenditure does not lead to rising prices and inflation. If that should be the case, demands for funds to spend before prices rise further can so increase the demand that interest rates are forced up.

Capital, Productivity, and Time

Capital differs from land as a factor of production in that it can be produced and therefore has a cost. Capital is worth producing as long as it adds enough to output, through roundabout production, to overcome the cost. A peculiarity of measuring how much capital adds is that the additions to output are expected in the future. One may say that these additions are worth something less in the present because of the necessity of waiting for them; or one may say that the necessity of waiting is one of the costs of using capital.

As was noted earlier in reference to the net productivity of capital goods, this *net productivity of capital* is the addition to output after considering all operating costs and also after recovering the original investment.

Consider the construction or purchase of a machine that would cost $10,000 and that would add $1,000 to costs annually and $2,000 to revenues for ten years, after which the machine would be worthless. Over the ten-year period the machine is expected to just return the investment in it. Consequently, no one would consider it a good investment, as there would be no net return. In fact, the element of time means that in this case there would be a negative return. This is because future receipts or incomes are worth less than present ones.

How much less a future receipt is worth than a present receipt of an equal number of dollars depends upon the rate of time preference expressed in the market through the interest rate. Suppose the interest rate is 5 percent a year; this is the market reward people can gain by postponing consumption for one year. Instead of spending $1,000 for consumption, one may lend $1,000 to others at the going rate and a year later be paid $1,050 — interest plus principal. If the same rate applies to loans of two years, the lender receives $50 after one year and $1,050 after the second year, and so on with longer maturities.

This example may be turned around in order to show how much a future payment is worth today. It is obvious that a payment of $1,050 a year from now is worth $1,000 now, assuming a rate of 5 percent, because an investment of $1,000 now will become a payment of $1,050 a year later. Or we may say that a future payment of $1,000 is worth $952.38 today because an investment of that amount at 5 percent interest becomes $1,000 a year later ($952.38 × 1.05 = $1,000). Thus the market *discounts* future payments to their *present value*. In this example, $1,000 ÷ 1.05 = $952.38. This is why the $10,000 the machine would cost is worth more today than the future net additions to revenue provided by the machine. Each net addition of $1,000 has to be discounted for the applicable length of time. The first year's $1,000 is worth $952.38 if the going market rate is 5 percent; the second year's $1,000 is discounted by another 5 percent and is worth $907.03, and so on.[10] The ten annual payments have a total present value as follows:

$$
\begin{array}{r}
\$ \ \ 952.38 \\
907.03 \\
863.84 \\
822.70 \\
783.52 \\
746.21 \\
710.68 \\
676.84 \\
644.61 \\
\underline{613.91} \\
\$7,721.72
\end{array}
$$

The present value of the net returns to this $10,000 investment is only $7,721.72. It follows that the annual incomes must be large enough to overcome the discount and be worth at least $10,000 when the market rate is 5 percent. If the rate were higher, each annual income would be worth less today and thus each income would have to be higher to make the project worthwhile. The importance of time is shown by the fact that to raise $7,721.72 to $10,000, each annual income must be 29.5 percent greater. That is, each annual income must be expected to be $1,295 to make the investment just worthwhile at going interest rates. If there were many such competing projects on which the expected returns were even larger, the demand for funds would be greater in investment markets and the rate would be driven up. In this way the productivity of capital determines the demand and, along with supply, determines the rate.

It should be noted that capital goods may be rented and that these rentals are related to the investment through the rate of return. If, in the foregoing example, the capital good were rented for $1,295, which is the rental that competition would tend to bring about, the rental would provide a 5 percent *yield* to the owner on his investment. The rate of interest provides a shorthand method of comparing different yields on competing projects, so that those with the highest yields can be undertaken. Again, in order to express the return as a rate, it is necessary to consider a time period, such as 5 percent a year or 6 percent a year, in order to compare yields of projects with different lives.

Thus in markets for capital, the interest rate performs the functions of any price but with particular reference to time. Any price rations the available supply to those who are willing to pay that market price and rewards those who produce the supply. If there are many capital investment projects that promise high returns (because the marginal productivity of capital is high), the demand is high and the high market rate of interest rations the available supply of loan funds. This rationing process also

[10] Since the $1,000 of revenue each year may be expected to flow in evenly throughout the year, the calculation might be amended to show this refinement although the principle is just as clear if it is assumed that each receipt comes at the end of the year, as in this example.

means that real resources are directed to the production of those capital goods whose returns justify the high rate, and other potential projects are squeezed out.

A final comment about market rates of interest. For simplicity the foregoing explanation has been made in terms of a single market rate. In actuality, since different loan markets have many characteristics that affect the desirability of loans, different rates come about and are related to the characteristics of particular loans, such as safety, liquidity, marketability, maturity, and tax treatment. However, there is a general level of rates prevailing at any one time, and actual market rates are related to this level. For example, short-term borrowing by the federal government is done at about the lowest market rates because such loans are considered perfectly safe and the loan instrument (a treasury bill) can easily be sold if the holder wishes. Banks' loans to their best and most creditworthy corporate customers carry lower market rates than loans to other customers. State and municipal governments can borrow at even lower rates than can the federal Treasury because the interest income is tax-free to the lender. Mortgage loans usually are made at relatively high rates because such loans are less liquid—they are harder to dispose of if desired—and have long maturities.

PROFIT

The explanations of wages, interest, and rent have all been similar in that the demand side is explained by marginal productivity, although each of the three factors of production has peculiarities of supply. In the case of interest, the allowance of money into the problem introduces additional factors influencing both supply and demand. No one pays the entrepreneurial factor a contractual payment called profit. Hence the explanation of the profit income in functional distribution has to be different. Essentially, the explanation is simply that when market rates do not require the entrepreneur to pay out all his sales revenue as costs to the owners of land, labor, and capital, he retains a profit; when they require him to pay out more, he incurs a loss.

Economic Profit

It has already been noted that incomes usually called profit are not what the economist means by economic profit but include many implicit costs or returns to other factors of production. Land, labor, and capital of the entrepreneur himself may be contributed to an enterprise without any actual payment, or even accounting, of rent, wages, and interest; the whole income of the enterprise is called profit. Economic profit, as something over and above all these implicit costs, is much smaller than reported profits of corporations and unincorporated businesses. Many small businesses make no profit over and above the implicit costs.

Also, because of the conventional treatment of depreciation, reported profits are sometimes overstated during a period of rising prices. If a machine costs $10,000 and lasts for ten years, the annual charge to gross income necessary to recover the cost is $1,000. But if the machine, or a similar one, costs $15,000 at the end of the ten-year period, the business firm cannot replace it with its depreciation allowances. To be able to do so, the firm would have had to reduce its reported profit by more than $1,000 a year.

This is not to say that economic profit does not exist. Undoubtedly, some companies with high reported profits more than cover all implicit costs because their reported rates of return on invested capital are well above market rates. However, many small businessmen probably earn little more than their imputed wages of management because they prefer to be their own bosses. At the same time, many others are highly success- ful and earn far more than they could by working for other firms.

To illustrate further how profit tends to be absorbed into other costs, consider a highly successful restaurant. It has built up a large volume of business and a high reported profit. The location of the restaurant may be an important factor in its success, or at least it would be costly to start again in a different location. When the lease expires, the landlord will de- mand a higher rental and, after the rental is raised, more of the total revenue becomes rent and less of it remains as profit. Insurance com- panies and other large institutions that lend funds for building shopping centers now lend at a stated rate of interest but also participate in the earnings of such projects, if and when they exceed certain levels. The success of another enterprise may be due to an exceptionally talented hired manager. In this instance, the manager can demand a higher salary, go to another employer, or go into business for himself. In each pos- sibility, the wage goes up and the temporary profit declines.

Sources of Profit

Since profit is a residual, the sources of profit are, in effect, those con- ditions that permit the residual to exist. One reason for profit is changes that take place in the economy. Consumers' tastes and preferences change and so do their demands for individual products. When consumer demand increases considerably, those in a position to meet the demand can reap *windfall profits*. Each year enterprising companies bring out some new products that capture the fancy of the public. Examples over the years have been midget golf, the Hoola Hoop, Silly Putty, and a host of others. More fundamental changes in the economy have been reflected in rising demands for many kinds of recreational equipment — outboard motors, skis, snow vehicles, fishing equipment, cameras and film, and so on. Another example is the development of low-cost copying machines for office use.

The possibility of rapid changes in the economy brings about uncer- tainties and risks for business enterprises. Business uncertainty differs from other forms of risk, which can be insured against. Risk of damage from storms, fires, or vandals can be offset by insurance, but a business- man cannot buy insurance against a decline in the demand for his product or a rise in his costs. When the changes are favorable, a business profits; when they are unfavorable, it loses. Skill in business management lies partly in foreseeing changes and partly in taking steps to minimize the effects of unfavorable ones. Profit is sometimes defended as a reward for taking business risk, without which new products would not be developed and other advances made.

An entirely different occasion for residual revenues in the form of profit is oligopoly or monopoly. If competition is weak or absent because entry into an industry is difficult and expensive, prices may be maintained above costs. When such profits are obvious and large, governments often intervene or encourage the establishment of newcomers in the industry.

Some innovations are highly beneficial to the economy because they meet a need or because they reduce costs. An innovation is the adoption or adaptation of a discovery to business use. Innovation tends to be profitable in the short run, as when a business firm brings out a new product such as color television, and that is why innovations are made. If the demand is seen to be permanent, however, and the profits attractive, other firms tend to produce similar products. Many commonplace articles today were innovations not long ago.

SUMMARY

The process of production automatically creates the incomes with which production is purchased. Incomes reflect rates of return set in markets for different kinds of land, labor, and capital, and residual profit. Markets for products set prices and quantities through supply and demand. Supply is determined by costs, which are, in turn, incomes. In a market economy, what is to be produced, in what manner, and when are determined in product markets and who shares the product is determined in factor markets.

The operation of both product and factor markets is regulated and influenced by many external controls that have been mentioned in the early chapters and will receive additional comment at other points. Output, prices, and incomes are not determined solely in the manner outlined in this and the preceding chapter, but they follow closely the underlying influences described here. These are the *natural* tendencies of a market economy.

Economic Terms for Review

Ricardian rent theory	time preference
margin of cultivation	loan funds
rent as surplus	by sector
single tax	net productivity of capital
capitalization of rent	present value
quasi-rent	economic profit
interest	windfall profits
rate of interest	

Questions for Review

1. What did Ricardo mean when he said that rent is caused by the niggardliness of nature?
2. What is the margin of use in the case of urban land?
3. What is the basic argument for the single tax?
4. If you have a bond that will pay $60 interest forever and your bond is worth $1,200, what is the going rate of interest?
5. Why must there be a reward for saving?
6. Are households net suppliers or net demanders of loan funds? Which are businesses?

7. Is the supply of loan funds elastic or inelastic?
8. What are the sources or causes of economic profit?

Questions for Analysis

1. How can rent be considered not a cost of production but a kind of surplus?
2. Does diminishing returns explain rent as it does wages?
3. Why is the salary of a star athlete similar to rent?
4. How does the marginal productivity of capital affect the interest rate?
5. Why is a payment to be received in the future worth less than face value now?
6. Suppose you have a 6 percent bond that matures in thirty years at par, $1,000. How important to the present market price of the bond is the maturity value?
7. How does the interest rate perform the functions of any price?
8. Why is economic profit much less than reported or accounting profits?

Problem for Solution

Suppose that in a new country there are three grades of land. Diminishing returns to labor, as workers are added to the various plots, are shown in the following tabulation:

| | Grade 1 Land | | | Grade 2 Land | | | Grade 3 Land | | |
| | Output (Bushels) | | | Output (Bushels) | | | Output (Bushels) | | |
Number of Workers	Total	Aver-age	Mar-ginal	Total	Aver-age	Mar-ginal	Total	Aver-age	Mar-ginal
1	100	100	100	90	90	90	80	80	80
2	190	95	90	170	85	80	150	75	70
3	270	90	80	240	80	70	210	70	60
4	340	85	70	300	75	60	260	65	50

Any number of workers could be assumed, the problem being to discover what plots they would settle, in what numbers, and what the resulting land rent would be. The problem can also be solved step by step. A first immigrant would no doubt settle on the best land (Grade 1), where he could produce 100 bushels. A second immigrant would find it immaterial whether he joined the first worker on Grade 1 or worked alone on Grade 2. This is because he could command 90 bushels of output in either case. If no rent had to be paid, he would join the first worker because the average output would be 95 bushels, although the first worker might object to having his output drop from 100 to an average of 95. But the landlord can demand 10 bushels as rent if the worker goes on Grade 1 land, because the worker's best alternative is to go to Grade 2. If either worker refuses to pay any rent in order to stay on Grade 1 land, he can be dispossessed and his alternative is to go to Grade 2 land. So either one of the workers may stay and pay rent, or both may stay and bargain about how to share the rent of 10 bushels.

Note that rent arises because of diminishing returns on Grade 1 land. The existence of different grades is not necessary for rent to arise, but it measures how much the rent is to be. Assume for a moment that there is no Grade 2 land, only Grade 1 and Grade 3. The rent at this point would be 10 bushels because the workers are better off paying this rent than in going where marginal output would be 80 bushels. As soon as there is a third worker, however, someone would have to add 80 bushels by staying on first-grade land or by going to third-grade land.

Assuming a second worker goes to the first-grade land, a third would go to second-grade land because there he can produce 90 bushels, as against 80 on either first-grade or third-grade land. No rent can be charged on second-grade land, and rent remains at 10 bushels on first-grade land. But a fourth worker faces the choice of producing 80 bushels on either Grade 2 or Grade 3 land or 70 bushels on Grade 1. The first two offer a marginal choice, so we may arbitrarily assume he goes to Grade 2. When there are four workers, rent arises on Grade 2 land because the workers' alternative is for someone to move to Grade 3. Rent on Grade 1 land rises to 20 bushels, again because the alternatives are to produce 80 bushels elsewhere. The following tabulation shows how the workers distribute themselves. You may want to copy the table down through four workers and work the remainder out for yourself, through nine workers.

| | | Marginal | Rent | | |
Immigrant	Grade	Output	Grade 1	Grade 2	Grade 3
First	1	100	...	...	...
Second	1	90	10	...	...
Third	2	90	10	...	...
Fourth	2	80	20	10	...
Fifth	3	80	20	10	...
Sixth	1	80	20	10	...
Seventh	1	70	30	20	10
Eighth	2	70	30	20	10
Ninth	3	70	30	20	10

And so on.

9
National Income

Foregoing chapters have surveyed the economy primarily from the point of view of the individual firm or the individual industry. The focus has been the markets in which firms and industries operate and the prices that result from the forces of supply and demand. Chapters 7 and 8 have broadened the focus in order to consider how market forces determine the shares of income throughout the economy. We now move from the division of total output into shares to the problem of the size of the total output itself.

THE CONCEPT OF NATIONAL INCOME

The concept of gross national product was introduced in the first chapter as an overall measure of the performance of the economy. It was shown that _gross national product_ (GNP) describes total output, and it was implied that in real terms this output constitutes the incomes of the members of the economy in which it is produced. Thus the increases in GNP in recent decades were taken as measures of the progress of the American economy. A measure closely related to GNP is _national income,_ which is the net amount of income available to society out of the GNP. The difference in the two measures is the difference between gross income and net income; how this difference comes about will be explained shortly.

National income may be thought of as the incomes produced and available to the human and corporate persons making up the economy. Just as a family with a large income is better off materially than one with a small income, a nation with a large national income is better off materially than one with a small national income. A large part of economics is the study of the reasons why a national income is large or small, growing or stagnant. A study of the economy as a functioning organization leads to the formulation of principles that explain why the national income is at the level it is. Equally important, knowledge of what determines the level of the national income leads to the formulation of principles that help explain how to prevent unwanted fluctuations and how to stimulate growth in this income.

This study of the economy as a whole is called _macroeconomics_ because it focuses on aggregates of spending and output. _Microeconomics_ is concerned with segments of the economy—individual firms and industries and their prices and costs.

Gross National Product

The fact that output and income are the same thing would be readily apparent in a very small, uncomplicated economy. If there were an isolated pioneer family, with no contacts with an outside economy, it would be clear that the income of this family would be whatever it produces. The more it could produce by its own efforts, combined with the use of its work animals, buildings, and tools, the more goods it would be able to enjoy. The family would be unwise to consume its total, or gross, output, however. On the one hand, it would be necessary to replace the articles of past output that were being used up. Thus each year part of the crop would have to be set aside for the next year's planting. And, as animals aged or died, they would need to be replaced. On the other hand, it would be desirable to set aside even more production than just enough for replacement. Increasing the amount of seed set aside would permit growing larger crops in the future. Constructing additional buildings would permit storing larger amounts of food for human beings and animals, as well as a greater variety of tools and the like. Much of this accumulation of wealth, therefore, would require a diversion of productive efforts to make goods that are not intended for consumption. The family would spend some of its time and effort in putting up fences, draining fields, and building sheds rather than producing more goods that could be consumed directly.

The fact that in a more complicated society most people do not consume or save the same products that they produce tends to conceal this simple identity. In the modern economy we produce something that is sold to others; with the money, we buy goods that we elect to consume (durable goods, nondurable goods, and services) and we acquire various assets with the income we choose to save. To a large extent, these assets are types of financial claims issued by borrowers who wish to spend for capital goods. Thus the simple identity holds true—the American family or society receives as real income whatever it can produce with its labor, capital, and natural resources. Consequently, the gross national product, looked at as goods and services valued at market prices, and the sum of money incomes in society must be closely related. Indeed, they are essentially the same thing looked at from opposite points of view.

Since gross national product is measured in current market prices, whatever current output is sold for to final buyers this year is the gross national product for this year. Whatever final buyers pay becomes the gross incomes of the sellers, out of which they pay their costs, which become the gross incomes of the recipients. If inventories are built up during the year, GNP is greater than _final sales_ to that extent. We count only sales to final buyers because otherwise there would be double counting. Obviously, we should not count the same thing every time it is bought and sold; we should not count wheat as one product, the flour it yields as another, and the bread made from it as a third. By counting the bread only, the product bought by the final buyer, we automatically include the wheat and the milling of it as costs of production of the bread. The prices of the intermediate products and stages of production reflect the value added at each stage of production.

Components of Gross National Product

The number of different goods and services produced in a single year defies counting. The range covers the alphabet—from armchairs to zinc, from abacuses to zithers, from antennas to zippers. Some meaningful arrangement and classification of these hundreds of thousands of items is necessary. As we saw in Chapter 1, it is possible to classify them according to purchasers and uses. The bulk of total output consists of items purchased by households for personal consumption. Business firms purchase plant and equipment for investment purposes, and households purchase housing for similar reasons. Government purchases a wide variety of goods and services to carry on governmental operations. Finally, some of the output of the economy is purchased by residents of other countries (and some of their output is imported into the United States). It should be noted that this classification is neither strictly by purchaser nor strictly by use. Some consumer goods are purchased by governments and foreigners as well as by domestic households; investment goods are purchased by all four categories. But by raising the question, Who buys the output? we can go on to related questions such as why they buy as much as they do. In this way we can approach the problem of why total output is as great as it is.

Let us examine this classification in somewhat more detail than was done in the introductory material in Chapter 1. In 1969 gross national product was estimated to be $932.1 billion. As might be expected, the bulk of this output was taken by households. Personal consumption expenditures were $576.0 billion, or 61.6 percent of total GNP, and consisted of:

	Amount (Billions of Dollars)	Percentage of Total Consumption
Durable goods	$ 89.8	15.6
Nondurable goods	243.6	42.3
Services	242.6	42.1

Such a high proportion of consumer expenditures for services is a reflection of a high-income economy. Poor economies must devote the bulk of income to nondurable goods for immediate consumption. Major components of the expenditures for services include education, transportation, medical and dental care, and entertainment.

In the aggregate, households also make substantial expenditures for new housing. In order to clarify the similarity of this type of expenditure to other investments in capital goods, however, it is included in the classification *gross private domestic investment.* Each of the words in this term is significant: *gross,* because it includes all expenditures of this type without regard to depreciation of existing capital goods and therefore without regard to how much net growth there is in the existing stock of such goods; *private,* because government expenditures on capital goods such as dams and highways are classified separately; *domestic,* because all expenditures made by foreigners are classified in one place; and *investment,* because the money is invested rather than expended on consumption. The total for gross private domestic investment in 1969 was $139.4 billion and was broken down as follows:

Fixed investment	$131.4 billion
Nonresidential	99.2 billion
Structures	*33.4 billion*
Producers' durable equipment	*65.8 billion*
Residential structures	32.2 billion
Nonfarm	*31.7 billion*
Farm	*.5 billion*
Change in business inventories	8.0 billion

The only classification requiring explanation is the last one, change in business inventories. This item arises because production is a continual process and, in a given year, some goods do not reach their final buyers; they are still in the inventories of some businesses along the line of production and distribution. For the year in question, the last business firms to buy such goods may be thought of as the final buyers. Such firms purchased, or in many cases produced and kept, some goods for future sale. These goods are analogous to structures and other fixed investment, which business firms also purchased or produced and kept. In each case the goods were produced during the year, and their costs were paid out and constituted incomes for the recipients. Only the net increase or decrease in inventories is significant. If all additions to inventory were offset by withdrawals, the effect would be the same as if there were no inventories at all.

The GNP accounts next list that segment of gross national product accounted for by net exports, which amounted to $2.1 billion. Like the change in business inventories, this expenditure is subject to rather large changes in relation to its own size. Although it is relatively small, it is the result of much larger transactions because it is the net difference between exports ($55.3 billion) and imports ($53.2 billion) of goods and services. Net exports have been as high as $8.5 billion in 1964. The logic of including net exports as part of GNP is simply that some of the total output ($55.3 billion) was purchased by residents of other countries, thus making this sum available as earnings to residents of this country, but residents of this country made expenditures of $53.2 billion that did not become available as earnings here because the purchases were made abroad. Thus earnings in the United States were $2.1 billion larger than they would presumably have been without international transactions.[1]

Finally, the various levels of government purchased current output of goods and services to the extent of $214.6 billion. As we noted earlier, these purchases are not identical with all governmental expenditures, as the latter include transfer payments to other sectors of the economy, which in turn make the actual purchases. The breakdown of governmental purchases in 1969 was:

Governmental purchases	$214.6 billion
Federal	101.9 billion
National defense	79.2 billion
Other	22.7 billion
State and local	112.7 billion

These four principal categories of aggregate expenditures constitute the gross national product for 1969, as follows:

Personal consumption expenditures	$576.0 billion
Gross private domestic investment	139.4 billion
Net exports of goods and services	2.1 billion
Government purchases	214.6 billion
Total GNP	$932.1 billion

[1] One should not jump to the conclusion at this point that exports are good and imports are bad. The relationship is considerably more complex than the arithmetic that is relevant to national income accounting indicates and is examined later in the study of international trade.

We have thus seen that a total of $932.1 was spent by final buyers for the current output of goods and services produced in this period. This being the case, the next question is, Who received this sum? We now turn to this question.

National Income

Aside from transactions with foreigners, it is obvious that if the American people produce some $900 billion worth of goods and services in a given year, they somehow divide this flow of goods and services among themselves. Basically, this division is accomplished in a market economy by people earning incomes in the process of producing the output and then using these incomes to buy the output or, to some extent, sharing these incomes with others through transfer payments.

A final sale of a good or service provides the seller with gross receipts or gross income out of which he pays his costs, including his costs of producing or acquiring the good sold. If he had no costs whatever, all his gross income from sales would be net profit. Whatever costs he does have reduce his net income; the higher the costs, the lower his net income, which may actually be a negative figure. But the costs he must pay to others represent the gross incomes of others, and the same remarks may be made about these gross incomes. Some of these payments become incomes directly, such as the wages of clerks and other employees; other payments are the gross revenues of businesses which supply the businessman with materials, light, heat, and so on. What each business takes in must be divided between what it pays out as costs and what it keeps as profit or net income. The costs are either income to someone or gross receipts out of which costs are paid and some income kept. If it were statistically possible to trace all such payments to recipients who no longer pay any out as costs, all the costs would have become incomes. It is in this way that the aggregate expenditures made by final buyers on gross national product become incomes.

Aggregate expenditure, or GNP, would thus amount to the same thing as aggregate incomes if it were not for two kinds of cost that are incurred by producers but not paid out to others as incomes. These two costs are *capital consumption* allowances and indirect business taxes. When we stated in the preceding paragraph that a businessman must pay out his costs and may keep the remainder as profit, we omitted consideration of his costs for capital consumption. It is correct to say that GNP becomes gross incomes, out of which these two costs must be deducted in order to arrive at the net incomes earned by members of the economy.

Allowances or deductions for capital consumption must be made for three main reasons. One type of allowance is *depletion,* which is the using up of natural resources owned by the business. When a petroleum company takes oil from its reserves in the ground or when a mining company mines coal, it realizes that the value of this resource is part of the cost of production. Its wealth is reduced by this depletion just as much as by other costs that must be deducted from the sales revenues. A second type of allowance is *depreciation,* which is the decline in value of capital equipment caused by use and the passage of time. In calculating his net profit, a businessman must make allowance for wear and tear of his plant and equipment, which he must eventually replace in order to keep his investment intact. The third type of allowance is *obsolescence,* which is the decline in value of machinery and other equipment caused by its becoming outdated as new types are invented. To the extent that the value of the businessman's capital goods has been reduced by depletion, depreciation, and obsolescence, his net gain or income for the year is reduced. His wealth has not been increased, in other words, to the full extent of his gross income before such allowances.

Suppose that in the past a business has invested $1 million in various items of plant and equipment and that, on the average, these items have a useful life of ten years. Each year, therefore, they go down in value by $100,000. That amount must be reinvested each year in the business or the businessman would consider that much of his capital to be income. It is not necessary that $100,000 be spent on items that are identical with those wearing out; as long as this amount is invested each year, the total investment will remain at $1 million. The situation is the same as if the capital goods cost $100,000 and wore out and had to be replaced at the end of each year. The fact that they last ten years merely means that they do not add $1 million to costs for one year and then nothing to costs for nine years but that they add $1 million to costs over a ten-year period and this cost must be recovered over the ten-year period. The method of recovering the costs is the use of depreciation allowances each year which represent sums that can be reinvested in order to maintain the original $1 million investment. Thus, if the business has an income of $200,000 after all costs have been paid out to others as rent, interest, wages, and so on, and the total depreciation allowance is $100,000, the net income of this business (or its owners) is the remaining $100,000.[2]

The same kind of reasoning applies to the nation as a whole, which can be viewed as the summation of all the economic units within it. At the beginning of the year there is a certain stock of capital. During the year a certain amount of capital goods is produced and added to the total stock. But this production is not entirely a net gain in the accumulated stock because of the decline caused by depreciation and obsolescence. Incidentally, the same reasoning applies to inventories. Inventories of a certain size exist at the beginning of the year and some goods go into inventory during the year, but some goods also come out of inventory. If the reduction exceeds the increase, some of the investment in this form at the beginning of the year is not there at the end of the year. The sales made from this source should not be confused with net income; they are a using up of capital.

The total output (GNP) for a given year, then, may be thought of as consisting of three parts. One part consists of the consumption goods actually consumed during the year; another part consists of the goods produced to replace the capital goods and the goods in inventory that were used up during the year; and the third part consists of the net increase in the stock of capital, including inventories.

Depreciation and similar allowances are a special kind of cost because they are not paid out to others as income. The original expenditure for the capital goods was, of course, paid out and became incomes at that time. The other deduction from gross national product is different in that it is paid out, but not as incomes to persons or corporations. This deduc-

---

[2] The costs that are paid out currently are called *expenses,* in contrast to costs that are only incurred, such as depreciation.

tion is the indirect business taxes, such as sales and excise taxes, which represent costs that must come out of sales receipts. In contrast, the income tax is considered a division of income with the government; first the income is arrived at and then the tax, based on the income, is paid. But taxes on sales and on payrolls (and other similar taxes) represent costs of doing business and are like other expenses, such as wages. However, they are paid to government and thus do not flow to factors of production as shares of the sales price. Consequently, the incomes earned in the process of production must be correspondingly less than the aggregate expenditures that include these indirect business taxes.

Allowing for these two deductions, gross national product was reduced in 1969 as follows: [3]

Gross national product	$932.1 billion
Less:	
Capital consumption allowances	77.9 billion
Net national product	854.2 billion
Less:	
Indirect business tax and nontax liabilities	86.6 billion
Other adjustments [4]	+3.6 billion
National income	$771.2 billion

The figure remaining after the first deduction for capital consumption allowances is called *net national product* because it is gross national product net of depreciation, depletion, and obsolescence, or the using up of capital in the process. It is the amount of income available to be shared, including the share taken by governments through indirect taxes (but not through direct taxes). Deduction of the indirect business taxes and other adjustments leaves the amount available to be shared as private incomes — *national income.*

DIVISION OF NATIONAL INCOME

In Chapters 7 and 8 we examined the principles that determine how income is shared in a market economy. It was shown how consistent principles explain the division of income into wages, interest, rent, and profit. Unfortunately, it is not possible to put the national income accounts into categories completely consistent with these categories of income. The reason is largely that people receive income as combinations of these basic categories. As already noted, the farmer obtains an income that is partly wages for his own labor, partly a return on his investment in land and capital, and perhaps partly a profit. As an accounting matter, his net income from operating his farm is considered profit. Another complication

[3] These and subsequent figures for national income are from the *Federal Reserve Bulletin,* March, 1970, p. A-69.

[4] These adjustments are obviously minor. The largest are often what appear to be statistical discrepancies in the estimates. Others are business transfer payments, such as pensions (because these payments are not for contributions to current output), subsidies to business (because they are business income but are not included in sales prices of output), and profits of government enterprises (because they go to government and not to others as income).

in categorizing the national accounts is the fact that corporations have their own incomes, which they may or may not share completely with their stockholders.

National Income and Personal Income

Incomes received by persons are less than the total national income because of the existence of corporations and other reasons. If corporations paid no dividends whatever to their owners, no corporate income would be available as personal income. Of course, the owners of such corporations would benefit in the sense that their investment in the corporations would increase. It would be as if the corporations paid out their entire net earnings and then sold new stock to the owners for an equivalent amount. But statistically and legally, retained profits of corporations do not become *personal income* because the stockholders do not actually receive the flow of money income and do not have discretion over its use. On the average, corporations in the United States retain a fairly large fraction of corporate profits. This policy tends in the long run to benefit the stockholders because of the growth of the companies, but it is a factor affecting the amount of income that households can divide between consumption and saving in a given year. In 1969, corporate profits were $88.4 billion before taxes and $50.6 billion after taxes. Dividends paid to stockholders were $24.6 billion; thus $26.0 billion of the national income was retained by corporations.

A second deduction from the national income is contributions made by employers and employees for social insurance, which were $54.4 billion in 1969. Part of these social security taxes are deducted by employers from employees' wages and turned over to government for social security benefit payments, and part are paid by employing institutions themselves. Technically, since the employer acts merely as an agent in collecting these taxes from his employees, the former part is not considered taxes or costs paid by the employer. These taxes do not reach the wage- or salary-earner, however, so they do not become part of his personal income.

Certain payments increase personal income. As already noted, dividends offset some corporate income. Similarly, government *transfer payments* add to personal income. These are social security benefits, veterans' pensions, government employees' pensions, and the like. During the period examined, these payments added $61.9 billion to personal incomes. Another type of transfer payment is the interest paid by government on government debt. This interest is considered a transfer payment because of the difference between private and government debt. When a business borrows, it uses the funds in the process of production and the interest becomes one of the costs of production. The lender is considered to earn the interest much as the engineer or clerk earns his salary. The net amount of interest paid by consumers, in contrast to producers, is similarly counted as a transfer payment for national income accounting purposes. These two types of interest transfers amounted to $28.7 billion. The final transfer payment increasing personal incomes is business transfer payments, such as pensions based on past rather than current productive effort. These were $3.6 billion.

Subtracting the deductions from national income and adding the increments provided a figure in 1969 of $747.2 billion for personal income. It may be seen that this amount is $24.0 billion less than national income, not a great difference since some rather large adjustments nearly cancel out.

Disposable Personal Income

The figure for personal income, $747.2 billion, is that amount out of which people, from millionaires to the poor, pay their direct taxes, if any, and pay for their consumption expenditures. Direct taxes and related payments were $117.5 billion. Such taxes are largely based on income and, in this sense, are a sharing of income with the levels of government. The remainder of personal income, in this case $629.7 billion, is called disposable personal income because it is at the disposal of the recipients. It may be spent for consumption or it may be saved in some manner. Whatever is not spent for consumption is, by definition, saved. Since we are looking at the aggregate economy, we are including those whose saving is negative as well as those who do not consume all their incomes.

In analyzing the components of gross national product, we have already seen that expenditures on consumption were $576.0 billion. We have now made the circle from the aggregate expenditures on current output, to the incomes earned in the process, to the disposal of these incomes on part of this aggregate expenditure—consumption. Later, to complete the picture, we shall examine the disposition of business and government income on the other components of gross national product. First, however, we need to note that consumers make certain other payments which dispose of their incomes but which are not, strictly speaking, for consumer goods and services. For statistical purposes, the Department of Commerce notes two types: interest payments of $15.3 billion on consumer debt and transfer payments abroad of $0.8 billion, such as gifts to relatives. Thus, $37.6 billion of disposable personal income was not used for consumer expenditures or these two types of transfers. Personal saving, therefore, was $37.6 billion.

Personal Saving

In the year we are examining, personal saving was 5.9 percent of disposable personal income and just about 5 percent of personal income. These ratios are within the usual range, but within this range there may be significant swings from year to year. It is generally agreed that the amount of saving depends more on the amount of income than on anything else, but other factors can be important in the short run. For example, the lowest ratio of saving to disposable income since World War II—the highest ratio of consumption to income—came in 1947, when households were able to purchase many things that had been scarce during the war years and when rising prices made it appear unwise to postpone purchases. In 1947, saving was 4.3 percent of disposable personal income. The ratio has exceeded 7 percent in several postwar years. In 1967, for example, it was 7.1 percent, the highest in fourteen years. This high figure has been attributed to a combination of circumstances. Households generally had less liquidity (money, savings accounts, and easily marketable securities) and more consumer debt than usual because of high levels of consumption in 1965 and 1966; there were many uncertainties stemming from the Vietnam War, including the possibility of higher income taxes and less full employment; and the reward for saving, in terms of interest rates, was at an historically high level.

Even this ratio in 1967 and early 1968 was low, however, in comparison to that prevailing during World War II. At that time, in spite of sharp increases in direct taxes, disposable income rose rapidly — by more than 50 percent between those years. The shortages of durable goods, coupled with campaigns to encourage lending to government through the purchase of savings bonds, led to large amounts of personal saving. Although disposable personal income was $146.3 billion in 1944 (as compared with $629.7 billion in 1969), personal saving amounted to $37.3 billion ($37.6 billion in 1969), or 25.5 percent. At the other extreme was the situation in 1933, when incomes were very low. In that year of deep economic depression, gross national product was only $55.6 billion and disposable personal income was only $45.5 billion. Personal consumption and other personal outlays were $46.5 billion, so personal saving was actually negative. Consumption was financed by credit to some extent and by using up existing goods.

These comments about consumption and saving are based on the definitions used in the national income accounts prepared by the Department of Commerce, and they follow from the attempt to view the economy as a single entity and to account for all the income of this entity and for its disposition into consumption and saving. Obviously the statistical difficulties are great and, in many instances, it is necessary to rely on estimates and to cross-check them to ensure their compatibility. In estimating national income, the Department of Commerce includes some items not actually sold through markets — it *imputes* income from some nonmarket sources. For example, estimates for payments made in kind, in the form of meals or lodging, are included as well as cash payments. An important form of imputed income is the rent assumed to be earned by owner-occupied houses — that is, the amount home owners would receive by renting their houses to others or would pay for renting equivalent quarters. Thus the reported figure for personal saving is of necessity an estimate, but presumably reported changes in this figure are in the right direction.

An important characteristic of the Department of Commerce's definition of saving is that all expenditures on durable consumer goods are considered consumption expenditures. As we have seen, the figure for saving is the residual left after deducting all consumer outlays from personal income. For the purposes for which the national income accounts were developed, this definition is quite legitimate; its main purpose is to aid in the analysis of the components of aggregate expenditures on gross national product. But for other purposes it is relevant to realize that durable goods continue to yield income in the form of services and satisfactions for periods of varying length. For example, it is only a matter of degree that differentiates a house, whose imputed rent is included in income, from an automobile, which is considered an item of consumption in the year purchased.

It is also significant that personal saving need not entail the acquisition of any physical objects. A person can save by decreasing his debts. His net worth is increased whether he adds to his assets or decreases his liabilities. The same is true if all households are added together and thought of as the household sector of the economy. The household sector may reduce its debts owed to the business sector in a given year. To the extent that it does so, however, the assets owned by the business sector are reduced. Taking all sectors together—the economy as a single entity —saving must result in the production of nonconsumption goods. It is this identity that underlies the calculation of saving in the national income accounts. This situation will be analyzed further in Chapter 13, which deals with savings institutions.

Another source of data, the flow-of-funds accounts prepared by the Federal Reserve System, does include the net growth of durable goods in the saving of households. For example, as noted previously, personal saving derived as a residual was $37.6 billion in 1969. Households spent $89.8 billion on durable goods during the year, but the flow-of-funds accounts estimate that depreciation of such durable goods amounted to $82.7 billion. Thus households increased their investment in durable goods by a net amount of $7.1 billion.[5] Including this item and a few minor adjustments where the accounts differ, in the flow-of-funds accounts $63.9 billion is arrived at as the net saving of households in 1969.

The nature of income and saving of the other sectors—governments and businesses—is more appropriately discussed later in connection with the determination of the level of national income.

DIVISION OF PERSONAL INCOME

The preceding section, describing the division of national income, points out that the revenues derived from the sale of gross national product, after adjustment for capital consumption allowances, flow as incomes to governments (through direct and indirect taxes and contributions), to businesses (as retained profits), and to persons. It was mentioned at the beginning of the section that it is impossible to arrange the receipts of personal income in the same categories as those used in economics to explain the distribution of income, primarily because accounts are not kept in this manner. However, the national income accounts do divide personal incomes into certain broad categories that provide more information about the nature of the economy.

The categories of personal income can most easily be presented in tabular form, as is done in Table 9-1. The data for this table are those for 1969, in order to make comparison easy with the data that were used earlier.

It is clear that wages and salaries constitute the bulk of personal incomes, about 68 percent, and about 70 percent if other forms of labor income are included. Although the largest category of wages and salaries is that of commodity-producing industries, its preponderance may be less than would commonly be supposed. The distributive industries—retail and wholesale trade—provide a significant fraction, as do service industries and governments. All wages and salaries are included in the total, those of corporation presidents as well as those of other employees. The other categories listed in the table are probably self-evident.

[5] Board of Governors of the Federal Reserve System, *Federal Reserve Bulletin,* May, 1970, p. A-70.

Table 9-1
Distribution of Personal Income, 1969
(Billions of Dollars)

Total personal income	$747.2
Wage and salary disbursements	509.9
Commodity-producing industries	*197.7*
Manufacturing only	157.6
Distributive industries	*119.5*
Service industries	*88.1*
Government	*104.5*
Other labor income	26.2
Proprietors' income	66.3
Business and professional	*50.2*
Farm	*16.1*
Rental income	21.6
Dividends	24.6
Personal interest income	59.4
Transfer payments	65.5
Less: Personal contributions for social insurance	26.2

Source: *Federal Reserve Bulletin*, March, 1970, p. A-69.

SUMMARY

This chapter presents the concept of gross national product and its components. Gross national product is the total output of goods and services for a period of time, measured by the market prices at which it is sold. These sales revenues become the gross incomes of all those who have claims on the output. After the gross incomes, primarily those of businesses, are adjusted for capital consumption allowances, the amount left is the revenue available as net incomes (including that of government in the form of indirect business taxes). Governments claim some of the revenues through taxation and otherwise; businesses hold some as retained profits; and individuals obtain the rest as costs or passed-on profits of businesses. These incomes are available for disposition between consumption and saving; however, since governments and businesses do not consume in the same manner as do human beings, we followed the division of national income into personal income (after deductions for governmental and business incomes) and observed the division of personal income into consumption and saving. Personal saving may be thought of as a residual after all personal outlays, or as this residual plus the households' net additions to stocks of capital goods. With a picture in mind of what gross national product is and how its resulting monetary incomes are distributed, we may now turn, in the following chapter, to a study of the principles that determine the size of national income.

Economic Terms for Review

gross national product   net national product
national income   personal income
final sales   transfer payments
investment   disposable personal income
capital consumption   personal saving

Questions for Review

1. How important a part of total production are goods and services for consumption? Of this part, how important are services?
2. Why are net exports rather than total exports counted as part of GNP?
3. How much of total output is purchased by governments? How much of this part is purchased by state and local governments?
4. What two deductions keep GNP from becoming entirely net incomes? Explain why each is deducted.
5. National income does not all become incomes of persons. Why not?
6. Approximately how much of disposable personal income do households spend for consumption? What fraction is generally saved?

Questions for Analysis

1. Why is an increase in inventories counted as part of expenditures for investment? Why is only the increase counted rather than all goods going into inventory?.
2. Explain why the purchase of securities is not included in total saving in the national income accounts. Compare a purchase of 100 shares of corporate stock with (a) the purchase of a used car and (b) a swap of a tennis racket for a baseball glove.
3. If society is viewed as a whole, what is the only way it can save?
4. How do the national income accounts and the flow-of-funds accounts differ in what they include as saving?
5. Total purchases of current output, or expenditures on GNP, are categorized as those made by households for consumption, those made by businesses and households for investment, those made by governments, and those made in net foreign investment. How do households, businesses, and governments obtain the incomes from which these expenditures are made?

Problem for Solution

The two parts of this problem test your grasp of the concepts used in national income accounting. Each contains both relevant and irrelevant data.

1. Calculate national income and gross national product from the following (in billions):

Wages and salaries	$600
Corporate profits	60
Dividends	30
Unincorporated business income	40
Personal income taxes	70
Interest and rent	20
Increase in savings accounts	15
Government bonds purchased	15
Capital consumption allowances	35

2. Calculate personal saving from the national income derived in Part 1 and from the following (in billions):

Gross private domestic investment	$ 60
Government transfer payments	10
Personal income taxes	70
Personal consumption expenditures	600

Determination of National Income

Why do some nations enjoy gross national products that provide average incomes of several thousand dollars per person while other nations have gross national products that provide only bare subsistence for most of the people? Why does the volume of total output in the United States sometimes spurt ahead dramatically, sometimes gain only slightly, and sometimes actually decline? Why are there periods when virtually every-one who wants a job can find one and other periods when many people are out of work? How can a nation maximize its output and cause it to grow from year to year? These are the kinds of questions that are an-swered by the study of how the national income is determined.

THE CIRCUIT FLOW OF GOODS AND PAYMENTS

Gross national product may be thought of either as all the current out-put of goods and services or as the aggregate expenditure made to pur-chase this output at current prices. Both views amount to the same thing since the aggregate expenditure constitutes the dollar value of the real output. To approach the question of why GNP is as large as it is, then, one may ask why aggregate expenditure is as large as it is. Aggregate ex-penditure may be divided into its main categories and the same question asked of each. Thus we may examine expenditures for consumer pur-chases, business investment in producers' goods, and government pur-chases of goods and services. (Net foreign investment or net exports are a relatively small part of the total and are discussed in Chapter 21, which deals with international economics.)

An Income Model of the Economy

In analyzing the categories of expenditures, we shall take them up one at a time, proceeding from a simple model of the economy to more real-istic and inclusive models. That is, we shall first examine the economy as if it consisted solely of households and a few business firms that produce consumer goods and the requisite capital goods and later add the con-tributions to GNP created by government purchases.

A simple way to visualize the economy is to picture households as pro-viding labor, managerial, and ownership services to businesses, on the one hand, and as making purchases of consumer goods from businesses, on the other hand. Business firms obtain revenues by selling goods to households and, in turn, pay out these revenues as wages, salaries, and profits. Such an arrangement consists of a double *circuit flow,* as illus-trated in Figure 10-1. In the outer circuit is the flow of payments, with businesses paying households for services and households paying busi-

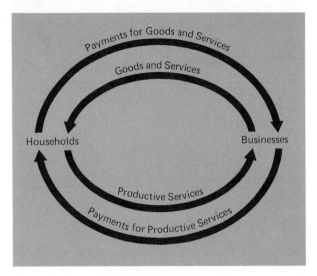

Figure 10-1. Circular flow.

nesses for their goods and services. In the inner circuit is the flow of goods and services, those bought by households from businesses and those bought by businesses from households.

We thus have a simple model of an economy, assuming that all the net national product consists of consumer goods. The business firms produce consumer goods and employ everyone involved in the process of production. They also have to replace capital goods when they wear out. The total cost of operation includes the costs of producing both types of goods; the costs incurred in replacing the capital equipment are reflected in the cost of the consumer goods through depreciation allowances, which are just sufficient to maintain the stock of capital. Suppose that the business firms pay $10,000 each month as wages, salaries, interest, rent, and profits. This sum is equal to the total costs and profits of producing the consumer goods sold to the households. The combined operating statements of the business firms would then look like this:

Sales revenues		$10,000
Additions to capital	+$1,000	
Depreciation	− 1,000	0
		$10,000
Wages	$7,000	
Salaries	1,000	
Rent	500	
Interest	500	9,000
Dividends		$ 1,000

In this example, GNP is $11,000 because total output includes $1,000 worth of capital goods kept for replacement by the companies rather than sold. But the business firms use up capital and thus reduce their gross incomes, which include retained output, by $1,000. If this $1,000 were not spent for replacing capital, dividends could be $2,000. The factors of production not needed to produce the capital goods could be used to produce another $1,000 worth of consumer goods. Net national product (NNP) is GNP less depreciation, or $10,000.

Since the businesses retain no profits but pay them out as earned, the $10,000 is also the sum of incomes received by households. So long as the households are willing to continue to purchase $10,000 worth of goods and services from businesses, individuals can continue to earn $10,000 each month by selling the services of labor, capital, and land. How much of this sum is received as wages, interest, rent, and profit depends upon the respective supplies and demands for the factors of production.

The net income of households is $10,000 per month. In this simple model, net national product equals national income because, since there is no government, there are no indirect business taxes. Depreciation just equals costs paid out in replacing capital, so it follows that net incomes are equal to the value—or the costs plus profits—of the output of consumer goods.

While we can see that this sort of an economy could be stable, with the net national product running at a monthly rate of $10,000, it is apparent that such stability is unlikely because it depends upon the willingness of households to continue to supply businesses with exactly this amount through purchases of goods and services.

Since the households are spending all their income, there is no personal saving. The only saving is being done by businesses, which devote an amount of gross income that is equal to depreciation allowances to maintaining the capital equipment. The businesses are not retaining any income in order to expand equipment or inventory. Similarly, households are not acquiring any permanent assets. As a realistic matter, it is likely that at least some of the households would like to postpone consumption of some of their income to the future. Or, they would like to acquire some income-producing wealth, as well as goods for current consumption. We need to introduce the process of net saving into the income model.

The Influence of Saving

Let us assume at first that some of the households decide to consume less than their total income. For illustration, we may assume that there are ten families, so the average household income is $1,000. Two of these families decide to save $200 each, so each expects to spend $800 on consumer goods in the following month. As a result, sales of consumer goods in that month fall by $400 to $9,600 and, as a further result, one of three things (or a combination of the three) must happen. First, if output remains at the same level, $400 of consumer goods are unsold and remain in the inventories of the businesses. Second, physical output may remain the same but prices are lowered just enough to sell all the goods for $9,600. Third, production may be cut by the amount of the reduction in sales.

In the first instance, if the unsold goods remain in the inventory of the businesses, the situation is the same as if the businesses rather than consumers had bought the output. Additions to inventory are a form of business investment, comparable to investment in fixed equipment. In this example, however, the investment is involuntary and unplanned; the households' decisions to save force businesses to make this *involuntary investment.* In the second instance, if businesses pay out the same costs but reduce prices, business income is $400 lower and dividends are reduced accordingly. Thus household income is reduced by the amount of the saving; if we assume for a moment that the same families are involved, they find that they are unable to save $400 as they planned. In the third instance, if production is cut, either the same costs are paid out (but for less output), reducing business and stockholder income as before, or people are paid proportionately less and their incomes are reduced. In either case, as in the second instance, consumption or saving must be reduced because of the decline in income.

These three possibilities illustrate an important point. In a period during which production is greater than consumption, investment necessarily takes place. The excess production is investment; in this example it takes the form of increase in inventory, but it could be output of plant or equipment. The production process involves the payment of incomes of equivalent value; if consumption is less than output, the difference has been saved. Thus, viewed as aggregates in the economy as a whole, saving and investment are the same thing. If output exceeds consumption, the excess output may be viewed as saving or as investment. There cannot be one without the other.

If people attempt to save without an equivalent amount of investment being made, incomes fall to eliminate the saving. The second and third possibilities in the example illustrate this situation. Incomes cannot continue to be paid out unless there is an equivalent output of consumer and capital goods. By the same token, as will be developed later, investment cannot take place without an equivalent amount of saving, since they are the same thing. If investment rises, incomes must rise accordingly to provide the saving. In the illustration just discussed, incomes fall because the associated investment is involuntary. There is no reason for businesses to continue to build up inventory, and they may be expected to reduce output and pay out less costs (incomes).

The situation would be different if the investment were planned simultaneously with the saving. Suppose that the two families who decide to save intend to lend $400 to businesses that wish to spend that amount in producing additional machines—machines that will go beyond replacement and add to the total stock of capital. In this case, sales of consumer goods fall by $400, but businesses continue to pay out $10,000 of incomes because they can utilize the labor and other resources released to produce the capital goods. Incomes remain at $10,000, but they are earned in producing $9,600 of consumer goods and $400 of investment goods. The consumer goods are purchased by households, and the capital goods are purchased by businesses with the savings of households.

Consumption and Saving

The model examined in the preceding sections illustrates a basic relationship that tends to be concealed in a complex money-using economy. For the economy as a whole, any output in excess of consumption is both saving and investment. In the case of the pioneer family, it is obvious that the only way the family can save is to produce output that is not consumed, and this is also the only way it can build up its stock of capital. In today's economy, however, it appears on the surface that some people save and others buy capital goods and that it must be a fantastic coincidence if the two quantities agree. The basic equality is such that they must agree. *Intended saving and investment* need not agree and probably never do, but *actual saving and investment* must. Intentions (*a priori* saving and investment) may not be realized as actual (*ex post*) saving and investment.

Recognizing how the money flow of saving is reconciled with the money flow of investment is the key to understanding many of the forces that determine the level of national income. In the model used so far, households make decisions about the disposition of their incomes between consumption and saving and businesses make decisions about purchasing investment goods. We recognize also that households may wish to purchase investment goods such as housing, rather than consumer goods, and save some of their incomes in this fashion. The next step in the analysis, then, is to inquire how households allocate income between consumption and saving.

Probably the basic factor in determining how much income is consumed and how much is saved is the amount of income itself. It is a matter of common observation that poor families save less than rich ones. There are, of course, exceptions; poor families may be very thrifty and rich families extravagant but, on the whole, far greater amounts of income are saved by those with large incomes. The reason is very simple. High-income families can afford more of everything; they can afford consumer goods low-income families cannot afford. In addition, they can divert income to the acquisition of income-producing assets, or savings. If a poor family saves a dollar, it may have to eliminate a necessity from its consumption, but if a rich family saves a dollar, it eliminates only an unimportant item from its consumption.

It follows as a general rule that high-income families save not only larger amounts of income but larger fractions of their income. If each of two families, one with an income of $20,000 and the other with an income of $5,000, saves 10 percent of its income, one saves $2,000 and the other $500. But the amounts saved are more typically something like $4,000 for the high-income family and $250 for the low-income family. Thus one family may save 20 percent of $20,000 and the other 5 percent of $5,000.

If saving is larger at higher incomes, it would seem to follow that if all incomes were to rise over a period of time, the proportion saved would also rise. We might expect the low-income family to save a larger fraction of its increased income and the high-income family to save an even larger fraction of its increased income. This does seem to be the situation in the short run. If the income of the $5,000 family rises to $6,000, the family is likely to save more than 5 percent of the extra $1,000 and thus also to raise the percentage of $6,000 saved to a figure somewhat above 5 percent. If this increase in income occurs in a relatively short period, a few months or years, the family tends to purchase more durable goods, better housing, new appliances, and also money-income-producing assets such as savings accounts or securities.

In the long run, the proportion of disposable personal income that becomes saving has been fairly stable. Two comments may be made about this apparent paradox. First, many expenditures that go up as income goes up are for durable goods and thus, in a sense, saving. Durable goods have an element of saving and are so recognized in the flow-of-funds accounts. Certain other types of expenditures also contain an element of saving. An outstanding example is education, in which the expenditure leads to the acquisition of knowledge and skills which, in turn, increase future income. Expenditures for durable goods, education, better health, and the like tend to rise more rapidly than income itself. It is true, therefore, that saving rises faster than income.

Secondly, as people see their incomes rising, they tend to live like people with similar incomes. They do not restrict their consumption to what it was previously but raise it to the level of other families with comparable incomes. They find it possible to enjoy a variety of consumer goods formerly out of reach. The proportion of income saved remains roughly the same although it rises in dollar amount. As just noted, however, some of the additional purchases contain elements of saving in that the families' holdings of material wealth increase.

The Consumption Function

In any event, since saving and consumption are the two components of income, the determining factor of their aggregate size is income. Other factors, some of which we noted in the discussion of the savings ratio in Chapter 9, influence the proportion of income saved in the short run. Nevertheless, saving is unlikely to rise when income falls or to fall when income rises. Saving is likely to rise, and at a faster rate, when income rises, and it is likely to fall at a faster rate than income when income falls.

Families with incomes of $1,000 per month in the model economy might normally save 10 percent of these incomes. This percentage is the *average propensity to save,* and the other 90 percent is the *average propensity to consume.* Aggregate consumption in the economy would then be $9,000, or 90 percent of income. Now suppose that for some reason aggregate incomes rise to $11,000 and that, in the aggregate, households save more than 10 percent of the $1,000 increase. If aggregate saving rises from $1,000 to $1,250, households are saving an additional $250, or 25 percent of the increase. Thus 25 percent is the *marginal propensity to save* (MPS). It follows that households increase their consumption expenditures by $750, or 75 percent of the increase in income. This percentage is the *marginal propensity to consume* (MPC). The average propensity to consume measures the tendency of the economy to consume 90 percent of income at present levels, and the marginal propensity to consume measures the tendency to consume 75 percent of additional income. When income shifts to $11,000, consumption shifts to $9,750 and a new average propensity to consume arises; it is now 88.6 percent, which is, of course, lower than before. Saving, on the other hand, is now $1,250, or 11.4 percent of income, and is higher than before. Since the two average propensities add up to 100 percent of consumption, as one rises the other must fall.

It is useful to visualize the relationship between consumption and income on a graph, as shown in Figure 10-2. The relationship is called the *consumption function* because it shows how consumption varies with, or depends on, income. In this graph a dotted line is drawn at an angle of 45°,

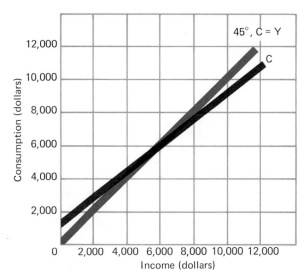

Figure 10-2. The consumption function.

equidistant between the two axes, to show what the consumption function would be if consumption were 100 percent of income. If this were the case, with each increase in income (shown on the horizontal scale) there would be an equal increase in consumption (shown on the vertical scale)—a one-to-one relationship. No matter what income is, consumption would be the same as income.

Consumption at normal levels of income is actually less than income. Consequently, a line drawn to connect several points showing the height of consumption at various income levels rises more slowly than the 45° line. If consumption tends to rise by 80 percent of a rise in income, the consumption function is $C = .8Y$ and the line rises by 80 percent of the increase in income. At very low levels of income, such as in 1933, households may spend more than current income on consumption. Hence Figure 10-2 shows consumption above income at very low income levels. At some point, consumption just equals income and, at higher income levels, consumption is some fraction of income.

The steepness of the rise of the consumption function, or how closely it follows the 45° line, depends upon the marginal propensity to consume. If the marginal propensity to consume is 90 percent, the functional line rises 90 percent as fast as income; if the marginal propensity is 50 percent, the line rises only half as fast as income. Note that the graph also shows what happens to saving as income rises. If the marginal propensity to consume is 90 percent, saving rises by 10 percent of an increase in income. At larger and larger incomes, saving becomes larger and larger. The amount of saving is shown by the distance between the consumption-function line and the 45° line because, at the 45° line, saving is zero (consumption is 100 percent). If the consumption line rises slowly, much saving appears between it and the 45° line. We could also show saving as a separate line or function. It would be drawn in the same manner but, of course, would lie much below the consumption line. The two added together would equal the 45° line.

For later reference, dollar figures have been supplied in Figure 10-2. It may be observed that consumption would equal income at about $5,000; below that income level, consumption would be larger than income. At income levels above $5,000, saving appears because consumption does not take all of income.[1]

The Importance of Investment

We have seen that aggregate expenditures in the model of the economy consist of expenditures on consumer goods and expenditures on investment goods. Using symbols and an equation, we may write this statement as $Y = C + I$. So far, we have an explanation of what determines the level of consumption (C). C is a function of income (Y), and the level of expenditure on consumption depends upon the marginal propensity to consume. At this point, it may appear as if we are involved in circular reasoning. C depends upon Y, and Y depends upon C. If investment expenditures (I) were determined by the level of Y, our reasoning would indeed be circular. Since there are other determinants of I, however, we shall discover that the level of these investment expenditures is very important and, along with MPC, determines the level of national income.

Investment Expenditures

What is the basic motive for business investment in plant, equipment, and other forms of capital goods? Essentially, such expenditures are made in order to reap the returns from these investments. Capital is productive. It increases output or it reduces costs. When a specific investment promises to increase profits in the future, business is tempted to make the investment.

Investments, especially in long-lived assets, must be made on the basis of estimates concerning the future.[2] The businessman must estimate the increase in sales, which involves estimating prices that will prevail in the future. He must also estimate or forecast operating costs in order to estimate future profits. In order to make these estimates, he must make judgments about other factors, such as population, prosperity, tastes, techniques, competition, and tax rates. He may make these estimates by hunch or by scientific methods of market research and other techniques of forecasting; he may be optimistic or pessimistic in his approach; he may turn

---

[1] What we have been saying may be stated algebraically. The consumption function is taken to be a straight line, or to have a linear relationship with income. The formula to describe such a relationship is $C = a + bY$. The quantity a is the quantity that consumption would equal if income (Y) were zero, about $1,000 in Figure 10-2; this is where the consumption function starts. The quantity b is the marginal propensity to consume, or the percentage of an increase in Y that is consumed. For example, if $a = \$1,000$ and $b = .8$, then when $Y = \$10,000$, C (the consumption function) would be $9,000. $C = \$1,000 + .8(\$10,000) = \$9,000$. If Y were $11,000, however, the equation would be $C = \$1,000 + .8(\$11,000) = \$9,880$ and, of course, S (saving) equals the remaining $1,120. C would equal Y when Y is $5,000. ($C = \$1,000 + .8[\$5,000] = \$5,000$.) Note that this form of equation provides for larger fractions of income to be saved when income is high even though MPC is held constant.

[2] In this context, since we are examining the determinants of output, the term investment refers to purchase of capital goods; it does not refer to purchase of securities or other paper claims. When a person invests in securities, he holds the debts of other economic units and there is no net increase in wealth. If the debtor uses the funds to purchase newly produced assets, however, there is a net increase in total wealth.

out to be accurate or inaccurate. But he must make forecasts in order to decide whether specific investment expenditures should be made.

Since the estimates involve uncertainty, they also involve risk. Some projects promise modest rates of return on the investment but rather high degrees of certainty that the rates will actually occur. Other projects promise much higher rates of profit if things turn out well but involve a high degree of uncertainty. These factors are taken into account even though they are evaluated differently by different businesses and under varying circumstances, and potential investments are ranked in some order of desirability. When estimates of future profitability are made, how does the businessman decide whether the prospective profit rates are high enough to justify the investments? Once the pros and cons have been determined and the prospective profits, adjusted for risk, have been estimated, the test of whether the profits are sufficiently attractive is the cost of the funds to be invested.

A business would not be expected to use funds that it could lend to others at 6 percent, or to borrow funds at 6 percent, in order to make investments that, over their lives, promised to yield 6 percent or only slightly more. If the interest cost is 6 percent but potential investments promise 10 or 15 percent rates of profit, however, the investments are much more likely to be made. They are even more likely to be made if the applicable interest rate is 4 percent but are somewhat less attractive if the rate is 8 percent.

At any moment in time, there are numerous investment projects that might be undertaken. Some are clearly desirable, others are less so, still others are just marginal at the current cost of funds, and others are not worth undertaking. The volume of investment spending, then, can be related to the cost of funds, or the level of interest rates. The interest rate provides a cut-off point below which projects will not be undertaken because their prospective profits are insufficient. At lower interest rates some of these projects would become feasible, and at higher rates some would become submarginal.

The relationship can be illustrated graphically by comparing the volume of investment expenditure with the interest rate, as in Figure 10-3. The _marginal efficiency of capital_ describes the situation with respect to the anticipated profitability of capital projects.[3] If expectations are great, the curve lies far to the right and shows (on the horizontal axis) a large volume of investment at a given interest rate (r, on the vertical axis). In other words, the curve for the marginal efficiency of capital is essentially a demand curve because it shows the amount of capital investment demanded at various interest rates. The vertical axis also measures the anticipated profitability of different investment projects. The curve slopes downward to the right, like other demand curves, because at any one time there are many projects to be ranked in order of their potential profitability. The more projects included, the lower the profit return for the marginal projects. If only a very few projects could be undertaken, they would presumably be the ones with the highest prospective returns.

[3] This term and several others used in this chapter were introduced by J. M. Keynes, especially in his _General Theory of Employment, Interest, and Money,_ Harcourt, Brace and Company, Inc., New York, 1936. This book was a pioneer work in the analysis of national income.

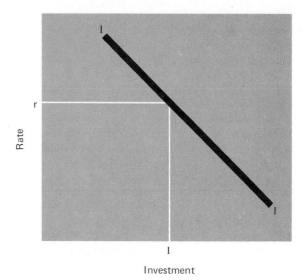

Figure 10-3. Marginal efficiency of capital.

On the graph in Figure 10-3, an assumed rate of interest, *r*, is shown, and lines connect *r* with the amount of investment, *I*, that would take place. It must be remembered that, like other demand curves, this one may shift. For reasons affecting either the real future profitability of investments or the psychology of businessmen, the demand may increase (shift to the right) or decrease (shift to the left) at a given interest rate. When business prospects appear bright, the investment demand tends to be greater; when pessimism is prevalent, the demand is less.

The Effects of Investment

Since the level of investment expenditure depends so crucially on the marginal efficiency of capital and the interest rate, it is not determined automatically, as consumption is, by the current level of GNP. Rather, investment expenditures may change quite independently and thus have a strong influence on the level of income itself. Business conditions may be very good, but businessmen may come to realize that, during a period of prosperity, capacity in their industries has been built up to the point where further additions appear unwise. Business conditions may be rather poor, but businessmen may see signs of recovery and decide that now is the time to modernize and expand plant and equipment.

Consumption expenditures and investment expenditures may thus be distinguished in that the former are largely *induced* by the level of income itself while the latter are *autonomous* and subject to change. The distinction is not absolute; current conditions do have some influence on investment expenditures, and consumers may change the savings ratio because of their anticipations. But the distinction is generally valid, and it is helpful in analyzing the level of GNP.

We may illustrate the importance of the autonomous nature of investment expenditures through further reference to the model of the economy. As we have already noted, as long as the ten families are willing to continue to spend $10,000 per month for consumer goods, their incomes continue at that level. However, if some of the families wish to save some of their income, aggregate expenditures decline; therefore, incomes decline unless another form of aggregate expenditure substitutes for the foregone consumption. If investment expenditures replace the foregone consumption (saving), aggregate demand remains the same and $10,000 of incomes continue to be earned.

To change the illustration a bit, assume that the businesses decide independently to increase their expenditures on investment goods by $400 and that there is no associated decision on the part of households to save this amount. Then, as soon as the businesses start to pay out the additional $400 per month, someone starts receiving this sum as income. Incomes are no longer running at the rate of $10,000 per month but are $10,400 per month. According to the marginal propensity to consume, these increased incomes should lead to increased consumption, but by something less than $400 per month. If the MPC is .8, consumption expenditures should rise by a monthly rate of $320, and saving automatically increases by $80, to $1,080 (.2 × $400).

But the sellers of the extra $320 of consumer goods – whether through higher prices or increased output – now receive this additional gross income and, to the extent that they have additional costs, they share it with other factors of production. Incomes, then, are increased by $320, and this increase leads to another increase in consumption. This increase should be 80 percent of the increased income, or $256, while saving rises by the other 20 percent, or $64. Total consumer expenditures in the economy are now running at the monthly rate of $10,000 + $320 + $256, or $10,576. Households are earning larger incomes, $400 per month by producing additional capital goods for businesses and the remainder by producing consumer goods.

There is a constant instability, or disequilibrium, in the model as long as businesses are paying out costs of $400 per month for investment and this sum is larger than the amount of saving households want to make at their present level of income. Every time income rises, consumption rises and adds to income, which leads to another rise in consumption, and so on. The rise in income is caused by the rise in consumption, and consumption rises because the households are unwilling to save all their increased incomes. They are willing to save only 20 percent of increased incomes. Consequently, this process must continue until the successive increments of 20 percent add up to $400. At that point, the additional incomes being created by the investment expenditures are being offset by voluntary saving rather than adding further to consumption.

The Multiplier

This expansion of income through successive increments of consumption may be summarized in a table. Table 10-1 is designed to illustrate the expansion in a step-by-step manner. If we use the original data for the model, we have a GNP of $11,000, consisting of $10,000 of consumption goods and $1,000 of investment goods for replacement and providing a national income after capital consumption of $10,000. Gross investment and gross saving are each $1,000; there is no net investment or net saving because capital consumption is also $1,000 and all net output is consumer goods.

Table 10-1
The Multiplier

Period	C	I	Y	S
1	$10,000.00	$1,000.00	$11,000.00	$1,000.00
2	10,000.00	1,400.00	11,400.00	1,000.00
3	10,320.00	1,400.00	11,720.00	1,080.00
4	10,576.00	1,400.00	11,976.00	1,144.00
5	10,780.80	1,400.00	12,180.80	1,195.20
...	....	....	....	....
n	11,600.00	1,400.00	13,000.00	1,400.00

In order to tabulate the steps in the process, it is necessary to use arbitrary periods of time, rather than a smooth progression. Thus, in Period 1 we have the original situation. In Period 2 investment expenditures are increased to $1,400. This increase makes GNP $11,400, but households have not had time to dispose of the additional income between consumption and saving. In Period 3 households increase consumer expenditures by $320 and thus increase saving by $80. The increase in consumer expenditures raises GNP to $11,720. In Period 4 households use this increased income to increase consumption by $256 and saving by $64. Thus GNP is also increased by $256. And so on, until the process ends.

But where does the process end? Given two pieces of information, we can find the answer. First, the increase in I is $400, and second, the MPC is .8. It follows from this information that Y will first rise by $400, that C will rise by .8, or four-fifths, of this amount ($320), that Y will then rise by $320, that C will rise by four-fifths of this amount, and so on. Consequently, there must be an infinite series of increases that ends when C has grown to four times $400. At that point, the additional C is $1,600 and, with the increased I, makes Y $2,000 larger.

We can explain this situation simply. As long as households are unwilling to save all their additional income, they must increase C and thus Y. The basic cause of the increased income is the additional I. If households would immediately increase S by an equivalent $400, there would be no increase in C and the only increase in Y would be the $400 of I. But the consumption function ($1,000 + .8Y$) tells us that households will save only one-fifth of the increased Y. Thus households keep on increasing GNP by additional consumption expenditures until Y has increased enough to allow additional saving of $400. Since the additional saving is one-fifth of the increase in Y, the additional Y must grow by $2,000. At that point, according to the consumption function, C will be four-fifths as much ($1,600) and S will be one-fifth ($400).

The MPC is therefore valuable in helping to determine how much Y will change when there is a change in I. Y is increased not only by the additional expenditure on I but also by the *induced expenditures* on C. It follows that the higher the MPC, the greater the increase in GNP. If MPC were .9, each increment of income would lead to additional C of nine-tenths as much. Y would have to rise by ten times the additional I before it would be large enough to provide an equivalent amount of S, S in this case being one-tenth. If MPC were only .5, an increase in income of twice as much would suffice because, at that point, half of it would be saved and would equal the increase in I.

This relationship is called the *multiplier effect* because a change in I is multiplied in its effect on Y. The size of the multiplier obviously depends upon the size of the fraction that represents MPC. The larger the MPC, the smaller the MPS, and the multiplier is the reciprocal of the MPS. When MPS is one-half, the multiplier is two; when it is three-fourths (.75), the multiplier is four, and so on. The multiplier may be written as $\frac{1}{MPS}$.

We have now surveyed the skeleton of the theory of the determination of national income. In terms of the equation $Y = C + I$, we may say that the level of I, working through the multiplier effects on C, determines the level of Y. Having stated the principle rather flatly, we should add some qualifications and elaborations of this simple proposition.

First, a distinction should be drawn between a "one-shot" increase in I and a more permanent increase. In the example just discussed, the increase in I was not a single investment expenditure of $400; it was an increase in the level of investment expenditures from $1,000 to $1,400 per month. Had there been a single expenditure of $400, covering perhaps a single month, income would have risen by this amount and the process of increasing consumption through the multiplier effect would have started. But in the subsequent month, income would have fallen back to the original level and the multiplier increases in consumption would not have been sustained.

Because the model used in this explanation is purposely simplified, several qualifications should be noted. In order to bring out relationships more clearly, the multiplier used in the example is probably unrealistically high. Recent experience in the United States suggests that the multiplier tends to be between two and three. The extent to which an autonomous increase in aggregate expenditure may lead to further induced expenditures for consumption depends upon the multiplier in effect at the time. In turn, the multiplier may vary with the distribution of income between low-income and high-income families, the tax structure and how it affects those who receive the additional income, and similar factors. In other words, MPC may change for autonomous reasons, although it was necessary to hold it constant in the example in order to bring out the principle.

Another important qualification is that the effects of government revenue and spending have been ignored. While these effects are obviously important in changing the quantities involved, they do not change the basic principle.

In addition, the example should be interpreted in terms of the economist's meaning of the word *equilibrium*. It is impossible to perform laboratory experiments in economics. We cannot hold all variables but one constant and measure the changes that ensue. However, we can see in the example that when investment expenditures rise by $400, there is disequilibrium. Planned investment exceeds planned saving at the existing level of income; consequently, we expect consumption to keep rising until income has reached a level where voluntary saving will offset the investment. Given the essentials of the problem, we can see what this new *equilibrium income* must be. But this particular equilibrium may never actually be reached. It is a situation toward which the economy tends to move but, before it reaches equilibrium, there are likely to be further changes that establish a new equilibrium goal. The economy is always in a state of flux, moving toward equilibrium situations but always being nudged toward new equilibrium situations as they are created.

These qualifications in no way detract from the usefulness of the principle involved. While economics cannot yet be said to have attained the precision of many natural sciences, an understanding of the basic forces at work in the economy is still very useful. Autonomous increases in expenditures are expansionary—and vice versa—and the multiplier principle is at work. Different results should be expected when the original impetus comes from business expenditure for plant and equipment, from increased consumer expenditures stemming from a cut in personal income taxes, from an increase in transfer payments, or from an increase in government expenditures. But these differences can be taken into account and allowed for in considering the wisdom of various measures. A selection of measures is available for increasing aggregate expenditures in time of unemployment or for decreasing them in time of inflation. The multiplier effect should obviously be considered in all such instances.

Production and Prices

In the model we have just analyzed, no distinction was made between a situation in which the additional expenditures lead to additional output and one in which they lead mainly to higher prices. Whether one or the other happens depends largely on whether there are unemployed resources in the economy. When the labor force is already fully employed and there is little excess capacity in industry, producers of capital goods respond to increased orders by trying to add employees and increase capacity. They can get more labor and buy more equipment only by bidding these from other employers. When they raise wages in order to attract labor, they must pay *all* their employees the new rates. They must bid higher prices for raw materials and other resources, which could otherwise be used by producers of consumer goods. Thus these other producers' costs are also increased as they raise wages in order to hold workers and raise prices to try to recover the added costs.

On the other hand, if there is unemployment of labor and capital, there is no need to raise prices and wages. The new orders can be filled by hiring labor otherwise unemployed. At the same time, competition from other employers who have idle capacity they want to use makes it difficult for any of the employers to raise prices. Under these circumstances the additional expenditures, whether for capital goods or consumer goods, result mainly in increased output. The rise in national income is a rise in real incomes as well as in money incomes.

These two situations are illustrated by developments during the long period of expansion of business that began in early 1961. Between 1961 and 1969, aggregate expenditures rose substantially as a result of rising business investment (and government expenditures), which led to induced expenditures for consumption. A growing labor force, combined with an unemployment percentage of some 6 percent in 1960, provided the

Table 10-2

Dollar and Real Increases in GNP, 1962–1969

(Billions of Dollars)

	Increase in Dollar GNP	Increase in Real GNP	Percentage of Real to Dollar
1962	$40.2	$32.7	81.4
1963	30.2	21.0	69.2
1964	41.9	30.1	72.1
1965	52.5	36.7	69.9
1966	62.7	39.3	62.6
1967	41.1	16.0	38.9
1968	80.9	33.6	40.3
1969	66.4	19.9	29.9

Source: *Federal Reserve Bulletins.*

additional labor resource needed for this expansion. Unemployment did not fall to 4 percent, which is considered close to the practical minimum, until 1966. While there were some increases in general prices throughout the period, increases began to accumulate after several years of rising employment. Table 10-2 shows the annual increments to gross national product in actual or current prices and the real increases when price increases are taken out of aggregate expenditures. It may be observed that price increases accounted for less than 20 percent of the increase in dollar GNP in 1962, with the real increase accounting for 81.4 percent. In each of the next three years, the real increase amounted to approximately 70 percent of the dollar increase. But in 1966, when there was also a large increase in investment expenditures, production was pressing more strongly against available resources and pushing up prices. In that year, real output constituted less than two-thirds of the increase in GNP, and in subsequent years it became much less.

These figures reflect the fact that when investment (or government) expenditures rise, GNP tends to rise even more because of the resulting increases in incomes and consumption expenditures. When these aggregate expenditures exceed the physical capacity of the economy to produce, they result in rising prices as well as in rising output.

GOVERNMENT EXPENDITURES AND REVENUES

We may now introduce into the model of the economy the flow of income to government and the flow of expenditures from government. All three sectors of the domestic economy — households, businesses, and governments — may add to aggregate demand by increasing expenditures or reduce aggregate demand by spending less.

Government expenditures (G) may be added to the equation for GNP by writing it as $Y = C + I + G$. Government purchases of goods and services add to GNP in the same manner as any other expenditures for current output, and the expenditures become incomes in the same fashion. Whether United States Steel Corporation purchases a ship to carry iron ore or the United States Navy purchases a destroyer, the purchase price represents part of GNP. Government expenditures are logically considered autonomous expenditures, akin to investment expenditures. That is, they do not follow automatically, nor are they a function of, the current level of income but may change in response to governmental decisions. Indeed, government expenditures tend to move quite independently of the current level of GNP for the simple reason that they may be used to affect the direction of movements in GNP. When GNP is sluggish, government may increase its expenditures or, as in 1968 and 1969, Congress may adopt economy measures in order to reduce the inflationary effects of government expenditures.

The influence of government is not confined to the amount of its own expenditures. Government affects the expenditures of the household and business sectors by taking larger or smaller amounts of income from these sectors. A reduction in personal income taxes, for example, is the equivalent of an increase in disposable personal incomes and normally leads to additional consumer expenditures. A reduction in corporate income tax rates tends to increase the profitability of investment projects and thus to lead to increased investment expenditures at given levels of interest rates. These two types of tax reduction probably would not have identical effects on GNP, nor would an equivalent increase in government expenditures.

The latter difference may be illustrated by comparing an increase of $10 billion in government expenditures with a reduction of $10 billion in personal income taxes. The government expenditure should increase incomes by roughly $10 billion and be followed by increases in consumer expenditures. In about a year, assuming a multiplier of two, GNP should be about $20 billion higher, the increase consisting of about $10 billion of G and $10 billion of C. If personal taxes are reduced by $10 billion, however, there is no immediate purchase of current output. Consumption should rise, but by something less than the $10 billion of disposable income since saving would also rise. Since disposable personal income would be increased directly, however, a high fraction of the increase would probably be devoted to consumption. The initial impact on GNP, then, might be an increase in C of some $9 billion. This initial impact might be doubled by the multiplier, as in the first case, but would total $18 billion.

In the other case, corporate income tax rates might be reduced. Suppose that the result is to raise profit expectations by the equivalent of one percentage point; that is, all projects are potentially this much more profitable than before. Some additional projects would be undertaken; how many would depend upon the slope of the curve of marginal efficiency of capital. It is even possible that the increased I would lead to sufficiently higher incomes so that the taxes on these incomes would compensate for the original reduction in tax rates.

SUMMARY

The material in this chapter provides a broad outline of the generally accepted modern theory of determination of the national income. The concepts discussed here provide a basis for further development of public and private policies designed to stabilize and promote the growth of the economy. The basic principles described here help one understand the underlying trends taking place in the economy as a whole, whether it be expanding or contracting.

Admittedly, there are disagreements in advanced economic thought concerning the relative importance of some of the variables described in this chapter. Some economists, for example, are convinced that changes in the stock of money are more important in determining the level of aggregate demand than are the autonomous changes in investment and government expenditures emphasized in this chapter. Nevertheless, the general principles explained in this chapter enjoy wide acceptance and, whether or not future research alters the emphasis placed on different factors, provide a foundation for such advances in knowledge.

To summarize, total expenditures on current output—gross national product—are the purchases of final buyers. Goods and services are purchased for consumption, investment, and government purposes. Consumption expenditures depend largely on the existing level of income; as a rule, they cannot initiate changes in the level of income. Investment expenditures, however, depend mainly on the current estimates of future profit possibilities and on the cost of raising funds—the interest rate. Thus investment expenditures are apt to change and, when they do, they lead to further changes in the level of income. The initial effects are magnified by the multiplier effect, which stems from the additional expenditures on consumption that follow an increase in income.

Government expenditures may also initiate changes in gross national product. They are similar to investment expenditures in that they need not depend on the current level of income. They may make an inflationary situation worse if they are large, or they may be manipulated to adjust aggregate expenditures to an equilibrium level. Government can also affect the expenditures of the household and business sectors through its powers of taxing and borrowing. It may encourage expenditures by these sectors by leaving them with more disposable income, or it may reduce this income by taking more of it away.

APPENDIX

Many of the principles and relationships described in this chapter can be stated with considerably greater precision algebraically. The use of equations makes possible concise statements that are difficult to frame in words. This appendix serves both to review the foregoing textual material and to carry somewhat further the analysis of the determinants of national income.

At the beginning of the chapter, we described the economy without government as $Y = C + I$. The consumption function was presented as $C = a + bY$. We may thus rewrite the first equation as $Y = a + bY + I$. If we take a to be 100, b (the marginal propensity to consume) to be .75, and I to be 200, we have

$$Y = 100 + .75Y + 200$$
$$Y - .75Y = 300$$
$$Y = 1,200$$

since $I = 200$ and $C = 1,000$, or $100 + .75$ (1,200).

This equation illustrates how investment expenditures of 200 lead to a GNP of 1,200, with the given consumption function. A different consumption function would lead to a different Y. (Note: What is Y when $I = 0$?)

We may introduce government in two steps: first, through taxes and secondly, through expenditures. Since taxes reduce income available for consumption, we rewrite the equation for the consumption function to relate consumption to disposable income, as follows: $C = a + bY_d$, and $Y_d = Y - T$. If we assume that $T = 60$, the original equation becomes

$$Y = 100 + .75(Y - T) + 200$$
$$Y = 100 + .75Y - 45 + 200$$
$$Y = 1,020$$

It follows that C is now 820, which we can derive by subtracting I from Y or through the consumption function, $C = 100 + .75(1,020 - 60)$. The introduction of T of 60 reduces C from 1,000 to 820, or by 180. This is the multiplier effect; 180 is three times 60 because the MPC is three-fourths.

Adding government purchases to the equation, we have $Y = C + I + G$, or $Y = a + b(Y - T) + I + G$. Substituting the same values as previously and 70 for G, we obtain

$$Y = 100 + .75Y - 45 + 200 + 70$$
$$.25Y = 325$$
$$Y = 1,300$$

We see that Y is 280 larger than before and that this increase is four times the new G. Thus the multiplier effect is to add to the original 70 three times as much $(70 + 210 = 280)$. Consumption, consequently, is 210 higher, and the consumption function shows that it is $100 + .75(1,300 - 60) = 1,030$. (Note: For practice see what Y and C are when $G = 60$.)

In this model T has been taken to be a constant and to affect C as a constant. More realistically, T should be taken as varying with income. This refinement is not difficult, as we may define tax revenues as some constant base (T) plus a percentage (t) of Y. Taxes may be defined as $T + tY$, or $20 + .2Y$. The consumption function would then be written as $C = a - bT + b(1 - tY)$ and, substituting, we would have

$$Y = 100 - .75(20) + .75(.8Y) + 200 + 70$$
$$Y = 100 - 15 + .6Y + 200 + 70$$
$$.4Y = 355$$
$$Y = 887.5$$

The foregoing model may be pictured graphically, as in Figure 10-4. This graph shows the consumption function and, in addition,

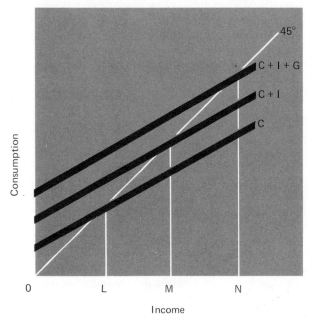

Figure 10-4. The consumption function with investment and government added.

amounts of investment and government expenditures. The consumption function shows the amount of C taking place at various levels of Y. The addition of a given amount of I produces the C + I line. The multiplier effect is illustrated by the movement of Y from L to M, a larger amount than the amount of I. Similarly, the addition of a given amount of G, providing the C + I + G line, moves Y out to N. The points L, M, and N are found by reading off the height of the three curves respectively since, for example, Y = C + I + G. This height can be shown on the vertical axis, or it is located equally well by the 45° line. (Of course, this implies that the scales on both axes are equal; $1 million is the same distance on the vertical scale as on the horizontal.)

Economic Terms for Review

circuit flow   expenditures
involuntary investment   induced
intended saving and investment   autonomous
marginal propensity to consume   multiplier
consumption function   equilibrium income
marginal efficiency of capital

Questions for Review

1. Describe the circuit flow of goods and services.
2. What is the effect of saving, taken by itself, on GNP?
3. Why may the public's plans or intentions to save not be carried out?

4. How would your family divide a 20 percent increase in income between consumption and saving? Would the answer differ if the increase were only for a single year rather than a permanent one?
5. What determines the level of investment expenditures?
6. If investment expenditures were to rise from $70 billion to $80 billion, what would be the effect on GNP?
7. How can GNP rise when there is already full employment?

Questions for Analysis

1. Suppose that everyone decides to build up his savings to twice the present level. Would this stimulate or depress GNP?
2. How can expenditure for education be called a form of saving?
3. Why is the marginal propensity to consume less than one?
4. Suppose the government tries to improve a situation of high unemployment by reducing all taxes by 20 percent. Would the action be more effective if the MPC were .5 or .75?
5. Business investment was higher in 1968 than in 1967 and interest rates were also higher. Illustrate this situation by drawing a marginal-efficiency-of-capital curve for each year.
6. Suppose business investment expenditures rise by $1 billion and the MPC is .66, or two-thirds. What is the equilibrium change in GNP? In consumption? In saving?
7. Judging from the data in Table 10-2, why was the government bringing about high interest rates in 1969?

Case for Decision [4]

In the spring of 1969 several congressmen were meeting informally at lunch to discuss the inflationary situation and what legislation might be desirable. Congressman Adams, from a rural district in the Midwest, noted that actions by the Federal Reserve System had brought interest rates to the highest levels in one hundred years. "For the last several months, prices have been going up at an annual rate of 8 or 10 percent, and I think the high interest rates have been a main cause. Interest is a cost of doing business, and businessmen have to recoup these high rates in the prices they charge," he argued. He suggested that Congress should pass a resolution in favor of lower interest rates.

Congressman Brown, from a middle-income district in New York City, believed that personal income taxes should be reduced. "Prices of food and clothing and all sorts of necessities have been rising steadily. People in my district are finding it harder and harder to make ends meet. If they didn't have to pay such high income-tax rates, they would have more left over to live on. I'm going to introduce a bill to cut personal tax rates 15 percent."

Congressman Chance, from an industrial city in the Midwest, said, "I could make myself unpopular by saying this, but I think tax rates should be raised. People have too much money to spend; that's why prices are being bid up. There aren't any real scarcities of

[4] This case anticipates in some respects material to be presented in subsequent chapters. However, enough basic principles are presented in Chapter 10 to permit some sound conclusions to be drawn.

meat, bread, or other things to make them expensive. Government expenditures are high because of Vietnam, and these expenditures are creating lots of jobs. This money has to be drawn back into the Treasury or it is spent for goods that can't be increased fast enough."

Congressman Adams seemed to agree partly with Congressman Chance, but they differed over which taxes should be raised. Adams argued that the corporate income tax should go up, but Chance claimed that this would only add to business expenses and lead to still higher prices; he favored raising personal taxes. Brown insisted that personal taxes were already too high and were leading workers to demand higher wages.

On the basis of how each proposal would probably affect gross national product, with which Congressman do you tend to agree?

Part 4
Financing
the Economy

11
The Monetary System

The point that ours is a monetary economy needs no great emphasis. Throughout the preceding chapters it has been taken for granted that the economy relies on the use of money. Prices, costs, wages, profits, and valuations of gross national product are expressed in terms of dollars and cents. We have referred to investment, saving, consumption, government spending, and other quantities, all measured in monetary terms. Having taken the existence and use of money for granted up to this point, it is now appropriate to examine more closely the operation of the monetary system. We need to ask such questions as: What is money? Where does it come from? How much is there? How much should there be? Who controls its quantity? Answers to these and related questions throw much light on the way the modern economy operates.

FUNCTIONS OF MONEY

As we have seen, the total flow of finished goods and services — gross national product — comes into the hands of final buyers through the market system. Incomes are earned through the sale of the services of labor and property used in the process of production, and these incomes are used to purchase the output of consumer goods and producers' goods. What makes possible the countless transactions by which this process takes place is money. Without money it would be necessary for people to barter, or "swap," one thing for another. A little reflection shows how difficult barter would be in anything but a very simple and primitive society.

Money as a Medium of Exchange

Two aborigines — or, for that matter, several — might have no difficulty exchanging their output with one another. The fisherman could trade fish for the chickens of the farmer, for the skins of the hunter, for the iron pots of the craftsman, and for the services of the medicine man. But the specialization and division of labor of the modern economy could hardly exist on a basis of barter. How could the mechanic, physician, lawyer, or policeman trade his specialized services for the products of all the other people whose goods and services he wants? This reliance on the use of money is not peculiar to an economy relying heavily on free markets. A communistic economy, even though it determines by governmental edict what will be produced, must also see that incomes are received in the form of money, which is then exchanged for goods.

The difficulty with barter is often called "the double coincidence of wants." This phrase refers to the fact that in order for two people to trade, each must want what the other has. If I have fish but want rabbits and you have rabbits but want eggs, we cannot trade, nor can we trade if you want fish but do not have rabbits. In a society using money, I can sell my fish to anyone who will buy and then buy rabbits from anyone who will sell. I am willing to accept the money because I know I can spend it for anything I want, at any time, from anyone, subject of course to prevailing prices. The person who sells me rabbits accepts my money for the same reasons.

Thus money is a *medium of exchange*. It makes it possible to split transactions into two parts, which are easier to carry out than barter would be. Selling fish and buying rabbits are easier than finding someone who will swap his rabbits for my fish. And another difficulty is also eliminated. It might be that a cow is worth five goats, but it is impossible to trade a fifth of a cow for a single goat. Money representing the price of a cow, however, can be spent on numerous things. One way to define money is simply to call anything money that serves as our medium of exchange. As we will see in more detail shortly, the principal medium of exchange in the United States today is checking accounts or demand deposits at commercial banks, and the second most important medium is our coins and paper money.

Money as a Unit of Account

As soon as one speaks of money, one implies prices. If $4,000 is required to purchase an automobile, money not only serves as the medium of exchange whereby ownership of the automobile changes hands but also measures the value of the automobile. In this transaction the automobile is "worth" $4,000. In the United States the dollar is the *unit of account* by means of which the values of all goods and services can be compared. People generally are not aware that there is an *abstract unit* called a dollar as well as physical things called dollars. The medium of exchange is a physical thing—a dollar bill or coins—or at least a physical bank record that can be transferred by means of a bank check drawn by a depositor. But the unit of account is just that—an abstract unit. There are many other units of measurement of things other than value. An inch is an abstract concept of a certain length; a pint is an abstract concept of a certain volume; a pound is an abstract concept of a certain weight.

We tend to forget that these units of measurement are abstract because we see them in physical forms. We can see what an inch is on a yardstick; we can see a pint bottle; we can see a pound of butter. But what we really see is an inch of wood, a bottle that holds a pint of liquid, and a block of butter that weighs a pound. These units did evolve historically from physical things that became accepted as standards. The foot, for example, was originally the length of the king's foot, but it became standardized as a certain length quite independent of any king's foot.

The monetary unit for measuring values evolved similarly. Money seems to have evolved naturally as generally acceptable commodities began to be used as money. That is, in a fishing society where everyone had or could easily get fishhooks, anyone who wanted to trade rabbits for eggs could eliminate the problem of double coincidence by trading his rabbits for fishhooks and then trading his fishhooks for eggs. Anyone who wanted to trade eggs for something else would reason similarly:

If he accepted fishhooks, he could more easily find someone who would accept them for what he wanted. For centuries the most generally acceptable commodities used in this way were gold and silver.

So the word money has come to have two meanings. On the one hand, we use the word to describe what we use as a medium of exchange and, on the other, we use it to describe the abstract unit by which we measure values. The difference is illustrated by the kind of barter that usually takes place in modern society, where money exists. Suppose you have a tennis racket but would rather have a first baseman's mitt. If you can arrange a swap, it is because both you and the other party consider the two items to have about equal value—say $15. You are thus using the dollar to measure the values of the racket and the mitt, but you do not need a medium of exchange. In fact, both of you may be "broke"! Or, if you agree that the racket is worth $20 and the mitt $15, you can trade the racket for the mitt plus $5, and the dollar will serve both as a unit of measurement and as a medium of exchange.

Because of this dual use of the word money, it is possible to define it more meaningfully. Money always has the same price in terms of the unit of account. This merely means that a dollar is always a dollar, but it has important implications. If you have a dollar bill or a dollar in a bank account, that dollar will be a dollar tomorrow, next week, or next year—whether you have it or someone else. Whether it will buy as much, more, or less next year is another question. The price of the dollar will remain a dollar, but the prices of other things may vary so that it will take more or less than a dollar to buy the same amount.

You may think of two apparent exceptions to this identity. We all know that rare coins and pieces of currency may be worth more than their "face" value. In such instances, however, they are usually no longer used as money. A person owning a gold piece or a rare half-dollar would be foolish to spend it. If he prefers not to keep it, he should *sell* it, and this means he would be exchanging it *for money*. Money, as a unit of account, would tell us that the $20 gold piece is worth $50, and it would take fifty of the units of the medium of exchange to buy it.

Another apparent exception relates to savings accounts. Instead of a checking account, you might have a savings account of $100 and know that, at the end of the year, the bank will credit $4 of interest to your account. Your account will then be $104, not $100. This is why we do not generally include savings accounts—and all the other interest-bearing financial assets—in the definition of money. They do change in price or value, and therefore they are generally not used as a medium of exchange. For one thing, a savings account is simply not transferable. There is no way for me to give you my savings account; the passbook is registered in my name, and only I can make withdrawals from the account with my signature. What I can do is withdraw *money* from the bank, either as currency or as a check drawn by the bank, and give it to you. Thus we cannot spend our savings accounts; we can only have the bank exchange them for money and then spend the money. Similarly, we do not give the storekeeper shares of stock, bonds, treasury notes, or other such evidences of debt when we buy groceries. These things are financial assets but they are not money; like everything else, they are bought and sold for money.

Other Uses of Money

The existence of a unit of account by means of which values of all other goods and services are measured leads to another use of this unit. This use is called the *standard of deferred payments;* it is simply an extension of the use as a measure of values. Many transactions involve credit, either through the actual lending of money or through postponement of payment for goods. The eventual repayment of a loan or payment for a purchase is made in accordance with the original agreement, which states the number of dollars to be paid. Thus debts of all kinds are almost universally stated in terms of the unit of account, and the appropriate number of units of the medium of exchange are paid in the future.

The existence of the medium of exchange also leads to another use of money closely related to it. Money need not be spent immediately, as soon as it is received. It may be held for a short or a long time before being spent. While it is held, it is one of the holder's assets, and it has the very useful characteristic that it can be spent whenever the holder wishes. People and institutions do hold money for a variety of reasons. One reason is that they have to correlate the timing of receipts and expenditures. A family breadwinner may be paid once a month, but he has to spread expenditures throughout the month; a business may receive money sporadically but have to make regular expenditures. Another reason for holding money is that it permits the holder to meet unexpected outlays and to take advantage of bargains. A third reason is that the holder may expect better opportunities in the future to purchase goods or securities. Money is thus a *liquid asset* held by all economic units to a certain extent; while being held, it serves the function of being a *store of value.*

There are numerous other liquid assets, however, the existence of which make unnecessary or less desirable the holding of money itself. Money can be exchanged for savings accounts or highly liquid securities without much loss of liquidity but at the gain of interest income.

MONEY IN THE UNITED STATES

It follows from the foregoing discussion that only certain things serve as the medium of exchange and are money in the sense that they are always worth their face amount in terms of other units of money. Much confusion has arisen over the nature of money because of its historical evolution. Like other things, monetary units once were physical standards, like the fishhooks alluded to previously. The British pound, for example, is called a pound because originally it was literally a pound of silver. The biblical coin, the shekel, took its name from a weight also. In Sweden, the monetary unit was once a given weight of copper. In the United States, the dollar was once legally defined as 24.75 grains of fine gold and later as other weights, and it still has a definition in terms of gold for official transactions with other countries.[1] But this does not negate the fact that the dollar has become an abstract unit by which we measure all values. The question now becomes: What are the dollars we use as our medium of exchange?

[1] Fine gold is 90 percent gold and 10 percent alloy, for hardness.

Table 11-1
Stock of Money in the United States, 1930, 1950, 1970
(Millions of Dollars)

	June 30, 1930	Dec. 31, 1950	Jan. 28, 1970
Currency	$ 3.4	$25.4	$ 46.3
Demand deposits	21.7	92.3	152.9
U.S. government demand deposits°	.3	3.0	6.0

°Not included in other demand deposits. Interbank deposits are also excluded.

Source: *Federal Reserve Bulletin*, February, 1970, p. A-17, and June, 1960, p. 648; *Banking and Monetary Statistics*, 1943, p. 34.

The stock of money in the United States is shown in Table 11-1 for two dates in the past and for a recent date in order to show how much the stock of money has increased over recent decades. In 1930 the country was falling into the severe and long depression of that decade. In 1950 we had passed through the depression, World War II, and the ensuing period of reconversion to peacetime production and rising price levels.

Coins and Currency

The system whereby coins and currency are supplied has changed in many respects over the history of the United States. In our early history coins and currency made up most of the money supply; the present system of payment by check developed mostly after the Civil War. The federal government supplied most of the coins, and the commercial banks supplied most of the currency in the form of banknotes. The latter process we will examine in some detail later; first, it is helpful to survey the system that provides us with coins and currency.

The relationship between currency and bank deposits is the opposite of what it appears on the surface. Rather than bank deposits resulting from people putting money in the bank, the volume of currency results from people taking it out of the bank. There is now a smoothly functioning system that permits the public to have whatever proportion of the total money supply it desires in the form of currency. On any given day, some people accumulate more currency than they want to have in that form, so they deposit the currency in order to have bank deposits on which they can draw checks. Examples are those businesses that receive *cash* in their normal operations—retail stores, filling stations, cafeterias, buses, and the like. At the same time, other people require cash and obtain it by cashing checks at their banks; they convert their checking account money to currency. Examples are housewives about to go shopping, people embarking on trips, and anyone replacing the usual amount of cash he carries for those daily expenditures made in coin or currency. How much currency there is in use at any given time, then, depends upon such factors as the amount of business being done, the price level, the number of people using currency, and the relative convenience of paying in cash or paying by check, either immediately or later. Many people can remember when they needed to take only $5 or $10 to the market to purchase a week's groceries at the prices that prevailed in the 1930s; today, to purchase approximately the same things, they would need to take $20 or more. There are now considerably more people and families, each of whom, on the average, is carrying more currency than was true a few decades ago. Working in the contrary direction is the increased use of charge accounts and credit cards. Many transactions are *charged,* and the buyer pays with a single check drawn on his bank once a month. But the net effect of all the influences on the need for coin and currency is to make the volume larger than in the past.

The monetary system makes it possible for the public to have not only that volume of currency that is most convenient but also those denominations of coins and paper money that the public needs. This we can see by tracing the source of the money. Although many people deposit currency and others withdraw it from their banks, the long-run tendency is for the banks to pay out more in cashing checks than they take in. Thus, unless they had some source of additional currency, they would run out of it. Banks which are members of the Federal Reserve System have deposits at Federal Reserve banks, of which there are twelve. These banks are "bankers' banks," meaning other banks use them as much as the public uses regular banks. Member banks can withdraw currency, and thus maintain their supplies of *till money,* from their deposits at the Federal Reserve banks in the same way the public withdraws currency from commercial banks. Other banks not members of the system rely on *correspondent banks* for the same service; that is, they carry deposits at large city banks where they can send extra funds, withdraw currency, or draw checks for the purchase of securities or other uses. But whether banks obtain the currency directly or indirectly, it comes from the Federal Reserve banks.

The natural question then is, Where do the Federal Reserve banks get cash? The answer is different for coins than it is for currency. The reserve banks are empowered to *issue* currency, or paper money, as it is needed. At one time it was a normal function of any commercial bank to make loans in the form of its own notes, but for some time the only banks empowered to extend credit in the form of banknotes have been the reserve banks. When a member bank needs more till money, it simply withdraws the notes from its account at its Federal Reserve bank, thus lowering its deposit there. Practically all the paper money in use today consists of Federal Reserve notes. What happens, therefore, is that the Federal Reserve bank simply exchanges its deposit liability to its member bank for a note liability, which is soon in the hands of the public. (How the banks' deposits at the reserve banks arise and can be replenished will be described later.)

For historical reasons the supply of coins is provided somewhat differently. Coinage has always been a function of the federal government, which established mints for the purpose. Although coins were the principal form of money in colonial days and in the early period of the nation, today they are primarily a convenience for making change, using parking meters, buying from vending machines, and the like. The decimal system and the use of the cent, nickel, dime, quarter, and half-dollar make it very simple to make change with a minimum of coins. The mints manufacture whatever quantity of coin is needed. As the public withdraws coins from banks and the banks withdraw them from Federal Reserve banks, the United States Treasury purchases the necessary copper, nickel, and silver and produces the coins in demand. It then deposits these coins to its account at the Federal Reserve banks, which are then able to meet the withdrawals of their member banks.

In the early days of the country, most coins were *standard money*. This expression means that the government established a fixed price (sometimes for gold, sometimes for silver, and sometimes for both) at which it would buy metal and coin it. The coins were "full-bodied" in the sense that they were made of the same value of metal as the face value of the coins. For example, when the mint price of silver was $1.29 an ounce, the mints used an ounce of silver to make $1.29 in coins. For many years, however, coins have been *token money*. That is, they have been produced as a convenience in trade and as a means of making change for full dollars. Thus the Treasury has purchased whatever quantities have been necessary and has paid market prices rather then *mint* prices; whatever the market price of copper or silver has happened to be, that is what the metal has cost the Treasury. Gold coins, which would be standard money if made, have not been made since the early 1930s.

Normally there has been a profit (called *seigniorage*) in the manufacture of coins, but this has been incidental and not the purpose of coinage. However, an interesting situation developed in the mid-1960s, when greatly increasing industrial uses for silver pushed up its price to the point at which the profit disappeared. That is, in order to make four quarters, two half-dollars, or ten dimes, the Treasury had to spend $1 for the silver. At this point the price was $1.29 an ounce. The Coinage Act of 1965 consequently was passed by the Congress in order to change the composition of the old silver coins. Dimes and quarters no longer contain silver but are made of a "sandwich" of copper and copper-nickel alloy (the same alloy as is used for nickels), and the half-dollar now contains 40 percent silver and the remainder copper. Before this change, these three coins were made of an alloy of 90 percent silver. The definition of the silver dollar—90 percent silver—was not changed, but this coin has virtually disappeared from circulation as it is more convenient to use the paper dollar.

Debts Used as Money

We have surveyed briefly the uses of coin and currency and how this form of the medium of exchange is supplied before discussing the larger component of the money supply, bank deposits, for several reasons. Everyone is familiar with "pocketbook money," in fact, so familiar that the general impression is that it is "real" money and in some sense bank deposits are not. It is important to make the point that our currency is the minor part of the total money supply and that it comes to us out of our bank deposits. The much more important question, then, is: Where do bank deposits come from? How is the money supply created in this form? We shall see that, by and large, bank deposits do not arise because people put money in the banks but because they borrow from the banking system.

The reason that this characteristic of the money system has been able to develop is that debts have become acceptable means of payment, or a medium of exchange. Coin and currency are actually debts, owed to the holder by the federal government or the Federal Reserve banks. These debts are somewhat different from most debts, largely in that we do use them as money. They are non—interest-bearing debts, but they are debts nonetheless. The situation is somewhat confusing because all other debts are payable in these debts which are used as money. There is no additional form of money in which these monetary debts are payable. But the holder of a $10 Federal Reserve note, even if he is aware that technically he holds a debt of a Federal Reserve bank, is not interested in having the debt "paid" because if it were, he would have money, which he already has! However, the fact that governmentally issued money is government debt is illustrated by the ability to pay debts owed to the government with it. That is, a $100 tax liability to the government can be paid — or canceled — by giving the government its debt to the holder of its currency.

To illustrate further how debts serve as money and to introduce the manner in which banks have developed to make this possible, let us consider first a situation in which other kinds of debts might have developed into this role. Imagine, for instance, that all the business in the country is handled by five giant corporations. These five corporations produce everything that is produced and employ everyone who is employed. As they turn out goods, they issue to their employees and stockholders claims on their output. These claims are expressed in the unit of account — dollars. In a given month, Corporation A produces goods valued at $1 million and gives to its employees and stockholders claims on that amount of output, that is, $1 million. Now these claims are essentially debts and the holders — the creditors — can collect the debts by claiming their goods. In this way the wages and profits would just pay for the output.

No doubt the employees and stockholders of Corporation A do not wish to spend all their incomes on the output of that company but want to buy output from Corporations B, C, D, and E as well. The economy might have developed in a way to make this possible. If each corporation would accept claims on other corporations in payment for its output, the debts of each corporation would serve as money. Suppose, to make the arithmetic easy, that the claims of each corporation are spent equally on the output of all five corporations. Then Corporation A would receive $200,000 of its own debts from its own employees and stockholders, and it would receive $200,000 from employees and stockholders of each of the other corporations, or $1 million in all. What would Corporation A do with the $800,000 of debts owed by the other four corporations? Each corporation would hold $800,000 of the debts of other corporations; each corporation would also owe $200,000 to each of four other corporations. It would be a simple matter for each pair of corporations to cancel the debts owed each other! Thus the debts issued by each corporation for wages and dividends would have served as the medium of exchange whereby the output was distributed.

If such a system had developed, there would be certain complications but not such as to make the scheme impossible. If one corporation failed to attract its fifth of total expenditures, its debts would pile up in the hands of other corporations and debts would not cancel out in the short run. However, this happens in the real world; such a company would have to attract customers by lowering its prices or reduce its issuance of debts by cutting its costs. There would no doubt have to be provision for someone to hold the debts of some corporations temporarily until the companies could redeem them by selling their output, but this is merely a question of timing.

The purpose of this illustration is to make the point that money could have developed as these claims on the output of the issuing companies. Instead of "paying" employees, the companies would in effect be saying, "We owe you for your services and will pay you with part of the output. If you want to have the output of another company instead, you may do so because some of their employees will want our output." Actually, the operation of the monetary system is much closer to this imaginary example than is generally realized. Because of the great number of producers and employers, it is not practical for each to issue its own debts. But if a generally recognized and trusted individual or institution assumed these debts, so that everyone would accept them, knowing that they could be used to claim the output of any producer, the scheme would work. And in fact, that is about what happens in the real world. Producers do not issue their debts to their employees and stockholders; they issue them to an intermediary institution, the commercial banks. In exchange for these debts, the banks issue their own debts in the form of deposits, and producers use these deposit-debts to pay their own debts to employees, suppliers, and others. In the modern world it is bank debts that serve as the principal medium of exchange, and these bank debts have come into existence in exchange for the debts of businesses, households, and governments. How this process of borrowing from banks gives rise to deposits, and thus the major portion of the money supply, is the principal topic of this chapter.

Demand Deposits as Money

The amount of funds transferred by check runs into several trillion dollars each year, and several million checks are drawn on their accounts by holders of demand deposits. Far more expenditures, measured by dollar volume, are made by check than by coin and currency. A principal function of the system of commercial banks is handling this great volume of paper, keeping accurate track of thousands and thousands of balances in the process of *check clearing*. Only the development of sophisticated electronic equipment has made possible this volume of traffic without heavy cost to depositors.

If we assume for the moment the existence of demand deposits and postpone the inquiry into how they arise, we may survey briefly the nature of bank operations. Essentially, a bank is a business venture like a store, manufacturing company, or other venture. Its basic function is to collect funds from depositors and lend these funds to borrowers or otherwise invest them. From the point of view of the individual bank, it obtains funds from its depositors. There are two broad types of deposits, time, or savings, and demand. _Demand deposits_ are those against which checks may be drawn, so the bank must always stand ready to honor checks. The depositor may want currency over the counter, but in far greater volume the checks order the bank to pay another person, the _drawee_. The drawee might, on occasion, wish to cash his check, but much more often he deposits it in order to build up his own deposit, against which he can draw checks. Since there are over 13,000 banks in the United States, the drawee is likely to deposit a check in a bank other than the one on which it is drawn. In such cases, the recipient bank must have a method of collecting from the bank of the drawer of the check.

The checks deposited at a bank on a given day, therefore, can be described as those drawn on the same bank, those drawn on other nearby banks, and those drawn on banks at some distance. The first group, those drawn by depositors of the same bank, does not require the bank to pay out any funds. It simply credits the accounts of the depositors and charges the accounts of those who drew the checks. Its total deposits remain the same, and it simply owes different amounts of deposits to its customers.

Checks drawn on other banks require that the drawers' bank pay the depositors' banks. Some generally acceptable form of money has to exist whereby banks can quickly and easily make these payments. Before the Federal Reserve banks, which were established by the Federal Reserve Act of 1913, banks paid each other what they owed in two ways. Sometimes they would ship currency, but this was risky and expensive. Consequently, banks developed the system of correspondent banks, mentioned earlier. A bank in a small town or rural area carried a deposit in a nearby city. When it received checks on out-of-town banks, it sent them to the city correspondent for deposit and, when it owed other banks, it paid with checks on this deposit. The city correspondent, in turn, had a correspondent bank in a larger city, and it might send these checks there to build up its balance. Thus a given check might be sent to many banks before it arrived at a bank that did business with the one on which it was drawn, and this method, too, was inefficient and expensive.

Establishment of the Federal Reserve banks provided _central banks_ where banks that joined the system could keep such deposits, similar to the old correspondent balances. When a member bank receives a check drawn on a bank located at some distance, it sends that check on to be deposited at its Federal Reserve bank. If the drawer's bank is located in the same Federal Reserve district—there are twelve such districts—the reserve bank sends it to that bank and, under authorization from the latter, charges the check to that bank's account. If the drawer's bank is in another Federal Reserve district, the check goes to the other reserve bank, which sends it to the drawer's bank and charges its account. When the drawer's bank receives the check, it charges the account of the drawer. Actually, there are shortcuts that eliminate some of these mailings, but the effect is as described here. The debits and credits to the various accounts can be summarized in an example. Suppose that Mr. Smith lives in Philadelphia and has received a check for $100 from Mr. Jones in San Francisco, which he deposits at his bank. The successive transactions would look something like those at the top of page 218.

Federal Reserve Bank of Philadelphia
Deposits
Philadelphia
State Bank +$100

Federal Reserve Bank of San Francisco
Deposits
San Francisco
Citizens Bank −$100

Philadelphia State Bank	
Account at	Deposits
F.R. bank +$100	Mr. Smith +$100

San Francisco Citizens Bank	
Account at	Deposits
F.R. bank −$100	Mr. Jones −$100

In addition to the accounts shown here, the Federal Reserve Bank of Philadelphia would gain $100 at the Interdistrict Settlement Fund, set up to clear such transactions as this, while the Federal Reserve Bank of San Francisco would lose $100. Of course, one should realize that each day thousands of checks are handled in this way, so that the net result for any one bank is the difference between the checks it receives and sends to its reserve bank and the checks drawn on it that have been deposited in other banks. To a large extent, the two figures cancel out, if not each day, at least over a longer period of time.

Checks drawn on nearby banks are handled much as those just described — in fact, frequently the same — but they are often subject to a preliminary canceling-out process through an institution called a clearing house. Suppose four banks in a city, A, B, C, and D, establish a clearing house. Each day or oftener each bank takes to a central place, the clearing house, the checks drawn on each of the others. Bank A has checks drawn on B, C, and D, as each of the others has checks drawn on it, but the debts are considered owed to or by the clearing house. For example, suppose that the banks have received checks drawn on each other as shown in the rows of the tabulation that follows. Bank A has received checks totaling $100 drawn on B, $150 drawn on C, and $125 drawn on D. These checks may be totaled for a single claim on the clearing house of $375. The vertical columns show how much other banks have of checks drawn on a given bank. It may be seen that the other banks have checks drawn on A totaling $320. Thus Bank A has a net gain of $55 at the clearing house. What one bank gains others lose, so the total gains and losses must be equal. Bank B gains $20 ($350 minus $330), Bank C loses $25, and Bank D loses $50. The losing banks may pay the clearing house with Federal Reserve funds, and the clearing house pays the gaining banks with these funds.

	A	B	C	D	Total
A	.....	$100	$150	$125	$ 375
B	$ 90	.....	120	140	350
C	110	115	.....	120	345
D	120	115	100	.....	335
Total	320	330	370	385	1,405

One thing that should be observed about the tremendous turnover of demand deposits is that it does not affect their total. Every deposit of a check also represents a withdrawal. When somebody's account goes up because he has made a deposit, somebody else's account goes down because he has drawn a check. We now turn to the crux of the question posed earlier: Where do deposits come from? To answer this question, we start with another: What kinds of transactions add to deposits without reducing them equally?

There are three such kinds of transactions. These are:

1. Deposits of currency
2. Bank loans and investments
3. Loans and investments of the Federal Reserve banks

Clearly, if someone takes $100 of currency to his bank and deposits it, his deposit rises and the deposit of no one else is affected. We should note in passing that the depositor has no more and no less money; he has less currency and more deposit. But this transaction would increase the total of bank deposits in the system of banks. However, we have already seen earlier in this chapter that the net effect of deposits of currency and withdrawals of currency is to increase the amount of currency in circulation. In actual practice, therefore, this kind of transaction is constantly tending to reduce deposits, not increase them. In short periods of time currency may flow back to banks, as it does after the Christmas shopping season each year, but to understand the functioning of the banking system it is very important to understand that bank deposits do not rise in any real sense because people deposit currency.

The principal factor affecting bank deposits is bank loans and, to a lesser extent, bank investments in bonds and similar securities. This is the point at which knowledge about how a given bank operates tends to obscure understanding of the way in which the *system of banks* works. Let us take an example.

Bank Loans and Deposits

Mr. Brown operates a factory that produces ladies' handbags. He knows that the biggest selling season is around Easter and that if he is to have his handbags in the stores for Easter, he must manufacture them months earlier so storekeepers can buy them before the season. To produce as many handbags as he thinks he can sell would cost a significant sum of money for raw materials, wages, and other costs. But he will not get paid for the handbags until he sells them and, in fact, his customers may not be able to pay until they have resold them. Let us say he wants to produce the handbags in February, sell them in March, and collect thirty days after he sells them. In other words, he plans to collect from his customers during April. At the end of February he will have funds tied up in inventory, and at the end of March he will have funds tied up in accounts receivable. We may assume that he will spend $10,000 in February for materials, labor, and other costs and that he will sell the handbags for $12,000. He does not have the $10,000, but he knows that his bank will lend the money to him, as he has obtained such a loan for each of the past several years. He has, perhaps, $2,000, but he can never afford to be completely without money so he asks his bank for $10,000 on February 1 to be repaid May 1, ninety days later.

Obviously, Mr. Brown does not want a bundle of $10 bills when he gets the loan. He wants the "proceeds of the loan credited to his account," to use banking terminology. Consequently, he signs a promissory note and gives it to the bank; this note is for a sum amounting to $10,000 plus interest for three months—perhaps $10,150. The banker in turn credits the proceeds—$10,000—to Mr. Brown's account, which is now $12,000 since he previously had $2,000. During the month of February, Mr. Brown draws checks and disburses the $10,000. In real life some of these checks would go to people who would deposit them at the same bank and others would go to people who would deposit them elsewhere. To simplify the example, however, let us assume that all the checks are disbursed to recipients who deposit them in other banks. Thus Mr. Brown's bank must have funds of this amount that it can afford to lose to other banks. In order to make the loan, the bank must have what are called *excess reserves* in the amount of $10,000 because the amount of checks drawn on it will be that much larger than if it did not make the loan.

Let us look at the bank's balance sheet just before the bank makes the loan:

Brownsville National Bank

Assets		Liabilities	
Cash in vault	$ 50,000	Demand deposits	$ 900,000
Deposit at Federal Reserve	145,000	Time deposits	900,000
Loans	1,330,000	Capital	100,000
Investments	435,000	Surplus	80,000
Bank building, etc.	40,000	Undivided profits	20,000
Total	$2,000,000	Total	$2,000,000

Of course, this balance sheet is somewhat simplified for our purposes and we have supplied nice round figures, but the significant data are present. The bank has $50,000 of coin and currency to take care of short-run discrepancies in its inflow and outflow of cash. Its deposit at its Federal Reserve bank is $145,000. This figure is important because, under law and regulation, the bank is required to have *cash reserves* of at least certain percentages of its demand and time deposits. In counting its cash reserves, or *legal reserves,* the bank may include its coin and currency and its balance at the Federal Reserve bank. We assume here that it is required to have 10 percent of its demand deposits and 5 percent of its savings and time deposits ($135,000) and that the bank likes to have in addition about $50,000 of vault cash. These percentages are not exactly what member banks are required to have at the present time, but they are reasonable approximations. Thus the bank is required to have $90,000 of reserves for its demand deposits and $45,000 for its savings and time deposits, or a total of $135,000. In anticipation of losing $10,000 after lending this sum to Mr. Brown, the bank is currently holding about $10,000 of excess reserves plus its desired vault cash.

Now let us look at the balance sheet after the loan has been made to Mr. Brown:

Brownsville National Bank

Assets		Liabilities	
Cash in vault	$ 50,000	Demand deposits	$ 910,000
Deposit at Federal Reserve	145,000	Time deposits	900,000
Loans	1,340,150	Capital	100,000
Investments	435,000	Surplus	80,000
Bank building, etc.	40,000	Undivided profits	20,000
		Unearned discount	150
Total	$2,010,150	Total	$2,010,150

Several significant changes have been brought about by the making of
the loan. First, loans have increased by $10,150. The reason for this is that
the bank now holds Mr. Brown's promissory note for that amount. The
sum of $10,000 has been added to Mr. Brown's demand deposit, increas-
ing the total of such deposits to $910,000. There is now needed a bal-
ancing item, the difference between the increase in loans and the increase in deposits. This is the interest or discount that Mr. Brown will pay
at the maturity of the loan. Since the bank has not yet earned this payment
but will earn it by lending the funds for three months, it is called in bank accounting *unearned* discount. Actually, since the bank has a portfolio of
loans, there was such an item before the loan to Mr. Brown, but we ignored it in order to introduce it here.

Now Mr. Brown has his money and is prepared to proceed with producing the handbags. Over a period of time he therefore disburses the
$10,000. In order to bring out most clearly the principle involved, we con-
tinue to hold to the assumption that all the checks he draws go to people
who deposit them in other banks. Thus, after these checks have been
cleared through the banking system (and if we ignore any other changes
that affect the bank during this time), the bank's balance sheet at the end
of February would look like this:

Brownsville National Bank

Assets		Liabilities	
Cash in vault	$ 50,000	Demand deposits	$ 900,000
Deposit at Federal Reserve	135,000	Time deposits	900,000
Loans	1,340,150	Capital	100,000
Investments	435,000	Surplus	80,000
Bank building, etc.	40,000	Undivided profits	20,000
		Unearned discount	150
Total	$2,000,150	Total	$2,000,150

The changes are fairly obvious. The bank has lost its reserve balance at
the Federal Reserve bank to other banks to the extent of $10,000 because
Mr. Brown has drawn checks for this amount against his borrowed account at the bank. Of course, it is somewhat unrealistic to assume that
no other changes occur during this period of time, but it is probably obvious that it is necessary to do so in order to illustrate the effect of this
loan. To attempt to combine many loans and other transactions in a single
example would hopelessly complicate what is essentially a simple prin-

ciple. It may be noted that the bank still holds Mr. Brown's promissory note and that the unearned, or to-be-earned, discount is still on the books.

The next step is to see what happens as Mr. Brown sells the handbags for $12,000, as he hoped to do. During March he makes sales, and during April he receives payments for these sales. Consequently, at the end of April, the bank's books will reflect these deposits made by Mr. Brown as follows:

Brownsville National Bank

Assets		Liabilities	
Cash in vault	$ 50,000	Demand deposits	$ 912,000
Deposit at Federal Reserve	147,000	Time deposits	900,000
Loans	1,340,150	Capital	100,000
Investments	435,000	Surplus	80,000
Bank building, etc.	40,000	Undivided profits	20,000
		Unearned discount	150
Total	$2,012,150	Total	$2,012,150

It is clear that Mr. Brown's account has risen by $12,000 and increased total demand deposits by this amount to $912,000. As the bank received these deposits, it collected the checks through the Federal Reserve System and thus increased its reserve balance by an equal amount.

The final step in Mr. Brown's story comes on May 1, when he pays his note. He owes the bank $10,150, so he draws a check for that amount against his deposit and gives it to the bank in exchange for his canceled promissory note. Now see what happens to the accounts of the bank:

Brownsville National Bank

Assets		Liabilities	
Cash in vault	$ 50,000	Demand deposits	$ 901,850
Deposit at Federal Reserve	147,000	Time deposits	900,000
Loans	1,330,000	Capital	100,000
Investments	435,000	Surplus	80,000
Bank building, etc.	40,000	Undivided profits	20,150
Total	$2,002,000	Total	$2,002,000

This is the end of the story or, more accurately, this chapter of it. Mr. Brown made a gross profit of $2,000 but paid the bank interest of $150 out of that profit, so his account is now $1,850 more than when the story started. Since this is the only factor we have allowed to take place, total demand deposits reflect this rise in Mr. Brown's account. The bank has restored its excess reserves and is now in a position to lend again to someone else. And its unearned discount has been earned and thus taken into undivided profits.

Creation of Bank-Deposit Money

All the figures in the last balance sheet are the same as in the first balance sheet except that Mr. Brown's deposit is $1,850 larger, the bank's undivided profits are $150 larger on the liability side, and the bank has $2,000 more cash reserves, in the form of balance at the reserve bank, on the asset side. It is important to realize that these increases represent a *shift* of funds from other banks to the Brownsville National Bank. Mr. Brown now has bank-deposit money that formerly belonged to the storekeepers who paid him for the handbags, and his bank now has some of the deposits at the Federal Reserve bank formerly held by the storekeepers' banks. In addition, Mr. Brown has transferred $150 of his deposit to the bank itself. Since the bank no longer owes this sum to a depositor, it is shown as part of what the bank itself owns — in the form of undivided profits. If the directors of the bank so decide, the undivided-profits figure could be transferred to the deposits of the stockholders; this would be a payment of dividends. Or the directors may decide to keep these earnings invested in the bank and transfer the sum to surplus.

We should now observe that when the bank originally made the loan to Mr. Brown, it did so by increasing his deposit. It was able to do so because it could meet the anticipated drain on its cash reserves, when he drew checks on this new deposit, by having excess reserves of $10,000. When the bank loses these excess reserves, it is obviously because other banks have gained them, through the process of collecting checks deposited by those to whom Mr. Brown gave them. We must therefore examine what happens at these other banks in order to grasp the process whereby commercial banks expand their deposits when there are excess reserves in the system. This *deposit creation* is the process by which banks create money.

It is easier to examine this process if we concentrate attention on the excess reserves themselves. The Brownsville National Bank has received these funds in one of the three ways listed earlier: deposit of currency, deposit of checks drawn on other banks, or deposit of checks drawn on Federal Reserve banks. Although the last-named process has not as yet been described, it is the one most likely to have brought new cash reserves into the banking system. Therefore, we will start by assuming that a Federal Reserve bank has purchased $11,111 of securities from someone who was willing to sell and that this seller deposited his check in the Brownsville National Bank. The reason for assuming this peculiar amount is both important and simple. Notice that the Brownsville National Bank's balance sheet will be affected by two changes as a result of the deposit of this check. It will have additional deposits of $11,111, and it will have a check drawn on the Federal Reserve bank for that amount. It will send this check on to its reserve bank to be added to its reserve balance there. Thus its balance sheet will have these two additions:

Assets	*Liabilities*
Deposit at Federal Reserve $11,111	Demand deposits $11,111

The reason for assuming this peculiar amount may now be apparent. If we assume, as we did earlier, that banks like Brownsville National are required to have legal reserves of at least 10 percent of demand deposits, this increase in demand deposits raises the bank's *reserve requirement* by $1,111. Thus it has excess reserves of $10,000, which is the amount with which we started. Any net increase in a bank's demand deposits brought about by the deposit of funds must increase the bank's excess reserves by 90 percent of that amount if the reserve requirement is 10 percent. If the requirement were 50 percent, only half of the new funds would be excess.

When the loan to Mr. Brown is first made, the additions to the bank's balance sheet are:

Assets		Liabilities	
Deposit at Federal Reserve	$11,111	Demand deposits	$21,111
Loans	10,000		

The interest or discount on the loan will be ignored hereafter, so the loan is added to the assets of the bank as $10,000 and, as before, this amount is credited to Mr. Brown, so that demand deposits have risen by $21,111 in all. Now, when Mr. Brown spends his $10,000 and these checks are deposited in other banks, the Brownsville National Bank loses this amount and reduces Mr. Brown's account accordingly. We thus have:

Assets		Liabilities	
Deposit at Federal Reserve	$ 1,111	Demand deposits	$11,111
Loans	10,000		

The significant point at this stage is that the Brownsville National Bank has lost its excess reserves and therefore it has exactly the required reserves. Its remaining deposit at its reserve bank is 10 percent of its additional deposits.

Since the Brownsville National Bank has lost its excess reserves to other banks in the system, these other banks have gained deposits and reserve balances at their reserve banks. Let us treat these other banks as a single bank, for purposes of simplifying the figures. This other bank, which we will call the Second National, has increases in its accounts like this:

Assets		Liabilities	
Deposit at Federal Reserve	$10,000	Demand deposits	$10,000

The Second National now has excess reserves, and it is in a position to make additional loans or, if there is no one to whom it wishes to lend, it may purchase investments. How much can it lend? If its reserve requirement is 10 percent of demand deposits, it must hold $1,000 so it has $9,000, or 90 percent of excess reserves. Thus it can increase its loans by this amount, as follows:

Assets		Liabilities	
Deposit at Federal Reserve	$10,000	Demand deposits	$19,000
Loans	9,000		

To repeat the process just described with respect to the Brownsville National Bank, the borrower at Second National disburses his new $9,000, deposits at Second National fall back to $10,000, and Second National loses $9,000 of its reserve balance at its reserve bank to other banks. It now has loans of $9,000 and legal reserves of $1,000. This last amount is 10 percent of its additional deposits. To go one step further, suppose all the checks drawn on the $9,000 deposit at Second National are deposited in the Third National Bank. Its balance sheet will show these additions:

Assets	*Liabilities*
Deposit at Federal Reserve $9,000	Demand deposits $9,000

Its excess reserves, after deducting the required 10 percent, or $900, are $8,100. Third National can increase its loans by $8,100 and credit the proceeds to borrowers' accounts, as follows:

Assets		*Liabilities*
Deposit at Federal Reserve	$9,000	Demand deposits $17,100
Loans	8,100	

When the borrowed $8,100 is disbursed, Third National will have reserve funds of $900 remaining, 10 percent of its remaining deposits of $9,000, as well as loans of $8,100.

At this point, let us review how the three banks stand. This may be done tabularly:

Bank	*Cash Reserves*	*Loans*	*Deposits*
Brownsville	$1,111	$10,000	$11,111
Second National	1,000	9,000	10,000
Third National	900	8,100	9,000

Each bank has received deposits, set aside the required reserve, and lent an amount equal to the excess reserve. It has then lost this excess reserve to other banks in the system. It is reasonably simple to visualize the remainder of the process of deposit creation by bank lending. The Fourth National Bank receives deposits of $8,100, keeps $810 as required reserve, and lends $7,290. The Fifth National obtains deposits of $7,290, keeps $729, and lends $6,561, and so on and on. Where does the process end? The answer is clear when one realizes that each bank keeps reserves of 10 percent of its deposits and that the original amount of reserves available to the system is $11,111. Therefore, there will no longer be any excess reserves when all the $11,111 is required reserves; this will be when deposits have grown to $111,111 or ten times the original reserves.

This is the situation if the required reserve ratio is 10 percent. If it were 20 percent, deposits could grow to only five times the original excess reserves. When deposits have grown to $111,111, they will have been increased by $100,000 over the original deposit of funds in the Brownsville National Bank, and this sum, of course, is ten times the original excess reserves. To carry the last tabulation a bit further, we would have:

Bank	*Cash Reserves*	*Loans*	*Deposits*
Brownsville	$ 1,111.00	$ 10,000.00	$ 11,111.00
Second National	1,000.00	9,000.00	10,000.00
Third National	900.00	8,100.00	9,000.00
Fourth National	810.00	7,290.00	8,100.00
Fifth National	729.00	6,561.00	7,290.00
Sixth National	656.10	5,904.90	6,561.00
Seventh National	590.49	5,314.41	5,904.90
Total, seven banks	$ 5,796.59	$ 52,170.31	$ 57,966.90
All subsequent banks	5,314.41	47,829.69	53,144.10
Total	$11,111.00	$100,000.00	$111,111.00

This example illustrates the principle of the expansion of bank deposits through the loan process. It is a bit simplified because, in order to bring out the arithmetic of the process, it has been necessary to make some clarifying assumptions, such as that all the checks on a bank go to a single other bank. But it should be clear that these assumptions are only simplifications. The principle would be the same if, for example, half of the $9,000 withdrawn from Second National went back to Brownsville and half were deposited at Second National itself. In this case, Brownsville would gain deposits of $4,500 and could expand its loans accordingly. Similarly, Second National could expand its loans further. The ultimate total expansion would be the same.

The Expansion Process

Actually, all banks tend to expand at more or less the same time, rather than in the step-by-step manner that is necessary for a textbook explanation. When many banks have excess reserves, they expand loans, lose reserves to each other, and continue to expand. But the ultimate limit is the point at which none of the banks has excess reserves, just as in the preceding example.

What makes this process possible is the ability of banks to operate with fractional reserves—reserves that represent some fraction less than 100 percent of their deposits. They can do this because, on any given day, each bank gains as well as loses deposits and reserves. The net loss on any day tends to be a small fraction of its total reserves and, of course, an even smaller fraction of its deposits. On other days it tends to have a net gain. For that reason, banks are required to have minimum reserves *on the average* over a period of one week rather than at all times, as implied in the foregoing example.

The fact that banks do have to keep minimum legal reserves and that the volume of these reserves (deposits at reserve banks and currency) is subject to regulation by the Federal Reserve System makes it possible for the Federal Reserve banks to influence strongly the volume of loans and investments banks can make and thus the volume of money available to the public. How this regulation is carried out is largely the subject of the next chapter, but there are a few loose ends to tidy up before taking up that subject.

One detail is to explain how the acquisition of investments by banks operates to expand bank deposits. The process is virtually the same as for loans. If a bank has excess reserves and no satisfactory loan demand, it tends to purchase interest-bearing investments rather than hold non–interest-bearing balances at the reserve bank. It pays for these bonds in either of two ways. It may issue a check drawn on itself and, when the seller of the securities deposits this check, his account rises just as if he had obtained a bank loan. The excess reserves of the buying bank shift to the bank where its check was deposited, and the recipient bank has excess reserves. Or the bank may purchase the securities with a check it draws on its balance at its reserve bank. The results are the same, as the seller of the securities deposits the check in his bank and his bank gets the excess reserves of the buying bank.

Other complications involve limitations on the process as it was just described. In real life the arithmetic is not quite so precise and simple. We may observe three complications in particular. First, many banks do keep some excess reserves at all or most times. The profit motive does impel banks to minimize excess reserves but, at the same time, some banks will be holding them for a variety of reasons. Some may be awaiting better loan or investment opportunities, and others may have such small amounts as not to bother with eliminating them. But since excess reserves do exist, the arithmetic of the relationship between reserves and deposits is not precise. It is a good general rule, as illustrated by the foregoing example, that in the banking system (and in each bank) reserves plus loans and investments equal deposits, but the relationship need not be exactly 10 plus 90 equal 100, given a 10 percent reserve ratio.

A second factor that complicates the precise arithmetic relationship is the fact that some of the expanded deposits will probably be withdrawn as currency. Thus, if an additional $10,000 of bank reserves were to enter the system through operations of the Federal Reserve banks, deposits would start to rise but, as they did so, some of them would be converted to currency and the banks would lose some of the additional $10,000. If this *cash drain* should amount to, say, $2,000, the banks would be left with $8,000 of additional reserves and deposits could rise to $80,000 if the reserve ratio were 10 percent.

A third complication of the arithmetic is the existence of savings or other time deposits. As bank deposits are expanded by the loan process, some of the recipients may wish to shift some of their demand deposits to the time category. This shift brings no new reserves to the banks for the simple reason that what is "deposited" in a savings account is a demand deposit already on the books of a bank.[2] For the bank receiving the savings deposit, however, the effect is somewhat similar to receiving new funds. The reason is that savings deposits have lower reserve requirements than do demand deposits. Thus a shift of $1,000 from demand to savings might "free" $50 of excess reserves if the required ratio for demand deposits were 10 percent ($100) and that for savings deposits 5 percent ($50). Actually, under present regulations the required ratio for demand deposits averages closer to 15 percent, so such a shift would produce nearer $100 of excess reserves. This amount can spread through the banking system and lead to a greater expansion of loans than would otherwise occur, even though demand deposits themselves would expand less.

Loan Repayments and Deposits

It follows from the principles explained in this chapter that since we use checking accounts as money and since banks credit the proceeds of loans to customers' accounts, an expansion of commercial bank loans expands the money supply. The statement is true of the expansion of

---

[2] Of course, it does happen that people deposit currency into savings accounts, but this fact should not obscure the general rule that, in the long run, the public withdraws more currency than it deposits.

any bank assets, not only *loan expansion*. As we have seen, acquisition of securities by banks has the same effect. Whether the banks "lend" to the federal government by buying its newly issued bonds or whether they extend credit to other levels of government, to businesses, or to consumers, all these acquisitions of assets by the commercial banks add to the volume of deposits.

When banks dispose of assets, deposits shrink correspondingly. We have already seen that when Mr. Brown repaid his bank loan, he did so by drawing a check on his account in favor of the bank. The bank collects by canceling that much of the deposit it owes him. Just as extending loans expands deposits, the payment of loans contracts them. But *deposit contraction* creates excess reserves again so that the banks are again in position to expand loans. There is a constant process of repayment of old loans and extension of new loans going on so that, in general, the level of deposits and money supply tends to remain the allowable multiple of available bank reserves.

SUMMARY

We conclude this chapter by referring to the example of the five huge corporations whose debts might be used as money in an imaginary society. These corporations "paid" their employees and stockholders with claims on their output, and these claims could be used to purchase the output of any corporation because the corporations could cancel the debts held against each other. It may now be clearer how, in effect, the commercial banks provide a system that approximates this imaginary one. Corporations, governments, and individuals do not issue claims against themselves which they give to others in exchange for goods but, instead, they issue claims against themselves to their banks. The banks exchange one claim for another. They accept a promissory note, as in the example of Mr. Brown, or some other type of evidence of debt, and they give for it a claim on themselves, a demand deposit. Other businesses and individuals will accept checks or claims drawn on the bank deposit where they might hesitate to accept the claims on unknown or numerous other businesses and individuals. Once put in circulation in this way, the bank-deposit money may be used several times until eventually an equivalent amount is eliminated by the payment of the loan that gave rise to it.

The money system has evolved greatly from the times when money was a generally acceptable commodity which people accepted because it was a valuable physical thing. Many people still think of money in these terms and relate the dollar in their wallet or checking account to gold, silver, or some other commodity. But, as we have seen in this chapter, the money supply is mainly peoples' claims on banks which they can transfer to other people by the use of checks. And the remainder of the money supply, our coins and currency, is provided through a machinery which basically allows us to have our money in whichever form is more convenient.

Economic Terms for Review

medium of exchange	demand deposits
unit of account	excess reserves
standard of deferred payments	deposit creation
store of value	reserve requirement
coins and currency	cash drain
standard money	loan expansion
check clearing	deposit contraction

Questions for Review

1. Why is barter difficult in a modern society?
2. Give an example of a transaction in which you might use money as a unit of account but not as a medium of exchange.
3. Explain: "Money always has the same price."
4. What characterizes a demand deposit?
5. What has given rise to the present volume of demand deposits?
6. Suppose a bank's balance sheet shows cash reserves, $100,000, and demand deposits, $800,000, and no other relevant figures. If its reserve requirement is 10 percent, how much can it lend?
7. If no other bank has any excess reserves and the bank in Question 6 lends all it can, by how much can loans of all banks expand?

Questions for Analysis

1. Suppose the Federal Reserve banks purchase $1 million of securities in the market. How are commercial banks affected?
2. With what does a borrower repay a loan to his bank? How are total bank deposits affected by the repayment?
3. Suppose Mr. Smith repays a loan to Mr. Jones by giving him a check for $500. Compare with Question 2.
4. Why does the volume of currency in circulation rise in the long run?
5. If your city should introduce parking meters, how would the volume of coin and currency be affected?
6. Suppose there are no excess reserves in the banking system and the Federal Reserve buys $100 million of securities. If the required reserve ratio is 10 percent, by how much may member bank deposits subsequently rise?
7. Why does a commercial bank compete for time deposits?

Case for Decision

Citizens National Bank is a small bank in a suburb of a midwestern city. It has been operating only a few years, in which time it has grown to $11 million of assets. It has $10 million of deposits and $1 million of capital.

The directors of the bank have been wondering whether they have been competing aggressively enough for savings accounts. Dr. Drill, a major stockholder and a dentist, argues that the bank should attract at least $5 million of additional savings accounts from the suburban area. The bank now has about half demand and half savings accounts. The bank has been paying 3 percent on savings accounts, and Dr. Drill argues that this rate has been too low because savers can get 4 percent in the city banks and 4.5 percent at the local savings and loan association.

Mr. Count, president of the bank, agrees that the bank would have no difficulty in lending an additional $5 million at 6 percent, but he is skeptical that going to the 4-percent rate on savings would boost deposits by that amount. He suggests that since people can get 4.5 percent at the savings and loan, they probably keep accounts at Citizens National only because of greater convenience. He also wonders how much of any growth in savings accounts would merely be a shift from demand deposits already at Citizens. He notes that boosting the rate would increase the amount of interest paid for the $5 million of savings deposits Citizens already has.

The directors decide they need more information and ask John Derby, a recent college graduate who has been working at the bank for about a year, to collect some relevant information. He finds that, as a national average, savings accounts in areas like Citizens is in are about $500 per person, that the local population is about 20,000 and growing, and that the local savings and loan association has about $5 million of share accounts. He has sampled the existing savings accounts at Citizens and finds that they are generally held by people who also have demand deposits and live near by.

Mr. Derby knows that he will probably be asked to make a recommendation on whether to raise the savings rate to 4 percent when he presents his findings. What are the pros and cons of doing so?

The Federal Reserve System

The Federal Reserve Act was passed in 1913 to provide for the United States the services of a *central bank*. Central banks had evolved naturally in older countries, and indeed the United States had twice in its early days established such banks (the First Bank of the United States, 1791–1811, and the Second Bank of the United States, 1816–1836). Both of these early American central banks ceased operation when their original twenty-year charters were allowed to expire, as there was much political opposition to them. Since commercial banks do need some facilities for clearing checks, occasional borrowing from one other, and other services, they developed the system of correspondent banks mentioned in Chapter 11. The larger city banks came to act somewhat as central banks for their country correspondents, but they lacked the one basic power of a true central bank—they were unable to create additional bank reserves when they were needed. This deficiency in the American system led to severe financial strigencies periodically and to the passage of the Federal Reserve Act.

FEDERAL RESERVE BANKS

Opposition to the early Banks of the United States was mainly due to the fear of having control of bank loans and the money supply in the hands of a single institution. This popular fear was still strong when the Federal Reserve Act was being debated. This fact largely explains the manner in which the Federal Reserve System was organized and the functions originally assigned to it.

Board of Governors

Instead of a single Federal Reserve bank, the Congress provided for regional central banks to be coordinated by a Federal Reserve Board. Today, however, the coordination is such that, in effect, there is a single central bank that operates in 12 major cities and other branch cities of the nation. The geographical organization of the System is shown in Figure 12-1; the map gives the location of the 12 banks and their branches.

Politically, the system was a compromise between a governmental central bank and a central bank owned and operated by private banking interests. The original membership of the Federal Reserve Board consisted of the Secretary of the Treasury, the Comptroller of the Currency,[1]

---

[1] The Comptroller of the Currency is a Treasury official responsible for the supervision of commercial banks chartered by the federal government. His title comes from the fact that the National Banking Act (1863), which provides for such chartering, also established the rules under which such banks could issue banknotes.

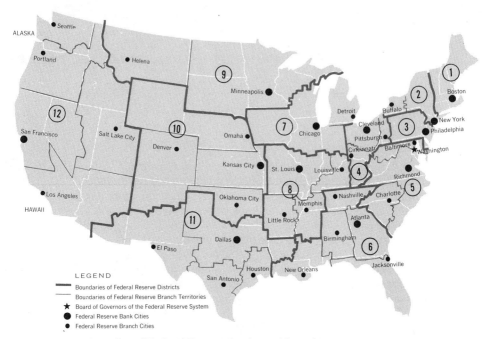

Figure 12-1. Location of Federal Reserve banks and branches.   Source: Federal Reserve System.

and five others appointed by the President to staggered ten-year terms providing a degree of continuity and independence. It was later decided that the Treasury, which might be a very large borrower from the banking system, should not have membership on the Board, and the ex officio members were removed. The composition and number of the Board's members have been changed a few times, but since 1935, when the Secretary of the Treasury and the Comptroller of the Currency were dropped in an extensive revision of the act, the Board has consisted of seven members appointed for overlapping fourteen-year terms. It was also renamed the *Board of Governors* of the Federal Reserve System. There has been much debate in recent years over whether the President should appoint the members for shorter terms, perhaps for four-year terms coincident with his own, and whether he should appoint the chairman at the beginning of each presidential term. The chairman now serves for four years but is appointed when the preceding term expires rather than when a President of the United States is elected.

Federal Open Market Committee

In many ways another group may be considered as important in determining Federal Reserve policies as the Board itself. This is the Federal Open Market Committee. The System carries out its policies largely through purchasing and selling government securities in the open market. Decisions on these actions are taken at meetings held every three weeks by this committee. It consists of the Board of Governors plus five of the twelve presidents of the reserve banks. The President of the Federal Reserve Bank of New York is always one of the five because of the importance of that reserve bank in carrying out both domestic and international transactions. The other four presidents represent banks set up in groups, but in practice all twelve presidents attend and participate in discussions prior to action taken by the twelve members of the committee (seven governors and five presidents). The presidents are also accompanied by their chief economic advisers so that meetings of the Federal Open Market Committee reflect the judgment and knowledge of regional business conditions of representatives of all twelve banks.

Other Committees

Besides the Board of Governors and the Federal Open Market Committee, several other organizations facilitate exchange of information and judgments. The Federal Advisory Council consists of a representative from each Federal Reserve district and meets with the Board at least four times a year. The representatives are usually prominent bankers, and they are selected by the respective Federal Reserve banks. The name of the committee is descriptive; the committee advises the Board in accordance with its views of business and financial conditions and recommends policy actions.

To coordinate the operations of the reserve banks, the Board also utilizes the Conference of Presidents of the reserve banks and the Conference of Chairmen of the reserve banks. These groups meet from time to time to discuss problems of operation in contrast to problems of monetary and credit policy. There are also several committees consisting of representatives of the banks and the Board that coordinate research, study special problems, and the like.

Organization of the Reserve Banks

It was originally planned that each reserve bank would be semi-independent and autonomous, so these banks are organized with their own boards of directors and officers. Each reserve bank has a board of directors of nine members, of whom six are elected by the member banks of the district. Three Class A directors are representatives of the banking community and are nearly always bankers. Member banks are classified into three size groups, each group electing one Class A director. Each group also elects one Class B director, who may not be a director, an officer, or an employee of a bank but who represents the business, agricultural, or industrial sector of the district. The three remaining directors—the Class C directors—are selected by the Board of Governors to represent the public generally. They, too, cannot be bankers. The Board of Governors designates one of the Class C directors as chairman.

As in any corporation, the directors select the officers of the Federal Reserve bank, but the selections for president and first vice-president must be approved by the Board of Governors. Each branch of a reserve bank also has a board of directors selected in part by the district reserve bank and in part by the Board of Governors.

In order to establish the reserve banks as nongovernmental banks, it was decided that the member banks would buy the stock of the reserve banks. While in a technical sense, therefore, the member banks are the stockholders of the reserve banks, they do not own them in the usual sense of controlling their policies and having unlimited claims on their earnings. A member bank must purchase stock in its reserve bank equal to 3 percent of its own capital and surplus; the law provides that this figure can be as high as 6 percent, but only 3 percent has been called. In return, the member bank receives a limited dividend of 6 percent on its investment.

The reserve banks are not intended to operate for profit but to follow monetary policies that are in the public interest and that achieve or maintain price-level stability, economic growth, and high employment. They are now so large and hold such large quantities of government securities purchased in the open market that they have much larger incomes than were contemplated at the beginning. The reserve banks therefore return to the Treasury, as a kind of tax, most of their earnings after expenses.

Member Banks

When the Federal Reserve System was established, the act required all federally chartered commercial banks—the national banks—to become members. Those banks chartered by their respective states are more numerous, but in general the national banks are larger. State banks may join the System, upon approval and acceptance by their reserve banks. Some, especially the larger ones, have done so. Consequently, the bulk of the commercial banking system, measured by assets or deposits, is in the System, but in terms of numbers of banks there are more nonmembers.

The principal advantages of membership are access to the check-clearing system, described in Chapter 11, and to the *discount window*. The latter refers to the fact that, under certain circumstances and limitations, member banks may borrow from their reserve banks. This is called *discounting*. The disadvantage is that in most states the member banks must carry higher reserve ratios than are required by state law for non-member banks. Since a small state bank can generally obtain the same check-clearing and borrowing services, along with certain others such as advice on investments, from a correspondent bank, many of the smaller banks remain outside the system. In fact, nonmember banks may also arrange to clear checks through the system.

The Banking System

To foreign observers the American banking system seems a rather unorganized one. In the first place, American business traditions and preferences have led to the establishment of many local banks, totaling over 13,000, while in most countries there are very few banks but these few operate many branches. In England, for example, there are eleven chartered banks that are members of the London Clearing House, and five of these do the bulk of the banking business in that country, while in Canada there are nine chartered banks.

Since there are so many banks, there is considerable heterogeneity in the American banking system. A few banks are very large, operate all over the world, and have many branches. Their deposits run into the billions of dollars. Then there are a few hundred banks that cannot be called small because their deposits are in the hundreds of millions, but neither are they huge. Most banks are considerably smaller, and many local banks have deposits totaling only a few million. About a third of the states permit banks to operate branches anywhere in the state, another third permit branches in restricted areas, and the remaining states prohibit branch banking altogether.

Banks may be classified as state or national, according to their charter, and as members or nonmembers of the Federal Reserve System, the members including all national banks and some state banks. In addition, since the Federal Deposit Insurance Corporation (FDIC) was established in the 1930s, they can be classified as members and nonmembers of this institution. The FDIC insures the deposits of banks, at present up to $20,000 per account. All member banks must join the FDIC and others may be accepted. Nearly all banks have joined, so a considerably greater degree of uniformity of regulations and supervision has been achieved than appears on the surface. The data on the structure of the banking system at the end of 1969 are shown in Table 12-1. Of course, the figures on the commercial banks do not approach describing the whole financial system, which includes such other deposit-type institutions as savings and loan associations, mutual savings banks, and credit unions, and also many other *financial intermediaries* such as pension funds and life insurance companies.

The uniformity just mentioned comes from the system of examining and supervising the banks. The basic legal responsibility for supervising banks lies with the Comptroller of the Currency for national banks, with the Federal Reserve System for member banks, with the state authorities (the Commissioner or Superintendent of Banks) for state banks, and with the FDIC for insured banks. Thus many banks would be subject to numerous examinations and supervisory rulings were it not for the fact that these agencies have arranged for the Comptroller of the Currency to take primary responsibility for examining national banks, the Federal Reserve banks for examining state member banks, and the FDIC for examining state nonmember banks; those state banks that have not joined the FDIC are responsible only to their state authorities. Even though these arrangements greatly simplify the procedure for examinations, banks may still be subject to conflicting rulings. For example, the Comptroller might rule that some action is legal for national banks, but the Federal Reserve might rule that the action is illegal for member banks.

Table 12-1
Number, Assets, and Demand and Time Deposits,*
Classes of Commercial Banks, Dec. 31, 1969
(Billions of Dollars)

Class of Bank	Number of Banks	Total Assets	Demand Deposits	Time Deposits
All commercial banks	13,661	$530.7	$208.8	$193.7
All insured commercial banks	13,464	527.6	207.3	193.1
National banks	4,668	313.9	121.7	114.2
State member banks	1,201	119.2	48.0	35.4
Nonmember banks	7,595	94.5	37.6	43.5

° Deposits are exclusive of interbank and U.S. government deposits. Hypothecated deposits have been deducted from time deposits; these consist of funds repaid on installment loans ($1.1 billion for all banks).
Source: *Federal Reserve Bulletin*, July, 1970, pp. A-21 to A-23.

SERVICE FUNCTIONS

When the Federal Reserve banks were established, they were not thought of as institutions to control the money supply or to attempt to regulate business conditions to the extent that they are today. These functions have developed with time and with the growth of knowledge of how the monetary system affects the economy generally. Rather, the reserve banks were designed to perform certain services for banks, some of which were inadequately performed before and some of which were to be new. The former group of services consisted largely of clearing and collecting checks, transferring funds around the country, and handling the issuance of new debt by the Treasury. The second group related mainly to the loans the reserve banks were empowered to make to their member banks. One of the important functions of the new system was to provide the mechanism for supplying currency.

Transferring Funds

The manner in which demand deposits are transferred by check through the Federal Reserve banks was described in Chapter 11, but there are other ways in which the reserve banks facilitate the movement of funds. In 1966, the reserve banks in one way or another transferred over $5.5 trillion of funds in addition to $2.5 trillion in checks. The System operates a wire transfer whereby a commercial bank can "send" a depositor's funds to a recipient in another Federal Reserve district. Funds are also transferred when the Treasury spends from its balance at the reserve banks and its checks are received by commercial banks from depositors. Besides checks, other kinds of money orders are collected through the System. Coupons for bond interest and postal money orders are two examples.

Fiscal Agency

As _fiscal agent_ for the United States Treasury, the reserve banks handle the Treasury's deposit at these banks and many of the details of management of the public debt. Many of the taxes collected by the Treasury, as well as proceeds of sales of securities, are deposited first in _tax and loan accounts_ at commercial banks. The Treasury then transfers these funds to its Federal Reserve deposit at about the rate it is drawing checks against this deposit. As is explained a little later, the purpose of this arrangement is to minimize the effect on bank reserves of Treasury funds moving into and out of the deposit at the Federal Reserve.

When the Treasury is about to sell a new issue of securities, the Federal Reserve banks accept applications for the securities from banks and other buyers. Generally the applications exceed the available offering and the Federal Reserve allots the securities in accordance with Treasury instructions, collects for them, and distributes the securities. The reserve banks also redeem securities for the Treasury, make exchanges when holders want different denominations, transmit securities across the country (by canceling them in one place and issuing replacements in another), issue and redeem savings bonds, and perform other tasks required by the existence of the federal debt.

Coin and Currency

Chapter 11 also explained that the reserve banks are the reservoir for the nation's coin and currency. The Treasury mints and then deposits coins at the Federal Reserve, which is thus able to pay them out when banks wish to make withdrawals from their own deposit accounts. There is a large flow of coins between the banks and their reserve banks. Banks seasonally receive coins in excess of what they wish to hold, so just as a person or business would, they send them on to their (reserve) banks. This coin has to be counted—usually by mechanical means—and the proper amounts credited. Each year the reserve banks handle approximately 10 trillion coins worth about a trillion dollars. When needed in circulation, the coins again flow back to the banks and from them to the public.

The development of the present method of issuing currency illustrates one of the principal reasons for the establishment of the reserve banks. Under the old system, national banks could issue notes by depositing an equivalent amount of government bonds with the Comptroller of the Currency. This system was designed to make the banknotes as safe as the government bonds, but it did not work well because there was no assurance that the banks could provide the proper amount of hand-to-hand money. It should be understood that a bank might issue notes for two reasons. First, when the use of currency in retail and similar transactions rose, people would cash checks in order to obtain the banknotes. The national bank would merely exchange its deposit liability for a note liability. Second, the bank might issue notes if that was the form in which a borrower wanted his funds. Half a century ago and earlier, this was often the case.

Several times—principally in 1873, 1893, and 1907—it happened that the demands for currency exceeded the amounts that the banks could supply in the form of national banknotes. At these times the banks had to dip into their supplies of federal government currency that they could count as bank reserves. When these Treasury issues flowed into the hands of the public, the banks ran short of required reserves and had to restrict their loans. Attempts to obtain funds to lend by selling securities caused chaos in bond markets because many banks were trying to sell with few or none buying. Businesses could not get financing, securities prices and commodity prices fell and, at the worst, there was financial panic. Obviously, a better way for both currency to be supplied and additional bank reserves to be obtainable at such times was needed.

SUPPLYING BANK RESERVES

The foregoing twin objectives were related in the provision that member banks might borrow from their reserve banks when in need of additional reserves and they might withdraw these additional reserve balances as currency if there was an outflow of banknotes to the public. The function of issuing notes was transferred to the reserve banks and a new basis for their issuance worked out.[2] The new *Federal Reserve notes*

[2] Actually, the power of national banks to issue notes was not withdrawn, but by the 1930s the last Treasury bonds which carried the so-called circulation privilege (eligibility as collateral for banknotes) were retired.

were based on the theory then widely held that the volume of money should automatically fluctuate with the uses of money in the production of goods. This was the commercial loan principle, which held, in effect, that if banks made loans only for productive purposes, the money supply could not become excessive.

Discounting

Thus it was written into the law that banks could borrow from the reserve banks when they were short of reserves because of expanding deposits to finance production. Evidence of this condition was supposed to be the fact that such banks would hold the loans of businessmen, farmers, and others for short-term productive purposes. These loans were called *eligible paper* because they were eligible for discount at the reserve banks. By thus *discounting,* or borrowing on, this paper, the member banks could expand their reserve balances at the reserve banks (just as a customer of a bank could expand his deposit by borrowing from the bank) and, if need be, the banks could withdraw Federal Reserve notes from these new balances.

Accordingly, the issuance of these notes was related to the concept of eligibility. If the banks had been discounting, the reserve banks would be holding eligible paper. They could issue Federal Reserve notes as needed by using this eligible paper as collateral. Since the United States was on a gold standard, it was also provided that the notes would have reserves of gold. Under the first rules established, the reserve banks would set aside gold reserves equal to 40 percent and eligible paper equal to 100 percent of the notes they issued. Later the eligible paper percentage was reduced to 60 percent.

The idea of issuing currency on the basis of eligible paper was one of those apparently sound principles that did not work out. First, it was learned that the money supply would not automatically be right under this principle. As one example, in a period of full employment and rising prices, many businesses would want loans, banks would have plenty of eligible paper and, if they could automatically borrow from the reserve banks, they could continue to make more loans and permit more inflation. But what led to change in the arrangements was the opposite condition. In the severe depression of the 1930s, business was stagnant and, as a result of many unpaid loans and depressed security prices, many banks failed. People became afraid of holding bank deposits and, as had happened in past serious depressions, there was a great deal of hoarding. Paying out this currency further depleted the banks' funds and more failed, but they were unable to borrow from their reserve banks because, not having many business loans, they had little eligible paper.

Actually, government securities had been defined as eligible paper from the beginning but, except during World War I, the banks did not have large quantities of such securities. But, as will be clearer after we discuss open-market operations, if the reserve banks would purchase government securities, bank reserves would rise. In order to bring this about and also to permit the banks then to acquire currency, the law was changed so that the reserve banks could use federal government securities as well as eligible paper as collateral. Since the 1930s, then, the Federal Reserve notes have been issued as needed with the required collateral consisting of government securities. This is an interesting throwback to the system in use under the national banking system, with the great difference that under current conditions there is little possibility of a shortage of currency caused by a shortage of government securities. However, the declining relative importance of the government's gold stock has led to the final change in the rules. As the currency supply grew, especially during World War II, it was necessary to lower the reserve of gold to 25 percent and, more recently, to eliminate the requirement, first from deposits at the reserve banks and finally from the Federal Reserve notes.

The original method of issuing currency was said to provide *elasticity* because it was based on eligible paper and the commercial loan principle. The term elasticity meant that the volume of currency would expand and contract with the needs for it. We have now seen that elasticity does not have to be provided by some formula. Rather, it exists if the public can withdraw whatever amount is required and the reserve banks can supply this amount and, when currency is redundant, if the public can deposit it and the banks can send it back to the reserve banks. But it remains true, as it was in the old days, that this flow of currency does affect the banks' reserves. When they pay out currency, they withdraw it from their reserve balances and, when it flows back, they deposit it there. And to the extent that they hold currency, they may count it as legal reserves.[3]

Open-Market Operations

Although the reserve banks were not designed to operate for profit, in the earlier days they did occasionally have to give thought to earning enough to cover expenses. Soon after their establishment, World War I broke out and, during the war, the reserve banks discounted heavily for member banks so that the latter had plenty of funds to lend to business, to government, and to individuals for the purpose of buying the Liberty and Victory loans. Later the member banks began to repay these advances, and the reserve banks sometimes purchased securities in the open market in order to sustain their income from interest payments. It soon became clear that the more they purchased, the more rapidly the member banks repaid their indebtedness. From this experience came the realization, not fully grasped before, that the reserve banks could control the volume of bank reserves through purchasing and selling securities.

It is important to understand how this process works because it has become the principal tool of the Federal Reserve System. Fortunately, it is a simple process. Assume that a Federal Reserve bank purchases a bond for $1,000 and that you are the seller. Actually, virtually all purchases are made from dealers in such securities, but the dealer replaces his inventory by purchasing from others, so in this example the dealer can be left out. The reserve bank makes the purchase by issuing a check drawn on itself. It expands its *Federal Reserve credit* just as a bank expands its bank credit when it credits the proceeds of a loan to a borrower's deposit account. As the seller of the bond, you receive the

[3] Banks generally do not hold more currency than they think they need, including a safety factor, for the same reasons individuals do not. Excess currency is vulnerable to theft, fire, and other forms of loss.

check and presumably deposit it at your bank, which we will assume is a member bank. (If your bank were not a member bank, it would deposit the check at a correspondent bank that is a member.) Your bank sends the check, along with the others it has received on out-of-town banks, to its reserve bank and has them credited to its account there. The other checks will be charged to other banks and reduce their reserves, but this check is different; it is not drawn on another commercial bank but on the reserve bank itself. Consequently, the reserve bank credits it to your bank but cannot charge it to another bank. Therefore, bank reserves in total rise as your bank's reserves go up. This process is shown as follows:

Your Bank		Federal Reserve Bank	
Assets	*Liabilities*	*Assets*	*Liabilities*
Deposit at	Deposits +$1,000	Securities +$1,000	Member bank
Federal Reserve +$1,000			deposits +$1,000

As a matter of fact, the reserve banks could purchase anything under the sun and the results would be the same. The increase in deposits at the reserve bank results from the extension of Federal Reserve credit, not from any magical quality of government securities. As a matter of practice, however, the central bank deals almost exclusively in government securities, but it is revealing to realize that it is the fact that it has added to its assets that permits it to expand its liabilities (deposits).

It is also possible for the seller of securities to be a commercial bank. Sometimes when an individual bank wishes to add to its reserves, it does sell securities which it has been holding for just such a purpose. We may distinguish three possibilities, depending upon the buyer of the securities. The buyer may be another bank which happens to have excess reserves. In this case the buying bank draws a check on its reserve balance, the selling bank deposits the check at the reserve bank, and the first bank's reserves shift to the second bank. Secondly, the buyer may be an individual, a company, a trust, or a savings institution—any member of the public. In this case the buyer draws a check on his bank, and again the selling bank gains reserves from another bank. Thirdly, the buyer may be a Federal Reserve bank, and again it draws a check against itself, which when deposited by the selling bank, adds to the total of bank reserves. No matter who sold the securities, when a Federal Reserve bank buys them, there is an extension of Federal Reserve credit and an expansion of member-bank reserve balances.

Naturally, the process works in reverse. If the reserve bank were to sell and you to buy, you would draw a check on your bank and the reserve bank would collect the check by deducting it from your bank's reserve balance; then your bank would deduct it from your balance. In the foregoing illustration, the figures would be the same but each would be preceded by a minus sign. Again, no matter who buys securities, if the seller is a Federal Reserve bank, there is a contraction of Federal Reserve credit outstanding and a contraction of member-bank reserve balances.

Open-market operations have become the principal tool used by the System to affect member-bank reserves and thus their ability to lend because they are undertaken at the initiative of the System and because they can be exercised in any appropriate volume. In the case of discounting, the initiative is with the member banks who may or may not wish to borrow. The reserve banks can only make discounting more or less attractive by lowering or raising the rate at which they offer to lend.

Reserve Requirements

The third tool in the "tool kit" of the Federal Reserve System is the power of the Board of Governors to change the reserve ratios required of member banks. The Federal Reserve Act was amended in 1935 to permit the Board to require up to twice the percentages originally specified in the act. The minimum and maximum percentages now provided are shown in Table 12-2.

It may be noticed that the minimum is not necessarily half the maximum that may be required, as was just implied. This is because there have been subsequent changes in the legislation. At first there were three classes of cities for reserve purposes. Central reserve cities were New York, Chicago, and St. Louis, then for many years only the first two. Finally in 1962 this classification was dropped. New York and Chicago became reserve cities, along with most major cities which had already been in this classification. All other locations are called country, although they include some fairly large cities. The original reason for this classification was the system of correspondent banks in which country banks carried deposits in large cities and most big banks had deposits in New York and Chicago. Although this system still exists, there appears to be no sound reason to require the New York and Chicago banks to carry higher reserves because of it. In the process of changing requirements and of changing classifications, the figures shown in Table 12-2 finally resulted. The central reserve cities were required to have reserves for demand deposits of 13 percent in the original legislation, and by the 1935 amendment they could have been required to hold 26 percent. The other classifications were originally set at 10 percent and 7 percent, and these percentages still hold true.

The requirements have been changed about twenty times since 1950, so it would be fruitless to examine each change. Until recent years, the general purpose of changing the requirements was simply to increase or decrease excess reserves by a significant amount. While the changes average out to about once a year, it should be recognized that open-market operations are engaged in every day. A small change in reserve requirements is generally a significant change in the reserve situation.

	Table 12-2 Legal Reserve Requirements	
	Minimum Percentage	Maximum Percentage
Net demand deposits		
Reserve city banks	10	22
Country banks	7	14
Time deposits	3	10

For example, demand deposits are roughly $150 billion. A change of 1 percent in the reserve requirement would alter member banks' requirements by $1.5 billion. Total reserves are about $26 billion and, after subtracting reserves required by time and savings deposits, there are about $18 billion for demand deposits. More significant, however, is the fact that excess reserves are usually only a few hundred million. Thus a change of less than 1 percent could significantly change the volume of excess reserves. Consequently, this tool is not considered one that can be used frequently. But when excess reserves accumulate or are deficient in a persistent trend which the system prefers not to offset by large open-market operations, it is called into use.

In recent years, however, another use has come into play. This is the process of changing reserve requirements to make time and savings deposits either more or less attractive for commercial banks. Competition for savings deposits between commercial banks, on the one hand, and savings institutions like savings banks and savings and loan associations, on the other, has sometimes led to problems in markets where these institutions lend, particularly in the mortgage market. The System has consequently developed the ability to temper the willingness of commercial banks to compete by raising or lowering the reserve requirements for time and savings deposits. The higher the requirement, the less attractive such deposits become as more of the funds must be held idle rather than lent.

In recent years the Board has set requirements for demand deposits at about 16.5 percent in reserve cities and 12 percent in country banks. In 1968, in order to tighten up requirements without unduly affecting small banks, the Board raised the reserve city requirement from 16.5 percent to 17 percent on demand deposits in excess of $5 million per bank and the country requirements from 12 percent to 12.5 percent on demand deposits in excess of $5 million. Similarly, it set the requirement at 3 percent for savings and time deposits up to $5 million but at 6 percent for deposits above this level. The *Federal Reserve Bulletin* publishes each month in the statistical section the current requirements.[4]

Coordinating the Tools

Discounting, open-market operations, and changing reserve requirements have become the standard, basic tools of the Federal Reserve System. It has others, to be described shortly, but first it should be observed how these three tools are used in conjunction with each other.

To oversimplify at first: If the System wished to restrain or to contract bank reserves, it could:

1. Raise reserve requirements.
2. Sell in the open market.
3. Raise the discount rate.

We have seen how each of these would reduce excess reserves. The first action would not affect total reserves, but it would redefine some or all of existing excess reserves as required reserves. Open-market sales would

---

[4] All member banks and most libraries receive the *Bulletin*. It is a valuable source of information on financial matters.

contract the volume of total reserves. A higher discount rate would make it more costly to borrow reserves from reserve banks.

In actuality, the measures taken by the System would depend upon the degree of urgency and the degree of effect desired. As already noted, reserve requirements are not changed frequently. Rather, they tend to be a sort of frame of reference within which open-market operations are carried out. The use of the discount rate requires additional comment. It cannot be described accurately in a few sentences because the way in which the rate has been used has changed from time to time.

Originally, in 1913, it appeared that the only influence the reserve banks would have over the member banks would be through this rate. If the reserve banks wished to restrain a growth in bank reserves, they would charge more for discounts and vice versa. In fact, there was lack of agreement over whether the act gave the member banks the *right* to borrow or whether it gave them the *privilege,* which might be withheld by the reserve banks.

In any event, discounting was the principal and almost sole means of extending Federal Reserve credit for the first decade of the System's existence. As open-market operations became more important, however, the System succeeded in establishing the idea that discounting was a privilege. This meant that a member bank might borrow but only if it had sufficient reason in the opinion of the reserve bank. The Board issued Regulation A, setting forth the rules for discounting. This regulation made it clear that banks were not to borrow continuously but only when unusual events caused them to need reserves in excess of those provided by normal good management. For example, a bank in a locality greatly affected by seasonal factors might have an outflow of funds at one time of the year which would make it unable to serve its regular borrowers. The bank should anticipate this outflow, but it might easily miscalculate and run short. Such a situation would entitle it to borrow for a period of a few weeks. Or a bank might have a wholly unexpected period of heavy withdrawals.

Banks are expected to manage their reserve positions with future inflows and outflows of deposits and reserves in mind. They acquire *secondary reserve assets* when funds flow in which they expect to dispose of when they again need funds. These assets are highly liquid and stable in price, like Treasury bills.[5] A bank in need of reserves normally disposes of secondary reserve assets before going to the discount window. If it has to dispose of an asset that is earning 4 percent but would have to pay 5 percent at the discount window, discounting would also be more expensive. The discount rate has usually borne some such relationship as this to the yields on secondary reserve assets — that is, it would be more

[5] A Treasury bill is an obligation due in not over a year and sold at a discount that represents the interest. The Treasury sells bills each week, largely to replace those maturing that week but sometimes also for "new money." Some mature in three months, some in six months, some in a year, and some on particular tax dates. For example, a six-months bill might sell at the weekly auction for $975. The $25 by which the bill will appreciate when it is redeemed for $1,000 at maturity represents a discount rate of 5 percent, as the $25 is for a half year. The bill will be worth $1,000 at maturity, so its price can fluctuate very little over the six months of its life. There is an enormous market in these bills. A bank can buy bills that mature in any week of the coming year. Besides using bills and other short-term assets, banks sometimes borrow excess reserves from one another by dealing in *federal funds.*

expensive to discount than to dispose of such assets. This relationship has strengthened the banks' reluctance to borrow and the privilege aspect of the process. However, at other times the Board and the reserve banks have not raised the rate above those on secondary reserve assets when interest rates have been at high levels. Such a relationship generally indicates a greater willingness of the reserve banks to lend, but only for acceptable reasons.

In a period of rising unemployment and a general falling off of business activity, the System would presumably reverse the actions previously listed. While it might not change reserve requirements unless it wanted to make a drastic easing of the reserve situation, it would expand bank reserves by open-market purchases. As banks obtained excess reserves, they would repay any existing indebtedness to the reserve banks and, as excess reserves accumulated, they would purchase secondary reserve assets. The greater demand for such assets would raise their prices somewhat and thus lower the yields on such securities. As interest rates came down through these actions and through the banks' greater willingness to seek out borrowers, the reserve banks would lower the discount rate accordingly. The timing of the decline in the discount rate would tend to depend upon the effect the System wanted. The financial community considers a change in the rate an important indicator of the System's thinking. The *announcement effects* of a change may be very important, but unfortunately they may also be unpredictable. For example, if the Board should announce that the reserve banks are lowering the discount rate from 5 percent to 4.5 percent, the reaction might be that this action will lead to expansion, rising prices, higher profits, and prosperity in general. But at other times the action might be interpreted as a sign that the System anticipates a recession which it is trying to check and people might take the reduction as a signal of recession rather than recovery.

Recent Proposals

The operations of the discount mechanism have been the object of study by Federal Reserve officials, academicians, bankers, and others during the whole period of the System. After a recent special study lasting over three years, officials of the System announced in 1968 that they favored a drastic revision of the workings of the discount window. To a large extent, this revision would return to the earlier emphasis on discounting as a source of reserves for member banks and make the reserve banks more *lenders of last resort,* as they were thought to be in the early days of the System. It would also partially restore the idea that member banks have a right to borrow from their reserve banks.

If the proposed changes become general practice, discounting will become much more common. The arrangements will include:

1. Member banks will have quotas based on their size within which they may automatically borrow.
2. Loans may be made for periods of several months where banks have serious seasonal inflows and outflows of deposits, such as in resort areas and some farming districts.
3. The discount rate will be changed much more frequently than at present, to keep it in line with market rates.

4. In emergencies the reserve banks will lend to nonmember institutions, such as nonmember banks, savings and loan associations, and mutual savings banks, but at rates higher than those charged member banks.

As a result of these changes, the reserve banks would presumably need to rely less heavily on frequent open-market operations to adjust the supply of reserves because member banks could make their own adjustments more readily. At the same time, banks would probably do less trading in federal funds whereby they borrow excess reserves from one another.

Under the Regulation A restrictions currently in effect, borrowings have seldom approached $1 billion, usually being about $300 million when most banks have adequate reserves and about $700 million in periods when reserves are tight. It is expected that borrowings might vary between $2.5 and $4.0 billion under the proposed rules. To avoid having the reserve banks supply permanent capital to member banks, however, the prohibition against continual indebtedness would remain. Each bank could use its quota, if desired, perhaps half of the time. Since reserve requirements are calculated as an average over a period of time (one week), a bank could borrow a large amount for a few days or a smaller amount for a longer period.

Regulation Q

In recent years the Board's power to regulate the interest paid by member banks on their time and savings accounts has become a fourth tool of monetary control, along with discounting, open-market operations, and changing reserve requirements. This power was granted in the emergency banking legislation of the 1930s but was of little importance until the 1960s, when competition among financial institutions for such deposits became acute.

By changing the ceilings established under its Regulation Q, the Board can strongly influence the public's willingness to hold time and savings deposits. When the banks are permitted—and are willing—to pay higher rates than are available on competing open-market instruments such as three-to-five-year Treasury securities, the public tends to hold time deposits. This is especially true of large corporations, whose treasurers carefully compute the yields they can obtain for temporarily idle funds. If the Board limits the maximum rates banks can pay below those on competing assets, the public tends to invest in such assets rather than channeling funds through the banks.

Regulation Q is important also in directing the competition between commercial banks and savings institutions. Before 1966 there were no direct controls over the rates paid by savings banks and savings and loan associations. In that year there was unusually active competition for funds, and the Board permitted commercial banks to pay increased rates. Savings institutions were unable to attract funds and had to limit their lending, especially their mortgage loans in which they specialize. As a result of this situation, legislation was passed to give the Federal Home Loan Bank Board authority to regulate the interest rates paid by the savings and loans associations and the FDIC authority to regulate those paid by insured savings banks.

Other Regulations

From time to time, circumstances have led to legislation authorizing the Board of Governors to limit extension of bank credit to be used for specific purposes. One of the most widely known of these powers is that to set margin requirements for purchases of securities. The Board is empowered by the Securities Exchange Act of 1934 to prescribe maximum loan values for stocks beyond which loans may not be extended for the purchase of such stocks. If, for example, the maximum loan value is 20 percent of the current market price, the purchaser must *margin* a loan of this amount with at least 80 percent from his own funds.

During and for a time after World War II, the Board had authority to limit loans for installment purchases and mortgage loans. It did so by establishing loan values as percentages of purchase price and maximum periods within which loans must be repaid. The purpose was to reduce demands for goods and housing in short supply.

Besides these specific regulations, the Federal Reserve System has certain indirect influences on bank lending for various purposes through what is called *moral suasion* or, less respectfully, its "open-mouth policy." Reserve officials may try to lead the financial community to act in certain ways through speeches to gatherings and conventions, through articles in banking journals, and through letters to member banks. Sometimes moral suasion may be coupled with other controls; for example, the Board may imply that discounts will be refused to banks making too many loans of certain types.

In summary, one should note that Regulation Q and the regulations over certain kinds of loans do not operate by affecting the volume of bank reserves but by attempting to influence the *flow* of loans into certain uses. Open-market operations and discounting affect the total volume of reserves available for loans, and reserve requirements determine how much of the total is required and how much is excess.

SOURCES AND USES OF BANK RESERVES

It follows from the foregoing discussion that the reserve banks can create and destroy bank reserves, which are essentially member-bank deposits at the reserve banks. These deposits may be withdrawn as currency, which is also bank reserves if held by banks but a loss of reserves when paid out to the public for circulation. We have seen, therefore, that Federal Reserve credit is an important source of bank reserves and that currency in circulation is an important drain or use of reserves. In order to see why the Federal Reserve may be expanding or contracting its own credit, we need to survey all the factors that influence bank reserves. The System may merely be offsetting other factors in order to maintain a steady volume of reserves, or it may be attempting to change the total. Often, the System is a source of reserves in order to offset a use, so we look first at these uses.

Uses of Reserves

By far the most important factor that tends to reduce bank reserves is currency in circulation, as already described. There is at present over $50 billion in circulation. This is the grand total of the currency (and coin) in cash registers, pockets, parking meters, wallets, sugar bowls, mattresses, and desk drawers; statistically speaking it also undoubtedly includes sums buried, burned, or otherwise destroyed (but not stolen—that currency still exists). This currency has been withdrawn in gradually increasing amount from the banks. If suddenly the public no longer needed or wanted currency, it would flow back to the banks and be deposited in their reserve accounts.

The other uses of reserves are principally the other accounts that are held at the reserve banks. The reserve banks are not open to the general public, but they hold deposits of nonmember banks who wish to clear checks through the system and deposits of the United States Treasury, foreign governments and central banks, and international agencies. When funds flow on balance from depositors at commercial banks—the general public—to any of these institutions, there is a corresponding flow of member-bank reserves to these institutions' accounts.

As an illustration, consider what happens when taxes are paid to the Treasury. The Treasury may, and to a large extent does, deposit these funds at commercial banks in the first instance, but it also maintains a balance, often around $1 billion, at the reserve banks. As it depletes this balance by spending checks, the Treasury replenishes it partly by direct deposit of tax checks and partly by drawing on the tax and loan accounts at commercial banks. For simplicity, assume a tax check is deposited directly at the Federal Reserve. It is credited to the account of the Treasury and charged to the account of the bank on which it is drawn. The member bank balances its books by offsetting its loss of reserve balance with a reduction in the check-drawer's balance. Whenever the Treasury's balance rises, then, the effect is to reduce bank reserves unless the effect is offset by some other change. Increases in other accounts at the reserve banks work in the same manner.

Sources of Reserves

Federal Reserve credit is the principal source of bank reserves, and the next largest is the gold stock of the United States government. When the gold stock rises, bank reserves rise accordingly and when the gold stock declines, as it has in recent years, it reduces bank reserves.

This relationship exists because the United States has a gold standard—not the old type in which gold coins circulated and any money could be exchanged for gold, but the international gold standard. Monetary gold is used only to settle transactions with international agencies at the official price of $35 per ounce, and the Treasury exchanges gold for dollars at that price. Since an ounce of gold is thus defined as $35, the Treasury can spend $35 for an ounce of gold and still have $35, because that is what an ounce of gold is.

Gold may enter the gold stock either from domestic mines or from abroad. Suppose an American mining company has produced gold worth, at the official price, $100,000. When it sells this gold to the Treasury, it receives a check drawn by the Treasury on the reserve bank and deposits it at its own commercial bank. The bank sends it on to be credited to its reserve account, and the check is collected by being charged to the Treasury's balance. The reserve balance goes up, the Treasury's balance goes down. To this point, the example is the same as if the Treasury had purchased typewriters or paid salaries. Its balance (a use of reserves) has gone down, so reserves have gone up. But since gold is the monetary metal, the Treasury can deposit the amount involved to its account, thus building its balance back up to where it started. The way in which it does this is to place the gold in the Treasury vaults at Fort Knox or elsewhere and issue an equivalent amount of gold certificates, which it deposits at the reserve banks. Thus the effect of the rise in the gold stock is to increase bank reserves; it also increases the volume of bank deposits (of the mining company).

If the gold came from abroad, the process would be similar if the seller deposited his sales receipts in a commercial bank, which is usually the case. If the seller had an account at the reserve bank and deposited his funds there, foreign balances would rise rather than member-bank reserve balances. The gold (source) would be offset by the foreign balance (use) without affecting bank reserves in this case.

The transaction involving domestically mined gold may be summarized through the balance sheets of the commercial bank and the Federal Reserve bank:

Commercial Bank		*Federal Reserve Bank*	
Assets	*Liabilities*	*Assets*	*Liabilities*
Reserve balance +$100,000	Deposits +$100,000	Gold certificates +$100,000	Member-bank balances +$100,000

Since Federal Reserve credit and gold are the two largest sources and currency in circulation is the largest use, the three may be put together in the *bank-reserve equation.* Federal Reserve credit plus the gold stock minus currency in circulation equals member-bank reserves. Because of the existence of other sources and uses, this equation is far from accurate, but it does present a broad picture of the important factors affecting bank reserves in the United States. In January, 1970, for example, Federal Reserve credit amounted to $62.8 billion. This sum was accounted for by $56.3 billion of government securities held by the reserve banks as the result of open-market operations, by about $965 million of discounts, and by about $5.5 of other forms of Federal Reserve credit. The gold stock amounted to $11.1 billion. These two sources had created therefore $73.9 billion of bank reserves, but $52.7 had been withdrawn as currency in circulation. These three factors would thus account for member-bank reserve balances of $21.2 billion. Actually such balances were $23.6 billion. The discrepancy arises from the other sources and uses.

The principal remaining source to be mentioned is Treasury currency outstanding, which amounted to $6.9 billion. Nearly all this sum was fractional coin, supplied as we have described earlier, and the rest was small amounts of types of paper money no longer produced but still in circulation. Production of coin by the Treasury is a source of bank reserves because it represents dollars which must be somewhere—either in the other uses or else in bank reserves. Most of it, in fact, is included in currency in circulation, but if these dollars had not been provided as Treasury currency, they would have had to come from Federal Reserve credit.

A complete tabulation of sources and uses of bank reserves is shown in Table 12-3. It is not necessary to understand the operation of every factor in the table, but it is important to realize the table includes every factor a change in which affects bank reserves. The one factor that is subject to control is Federal Reserve credit. Consequently, the provision of Federal Reserve credit does not take place in a vacuum but with regard to changes in the other factors.

The balance of payments of the United States in recent years has resulted in an outflow of gold. To prevent a corresponding decline in mem-

---

Table 12-3
Sources and Uses of Bank Reserves, January, 1970 *
(Millions of Dollars)

Sources

Federal Reserve credit		
Government securities		$56,273
Discounts and advances		964
Float †		3,429
Other Federal Reserve assets		2,114
	Total Federal Reserve credit	$62,853
Gold stock		11,141
Treasury currency outstanding		6,856
	Total sources	$80,850

Uses

Currency in circulation		$52,722
Treasury cash holdings		655
Treasury deposit		1,206
Foreign deposits		170
Other deposits		642
Other liabilities and capital		2,044
	Total uses	$57,439

Member bank reserves

Balances at reserve banks		$23,566
Currency and coin		5,272
	Total reserves	$28,838

° The data are averages of daily figures for January, 1970. The totals are not precise because of rounding and minor omissions.

† Float is not explained in the text. It arises because of the time schedule according to which checks going through the Federal Reserve System are collected. Sometimes checks are credited to the accounts of recipient banks before they are charged to the drawers' banks. For a short time the balances are carried by both banks, and at any moment of time this is a significant amount.

Source: *Federal Reserve Bulletin*, February, 1970, p. A-4.

ber-bank reserves, the Federal Reserve has expanded its credit correspondingly through open-market purchases. Each year the volume of currency in circulation rises. This increase might be supplied as Treasury currency but, since it is not, the reserve banks replace the lost reserve balances by open-market purchases. Each year at the Christmas season, currency flows out and the effects are offset by open-market operations; early in the following year reverse flows usually occur. So the System is constantly *stabilizing* the supply of member-bank reserves but, at the same time, it is carrying out its policies of easing or tightening the supply for the purpose of affecting business conditions.

SUMMARY

The Federal Reserve System was established in 1913 to provide the services of a central bank. The Federal Reserve banks became the issuers of hand-to-hand currency. An important early function of the reserve banks was to lend to the member banks through the discount process, but in later years the reserve banks (under the direction of the Federal Open Market Committee) took a more active role in controlling the volume of bank reserves through open-market operations. By coordinating its powers of setting member-bank reserve requirements, adjusting the discount rate, and purchasing and selling securities in the open market, the Federal Reserve System can strongly influence the amount of excess reserves in the member banks. As a result, the System can greatly influence the ability of the banking system to expand loans and the money supply.

Bank reserves are also affected by the gold stock and by the volume of currency in circulation, as well as by relatively minor sources and uses of reserve funds. Consequently, the Federal Reserve banks are constantly either offsetting or augmenting the influence of these other sources and uses by changing the volume of Federal Reserve credit.

Economic Terms for Review

central bank
Board of Governors
Federal Open Market Committee
member banks
discounting
fiscal agent

open-market operations
Federal Reserve credit
secondary reserve assets
Regulation Q
uses of reserves
sources of reserves

Questions for Review

1. What is the power a central bank has that other banks do not have?
2. What decisions are made by the Federal Open Market Committee?
3. To what extent does the Federal Reserve System include all commercial banks?
4. In what ways does the American banking system lack uniformity?

5. What does the Federal Reserve System do as fiscal agent of the Treasury?
6. By what two processes may the reserve banks create additional bank reserves?
7. What is eligible paper? Why is it less important now than some fifty years ago?
8. What would the reserve system do to make bank reserves tight?

Questions for Analysis

1. Why did open-market operations replace discounting as the main tool of the Federal Reserve?
2. Why are many small banks not members of the reserve system?
3. How does the FDIC unify the banking system?
4. If you were a banker and knew that the reserve officials wanted bank reserves to rise, would you prefer the rise to come through discounts or through open-market operations?
5. In a period of tight money and high interest rates, how may the reserve officials restrain bank lending by use of Regulation Q?
6. Suppose that in a given year currency in circulation rises by $1 billion and the gold stock falls by $1 billion. If the reserve officials want bank reserves to rise by $1 billion during the year, what do they do?
7. Trace the path of a check drawn to pay your income tax, assuming the Treasury deposits it at the Federal Reserve. How are bank reserves and bank deposits affected?

Case for Decision

In June of 1969 the directors of Citizens National Bank were spending most of a weekly meeting discussing two applications for loans. Mr. Press, the local printer, was requesting a loan of $75,000 with which to buy some new equipment and supplies needed for a job he had won at competitive bidding. He intended to repay the loan over three years, one-third each year. Mr. Hall, head of a local trucking firm, also wanted to borrow $75,000 for several moving vans. He intended to repay equal installments over five years. Both applications were from men known to the bank, and each had made previous loans which were repaid on schedule.

The problem facing the directors was that in June, 1969, money was very tight. The Federal Reserve System had been restricting the growth of bank reserves for several months while the banking system had been faced with unusually large loan demands. Interest rates were higher than they had been since the Civil War. Prices of outstanding bonds were depressed. Many banks were discounting at the "Fed," and total discounts amounted to about $1 billion. Very few banks had excess reserves.

Citizens National was not in debt to the Fed, but its reserve balances were about as low as was possible to meet requirements and allow for normal weekly fluctuations of deposits. Deposits tended to decline at Citizens National nearly 10 percent between mid-summer and the end of September, after which each year they tended to rise seasonally.

Citizens National's balance sheet at the time of the directors' meeting showed:

Assets		Liabilities	
Cash assets	$ 800,000	Demand deposits	$5,000,000
Securities	3,000,000	Savings and time deposits	5,000,000
Loans	6,700,000	Capital and surplus	900,000
Bank building, etc.	500,000	Undivided profits	100,000

Since there were little or no excess reserves, the directors were discussing whether to (1) refuse the loans, (2) sell some Treasury bills, or (3) sell some other securities. The securities carried on the books at $3 million consisted of:

1. $500,000 of Treasury bills originally costing $498,000, due to mature at various times in the next three months. These bills were yielding 6 percent.
2. $960,000 market value of Treasury bonds originally costing $1 million, due in three to five years. At current prices the average yield of these bonds was 6.5 percent.
3. $1,430,000 market value of Treasury bonds originally costing $1,500,000, due in six to ten years. These bonds were yielding 6.75 percent.

Mr. Count favored refusing the loans because he did not want to sell any of the Treasury bonds at a loss and he felt that the bills were needed for liquidity purposes. Dr. Drill wanted to sell $150,000 of the Treasury bills and said that one reason the bank held liquid assets was to use them. Mr. Graves, the local undertaker, argued that the loans should be made because they were sound loans to good customers, the loss on the bonds already existed whether they were sold or not, and $150,000 of bonds yielding 6.75 percent should be sold in order to lend to Press and Hall at 8 percent. Dr. Drill then suggested that, instead of selling anything, the bank borrow from the Federal Reserve bank in order to make the two loans. A new director, Mr. Dull, asked why the bank didn't use some of the capital and surplus for the loans, but no one took him seriously.

If you were a member of the board, would you favor making the loans and, if so, with what funds?

13
Savings Institutions

The description of the commercial banking system in Chapters 11 and 12 makes clear that an important function of these banks is to handle the machinery for making payments. We have seen that these banks should not be thought of as places where people can put their money but rather as institutions that extend deposit credits in exchange for other debts and that these deposit credits comprise most of the money supply. But it is also true that individuals and corporations who have demand deposits larger than they wish to hold can shift these deposits to the savings- or time-deposit category. They can exchange their money-type deposits for nontransferable interest-bearing deposits. Many people build up their savings deposits by frequent additions to them. Commercial banks thus operate in the savings market as well as in the money market. They are the only institutions that have checking accounts, but in the savings market they compete with several other types of institutions.

DEPOSIT-TYPE SAVINGS INSTITUTIONS

There are three institutions in particular that resemble commercial banks in the sense that they hold deposits which they are obligated to repay either on request or according to contract at maturity dates. These are mutual savings banks, savings and loan associations, and credit unions. They differ from commercial banks, of course, in not having demand deposits transferable by check. In other words, their deposits are not used as money but as _financial assets_ that earn a return in the form of interest. In this section these institutions will be compared with commercial banks and with one another.

Commercial Banks

Since about 1950 commercial banks have become much more active in the savings field than they were previously. The underlying reason has been that at that time the Board of Governors of the Federal Reserve System became more restrictive of the growth of bank reserves to combat the postwar inflation. As a result, commercial banks have been inclined to seek funds wherever available more aggressively and have therefore competed more actively for deposits.

Since commercial-bank demand deposits are money, the commercial banks are in a peouliar position in competing for deposits. When a commercial bank competes for savings deposits, it is in a sense competing for deposits that it already has. This is because when a person deposits money to a savings account, he does so by shifting some of his demand deposit to the savings deposit. As we noted earlier, however, the reserve requirement for savings and time deposits is lower than that for demand deposits so, given a certain volume of reserves, the banks can hold a larger volume of deposits and thus assets if deposits are switched to the time category.

The principal motivation of commercial banks in seeking savings and time deposits, however, is a little different from simply recognizing that the reserve requirements are lower. Each commercial bank must look at the situation as an individual bank; it must attract all the deposits it can or is willing to pay for. If it loses deposits, it must contract its assets. When some commercial banks attempt to maintain or increase their total deposits by bidding for time deposits, then, all commercial banks must do so or lose funds to the more aggressive ones.

Because of the nature of their business, commercial banks' competition for these accounts is also somewhat different from that put forth by other savings institutions. This is because many of their time deposits are held as temporary substitutes for demand deposits. Before 1950 interest rates had been historically very low for about twenty years. If a corporation had funds that it intended to spend a month or two later, it tended simply to hold them as a demand deposit. As interest rates rose under the more restrictive policies of the Federal Reserve System, however, the income foregone as interest on these funds became more significant. Consequently, corporate treasurers became more interested in buying money-market instruments like Treasury bills, commercial paper, and other short-term obligations to hold until they again needed the money. Now, when someone buys a Treasury bill, he must buy it from someone, so the buyer's demand deposit shifts to the seller. The money is not destroyed unless the seller is a bank. But from the point of view of the buyer's bank there has been a loss of deposits. The buyer's bank would like to keep these deposits, so it offers interest on time deposits which would replace the demand deposits and also compete with open-market instruments.

In the early 1960s commercial banks greatly increased their use of a form of time deposit called the certificate of deposit, or CD. They offered these in large denominations to corporate treasurers and helped to create a market for them so that they could be bought and sold like other securities (in other words, they were *negotiable*). Thus, if a corporation had $1 million of excess funds temporarily and took a $1 million negotiable CD from its bank, payable at the end of sixty days, it not only would receive interest for sixty days if it held the CD until maturity but also could have the added assurance that it could sell the CD in the meantime to some other investor. Since the corporation would sell at a market price, it might or might not earn in the meantime the original rate of interest, but it would have the assurance of liquidity. Later, as the competition remained keen, commercial banks tailored the CDs to smaller amounts and offered them to individuals. The small CDs are generally not negotiable.

Therefore it is not correct to think of all the commercial banks' savings and time deposits as representing savings in the usual sense. Rather, to a large extent they are liquid assets offered to the public as substitutes for demand deposits, on the one hand, and for other financial assets they might hold, on the other.

Mutual Savings Banks

Mutual savings banks are virtually unknown in most parts of the country, but a hundred years ago and more, when most of the population and business activity was in the East and Northeast, they were actually the dominant form of financial institution. They have had an interesting history.[1] In the early days of the country, the problem of poverty in the cities was becoming acute as more and more of the population became wage earners rather than farmers or independent artisans. Public-spirited citizens sought, both from altruism and from a desire to prevent excessive taxes for poor relief, a means of making the poor more self-reliant. They adopted the idea of the savings bank, as such institutions had recently been started in Scotland through the efforts of the Rev. Henry Duncan of Ruthwell, and in 1816 savings banks were begun in Boston and Philadelphia. Soon banks were started in New York, Providence, Baltimore, and other places, and these were followed by additional ones in several of these cities. They then grew rapidly in this part of the country.

Since the people who started these banks were not seeking profits or starting business enterprises for themselves, they established the banks as mutual institutions. A mutual institution is operated for the benefit of its customers; profits are paid to the customers rather than to owners. A cooperative in the marketing of farm crops is another example of a mutual organization. The owners of a mutual organization may be the customers, who have established the organization to serve themselves. However, the founders of the savings banks were not, to any important extent, the prospective customers. They turned to a natural precedent, the trusteeship. These same people were usually the founders of the early hospitals, libraries, orphanages, and similar civic enterprises whose property was held by trustees for the benefit of the public. Hence, the mutual savings banks were set up as trusteeships. Technically, the banks are owned by trustees who cannot profit from their position; they may, of course, be paid for their actual services.

As the country grew to the west, the philanthropic reasons for establishing the early savings banks generally were not present, as people generally were farmers rather than wage earners. In addition, the smaller commercial banks that were established in the newer parts of the country were willing to accept small deposits, which as a rule the older and larger commercial banks along the East Coast were not. These older banks concentrated on serving merchants and other large customers. Hence, savings banking did not spread widely throughout the country, and only 18 states have laws providing for chartering them. In recent years, however, the savings banks as an industry have become much more interested in expanding. Accordingly they have proposed a federal law, such as commercial banks and savings and loan associations have, to permit federal charters. This proposal is naturally opposed by the competitors of the savings banks and, while it has progressed through several legislative stages, it has not been enacted.[2]

[1] See Weldon Welfling, *Mutual Savings Banks: The Evolution of a Financial Intermediary,* Case Western Reserve University Press, Cleveland, 1968.

[2] The savings and loan associations and savings banks reached agreement in 1967, and both backed a bill which, if enacted, would establish *Federal Savings Institutions* into which both could convert. It would have in general the powers separately held now by the two institutions.

Table 13-1
Assets and Liabilities of Mutual Savings Banks, Apr. 30, 1970 *
(Millions of Dollars)

Assets		Liabilities	
Mortgage loans	$56,279	Deposits	$67,861
Other loans	2,048	Other liabilities	1,905
U.S. government securities	3,294	General reserve accounts	5,599
State and municipal	188		
Corporate and other	11,319		
Cash	912		
Other assets	1,385		
Total	$75,366	Total	$75,366

* Totals are not accurate because of rounding.
Source: National Association of Mutual Savings Banks.

Historically the economic role of the mutual savings bank has been to accept the relatively small personal savings accounts of the public and to invest these funds in a variety of highly safe assets permitted by state laws. Since World War II, however, the market for mortgage loans has been so active that savings banks have invested virtually all their growth in assets in this form. Today the savings banks are to a very high degree mortgage lenders. They hold all kinds of mortgage loans and lend heavily in states other than their home states. They do not concentrate as exclusively on home loans as do the savings and loan associations but also make large commercial and multifamily loans.

Most savings banks currently in existence were originally chartered over a hundred years ago. There are consequently few new and, therefore, small savings banks although some of the older ones have remained small. In recent decades the number of savings banks has gradually fallen to about 500, as mergers have exceeded new charters. Savings banks seldom fail, and they had an extremely good record in the 1930s when failures among other institutions were numerous. There are more savings banks in Massachusetts than in any other state, but total deposits are larger in New York State. The principal categories of assets and liabilities of mutual savings banks are summarized in Table 13-1.

Savings and Loan Associations

Savings and loan associations began in Philadelphia in the 1830s as a cooperative arrangement for raising money for mortgage loans. In the last century many such mutual organizations were formed, often by people of the same ethnic origins in large cities. The arrangement was that people would pool their savings on a continuing basis and, as funds became adequate, they would borrow these funds to buy homes, either according to lot or by bidding. Repayments on early loans along with current savings provided funds for later borrowers. When all the group had obtained loans, the plan ceased under the original arrangements.

Later some of the associations began to accept savings from nonmembers and to lend to nonmembers, thus dealing with the public generally.

In the mutual savings and loan association, the "depositors" are technically shareholders because they are owners of the association rather than creditors of it. However, a 1969 law permits associations to call their share accounts deposits. Most savings and loan associations are mutual, but some states provide for stockholders' associations; these are essentially the same as any other business corporation. The stockholders risk their capital and earn profits on their invested funds.

In the 1930s the savings and loan business was drastically reorganized. Congress enacted legislation providing for federal charters; a system of central banking institutions to serve the member associations (the Federal Home Loan Banks); and a system of insurance comparable to the FDIC, the Federal Savings and Loan Insurance Corporation (FSLIC). The associations copied the savings banks' deposit arrangements—having passbooks and allowing deposits and withdrawals to be made at any time. They continued to specialize in mortgage loans and more specifically in single-family home loans. In fact, the federal and most state laws limit the amount of assets they can have other than in this form.

Few houses were built during the 1930s and World War II. Consequently, there was a considerable shortage of housing after the war, and this shortage was accentuated by rising population, movement of the population to suburbs, and the age distribution of the population. Construction was encouraged by government programs and general prosperity and high living standards. The savings and loan associations had a ready and expanding market in which to make mortgage loans, so they were able to attract savings with good interest rates. They grew very rapidly and soon surpassed the savings banks (which were important in only a few states) in terms of national totals. In the 1960s they went well over the $100 billion mark in assets.

Savings and loan assets and liabilities are shown in Table 13-2. In general proportions they are similar to the savings banks, but the savings and loan associations' assets are much more heavily concentrated in single-family home loans.

Roughly half of the total assets are held by state-chartered associations and half by federal. There are just about twice as many state-chartered as federally chartered associations, however, so on the average the former are smaller. There are approximately 6,000 associations, 4,000 state and 2,000 federal. All those with federal charters must be insured by the FSLIC, and about 2,400 of the state associations are insured, leaving about 1,600 not covered. Some states permit savings and loan associations to make a variety of loans, such as personal or consumer loans, but as a rule savings and loan associations are specialists in home-mortgage financing.

Credit Unions

Credit unions are cooperatives specializing in consumer credit. Not many decades ago financial institutions generally did not want to make small loans to individuals. It was thought that these loans were risky and it was true that, because of their small amounts, administrative costs were high. Personal-finance and small-loan companies did exist but did

Table 13-2
**Assets and Liabilities of Savings and Loan Associations,
Apr. 30, 1970**
(Millions of Dollars)

Assets

Cash		$ 2,371
U.S. government securities		8,405
Other assets		11,989
Mortgage loans		141,283
	Total	$164,048

Liabilities and reserves

Savings capital		$136,106
Reserves and undivided profits		11,237
Borrowings		10,079
Loans in process		2,216
Other		4,410
	Total	$164,048

Source: *Federal Reserve Bulletin,* June, 1970, p. A-38.

not cover the whole potential market. There were great abuses in this field, as many people in need of small loans got them from loan sharks, who were in fact racketeers and who charged enormous rates of interest and collected when necessary with strong-arm methods. Some of the market was also served by pawnshops. In only a few decades the situation has changed drastically. Commercial banks especially have entered the field and compete ambitiously for installment loans for the purchase of automobiles, appliances, and other durables. They also make many loans for vacations, education, and a host of other purposes. They offer credit-card and instant-credit plans whereby their depositors may charge purchases at stores and other establishments and pay in installments later at their banks or overdraw their accounts and automatically have loans restore their balances. But up through the 1930s reforms were needed in this field. One was the enactment of small-loan laws in the states, validating interest rates which appeared to be high but which were justified by the costs of making small loans. Such rates had been illegal under the general usury laws, which set a maximum of 6 or 7 percent per annum. Since small loans could not be made economically at these levels, the field was left open for the loan shark, who might charge 10 percent *per week* or more since he was willing to break the law.

Another reform was to encourage the growth of credit unions, cooperatives formed somewhat like the early savings and loan associations but for the purpose of making personal loans rather than mortgage loans. Credit unions may obtain state or federal charters and be supervised accordingly. They generally are organized to serve a group of persons having some common bond, which may be rather loose. Often they are employees of a single firm or members of a union, neighborhood, church, or other group. Often an employer will grant rent-free space for the credit union, and most small credit unions operate with volunteer officers and help so that costs are low. Generally they charge 1 percent per month for consumer credit loans, which is less than finance companies usually charge, and out of this revenue pay interest on deposits of members. If earnings exceed expectations, rebates are made to borrowers for some of the interest. There are some 22,000 credit unions, and they hold over $14 billion of assets, but their rate of growth is very rapid; in 1950 they represented only about $1 billion of assets. Nearly all the assets are consumer loans.

LIFE INSURANCE AND PENSIONS

By the time of the Civil War, life insurance companies were rivaling the savings banks in total size and handling an equivalent proportion of household savings. Today the life insurance companies hold tremendous amounts of assets accumulated through their plans for individuals' savings. In more recent decades the growth of pension plans has been spectacular. Under these plans, both private and governmental, assets are built up out of which pensions are paid in future years.

Life Insurance Savings

Life insurance is not necessarily a form of saving but, in actuality, it generally is. The reason for this lies in the nature of most insurance policies. It is possible to predict fairly accurately the number of deaths that will occur in a large population of a given age. Thus it is possible to establish premiums. Of course, there will be more deaths in a given year among 100,000 people aged seventy than in another group of 100,000 aged thirty. Suppose that the predictable number in a certain age group is 10 per thousand. If all the 1,000 would pay a premium of $100, there would be $100,000 to be divided among the estates of the 10 who die. Of course, these benefits would have to be reduced by the costs of operating the plan or the premiums would have to be raised to cover these costs plus a safety factor.

The following year the 990 survivors would face a slightly higher death rate. In order to assure the beneficiaries of those who die during the second year the same amount of benefits, a somewhat higher premium would have to be charged. Each year the survivors from preceding years would have to pay a little more to provide the amount necessary to cover the rising death rate. Theoretically, at some age around one hundred there should be only one survivor and, since his chance of dying that year is statistically almost 100 percent, he would have to pay a premium of about the same amount as the benefit to be paid at his death.

This is the way life insurance would work if all policies were for so-called term insurance. That is, if policies were sold anew each year, the premium would have to rise with the age of the insured. Most policies, however, are not term policies but whole life policies or some variant. For example, a policy bought by a man at age thirty may call for the payment of the same premium over his lifetime. The premium, therefore, must be too high for the first years considered by themselves in order to average out with later premiums that will be too low. Thus the insurance companies figure that this *level premium* exceeds the cost of pure insurance in the early years and they invest this excess. This investment yields income which helps reduce the need for future premiums, but in a sense these *life insurance reserves* belong to the policyholder. Consequently, the insurance companies calculate the *cash value* of policies as this cash value accumulates over the years. It is a form of saving because the policyholder can withdraw it by dropping the policy, he can use it to pay premiums in his old age, or he can let it accumulate and increase the benefit. He also has the right to borrow it at a rate of interest stated in the policy.

There are many variations of the way in which accumulations are made. For example, the policyholder may prefer a policy under which he pays premiums for thirty years rather than throughout his life. He may prefer an *endowment policy,* which matures at a certain time even though the policyholder is still living. It may, for example, pay $10,000 of benefits at any time if he dies but in any event will pay $10,000 at the end of twenty years even though he is alive. The premium must therefore be calculated to cover the pure insurance risk for twenty years and also to accumulate to $10,000 at the end of that time.

The amount an insurance company charges in premiums is consequently determined by its (1) death-rate experience, (2) earnings on investments, and (3) operating costs. The more favorable the experience with these three factors, the lower the cost of a given coverage of life insurance.

The American people have accumulated huge sums in the form of reserves of life insurance policies. In 1969, these policy reserves amounted to about $125 billion, roughly the same as the amount of savings at savings and loan associations.[3] In addition to regular life insurance policies, there are annuities and supplemental contracts. An annuity is a contract under which the insurance company agrees to pay a given amount each year as long as the recipient lives. It is insurance in reverse, in that the insured or annuitant pays the company a lump sum in exchange for the future annual payments. The amount of the annual payment is based on the annuitant's life expectancy; if he dies before that time, he receives less, but if he lives beyond his average life expectancy, he receives more. It is a way of living on one's accumulated capital without fear of using it up.

Most people think of their insurance policies in terms of the face amount—the benefit payment. This amount is naturally much greater than the amount that represents savings accumulated on these policies. The face amount of life insurance policies outstanding is about $1 trillion. It is estimated that "the head of the family has some form of life insurance in nine out of every ten families in the United States that include husband, wife and children under 18."[4]

Naturally, the life insurance companies hold assets equal to their policy reserves plus additional assets that represent their general surpluses. Insurance companies are important lenders to a wide variety of industrial and public-utility industries through purchases of bonds of such companies. They are also important mortgage lenders and hold

---

[3] Securities and Exchange Commission data.

[4] *1967 Life Insurance Fact Book,* Institute of Life Insurance, New York, 1967, p. 7.

Table 13-3
**Assets of Life Insurance Companies,
Mar. 31, 1970**
(Millions of Dollars)

Type	Amount
Bonds	
U.S. government	$ 4,505
Foreign government	3,194
State and local	3,242
Business	71,532
Stocks	13,812
Mortgages	72,616
Real estate	5,990
Policy loans	14,535
Miscellaneous assets	9,977
Total	$199,403

Source: Institute of Life Insurance.

significant portions of common and preferred stocks. Their assets are summarized in Table 13-3.

Pension Funds

Saving through life insurance plans differs from savings in deposit institutions in that it is contractual—the policyholder agrees to pay a stated premium over a period of time. The other principal contractual type of savings is pension plans. Pension plans have become widespread since World War II, when restrictions on wage increases shifted attention in union negotiations to fringe benefits. While it may have been contrary to federal controls to grant increased pay in the form of wages, it was often possible to increase fringe benefits such as the employer's contribution to a *pension fund.*

Pension funds are public and private, and the latter are insured and noninsured. Federal, state, and local governments provide plans whereby the employing institution and the employee jointly contribute to a fund out of which retirement benefits will be paid. Such funds exceeded $96 billion in 1969. Originally, state laws restricted investments of these funds to federal, state, or local securities, but more recently the laws have been liberalized to permit investment more in the manner of private funds. Such funds therefore may hold mortgages, corporate bonds, and other private obligations as well as governmental securities, but funds of federal plans may not.

The federal government covers millions of citizens through programs of the Social Security Administration.[5] Death benefits and payments to retired people are financed from contributions of employers and employees based on wages and salaries up to a stated maximum amount.

[5] These programs are described in Chapter 19.

However, there is a fundamental difference between a federal program and the program of a private corporation. The federal government can anticipate paying each year's benefits from governmental revenues of that year, but a corporation, in order to assure its present employees that they will receive benefits in the future, must accumulate a fund whose earnings will contribute all or a large part of the costs in future years. The federal government also has programs comparable to state and local plans, one for government employees and one for railroad employees. These involve the accumulation and management of pension funds.

Private plans are partly or completely *funded.* If a plan is completely funded, the current contributions (generally from the employer) are calculated to provide a fund sufficient to meet future obligations completely. A private plan may be insured or noninsured. If insured, it is administered by a life insurance company and the employer pays premiums calculated by the insurance company to be adequate to meet the payments it must make in the future. A noninsured plan is administered by a trustee, such as the trust department of a commercial bank, or by trustees agreed upon by the employer and the union. Noninsured plans have grown more rapidly than the insured plans for a variety of reasons. At first the insurance companies could not segregate their pension-fund assets but comingled the funds and invested them along with other reserves; more recent legislation has permitted them to segregate the funds and invest them to a greater degree in common stocks. Noninsured pension funds can generally invest more aggressively and grow through capital gains and thus reduce the amount the employer must contribute.

At the end of 1969 insurance companies held about $38 billion of pension-fund reserves. Noninsured plans, however, had assets of $96.5 billion. Thus, private plans currently represent funds of about $135 billion and with federal, state, and local plans amount to approximately $185 billion. Private pension funds have therefore become very significant

---

Table 13-4
Assets of Noninsured Pension Plans, Dec. 31, 1969
(Billions of Dollars)

Demand deposits and currency	$ 1.6
U.S. government securities	3.1
Corporate and foreign bonds	26.6
Corporate stock	57.0
Home mortgages	4.0
Miscellaneous	4.3
Total	$96.6

Source: Board of Governors, Flow of Funds Section, *Financial Assets and Liabilities* (mimeograph), May 15, 1970.

intermediaries in capital markets, receiving saved funds for the benefit of employees and investing these in a variety of assets. They are also a rapidly growing type of savings institution. The assets held by private noninsured pension funds at the end of 1969 are shown in Table 13-4.

MARKET-TYPE SAVINGS

All the institutions described so far are *financial intermediaries*. They intermediate between the individual saver and the borrowing individual, corporation, or government. The intermediary performs a valuable service because it provides not only a channel through which saved funds may flow from saver to borrower but also an asset that is generally better suited to the saver. When a household builds up a deposit at a savings bank, for example, it has a liquid asset. This asset earns interest for the depositor, but it may also be withdrawn should the depositor prefer. It can be any size the depositor wants to make it and remain as long as he desires. The individual saver would have difficulty making loans directly to the borrowers served by the intermediary. For one thing, many savers could not accumulate large-enough sums to make mortgage loans. For another, the mortgage loan would not be a liquid asset. There is much bypassing of intermediaries, however, by savers who are willing to hold financial assets bought and sold in the market rather than deposit-type assets. The public holds large quantities of open-market securities, both bonds and stocks.

Investment Companies

There is one institution that partakes of the nature of both the intermediaries and the market instruments—the investment company. An *investment company* sells shares of stock, like other corporations, but uses the funds to purchase securities of other corporations (and perhaps governments). Investment companies are of two general types, closed-end and open-end, the latter more commonly called the mutual fund. The closed-end fund has outstanding a given amount of its own stock, and this stock is traded like other shares of stock. The mutual fund issues new stock when purchasers wish and redeems stock when stockholders wish to liquidate. The issue and redemption prices are based on the value of the securities held by the fund. Mutual funds have grown at a rapid average annual rate in recent decades, as new issues have generally exceeded redemptions by a substantial margin. Some funds sell their shares directly to purchasers with little or no sales charge, but most sell theirs through dealers who retain a percentage, often about 8.5 percent, as commission.

Different funds have different investment policies and objectives and thus attempt to appeal to different potential investors. Some funds emphasize growth and try to invest in companies that will grow more rapidly than the average and provide capital gains in the market value of their stock; some emphasize income and seek investments in companies that pay good dividends; some are "balanced" in the sense that they hold both bonds and stocks; and some specialize in investing in specific industries such as electronics or oceanography. How much the

Table 13-5
Financial Intermediaries, 1947 and 1969
(Billions of Dollars)

		1947	1969
Commercial bank time and savings		$ 35.5	$192.8
Of households only	$31.9		$155.4
Savings and loan savings shares		9.8	135.5
Mutual savings bank deposits		17.8	67.1
Credit union shares		.5	13.7
Life insurance reserves		48.3	124.7 °
Pension fund reserves, total		13.9	210.8
U.S. government			
Employee retirement	2.7⎱		25.2
Railroad retirement	1.4⎰		
State and local governments	3.1		51.0
Insured private plans	3.6		38.1
Noninsured plans	3.1		96.5
Total		$125.8	$744.6

° Includes $7.3 billion of government life insurance.

Source: Board of Governors, *Flow of Funds Accounts*, 1945–1967, Washington, 1968, pp. 165–173, and *Financial Assets and Liabilities*, Dec. 31, 1969 (mimeograph), May 15, 1970.

public holds of the shares of investment companies at a given time depends on the current market prices of these shares. As stock prices have generally risen over recent years, the public's holdings have gone up faster than the amounts of annual purchases. That these funds hold primarily the stocks of other companies is indicated by the totals at the end of 1969: open-end companies held total assets of $48.3 billion and, of this amount, $40.9 billion was corporate stocks. The rapid recent growth of these investment companies is shown by the fact that their total holdings were only about $1 billion twenty years earlier.

Before the public's direct holdings of securities are examined, the use of financial intermediaries is summarized in Table 13-5, which shows the extent of the public's holdings at the end of 1947 and 1969. These data show the great growth in financial assets held in recent years.

Stocks and Bonds

Direct holdings of stocks and bonds by households are given in Table 13-6. This table shows that by far the largest type of financial asset held by households is corporate stocks, $749.3 billion at the end of 1969 (this figure includes the shares of investment companies described earlier and fell by $123.9 billion during the year).

A few words will suffice to explain the advantages and disadvantages for most people of the sorts of securities listed. Except for the United States savings bonds, the other securities are bought and sold at market prices. Savings bonds are not marketable but have redemption values.

The redemption values are set in such a way that the interest accrues faster in the later years; if a holder redeems his bond in the early years before maturity, he obtains a lower rate of interest. These bonds are issued at a discount so that interest is earned through the increase in the redemption and final maturity values. For instance, a bond might be issued at $75 and redeemed at maturity at $100, the length of time determining the annual rate of interest. Other series are issued at par and interest is paid by check, as on most bonds. Savings bonds were designed to permit more of the federal debt to be held by small savers and investors, especially during World War II. They have been popular, competing with deposit-type savings because of their redemption values, but in recent years have not yielded as much as many other securities. It may be noted that there is not much increase in the amount outstanding between 1947 and 1969 and, in fact, in 1969 the households' holdings were slowly declining.

When a security is marketable, the chance of gain or loss is introduced. Bonds almost universally are promises to pay a fixed amount of interest for a period of years at the end of which the principal amount will be paid. When issued, they are usually sold at or close to par, or face, value, so the amount of interest is determined by market conditions at that time. A bond with a par value of $1,000 may thus pay the holder $50 a year (or $25 twice a year) for ten years and, on the final interest-payment date, the principal of $1,000 would also be paid. In this example the interest rate for ten-year obligations of this particular degree of risk would be 5 percent.

If the bondholder keeps the bond for the full period of ten years and if there are no credit problems whereby payments are not made or are delayed, he is assured of earning 5 percent for the whole period, regardless of what happens to interest rates in the interval. If sometime during

---

Table 13-6

Credit and Equity Market Instruments of Households,

1947 and 1969 °

(Billions of Dollars)

	1947	1969
U.S. government		
Marketable bonds	$ 19.5	$ 53.8
Savings bonds	46.2	51.2
State and local obligations	7.6	41.1
Corporate and foreign bonds	6.0	25.4
Corporate stock (market value)	100.3	749.3
Mortgages	6.8	39.7
Total	$186.2	$960.5

° Holdings of personal trusts and nonprofit organizations are included.

Source: Board of Governors, Flow of Funds Accounts, 1945–1967, Washington, 1968, p. 160, and *Financial Assets and Liabilities*, Dec. 31, 1969 (mimeograph), May 15, 1970.

the decade interest rates go down, he will be fortunate in having a bond that pays 5 percent, but if interest rates at which he could invest anew go up, he nevertheless will continue to get only his $50 per year. Such changes in market rates, however, are reflected in the market value of his bond. Thus he cannot count on always having exactly $1,000 as he could with a deposit-type asset.

Suppose that five years after this bond was issued, interest rates are higher. There are now five years left to the maturity of the bond. If people can invest funds for five years at 6 percent, they will not pay $1,000 for this bond because it pays only $50 per year, not $60. But there is a price at which this bond yields 6 percent, considering the combination of appreciation to par at maturity along with the annual interest. This price is $957.30. A purchaser at this price will receive $50 per year and if he, in turn, holds the bond to maturity, he will have a capital gain of $42.70, or an average of $8.54 per year. The total of $58.54 represents a *yield to maturity* of 6 percent at compound interest on the current price of $957.30.[6] By the same token, if the market rate on five-year bonds had fallen to 4 percent, the outstanding bond would be more valuable. At a market price of $1,044.90, the combination of $50 interest and average annual decline in value of $8.98 would represent a yield to maturity of 4 percent on the investment. When interest rates seem historically high, more people are interested in acquiring bonds at these yields because, even though deposit institutions may be paying relatively high rates, there is no assurance that they will continue to do so throughout the life of the bond.

It may be observed that households generally do not hold large quantities of marketable bonds, at least in relation to their holdings of stocks and of accounts at savings institutions. Most people prefer the liquidity of the deposit-type asset and prefer to avoid the changes in the market value of bonds. If they are willing and able to assume the risks of changes in market value, they are more apt to purchase stocks, where the chances of appreciation are much greater than with bonds. Another drawback to bonds is the fact that most corporate bonds are issued in units and multiples of $1,000, which may be rather large for most people. The fact that deposits are insured makes them more attractive also to some people.

There is one special reason for holding state and local government bonds, and it may be observed that households have nearly as many of them as of marketable federal government and corporate combined. This is the tax-exemption feature of state and local government obligations. According to a constitutional interpretation of the Supreme Court many years ago, the federal income tax does not apply to the interest from these securities. The nature of the income tax has changed greatly since the 1930s and the rates are much higher and more progressive (rise faster as income is larger). If a person had both a corporate bond and a municipal bond paying the same rate of interest, he would pay income tax on the interest from the former but not from the latter. Hence the municipal bond is worth more to him, and the value of the tax exemption is greater the greater is his income. People with relatively large incomes therefore tend to own municipal bonds, but this being the case they have little

---

[6] There are books of bond values tables which make unnecessary calculating prices and yields for different maturities.

reason to hold corporate bonds. Because of this advantage, municipalities can borrow at even lower rates than can the federal government. People with smaller incomes, if they wish to hold bonds at all, are more likely to buy Treasury obligations since the after-tax income may be as high.

Before the rapid rise of savings and loan associations and the increased interest of commercial and savings banks and other lenders in mortgage loans, individuals were the principal lenders on this type of security. The wealthier citizens of small towns and rural areas often held much of their wealth in the form of mortgage loans on local property, and often when one sold property, he held a mortgage on it until it was fully paid for. Today, however, most mortgage loans are made by financial intermediaries. Most mortgages have little liquidity, in the sense that there is no organized market for them as there is for stocks and bonds.[7] Generally, if a person makes a mortgage loan, he must expect to keep it until maturity.

Household Financial Assets and Debts

A kind of a summary or overview of the great network of debt and credit in this country can be obtained by looking at the financial position of households. How the three principal sectors—households, business, and governments—fit together we will examine in a final section of this chapter. The United States is such a large and rich country that the dollar figures necessary to describe it are almost beyond comprehension, like the number of miles to some planet. Table 13-7 summarizes the financial assets and liabilities of households. Note that this table says nothing about the real, or nonfinancial, assets owned by the American people. These financial assets are only the debts or other claims that households have on governments and businesses (and to some extent on each other).

The data in Table 13-7 indicate that American families are not the debt-ridden, free-spending people that they are commonly thought to be. If one looked only at the figures for financial liabilities, he might be impressed that household debt for one- to four-family mortgages had increased tenfold in twenty-two years, to the huge sum of $260.4 billion. He might forget that these mortgage debts permitted the purchase of homes worth well over this sum. Or he might observe the increase in consumer credit at virtually as great a rate. If one simply said that Americans are in debt for over $120 billion for automobiles, appliances, furniture, and a host of other things, he would be telling the truth but giving a misleading impression of the financial position of households.

Household holdings of money—demand deposits and currency—were virtually the same amounts in 1967 and 1969 as household debts for consumer credit. Household savings accounts were three times as much as these consumer debts. Financial assets totaled the incomprehensible sum of $1.8 trillion. Taken as aggregates, household financial assets were about four times as great as household debts.

All this is not to say that people cannot abuse debt or have too much of it. Certainly, some families each year realize that they have gone over-

---

[7] A market among large institutional investors has developed for governmentally insured or guaranteed mortgages.

Table 13-7
Financial Assets and Liabilities of Households, 1947, 1967, and 1969
(Billions of Dollars)

	1947	1967	1969
Financial assets			
Demand deposits and currency	$ 57.6	$ 96.9	$ 114.7
Savings accounts	59.8	329.4	370.9
Life insurance reserves	46.5	115.7	124.7
Pension fund reserves	13.9	181.9	210.8
Bonds	79.3	135.1	171.5
Stocks	100.3	727.5	749.3
Mortgages	6.8	9.3	39.7
Other financial assets	7.2	22.4	26.3
Total	$371.2 °	$1,618.2	$1,807.9
Financial liabilities			
One- to four-family mortgages	$ 21.6	$ 226.1	$ 260.4
Other mortgages	.9	15.8	18.9
Consumer credit	11.6	99.6	122.5
Other debts	8.6	44.2	58.9
Total	$ 42.7	$ 385.7	$ 460.7

° Total does not check because of rounding.

Source: Board of Governors, *Flow of Funds Accounts*, 1945–1967, Washington, 1968, p. 160; *Financial Assets and Liabilities*, Dec. 31, 1969 (mimeograph), May 15, 1970.

board in spending beyond their current income and have great difficulty in restricting their consumption enough to pay off these debts. Many families have debt and very few assets; others have many assets but few debts. Most families have both, and the important factor is the proportion of current income required to service the debts. While debt has risen rapidly in recent decades, so have incomes. In recent years, aggregate payments of household debts have required about 15 percent of household incomes. Again, of course, this is an average figure.

DEBT, CREDIT, AND REAL ASSETS

Without debt there could be no credit; they are the two sides of the same transaction. Many people seem to believe in the adage "Neither a borrower nor a lender be" yet, if there were no borrowing and lending, there could be no saving. More accurately, saving would be very difficult in a modern society where most exchanges of goods and services are monetary transactions.

Flows of Savings

In more primitive societies people saved by producing capital and durable goods. When a farmer set aside some of the harvest as seed for next year, he was saving by diverting some current income (output) to

future use. When he built a fence or barn or kept a cow instead of slaugh-
tering it, he was saving. He was building up his capital goods or *real assets*
by not consuming all his current income.

Today, in a monetary society, most people receive their incomes in
the form of money and have no convenient way to build up capital goods.
A person who wishes to save today must choose between accumulating
money, durable consumer goods, and claims on other members of society.
Of course, it is possible to buy farmland or some other real assets, but this
course is often impracticable. Unless he is willing to hoard money or
accumulate consumer goods, then, modern man must lend to someone
else if he wishes to save. He may lend in numerous ways, as illustrated
by the foregoing discussion in this chapter. He may acquire a very liquid
asset, like a savings deposit; a somewhat less liquid asset, like a government bond; or an even less liquid asset (because of its potential changes
in market value), like shares of stock.[8]

While some people desire to save part of their current income, others
have good reason for spending more than theirs. A family buying a
house is very likely to spend considerably more than its annual income
in that year. Buying a house is not necessarily a spendthrift act, however, as the family will have an asset—the house—to offset the debt it
has taken on. Presumably the house will provide income in the form of
shelter that warrants the annual debt service. Similarly, a businessman
may want to double the size of his store or shop and may have to spend
considerably more than his income that year in order to make the expenditure. On a larger scale, a manufacturing corporation may want to
invest in plant, equipment, or inventory and need to borrow funds from
others in order to do so.

Debt is the machinery which makes possible the transfer of income
from savers to spenders. Some of the spenders wish to spend for consumption, others for investment. One borrower wants to buy a car or
take a vacation, another to build a steel mill or buy a fleet of trucks. In
the first instance, the saver and spender cancel out as far as social or
national totals are concerned. Total consumption is not reduced by the
saving of the first, as his saving is offset by the borrower's consumption.
But when the borrower spends for capital goods of some kind, the saver's
consumption is replaced by the production of investment goods. In this
way capital goods are produced in response to market demands and it is
true, as in a primitive society, that current output is diverted to the production of capital and other durable goods by saving.

This flow of saving from saver to spender could not take place without
the establishment of claims on the spender's future income. If the saver
lent directly to the spender, his loan would be such a claim. As we have
seen, however, most such flows go through intermediaries. Thus more
than a single layer of claims or debts is created. For example, a depositor
increases his savings deposit rather than buying consumer goods; the
savings bank lends to a customer who is having a house built. There are
two debts, one from the savings bank to the depositor and one from the
borrower to the savings bank. Without these debts, the borrower might

[8] Legally and technically, a share of stock does not represent a loan but a share of ownership.
However, since it does represent a claim on the corporation and since new shares provide
funds for the business, such claims are included in the discussion.

not be able to raise the funds with which to buy a new house. Thus each year, as some of the total output is purchased with borrowed funds, the total of outstanding debt grows. If gross national product rises by 10 percent, debts probably must grow by something more than 10 percent.

This discussion does not imply that debt is never paid off. Individual debts are paid off, but new ones are created at a somewhat faster rate. The only times in modern history when total debt in the economy has declined have been periods of severe depression. The fact that output and debt both decline is not accidental.

Sector Debts and Ownership

As we have seen, the household sector owns much more debt than it owes. Businesses generally increase their debt each year in the aggregate, and this is normal, as we have just seen. Business corporations get much of the funds they spend for plant and equipment from their own net profits and from the depreciation charges taken out of gross receipts to offset the wearing out of existing capital goods, but they normally also raise additional funds by selling bonds and stock and from bank loans. As a general rule, the total of federal, state, and local debts rises each year although there are years in which one or more of these levels of government reduces its outstanding debt. The general relationship is that business and government borrow and households lend. This is why households are seen to have such huge accumulations of financial assets, as shown in Table 13-7.

Every debt is two-faced: It is owed by someone and owed to someone. Consequently, financial assets do not add to the total wealth of a society. Debt makes possible the production of real wealth, but it itself is not wealth except to its owner. If we added up the balance sheets of all the households, businesses, and governments, we would find each debt appearing twice. It would be an asset for its owner but a liability for its issuer. Thus it reduces the net worth or wealth of the issuer as much as it increases that of the holder. (We should remember that the debtor may also hold an offsetting asset.) If we aggregated all the balance sheets of all economic units into a grand total — a balance sheet for the United States economy — the debts would appear on both the asset and liability side and would cancel out. What would be left, then, would be the real assets and the net worth. Real assets have to be owned by someone and contribute to his net worth. A simple example of this relationship may be illustrated by taking just two families to represent the whole economy. Their balance sheets might look something like this:

Family A				Family B			
Assets		*Liabilities*		*Assets*		*Liabilities*	
House	$20,000	Mortgage	$15,000	House	$25,000	Loans	$10,000
Car	5,000			Car	6,000		
Securities	10,000	Net worth	20,000	Securities	15,000	Net worth	36,000
Total	$35,000	Total	$35,000	Total	$46,000	Total	$46,000

Since there are only two units in the economy, it is obvious that if Family A owes a $15,000 mortgage, it must be to Family B. This mortgage is the securities shown among the assets of Family B. If Family B has loans outstanding of $10,000, it must owe this sum to Family A, and this is shown by Family A's assets. If we combine the two balance sheets, we have:

Social or National Balance Sheet

Families A and B

Assets		Liabilities	
Houses	$45,000	Mortgage	$15,000
Cars	11,000	Loans	10,000
Securities	25,000	Total debts	$25,000
Total	$81,000	Net worth	56,000
		Total	$81,000

It is obvious that the net worth of all the families and other economic units in society is equal to the total real assets, the houses and cars. In this simple example, the units of society have total debts of $25,000 and own total debts of this amount, so the total net worth is unaffected by their existence.

Of course, the net worth of each unit is probably not equal to its real wealth. In this example Family A has real assets of $25,000, but since its financial liabilities exceed its financial assets, its net worth is $20,000, not $25,000. Family B has acquired more financial assets than financial liabilities, so its net worth is greater than its real assets. It has increased its net worth by accumulating claims on Family B, which is also the reason why Family B's net worth is reduced. This simple example illustrates how most families have accumulated wealth in the form of financial assets, except that most of the claims are on businesses and governments rather than on other households. Many of the claims are on financial inter- mediaries who, in turn, hold the claims on governments and businesses. Most businesses are debtors, but these debts have permitted them to acquire the real assets with which they operate.

SUMMARY

In a modern monetary economy most people cannot conveniently save by accumulating real assets and instead accumulate financial assets, which are claims on other members of the economy. Some of these claims are issued by financial intermediaries which serve the function of accepting savings, on the one hand, and lending them, on the other. Those whose claims are deposits or similar to deposits are commercial banks, savings banks, savings and loan associations, and credit unions.

Other financial intermediaries or savings institutions are related to life insurance and pensions. In recent years savings in the form of pension reserves have grown very rapidly.

Many times, savings take the form of direct claims on issuers of debt rather than indirect claims through intermediaries. Both the business sector and the government sector are, on balance, debtors of the household sector. At the end of 1969 the household sector held over four times as much in financial assets as in household debts.

Economic Terms for Review

financial assets	financial intermediaries
mutual savings banks	investment company
life insurance reserves	yield to maturity
pension fund	real assets

Questions for Review

1. Why were mutual savings banks originally started? Why were they organized as mutual organizations?
2. Why were savings and loan associations started? Why were they mutual?
3. Why do insurance companies have policy reserves?
4. Why are many pension plans not insured?
5. What are some reasons for the popularity of mutual fund shares?
6. Why do some people have more state and local bonds than federal government bonds?
7. Compare the amount of household financial assets with household debts.

Questions for Analysis

1. What characteristics have made mutual savings banks unusually safe depositories?
2. How is a level premium computed for a whole-life policy?
3. Why do you think life insurance companies invest largely in corporate bonds while most other financial intermediaries do not?
4. Why do people buy common stocks that yield 3 percent when they could buy high-quality bonds that yield 6?
5. In mid-1969 Treasury bonds paying $40 per year interest and maturing in 1972 were selling at $920. What does this say about interest rates at that time?
6. What are the largest forms of households' financial assets? Why do households have these?
7. Why is debt necessary if people are going to save? How is debt related to real assets?

Case for Decision

Harry Wright is thirty years old and has a wife and two small children. He earns $9,500 per year as manager of a branch of a department store and expects to progress with the company. He lives in a house worth about $25,000, on which there is a $15,000 mortgage with a 6 percent interest rate. He believes that his insurance program is adequate.

Wright has recently learned that he is about to receive an inheritance of about $10,000 from an aunt. He has attempted to save fairly regularly and has accumulated about $1,000 in a regular savings account on which 4.5 percent interest is currently being paid, but he has never felt that he had adequate capital with which to make market investments.

While aware that interest rates are unusually high, Wright is not familiar with specific market yields so he has been jotting down some figures to help him decide what to do with the inheritance. From the financial press, he finds a wide choice. His list shows:

One-year Treasury bills	6.8 percent
Three-to-five-year Treasury bonds	6.4
Five-to-ten-year Treasury bonds	6.3
One-year certificate of deposit	5.0
Corporate bonds, various maturities	7.5 to 7.75
Municipal bonds, various maturities	6.1 to 6.4

As some indication of yields on common stocks, Wright has jotted down at random:

Ford Motor—dividend $2.40, price $49
Westinghouse Electric—dividend $1.80, price $58.50
Recognition Equipment—no dividend, price $57

He has also looked up a mutual fund in which a friend is investing, which the friend calls a conservative balanced fund. It is being offered at $16.25, and in the last couple of years the annual dividend from income has been 48 cents and the annual dividend from capital gains—paid in additional shares of the fund—$1.20.

Wright intends to ask the president of the local bank for his advice on what to do with his inheritance, but before doing so he wants to be able to narrow down his own preferences. He has decided to make a list of the advantages and disadvantages for him of each of the investments on his list.

If you were Wright, what would be your preference?

14
Government Finance

Governments are a truly important sector of the American economy. In 1969 purchases made by federal, state, and local governments amounted to 23 percent of total GNP. This percentage is less than in several other countries, but it is obviously sufficient to exert a strong influence on the economy. How these expenditures, amounting to $215 billion, are made and how the revenues to match them are obtained affect virtually every citizen. In examining this sector of the economy, we note two broad areas of study. The first deals with the many facts of governmental revenues and expenditures, the effects of specific taxes, the principles applied in this country in selecting among alternative sources of revenue, and related questions. This area is commonly called *public finance,* or governmental finance. The other area is concerned with the public policies that may be adopted in order to promote the stability and growth of the economy through government spending and taxing. This aspect of the subject is called *fiscal policy.* This chapter is devoted primarily to public finance, while fiscal policy is discussed in Chapter 16.

GOVERNMENTAL EXPENDITURES

The budget document for the federal government alone is a publication as large as the telephone directory of a major city. Supporting documents add hundreds of pages more. Expenditures of nearly equal total volume are made by the states, cities, towns, counties, and other governmental units. Consequently, any survey of this mass of data must be confined to broad categories.

Federal Budget Process

The budget is the instrument by which the President presents his financial proposals for the ensuing year to the Congress. The federal government uses a fiscal year starting on July 1, and work in the many administrative branches of government must start nearly a year and a half before expenditures are planned to begin. That is, early in the calendar year, usually February, the administrative branches and agencies begin to collect data to go into the budget message delivered the following January, recommending the budget for the fiscal year beginning July 1 and ending June 30 of the following year. For the fiscal year beginning July 1, 1970, for example, preliminary estimates had to be started in February of 1969.

The central coordinating agency for the plans of the administration is the Office of Management and Budget, created in 1970 to absorb the old Budget Bureau. As the budget begins to take shape and the President's wishes take form, the Budget Bureau provides the departments with guidelines. During the summer the Budget Bureau, the Treasury Department, and the President's Council of Economic Advisers estimate the effects of the forthcoming budget on the economy and the effects of economic conditions on revenues. As January nears, these estimates are made more precise and the detailed budget requests from each department are made formal.

The Congress is given the proposed budget in the President's budget message, along with a voluminous explanatory appendix and several publications called "Special Analyses" that are designed to clarify budget requests that do not fit neatly into departmental lines but pertain to similar functions. For public consumption and general information, the Bureau of the Budget also publishes *The Budget in Brief.*

Congress does not adopt a budget as such, a point not generally understood. It considers and passes appropriation bills. Enactment of these bills authorizes the expenditure of funds by appropriate agencies. Congress also separately considers revenue bills. A common criticism of the budget process, therefore, is this piecemeal approach. In nations with the parliamentary form of government, it is often the practice to adopt the overall revenue and expenditure measures together in a unified budget. In the United States, the President must approve or veto each appropriation act, and he lacks the power to approve some items and disapprove others (the item veto).

The Constitution requires that action on these matters originate in the House of Representatives. More than a dozen subcommittees take up the appropriation requests of specific agencies and report to the House Appropriations Committee. This committee's recommendations are acted upon by the full House. The Senate then goes through the budget requests by a similar process. If it fails to accept the House bill, joint conferences work out a compromise that goes back to the two houses for enactment.

Once the appropriation bills have been passed, the Budget Bureau reviews each department's requests and passes on them in light of the appropriations.

Types of Budgets

As the volume of governmental operations grew, the traditional type of budget just described, called the *administrative budget,* became less and less adapted to use in interpreting the economic effects of government expenditures and revenues. The main defect was that it did not include the operations of government trust funds because the revenues and expenditures of these funds do not depend upon annual action by the Congress. A principal example is the social security funds, which in recent years have taken in and expended sums in the neighborhood of $40 billion. Also, the federal government might have budget outlays for land or other existing assets, rather than for current output of goods and services, and many of its outlays are loans rather than expenditures. Consequently various analysts began to rearrange the information of federal finance, and the Budget Bureau followed suit. It prepared not only the traditional administrative budget but also the *cash budget* and the *national income accounts budget*. The former put together all the finan-

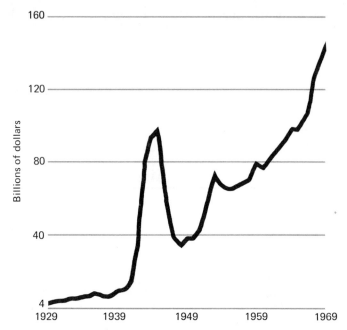

Figure 14-1. Federal expenditures, 1929–1969.   Source: President's Council of Economic Advisers, *Annual Report,* 1968, p. 284.

cial transactions of government with the public, in order to compare the volume of funds taken away from and the volume restored to the public. The latter attempted to measure more accurately the influence of the federal government on GNP. An important adjustment in the latter, for example, was to enter tax liabilities as they accrued, rather than as they were paid, because the economic effects of taxes, especially on corporations, occur as the taxes accrue.

Beginning with the 1969 budget, presented in January, 1968, a new form of budget was adopted, following largely the recommendations of a commission appointed by the President for this purpose. The budget is now unified in that it includes the operations of trust funds, separates loan outlays from current expenditures, nets out the revenues and expenditures of government business operations, and considers the sale of *participation certificates* a means of financing rather than revenue.[1] References to specific data subsequently in this chapter are based on the *unified budget* concept wherever possible.

Federal Expenditures

The dollar volume of federal expenditures has increased greatly over what it was in past years (see Figure 14-1). There are many reasons for this increase. Not all of them involve the growth of government relative to the economy as a whole. In recent decades, people have added to their budgets many items unknown to other generations—airplane travel, automobiles, radio, television, higher education, new drugs and medical

[1] An example of participation certificates: Some government agencies have acquired mortgage loans by purchase from lending institutions, issued securities using the mortgages as collateral, and sold the securities (participation certificates) to the public.

treatments, and so on—and it would be surprising if governmental functions had remained the same and expenditures had remained at the old levels.

The long-run rise in incomes and the standard of living affects the role of government in numerous ways. The public demands more goods and services obtained through government, as well as those obtained through the marketplace. As citizens, we have directly and indirectly approved of governmental functions in such new fields as social security and its extensions, such as Medicare; in the regulation of airlines and television stations; in research and the exploration of outer space; in the development of atomic energy; in giving foreign aid; and so forth. The urbanization of the population and the development of suburbs have probably had more direct effect on state and local governments, but they have also involved the federal government in highway construction, railroad transportation, slum-clearance projects, and health programs.

A principal cause of the present level of federal expenditures and of past increases in it is war. In each war there has been a sharp rise in expenditures which has not completely disappeared afterwards, partly because of wartime inflation of prices. Defense against war is a principal part of federal expenditures during peacetime. The expensive installations of electronic detection equipment in the radar network of the defense system and in the retaliatory bombers constantly in the air are only one example of this expense. War and defense add to the budget in other ways, through interest on a larger federal debt and through veterans' pensions, survivors' pensions, benefit payments to veterans for education or for entering business, and medical care.

Although federal expenditures have risen steeply since 1929, the postwar increase has approximately matched the growth of the economy. in Figure 14-2 are shown the trends of GNP and federal budget outlays. Two scales are used on this chart. The left-hand scale, which measures budget outlays, is one-fifth that of the right-hand scale, which measures GNP. It is plain that outlays have not fluctuated widely from one-fifth of GNP, once federal outlays fell from their wartime levels following 1945. The steeper rise in outlays after 1965, pushing them above the GNP line, is attributable to expenses of the war in Vietnam.

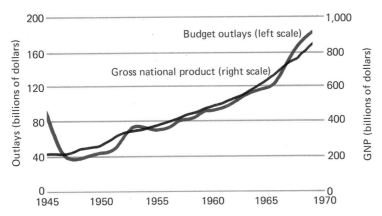

Figure 14-2. Federal outlays and GNP, 1945–1969.   Source: U.S. Department of the Treasury.

Types of Federal Expenditures

Governmental goods and services are received by the public in two broad ways. A relatively small portion of them is produced by the government sector itself, but most public goods are purchased by governments from the private sector. Governmental services are produced by government agencies much as private services are produced. Judges, army personnel, legislators, administrators, and numerous governmental employees such as teachers, social workers, agricultural agents, and others provide services that are paid for through government revenues rather than through market prices. Most of the government expenditure for this type of output takes the form of salaries and wages.

A large fraction of governmental expenditure, however, takes the form of purchases of output of private industries. Wages, salaries, and other incomes are thus obtained out of the sales prices paid by government. The government buys limousines for the justices, armament for the army, supplies for the legislators and administrators, and buildings, equipment, and so on for all these groups. The government does not have an army of employees who build highways, but it provides funds directly and through the states for the purchase of highway construction.

As was noted in an earlier chapter, another significant fraction of the federal government's outlays takes the form of transfer payments rather than purchase of current production. The principal items are social security and other benefits and interest on the federal debt.

Principal Federal Expenditures

The principal broad categories of federal outlays budgeted for fiscal 1970 are shown in Table 14-1. This table shows outlays by function,

Table 14-1
Federal Budget Outlays, Fiscal 1970

(Millions of Dollars)

	Amount	Percentage
National defense	$ 79,432	38.8
Health and welfare	57,097	28.0
Interest	17,821	8.7
Commerce and transportation	9,436	4.6
Veterans	8,681	4.3
Education and manpower	7,538	3.7
Agriculture	6,343	3.1
International affairs	4,113	2.0
Space research	3,886	1.9
Housing and community development	3,781	1.9
General government	3,620	1.8
Natural resources	2,485	1.2
Total °	$204,233	100.0

° Total shown here is exclusive of intragovernmental transfers.
Source: *Federal Reserve Bulletin*, February, 1970, p. A-41.

Table 14-2
State and Local Governmental Expenditures, 1967

	Amount (Millions of Dollars)		Percentage of Total	
	State	Local	State	Local
Education	$21,229	$28,552	39.8	48.0
Highways	11,284	4,552	21.2	7.7
Public welfare	7,188	4,022	13.5	6.8
Health and hospitals	3,659	3,374	6.9	5.7
Housing and urban renewal	95	1,441	.2	2.4
Natural resources	1,847	548	3.5	.9
Air transportation	88	400	.2	.7
Social insurance administration	545	2	1.0	....
Interest on general debt	1,026	2,007	1.9	3.4
Other	6,344	14,578	11.9	24.5
Total	$53,305	$59,476	100.0	100.0

rather than by the department or agency making the expenditures. The predominance of national defense in the total outlay is obvious and, if a goodly proportion of the expenditures for interest, veterans' affairs, and space research—all closely related to defense—were added, a very large part of the total budget would be seen to be defense-related.

State and Local Expenditures

There are more than 3,000 counties, 18,000 municipalities, and 17,000 townships in the United States, and over 22,000 school districts and 21,000 special taxing and spending districts providing sewers, water, parks, and other governmental goods and services.[2] Altogether, there are more than 81,000 such governmental units, of which nearly 71,000 have the power to tax property. With such a variety of local spending units, any discussion of their expenditures can only be summarized. A summary of state and local expenditures in 1967 is given in Table 14-2, with the expenditures listed in order of their importance for local governments.[3] Education tops the list for both state and local governments, and highways are second; public welfare is also a significant fraction. Many types of expenditures are included in the "other" category, such as those for police and fire protection, sanitation, parks and playgrounds, utilities (water, gas, electricity, and transit), and liquor stores.

Although much of federal expenditures is for capital goods, like dams, buildings, and defense installations, no effort is made, for budgeting purposes, to classify federal expenditures into current expenses and capital investments. A considerable amount of state and local expenditures, however, is budgeted for capital outlays—in 1967 over $11 billion for the states and $12 billion for the local governments. The largest capital item for the states is highways and, for the local governments, educational institutions.

[2] U.S. Bureau of the Census, *Statistical Abstract of the United States,* 1968, p. 406.

[3] *Ibid.,* 1969, pp. 412–413.

The forces leading to increased governmental expenditures have in some cases operated more directly on state and local governments than on the federal government. The principal expenditures, education and highways, for example, are ones for which modern society demands much more governmental service than used to be the case. As occurs in the private sector, the public directs more expenditures toward services as living standards rise. Since the provision of services is often less subject to economies of rising productivity than is the manufacture of commodities, the expansion of state and local expenditures tends to be costly. For example, the expansion of higher education, provision of facilities and services for the mentally ill, traffic control, and many other services are relatively expensive.

Direct expenditures of state and local governments have thus tended to rise at a fairly rapid rate. Such expenditures were $11 billion in 1942, as compared with $115 billion in 1967. By 1955, expenditures on education alone exceeded the total of all expenditures in 1942, and by 1965 such expenditures exceeded the total of all expenditures in 1950. The bulk of educational expenditures is for local schools, usually a responsibility of local governments, but the expenditures on higher education have pushed up state spending rapidly. Virtually all types of state and local expenditures are considerably higher than they were at the end of World War II.

Criteria for Governmental Expenditures

The problem of what services government should undertake, and to what extent, is an extremely old one. Basically it is a problem in economics because in essence it is a problem in the allocation of resources. Goods and services can be produced in response to demands expressed through private expenditures in the marketplace or in response to public expenditures financed through tax levies. Since hardly anyone welcomes the arrival of forms demanding payment of federal, state, and local taxes, there is a natural tendency for citizens to be more aware of the tax side of the equation than the expenditure, or benefit, side. The reduction of income and of the power to spend for consumption or to save is obvious, while the benefits received from the public use of the tax dollars are less obvious.

The element of compulsion in public expenditures also adds to the natural resistance to paying taxes. The citizen freely chooses whether to spend his income on sirloin steak or hamburger, or on a television set, cosmetics, clothing, vacations, or whatnot, but he is compelled to pay taxes and has no direct choice in how his tax money is spent. The determination of the "proper" level of expenditure by the several levels of government, and of the "proper" mix of expenditures within that level, consequently becomes primarily a problem in politics and sociology and not merely an exercise in economic theory.

The citizenry consequently tend to have divergent views of the necessity or desirability of proposed additions to public expenditures, and these views tend to become associated with other political beliefs. On the one hand, there is a tendency to believe that government expenditures are too high. This belief stems largely from the fact that the individual citizen is unlikely to be in favor of all the individual expenditures;

in his scale of values, some of them are of less importance than the things he would buy if he had a larger disposable income. One citizen considers better highways and access streets important because he is annoyed by traffic congestion, and he willingly pays taxes for highway construction. Another citizen is less concerned with this problem but is much interested in conservation of forests and trout streams. If government both builds highways and provides national and state forests and wilderness areas, both citizens feel that they are paying taxes for unnecessary governmental expenditures.

On the other hand, there are those who are greatly impressed by the general affluence of most private citizens and by the unmet needs of society that require public action. As Professor J. K. Galbraith argues in *The Affluent Society,*[4] traditional thinking, rooted in a past period when production was barely able to provide minimum standards of living for most of the population, puts a high social value on private production but considers most public expenditure a necessary evil. The "conventional wisdom" is that provision of public services is not so much a net increase in total output as it is a drag on private production. Thus people buy automobiles but resist public expenditure for adequate highways and parking lots, expand expenditures on telephone calls but demand reductions in postal expenditures, buy vacuum cleaners for home use but stint on sanitation departments' purchases of sweepers for the streets.

The economist's approach to the problem of how much of society's resources to allocate to public expenditures and how much to private is, of course, to attempt to allocate values and costs to public services. The difficulty, and the source of conflicting political opinions, is the lack of objective measures for the value of public services. By their nature, public services must be provided publicly or—in most cases—not at all. It is socially impossible, for example, for a city government to provide a sewer system yet allow some citizens to continue using outhouses rather than to pay for connecting to the system. It is impossible to provide police or fire protection only to those who want to buy it—if one house burns, others are threatened. Thus the ballot box has to be substituted for the marketplace and majority rule applied.

Needless to say, once a level of government adopts a function and expands its expenditures, the function should be carried out as efficiently as possible. Just as in private enterprise, public enterprise is wasteful of resources if it is not carried on with due regard to costs and modern methods of management.

In recent years the federal government has experimented extensively with *Planning-Programming-Budgeting Analysis,* or attempts to weigh costs and benefits of particular programs, especially in the Department of Defense. Such an analysis involves assigning benefits to a program, which are often necessarily rather arbitrarily valued in dollar terms, and then comparing the calculated benefits with the costs. Sometimes benefits are reasonably measurable, such as in the case of a dam that will provide water for irrigation. Other uses of the same project, such as boating and fishing, are more difficult to evaluate but clearly have some value. The Chairman of the House Ways and Means Committee, Wilbur D. Mills,

[4] Houghton Mifflin Company, Boston, 1958.

has stated, "We must continually re-evaluate existing expenditure programs in the light of a very objective measurement of the benefits which they convey and the costs which they will impose."[5]

The *benefit-cost analysis* tends in two ways to make governmental expenditures more economical in their allocation of resources. It may seem virtually impossible to assign dollar benefits to a program such as a defense system against missile attack, as the benefits include the saving of some assumed number of lives, weighed against other possible methods of accomplishing the same thing. Yet the discipline of being forced to put dollar values on such benefits helps to put various proposals in some sort of order of urgency. If the benefits clearly outweigh the costs in the case of one proposal but benefits barely outweigh costs in another, the choice between them is easy to make and the question of which should be done first is largely answered. Where the benefits cannot be shown to outweigh the costs, the presumption is that government should not undertake that project.

A second result of carefully weighing costs and benefits is that the economist's concern with marginal values and costs tends to be emphasized. The problem is not whether the Department of Defense should have bombers or whether a local government should provide schools; rather, the problem is how many bombers and how many schools? Ideally, the calculation should weigh the benefits of one more bomber against its costs, one more school against its costs. In this way, the calculation helps to determine whether another bomber is a better purchase than a few more pursuit planes or something even less closely related. The calculation also helps to determine whether more benefit would be gained from improving facilities within existing school buildings than from building a new school. In this way public officials and legislators can imitate, in a general way, the process of valuation that takes place in private markets. The housewife does not decide between buying some bread and no bread, but between more bread and less bread, in the light of other things that might provide more satisfaction at the same cost than another loaf of bread.

GOVERNMENTAL REVENUES

Public expenditures require equivalent revenues, whether from taxes, other sources of revenue, or borrowing. Sources of governmental revenues are shown in Figures 14-3 and 14-4. Different levels of government have developed reliance on different types of taxes, largely by historical accident.

Federal Revenues

In the early days of this country, the federal government relied heavily on tariff duties. By modern standards, federal expenditures were very small, and this form of indirect taxation generally provided adequate revenues. During the Civil War an income tax was adopted, but it was declared unconstitutional. The Sixteenth Amendment was adopted in 1913 in order to permit *direct* taxes to be levied without regard to the population of the

[5] Quoted in *NAM Reports,* Aug. 19, 1968.

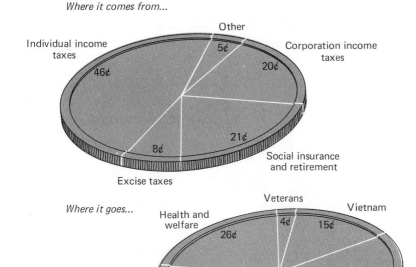

*Excludes interest paid to trust funds.

Figure 14-3. The federal government dollar, fiscal year 1969.   Source: *Your Federal Income Tax,* 1970 ed., U.S. Department of the Treasury.

different states.[6] Since then income taxes on individuals and corporations have become the principal source of federal revenue.

Governmental revenues have naturally grown in step with expenditures. Federal revenues from taxes first exceeded $100 billion in fiscal 1966. This figure amounted to $531 per capita, or roughly $2,000 per family. Individual income taxes provide over half of the total tax revenue, and corporate income taxes nearly a third. (These fractions are higher than those shown in Figure 14-3 because they apply to tax revenues only, not total revenues.)

State and Local Revenues

Originally the state governments relied heavily on property taxes, as did the local governments. However, the difficulty of assessing property fairly across the state and the growing load on this single source of revenue led the states to develop other taxes, particularly sales or gross-receipts taxes and income taxes. The property tax remains the principal form of local taxation. (See Figure 14-4.)

State and local revenues from taxes amounted to $308 per capita in 1967. Other sources of revenue such as liquor stores, utilities, and trust

---

[6] A direct tax is one levied directly on the taxpayer who pays it, rather than indirectly as through a sales tax, which may in terms of law be levied on the seller.

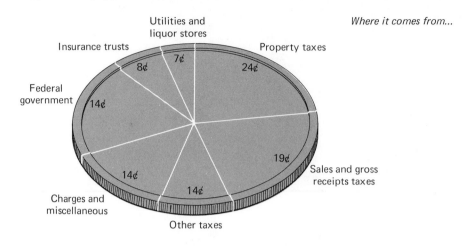

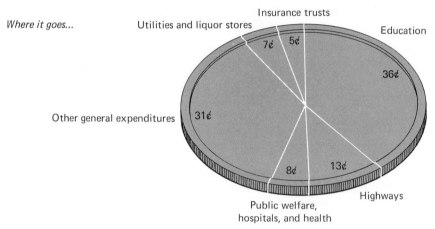

Figure 14-4. State and local government dollars, 1967. Source: U.S. Bureau of the Census, *Statistical Abstract of the United States,* 1969, p. 402.

funds increased the per capita amount to $539. Property taxes provided about $25 billion for local governments but only about $1 billion for state governments. In contrast, sales and gross-receipts taxes provided $19 billion for state governments and $2 billion for local governments. Many local governments rely on grants from their states and the federal government for part of their income, and states receive grants from the latter. State grants to localities are often for educational purposes. Federal grants give financial assistance for welfare, highways, education, and parts of the social security programs.

Criteria for Taxes

In general, two principles have developed over the years as criteria for the fairness of specific taxes. The older one is the *benefit principle,* that people should pay taxes according to the benefits received from government. This principle grew up partly because of the reliance in the early days on the property tax. It was argued that if one person paid taxes on

Table 14-3
Progressive, Proportional, and Regressive Taxes

Tax Base (e.g., Income)	Progressive		Proportional		Regressive	
	Amount of Tax	Per-centage	Amount of Tax	Per-centage	Amount of Tax	Per-centage
$ 1,000	$ 30	3	$ 50	5	$ 50	5
3,000	150	5	150	5	120	4
5,000	500	10	250	5	150	3
10,000	1,500	15	500	5	200	2
20,000	4,000	20	1,000	5	200	1

twice as much property as another, he also received twice as much bene-fit. But it is very difficult to measure the benefits received and, in many instances, it is not desirable to follow the rule. It is difficult to say how much benefit any one citizen derives from the space program or national defense, or how it compares with the benefit received by others. Also, if it is accepted policy that all children should receive an education, a young family with three or four children receives more benefit than does an older family whose children have finished school. The benefits of free public schools have to be considered general benefits for society, not specific benefits for only those who are educated.

The other principle came into prominence with the increased use of income taxes. It holds that people should pay taxes in accordance with their *ability to pay,* but it goes far back in history.[7] The same difficulty of measurement is encountered, this time of ability to pay. Ability to pay is undoubtedly related in some way to income, but what is the relationship? Does twice the income provide twice the ability — or more? In other words, the problem is introduced of whether the tax should be *proportional* (the same rate regardless of the size of the income base) or *progressive* (the rate rising as the income base rises). And if the principle of progres-sion is adopted, there is still the question of how rapidly the rates should rise on larger incomes. There is also the difficulty that people with similar incomes may not be considered to have similar tax-paying ability. A single man may have an income of $15,000, as may a family with several young children, a mortgage on the home, and perhaps considerable expenses for doctors and medicines.

Examples of progressive, proportional, and regressive taxes are shown in Table 14-3. A *regressive tax* is one in which the rate of tax goes down as the tax base rises. A tax is sometimes called regressive also if it is a larger proportion of small incomes than of large incomes regardless of the ac-tual base of the tax. For example, an excise tax such as that on ciga-rettes tends to take more of the income of a poor man who smokes than of

[7] Adam Smith wrote in 1776 (*Wealth of Nations,* Book V), "The subjects of every state ought to contribute towards the support of government, as nearly as possible, in proportion to their re-spective abilities; that is, in proportion to the revenue which they respectively enjoy under the protection of the state."

a rich man who smokes. The property tax is an example of a *proportional tax* because the amount of tax is proportional to the value of the property. However, it is sometimes said that this tax tends to be regressive because small properties may be valued for tax purposes closer to their market values than are large properties. The income tax is the principal example of a *progressive tax,* as the tax rate rises on higher incomes. Again, however, the income tax may not be as progressive as the rates indicate because recipients of high incomes may be able to find tax shelters for some of their income. For example, income in the form of capital gains is subject to rates below those on regular income, and interest on state and municipal bonds is not taxed by the federal government.

There is no satisfactory way in which to measure such subjective criteria as benefit and ability, but in broad, general ways these principles do affect the selection of taxes and tax rates. In the case of property taxes, it is generally felt that the same rate should apply to all real estate, or at least to all real estate of the same general type (such as housing), and that to charge different people different rates would be unfair. Similarly, it is generally felt that people with high incomes can afford (and should pay at) higher income-tax rates than those with lower incomes. It is probably impossible to devise a system of taxes that is completely fair to everyone, but the complex set of taxes in use probably cannot be characterized as particularly unfair to any group.

Besides these considerations of fairness, there are other criteria by which a given tax may be judged. So far as possible, a tax should be economical to administer; that is, a large part of the tax revenue should not be lost in collection costs. Also, it is desirable that a tax be as simple as possible to compute. This is one of the criticisms of the federal income tax; in spite of efforts of the Internal Revenue Service to make computations simple, the complexities of the law still make computation difficult for many taxpayers. A flat rate for everyone, regardless of income and dependents, would be simple but would violate other principles of fairness. From the point of view of the governments involved, it is desirable that a tax provide a stable source of revenue. The property tax ranks high in this regard, the state inheritance tax rather low because deaths of people with large estates do not occur at a steady annual rate. And from a broader point of view, it is also desirable that taxes be drawn in such a way that they do not reduce incentives to work and to earn, or otherwise lead people to act uneconomically. This is one of the problems of progressive income-tax rates, and there are other examples, such as the taxes on forest property. If a tax must be paid annually on the value of the trees, the owner may be tempted to cut the trees before the best time whereas if, instead, he were to pay a "severance" tax at the time the trees were cut, he would not be under pressure to obtain the revenue too soon.

INCIDENCE OF TAXES

A major problem of taxation is the question of the ultimate effects of different taxes and whether the taxpayer on whom a tax is levied actually bears the tax or is able to shift the burden, such as through charging a higher price, to someone else.

Shifting of Taxes

Whether a tax, such as one on gasoline, cigarettes, or telephone messages, can be shifted can be answered by reference to the principles developed in Chapters 3 and 4. The purchaser of cigarettes does not pay a tax directly to the government, but the manufacturer must pay the excise tax in order to sell the cigarettes. From his point of view, this tax is like any other variable cost in that the more packs he sells, the higher the total tax, and this cost must be covered by the price in the long run. If the amount of the tax is covered in the price, the seller who *pays* the tax does not *bear* the tax; the purchaser of the commodity bears it, along with the other costs of production covered by the market price. As we noted in Chapter 4, the imposition of such a tax raises the supply curve, in the sense that any given amount of output can now be produced only at a higher cost than before the tax. Taken by itself, the imposition of a tax should not affect the position of the demand curve, but the higher-cost supply curve now cuts the demand curve at a point indicating a higher price and a reduced volume of sales. At this quantity, the marginal cost exclusive of the tax is lower than it was for the larger quantity.

The general rules that evolve from this analysis are:

1. If a tax represents a cost of production, it reduces supply and raises price. See Figure 14-5, in which a tax is levied on the output or sales of a commodity. The amount of the tax is measured by the distance between P_1 and P_3. The supply curve shifts upward by the amount of the tax. If the old quantity Q_1 could be sold at the old price plus the tax, the new price would be P_3 but, since the demand curve has some elasticity, only some smaller quantity can be sold. The new supply curve intersects the demand curve at P_2 and Q_2. In this particular case something over half of the tax is reflected in the higher price. However, notice that all the tax is covered by the new price because the tax is now added to a lower point on the old supply curve.

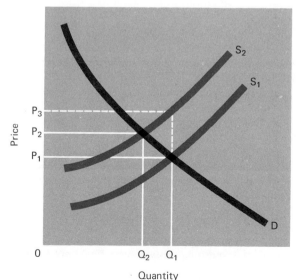

Figure 14-5. Incidence of a tax.

2. To the extent that the demand is inelastic, the price rises by a larger proportion of the tax; if demand were perfectly inelastic (the demand curve vertical), all the tax would be passed on in higher price and there would be no reduction in sales.

3. To the extent that the supply of a commodity is inelastic, however, suppliers continue to supply nearly as much as before the tax was levied on it and they are therefore unable to raise price very much; in this case, less of the tax is passed on to purchasers.

Another possibility is that the producer or seller on whom the tax is levied may be able to shift some of the tax backward, that is, on his suppliers, by paying less for his materials or labor. This could take place if his sales are reduced by the higher price charged and, consequently, his purchases are curtailed also. If this reduction in demand for things he buys reduces the prices of these things, some of the tax is borne by suppliers in the form of lower prices received.

It follows from these comments that if a tax is not in some manner a cost, it cannot affect supply and therefore it cannot affect price. In a perfectly competitive economy, a tax on personal or corporate income would not affect price. If we assume that everyone is already maximizing his income, the imposition of a tax based on that income would not lead anyone to change the amount produced and offered for sale, because to do so would reduce income even further. The greatest possible income would still be gained at the optimum amount of output. But there is some question in the real world whether high income-tax rates may in fact have some effect on output when they reduce after-tax income sufficiently to make leisure more desirable than the extra income available from maximizing income.

It may be, therefore, that there are instances of income taxes being shifted if they impinge sufficiently on income to affect total supply. A prominent surgeon, for example, may be able to earn $100,000 before taxes by performing a certain number of operations but, when he considers the after-tax "take-home pay" available from doing a fourth of these operations, decide to earn $75,000 before taxes and enjoy a greater amount of leisure. If enough surgeons behave similarly, the supply of their services is reduced and the price of surgeons' services tends to rise. The reduction in supply enables surgeons to charge more and in effect shift some of their income taxes to their patients.

Various studies of the reactions of high-income recipients to progressive tax rates have been made and suggest that this reduction of the supply of their services may be considerably less than might be supposed. People often have noneconomic motives for working or for working as hard as they do, and this is often true of people with sufficient talent and ability to earn high incomes. In a study covering nearly a thousand persons whose incomes ranged from $10,000 to over $1 million in 1961, it was found that high tax rates on marginal income had surprisingly little effect on the amount of work done.[8] The findings of this study suggest that few people subject to rates on the highest brackets of their income of 70 percent and more work less because of the tax. More people whose incomes are subject to marginal rates between 50 percent and 70 percent

---

[8] Robin Barlow, Harvey E. Brazer, and James N. Morgan, *Economic Behavior of the Affluent*, The Brookings Institution, Washington, 1966.

seem to, however. The reason may be that as a person increases his income to where additional income is taxed at 50 percent or more, he is at first resentful and does not want to become subject to even higher tax rates; later, as he gets used to the rate, the disincentive to work weakens and other motives, perhaps, prevail.

PUBLIC DEBT

Many people are concerned about the federal government's debt. Much of the public's concern about the debt stems from the failure to distinguish between the current deficit that adds to the debt and the existing debt itself. The effects of a deficit in a given year are not the same as the effects of the existence of a public debt created by past deficits. Recent periods of growth in the federal debt have led to considerable public interest and have given rise to many opinions that economists consider naïve. Much of the popular fear of debt arises from periods in history when great deficits (in this and other countries) had serious inflationary effects. The following discussion consequently distinguishes between problems created by deficits and problems created by existing debts of governments.

Growth of the Public Debt

Government debt seems to be synonymous in much public discussion with the debt of the federal government, but it should be remembered that a substantial part of government debt in this country is owed by state and local governments. At year-end 1968, state and local debts were $129 billion, while the federal debt was $292 billion. Since the end of World War II, the growth of state and local debt has been much more rapid than the growth of federal debt. These debts on various dates are shown in Table 14-4, along with corporate and individual debts for perspective.

Some interesting relationships are revealed in Table 14-4. It may be seen that corporate debts declined in the 1930s. This decline did not result from prosperity that enabled corporations to repay debt but from just the opposite. These debts declined as a result of the great depression, during which there was little incentive to borrow funds for expansion of business. Similarly, the decline in noncorporate debt represents mainly a gradual repayment while little new debt for purchasing homes and other durables was taken on. The only sector that felt able to expand expenditures during the 1930s was the federal government, and here, as a result, was an increase in debt. The slight increase in state and local debt resulted more from a decline in revenues than from increased expenditures.

During the war years 1940–1945, there was little opportunity for state and local governments, corporations, or individuals to expand their debts because construction of highways, schools, commercial buildings, and homes was controlled, but the federal government borrowed heavily for war purposes. It may be seen that the federal debt declined after the war and was still below the 1945 figure in 1960, while many demands on state and local governments led to a rapid expansion of their debts. Similarly, there has been rapid growth of private debt, largely to finance construction of homes and industry.

Table 14-4
Net Public and Private Debt, Selected Dates
(Billions of Dollars)

End of Year	Public Federal Government and Agency	Public State and Local	Private Corporate	Private Individual and Noncorporate
1930	$ 16.5	$ 14.7	$ 89.3	$ 71.8
1935	34.4	16.1	74.8	49.7
1940	44.8	16.4	75.6	53.0
1945	252.5	13.4	85.3	54.7
1950	217.4	21.7	142.1	104.3
1955	229.6	40.2	212.1	180.1
1960	239.8	63.0	302.8	263.3
1965	266.4	99.9	454.3	416.1
1968	291.9	128.6	604.5	522.2

Source: President's Council of Economic Advisers, *Economic Report of the President*, 1970, p. 248. Net debt is total debt minus any of the debt held by the debtors themselves.

The figures in Table 14-4 show the *net public debt* rather than the gross debt because they allow for that part of the debt that is owned by government agencies themselves. Government trust funds, such as the social security funds, generally invest only in Treasury securities. The Federal Reserve banks also hold a substantial part of the debt. Most of the interest received by the Federal Reserve banks is returned to the Treasury as a kind of tax. On the other hand, the figures in Table 14-4 include the debts of government agencies although they are not direct obligations of the Treasury. At the end of 1968, the gross debt of the Treasury itself was $358.0 billion, but government investment accounts held $76.6 billion and the reserve banks $52.9 billion, leaving $228.5 billion owed to "the public." The largest holders of the debt, in order, are individuals, commercial banks, and a miscellaneous group including savings and loan associations, pension funds, trust companies, and foreigners.

Effects of Growth of Debt

As we have just seen, private debts tend to grow in periods of prosperity, not in periods of recession. This is neither strange nor accidental, as it is partly with borrowed funds that businesses expand their plant and equipment and households add to their durable possessions. Indeed, if this output were not purchased with funds made available by savers, the prosperous period would probably not occur at all, since saving by itself reduces total market demands. Debt is the mechanism by which savers make available the saved funds to those who wish to use them, as we examined in Chapter 13.

Public debts differ from private debts in that there is a less close connection between the debts and productive uses of the funds. No one sees anything uneconomic or foolish about a corporation borrowing funds at 6 percent to help finance a plant that is expected to earn 15 percent. Whether governmental borrowing is equally sensible depends upon the uses of the funds. If a city fails to tax its citizens enough to cover the costs of its annual current expenses, a debt builds up that eventually requires heavy interest payments as one of the annual expenses as well as eventual payments for debt retirement. Unless the local citizens buy the bonds themselves, in which case they will eventually pay interest and repayments to themselves, they will have to make these payments to outsiders. The example is comparable to that of a business whose current revenues fail to cover its current expenditures; rather than earning a profit it has a deficit, which must be covered either by debt or by using past savings.

In another situation, however, a local government may be completely justified in borrowing. This is especially true when it is about to make a large capital expenditure. When a small town builds a school building, it would perhaps have to tax itself very heavily—perhaps impossibly so—in order to raise the cost of the building in the same year. The building will serve the town for perhaps thirty years, and there is no more reason why the townspeople should pay for the building in one year than there is for a household to have to pay for a house out of a single year's income. The situation is different if a city is so large that it finds it necessary to build a school building every year, either because of its growth or to replace old buildings. In this case, expenditures for school buildings are annual expenditures and borrowing funds for the purpose would not spread the cost over a longer period, because the costs arise every year anyway.

The situation also differs with respect to the federal government because, as we have noted, the distinction between capital and current expenditures is more difficult to make. Whether the federal government should cover a year's expenditures entirely with tax revenues or resort to borrowing becomes a matter of fiscal policy. As we shall examine more closely in Chapter 16, the economic effects of federal expenditures and taxes are so great that they can be used to affect business conditions in general. Expenditures in excess of tax revenues can be beneficial to the economy when private purchases are not providing a gross national product sufficient to provide high levels of employment. If the federal government refuses to permit a deficit to occur under these circumstances, it refuses to use one of its most important means of affecting the economy. More accurately stated, it *is* using it, but in the wrong direction.

When there are unemployed resources of plant, equipment, and labor, there is no real cost to the economy when the government borrows otherwise idle funds or newly created funds from the banking system and spends them on public works. The real cost of anything is what must be given up in order to obtain it. If a federal deficit results in a net addition to total output, nothing is given up to obtain this output and income. In a period of full employment, however, the resources devoted to construction of a school building or other public project must be diverted from other uses. The real cost of the school building, as measured by the dollar costs, is the other things that could have been produced with an equivalent expenditure.

When governments have deficits in periods of full employment, the deficits tend to be inflationary. In this respect, government debt is not different from private debts. Any borrowing can be excessive, just as it can also be inadequate. The federal government is in a better position to adjust its own borrowing (by adjusting its expenditures and tax revenues) to the needs of the overall economy than are businesses and households. If the government permits a deficit to develop when there are already heavy market demands for output, and if it raises the funds by selling securities to the banking system for new deposits, its expenditures draw resources away from other uses and tend to cause a general rise in prices.

It follows that borrowing or debt is neither good nor bad in itself. The economic effects depend upon the circumstances. State and local governments have much the same reasons for using debt as do households. The federal government is in a position to finance expenditures through debt when the additional expenditures are appropriate and to cover its expenditures by taxes when taxes should be used to restrain others' expenditures.

The Burden of Public Debt

One of the most widely held notions about government debt is that it must constitute a burden on future generations. Whatever the merits of a current deficit under varying circumstances, this idea of the nature of an existing debt is incorrect. This can be illustrated by reference to a specific debt, such as that created during World War II.

Whether the government obtains the funds it spends for war purposes entirely from taxation or partly from borrowing depends on the sources of funds it taps during the war. Debt is a mechanism for determining which citizens provide the dollars to be spent by the government. It is possible that the same citizens would provide the same amounts whether through taxes or through bonds. Suppose that $100 million is to be raised from 1 million citizens. The government might tax each citizen, on the average, $100. Or it might tax each citizen $50 and sell each a $50 bond. If each citizen buys a $50 bond, the government will later have to pay him interest and eventually repay the debt. If the interest is $2 a year, or $2 million in total, the government must raise this sum through taxation. It is conceivable that each citizen would pay $2 more in taxes and get back $2 in interest. The same reasoning applies to repayment of the debt. Any taxes raised from the citizens for debt repayment are paid back to the citizens for their bonds.

Presumably, however, people (and financial institutions) do not buy the bonds in the same proportions as they pay taxes. In this example, each of the 1 million citizens might pay $50 in taxes and half of the citizens might buy $100 bonds. In the future, all the citizens will pay $2 in taxes for interest on the public debt and half of them will receive $4 in interest. One result of a large public debt, then, is this *transfer effect,* whereby some citizens transfer income as taxes to others as interest. But it does not follow from this fact that the failure of the citizens to pay for the war without borrowing creates a burden for a future *generation.* The generation that lived during 1941–1945 paid for the war. Some people paid less than they would have paid if all the expenditures had been covered by taxes; others paid more at that time by purchasing bonds as well as paying taxes. These bondholders received indirect claims on the taxpayers (including themselves) for future interest payments and return of the borrowed funds. A quarter of a century later, in 1970, when we may assume the bonds mature, any payments that must be *made* by the new generation must also be *received* by the new generation. Any payments made to bondholders in 1970 must be raised from taxpayers in 1970. The 1970 generation pays, but it also receives. If we look at the 1945 generation as a whole and the 1970 generation as a whole, we see that there was a shift of the financial burden between groups of the 1945 generation and that there is a shift of income between groups of the 1970 generation.

All this is not to say that the existence of the debt is entirely free from problems. But it should be clear that it is a physical and logical impossibility for one generation to shift a financial burden to a future generation. This impossibility stems from the simple fact that future taxpayers pay future bondholders; future taxpayers do not pay past bondholders. If the future generation inherits the tax liabilities, the members of the future generation also inherit the bonds entitling them to payment. The only exception to this statement would occur if a significant fraction of the bonds had originally been sold to foreigners. In that case, the old generation would have avoided payment for some of the costs of the war (by not purchasing bonds), and the new generation would pay taxes, in effect, to foreigners.

In this respect, state and local debt resembles private debt more than federal debt does. Much of a local debt is likely to be sold to residents of other parts of the country, and some years later the local citizens are paying interest to "foreigners." It does not follow, of course, that the locality should not have borrowed. The citizens may be sending their children to a school built with the borrowed funds and, while they are still paying for the school building, it is still currently benefiting them. It might be that the funds were borrowed to pay for a statue of a local hero, in which case the citizens today might regret the necessity of still paying interest on the debt. But in this case their complaint should be against the unwise expenditure, rather than the debt itself. By the same token, if the earlier citizens had raised the funds for the statue through taxation at the time, today's citizens might wish that they had built a memorial school building instead.

Problems Related to the Debt

While the public debt is not a burden in the usual sense of the word, its existence may create problems for the economy. We may reverse the usual opinion of the existence of a burden by turning it around and thinking only of the crisp, beautifully engraved bonds that the present generation is lucky enough to have inherited from thrifty ancestors who bought the bonds long ago! This would leave out half the problem, just as is done by those who think only of the tax side. But while this aspect of the debt is greatly exaggerated, other problems should not be overlooked.

A principal problem, as already suggested, is the fact that a considerable transfer of income from taxpayers to bondholders is required. While it is true that we "pay it to ourselves" insofar as the entire generation or population is concerned, the transfer may not be easy. It should be noted, however, that this shift in incomes may not be as great as might be supposed. Both tax payments and government debt are widely diffused. Perhaps the wealthy own most of the government bonds (although this is not necessarily true; the wealthy usually prefer other assets), but they also pay higher taxes. Much of the federal debt is held by government agencies and the Federal Reserve banks, and this part does not represent a burden on the public. Much of the debt is also owned by banks, insurance companies, business corporations, and pension funds. Indirectly, the interest paid to these holders goes to numerous ultimate recipients. It is virtually impossible to trace whether a given person pays more in taxes for debt service than he regains directly and indirectly.

The fact that the transfer must be made leads to other potential problems. For one, the existence of the debt rigidifies the federal budget in that there is a continuing expenditure item for interest and, to this extent, the general level of tax rates must be higher than would otherwise be necessary. There is probably, therefore, some tendency to limit the government's choices among uses of funds; to adopt some additional but socially desirable program would push taxes up even higher. It is also possible that the deflationary effects of the taxes are greater than the inflationary effects of the interest or transfer payments. The individual bondholder sees no direct connection between the interest he receives and the taxes he pays. If he were to stop earning other income, he would continue to receive the interest. Some people may be tempted to cease earning marginal income for the twin reasons that they have the interest income anyway and that tax rates are higher than they would be without this cost to the government. But if there is such an effect, it must be slight.

It should also be noted that a public debt has some advantages. Government bonds are desirable financial assets; in fact, some of the loudest critics of the debt may have some of the bonds safely locked up in their safe-deposit boxes. The fact that financial institutions and individuals hold government bonds when they could obtain higher yields from other securities indicates that they consider them safer assets. Government securities help make possible the existence of an efficient money market through which funds can be shifted easily from those who have excess funds to those who need them. For example, financial institutions buy government bonds from other holders when loan demands do not use up all their available funds, and they sell these securities to other holders when they need funds for additional loans. Through this and related markets for short-term funds, money flows freely to those with the most urgent needs as represented by a willingness to pay the highest interest rates.

SUMMARY

As we have seen, public debt is like private debt in some respects but entirely different in others. It is like private debt in that it is one means of financing, and it may be appropriate or not in a particular case. Public debt, especially that of the federal government, differs in that it involves the whole economy, not just one segment of it. Some of the widespread aversion to public debt is due to a failure to make this distinction. When a household uses debt to purchase offsetting assets, it is not criticized, but financing ordinary consumption in excess of income is considered unwise because consumption will later have to be curtailed in order to reduce the debt. It is also true that a government can abuse debt, and irresponsible governments have done so throughout history. Such borrowing, added to private expenditures, can strain the economy to the point of maximum potential output and into a condition of inflation. There have been examples of such borrowing, first from willing lenders, then from a captive banking system, and finally by printing money. The excesses of irresponsible governments, from Nero to the French kings at Fontainebleau and Versailles, and many examples of failure to tax adequately in time of war have created widespread disapproval of government deficits.

Yet, a responsible modern government has options open to it that are not open to individual parts of the economy. It is sometimes better economics to add to total expenditures in the economy than not to do so, just as at other times it makes better sense to reduce the total expenditures by reducing those of government. The fact that the federal debt remains in existence should cause no more alarm than the fact that corporate debt is never entirely eliminated but, in fact, grows. Individual debts are paid, but new ones are created at a somewhat faster rate. Similarly, individual government bond issues are always paid, but sometimes with money raised by selling other bonds. Sometimes the holder of a maturing bond would rather accept a new bond than receive payment in money.

Again, these comments do not imply that there is no economic limit to the size of the public debt. There are times when creation of debt is wise and others when it would be inflationary. As we saw in Chapter 13, if there is saving by some sectors of the economy, there must be debt to transfer the saved funds to others. Often, it may be preferable for these funds to be borrowed by business corporations or by state and local governments; if these demands are inadequate, it may be wise for the federal government to borrow them in order to return them to the income stream.

Economic Terms for Review

national income accounts budget	progressive tax
unified budget	shifting of taxes
benefit-cost analysis	net public debt
benefit principle	burden of public debt
ability to pay	transfer effect

Questions for Review

1. How does the American budget-making process differ from that in many parliamentary governments?
2. What are some of the recently added functions of government?
3. What are the largest types of federal expenditures?
4. What are the largest types of state and local expenditures?
5. Do you think governments spend too much or too little? Why?
6. What is Planning-Programming-Budgeting analysis?
7. On what principle of taxation is the income tax based?

Questions for Analysis

1. If the excise tax on gasoline were raised by 5 cents a gallon, would the price probably rise by more, less, or exactly 5 cents?
2. The federal debt is about $1,500 per person in the United States. Does this fact indicate that the debt should rapidly be reduced?
3. Why did government debt rise and corporate debt fall in the 1930s?
4. Why might a large city be foolish to finance a new school with bonds, but not a small town?
5. The federal debt rose by some $200 billion during World War II. Did this financing shift the cost of the war to future generations?
6. What are some of the problems that exist because of a large government debt?

Case for Decision

In June, 1969, President Nixon sent to the Congress a special message in which he recommended that the federal government spend $5.6 billion on airports and other air-transport facilities over the next ten years. He coupled this recommendation with another for special taxes and fees to raise the required revenue: a tax of $3 on international flight tickets, a tax of 5 percent on air freight, and a tax of 9 cents per gallon on jet fuel used in general aviation (as compared with commercial aviation). He also recommended raising two existing taxes: the tax on aviation gasoline used in general aviation and the tax on domestic flight tickets.

The expenditures would be for increased outlays on air-traffic control, airport construction, and research and development. The new level of expenditures would be more than twice that of current outlays.

The Nixon proposals resulted from dissatisfaction with congestion and delays at airports and complaints over the apparent decline in safety caused by these conditions. Senator Magnuson (D., Washington) had already introduced a bill, referred to the Senate Commerce Committee, containing similar provisions.

While the other provisions of both bills would be considered by the House and Senate Commerce Committees, the revenue provisions would have to be considered by the House Ways and Means Committee and the Senate Finance Committee. In the past, proposals for levying or increasing so-called user taxes generally died in these committees.

The Nixon and Magnuson proposals suggest several areas of discussion. Should the federal government be concerned with providing airport facilities and traffic control? If these are important federal concerns, should the funds be raised from these specific sources or from general revenues? How are the benefits from these expenditures to be calculated? Who gets the benefits? Who should pay for them?

Part 5
Stability and Growth
of the Economy

15
Economic Fluctuations and Growth

The level of economic activity, as measured by output, employment, or production of income, does not remain the same month after month and year after year. Neither does it rise at a steady pace. There is a maximum level of output and employment at any given time, but seldom does the economy reach it. Actual output and employment are sometimes substantially below this point of full employment, at other times virtually at this point. Sometimes they are below because output has actually declined, while at other times it is because output has failed to grow as fast as employable resources would permit. But while there are ups and downs in total economic activity, in the long run expansions of output exceed contractions. As a result, there is long-run growth of the economy. The discussion of the national income and its determination in Chapters 9 and 10 suggests reasons for fluctuations in national income. These reasons are examined more closely in this chapter.

ECONOMIC FLUCTUATIONS

Three major categories of economic fluctuations have been identified by statisticians. These are called seasonal fluctuations, cyclical fluctuations, and the long-run trend. The influence of each of these can be isolated by techniques of statistical analysis,[1] but at any given point in time most measures of economic activity reflect all three influences; they may also reflect a fourth type of influence, called random or sporadic.

In many industries output and employment vary from season to season for natural reasons. Agricultural production provides an obvious example, but residential and highway construction, tourism, automobile production, and many other industries also exhibit seasonal variations. These variations do not all cancel out, so there is also some *seasonal variation* in total output or GNP.

A *cyclical variation* is one associated with the business cycle. Some industries have cycles of their own, but the term is more commonly applied to the tendency of the economy to expand or contract in total. One of the better known single-industry cycles is that related to corn and hog production and prices. When hog prices are high, production is stimulated. The demand for corn to be used for feed is also stimulated, its price rises and, in turn, plantings of corn increase. As production of hogs catches up with demand, prices decline, production declines, and

[1] For an explanation of these techniques, see any elementary textbook in statistics, for example, Lawrence J. Kaplan, *Elementary Statistics for Economics and Business,* Pitman Publishing Corporation, New York, 1966.

there is less demand for corn, so its production and price follow a similar pattern. Once such a cycle is started, there is some tendency for it to persist. For example, if an unusually large number of automobiles is produced in one year, a few years later these cars tend to be scrapped at about the same time, leading to a repetition of high demand for new cars. The term business cycle, however, is applied to the tendency of the economy as a whole to pass through periods of alternate expansion and contraction — periods in which output is rising and unemployment is falling alternating with periods in which output is leveling off or falling and unemployment is rising.

In a given month a particular industry may be at a seasonal high point of output while, at the same time, it is affected by a recession in the economy generally. In such a case, output of the industry may be near its peak for the year but below the level reached in the same month of the previous year. The industry may be one that is growing on a _long-run_ _trend,_ so that its capacity has been built up considerably over the past decade; thus its output is well above that of a decade ago although below both its capacity and last year's output. This situation is applicable to the economy as a whole in that there are more growing industries than declining ones and total output is virtually always higher than it was a decade earlier even when it is at the low point of a business cycle. Only in recessions of unusual severity has the reverse been true.

Seasonal Fluctuations

A comparison of college enrollments in August with those in the previous October would obviously not truly indicate a great drop in the number of people attending college. Only the figures for the ensuing college year would reflect the true rise or fall without distortion from the seasonal influence. The same is true of many industries and, if these industries are sufficiently important in a country's economy, the national economy probably reflects a decided seasonal variation in output and employment.

Agricultural countries tend to exhibit these natural seasonal fluctuations.[2] There is naturally more employment in the busy seasons of planting and harvesting, not only in agriculture itself but in related industries such as transportation and trade. But these fluctuations are not of prime economic concern because they reverse themselves each year and they do not automatically lead to cumulative movements of the economy in the same direction. When the United States was more heavily dependent on agriculture, however, there were instances when seasonal peaks in agriculture coincided with high points of the business cycle and resulted in more demands for financing than the banking system could supply. The results in a few of these instances were bank failures and financial panic, leading in turn to serious recessions.

Since the seasonal fluctuations in different industries are the result of different natural and man-made causes, many of them tend to offset each other. When the coal furnace and the icebox were common household items, the coal and ice dealer was a classic example of two busi-

---

[2] Not all seasonal fluctuations stem from natural forces; some are man-made. Examples are the bulge in retail sales around Christmas time, another bulge around Easter, and the practice of bringing out new car models in the fall.

nesses with offsetting seasonal factors being combined. Today the electric utilities attempt to sell more current in the summer to power air conditioners, in order to use generating equipment needed for illumination during the longer winter evenings. If management fails to combine businesses with offsetting seasonal patterns or if labor is not mobile between such businesses, the labor in each industry tends to be seasonally unemployed and total output for the year does not reach its potential.

Seasonal factors for many widely used measures of the economy have been computed by the Bureau of the Census, and many others have been computed by those directly interested (for example, for bank deposits, soft-drink consumption, and many others). The seasonal influence is both recurrent and periodic, so it is not difficult to measure the month-by-month change that would tend to take place without the influence of the cycle and the trend. A store might find, for example, that its sales in December tend to be about 10 percent above the average sales for all twelve months. If this year, then, sales are 115 percent of the monthly average, more than the seasonal effect alone appears to be at work. Dividing the actual sales by 1.10 gives the figure for what sales would be without any seasonal influence and indicates that they have in fact grown by about 4.5 percent more than the seasonal influence accounts for.

Cyclical Fluctuations

Business fluctuations caused by the seasons are important to the industries involved but are not of general concern except that overall output is reduced by the seasonal unemployment. Cyclical fluctuations, in contrast, have received a great deal of attention from economists and are of substantial public interest. Recessions in economic activity create serious problems of unemployment, financial losses to business, and revenue losses for governments while booms in business activity create problems of inflation, distress to those on fixed incomes, and over-optimistic investments.

Figure 15-1 illustrates the fact that business activity does not follow a plateau but constantly rises and falls. This chart reproduces an overall measure of business activity computed by the Cleveland Trust Company by combining several specific measures. It should be noted that the long-run growth trend of the economy has been computed and removed before plotting the data. In other words, the fluctuations shown are the fluctuations around a rising trend, but the trend is drawn as a horizontal line. The broken line on the chart shows changes in wholesales prices.

This chart also illustrates an important point about the so-called business cycle—it is not really cyclical. The word *cycle* implies that there is a regularity to the alternate rise and fall of business activity that is actually nonexistent. Only a cursory reading of the chart reveals that neither the timing (periodicity) nor the severity (amplitude) of the rises and falls is at all regular. Nevertheless, it can be said that rises and falls do alternate, and that is the nature of the business cycle. Output does not grow forever without slowing down considerably or actually declining, but when it declines it does not decline forever, either, but eventually turns back up. The ideal situation, of course, would be to have output and employment grow fairly regularly year after year, keeping output at virtually a full-employment level, but the economy has never behaved in this manner. It may be noted, however, that the expansion that began in early 1961 had the longest duration of any expansion to date and that all the recessions since World War II have been much milder than was typically true of earlier recessions.

Measuring the Cycle

The National Bureau of Economic Research, a private institution that devotes much of its efforts to analyzing the business cycle, has studied hundreds of series of economic data in order to decide how to tell when the economy as a whole is expanding or contracting. It defines a recession as a period in which GNP declines for two consecutive quarters or longer.[3] The stages of the business cycle are not easy to define, but two pairs of concepts have been adopted that are generally used. One pair is *contraction* and *expansion,* the other *recession* and *prosperity.* These are often confused and should be carefully defined. A contraction is a period in which the majority of significant economic *indicators* are contracting or falling; an expansion is a period in which the majority are rising. The periods of contraction since World War II are shown by the shaded areas in Figure 15-2. These are often mistakenly called recessions; they actually measure the *cyclical turning points* where the economy turns down and up. For example, Figure 15-2 shows one of the numerous indicators used, the index of industrial production produced by the Board of Governors of the Federal Reserve System. It can be seen from the chart that this measure turns down at just about (but not precisely) the times decided upon by the National Bureau as the upper turning points, where the economy turns down. The same is true of the lower turning points, where the economy is deemed to have turned up.

The period of contraction should not be confused with a recession because the contraction presumably begins at the peak of a business cycle (at the height of prosperity), and it must continue for some time before the economy can be said to have shifted from prosperity to recession. Similarly, when the economy turns up (at the end of a shaded area), it remains in a period of recession for some time, until enough indicators have risen to bring about a period of prosperity. In other words, various kinds of production may be rising but not enough to bring about a rise in GNP in a given quarter. *Recession* and *prosperity* are not precise terms, but *contraction* and *expansion* are more precise. *Prosperity* has a kind of general meaning—high output by previous standards accompanied by a very low level of unemployment. *Recession,* of course, has the opposite meaning.

Before World War II many analysts used four stages to describe the typical business cycle. When the upturn came, the ensuing period was called recovery, which was followed by prosperity or boom; the downturn was followed by recession and then eventually by depression. These uses of the terms have fallen into disuse, largely because the postwar recessions did not develop into anything like the serious and prolonged depressions of earlier periods and some of the postwar expansions turned

---

[3] The definition was originated by Arthur Okun when he was a member of the late President Kennedy's Council of Economic Advisers.

AMERICAN BUSINESS ACTIVITY SINCE 1790

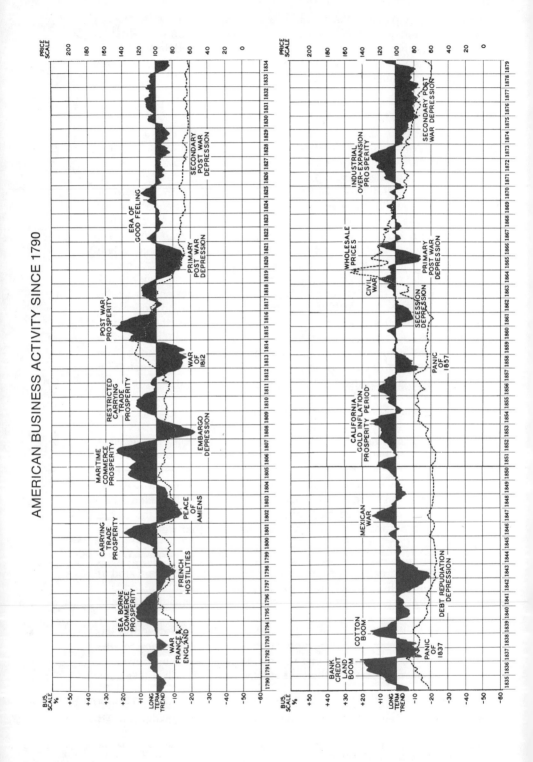

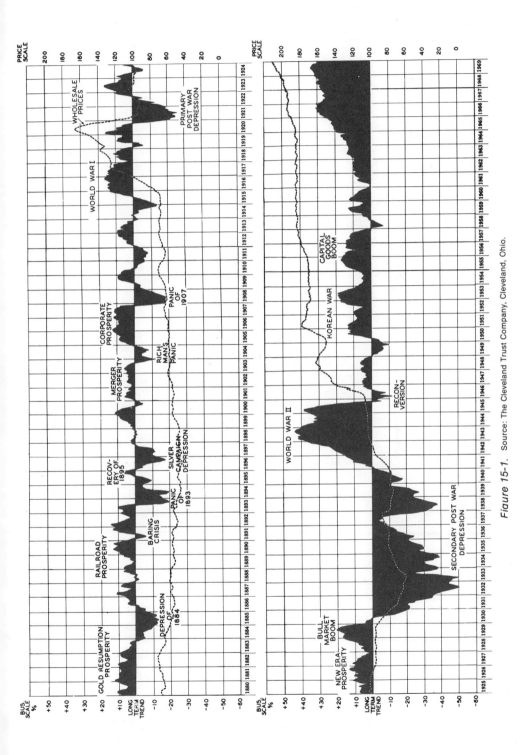

Figure 15-1. Source: The Cleveland Trust Company, Cleveland, Ohio.

305

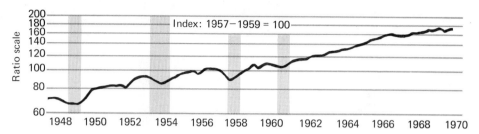

Figure 15-2. Federal Reserve index of industrial production, 1948–1969.   Source: *Business Conditions Digest,* May, 1970, p. 63.

down before they reached typical boom proportions (unemployment remained high).

Cyclical Indicators

From the many measures of industries' output, prices, and employment and from many other measures such as stock-market prices, interest rates, and bank loans, the National Bureau has selected a limited number in three categories called leading, roughly coincident,. and lagging indicators. The names are descriptive: the *leading indicators* are those which more often than not turn down or up before the majority of the others; the *roughly coincident indicators* are those deemed to behave roughly with the economy as a whole; and the *lagging indicators* are those that turn up or down after most of the economy has already moved in that direction. Figure 15-2 shows one of the important roughly coincident indicators, the Federal Reserve index. Industrial production is naturally tied closely to business conditions in general, so it tends to fluctuate much as does the economy. Other roughly coincident indicators are gross national product (which in a sense measures the whole economy), personal income, bank debits, and retail sales.

Some of the fairly obvious leading indicators are the accession rate in manufacturing (the rate at which new workers are added), new orders for durable goods, nonfarm housing starts, changes in business inventories, corporate profits, and changes in the money supply. Some of the lagging indicators are labor cost per unit of output (which tends to rise after a period of expansion), consumer installment debt, and certain interest rates.

Perhaps it should be emphasized that none of these indicators is highly reliable as a predictor; if it were, none of the others would need to be used. Many have false starts that are reversed before they go far. However, they are good starting points for making analyses of the business situation. If, for example, many of the leading indicators are declining from month to month, there is certainly good reason to investigate why they are and whether they are likely to be followed by the roughly coincident ones.[4]

[4] The principal source of current data on these indicators and other business-cycle data is *Business Conditions Digest,* formerly *Business Cycle Developments,* published monthly by the Bureau of the Census. Another good source of such information is the monthly *Economic Indicators,* prepared for the Joint Economic Committee by the Council of Economic Advisers. Both are sold by the Superintendent of Documents.

Severity and Length

Whether a contraction in business activity is severe or not depends upon two dimensions, its length and its depth, or its duration and its amplitude. The great depression that occurred in the 1930s was noteworthy on both counts (see Figure 15-1).[5] After the contraction began in July, 1929, per capita output did not again reach its former level until the end of the decade, under the spur of demands for output coming from the defense program. In this period, output, prices, and employment all fell drastically from their 1929 peaks. The distress and losses associated with widespread unemployment and bankruptcies were tremendous.

The duration and amplitude of the cycles since the one beginning with a downturn in March, 1892, are listed in Table 15-1.[6] The peaks listed are the upper turning points, where the economy started to contract, and the troughs are the lower turning points, where expansion began. The duration of the whole cycle is measured from peak to peak, the cycle consisting of the two phases of contraction and expansion, and is listed in terms of the number of months. The amplitude is measured by taking the percentage of monthly decline in industrial production in contractions and rise in expansions. A mild depression is one in which the monthly decline during the contraction is not severe and does not last for many months. Considering the cycle from July, 1929, to May, 1937, as a single cycle, the table shows that the duration was ninety-four months and that the average monthly change during the complete cycle was 1.6 percent. Since the downturn lasted until July, 1932, the cumulative effect was severe. The expansion that began in February, 1961, was apparently ending in early 1970 when this book went to press.

An important fact that can be deduced from Table 15-1 is that the duration of the contraction phase is usually shorter than that of the expansion phase. Thus, the business cycle usually consists of a longer period of expansion than of contraction and the economy tends to reach a higher level of output at each subsequent peak.

Unemployment

When output declines, there is less real income for the members of society to enjoy and to accumulate, but unemployment is a better measure of the distress caused by recessions. The real losses of a recession are not spread evenly over the population, and some people, such as those who have fixed incomes or have investable funds, may actually benefit. But the unemployed are unable to earn incomes at all and must depend upon unemployment benefits and past savings. Data on employment and unemployment are plotted in Figure 15-3. The extent of unemployment may be seen as the difference between employment and the labor force in the top part of the chart or as specific amounts and rates in the bottom part.

[5] Some say there were actually two depressions, one occurring in 1930–1936 and another in 1937–1938.

[6] The table is separated at January–February, 1920, because a new index was introduced for later periods. The cycle of 1943–1948 is omitted because of distortions caused by the ending of World War II and reconversion.

Table 15-1
Seventeen Cycles in Industrial Production

Trough	Peak	Months	Average Percent Change per Month
	March 1892		
October 1892	November 1895	44	1.3
September 1896	June 1900	55	0.9
October 1900	July 1903	37	1.0
December 1903	May 1907	46	1.1
May 1908	March 1910	34	1.8
January 1911	January 1913	34	0.8
November 1914	May 1917	52	1.1
March 1919	January 1920	32	1.3
	February 1920		
April 1921	May 1923	39	2.2
July 1924	March 1927	46	0.9
November 1927	July 1929	28	1.0
July 1932	May 1937	94	1.6
May 1938	November 1943	78	1.7
	July 1948		
October 1949	July 1953	60	0.8
April 1954	February 1957	43	0.6
April 1958	January 1960	35	1.0
February 1961	March 1966 °	74	0.6

° Latest month of table, but not a peak month.

Source: U.S. Bureau of the Census, *Long Term Economic Growth*, 1966.

The Price Level

Since market demands for nearly all goods and services fall off in a recession of any severity, it might be expected that market prices would also fall. This reaction was typical of prewar business cycles, but it has not held true since the recession of 1948. The decline in aggregate spending typically was reflected in declines in both real GNP and the price level. Wholesale prices were also considerably more sensitive to business conditions and changes in demand than were consumer prices. Since World War II, the declines in wholesale prices have been considerably moderated and, with the exception of 1948, consumer prices have not fallen but, at the most, only leveled off in recessions. These changes are highlighted in Figure 15-4. Since this chart is plotted on a ratio scale, it shows rates of change, and it can be seen that wholesale prices fell by 1932 to about a half of their pre-depression level. Since 1950, there has been no appreciable decline in consumer prices, but a leveling off occurred in the recession of 1954.

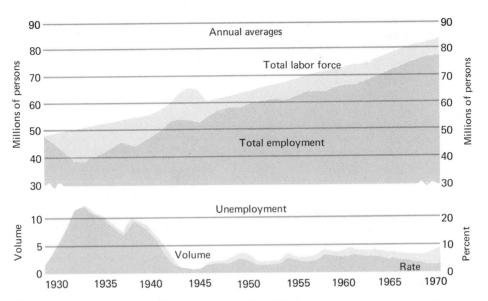

Figure 15-3. Unemployment rate and volume, 1929–1970.   Source: *Federal Reserve Historical Chart Book,* 1969, p. 78; *Federal Reserve Monthly Chart Book,* April, 1970, p. 55; *Economic Indicators,* May, 1970, p. 10.

This general stability of prices can be attributed to several differences between the prewar and postwar economies. Several of these differences will receive attention in the following chapter, which deals with stabilization policies. Some of the more obvious developments that help to maintain incomes and thus expenditures are unemployment compensation; government expenditure programs; the automatic decline of income taxes when incomes fall; longer-range business-investment planning; and, to some extent, less cyclical expenditure patterns of households.

There has been a persistent upward trend of the consumer price level for two decades, but whether there is actually as much rise as is shown in Figure 15-4 is questionable. Improvements in quality are important in

Figure 15-4. Indexes of wholesale and consumer prices, 1913–1970.
Source: *Federal Reserve Historical Chart Book,* 1969, pp. 97, 99, 101.

consumer goods, no doubt more so than is true of basic wholesale commodities. If the quality of an item is deemed to have increased by 2 percent
in a year while its price rises by 2 percent, there is no real increase in its
price. But improvements in quality are extremely difficult to measure,
especially because many of them are subjective.

Two statistical difficulties arise in measuring changes in quality and
relating them to changes in prices. One is related to the substitution of
new goods for old, such as gas lights for kerosene lamps and electric
lights for gas lights. Should they all be considered "illumination" and, if
different, how much better is the new? The other difficulty relates to the
gradual improvement in goods in continuous use. There is a common
notion that goods used to be better-made than they are today, but few
people would prefer the automobiles, refrigerators, radios, and other
things of the "good old days." It has been suggested that if people were
given $1,000 and two Sears, Roebuck catalogs, one of twenty years ago
and one new, and allowed to spend the $1,000 as they choose on goods
from the old catalog at the old prices or goods in the new catalog at the
new prices, most of the money would be spent on goods in the new
catalog. If this were the case, people would unconsciously be valuing the
changes as worth at least as much as the increases in prices and inflation
would not have taken place. These two statistical problems probably
cause the rise in consumer prices to be overstated. However, they do not
destroy the fact that both consumer and wholesale prices are much more
stable than formerly.

Money and the Cycle

The ability of the Federal Reserve System to control the volume of
reserves available to commercial banks, and thus to influence strongly
the supply of money, was noted in Chapter 12. This power is exerted
largely in ways designed to stabilize the economy, so it is to be expected
that close correspondence may be found between cyclical changes in
the economy and in monetary conditions.

That there is a close correspondence between the money supply and
gross national product is shown by Figure 15-5, which traces these two
series on a ratio scale. Although the correspondence appears to be very
close in the top part of the chart, closer inspection shows that the slowing
down of the rate of growth in the money supply after World War II was
reflected in a rapidly declining ratio of money supply to GNP (in the
lower part of the chart). That the money supply was overadequate in
1945, following the expansions carried out in both the depression and
World War II, is indicated by the fact that more and more transactions
could be carried on at rising prices in subsequent years. Thus GNP
continued to grow while the money supply was allowed to grow at a
slower rate.

Figure 15-6 shows more clearly the *changes* in the money stock instead
of the total stock itself. Here the changes are expressed as monthly
changes at annual percentage rates and the curve is "smoothed" by
plotting consecutive six-months averages. It may be seen that most of
the monthly fluctuation is confined to between plus 5 percent and minus
5 percent annual rates. More significant, however, is the tendency of
the series to behave as a leading indicator.

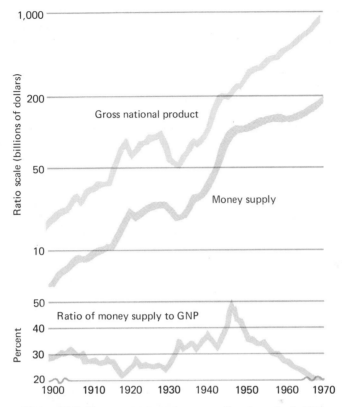

Figure 15-5. Money supply and gross national product, 1900–1969.   Source: *Federal Reserve Historical Chart Book*, 1969, p. 66; *Federal Reserve Bulletin*, May, 1970. pp. A-17, A-68.

When the curve in this chart declines, it indicates a slowing down of the rate of growth of the money supply; it does not indicate a decline in the money supply unless the change is negative (below the zero line). It may be seen that the typical pattern is for the rate of growth to speed up during a contraction, then to hold a level rate for a while, and then to slow down and perhaps even to cause a decline in the money supply (1959 and 1969). This pattern reflects the Federal Reserve System's efforts to "lean against the wind" in business cycles. That is, as a recession occurs, the System expands bank reserves and the banks expand

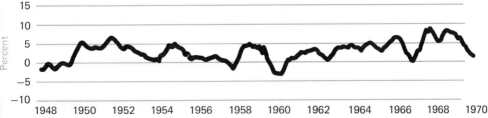

Figure 15-6. Change in the money supply, 1948–1970.   Source: *Business Conditions Digest*, February, 1970 p. 30.

their earning assets (mostly investments), thus expanding demand deposits. But as the expansion phase gradually absorbs unemployed resources, the System slows down the rate of growth of the money supply and, if inflationary tendencies arise, it opposes them, perhaps to the extent of actually decreasing the money supply.

The rather large declines in 1966, in 1967, and again in 1969 are interesting because they represent drastic measures on the part of the Federal Reserve System to stop the inflation that first became obvious in 1966 (see Figure 15-4) when accelerated expenditures for the Vietnam War were coming on top of a civilian boom. (A tax increase was widely recommended by economists at that time but was not encouraged by the Administration or adopted by the Congress then.) This complete stoppage of the growth of the money supply, and attendant high interest rates, slowed down the rate of aggregate expenditures and threatened to start a period of contraction. It may be seen that the Federal Reserve System quickly reversed itself in 1968 and brought about a rapid increase in the money stock.

Interest Rates

These and similar actions in the monetary sector are reflected in the behavior of interest rates. In the early stages of a contraction, the System is generally adding to the supply of bank reserves through open-market purchases. Loan demand is low, so banks use the excess reserves to acquire securities (secondary reserve assets which they expect to dispose of eventually when loan demands are greater). These purchases tend to raise securities prices and lower market rates of interest. Market yields on short-term securities tend to fall faster than rates on long-term securities because banks concentrate their purchases in this area, but long-term rates fall also. Later on, in the expansion phase, loan demands increase, banks let their short-term securities mature without replacing them, and interest rates on loans and short-term securities begin to rise. Concurrently, corporations again wish to sell long-term bonds in order to finance expansion and the demands for these funds also push up the longer-term rates. Thus interest rates generally follow along after business conditions have set a new direction; they are a lagging indicator.

Timing of the Turning Points

As noted above, the level of economic activity rises and falls but with no particular regularity. Periods of expansion may last less than two years, as did the one ending in January, 1960, or as long as eight years or more. Similarly, declines in economic activity may end after a year or less or they may extend over several years. The puzzling question about this behavior is why the turning points come at such erratic intervals. No two business cycles are alike, and the forces that expand or contract output are of different degrees of strength in successive cycles. But there is sufficient similarity in succeeding cycles to warrant using the term, and the fact remains that expansion and contraction do alternate—or always have—even if at irregular intervals.

A review of the categories of aggregate expenditure provides a starting point for understanding why the level of output is unlikely to remain at a given height or to rise at a steady rate. As we have seen, gross national product consists of durable and nondurable consumer goods; investment goods in the form of inventories, plant and equipment, and residential construction; goods and services purchased by governments; and net purchases of exports. Considering primarily the domestic private economy, it is clear that expenditures for gross private domestic investment are likely to fluctuate. For example, after some period of contraction, conditions become more and more favorable for an expansion of expenditures on plant and equipment. Although, at the upper turning point, capacity in most industries may have been adequate to produce all that is being sold, depreciation and obsolescence operate during a contraction to reduce some capacity and to make some of it high-cost. At the same time, businesses are able to raise funds for additional investment at relatively low interest rates and prices of machinery and equipment may have fallen. Labor is more readily available for construction projects, and other similar conditions make expansion and modernization more attractive than they have been. In the background of business decision-making is the realization that the economy grows in the long run and that new capacity that will be wanted in the future may be available now on more favorable terms than may prevail later.

Many of these factors reverse themselves after a period of expansion has existed for a while. Interest rates are forced up by larger demands for loanable funds and perhaps also by actions of the Federal Reserve System. Some projects that would have been marginal at lower rates are discarded or postponed. Producers of machinery and equipment may be able to charge somewhat higher prices than during the recession. As full employment is approached, labor is less available for additional construction projects and contractors can choose to bid for only those projects that promise to be the most profitable. Furthermore, labor to operate the newly added plant and equipment may be in short supply and available only at higher wages necessary to draw labor from other occupations. Although the level of business activity is high, rising costs may be squeezing profit margins and making further commitments less attractive.

Some of the other components of gross national product behave in the same fashion, while others tend to have offsetting characteristics. Residential construction, for example, might be expected to rise and fall with general business conditions, as incomes rise and fall. However, other factors have operated to make housing behave in a contracyclical fashion, at least since World War II. As incomes rise people tend to devote more expenditure to housing, but financing is very important in this industry. The availability of mortgage funds from savings institutions at relatively low interest rates tends to stimulate housing in recessions; this relationship has been relied on by the central bank and other government agencies in making funds available during downturns in business. The federal government has considered construction a countercyclical weapon and through a variety of means, such as liberalizing the terms of mortgages it will accept for mortgage insurance, has stimulated housing construction in recessions. On the other hand, restrictive monetary measures are particularly effective in restraining construction. The restrictions and resulting shortages of mortgage funds and high interest rates in 1966 were reflected in a decline in expenditures on new housing units from $21.6 billion early in the year to $14 billion late in the year (seasonally adjusted annual rates), and the situation in 1969 was similar.

In contrast to residential construction, production for inventory tends to fluctuate in a cyclical fashion. The significant change here is the change in the rate at which inventories are being accumulated; when this rate changes, it tends to have magnified effects on orders and thus on output. In the expansion phase, producers and merchants tend to build up inventories because they need inventories in some relationship to sales, which are rising, and they may also wish to stock up in expectation of higher prices. When inventories are finally brought up to desired levels, orders are cut back accordingly. The production of goods for inventories, like any other production, creates incomes and adds to aggregate expenditures on output; a reduction in accumulation has the same effect as a reduction in output for sale to others. Consider a store that has monthly sales of goods that have cost $10,000 and that is bringing its inventories up from $3,000 to $5,000 by purchasing each month $500 more than it sells. Thus it buys $10,500 of goods each month but, when its inventory reaches $5,000, it cuts back its purchases to $10,000. Its suppliers, in turn, find that they need smaller inventories in order to be able to fill their incoming orders, and they cut back on orders. Thus these reductions in the rate of increase in inventory tend to become cumulative, all down the line. When inventories are actually decreased, the effect is, of course, even greater. Changes in business inventories are shown in Figure 15-7.

Consumer expenditures respond in some ways to the influence of current business conditions. Sales of durable goods, especially, tend to fluctuate with household incomes and expectations of income. These goods are often sold through the use of installment credit, and households tend to be more willing to take on additional debt when incomes are rising; they are also more willing to spend accumulated funds. When households anticipate less income, such as less overtime pay, they tend to build up their savings accounts, continue to pay off installment debt, and refrain from borrowing more. Sales of automobiles, furniture, household appliances, and other durables thus tend to rise in periods of rising or full employment. If the expansion phase is rapid enough or long enough, saturation points tend to be reached; replacement of old items plus expansion of ownership can no longer serve to produce rising levels of sales. The fact that purchases of durable goods are postponable contributes to this instability; sales of nondurable goods tend to be more stable throughout the business cycle.

The labor supply is another factor that affects the timing of the turning points. An expansion that has been possible because of the absorption of the unemployed cannot continue, at least at its previous rate, once a condition of full employment has been reached. If the labor force is growing at a rate of 3 percent per year and output has been rising at 8 percent per year, once full employment is reached output cannot continue to rise at 8 percent, and the mere slowing down is likely to have cumulative effects (such as through the rate of inventory accumulation). When the overall figure for unemployment reaches some historically low point such as 3 percent, there are almost certainly shortages of particular kinds of labor. Wages tend to begin to be bid up, and further additions to wage costs appear in increased use of overtime. Costs per unit of output tend to rise and profit margins tend to fall except in those lines where prices can be raised — and these increased prices may raise costs in other lines. This squeeze on profit margins tends to reduce the attractiveness of additional expenditures for expanded capacity, and orders for plant and equipment may fall.

In addition to the built-in reasons for instability in the private sectors of the economy, expenditure or revenue actions by government may contribute to economic fluctuation. While we tend to think of these actions as intended to minimize instability, sometimes conditions may lead the federal government to spend or tax in ways that are destabilizing. State and local governments are seldom concerned with the overall

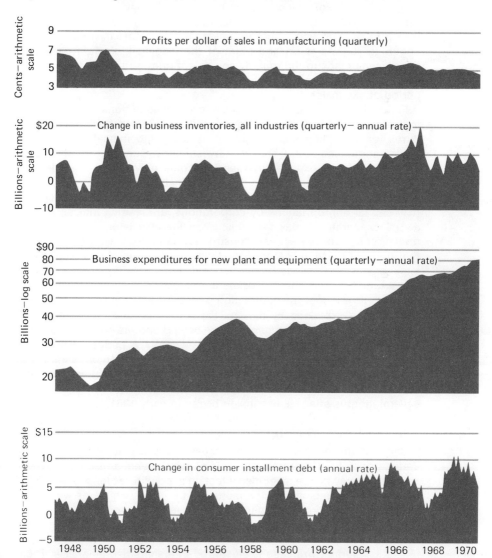

Figure 15-7. Four indicators of the business cycle.   Source: *Business Conditions Digest,* May, 1970, pp. 12, 25, 28, 37.

economic effects of their activities, resembling households and business units in this respect. Government purchases, of course, add to aggregate demand just as do private purchases and may come at a time when they strain productive facilities, and ill-considered changes in tax rates can affect private expenditures in the wrong direction.

While this discussion of the behavior of various segments of the economy is far from comprehensive, it does suggest reasons for the twin facts that an expansion or contraction tends to cumulate and that the cumulation ends and sooner or later reverses itself. The expansion phase of the cycle is over when the majority of the specific measures of economic activity have leveled off or begun to decline. Even as most indicators may be falling, some segments of the economy may still be expanding. After a period of contraction, some of the leading indicators may have begun to turn up and some of the lagging indicators may not yet have begun to fall. As more and more of the leading indicators rise, their influence spreads to the roughly coincident ones and, at some point, the majority of the segments of the economy are moving upward into a new period of expansion.

Figure 15-7 shows four indicators of cyclical conditions. Three of these indicators are considered leading indicators; the fourth, business expenditures for new plant and equipment, is a lagging indicator. In view of earlier comments about business investment expenditure, it should be noted that actual expenditures tend to come only after a considerable delay, once decisions to make them are initiated. Certain other statistical series related to investment, such as construction contracts awarded and new capital appropriations by corporations, are leading indicators. The actual expenditures may take place considerably later, after plans are drawn, contracts are let, and construction is under way. It can be seen that none of these indicators fits exactly the periods of contraction and expansion as determined by the National Bureau of Economic Research. For example, consumer installment debt grew by increasingly large amounts throughout the contraction period in 1949, instead of declining. This can be explained by the fact that such debt was extremely small after World War II and consumers were buying durable goods in quantity; that period of contraction was almost entirely a period of inventory adjustment, as is suggested by the liquidation of inventories shown in the chart. Although changes in consumer installment debt are a leading indicator, it may be observed that such debt did not begin to rise until several months after the expansion began in early 1961.

The Accelerator Principle

Some of the relationships just discussed are explained by the accelerator principle. This principle explains why changes in consumer expenditures may have a magnified effect on expenditures for capital goods. In a sense it complements the multiplier principle, which, as we saw in Chapter 10, explains how changes in investment spending tend to have a magnified effect on consumer spending. Both principles help explain the instability in the level of total output.

The accelerator principle is illustrated in a simplified manner in Table 15-2. We assume that sales of some consumer good are 1,000 units per

Table 15-2
The Accelerator Principle

Year	Sales of Consumer Good	Number of Machines Used	New Machines Bought
1	1,000	100	10
2	1,000	100	10
3	1,100	110	20
4	1,100	110	10
5	1,200	120	20
6	1,300	130	20

year and that 100 machines are required to produce this output. We also assume that these machines wear out in ten years and that they need replacement at a fairly even rate, about 10 each year. Now, if sales of the consumer good rise (Year 3), there will be a magnified (accelerated) effect on production of machines. The rise in sales of the consumer good may result from an autonomous change in consumer expenditures or from the multiplier principle operating on prior business or government expenditure.

When sales increase from 1,000 to 1,100, or by 10 percent, another 10 machines are required to produce the extra 100 units. Consequently, in Year 3 producers order not only the usual 10 machines to replace those wearing out but an additional 10 machines to bring the stock up to 110. Thus production of machines does not rise by 10 percent, in line with the stock of machines, but it doubles from 10 in Year 2 to 20 in Year 3. If sales of the consumer good remain at the new level of 1,100 in Year 4, an adequate number of machines is available if only the 10 that wear out are replaced. Even though there is no decline in sales of the consumer good, sales of the machines must drop back from 20 to 10 – a drop of 50 percent. Years 5 and 6 illustrate that, in order for production of machines to stay at 20, there must be an annual increase in sales of the consumer good. If sales fail to rise by 100 units in any year, a decline in orders for machines will result. Of course, eventually there will be a year in which 20 machines wear out and the assumptions of the problem have to be changed.

A single example cannot be taken as representative of the operation of the principle in the economy generally, for several reasons. One reason has just been mentioned: The repercussions are complicated by uneven amounts of depreciation in different years. Another reason is that there are different ratios between output and capital goods in different industries. Some types of capital equipment may be replaced in five years, other types in twenty years. But the example does illustrate that, in a country using a large stock of capital goods, there is an inherent element of instability in that only constant increases in the output of consumer goods can maintain stability in the output of producers' goods and, in the long run, even this stability would not be sufficient.

ECONOMIC GROWTH

It was noted in the preceding discussion of economic fluctuations that, typically, periods of expansion exceed periods of contraction in both duration and amplitude. This situation is virtually a necessity if the economy is to grow. Only an economy that is growing faster than the population can provide a rising standard of living. The alternating ups and downs of the business cycle take place around a rising trend line, so that each upper turning point tends to be at a higher level of total output than the preceding one and, unless a contraction is unusually severe, it ends at a trough higher than the preceding trough. This trend, however, is a statistical abstraction; only after the fact is it apparent that during some preceding period, such as a decade, the economy has grown by a given rate. It is obvious that gross national product has not grown by any constant rate since 1900 (see Figure 1-1, page 17). By using different beginning and ending dates, we could obtain a variety of long-run economic growth rates. Reasons for variation in the long-run rate are partly related to the same explanations that apply to cyclical fluctuations and partly independent of them. Before turning to policies that may be adopted to minimize fluctuations and maximize growth (Chapter 16), we briefly survey some of the principal determinants of long-term growth.

Factors in Economic Growth

Several factors determine the general level of the gross national product of a country and whether it increases or remains stagnant. The principal ones may be outlined as follows:

1. Population and Labor Supply. Other conditions being equal, a large population can produce a larger total output than can a smaller one. One of the conditions taken as being equal is the percentage of the total population in the labor force and contributing to output. In the United States, the growing number of women in the labor force tends to increase total output while the gradual lengthening of the average period of education tends to hold people out of the labor force and, in the short run at least, restrain output. The age distribution of the population often becomes a factor in determining the proportion of the population in the labor force. When there is a period of many births, such as during and immediately after World War II, a larger proportion of the population is nonworking. Similarly, as a larger proportion of the population moves into ages over sixty-five, the proportion in the labor force is reduced.

Other factors influence how much work is actually done, or the input of labor and capital services. The labor force may work few or many hours in a period of time. The average workday and the average workweek have gradually shortened in the United States, and this shortening has presumably had some restrictive effect on output. The real effect is not clear, however, because it is difficult to say how much more efficiently people can work over a shorter period. The grade school arithmetic book may assume that if a man can produce 80 units in an eight-hour day, he can produce 90 in a nine-hour day, but this may not be true in actuality. The smaller number of hours devoted to work both contributes to productivity (up to some point) and is a result of rising productivity. That is, it is now possible to produce more in less time and to have more leisure. Leisure may be as socially desirable as additional output of goods and services; at least social pressures have indicated a preference for additional leisure over taking all gains in productivity in goods and services.

2. Quality of the Labor Force. Some labor is more productive than others; a given labor force may be capable of turning out a great deal of output because it is familiar with machinery, is willing to work regularly and conscientiously, and for other reasons. Many characteristics of the labor force determine whether it is highly productive or not. Desirable characteristics include general education and specific training, skills, good health, longevity, and motivation of various kinds.

3. Capital. Advanced economies are all characterized by the use of considerable amounts of capital equipment and nonhuman power. Those countries where output per capita is very low are all characterized by very little use of capital. When each person in the work force is able to work with capital goods that make his output per hour much higher, total output will naturally be greater and, when divided through the market process, will represent greater incomes.

4. Technology. Like labor, capital may be more or less efficient. Some machines are more productive than others, and advancing technology constantly uncovers new and better ways of doing things, as well as completely new things to be done. Each generation of computers, for example, can do more jobs and more quickly than its predecessors. Less dramatic improvements take place all the time in virtually all processes of production. The design of various kinds of engines is constantly improved in order to utilize a higher percentage of the input of fuel; they are improved in being made lighter, more mobile, or more adaptable; and the spread of automation leads to less need for human labor and supervision while a machine is in operation.

5. Effective Demand. The foregoing factors are similar in that they set limits to potential output and to its potential growth. They may be thought of as the supply side of the equation. Whether output actually approaches its physical potential in modern market economies depends crucially on whether there is sufficient market demand to call forth the required output. Aggregate expenditures must be adequate to absorb maximum output or the output will not be forthcoming. This is a problem that individual businesses and households can do little to solve, as it devolves largely on government to foster proper monetary and fiscal policies.

Measurements of Economic Growth

The growth of the American economy has reflected the influence of each of the factors just listed. Some analysts think of population, modified by the proportion in the labor force and the number of hours worked, and capital as the inputs and of technology and quality of the labor force as qualitative factors that determine how productive the inputs are. We may also consider these qualitative factors as increasing the available inputs and thus consider total output as rising with increasing inputs.

Over the history of the United States, the population has increased enormously. Originally settled thinly along the Atlantic Coast, the population has spread across the continent, establishing first farms and mining and lumbering operations, and then sprawling metropolitan centers.

Both New York and Philadelphia had about 37,000 people in 1790; Philadelphia had a half million by the time of the Civil War and New York still well under a million; and at that time the population of Chicago was 100,000 and that of Pittsburgh, 50,000. In 1860 the total population was about 31.5 million; by the turn of the century, 76.1 million; by the late 1960s, 200 million. The labor force has grown accordingly: It was about 28 million in 1900 and 50 million in 1930, and increased subsequently as follows:

1940	56,180,000
1950	64,749,000
1960	73,126,000
1965	78,357,000

The development, as contrasted to simple expansion, of the economy is reflected in shifts of the labor force into different occupations. These shifts are illustrated in Figure 15-8, showing trends in four major classifications. Because of the scarcity of data before 1940, the lines on the chart are not precise but connect decennial census figures or other estimates. The decline in the percentage of the labor force on farms and the rise in the percentage of white-collar workers are particularly apparent.

Total private man-hours of work are estimated to have been a little over three times as great in 1929 as in the decade 1869–1878 and a little over four times as great in nonagricultural activities alone. Although there was a considerable increase in population and the labor force between 1929 and 1957–1959, the increase in man-hours was only about 6 percent, reflecting a considerable decline in the length of the workweek.[7] In the last hundred years—since the Civil War—the number of man-hours of input has increased gradually, the increase being interrupted only in periods of severe depression. Such interruptions occurred in 1893, in 1907, and in the depression of the 1930s; the level reached in 1929 did not recur until 1942, and in 1934 the number was only 72 percent of the 1929 level.

Productivity of the labor inputs may be measured in various ways, the usual measure being output per man-hour. Indexes representing two estimates of output per man-hour are shown in Figure 15-9. Two indexes are used because one of them, prepared by the National Bureau of Economic Research, goes back to 1890 but ends in the 1950s. Behind the rise in productivity lie many advances not only in technology and industrial research but also in health and education.

The rate at which productivity rises is influenced by the relative growth of different industries. There is some tendency for industries in which productivity may be improved sharply to grow rapidly simply because they are often new industries in which technological progress is rapid and because the rising productivity reduces costs and expands markets. In the contrary direction, however, is the tendency of the American economy to expand more rapidly in the production of services than in output of tangible goods. Services are generally thought to be less susceptible to improvements in productivity, but part of this opinion is undoubtedly

[7] U.S. Bureau of the Census, *Long Term Economic Growth, 1860–1965*, p. 174.

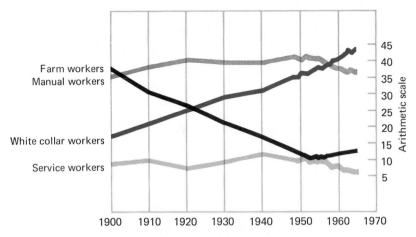

Figure 15-8. Proportions of the labor force, 1900–1965.   Source: U.S. Bureau of the Census, *Long Term Economic Growth*, 1966.

based on the difficulty of measuring productivity. For example, it is a common-sense conclusion that physicians are more productive than in the past simply because, with improved diagnostic techniques and medicines, they can usually cure an ailment more rapidly than in past years. Similarly, a stay in a hospital is generally shorter than was formerly true. But productivity is generally measured, for example, by comparing the number of nurses with the number of beds tended, rather than with the number of patients that may use the beds in a year. Clearly, it is difficult to measure the productivity of a teacher or a government employee because much more than the quantity of work performed is involved. In any event, there is some concern that the overall rate of improvement may be slowed down by the shift of resources into service industries, although it is far from clear that this concern is well-founded.

The degree to which this shift has been taking place in the period since World War II is indicated by Table 15-3 and Figure 15-10. Table 15-3

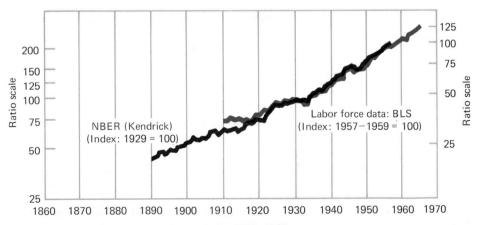

Figure 15-9. Indexes of output per man-hour, 1890–1965.   Source: U.S. Bureau of the Census, *Long Term Economic Growth*, 1966.

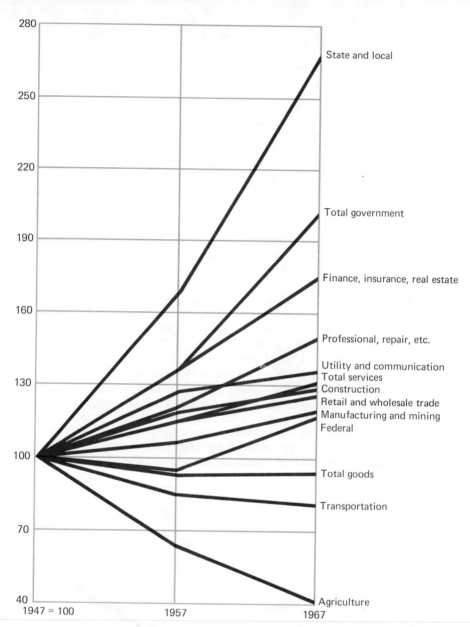

Figure 15-10. Indexes of man-hours in various occupations, 1947, 1957, 1967.

shows in absolute numbers the billions of man-hours devoted to various occupations in 1947, 1957, and 1967.[8] For example, it shows that the number of man-hours devoted to production of tangible goods declined from 64.2 billion to 60.1 billion over the twenty years while the number devoted to production of services rose from 57.1 billion to 75.5 billion. Man-hours in government increased from 11.8 billion to 24.1 billion.

[8] The data for this table and for Figure 15-10 are the Department of Commerce data used by *Fortune* in October, 1968, in somewhat different form.

Table 15-3
Man-Hours in Various Occupations, 1947, 1957, 1967
(Billions)

	1947	1957	1967
Production of goods	64.2	59.9	60.1
Manufacturing and mining	35.9	38.4	43.0
Agriculture	22.0	14.0	9.0
Construction	6.3	7.5	8.1
Production of services	57.1	65.6	75.5
Retail and wholesale trade	24.9	28.7	31.7
Professional, repair, etc.	18.3	21.9	27.4
Transportation	7.4	6.3	6.0
Finance, insurance, real estate	4.0	5.5	7.0
Utility and communication	2.5	3.2	3.4
Government	11.8	16.1	24.1
Federal	5.1	4.8	6.0
State and local	6.7	11.3	18.1

The rates of change in various occupations are obviously quite diverse, and this diversity is illustrated in Figure 15-10. This chart shows, for example, that the number of man-hours in agriculture fell to 41 percent of the 1947 level and the number in state and local governments rose to 270 percent by 1967.

The concepts of inputs of labor and capital, as well as some concepts of output, are slippery ones and difficult for statisticians to measure objectively. An hour of work performed by a trained operator of a complicated machine in the 1970s is not the same thing as an hour of work performed by an unschooled field hand in the 1870s. A given amount of investment in capital is similarly unlike one made in a previous era. A truck purchased in the 1970s is quite unlike one purchased in the 1920s. However, estimates of the inputs of labor and capital have been derived, and while different analysts obtain different measures because of the assumptions they adopt, it may be observed in Figure 15-11 that these measures agree in general direction. Unfortunately, these measures have not been updated, but they indicate the general trend toward using more capital, as the capital inputs may be seen as rising more rapidly than the labor inputs.

As we have already noted, advances in output per man-hour stem from advances in scientific and technological research, in medical and health sciences, and in education. These advances bring improvements through increasing the productivity of labor as a result of improvements in labor itself, through increasing the productivity of the capital with which the labor works, and through improving the techniques of business and industrial management. Universal elementary and secondary education has been standard in the United States for many decades, and higher education constantly becomes more common among the population. About three-fourths of the population aged 5 to 17 were enrolled in school at the turn of the century, and today the figure is virtually 100 percent. Only 4.0 percent of those between 18 and 21 were enrolled in 1900—and fewer in earlier years—but this percentage has climbed rapidly until today it is

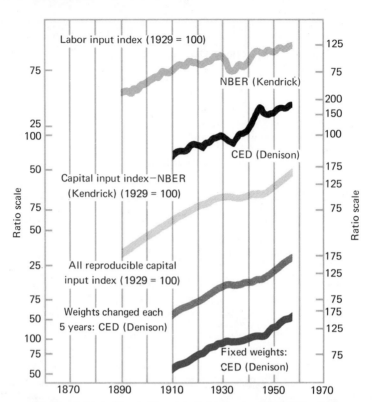

Figure 15-11. Indexes of inputs of labor and capital, 1890–1957.
Source: U.S. Bureau of the Census, *Long Term Economic Growth,* 1966.

about 45 percent. Also, more days per year are spent in school, as the length of the school year has increased. In terms of expenditures, the total for education has increased from around $3 billion in 1930 to about $40 billion in the late 1960s while the expenditure per student has increased from $90 to about $550 in public schools and from about $575 to $2,450 in institutions of higher education. In spite of these increases, however, the median number of years of education completed by the population aged 25 and older has risen only from 8.1 years in 1910 to 11.8 years in 1965.[9]

It is well recognized that expenditures on scientific research and development and on medical research have increased rapidly in recent decades, but data on these subjects have not been collected very far back in the past. Public expenditures on medical research are estimated to have been about $1.25 billion in 1965, as compared with only $3 million in 1940. Average life expectancy in the United States, one measure of general health standards, has increased from 47.3 years in 1900 to over 70 years. Expenditures for scientific research and development, while partly estimates, show an increase from $166 million in 1930 to $5.16 billion in 1953, and to about $20 billion at present.

[9] See *Statistical Abstracts of the United States* and *Long Term Economic Growth.*

SUMMARY

In the American economy there are some 200 million people; hundreds of thousands of business enterprises of all kinds and sizes; about $5 trillion of total assets, both real assets and financial claims; and thousands of governmental units. Considering the freedom of the households and businesses to make decisions about what to produce, and how, and when to purchase and how much, it is inconceivable that the level of economic activity should pursue a level course.

From the earliest days of this country—and the same is true of other advanced economies—the level of economic activity, as measured by a variety of overall indicators, has fluctuated. While some economic statistical series indicate a rather high degree of regularity, the economy as a whole exhibits very little in the timing of its upturns and downturns. In either direction, economic activity tends to cumulate but sooner or later to turn in the other direction. While the irregularity suggest that *fluctuations* is a better word than *cycles* to describe it, the latter has become pretty well established in general use.

In the modern economy production, and therefore most indicators of the level of business activity, responds to demands expressed in the market. Thus explanations for the ups and downs of business can be sought in the reasons for changes in aggregate demand. In this chapter and in earlier ones dealing with gross national product, we have observed that various factors affect aggregate expenditure through the expenditures of different sectors of the economy. While these variations take place in the short run, they fluctuate about a rising long-run trend of gross national product. While the economy may be in a slack period, with output and employment well below capacity, output—both total and per capita—may be well above what it was a decade or two earlier.

The existence of these fluctuations and the long-run growth trend suggest the desirability of public policies designed to minimize the severity of economic fluctuations and to maximize the rate of long-run growth. The development of such policies is discussed in the following chapter.

Economic Terms for Review

seasonal variation	leading and lagging indicators
cyclical variation	accelerator principle
long-run trend	economic growth
cyclical turning points	productivity

Questions for Review

1. Why are seasonal fluctuations less important than cyclical ones?
2. Are cyclical fluctuations really cyclical? What is a better adjective?
3. What are some leading indicators? Why do they tend to lead?
4. How have prices behaved in the most recent recessions?

    5. Explain why interest rates behave as they do over the business cycle.

Questions for Analysis

    1. What are some reasons why expansions and contractions reverse themselves?

    2. Why do business analysts carefully watch the behavior of inventories?

    3. Describe the accelerator principle. How is it related to the multiplier principle?

    4. How are some of the principal determinants of economic growth illustrated by the American economy?

    5. How has the allocation of the labor force been altered by the growth of the American economy?

Case for Decision

    The directors of Citizens National Bank are having one of their fairly frequent differences of opinion. This time the problem is whether funds received because of the maturity of some government bonds should be used for short-term investments or some long maturities. At the present time the bank has no unsatisfied loan demand—loan repayments are about equal to new loans being made—and all the directors are agreed that the $300,000 from maturing bonds can be reinvested in virtually any manner they consider the most profitable.

    Mr. Counts, the president, argues that the bank should take advantage of the unusually high short-term rates existing in the market. He points out that it is most unusual for Treasury bills to yield 6 percent or more. He considers bills an unusual bargain combining liquidity and yield. He also fears that the restrictive measures being employed by the Federal Reserve may lead to further declines in bond prices, which are already at historic lows.

    Dr. Drill, on the other hand, is impressed by the possibility of the bank earning some attractive rates of income from its bond portfolio. Normally, the bond portfolio uses funds not otherwise in demand for loans, and it typically provides yields considerably less than those on loans. He is struck by the possibility of buying high-quality corporate bonds that yield 7 percent or even more, or even Treasury bonds that yield over 6 percent.

    Mr. Graves is interested in bonds, but his reasons differ from those of Dr. Drill. He realizes that current low prices of outstanding bonds are a reflection of the current high yields, but he is more impressed by the prices than by the yields. That is, he thinks that what is more important than the yield *to maturity* is the possibility of selling the bonds at a profit once interest rates fall again.

    The difficulty of reconciling the different points of view lies mainly in the uncertainty of when, if ever, interest rates will fall again. As businessmen, the directors seem to have different opinions about how long business will stay at a high level, with high demands for loan funds and thus high interest rates. Finally, they decide to ask

Mr. Derby to compile some data from which they might draw some conclusions on this point.

At the subsequent meeting Mr. Derby shows several charts (see Figures 15-12 through 15-19), which he has found in a publication of a business advisory service. After explaining briefly how each chart is prepared, Mr. Derby is asked by Dr. Drill what he thinks the charts indicate about the duration of the current level of interest rates.

As Mr. Derby, how would you answer Dr. Drill?

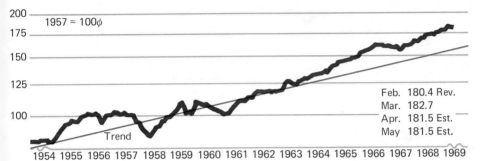

Figure 15-12. The growth of industrial activity in the United States.

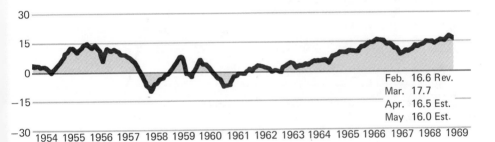

Figure 15-13. Industrial activity—percent deviations from trend.

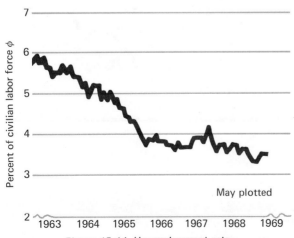

Figure 15-14. Unemployment rate.

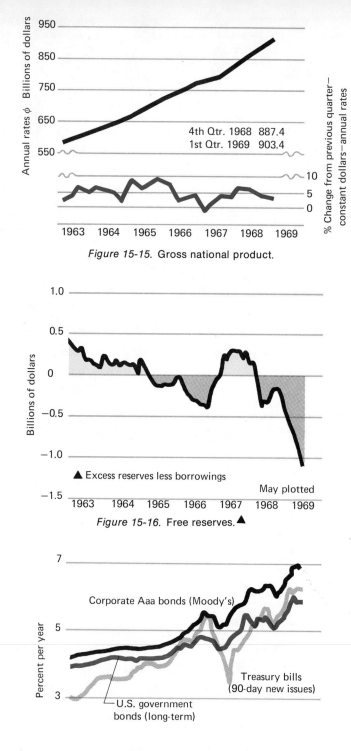

Figure 15-15. Gross national product.

4th Qtr. 1968 887.4
1st Qtr. 1969 903.4

▲ Excess reserves less borrowings

May plotted

Figure 15-16. Free reserves. ▲

Corporate Aaa bonds (Moody's)

Treasury bills
(90-day new issues)

U.S. government
bonds (long-term)

May plotted

Figure 15-17. Selected money rates.

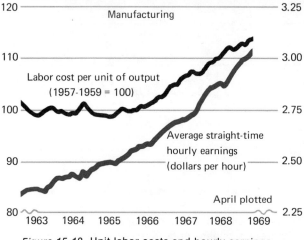

Figure 15-18. Unit labor costs and hourly earnings.

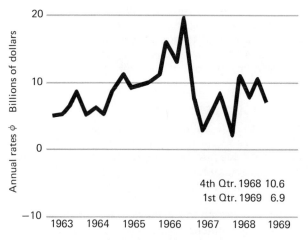

4th Qtr. 1968 10.6
1st Qtr. 1969 6.9

Figure 15-19. Changes in business inventories.

Source: *Economic Charts,* Economic Analysis Section, American Telephone
and Telegraph Company, New York, June, 1969.

16
Policies for Stabilization and Growth

The notion that government might have a principal responsibility for reducing cyclical fluctuations and for stimulating economic growth is relatively recent. Although there has long been agreement that national policies could improve business conditions, in general the accepted opinion was that the less the government did the better. The great depression occurring in the 1930s was so severe, however, that people looked to the government for assistance. Since that time it has been widely assumed that the federal government would attempt to reduce unemployment when it appeared and that it would at least attempt not to aggravate cyclical fluctuations by its own measures of spending and taxing. Since the 1950s, interest in promoting economic growth has also developed.

DEVELOPMENT OF POLICIES

It is easy to exaggerate the extent to which government was expected to follow a laissez-faire policy in the past. Even in the earliest days of the nation, policies were debated and adopted in terms of their effects on the economy. Alexander Hamilton succeeded in having established the first Bank of the United States, which he thought would aid greatly in the economic development of the country—Thomas Jefferson was opposed largely because he preferred to see the country remain a nation of farmers and artisans. The government built post roads and turnpikes and established a postal system largely for their economic benefits. Millions of acres of land were given to railroad companies or opened to homesteading to stimulate the development and settlement of the western lands. Tariffs were imposed on imports in the belief that such protection would speed the development of industry, and many other examples could be cited, such as the adoption of a system of patents and copyrights, creation of cabinet departments for agriculture, commerce, and labor, and support for the land-grant colleges. Various measures were taken to reduce the imperfections in the system of money and banks. But while all these things took place, there remained a climate of opinion in which the business cycle was considered virtually inevitable, in which depressions were thought of as necessary for adjustments which would bring subsequent recoveries, and in which most people believed that well-intentioned "interferences" by the government merely upset the "natural workings" of the economy and did more harm than good.

Monetary Policy

Even before the great depression, it had become obvious that a malfunctioning financial system could create financial panics and severe depressions. Consequently, control of the banking system and operation of a central bank have traditionally been among the generally accepted functions of government. Even here, however, tradition led to the establishment of a Federal Reserve System that was largely insulated from direct federal control. A principal reason for virtually all the legislation in the financial field has been to avoid bank failures, financial panics, and resulting economic crises.

Controlling the supply of money and guarding against unsafe banking were accepted early as proper governmental policies. It was generally believed that proper regulation of the growth of the money supply would provide a correct relationship between money and output and minimize economic fluctuations, mostly by preventing financial panics. Both professional economists and the general public agreed that the economy had a natural tendency toward full employment and that depressions were variations from the natural equilibrium, caused by some outside or sporadic factor like the breakdown of the banking system. Thus a principal function of the traditional central bank, both here and abroad, was to provide all the funds in demand in a financial panic so that banks could continue to operate and finance trade and commerce.

Priming the Pump

The great depression of the 1930s brought a drastic change in both professional economists' and the general public's thinking about the nature of unemployment. In that long and severe depression, it began to appear that monetary measures could not initiate any significant increase in production and employment; no matter how low interest rates were pushed or how freely available loanable funds became, there was little demand for investment goods. Economists turned their attention from analyzing the nature of economic equilibrium at full employment to analyzing the reasons for the low levels of output and prices. As we have surveyed in Chapter 10, the general tenor of thinking involved these ideas:

1. There is no necessary built-in tendency for the economy to adjust itself to full employment. Rather, the level of output and thus of employment depends upon the level of aggregate demand. This level might be inadequate to provide a satisfactory level of output and employment.

2. Given the propensities to consume and to save, the level of aggregate demand is determined largely by the level of investment expenditures. Thus a depression is the result of an inadequate level of investment.

3. When profit prospects are exceptionally pessimistic, no increase in the supply of money can lower interest rates sufficiently to encourage investment spending. Increased supplies of money, brought about by open-market operations of the central bank, drift into the hands of those who prefer to hold them as idle cash balances. Interest rates are too low to attract purchasers to securities, yet they are still too high to attract borrowers who would spend the funds for capital goods.[1]

Since, under these circumstances, investment demand could not be expected to initiate a recovery, an increase in aggregate demand had to be sought elsewhere. The answer lay in increasing government expendi-

[1] To be attractive to business borrowers, interest rates might have to be below zero under these severe conditions. This situation was called the *liquidity trap* by J. M. Keynes, by which he meant that as interest rates got down to very low levels, people and businesses preferred to hold idle money rather than to lend and there was insufficient demand for loans to raise rates.

ture as a substitute for private investment. But the increase in government expenditure would provide no real improvement if the government financed the expenditure through additional taxes. This would only reduce private expenditures. Thus was made the proposal, revolutionary for the time, that the government should intentionally create a deficit in its budget, borrow the needed funds either from those who would not otherwise spend them anyway or, better yet, from the banking system, and either purchase current output (public works programs) or make transfer payments to those who would increase their consumption expenditures. This proposal was called *priming the pump,* as it was thought that once the economy started upward, it would proceed under the natural forces of recovery.

This proposal was revolutionary for the 1930s because, until that time, little distinction had been drawn between public and private debt; a government was supposed to be as careful to balance its budget year by year as was a prudent householder. The conviction that governments should avoid deficits stemmed largely from the historical fact that major inflations had always stemmed from great government deficits, which governments had covered by creating money. Examples were, in this country, the Revolutionary War, the War of 1812, the Civil War, and World War I. The distinction that was not immediately adopted by the public is that in these war periods there was already full employment, and government deficit spending was added to an economy already at or near capacity output, while in the 1930s there was a deficiency of aggregate expenditure rather than an excess. In any event, the proposal was so contrary to generally accepted notions of sound economics that many businessmen were shocked at the "irresponsibility" of the New Deal administration and probably postponed some investment commitments that they might have adopted had they considered the political situation normal.[2]

The great depression did not come to a complete end until the stimulus of defense spending before and during World War II finally brought about full employment. Because this stimulus was obviously fortuitous and because the depression had been so severe, it was widely believed that the normal long-run problem of the economy was thereafter to be deflation, rather than inflation. It appeared to some students of the situation that the economy could produce such a high level of income that saving would tend to outrun opportunities for profitable investment. There would thus be a continuing tendency for aggregate demand to be inadequate, for gross national product to fall, and for unemployment to persist—unless government assumed the responsibility of ensuring that aggregate demand was made adequate.

As a reflection of this widespread opinion, the Congress adopted the Employment Act of 1946, at a time when it was widely feared that the cessation of wartime spending would lead to widespread unemployment. This act was in effect a directive to governmental agencies and departments to follow policies that would "coordinate and utilize all (govern-

---

[2] It is revealing, for example, that in his campaign for election in 1932, Franklin D. Roosevelt was highly critical of Herbert Hoover for the deficit that had crept into the federal budget because of declining revenues and promised to balance the federal budget as a necessary step before recovery could begin. After he was elected, he was persuaded that balancing the budget would require taxes that would make the depression worse.

ment) plans, functions, and resources for the purpose of creating and maintaining, in a manner calculated to foster and promote free competitive enterprise and the general welfare, conditions under which there will be afforded useful employment opportunities . . . and promote maximum employment, production and purchasing power." The language of the act is obviously very carefully drawn and reflects the fact that there was sharp disagreement over the law. It is significant that it was not called the Full Employment Act. One of its principal provisions was to set up the Council of Economic Advisers to assist the President in formulating economic policies and the Joint Economic Committee of the two houses of the Congress.

Compensatory Finance

Instead of returning after the war to depression conditions, the economy soon entered into an expansion phase of considerable proportions. Contemporary opinion had overlooked the influence of two important conditions. First, there had been a tremendous increase in the liquidity of the economy during the war. Government deficits had led to a greatly expanded money supply, held largely by households and businesses that expected to make postponed expenditures as soon as possible after the war. Households also held large quantities of government securities which made their holdings of cash even more redundant, and the large holdings of government securities of all sorts of financial institutions made them unnecessarily liquid and willing to lend.

Second, behind this large accumulation of actual money and other liquid assets lay large pent-up demands for all sorts of durable goods and housing. People wanted automobiles, refrigerators, radios, washing machines and ironers, and houses, and had the funds and borrowing ability to get them. Consequently, reconversion to peacetime production took place with surprising ease and swiftness. The economy enjoyed a general postwar expansion, although there were slowdowns in 1949, 1954, and 1958. In each of these, the downturn came before unemployment had been reduced to its previous low point. Interest in stabilization policies therefore remained high and, because of the cyclical behavior of the economy, the idea of priming the pump in recessions was superceded by a new concept called *compensatory finance*.

As the name implies, compensatory finance refers to the offsetting of excessive or deficient levels of aggregate demand through federal fiscal policy. Under this concept, a deficit in federal finances is acceptable if needed for full employment but, in periods of full employment, tax rates are supposed to provide a federal budget surplus with which to reduce the previously created debt.

Along with compensatory finance came a related development, that of *automatic stabilizers*. These are measures that more or less automatically affect governmental revenues or expenditures in the direction of offsetting a boom or a recession. Some of the actual measures were adopted before the war, but for other reasons. For example, one of the principal automatic stabilizers is the personal income tax. As incomes rise, tax revenues tend to rise even faster, as incomes move into higher tax brackets; and as incomes fall, the amount of tax tends to fall more rapidly. On the expenditure side, several types of government outlays tend to rise automatically in a recession; examples are payments for unemployment compensation, payments under agricultural price-support programs, and certain welfare payments under the social security programs. In addition to these automatic adjustments, of course, the Congress may decide to legislate changes in tax rates or in total expenditures.

Economic Growth

Economic growth became a goal of economic policies as a result of several developments in the 1950s. One development was the effort of the more advanced nations to assist the less developed nations to stimulate their growth rates. This development helped to focus attention on the problem of economic growth, and it increased interest in the advanced countries themselves. Also, after World War II several countries showed rather rapid rates of growth, partly for the simple reason that they were starting from rather low bases. European nations that were recovering from the destruction of the war and rebuilding virtually new industrial organizations with American support, and countries like Japan that were able to adapt advanced technology to their own economies, were showing annual increases in gross national product at considerably higher rates than those in the United States.[3] The public became particularly interested in economic growth after the Soviet Union succeeded in launching the first sputnik, exhibiting a rapid advance in technology in that country.

In the United States, public policies were directed in the 1950s to restraining inflation. As we have noted, there were three short recessions between the end of the war and 1958, and each occurred before unemployment had been eliminated in the preceding recovery. The average annual rate of growth during the decade was slow, when the recession years are included. The contrast with other countries led to the suspicion that the United States was not using the proper mix of fiscal and monetary policies to achieve both stability and long-term growth. The situation also gave rise to the question of the extent to which the two goals are compatible and the extent to which they conflict—how much growth might have to be given up to achieve stability (especially of the price level) and vice versa.

Political and academic debates over these problems led to a wider acceptance of the idea that stabilization policies should not be limited merely to trying to smooth out the business cycle by leveling up activity in recessions and leveling it off in booms. Such a policy implies a level underlying trend of activity, but there must be a rising trend if the economy is to grow over the long pull. Thus, the intent of governmental policies should be to encourage a rising trend line for GNP and to keep output in the short run close to the full-employment level. The concept of _potential gross national product_ was adopted by the President's Council of Economic Advisers. Potential GNP is defined as that GNP that would result from a practical minimum (about 3.5 or 4.0 percent) of unemployment. GNP should rise from year to year with greater population, labor force, technological advances, and the like.

---

[3] While the rates of increase were more rapid, the amounts involved were relatively small; a country's GNP might rise from $50 billion to $55 billion (10 percent) while, in the United States, the rise was from $447 billion to $476 billion (1958 to 1959 in stable prices, about 6 percent).

The relationship of GNP to potential gross national product is shown in Figure 16-1. Here, potential gross national product is defined as the actual GNP in 1955 rising at the rate of 3.5 percent to 1962 and at higher percentages thereafter (the earlier rate was seen to be inadequate to absorb both the unemployed and the growing labor force). This chart shows the apparent anomaly of actual output exceeding potential, but this result, of course, stems from the definition of potential output and the fact that output rose rapidly enough, in 1965 especially, to outpace the defined rate. The closeness of the two lines from 1965 on illustrates the low level of unemployment reached at that time. The projections on the chart reflect the opinion of the council in January, 1970, that anti-inflation measures taken in 1969 would depress actual GNP below its potential but that longer-run projections of demands indicated no lack of aggregate demands.

The concept of potential gross national product implies that in a recovery period the automatic stabilizers begin to take effect and to retard growth. Expansion of the curve of the cycle is restrained, but so is expansion along the trend line. The Council of Economic Advisers developed the concept of the *high-employment budget,* which is an estimate of what the federal budget would be if there were virtually full employment, assuming the actual level of expenditures and tax rates. The tax rates would apply to higher incomes, both individual and corporate, and (it was estimated in 1963) would actually provide a surplus in the budget. But this surplus would be deflationary and, coupled with the level of private spending, would not permit the high employment GNP to come about. In other words, recoveries could be choked off before they reached

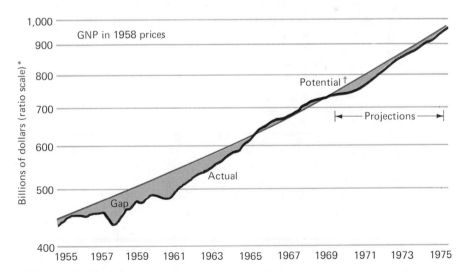

* Seasonally adjusted annual rates.

† Trend line of 3.5 percent from middle of 1955 to 1962 IV, 3.75 percent from 1962 IV to 1965 IV, 4 percent from 1965 IV to 1969 IV, 4.3 percent from 1969 IV to 1970 IV, 4.4 percent from 1970 IV to 1971 IV, and 4.3 percent from 1971 IV to 1975 IV.

Figure 16-1. Actual and potential gross national product, 1955–1975. Source: President's Council of Economic Advisers, *Annual Report,* 1968, p. 61, and 1970, p. 85.

the point of eliminating unemployment, as a result of this *fiscal drag*. Consequently, it was felt that the stabilization measures being applied in the 1950s were choking off recoveries before they reached full employment and thus preventing the full measure of long-term growth to occur. This concept led to certain recommendations on federal tax and expenditure policies. These will be discussed later.

MONETARY POLICY MEASURES

The types of policies aimed at stabilization and growth that receive most attention are monetary policies and fiscal policies, but there may be a variety of others. At the present time there is disagreement over the effectiveness of monetary policy measures as compared with fiscal policy measures. The preference for one or the other depends mainly on one's opinion on the relative effectiveness of changes in the money supply versus changes in the government's budget surplus or deficit. An example of this uncertainty illustrates the situation. In late 1968 economic forecasters were divided between those who anticipated a considerable slowdown in business activity in 1969 because of the effects of the income tax surcharge that had recently gone into effect and those who anticipated an upsurge because of the expansion of the money supply that had recently been permitted by the Federal Reserve System.[4] A complete examination of the debate would take us further into monetary theory than is possible here, but we take the position that both types of measures do have repercussions, that one or the other may be more effective in different circumstances, and that a combination of both types is more effective in most instances than is reliance on only one.

The monetary approach to stabilization is based essentially on the idea that there is an appropriate supply of money to support a given level of national income and level of interest rates. The problem is basically one of analyzing the demand for money and providing the appropriate supply of money to match the demand at a full-employment level of gross national product.

The *demand for money* consists of two types of demand, characterized by the demand for money for transactions and the demand for money for liquid balances. Some given quantity of money is needed simply to finance the transactions that take place, given the volume of transactions and the price level. Each household, business unit, and government needs to have a balance of this sort, largely because its income and expenditures are not perfectly synchronized. For example, if income is $1,000 per month and if expenditures take place evenly over the month, one's cash balance would decline by $33.33 each day. Even if the income recipient were willing to run out of money on the thirtieth day, on any other day he would be holding some sort of cash balance, and his average holding over the month would be $500 (if he started with $1,000).

---

[4] Unfortunately, the problem was not so simple that it permitted waiting for the events of 1969 to unfold and expecting them to provide a complete answer. Economic experiments cannot be performed in a laboratory. Later developments do not completely prove that a policy was right or wrong, because they are influenced to some extent by conditions that did not exist when the policy was adopted. As events unfolded, 1969 proved to be a year of inflation.

At any moment of time, all the money supply is in various cash balances. People cannot decide to get rid of all their money, because of this *transactions motive* for holding money. And to the extent that all economic units—or many of them—do want to get rid of money, it is obvious that the money must flow into the balances of others, through such transactions as sales of goods, repayments of debts, and sales of securities or other assets.

Under these circumstances, some changes in prices or other variables have to take place to make the public willing to hold the supply of money; this is why it is necessary to examine the determinants of the demand for money. The transactions demand explains part of it: if income is received and payments are made infrequently, if the price level is high, and if the clearing of checks is slow, this demand for money is large. A larger population, consisting of more households and a greater number of business units, along with a higher level of physical output, tends to require a larger supply of money for transactions.

The second type of demand for money consists of the demands for it as a highly desirable asset. Money is the most liquid of all assets because it can be spent at any time for anything on sale. It is therefore desirable for the *precautionary* and *speculative* motives. There are certain risks involved in running out of money, both in actual costs that may be incurred and in foregone opportunities. For example, a person embarking on a vacation trip by automobile will calculate not only how much money he should take for expected outlays but also a margin for unexpected ones, such as replacing a tire, or a dozen others. (He may rely on the use of credit cards for these purchases, but he will have to make settlement later.) [5] He may take along (or keep in his checking account to pay for charged purchases) another margin of money in case he finds bargains that tempt him. For these and many comparable reasons, most people like to hold at least some money in addition to the minimum required for transactions—for precautionary reasons.

The characteristics of money as a liquid asset (a store of wealth rather than a medium of exchange) make it also subject to changes in demand for speculative reasons. The speculative demand for money is comparable to the speculative demand for other things, especially securities. The demand increases when it is anticipated that its value will increase. The value of money may increase in terms of prices—prices of goods or of securities. If the prices of goods or securities are expected to fall, people tend to hold money until the fall takes place or the expectation changes.

Since the prices of securities reflect interest rates, as market yields on the securities, it follows that the speculative demand is related to the levels of present and anticipated interest rates. When expectations are for higher rates in the future (lower securities prices), more people prefer to hold cash but, when interest rates are considered high, it becomes expensive to hold cash. When money can be lent at high rates or can pur-

---

[5] Note that the inability to purchase a new tire, for a simple example, could lead to expenses considerably greater than the price of a tire—the cost of contacting someone from whom to borrow the money, delays and expenses for accomodations, and so on. The same sort of repercussions on a larger scale could result if a business were to run out of cash. Note also that the availability of borrowing reduces the need to hold cash for these possibilities, but of course at the potential expense of interest charges.

chase securities at low prices, preferences shift from cash to loans and securities.

A demand curve for money can be drawn to incorporate the two kinds of demand, transactions and liquidity. Since the transactions demand increases with the level of GNP and the liquidity demand is a function of interest rates, the demand curve can be drawn to illustrate the latter relationship at a *given level* of GNP. Thus Figure 16-2 shows two demand curves for two different levels of GNP. The curve D_1 illustrates the demand for money at a low level of GNP. The curve starts at a point above M_1, which is the amount of money required to finance the transactions involved in this level of GNP. If the total stock of money happened to be only M_1, none would be left over from transactions balances for liquidity balances. Thus interest rates would have to be high in order for people who need money for transactions balances to attract it away from people who desire it for liquidity.

If the stock of money were larger, such as M_2, money could be held in idle balances as well as in transactions balances. Interest rates would be lower, to reflect the relative availability of funds, such as r_1 rather than r_2. The other curve, D_2, reflects the situation at a higher level of GNP. The transactions demand is greater and a stock of at least M_2 is necessary if the higher level of GNP is to be possible. With a stock of M_2, interest rates would be as high as with a smaller stock at a lower GNP, since money would have to be attracted from liquidity balances. In order to maintain an interest rate as low as r_1, the money stock would have to be increased to M_3—if the higher level of GNP is to be maintained.

This analysis fits into that of the determination of national income developed in Chapter 10. Suppose the higher level of GNP is the desired one in terms of full employment, and suppose further that the necessary amount of investment spending would be forthcoming at r_1 but would be insufficient at higher rates of interest. Then, given the demand for

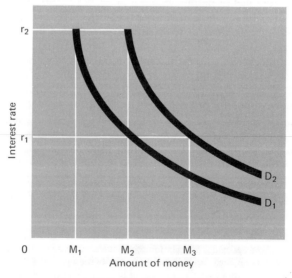

Figure 16-2. The demand for money.

money, the supply would have to be adjusted to M_3 in order to provide the interest rate that is consistent with the desired level of GNP. Similarly, if the higher level of GNP reflected an inflationary situation and the lower level of GNP would provide full employment without rising prices, the supply of money should be adjusted backward to M_2, if r_1 were the appropriate interest rate to bring out the proper amount of investment spending. As can be seen on the chart, the supply M_3 would provide more money than is demanded at r_1 and this extra money would be used to purchase securities and make loans until the interest rate settled at a level below r_1. Such a rate would stimulate further investment spending and bring about an excessive GNP.

The Monetary Equation

The relationships of supply and demand pertaining to money can also be illustrated by the monetary equation, usually called the *equation of exchange*. Like any equation, it illustrates a truism and, taken by itself, does not explain the relationships involved but does provide a framework for an explanation. We may think of GNP as all the goods and services going into final sales multiplied by their prices, or *PQ*. The expenditures that buy *PQ* must obviously be the same amount. If total sales, or *PQ*, in a period of time were $1,000, $1,000 must have been spent on these goods and services. If, during this period, the total stock of money was $100, each dollar on the average must have been spent ten times; if the stock was $250, each dollar on the average must have been spent four times. The money stock multiplied by its turnover or velocity equals aggregate expenditures, so the equation may be written $MV = PQ$.

Comparing the stock of money existing in a period of time with the GNP of that period yields the *income velocity* of money, or the number of times each dollar becomes income during the period. During the period, however, there are many transactions other than final sales—all the intermediate transactions that move goods and services through the processes of production and distribution. These transactions are also the means by which incomes are distributed as portions of national income. These transactions are more numerous and constitute a much larger total than final sales only, so money is used much more frequently than its income velocity. Its *transactions velocity* is considerably higher.

The identity between *MV* and *PQ* might suggest that, in determining monetary policy, all that one has to do is to calculate the *PQ* or gross national product that produces full employment at the existing price level and then supply the appropriate volume of money to finance these transactions. But there are numerous complications that must be considered.

Problems of Monetary Policy

There are several types of problems that complicate the choice and application of monetary policies. The demand for money is not stable but subject to shifts, as well as being somewhat elastic in terms of interest rates. The demand for money may increase, for example, not only because more is needed for transactions but also because of changes in preference for cash over interest-bearing assets. Such a change would be illustrated in Figure 16-2 if the curve D_2 began at the same point as

D_1 but thereafter stayed to the right of D_1; at any level of interest rates, people would prefer to hold larger cash balances than before the increase in demand.

Suppose that statistics show that the current equation of exchange is $250 \times 4 = 10×100, or that a money stock of $250 is financing the flow of 100 units of output at an average price of $10. Suppose further that there is a decline in the demand for money because expectations of future prices make goods and securities more desirable at present prices than they have been. In the past perhaps $50 of the money stock has been held in idle balances (in other words, the *active* money stock has had a velocity of turnover of 5). Now, with the lesser demand for money, all the money stock may be offered in markets for goods and securities, increasing demands for them and pushing up their prices. Spending the previously idle balances increases the V in the equation and has the same general effect as would an increase in M.

The difficulty created by such shifts in demand lies in the fact that it is difficult to estimate the extent to which money is kept in idle balances. A strong clue is provided by the size of V because, if it is low by usual standards, there is a strong implication that some balances, or parts of them, are not turning over at all. But businesses and households do not keep separate balances, labeled active and inactive, and the principal evidence available to the authorities is that total spending is rising or falling. If spending increases and the authorities are already satisfied with the level of output and prices, they must attempt to reduce the monetary stimulus to spending, but just how much restraint to apply to the growth in the money supply remains a question of judgment. The Federal Reserve System must decide by how much to reduce the volume of bank reserves, or their rate of growth, in order to require banks to reduce the volume of lending and thus of deposits.

In the real world the monetary authorities must feel their way, largely because banks do not respond automatically or mechanically to pressures on their reserve positions. Banks may attempt to offset the pressures by competing for time deposits in order to maintain their loan volume. There will be a reduction in demand deposits to some extent, but higher interest rates, reflecting the competition for funds, may draw more funds out of idle balances into the stream of spending. The use of money may accelerate although its quantity is restricted. This is not to say that the central bank is unable to affect the situation materially, only that there are no mechanical rules that make the choice of actions simple.

Monetary Lags

Related to these considerations are the complications introduced by *lags*, of which there are several kinds. One kind is the *recognition lag*, which results from the fact that economic data are not instantaneous or unanimous in their direction. It is often not very clear in what stage of the cycle the economy currently is. The fact that an upper or lower turning point has been reached is not known with any degree of certainty for at least two or three months after it has happened. In the meantime, however, the monetary authorities must make decisions about the direction in which they should be exerting pressure. The authorities are not likely, for example, to switch to an easy money policy before they are fairly sure that a downturn has started because, if they are wrong, they will aggravate the tendency of an expansion to turn into a boom period.

Another type of lag is the time period required to put a policy into action, the *implementation lag.* This lag need not be long in the case of monetary policy since monetary measures may be taken quickly, but it tends to be more important in the case of fiscal policies, as will be noted later. A third and more important type of lag is that required by the length of time before monetary measures begin to take effect throughout the economy, sometimes called the *linkage lag* because it refers to the linkages between monetary actions and the production of goods and services. Steps that the reserve authorities may take today cannot be fully reflected in the economy for perhaps several months. Consequently, it is necessary for the authorities to attempt to forecast conditions some months ahead and to avoid actions that will turn out to have been inappropriate.

For example, the Federal Reserve banks might increase bank reserves through open-market purchases. Sellers of the securities deposit the checks drawn on the reserve banks at their own banks, which thus obtain the additional reserve balances. The sellers of the securities now have larger cash balances. They may use this money to purchase other securities (tending to lower interest rates) or to purchase goods and services, or they may hold the money. If they buy securities or goods, the sellers of these will also do something with the money received. In the meantime, the banks with excess reserves presumably increase their loans and investments, and there is the question of what the borrowers and sellers of securities want the money for. It is apparent that the chain of events through which the effects of the increased money supply operate are going to be different each time, and the linkages between changes in the money supply and its eventual effects on output, prices, and employment may require from a few months to a year or more to work through.

Conflicting Objectives

Another type of problem that may complicate the operation of monetary policy is the conflict among different economic objectives. There may be a conflict in the sense that prevention of price inflation may involve a cost in terms of unemployment or perhaps in terms of growth. A constant problem throughout the 1950s was that of balancing the resistance to inflation against the persistence of unemployment. If the reserve authorities had taken price stability as their sole objective, they would have adopted more stringent restrictions on the money supply, but these restrictions would probably have aggravated the problem of unemployment. Later, in the 1960s, the problem of the balance of payments came to the fore and led the reserve authorities to try to hold up short-term interest rates in order to make investment of foreign-owned dollars in American securities attractive and, at the same time, to try to hold down long-term rates in order to encourage expansion and growth. Had the authorities been willing to overlook unemployment and stagnation, they might have pursued a tight money policy that would have raised interest rates and lowered prices in this country.

FISCAL POLICY MEASURES

The economic effects of federal revenue and expenditure measures are extensive. It is inevitable that these effects receive attention when revenue and expenditure proposals are considered by the Congress. Stabilization and other economic policies have supplanted the belief that the proper fiscal policy of government is to seek a balanced budget each year. Government taxing and spending lie at the heart of the political process, so it should not be surprising that much political disagreement arises over the proper size of the total budget and the relative priorities of various governmental programs. There is also room for disagreement over the expected effects of changes in taxes or expenditures, largely because these effects take time to come about and thus are viewed in the context of forecasts of later conditions.

Taxes and Expenditures

Although some economists consider that the principal effect of government purchases is to alter the composition of gross national product more than to alter its total size, fiscal policy measures are thought by many to be important determinants of the level of GNP. The President's Council of Economic Advisers has stated:

> The instruments of fiscal policy—purchases of goods and services, transfer payments, subsidies, grants-in-aid, and taxes—are the government's most powerful tools for expanding or restraining overall demand. Federal purchases of goods and services are directly part of market demand, and—through their impact on production, employment, and income—encourage further private investment expenditures. Taxes, transfers, subsidies, and grants-in-aid affect consumption and investment through their influence on disposable personal income, after-tax profits, incentives, and state and local expenditures.[6]

The nature of fiscal policy measures has already been indicated in Chapter 10, so the description here may be brief. We shall review separately the general effects of changes in tax revenues and expenditures during periods of expansion and contraction, and illustrate the discussion with a summary of fiscal policy actions adopted in recent years.

During a recession aggregate expenditures are insufficient to call forth a full-employment output. $C + I + G$ constitute an inadequate total. Consumer expenditures are not likely to provide an upward impetus because they are primarily a function of disposable income, which in turn depends upon GNP. Investment expenditures depend upon profit prospects and interest rates. Interest rates may be lowered through monetary measures, but recovery may depend more upon improved profit prospects. Some types of government expenditures may be de-

---

[6] President's Council of Economic Advisers, *Annual Report,* January, 1965, p. 62.

signed for this purpose. Federal purchases of public works, such as roads, dams, post offices, and other construction, may make attractive investment in bulldozers, scrapers, hauling equipment, and other construction items. Federal investment in these public works tends to have the same stimulative effects as would private investment in comparable items. Similarly, federal grants-in-aid to state and local governments may increase their expenditures.

By the same token, government transfer payments to households support or stimulate consumption expenditures through increasing disposable personal income. Such payments consist of social security benefits, pensions, veterans' benefits, and the like. They are distinguished from other forms of personal income in that they are not payments for contributions to current output. They are not purchases and thus do not directly increase GNP, but they lead to subsequent purchases of current output of consumer goods. Closely related to transfer payments are some types of direct employment by government, such as the projects adopted during the great depression in which youths were hired to clean up debris from forests and build hiking and fire trails (Civilian Conservation Corps) and in which buildings were cleaned and parks and beaches improved. These projects were adopted because of the general public disapproval of straight "handouts" at that time and because they could be inaugurated without long prior planning; they were often referred to as *leaf-raking* and, because the value of the finished work was sometimes not great, the wages paid were somewhat in the nature of transfer payments.

On the tax side of the situation, the effect of personal taxes on disposable personal income and thus consumption in a recession is somewhat reduced by the progressive structure of the tax system (the automatic stabilizer feature). Further, if the Congress considers the stimulus to be required, tax rates may be cut further. Reductions in personal taxes increase disposable personal income and presumably consumption, while reductions in corporate tax rates improve the profitability of investment projects and increase the likelihood that additional investments will be made.[7]

The principle of the multiplier should be kept in mind when one considers the probable effects of changes in tax rates or expenditures. Additional government expenditures represent direct increases in incomes, which lead to additional expenditures for consumption. Tax reductions increase disposable personal incomes and similarly lead to secondary rounds of consumption expenditures. The increased consumption expenditures may, in turn, lead to additional investment expenditures through the accelerator principle.

When full employment exists and inflationary pressures on prices are present, these fiscal tools can be used to restrain aggregate demand. Progressive tax rates can be allowed to restrain incomes automatically, and government expenditures can be postponed until more appropriate times. However, as in the case of monetary policy, the existence of lags

---

[7] An interesting question arose as a result of the tax increase imposed in 1968, which was legislated to be in effect for one year. For some months after its enactment, there was much less reduction in both consumer and business spending than had been expected. It may be that when a change in tax rates is expected to be temporary, people look beyond the period and do not adjust either type of spending significantly.

complicates the application of fiscal policy. Proposals for change normally originate in the administrative branch of government and are then considered by the Congress. In both branches there may be a recognition lag comparable to that in monetary policy. The legislative process itself may take up a considerable amount of time if there is general disagreement over the need for a change in taxes or expenditures. Realization that the effects of such a change will be felt some months in the future raises another area of uncertainty; some may feel that a change in taxes will turn out to be inappropriate by the time the full effects occur. For example, some Congressmen — and economists — believed that taxes should have been higher in early 1968 but hesitated to recommend increases because they feared a slowdown in business would occur in any event. As in the case of monetary policy, selection of today's measures depends largely on one's forecast of business conditions six months or a year later.

Fiscal Policies in the 1960s

The decade of the 1960s provides a good illustration of the use of changes in federal financing to affect economic conditions. Both selective measures — those designed to affect certain kinds of spending — and aggregative measures were employed on the revenue side. Less attention was paid to the level of government expenditures until late in the decade.

In the early years of the decade, the principal problems seemed to be associated with a growth rate that was inadequate to absorb the growing labor force. A direct approach to this problem was taken by an act in 1962 that provided business corporations with an *investment tax credit* to stimulate investment in plant and equipment. Businesses could take a credit against income tax liabilities up to 7 percent of such expenditures for machinery and equipment. At the same time, the Treasury issued new regulations permitting depreciation of such assets to be computed over a shorter period of years.[8] These measures were estimated to have long-run benefits on the rate of economic growth.

It was at this time that the Council of Economic Advisers and others responsible for fiscal planning developed the idea of fiscal drag. As noted earlier, this concept held that existing corporate and personal tax rates would create an excessive federal surplus in a high-employment economy, taking too much income out of the expenditure stream and leading to a downturn. It was believed that as the economy neared full employment, these effects began to apply and thus actually prevented the economy from reaching full employment. It was estimated that, at a high level of employment, existing tax rates, with actual expenditures, would have produced a budget surplus of some $12 billion.

Consequently, in 1963 the administration recommended a reduction in corporate and personal income tax rates. This was an unprecedented move because at the time there was a budget deficit. The argument was that a deficit was inevitable at existing rates because these rates exerted

[8] Such a computation does not reduce the total tax liability over the life of the asset but does have certain advantages to the taxpayer. If an asset is depreciated in five years instead of six, no more depreciation can be taken as a cost after the fifth year. But taxable income and tax liabilities are reduced for five years, and the amounts saved can be reinvested for further income, used to reduce debt, or used for other purposes.

so much fiscal drag that full employment could not be reached; for that matter, neither could a level of national income adequate to yield revenues sufficient to balance the budget be reached. Reducing expenditures would have increased the fiscal drag, as well as cut into programs considered socially desirable by the administration. It was further argued that lower tax rates would permit a sufficient growth in the economy to produce higher total revenues — perhaps enough higher to balance the budget at high employment.

There was considerable debate in the Congress over the proposal, but in early 1964 the Revenue Act of 1964 was passed. It provided a two-stage cut in personal tax rates in 1964 and 1965, lowering the rate on the first bracket of personal income from 20 percent to 14 percent and the top rate from 91 percent to 70 percent. In general, the effective rate for corporations was lowered from 52 percent to 48 percent. At the level of income in 1964, these reductions were calculated to lower total tax revenues by about $13 billion; at the level prevailing in 1967, the difference was about $18 billion.[9]

The anticipated stimulus to the economy appeared to materialize on schedule. By the following year the disparity between potential gross national product and actual was about half of its previous figure, a cut of about $15 billion (GNP was $684.9 billion in 1965, up from $632.4 billion in 1964). The effects of the investment tax credit (also liberalized in 1964) were probably also being felt. Business expenditures on durable equipment had been $34.8 billion in 1963 but were $45.8 billion in 1965.

The reduction in tax rates called attention to the fact that these rates were still much higher than had ever been considered normal before World War II and that there were also many "nuisance" taxes still in effect — excise taxes enacted to raise revenue during that war and the Korean War. Consequently, as there was still a gap below potential GNP, an act was passed in 1965 to eliminate or reduce many of these taxes on consumer durable goods, telephone messages, and other items.

In 1965 the experiment with more active manipulation of fiscal policy measures appeared to be highly successful. Gross national product was growing at a more satisfactory pace, although it had not quite reached its calculated potential; unemployment was reduced below 5 percent although still above a target level; and it was gratifying that this expansion had occurred with virtually no increase in wholesale and retail price levels. Other developments in the latter part of the decade complicated the situation, however.

The major complication was acceleration of expenditures for an escalated level of warfare in Vietnam. Inflationary pressures were absent in 1965 partly because there was a general expectation that the growth of business activity would slow down in the near future but, as it became clearer that government spending was about to rise, analysts foresaw further expansion and development of bottlenecks in production. Budget Bureau forecasts of defense, and thus total, spending were surprisingly incorrect on the low side at this time; such expenditures rose much more

[9] This and other proposals originating in the Council of Economic Advisers added several terms to the American vocabulary. The general approach was popularly labeled *the new economics,* although all that was new was a wider measure of acceptance, and the willingness to make frequent changes came to be called *fine tuning of the economy.*

rapidly than the Department of Defense apparently anticipated. Defense purchases rose rapidly, beginning in mid-1965. In several nondefense areas, government spending was also accelerated in accordance with programs adopted earlier. Total expenditures rose much more rapidly after 1965 than in the first half of the decade. As one example, social security payments under old-age insurance increased from $16.6 billion in 1965 to $29.2 billion in 1968 (both being annual rates for the first half-year). Social security taxes were also increased during this period, but not in close step with benefits. Federal lending was also considerably increased.

Although many business and academic economists began to call for tax increases in 1965, the administration apparently relied on the hope that defense expenditures would rise only temporarily. As the administrative deficit increased, price rises became persistent, and the balance of payments with other countries deteriorated, however, the administration moved to the side of restriction. Administration economists had been impressed by the fact that the budget was in slight surplus, on a national-income-accounts basis, that revenues were rising with incomes, and that social security taxes had been sharply increased. However, it became clear that federal outlays were also on a sharp upswing.

Early in 1966 the administration proposed several measures to increase revenues without actually canceling the previous cuts in income taxes. Tax collections were speeded up by requiring corporations to pay taxes sooner than had been the case, and withholding of personal taxes was put on a partially progressive-rate basis. The part of the reduction in excise taxes that hau not yet gone into effect was postponed. These measures increased federal revenues in fiscal years 1966 and 1967 (ending June 30), but the effects then dissipated themselves because they were only accelerations of tax payments, not increases in liabilities. The necessity for heavy government borrowing in 1966 added to heavy business demands for credit from lending institutions and, coupled with restrictive measures taken by the Federal Reserve System because of inflation, put heavy pressures on credit markets and led to the highest interest rates in some hundred years. At this point, the Congress suspended the investment tax credit for fifteen months and the administration announced cutbacks in federal spending.

By early 1967 the administration expected another surge in economic expansion later in the year and consequently proposed an increase in income taxes in the form of a temporary surcharge to be added to tax liabilities. The fate of this proposal illustrates the nature of the lags in fiscal policy. The surcharge was proposed to become effective July 1, 1967, and to remain in effect for two years or until Vietnam expenditures could be substantially reduced. Business activity in early 1967, however, was considerably slowed down by the restrictive measures taken to stop the inflation of 1966, and many Congressmen were inclined to think that a tax increase in 1967 would be poorly timed. As a matter of fact, at the request of the administration, the Congress did restore the investment tax credit at this time.

By mid-year 1967 it was apparent that the federal deficit would be large, requiring a considerable amount of federal borrowing. Remembering the *credit crunch* of 1966 and the difficulties of obtaining funds then, many businesses began to prepare for a repetition by entering the bond market for funds, and again interest rates rose to unprecedented heights, even though the Federal Reserve was not restrictive. The administration renewed its request for a tax surcharge, this time at 10 percent rather than 6 percent because it could apply to less of the calendar year. Disagreements over many aspects of the problem delayed disposition of the proposal in the Congress for several months. Since the proposal was based on a forecast, some congressmen disagreed with the need for the increase even though a large deficit was inevitable. Some felt strongly that the costs of the war in Vietnam should be met by postponing various domestic programs with which they were not greatly in sympathy, and others wanted to force the administration to end the war. Still others remained unconvinced that it was possible or desirable to fine-tune the economy with frequent changes in tax rates.

Probably what brought about eventual action was a crisis in the balance of payments, aggravated by a clear trend toward domestic inflation. The nation's deficit in the balance of payments had permitted foreign governments to acquire large holdings of dollars, which many of them were now using to demand gold from the Treasury.[10] It appeared that devaluation of the dollar would be forced unless fiscal action was taken to reduce the inflationary pressures that were becoming constantly more apparent. But the proponents of reduced spending were able to demand as the price of their support for the tax surcharge a reduction in most federal spending programs. Consequently, the compromise reached—the tax surcharge plus a cut in federal spending—was considerably more restrictive than had been proposed. A large part of the projected deficit was estimated to be eliminated by roughly $10 billion of additional revenue and about the same amount of reduction in expenditures.

In spite of these measures, inflationary pressures continued. An inflationary psychology had taken hold. Businesses were willing to borrow, even at very high interest rates, in order to buy equipment they expected to become more expensive later. The surtax did not materially dampen consumer expenditures. The price level continued to rise throughout 1969, but there was an impact on the amount of real output. The increase in real GNP became smaller each quarter (see the chart in the case at the end of Chapter 14) and disappeared by early 1970. In the summer of 1969 the Congress voted to discontinue the surtax in 1970.

NONFINANCIAL MEASURES

Besides monetary and fiscal policy measures there are many specific steps that government can take to improve the productivity of the economy. We call these *nonfinancial* not because they may be costless in terms of governmental expenditures but because they are aimed specifically at encouraging economic growth from the supply side; monetary and fiscal policy measures are designed in the main to operate through aggregate demand. The following list of programs is brief and is included primarily to emphasize that the supply side should not be overlooked

[10] This situation is explained more fully in Chapter 20.

while the bulk of attention is given to measures designed to affect aggregate demand.

1. The Mobility of Labor. If labor is able to move easily from lower-paying to higher-paying jobs, productivity is presumably increased. The higher pay normally reflects the greater output (in terms of value) possible in the new job and the willingness of employers to attract labor. Impediments to mobility keep labor in the less productive jobs. Mobility tends to increase with education, accumulated savings, information, and specialized institutions in the labor market. One such institution is the U.S. Employment Service, which serves to bring employers and workers together.

2. Social Programs. Some types of social welfare programs can serve to increase individuals' productivity and value in the labor market through training and basic education. A wide variety of programs could be included in this category, such as grants for training programs, aid to dependent children, and the like.

3. Urban Redevelopment. Many cities are currently working with aid from federal sources to stem the decline of central cities and to rebuild them as centers of industry and commerce, making these areas productive rather than a drain on public revenues.

4. Conservation and Development of Natural Resources. Conservation involves more than merely setting aside lands and forests for recreation and preventing their use for other purposes. For example, it is often possible to develop multiple uses for government property, such as for controlled cutting of timber, grazing, mineral exploration, and hunting, fishing, and camping. It may be economically impossible for private users of water from a river to purify it for their own use if other users pollute it, but the availability of pure water is necessary not only for human consumption but for many industrial uses. Many problems of this sort are created by the complexities of modern society and do not lend themselves to solution except through the actions of some level of government.[11]

5. Research and Development. American industry is well known for its willingness to spend large sums in order to develop new processes and products. A large part of the total output of some large companies consists of products that were unknown only a few years ago. Many Europeans believe that these expenditures for research and development are the principal reason for the superior productivity of the modern American economy. In some fields, private interests are not sufficiently direct to bear the costs of research, which may be very great. In others, the firms are too small to shoulder such expenditures. In these situations government has sometimes stepped in to finance research and development, as in aerospace and agriculture.

6. Public Health. Urbanization of society has made many problems of health and sanitation of public concern although, in earlier days, they were

---

[11] Some of these problems are examples of *social costs* of production. A factory that dumps pollutants into the water or the air creates costs for others, either in the disadvantages of pollution or in the costs of removing it. In a real sense, these costs are part of the costs society has to pay for the products. An argument for requiring measures to reduce such pollution is that they place the costs on the producer, who must reflect them in the price. If the price is more than consumers will pay, the goods should not be produced.

essentially of private interest. Our rural grandfathers were not concerned about air pollution, sewage disposal, traffic control, water purification, and other matters affecting the general health of the public. Advanced research in the medical and related sciences must be paid for by someone if it is to take place and, while many private sources of funds exist, much of the total expenditure in this area is made by government.

Many of the measures just listed account for the relatively large proportion of gross national product that government purchases represent in modern industrial countries, a subject discussed in Chapter 14. To the extent that measures like these succeed in raising the level of productivity, they tend to pay for themselves in the resulting output.

SUMMARY

There is now widespread acceptance of the idea that government should try to stabilize the economy and encourage its growth. It has long been agreed that a nation's monetary policies should be stabilizing, but the use of fiscal policy measures is relatively recent. Such measures began with the attempts to prime the pump in the New Deal days. Later the idea grew that government spending and taxes could compensate for excess or deficient spending in the private sector at all times, not only during depressions. Some fiscal measures, such as unemployment compensation, were built into the economy to serve as automatic stabilizers. More recently the focus has been on attempting to keep the economy close to its potential GNP by minimizing unemployment. In the 1960s the administration used the idea of the high-employment budget in pursuing this goal.

The essence of monetary policy is to adjust the supply of money to the demand for it. Supply and demand must be in equilibrium, just as in commodity markets, if the value of money is to be stable. When supply exceeds demand, people attempt to get rid of their excess money by buying goods, thus pushing up prices, or securities, and pushing down interest rates. Both rising prices and falling interest rates tend to encourage business investment.

Fiscal policy measures rely on the impact of government spending and taxation. Government spending financed by a deficit rather than by taxes tends to increase the total amount of spending and thus be expansionary.

Efforts to fine-tune the economy, especially with fiscal measures, seemed to work well in the first half of the decade of the 1960s. In the second half, inflation became a serious problem. Large expenditures for the war in Vietnam complicated the task of adjusting the amount of government spending to that needed by the economy. The task of stabilization fell largely to the Federal Reserve System. By the time the federal budget was brought into balance, it was very difficult to restrain inflation even with highly restrictive monetary policies.

Economic Terms for Review

priming the pump	demand for money
compensatory finance	equation of exchange
automatic stabilizers	income velocity
potential gross national product	transactions velocity
high-employment budget	monetary lags
fiscal drag	credit crunch

Questions for Review

1. How does compensatory finance differ from priming the pump?
2. What was the Employment Act of 1946?
3. How does the high-employment budget differ from the actual budget? How is it used?
4. What are the three types of demand for money?
5. Why is there a delay before monetary policy measures take effect?
6. How successful were government economic policies in the late 1960s?

Questions for Analysis

1. Why did the President's Council of Economic Advisers believe that the tax system was making full employment impossible?
2. Why is more money needed when GNP is large?
3. Suppose the business community is convinced that a fall in the price level and a rise in interest rates are likely. What happens to the demand for money? How is this change related to the demand for goods? for securities?
4. Suppose that the Federal Reserve increases bank reserves. How is this increase supposed to affect the real economy? How long may it take?
5. Why did the Federal Reserve have most of the job of stabilization in 1966–1967?
6. Why were the fiscal measures of 1968 not more effective?

Case for Decision

Toward the end of the 1969 fiscal year (June 30), the President and the Congress were concerned with much the same problem that was puzzling the directors of Citizens National Bank (see Chapter 15). That is, they were attempting to determine whether underlying business conditions indicated a decline in inflation, whether the surtax enacted in 1968 had been beneficial, and whether it should be allowed to expire on June 30 or be extended.

The Nixon administration strongly favored extension of the surtax at 10 percent until December 31, 1969, and then at 5 percent to June 30, 1970. (That is, each person's tax would be increased by 10 percent in 1969 and by 5 percent for half of 1970.) The Chairman of the House Ways and Means Committee, Democrat Wilbur Mills of Arkansas, also favored extension, but a majority of Democrats on the committee were opposed. In general, they had two reasons, (1) the belief that the surtax had not been effective, and (2) the belief that many fundamental reforms of the personal income tax structure were more important. Partly to obtain bipartisan support, President

Nixon also proposed that low-income people be given greater deductions in calculating taxable income. For example, a single person earning $1,735 would normally have a tax of $117, but Nixon proposed that all tax be eliminated at that income. The amount of deduction would decline by half of increased income up to an income of $3,300, where the usual rates would again apply. This provision would eliminate about $665 million of tax revenue.

On June 17 the House Ways and Means Committee voted 16 to 9 to report the administration bill to the full House. On the following day the President told a press conference that if the Congress passed the bill, the economy should "cool off" within two or three months. He said that there is usually a lead time of several months before the results of economic measures show up, that the basic decisions to extend the surtax, hold back on spending, and maintain tight money had been made, and that the effects should appear in two or three months.

In the meantime, Chairman Patman (D., Texas) of the House Banking Committee, long known as a critic of the banking industry, was asking Secretary of the Treasury Kennedy why he was not taking greater action to force banks to hold down interest rates. Kennedy answered that he had no control over bank rates but that he did hope, with Patman, that banks would try to ration loans without raising rates further. Kennedy added, however, that interest rates tend to reflect anticipations of future credit conditions and that the prime rate had recently risen to 8.5 percent because there was doubt that the surtax would be extended. "We are entitled to expect responsible behavior from the banks," he said, "but bankers are entitled to expect the government to take the actions necessary to restrain inflation."

If you were a member of the House Ways and Means Committee, would you have voted to report the administration bill to the House? Why or why not?

Part 6
Current Economic Issues

17
Government and Business

The influence of government pervades the economy. The United States has far from a laissez-fair economy, and yet it has the closest to a free-enterprise economy of any nation. This situation can be explained by the fact that, although public opinion generally favors production by private enterprise, it also favors in many instances governmental interference with the operation of completely free markets. There are many reasons for this dual approach. The early development of the capitalistic economy in England and the United States brought many results that a democratic society would not accept as morally right. For example, the plight of women and young children working long hours in mines and textile mills led to the enactment of legislation prohibiting or regulating these labor practices. As time has gone on and conditions have changed, social problems have arisen with increasing urbanization and have led to other controls over the economy. Some relatively recent examples are the adoption of the social security program in the 1930s and many subsequent amendments, federal minimum-wage laws, and laws regulating transactions in such diverse markets as residential housing (to attack discriminatory practices) and securities (to require full disclosure of relevant information). Besides these and many other examples of legislative influence on specific markets and industries, monetary and fiscal policies have been designed by government to influence the behavior of the economy in the aggregate.

REGULATION OF MONOPOLY

This chapter is concerned with a specific segment of the broad subject of government-business relations, the regulation of business practices. More specifically, it is concerned with the development of governmental regulation of competitive practices. This subject, in turn, logically comprises two areas. One deals with the problem of monopoly and its prevention, and the other deals with competitive practices that may be considered injurious to consumers or competitors or likely to lead to monopoly.

The Monopoly Problem

Monopolies became an economic and political problem in the United States during the period after the Civil War when the economy was expanding rapidly and shifting from agriculture to industry. With the rise of metal-producing and metal-using industries and other industries related to them, such as petroleum, many situations of high concentration of output in a few firms developed. These situations were partly a result of the fact that the new industries required large amounts of invested capital. This requirement not only led to the establishment of large companies in industries like iron and steel and the railroads but also encouraged their managements to seek protection against the risks of competition.

The situation was also partly a result of the fact that there was no federal legislation and virtually no state legislation dealing specifically with monopoly. If the managements of several large manufacturing companies wanted to protect the large investments in their companies against the risks of competition by agreeing among themselves to share markets or not to sell below certain prices, they were not breaking any specific laws. Under the common law — that is, the unwritten laws that develop as the result of court decisions in specific cases — such agreements were conspiracies and therefore not enforceable at law, but it was not illegal to make the agreements. If one participant broke the agreement, the others could not call on the courts to require him to live up to it.

The Railroad Problem

In the second half of the nineteenth century, the monopoly problem arose spectacularly in the railroad industry. The railroads were a prime example of an industry with heavy fixed costs, related to the investment in roadbed and rolling stock. Each railroad was tempted to try to increase traffic because marginal costs were not high in relation to total costs. Adding more cars to a train or adding additional trains increased costs only by the specific additional costs of hauling the extra cars. Thus the railroads frequently got into rate wars in attempts to take traffic away from each other. But the rate competition naturally arose only where two or more lines served the same territories. Each railroad system had some points along its lines where it was the only railroad and where it did not have to compete for traffic. Thus the roads tended to charge low rates on long hauls where there was competition and high rates on short hauls where they had monopolies.

This practice led to much criticism of the railroads, especially by shippers who were hurt by the high rates and by farmers who were served by single lines. Regulation of the railroads became an active political issue, and in 1888 the Congress passed the Interstate Commerce Commission Act. By this act, it was decided that competition was unworkable in the railroad industry and that the railroads should be treated as public utilities. Thus, the Interstate Commerce Commission (ICC) was given jurisdiction over requirements of service and rates for interstate shipments. The situation may be considerably different now in that the railroads face competition from other means of transportation that did not formerly exist, especially automobiles, trucks, buses, and airplanes. Perhaps, in light of this competition, resources could be allocated more efficiently among the competing uses without regulation of rates, but the practice is well-established today — the airlines, trucking companies, and buses are regulated with regard to service and charges, as well as the railroads.

Monopoly in Other Industries

The large companies in various other industries also developed collusive practices. Managements often arranged for stockholders to deposit their stock in a voting trust, so that management of all the companies could be unified. As a result, virtually any monopolistic group or company came to be called a *trust*. Around the turn of the century, this situation attracted a great deal of public attention. Several reporters and writers publicized not only the business practices of the day but also many of the political evils of the time, especially corruption in the governments of the big cities. Such writers as Lincoln Steffens and Ida Tarbell came to be known as the Muckrakers and, through their magazine articles and books, they did much to arouse public interest in *trust busting* and civic reforms.

Many of the leading industries were trusts, according to the use of the word at that time. Combinations of steel companies, and combinations of these with companies producing iron ore and coal, brought a high degree of concentration in the steel industry. There was a meat trust, a whiskey trust, and a sugar trust, each of which produced in the neighborhood of 90 percent of the total output of the industry. In the rapidly growing petroleum industry, the original Standard Oil Company put together a virtually complete monopoly of the refining and marketing end of the business.

The Sherman Antitrust Act

In this environment, the *Sherman Act* was passed in 1890. There was surprisingly little debate prior to its passage, and it may be that the Congress was not fully aware of the import of the law. It became and still remains the basic legislation in the control of monopoly in the United States. The act is brief and simple in language, and its actual meaning and applicability to specific instances have had to be interpreted by the courts.

Section 1 of the original act stated, "Every contract, combination in the form of trust or otherwise, or conspiracy, in restraint of trade or commerce among the several States, or with foreign nations, is hereby declared to be illegal." Section 2 provided:

> Every person who shall monopolize, or attempt to monopolize or combine or conspire with any other person or persons, to monopolize any part of the trade or commerce among the several States, or with foreign nations, shall be deemed guilty of a misdemeanor, and, on conviction thereof, shall be punished by fine not exceeding five thousand dollars, or by imprisonment not exceeding one year, or by both said punishments, in the discretion of the court.

The act also provided that property owned by such contracting parties or conspiracy would be forfeited, and it provided that parties injured by such conspiracies could sue the guilty parties for three times the amount of the damages.

There have been many court cases under the Sherman Act and other subsequent laws. Theodore Roosevelt became President shortly after its passage and immediately used it to prevent combinations of railroads.

But a great deal of interpretation was necessary, as is illustrated by brief reference to some of the important cases.

An early case that was important in shaping the judicial interpretation of the antitrust laws involved the Standard Oil Company of New Jersey as it was organized in 1911.[1] This company had been a trust in Ohio but was established as a holding company when New Jersey made such corporations legal.[2] The company had aggressively built up a dominant position in the refining industry. In doing so, it had followed practices that were generally considered normal business practices at the time but which also aroused much public criticism when publicized by the Muckrakers. For example, the company cut prices in localities served by small refiners, forcing these smaller companies to sell out to Standard Oil. It was also accused of setting up companies to compete with local refineries and of maintaining spies in other plants. Because of its size, it was able to obtain preferential shipping rates from railroads, but it not only received rebates on its own shipments but was able to demand rebates on shipments made by other companies.

Suit was brought against the company by the Department of Justice and reached the Supreme Court on appeal by the company. In deciding the case, the Supreme Court established the *rule of reason* which, in effect, held that the Sherman Act was aimed not so much against monopoly or great economic power itself as against the abuse of such power. In reviewing the history of the law, the Court found that "the dread of enhancement of prices and of other wrongs which it was thought would flow from the undue limitation on competitive conditions" led to the prohibition of acts that had not been "performed with the legitimate purpose of reasonably forwarding personal interest and developing trade but . . . had been entered into or done with the intent to do wrong to the general public and to limit the right of individuals." This excerpt indicates the importance of such words as *undue* and *reasonably* in the Court's interpretation.

The Court further found that, in this particular case, the acts of the company had been designed to restrain trade, not to advance it. The Court referred to the acquisitions of old companies, control of transportation, purchase of newly established firms, division of markets, and other exclusive practices and concluded that they "necessarily involved the intent to drive others from the field and to exclude them from their right to trade. . . ."

To remedy the situation, the Court found that it would not be sufficient merely to forbid further use of the outlawed practices, since they had already led to monopoly. It confirmed, therefore, the lower court's decision that the company had to be split up into several companies, in order to restore competition to the industry. In other words, in the Standard Oil case it was found that the company had "unreasonably" restrained trade and attained a dominant position in the industry by use of methods

---

[1] *Standard Oil Company of New Jersey v. United States,* 221 U.S. 1 (1911).

[2] A *holding company* is a corporation that owns (holds) the shares of other corporations. A holding company is not necessarily a monopoly, and the device is widely used to bring operating companies together under a single top management. However, at the time of this case it was also used to bring together previously competing companies, as the trust device had been.

of excluding competition, rather than through its own superior competition.

The rule of reason was important in a subsequent case brought against United States Steel Corporation in 1920.[3] Again a holding company was involved, as United States Steel had put together many operating, mining, and fabricating companies in this manner. The Department of Justice failed to win the breakup of the company in lower courts and appealed to the Supreme Court. The four judges of the District Court had disagreed about whether the company actually possessed a monopoly in the steel industry and about the seriousness with which to regard price agreements that the company had made from time to time with competitors.

The Supreme Court held that the company had been unable to accomplish a monopoly by itself because ". . . competitors had to be persuaded by pools, associations, trade meetings, and through the social form of dinners, all of them, it may be, violations of the law, but transient in their purpose and effect." The Court further found that the company had recently abandoned these violations. It found that United States Steel was "greater in size and productive power than any of its competitors, equal or nearly equal to them all, but its power over prices was not and is not commensurate with its power to produce." The Court found, consequently, that the law did not require the breakup of this company.

> The corporation is undoubtedly of impressive size, and it takes an effort of resolution not to be affected by it or to exaggerate its influence. But we must adhere to the law, and the law does not make mere size an offense, or the existence of unexerted power an offense. It, we repeat, requires overt acts, and trusts to its prohibition of them and its power to repress or punish them. It does not compel competition, nor require all that is possible.

Mr. Justice Day dissented, saying that, "For many years, as the record discloses, this unlawful organization exerted its power to control and maintain prices by pools, associations, trade meetings, and as the result of discussion and agreements at the so-called 'Gary Dinners.' "

In effect, this decision in 1920 stated that mere size was not to be the criterion in antitrust cases but, rather, the behavior of the company. If it attained its size through economies and reasonable combinations, rather than restrictive practices and "unfair" practices, the Sherman Act was held not to outlaw it. As we shall see, this rule of reason has been altered by subsequent courts.

The Clayton and Federal Trade Commission Acts

In 1914 the Congress passed two pieces of legislation intended partly to clarify the brief and ambiguous Sherman Act. The *Clayton Act* made clear that the antitrust law did not apply to labor unions, and it also declared certain monopolistic practices illegal. The reason for exempting labor unions was that some court cases had resulted in unions being made subject to the Sherman Act because they had acted in restraint of

[3] *United States v. United States Steel Corporation et al.*, 251 U.S. 417 (1920).

trade. The Clayton Act denied this application of the Sherman Act by stating that "labor is not a commodity," implying that combinations of labor for legitimate ends are not illegal.

The Clayton Act enumerated four business practices that were now illegal if they resulted in lessening competition — an important proviso because in each case it is necessary to show that the practice has had this effect. Businesses were prohibited from:

1. Discriminating among different buyers in the prices charged. This provision was aimed at local price cutting designed to weaken competitors or to favor certain customers by lower prices, which gave them competitive advantages in their markets.

2. Making tying contracts. Under a tying contract or agreement, a dealer is prohibited from selling the products of another manufacturer and must therefore carry the full line of the single manufacturer. Such a contract might also apply to leased goods, such as machinery for manufacturing shoes or for making tin cans.

3. Combining competing firms through the holding-company device.

4. Having interlocking directorates. One method of reducing competition was to have the same people on the boards of directors of competing concerns. The same person serving on different boards of noncompetitive firms was not prohibited.

The companion law, the Federal Trade Commission Act, set up a federal commission of that name to oversee interstate business generally and to prohibit trade practices it found to be unfair. The law did not specify, however, what were to be considered unfair competitive practices.[4] As a result, the early orders of the Federal Trade Commission (FTC) were challenged in the courts and the courts accepted jurisdiction. In other words, the commission lost its role as the final arbiter of what is and what is not an unfair competitive practice. It may bring a *cease and desist order* against an offending company, but the order may be reviewed in the courts.

Subsequent Legislation

The evolution of the problem of monopoly and of interpretation of the Sherman and Clayton Acts led to subsequent legislation, largely designed to clarify existing law. Briefly, the principal pieces of legislation were as follows.

1. The Robinson-Patman Act of 1936. This law was a product of the depression of the 1930s and of antipathy to the growth of chain stores. The chains were bitterly resented by independent retailers, who could not match the chains in many kinds of economies. The independents blamed the power of the chains on the latters' ability to buy more cheaply than could the small independent. It was further argued that the chains had sufficient market power to demand price reductions that were greater than justified by the economies of selling to them in large quantities. Several states adopted punitive taxes on chain stores, such as a

---

[4] These practices were specified in the Wheeler-Lea Amendment of 1938. For example, issuing misleading advertising and engaging in dishonest labeling were declared illegal.

tax that became steeper with the number of outlets of the chain in the state. At the federal level, the Congress amended the Clayton Act to forbid suppliers from offering quantity discounts or similar price reductions greater than justified by lower costs of quantity sales. Such lower prices could be charged, however, where necessary to meet similar prices of another competitor.

2. The Anti-Merger Act of 1950. This act, also known as the Celler-Kefauver Act, was a response to another wave of mergers after World War II similar to that at the turn of the century. Existing legislation covered *combinations* of existing companies, such as through establishment of a holding company, but it did not specifically bar the outright purchase by one company of the *assets* of another company. The principal purpose of the new law was to include this type of merger when the effects would be to lessen competition.

Subsequent Interpretation of Antitrust

Subsequent cases brought under the antitrust laws are interesting in their efforts to arrive at a more satisfactory definition of monopoly, especially in terms of the market in which monopoly is alleged to exist and the degree of market power exercised by the monopoly. They are also interesting in that they illustrate the very difficult problem of drawing the line between those cases in which a company grows by legitimate and efficient practices and those in which its dominance is less defensible. The difficulty in the former instances is that legal prohibition of this type of growth really becomes a form of protection of the less competitive members of the industry; thus it does not really encourage competition but protects some members of the industry from the effects of aggressive competition.

On the whole, early interpretations of the Sherman Act tended to be narrow, in the sense that dissolution suits were not successful unless the combinations were clearly "unreasonable." The American Sugar Refining Company successfully defended itself in 1895, even though it produced almost 100 percent of all the refined sugar in the country; the Supreme Court held that the monopoly existed but was one of manufacturing and not commerce. In 1918 the government lost a suit against the United Shoe Machinery Company, which had been built up through the holding-company device and was requiring tying contracts for its machinery, which it was able to do because of patents.

More recent cases have taken a different view of market power, including the attitude that the mere existence of dominant power in a market is illegal, no matter how or whether it is used. Ownership of a large block of General Motors stock by Du Pont was declared illegal (under the 1950 amendment to the Clayton Act) even though Du Pont was apparently innocent of requiring General Motors to purchase Du Pont products, because the situation "tended to lessen competition." In the particular field of banking, the courts have blocked several mergers that had been approved by the supervisory banking authorities, on the grounds that the merged banks would control too large fractions of the markets in which they operated. We shall review briefly a few of these cases to illustrate how the law is applied in such situations.

The Aluminum Company of America

An attempt to dissolve the Aluminum Company of America (Alcoa) was settled in 1945.[5] In this case the court attempted to answer four questions: (1) whether Alcoa monopolized the market in virgin aluminum ingots, (2) whether Alcoa was guilty of illegal practices in establishing its monopoly in aluminum, (3) whether Alcoa had illegally conspired with Aluminum Company of Canada, and (4) what remedies were appropriate.

A lower court had decided that Alcoa's share of the market for aluminum ingots was about 33 percent. The Court agreed that this fraction did not constitute a monopoly. However, it disagreed with the manner of calculating the fraction. First, the Court did not agree to exclude secondary ingots made from scrap, and second, it did not agree to exclude ingots fabricated into finished products by Alcoa itself. The Court's reasoning illustrates the difficulties of applying broad legal concepts to specific economic problems. The Court held that "the ingot fabricated by 'Alcoa' necessarily had a direct effect upon the ingot market" because to the extent Alcoa sold fabricated products, there was that much less demand for ingot from other fabricators. The Court also pointed out that to the extent secondary ingots were acceptable to and purchased by fabricators, there was that much less demand for ingots, but it did not agree that this fact lessened Alcoa's monopoly. It argued that the present supply of ingot consisted of Alcoa's current production of virgin ingot plus the supply of scrap ingot which the company had produced in the past. It reasoned that a monopolist would always know "that the future supply of ingot would be made up in part of what it produced at the time, and, if it was as farsighted as it proclaims itself, that consideration must have had its share in determining how much to produce. . . . The competition of 'secondary' must therefore be disregarded, as soon as we consider the position of 'Alcoa' over a period of years; it was as much within 'Alcoa's' control as was the production of the 'virgin' from which it had been derived." The Court concluded that Alcoa therefore controlled 90 percent of the market for virgin ingot, the other 10 percent being imported.

The Court then raised the question of whether there was anything illegal in the existence of the monopoly, referring to past cases in which "size did not determine guilt" and in which there had been no wrongful use of power. "A single producer may be the survivor out of a group of active competitors, merely by virtue of his superior skill, foresight and industry. . . . The successful competitor, having been urged to compete, must not be turned upon when he wins. . . ." However, the Court decided that Alcoa had very successfully maintained its monopoly, based originally on ownership of bauxite ore, by providing for all increases in demand before others could enter the industry. Such action might be considered merely normal business practice, but the Court could "think of no more effective exclusion."

Since the Court found that a monopoly did exist, it felt that the question of whether illegal practices had occurred would normally be irrelevant. However, in this case it felt that the question was important in consider-

[5] In this case the Supreme Court was unable to have a quorum consider it because some Justices had been previously involved in it. Therefore, the case was decided by the Circuit Court of Appeals. *United States v. Aluminum Company of America*, 148 F. 2d 416 (1945).

ing the appropriate remedial action, because of the great changes in the industry that had just taken place during World War II. In view of the uncertainties of the shape of the industry after the war and the possibility of new government-supported producers entering the industry, the Court refrained from ordering the dissolution of the company. It did enjoin certain specific practices, those relating to pricing ingot in such a way as to discourage fabricators from competing with products fabricated by Alcoa, and those relating to imports. The case was left that if postwar developments did not establish competition in the aluminum ingot industry, the courts should reconsider dissolution.

The Cellophane Case

In the Du Pont Cellophane case the government contended that E. I. du Pont de Nemours & Company monopolized the production of cellophane.[6] The facts were clear that Du Pont, under patents held with a French company, produced 75 percent of the cellophane sold in the United States and that one other company, using partly licenses from Du Pont and partly other patents, produced the other 25 percent. The lower court had decided, however, that the *relevant market* to be considered was not cellophane alone but the market for packaging materials in general. Cellophane constituted only 20 percent of total sales of "flexible packaging materials." The Supreme Court consequently had to look into the nature of the demand for cellophane, particularly the cross-elasticity of demand with respect to the prices of substitute wrapping materials. This case is a good example of the trend towards looking to economic principles for help in determining the applicability of legal concepts to specific problems. The Court stated:

> An element for consideration as to cross-elasticity of demand between products is the responsiveness of the sales of one product to price changes of the other. If a slight decrease in the price of cellophane causes a considerable number of customers of other flexible wrappings to switch to cellophane, it would be an indication that a high cross-elasticity of demand exists between them; that the products compete in the same market. The [lower court] held that the great sensitivity of customers in the flexible packaging markets to price or quality changes prevented Du Pont from possessing monopoly control over price [and] the record sustains these findings.

The Court further stated that ". . . where there are market alternatives that buyers may readily use for their purposes, illegal monopoly does not exist merely because the product said to be monopolized differs from others. If it were not so, only physically identical products would be a part of the market." A minority of the Court remained unconvinced that flexible wrapping materials are generally so similar and interchangeable that cellophane could not be considered to have its own relevant market. They pointed out that cellophane had cost seven times as much as

[6] This case illustrates the time required to settle such cases. The case was begun in 1947 and the Supreme Court handed down its decision in 1956. *United States v. E. I. du Pont de Nemours & Company,* 351 U.S. 377 (1956).

glassine in 1929, four times as much in 1934, and twice as much in 1949 although sales of cellophane had grown enormously. "We cannot believe that buyers, practical businessmen, would have bought cellophane in increasing amounts over a quarter of a century if close substitutes were available at from one seventh to one half cellophane's prices. That they did so is testimony to cellophane's distinctiveness."

The Cellophane case is an important example of the development of economic analysis of the relevant market in order to define whether monopoly exists. Obviously, the Court's reasoning is closely related to the nature of many oligopolistic industries in which each important producer can be said to have a monopoly of his own product (Ford, Chrysler, General Motors) but at the same time to face competition from closely similar products.

The Brown Shoe Company Case

Shortly before the Cellophane case was decided, the government moved against a proposed merger between the Brown Shoe Company and the G. R. Kinney Company, under the 1950 amendments to the Clayton Act. This case involved both a *vertical merger* and a *horizontal merger*. It was vertical in that Brown Shoe Company was a manufacturer of shoes and Kinney was a retailer; it was horizontal in that Kinney also manufactured shoes. The case was decided in 1962.[7]

Brown Shoe Company had been extending into retail outlets, of which it had over 1,200; some it owned and others were operated under franchise. Its sales to retail outlets it acquired naturally increased after the acquisitions. Brown produced about 4 percent of the total footwear output of the country, making it the fourth largest shoe manufacturer. Kinney operated over 400 "family-style" shoe stores in some 270 cities. The chain's sales represented a little over 1 percent of total retail shoe sales. Kinney also manufactured one-half of 1 percent of the total footwear production, being the twelfth largest manufacturer.

In reviewing the legislative history of the antitrust laws, the Court found that the Congress had intended not only to cover merger by acquisition of assets by the 1950 law but also vertical and conglomerate mergers that might tend to lessen competition, as well as horizontal mergers of similar companies already clearly covered.[8] In addition, the intent of the Congress had been to check the merger movement before it led to the establishment of dominant companies. The Court's problem was to decide whether a merger of two companies controlling such small shares of the national market would violate the congressional intent of the Anti-Merger Act.

The Court found that, in spite of the relatively small share of total production and retail sales involved, the merger "may substantially lessen competition, or tend to create a monopoly in this market." Thus the Court declared the merger illegal. Although the respective shares were small, nevertheless Brown was the fourth largest manufacturer and Kinney was the largest independent chain of family shoe stores. The Court also reasoned that since the tendency would be for Kinney stores to sell

[7] *Brown Shoe Company v. U.S.*, 370 U.S. 294 (1962).

[8] A conglomerate merger involves companies in unrelated lines of business.

Brown shoes, other manufacturers would be foreclosed from markets otherwise open to them. Thus the vertical merger would tend to reduce competition in a substantial share of the market for shoes.

As a horizontal merger, the case needed to be studied on both the manufacturing and retail levels. The Court found that the combined share of manufacturing was too small to be a threat to competition but that the situation was different in retailing. This conclusion stemmed from the different definitions of the relevant markets the Court thought appropriate. For manufacturing, the Court thought that the entire nation represented the appropriate market, but for retailing it thought competition should be measured in much smaller areas — cities exceeding 10,000 population in which both Brown and Kinney had retail outlets. In 32 cities Brown and Kinney had over 20 percent of sales of women's shoes, and in 31 cities, over 20 percent of sales of children's shoes. In 118 cities the combined shares exceeded 5 percent of men's, women's, or children's shoes, and in 47 cities they exceeded 5 percent in all three.

Admitting, therefore, that the market share of Brown and Kinney was relatively small on a national basis, the Court still found that the merger was contrary to the antitrust laws. For one thing, approval of this merger, which would control about 5 percent of the national market, would require subsequent approval of similar mergers and "the oligopoly Congress sought to avoid would then be furthered." Also, the fact that the small share is held by a "strong national chain" can adversely affect competition because the chain can change styles in order to make it difficult for smaller retailers to maintain adequate inventories. On a final point, the Court faced the problem that a combination might be more efficient than its competitors, in this case by elimination of wholesalers:

> Of course, some of the results of large integrated or chain operations are beneficial to consumers. Their expansion is not rendered unlawful by the mere fact that small independent stores may be adversely affected. It is competition, not competitors, which the Act protects. . . . Congress appreciated that occasional higher costs and prices might result from the maintenance of fragmented industries and markets. It resolved these competing considerations in favor of decentralization.

The Philadelphia National Bank Case

One final case will be noted because it illustrates in another way the necessity of defining the relevant market and measuring the effects of a merger on competition in that market; this case is also interesting in that it involves a regulated industry, commercial banking.[9]

The second and third largest commercial banks in Philadelphia, Philadelphia National Bank and Girard Trust Corn Exchange Bank, agreed in 1960 to merge under the former's charter. A specific federal law, the Bank Merger Act of 1960, covered such mergers. It provided that the appropriate regulatory agency, in this case the Comptroller of the Currency because the surviving bank was a national bank, was charged with approving or disapproving the merger. The Comptroller was required to obtain opinions from the Federal Reserve Board and Federal Deposit Insurance Corpora-

---

[9] *United States v. Philadelphia National Bank,* 374 U.S. 321 (1963).

tion, as well as the Attorney General, but he was not bound by them. The act required him also to consider the effects on competition in deciding whether a given merger was desirable.

All three opinions stated that this merger would have "substantial anticompetitive effects in the Philadelphia metropolitan area," but the Comptroller authorized the merger because he believed that an adequate number of alternative sources of banking service would remain in that area and also that the merger would make the combined bank more able to compete in national and international markets (particularly with large New York City banks). The Attorney General then brought suit under the antitrust laws to prevent the merger. The District Court found for the banks, partly because it held that the Clayton Act was not applicable but also because, even if it were, the relevant market was the northeastern United States, in which the merged bank would not be a monopoly.

The Supreme Court decided otherwise. It agreed with the Attorney General that the relevant market was the four-county area including Philadelphia in which the banks were permitted by state law to have branches.[10] The Court admitted that the Philadelphia banks competed with New York City banks for some business but stated that the bulk of their business originated in the four-county area; the Court found that some large customers could seek accommodation in other areas while small customers could not. In defining the market, "a workable compromise must be found." Having so defined the market, the Court had little difficulty in then finding that the merger would lessen competition in that market. "The merger of appellees will result in a single bank's controlling at least 30 percent of the commercial banking business in the four-county Philadelphia metropolitan area. Without attempting to specify the smallest market share which would still be considered to threaten undue concentration, we are clear that 30 percent presents that threat." The Court noted that, before the merger, the two largest banks (Philadelphia National and the one larger bank) had 44 percent of the banking business in the market and that, after the merger, the two largest would have 59 percent.

RESALE PRICE MAINTENANCE

In the Brown Shoe case the Supreme Court commented that small independent stores might be harmed by the growth of large efficient competitors but that this harm did not make such growth illegal. "It is competition, not competitors, which the Act protects." This quotation identifies a very difficult line for the courts to draw. In the American form of government, it is natural that economic groups attempt to insulate themselves from competition through some form of legislation. When independent grocers or other retailers are hurt by the development of chain stores, they naturally attempt to strike back. In this attempt they are ably supported by their trade associations. These groups were able to obtain

---

[10] Another point settled by the District Court had involved the "relevant line of commerce." The banks contended that they competed with savings banks, savings and loan associations, personal-loan companies, and others for parts of their business and that any measure of their share of the market should include these institutions. The District Court found that commercial banking is sufficiently differentiated to be considered a specific line of commerce.

from the Congress another important piece of legislation with objectives similar to those of the Robinson-Patman Act during the great depression.

The Miller-Tydings Act

It would probably be against human nature for a small druggist or grocer to conclude that a chain store or discount house, for which customers are leaving his store, offers a more economical or desirable good or service. He would be more likely to rationalize that these stores offer "unfair" competition in that they do not have salesclerks, charge accounts, delivery service, complete lines, and other things he must provide in order to stay in business. Overlooking the probability that such stores would compete among themselves even if they attracted the bulk of the trade, he would feel that, once they drive smaller rivals out of business, they can then raise prices. This line of reasoning was pushed in obtaining passage of the Robinson-Patman Act and the subsequent (1937) Miller-Tydings Act.

The Miller-Tydings Act amended the Sherman Act to legalize contracts for *resale price maintenance* between manufacturers and retailers. Prior to this amendment, once a distributor or retailer purchased an item, he could resell it at any price he chose. The rise of the discount house, which sold standard brand-name articles substantially below usual retail prices, raised several questions. The regular retail outlets demanded that manufacturers protect them from this competition. Sometimes it was argued that a discount house merely sold some well-known goods at low prices as *loss leaders* to attract customers. Some manufacturers feared that the reputations of their goods would suffer if they were sold at cut-rate prices, and others feared that regular retailers would have to meet this competition and thus become less able to pay the established wholesale prices. Thus there was considerable pressure for legalization of maintaining retail prices.

The Miller-Tydings Act left it up to the states to enact, if they wished, laws which would allow manufacturers to enter into contracts with retail outlets to maintain selling prices set by the manufacturers. Shortly after the passage of the act, such arrangements became common under so-called fair-trade laws. Many nationally advertised and branded appliances and drugs were sold at fair-trade prices. At one point, all but three states had enacted fair-trade laws. However, these laws were somewhat less effective than might be imagined since the largest retailers could have their own brands manufactured and sold at prices that suited them. The large mail-order houses and city department stores thus offered the independent retailer a new form of competition.

A peculiarity of many of the state laws was a provision that when one retailer signed a resale-price-maintenance agreement, all other retailers in the state were bound by it, whether they signed or not. The legality of this provision was challenged early, but not until 1951 did the Supreme Court rule on it and find it not enforceable under the act.[11] The pressures for such legislation were strong, however, and a further amendment to the antitrust laws was passed in 1952, when the McGuire Act specifically covered the "nonsigner" clause in state laws. In the meantime, many re-

---

[11] *Schwegman Bros. v. Calvert Distillers,* 341 U.S. 384 (1951).

tailers who wished to charge lower prices had begun to do so. Thereafter, the problems of manufacturers in policing their retail outlets and bringing "violators" to court became more and more difficult.

By the late 1960s fair trade had largely broken down, partly because of the difficulties of enforcement and partly because of the more general acceptance of newer forms of retail competition. Several states repealed their laws, and many manufacturers stopped trying to enforce contracts. Where resale price maintenance is still employed, it is mostly in sales of cosmetics, drugs, liquors, and appliances, but in 1968 only 22 states still had fair-trade laws.

Most economists would undoubtedly agree with comments made by the President's Council of Economic Advisers in their report for January, 1969:

> One effect of resale price maintenance is to shift the focus of competition into less desirable forms. Retailers compete by providing more extensive consumer services, thereby increasing business costs. Manufacturers often set resale prices at levels providing generous markups to retailers, in order to induce them to favor the sale of their products. The principal objective of resale price maintenance is to protect smaller concerns from their larger competitors. The prohibition of predatory practices is a valid objective of public policy. In practice, however, lower prices reflecting greater efficiency and lower costs cannot be called predatory. Moreover, there is no evidence that the efficient small retailer needs such special protection, which can freeze an inefficient market structure.

With respect to the related Robinson-Patman Act, the Council observed:

> Although public policy should be concerned with preventing improper use of the advantages conferred by sheer size, some evidence indicates that the Act has had the unintended effect of accentuating price rigidities in some markets. A seller may refuse to bargain on price with an individual customer by contending that under the law any concession granted to one buyer would have to be made uniformly available to all others. . . . A careful reappraisal of the Act might suggest ways to focus its application more sharply on those particular forms of price discrimination that constitute a truly serious threat to competition.[12]

In many other fields besides antitrust legislation, the government also seems torn between the desire to protect competition and prevent monopoly and the conflicting desire to protect some competitors against their more aggressive, powerful, or innovative rivals. Evidences of this tug of war can be found in legislation that lowers tariff barriers to imports that compete with domestic industries and exceptions to this legislation in the form of import quotas or other restrictions. It is also illustrated in

[12] *Annual Report*, January, 1969, pp. 108–109. The close relationship between politics and economics, a theme of this chapter, is suggested by the fact that these comments appeared in the final report of the Council of outgoing President Johnson, rather than in earlier reports. They might be interpreted, therefore, as a suggestion of bipartisan support should the incoming President wish to pursue these suggestions.

farm policies, whereby the government encourages adoption of more efficient and larger-scale farming while, at the same time, it maintains farm prices in an effort to protect small farms. These inconsistencies are presumably a characteristic of democratic government, wherein various forces can be reflected in legislation. The real economy is not a textbook model but a mixture of policies adopted at different times, by different legislatures, under different conditions.

Current Status

In regard to the current status of antitrust and related legislation, an interesting recent development has been that of the *conglomerate merger*. The legal difficulties hindering corporate expansion through merger, when the merging corporations operate in the same or closely related markets, have become so great that the "urge to merge" has been reflected in acquisitions involving quite different lines of business. In the late 1960s a new merger movement was under way that differed from previous ones in involving conglomerates, or groupings of companies formerly quite unrelated.

The defenders of this type of merger base their arguments primarily on the claim that the acquiring company can supply better management and thus use more efficiently and economically capital invested in the acquired companies. There have been examples in which this has been true, in which relatively "sleepy" companies that have accumulated great assets over the years but that have low earnings have been revitalized.

On the other hand, it also seems obvious that some of the recent mergers have been motivated to some extent by the desire to enhance the market price of the acquiring companies' stock by showing a continuing record of growth in size and in per-share earnings. This trend has been stimulated by the public's greater interest in holding common stocks, especially those that appreciate with some rapidity.

A simple example illustrates how an improvement in earnings, and thus a continuation of "growth," can be accomplished. Suppose a corporation has 100,000 shares outstanding and is earning $1 per share. Because of its aggressiveness and recent growth, its shares are selling "on future prospects" at forty times earnings, or $40 per share. Another, less glamorous company also has 100,000 shares outstanding and has been earning more or less steadily about $2 per share. Since it exhibits no growth prospects, its shares are selling at perhaps ten times earnings, or $20. A "fair" exchange might seem to be for the first corporation to offer to issue one share in exchange for two of the second. But it can make a more attractive offer to the stockholders of the second company: it can offer two for three (making the second company's stock worth not one-half but two-thirds of a share of the first, or worth, at market prices, $26.66). For the 100,000 shares of the second company, the first would issue and exchange 66,666 shares, thus having outstanding a total of 166,666 shares. Combined earnings of the two companies (before any potential improvement) would be $100,000 + $200,000, or $300,000, and this amount divided among the 166,666 shares would be $1.80. Thus the acquiring company would immediately improve its earnings per share from $1 to $1.80 — and if the market continued to value its shares at forty times earnings, its stock would become worth about $72, making the next acquisition that much easier to finance.

At the time of writing, it appeared that the Congress might investigate the conglomerate type of merger in order to determine whether it should be brought under the antitrust laws and, if so, for what reasons.[13] A related problem is that of expansion by commercial banks into areas not legally open to them as banks, through the device of exchanging shares of the bank for shares of a holding company which thereafter owns the bank. Not being a bank, the holding company could operate in fields not clearly open to banks, such as purchasing and leasing equipment. When a holding company owns more than one bank, it is subject to the Bank Holding Company Act, which regulates the activities of the holding company to those closely related to banking but which also exempts holding companies owning a single bank. The rapid growth in the number of one-bank holding companies in the late 1960s raised the question of whether they should be brought under the banking laws. Such a bill was passed by the House of Representatives in 1969, but in early 1970 it appeared that the Senate would not adopt it without change.

SUMMARY

It is easy to conclude that free competiton is superior to monopoly as a characteristic of market behavior, but study of actual industries and real market structures illustrates that it may be difficult even to define competition and monopoly.

This chapter refers to a few, out of a great many, court decisions that have helped shape the meaning of the antitrust laws. The early cases involving the Sherman Act of 1890 emphasized the business practices followed by large business firms. Where these were considered "unfair" or "predatory," the market power of the companies was deemed illegal; where the companies competed with "reasonable" methods, their size alone did not make them illegal.

Mergers, in contrast to internal growth, have required the courts to think through the concepts of competition, oligopoly, and monopoly. In recent decades, the existence of dominant market power, however used, has been held contrary to the antitrust laws. But market power has to be related to the relevant market. Thus in the Cellophane case Du Pont was held not to monopolize the market for flexible packaging materials although it had a virtual monopoly of one type of such materials. But in the Philadelphia National Bank case, it was held that two merging banks would have too large a share of a market area consisting of four counties, although the banks claimed that their relevant market was the northeastern United States and that they competed with financial institutions other than commercial banks.

The great requirements for invested capital and for extensive marketing systems tend to bring about very large companies in some fields and thus the existence of only a few companies in such industries. The difficulties of other companies in competing with the Big Three of the automobile industry, for example, are well known. At the same time, the existence of keen rivalry among the

---

[13] In 1969 the Justice Department brought suit against Ling-Temco-Vought, a large conglomerate, for the acquisition of Jones and Laughlin Steel Company.

Big Three is also evident. In 1968 General Motors prepared a statement for a Senate subcommittee in which it argued:

The domestic passenger car companies which were brought into
General Motors, the most recent approximately 50 years ago,
gave it no competitive advantage in technology, products or markets and were of little significance to its ultimate success. At the
end of 1920, General Motors was on the verge of financial collapse and in 1921 had less than 14 percent of the market. Since
this turning point in its history, GM's growth has been from within.
Its success stems in major part from: (1) the development of new
concepts of internal administrative management, largely pioneered
by Alfred P. Sloan, Jr., and widely copied by many companies, including General Motors' competitors, and (2) its conviction that
the American consumer wanted improved products and a variety of
choices, not merely basic transportation in "any color as long as
it's black."

The paradox in attempting to maintain competition through legislation is often that the most innovative and successful competitors
naturally grow at the expense of other competitors. If the technology and size of the industry so determine, only a few major
companies survive. Each company then inevitably is a strong influence on the production and pricing practices of the others, and
each recognizes the potential reactions of its rivals to any steps it
might take. Legislators have a difficult problem in deciding whether
the resulting efficiencies in production and a type of "workable
competition" among the few are socially more desirable than protection of small business competitors even though the latter may
be less able to introduce economies. In other words, protecting
competition and protecting competitors are not the same thing,
but the line between them is difficult to draw.

Economic Terms for Review

trust	relevant market
Sherman Act	vertical merger
holding company	horizontal merger
rule of reason	resale price maintenance
Clayton Act	conglomerate merger

Questions for Review

1. What characteristics of the early railroads led to regulation?
2. How was the rule of reason applied in the Standard Oil and U.S. Steel cases?
3. What are some unfair trade practices?
4. How does the Cellophane case illustrate the nature of oligopoly?
5. How did the Court measure the relevant market in the Brown Shoe case?
6. How do conglomerate mergers differ from others?

Questions for Analysis

1. Compare the reasoning of the Court in the Cellophane case with that in the Brown Shoe case.
2. Suppose that virtually all retail sales were subject to resale price maintenance. How well would you expect the system to work?
3. What forces have led to the conglomerate-merger movement?
4. Why did many banks establish one-bank holding companies?
5. Should the banks in the Philadelphia Bank case have been allowed to increase their ability to compete with New York City banks?
6. What would you consider the relevant market in a case in which a company is charged with having a monopoly of the production of cornflakes?

Case for Decision

In 1969 the Justice Department brought a civil suit against the United States Steel Corporation, charging that the company violated the Sherman Antitrust Act by requiring companies from which it bought supplies to reciprocate by buying steel, cement, and other products from U.S. Steel. U.S. Steel agreed to a settlement by consent decree, in which it admitted no wrongdoing or illegal acts but agreed not to engage in such reciprocal deals in the future. (By bringing a civil suit, rather than a criminal suit, the government is able to obtain such consent agreements; the advantage to the accused company is that it admits to no illegal acts in the past and thus the suit cannot be used as evidence by other parties who might want to claim damages under the criminal sections of the Sherman Act.)

The Justice Department claimed that for many years the company had followed a practice of keeping detailed records of purchases from it by its suppliers and of keeping its buying agents informed of the companies who bought from U.S. Steel. The buying agents were also informed of the policy of reciprocity.

In its own announcement, the company stated that ". . . in its simplest form of buying from concerns who are your customer when all other conditions are equal, reciprocity is widespread and accepted in commerce and industry" and that "In and of itself, United States Steel does not believe this can be considered contrary to law." The Justice Department contended that reciprocity arrangements tended to monopolize that part of the market for steel, cement, and chemicals made up of "the requirements of actual and potential supplier-customers of" the company. In effect, the Justice Department argued that the reciprocity arrangements required some suppliers to buy from U.S. Steel when they might have preferred — even at identical prices — to buy elsewhere.

At about the same time as the suit, a working paper prepared for the Nixon administration by a leading academic authority on antitrust problems, Professor George G. Stigler of the University of Chicago, had noted that, to be acceptable to both parties, reciprocal deals had to be made on competitive terms — that is, at prices and other conditions set by the market. Professor Stigler noted that reciprocity occurs mostly where prices are set by government regulation or by a cartel.

Prior to this suit, the head of the Antitrust Division had made several speeches in which he had said the division would move against reciprocity arrangements, conglomerate mergers, and mergers affecting any of the 200 largest corporations.

Do you consider reciprocity arrangements contrary to competitive practice? Might they be a form of competition? Could a supplier find it advantageous to buy from a customer even at a slightly higher price? Are informal reciprocity arrangements common in small towns? Under what conditions might you agree with the Justice Department's position?

18
Labor and Unions

In Chapter 17 we examined some of the legal and political aspects of big business and traced the main threads of legislation and court decisions dealing with this economic problem. In the labor sector of the economy, related problems have developed, and these too have been reflected in legal and political reactions. There is a rough parallel in the two types of problems. Legislation dealing with the monopoly problem has sometimes protected the right to compete, even though some competitors must be injured in the process, but it has sometimes protected competitors from their rivals. Legislation dealing with labor problems is also two-sided. Sometimes it has been protective of labor, shielding laborers from the effects of unregulated competition in the labor market, but it has also sought to prevent organized labor itself from dominating the market. A brief history of the labor movement will illustrate the development of these two strands of labor economics.

THE LABOR MOVEMENT

As industrialism and the factory system began to provide the type of production and employment common to advanced nations, workers tended to join together in order to deal collectively with their employers. The weak bargaining position of the individual worker, in relation to that of his employer, made it clear that workers could bargain only as groups rather than as individuals. Early associations of workers, which developed into modern labor unions, appeared as one of the consequences of the Industrial Revolution. Even today most unionized workers are in industrial occupations, rather than in service industries, banking, retail trade, or agriculture—although there is some union strength in these fields.

The Basis of Labor Unions

The development of labor unions is therefore a reflection of the separation of the management function and the labor function in modern industry. After the Industrial Revolution, labor became purely an employed factor of production rather than sharing the role of the entrepreneur. The capital—factories, machines, and tools—came to be owned by one group while the labor group was employed to use this capital and was paid wages. The worker became isolated from both the employer and the user of the product. Workers consequently found that they had a group interest different from the interests of employers and customers. Essentially, this interest was in striking the best possible bargain that can be made in the markets for labor.

Interest in increasing income was not the sole reason for the development of collective action, however. Other aspects of the growth of modern industry also encouraged this development. The factory system brought the hazards of industrial accidents and unemployment, against which the worker needed protection. In addition, in many aspects of the terms of employment—ranging from the hours of work, the speed at which work takes place, and other aspects of the job itself to such matters as vacations, holidays, and fringe benefits—the worker wanted to have a voice.

The influence of all these matters on the attitudes of workers is greater where the distinction between labor and capital or management is sharp. In factory-type occupations there is usually less expectation on the part of workers of advancing to managerial positions than there is in other occupations where unions are less developed. When a worker expects to remain a laborer all his life, he is more concerned with the income and other terms of employment than he would be if he expected to move into the managerial ranks.

Types of Unions

The early unions in this country were usually organized along craft lines. Workers pursuing the same trade or craft felt the closest identity. In spite of the importance of factory organization, some of the early _craft unions_ arose among craftsmen working largely outside of factories, such as the carpenters. Whether they worked inside or outside of factory walls, however, such workmen as carpenters, machinists, engravers, and painters had obvious interests in common when dealing with employers. Where such a craft was basic to an employer's business, the employees tended to organize as members of this craft. Even when a craft was a small part of the organization, the individual workman still felt impelled to unite with his fellow craftsmen working for other employers rather than with other workers doing less skilled work.

The more recent development of the factory system, in which more and more work is being done by machines, has tended to reduce the importance of traditional crafts and skills. New skills develop as workers are highly trained to operate modern precision machinery, but these skills are closely related to the occupation, such as manufacturing automobile engines. This situation has brought about the establishment of _industrial unions,_ in contrast to craft unions. In an industrial union the members are employed in the manufacture of a given product, such as automobiles, steel, or electrical machinery. A union of all the steel workers, regardless of their particular occupations and skills, is a more potent bargaining agent with a large steel company than would be separate unions representing different kinds of labor.

Some years prior to the enactment of the labor legislation in the 1930s, a third type of union, called a company union, grew up under the encouragement or sponsorship of employers who preferred such a union to either of the independent types. These employers encouraged the establishment of unions of their own employees in order to forestall the establishment of independent unions in their plants. Such employer-dominated unions have been outlawed as bargaining agents for employees and, where they still exist, they are usually very restricted in their operations.

The Development of American Unions

The development of labor unions was slow in the early days of this country because the country was largely agricultural and continued to remain so as long as the frontier offered opportunities for migration. The growth of a wage-earning group which looked upon itself as such was therefore delayed. In the cities of the Eastern Seaboard, however, some craftsmen began to organize into unions, along the model provided by English workmen, and demanded that employers bargain for their services through these unions. As early as 1827 a loose federation of craft unions was formed—The Mechanics Union of Trade Associations. In the following decade a few craft unions reached national breadth, and by 1834 there was a national organization of them called The National Trades Union. In the mid-1830s there were some 300,000 members of separate local unions in the East. The severe depression in 1837 weakened their ability to hold together. Disagreements over political activity also weakened the organizations. Consequently, membership declined.

After the middle of the century, and especially after the Civil War, the pace of industrialization quickened. Several industries, such as the railroad and steel industries, began to evolve into large companies operating over regional, rather than local, areas. The individual worker became less and less able to cope with the employer in cases of disagreement over wages and other conditions of employment, and the union movement was stimulated.

The Noble Order of the Knights of Labor was organized in 1873. This union was intended to be an all-encompassing organization of labor in general and was founded by idealistic rather than practical labor leaders. It had a rapid but short period of growth. Cutting across craft lines, it included virtually all types of labor. It was concerned with political issues and public problems such as immigration, as well as with labor problems, and was therefore vulnerable to differences of opinion among the membership. After a brief period of growth, it lost membership to the American Federation of Labor, organized in 1886, which remained the principal central organization of labor groups until the mid-1930s.

The American Federation of Labor (AFL) was an organization of local craft unions. It was based on the principles of the craft union and local autonomy, because of its belief that the main role of a union was to bargain with employers, not to engage in political disputes. Leaders of the AFL believed that craft unions provided the bargaining strength needed, because of the importance of the skilled workers to the employer, and that the bargaining should be done between the local union and the employers involved. The AFL thus accepted the economic system as it was, rather than having revolutionary or reform objectives, and attempted to improve the lot of labor through "bread-and-butter" bargaining. In this sense, it was a conservative organization.

In general, over the hundred years from 1820 to 1920, unions tended to gain membership when times were good, employment rose, and bargaining could produce results. They lost membership during depressions when unemployment rose and workers sought jobs. Membership did not rise as might have been expected during the 1920s, and the unusually severe depression of the early 1930s initially caused a decline in union power, as shown in Figure 18-1. Part of the comprehensive New Deal

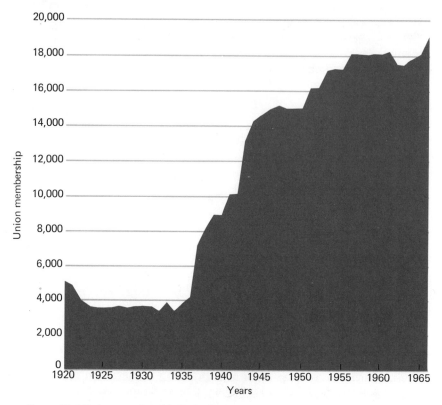

Figure 18-1. Union membership in the United States, 1920–1966. Source: 1920–1956: U.S. Bureau of the Census, *Historical Statistics of the U.S., Colonial Times to 1957*, pp. 97–98, 735–745. 1957–1966: U.S. Bureau of Labor Statistics, *Handbook of Labor Statistics*, 1969, p. 351.

legislation of that period, however, wrote into law the right of labor to bargain with employers collectively—that is, through unions. Union membership was encouraged by the federal government, both to improve labor's bargaining position and as part of a broad program to attempt to raise prices and wages.

This legislation (described in a subsequent section) provided a stimulus to membership and to the recruiting efforts of unions. Some labor leaders believed that the time had come to organize aggressively in the mass-production industries, where membership was low, and that industries like steel and automobiles had to be organized along industry lines. Officials of the traditional craft unions disagreed, and the AFL was basically an organization of the latter. Consequently, the industrial union group withdrew from the AFL and established the Congress of Industrial Organizations (CIO), which launched recruiting campaigns in a number of unorganized industries. In 1955 the two groups merged into the AFL-CIO, which included the bulk of the labor groups in the country. But disagreements again led to a split and, in 1968, under the leadership of the United Auto Workers (UAW), some of the industrial unions again withdrew. At about this time the UAW and the International Brotherhood of Teamsters, which had remained outside the AFL-CIO, formed a combination called the Alliance for Labor Action (ALA). The Teamsters Union had 1.9 million members and the UAW 1.5 million members, making an alliance of 3.4 million workers. The ALA is interested in organizing unions where unions are weak or nonexistent, as in service industries, and in pushing for welfare programs and other political action.

Union Membership

In recent years membership in American labor unions has been about 18 million. This figure is nearly a quarter of the civilian labor force, or 29 percent of employees other than agricultural. Although the number of union members is currently at a high point, the percentage in the labor force has declined slightly over the last decade. The reason for this is that employment has grown more rapidly in nonunionized occupations than in manufacturing. About half of all union members are in manufacturing industries.

The two largest unions are the auto workers and teamsters, both independent of the AFL-CIO. Altogether, independent unions have about 4 million members, of which 3.4 million are in these two unions. The growth in unions since the 1930s is indicated by the fact that all the unions had only about 3.6 million members in 1930. Total membership was nearly 9 million in 1940 and by 1950 it was 15 million.

The Legal Status of Unions

The attainment of the right to bargain collectively, as a result of New Deal legislation, was noted previously. This was a milestone in labor legislation because, speaking quite broadly, legislation in favor of unions and their bargaining power was virtually unknown before the 1930s. In the early days of unions, the early nineteenth century, in the absence of any specific legislation the unions were subject to court interpretations of the doctrine of conspiracy. Essentially, this doctrine of the common law holds that a person can legally do certain things individually that become illegal if done in concert with others. In the field of labor, this doctrine meant that a person could refuse to work in order to compel an employer to meet his wage demands but that, if a group of workers refused to work until their wage demands were met, they might be guilty of an illegal conspiracy because they were depriving the employer of his "right" to bargain with each worker. Some courts quite early held that when the workers were combining in order to promote their legitimate ends, such as improved wages and working conditions, their combinations were not illegal conspiracies, but other courts in other states sometimes held the opposite. In general, however, unions were considered legal organizations for pursuing legitimate ends, although specific actions were sometimes condemned.

We have already noted also that, at first, the Sherman Antitrust Act was held to apply to unions and thus they were regarded as illegal conspiracies or monopolies, but that the Clayton Act stated specifically that the antitrust laws did not apply to labor. (A union might run afoul of the law, however, if it were to conspire with an employer to restrain trade — for example, if it promised to keep workers from working for a competitor.)

Federal legislation prior to the New Deal worthy of mention includes the Railway Labor Act of 1926 because this law provided specifically that railroad workers had the right to bargain collectively. The act applied, of course, only to this one industry. In 1932 the federal government enacted the Norris–La Guardia Act in order to prevent the use of the *labor injunction* in local courts to hamper labor-union activities. Prior to this law, an employer could request a court to enjoin a union from certain practices if he could show, to the court's satisfaction, that he would be irreparably damaged by these practices. Such injunctions were often issued by friendly courts in order to prevent recruiting of union membership, strikes, picketing, or other union activities. The Norris–La Guardia Act reflected a swing of public sentiment in favor of unions in such situations by saying that such injunctions were not in the public interest where the union was pursuing legitimate ends.

The New Deal legislation previously referred to includes especially the National Industrial Recovery Act of 1933 and the National Labor Relations Act, or Wagner Act, of 1935. The NIRA was an attempt to attack the depression by a series of measures to raise prices and wages, and as such it raised many serious questions of whether it would do away with the competitive-market system. It amended the antitrust laws to permit industries to draw up codes under which they would operate. Among other things, these codes permitted the industries to adopt minimum prices or methods of calculating prices, as well as means of restricting production. Having made these concessions to industry, the Congress also enacted the famous Section 7a, which provided that all workers in interstate commerce had the right to bargain collectively. Shortly thereafter the Supreme Court found the NIRA unconstitutional, but the Congress reenacted this particular provision in the Wagner Act and also listed certain "unfair" labor practices on the part of employers that were henceforth to be banned. For example, establishing and dominating a company labor union and refusing to bargain with a union that represented a majority of the workers were no longer permitted.

The Taft-Hartley Act

The Wagner Act was passed largely on the premise that workers were at a serious disadvantage in bargaining with modern employers like giant corporations and that collective bargaining and abolition of antiunion practices were needed to restore a workable balance. Over the ensuing decade, especially when labor became scarce and obtained a strong bargaining position during World War II, sentiment swung the other way. Another effort towards restoring a balance was made in the Taft-Hartley Act of 1949.[1] It was felt that unions also required policing and that both parties had to be required to bargain in good faith. This act was an amendment to the Wagner Act.

In general, the Taft-Hartley Act retained the ban on unfair labor practices of employers, but it also banned certain practices by unions as well. For example, unions had been criticized for expelling members who had, perhaps, opposed union officers. Expulsion from the union meant that the worker could no longer be employed if the employer had an agreement to hire only union members. The Taft-Hartley Act required unions to admit workers to membership and prevented them from expelling members who paid their dues.

[1] Its official title is The Labor-Management Relations Act.

The Taft-Hartley Act recognized *union shop* agreements, which are contracts under which the employer may hire nonunion workers but, within a given period, these workers must join the union. The union shop is not legal in those states which have passed *right-to-work laws.* The Taft-Hartley Act also attacked—without complete success—certain other union practices considered unfair. Unions are banned, for example, from exerting influence on the employer in his choice of his bargaining agent and from demanding payment for work not actually performed (*featherbedding*).

Enforcement of the labor act is entrusted to a National Labor Relations Board, established by the Wagner Act. It holds elections for workers who wish to vote on selecting a union to be their bargaining agent and certifies that the winning union is the bargaining agent for that group. Many of its rulings have been controversial, and both unions and management have resented some of its applications of the law. The thorniest problems of enforcement have generally involved secondary boycotts, featherbedding, the closed shop, and union finances.

A secondary boycott is a refusal by the employees of one firm to work on the products of another employer, in order to exert pressure on him in his negotiations with his own employees. The pressure may simply be the unwillingness of the boycotting workers' employer to buy the products. The Taft-Hartley Act makes it illegal for the employees of one firm to refuse to handle the products of a struck firm. *Sympathy strikes* to enforce this refusal are also illegal. In specific cases, it is often difficult to draw a line between a secondary boycott of this type and the legitimate pursuit of their own ends by a group of workers.

The *closed shop* is an agreement whereby an employer will hire only members of a union. This kind of agreement is subject to much criticism when it is coupled with a *closed union,* which is a union that is restrictive in letting in new members. The restriction may take the form of excessive apprenticeship rules, high entrance fees and dues, or other forms. Such an arrangement obviously makes it difficult to get a job and constitutes a monopoly of the available jobs with that employer. The Taft-Hartley Act attempts to eliminate the closed shop and to encourage the union shop. (An *open shop* is one that has no union agreement.)

Union defense of the closed shop is based on the argument that it is necessary to protect the employment of the members. Unions have always feared that once they gain recognition from the employer, he may undermine their power by hiring nonunion workers—hence their preference for the closed shop. Unions contend that nonunion workers get a "free ride" by obtaining the same wages and other benefits but without paying their share of dues. (The union shop is one answer to this argument.) In some industries, the unions are able to show that the closed shop allows them to enforce regulations covering productivity and discipline, for the benefit of the employer. The employer might be unable to enforce such regulations himself, as seems to be the case with small manufacturers of ladies' garments, and at least would have some additional expense in doing so. The Taft-Hartley Act attacked the closed shop by making it illegal for the *employer* to discriminate between union and nonunion workers in hiring, but this is obviously a difficult provision to enforce.

Featherbedding has remained a controversial problem. Some union regulations are designed to protect members from losing their jobs when more efficient ways of getting work done are developed. An old example is the insistence of printers that they set type, even though cuts or preset type is actually to be used rather than the "bogus" type set by the printers. Unions may demand that prewired equipment be done over on the job; that not more than a given amount of work (number of bricks laid or amount of surface painted) be done in a day; that "full crews" be maintained on railroad trains (sometimes based on safety arguments), including a fireman on electric locomotives; or that a radio station pay for an orchestra while it broadcasts records. The Taft-Hartley Act outlawed demands for pay for work that was not actually performed or that could not be performed if suddenly required. This prohibition still allows the union to bargain with the radio station to hire and have present an orchestra, even if it does not intend to use it.

The Taft-Hartley Act also provided that when a labor dispute in a major industry created a national emergency, the President could request a federal court to issue an injunction which would require the parties to continue operations during an eighty-day "cooling-off" period. This provision has been used rarely and only in conjunction with the appointment of a Presidential commission to study the dispute and make a public report. Such a report naturally puts considerable pressure on the disputants to accept its findings. The law requires that the union members have a secret vote on the company's latest offer before the expiration of the eighty days.

The Landrum-Griffin Act

During the late 1950s congressional investigations disclosed that, in a minority of unions, there was considerable racketeering and misuse of union funds. This disclosure led the Congress to regulate the activities of unions more closely than in the past. The Landrum-Griffin Act of 1959 was designed to protect union members from malpractices of union officers by requiring disclosure of union finances, by limiting the length of terms of officers between elections and by requiring secret ballots in elections, and by prohibiting those who have been members of the Communist Party or who have been convicted of felonies from serving as union officers for a period of five years after conviction.

COLLECTIVE BARGAINING

The essence of unionism is that the union becomes the sole bargaining agent through which the members bargain collectively with the employer. The bargaining may take place between a union local and a single employer or, on a broader scale, between a union local and an association of employers, or between a national union and part or all of an industry, such as a large automobile company or several steel companies.

Union Goals

The general public impression of collective bargaining is that it takes place over wage questions. While wages are obviously very important, other objectives may be at least equally important to a union and its members.

When a group of employees is unorganized, the first objective is naturally that of forming a union and having it recognized as the bargaining agent by the employer. Under present law and other conditions, when a majority of workers in a plant or workers of an employer join a union—usually by forming a local of one of the national unions—recognition normally follows automatically. During the 1930s and earlier, however, recognition was often the first objective that the union had to win, as the employer could refuse to bargain with it. It was not unusual for organization to be followed by a strike to gain this recognition.

Once a union has become the recognized bargaining agent, its next objective is likely to be that of maintaining this position. Before the passage of the labor legislation discussed earlier, employers could attempt to undermine the union by hiring nonunion workers to fill vacancies. Consequently, labor agreements often contained provisions on hiring practices and preferences. Similarly, if an employer could let go anyone he chose when work was slack, he could let union workers go first; consequently, a principal union objective has always been obtaining adoption of the principle of seniority, whereby those workers with the longest time with the company are laid off last. Unions also bargain to obtain application of this principle to job openings involving promotion, so that the workers with the greatest seniority have claim to vacancies offering higher pay. Thus a union is interested in union security—maintaining its own position—and demands preferences for union workers, the union shop, or some other provision, and usually the checkoff, whereby union dues are deducted by the employer and transmitted to the union. Closely related to union security is the job security of the individual members, provided by many of the same means.

Other concerns of workers over which a labor agreement is worked out include the standard hours of work and the standard work load; working conditions, including a host of considerations such as the lunch period, rest breaks, sanitary facilities, and safety measures; and many non-wage monetary considerations such as pay for vacations and holidays, sick leave, insurance coverage, retirement benefits, and others, as well as when overtime rates and shift differentials apply.

This collection of goals suggests that the motives of workers in joining unions are far from being related solely to the issue of wages. Belonging to a union provides a worker with a sense of solidarity and community with a group that can assure all-around better treatment in terms of human dignity than individual industrial workers thought possible in earlier days. This is a basic reason why the bulk of union membership consists of industrial workers rather than clerical workers and those in similar occupations.

Union Weapons

The most obvious and best-known weapon of the union in collective bargaining is the strike. It should be emphasized that the strike is a last-resort weapon. The overwhelming bulk of industrial agreements is reached by the normal processes of collective bargaining and the strike occurs infrequently. Year after year statistics show that the percentage of man-hours of work lost through strikes is a small fraction of 1 percent. Yet strikes easily attract public attention, especially when they occur in a major industry, giving the impression that they are a common method of settling disputes.

A strike may occur because the union bargainers feel some kind of pressure to make wage or other demands that the employers feel equally strongly are impossible to grant. The union tends to compare the pay of its members with that of workers in other industries. If it is relatively low, the union officials' job is to bring it up. If it is high, the union tends to look at the ability of the industry to pay, which it gauges by the level of profits. The union is also concerned about changes in the cost of living, as rising prices erode past wage gains. If a settlement has recently been reached granting a sizable wage increase in one industry, union officials are under pressure to win at least as much in their industry or risk dissatisfaction among the membership.

Employers are motivated to consider their stockholders, the workers, their own position and, in the case of very large corporations, the public. Employers expect wages to rise as improvements in production methods raise the productivity of labor; at the same time, management wants to improve the earnings available for investors, so it is motivated to keep wage and other cost increases from being "excessive." Management may be adamant about denying union demands which it considers to infringe on "management prerogatives," such as those limiting management's rights in selecting people for promotion, in deciding in which plant certain work will be done, and the like.

A *strike* may be defined as a cessation of production by a group of workers, who expect to return to work without loss of any rights or privileges when a satisfactory settlement has been reached. In a strike involving a demand for an increase of only a few cents in hourly wages or other small gains, the newspapers often point out that it will take many months or longer for the workers to make up what they lose in pay during the strike. Such comments miss the point that if workers are never willing to go out on strike, threats of striking will carry little weight in collective bargaining. By the same token, the employer must also be willing to have a strike if necessary to make his point, or his bargaining is similarly handicapped.

A strike usually occurs, if at all, as part of reaching a labor agreement. While the agreement or contract is in force, it generally bans the use of strikes over matters that may come up in applying and interpreting the contract. The labor agreement provides methods of dealing with labor grievances as they come up. If workers decide to walk out as a result of a grievance, both the local and national union officers usually attempt to bring them back. It is essential to both sides that agreements be lived up to; otherwise the value of reaching agreement is greatly reduced. Grievances are brought by affected workers to the shop steward, who stands in relation to the union much as the foreman does to management. It is his job to bring up the matter with the foreman and attempt to have it settled under the terms of the agreement. If management and the union disagree in the application of the agreement to a particular problem, such as what piece rate or hourly rate should apply to a new job, who should be assigned to a job, or whether a firing was justified, it is common for the labor agreement to provide for calling in an outside arbitrator whose decision both sides must agree in advance to accept.

There is little question that workers have the right to strike against their own employer with whom an agreement is being negotiated. But if a union calls a strike against another employer who may supply or buy from the negotiating employer, the strike becomes a secondary strike or secondary boycott, which is banned by the Taft-Hartley Act and Landrum-Griffin Act.

A difficult type of strike in which to judge the public interest is the jurisdictional strike. This type of strike arises in a dispute in which two or more unions claim that a particular type of work should be done by their members and that their members must be paid even if the work is done by others. Such jurisdictional disputes arise, for example, in the building trades. A contractor may want metal moldings installed around doors, but if metalworkers do the installing, the carpenters may object that they have always installed doorway moldings. If the carpenters strike to force the employer to let them do the work, it is a jurisdictional strike. The employer is caught because if he gives the work to the carpenters, the metalworkers will strike. The present labor laws make this type of strike illegal.

A companion weapon to the strike is *picketing,* which is an effort to prevent or at least dissuade other workers from going to work at a struck plant. So long as picketing is done peacefully and is directed at the struck plant (not secondary employers), it is legal. Another weapon, generally of considerably less importance, is the *boycott.* If the workers themselves refuse to buy the products of their employer, the loss in sales is generally unimportant. Therefore, the workers often attempt to persuade others not to patronize the struck employer. This tactic is frequently used against retail and service establishments in what is loosely but inaccurately called picketing; workers out on strike parade in front of the establishment with placards asking the public not to enter. Again, if peaceful and directed against the primary employer, boycotting is legal.

Employer Weapons

The ability of the employer to withstand a period of strike has traditionally been greater than that of the worker. However, this is not always true today, especially when management is not the owners of the firm. Stockholders are usually more interested in the dollars and cents of the dispute than in a personal desire to beat the union. Workers may also obtain strike benefits from the treasury of the national union, and they may be eligible for unemployment compensation.

Prior to the labor legislation of the 1930s, when there was no legal right to collective bargaining and it had to be gained by bargaining itself, the employer could resist the organization of a union in several ways. Rather than recognize a union, the employer could shut down his plant in a *lockout*. He could refuse to reopen except as a nonunion plant. As mentioned earlier, the employer could often obtain from local courts injunctions that hampered the activities of union organizers or of striking or picketing workers.

Today it is difficult to understand the bitterness that often prevailed between employers and union groups in the 1930s and earlier. Many employers firmly believed that workers had no business negotiating the terms of their employment and certainly none in "interfering" with what managers considered their prerogatives. While many enlightened employers improved working conditions, wage rates, fringe benefits, and other terms of employment in the belief that such actions raised labor productivity, others believed that unions interfered with free-market forces. Rather than bargain with unions at all, many employers preferred to outlast the workers in costly strikes or to resort to lockouts. Some of the organizing campaigns in the mid-1930s were met with stubborn resistance, and bloody pitched battles took place at plant gates between organizers who wanted to reach workers and plant guards hired to keep them away. In some cases, striking workers refused to leave the plants (sit-in strikes), in order to make sure that strikebreakers were not brought in. However, some of the largest companies in the biggest industries accepted the fact that unions had the legal right to organize and that negotiations with "responsible" unions were preferable to the kind of antagonism that was the alternative. While it is still true that sometimes agreements cannot be reached without strikes, on the whole collective bargaining is carried on peacefully and with mutual benefit.

Mediation and Arbitration

When an industrial dispute reaches the stage of necessitating a strike, a difficult problem of public policy may arise. On the one hand, it is generally considered preferable for the disputants to settle their disagreement by themselves rather than have a settlement imposed on them by government. In a political system where there is basic reliance on free markets and freely arrived-at bargains, imposition of wage rates or other terms of employment by decree is a violation of the basic rules of the game. Fundamentally, it must be assumed that resources, including labor, are allocated best in response to decisions reached in the marketplace. On the other hand, disruption of production in an important industry can create serious inconvenience for the public. Some essential service, such as transportation, may become unavailable or some industries may be unable to purchase needed supplies from the struck industry and, consequently, workers not directly involved in the dispute may become unemployed.

This element of public interest in having industrial disputes settled expeditiously has led to experiments by both the states and the federal government aimed at facilitating agreements. In general, these efforts can be classified as either mediation or arbitration. _Mediation_ is the activity of a third party who attempts to bring the two sides together, taking back and forth offers and counteroffers, suggesting solutions and compromises, reminding the parties of the public interest, and in general smoothing the path towards an agreement. Some industries, through agreements with unions, have established the office of permanent mediator. Both federal and state governments have established such offices, the Federal Mediation and Conciliation Service having over 200 mediators. These mediators may be asked to intervene by the disputing parties, or they may enter the negotiations themselves and offer their services.

A mediator is a skilled person and must be well-informed about the labor problems of the industry in which he is dealing. He must be familiar with labor practices and with other business practices that bear on the attitude of the employer, as well as with the financial situation of the companies in the industry. A mediator can often point out directions in which negotiations can go in order to arrive at acceptable compromises; the parties may be more willing to consider a suggestion from a mediator than if it had come from the other party.

Arbitration is the actual making of a decision or settlement by a third party. The mediator tries to bring the parties to an agreement between themselves; the arbitrator imposes a decision. Arbitration may be voluntary or compulsory. In voluntary arbitration, the parties request an arbitrator—or board of arbitrators—to settle the dispute and agree in advance to accept the decision. Often each side may select perhaps two arbitrators, these four choosing a fifth arbitrator who, in effect, is likely to be the deciding member.

Some states have experimented with compulsory arbitration, but its history has not been successful. Its very existence may make the process of bargaining more difficult because one or both parties may feel that more can be gained by holding out than by reaching agreement. A union might hold out, for example, for a much higher wage increase than it would expect to get by agreement in hopes the arbitrator might somehow "split the difference" between its demands and the employer's offer.

Arbitration is more widely used in settlement of disputes that arise under labor agreements than it is in actually reaching agreements. Problems of interpretation are likely to arise in the life of the shop—who is entitled to do certain work? What piece rate applies to a certain new job? Who is entitled to a particular promotion? Can the employer fire a certain man? The labor agreement, originally reached by collective bargaining, is likely to provide that in cases in which the shop steward and the foreman (or their superiors) cannot agree, the case will be given to an arbitrator. The arbitrator hears evidence from both parties, considers the language of the agreement, and renders a decision. If one or both parties do not like the decisions that come from arbitration, they can attempt to modify the agreement when it is next negotiated.

Collective Bargaining and Wages

It is almost impossible to measure the effect the existence of unions has had on actual wage levels. Certainly union members believe that collective bargaining makes possible higher real wages, and the general public impression is that unions raise wages at the expense of other segments of the economy. Applying basic economic principles to the question, however, raises some doubts that these beliefs are justified.

In order to raise the price of anything, one must presumably reduce the supply or increase the demand. Unions tend to reduce the supply of labor, but here one must carefully distinguish between the supply in a given occupation and the total supply. By restricting entry into the union through a variety of apprenticeship rules and other regulations, by limiting the amount of work done by an individual, and by enforcing a closed shop, a given union could no doubt make its type of labor scarce and thus enforce a higher price for it. On the other hand, the workers who would enter the union and that occupation if free to do so—and thus reduce the scarcity—must seek other jobs, making labor more plentiful in those occupations than it would otherwise be.

There has long been a belief that any long-run effect unions have on general wage levels is through the indirect pressure they exert on employers to improve technology. Paradoxically, if employers are under continual pressure from union bargainers for wage increases, they are stimulated to economize on the labor factor by substituting machinery and other forms of capital. In the short run, this substitution would seem to reduce the demand for labor, but the greater efficiency with which labor can produce makes each laborer more valuable. The greater efficiency of labor in general tends to raise its marginal productivity and the level of wages. This is how the gains from technology are shared throughout the economy in a competitive society.

The wider the view one takes of the labor market, the less possible it appears for unions to "demand" a higher wage level, at least in real terms of what wages can buy. Certainly, in a nonunion industry in which there are few employers and a traditionally low wage level, unionization and collective bargaining could force up wages. If wages had prevailed at a level below marginal productivity because of the lack of competition among employers, the wage could rise without causing employers to reduce employment. Even if wages should be pushed up to where some unemployment would occur, the resulting scarcity of the final product could—depending upon the nature of demand for the product—force up its price and the employers' willingness to pay.

Collective bargaining cannot set some arbitrary wage level unrelated to productivity, however. If such were possible, Asian workers would merely have to unionize in order to bring their wages to the American level and Italian automobile workers could unionize to obtain the same wages as are paid in Detroit. All Italian workers could conceivably, by strike or political means, suddenly double their wages, but their employers could not retain them without raising prices. If the economy was in some kind of balance before the doubling of wages, incomes of other factors of production would have to be restored in order to maintain their supplies and the price level would tend to double.

Given free bargaining, competition among employers as well as among laborers, and mobility of labor, wages for similar work tend to equality in different occupations. If there are rapid technological advances in one industry that raise labor productivity and if that industry is growing because of expanding markets and declining costs, employers will seek to hire labor and will offer higher wages if necessary. Workers leaving other occupations will force employers there to raise wages and to strike a new balance of employment with fewer men at higher wages. The increasing productivity in the first industry thus tends to raise wages throughout the economy, at some sort of average of the rising productivity of the economy in general. The high profits in the first industry serve as a signal to invest capital and to hire labor in that industry until its expansion has tended to reduce the unusual profits to a normal level.

Actual labor negotiations seldom explicitly stress these underlying economic constraints. The arguments feature the ability of the company to pay, its profits, the cost of living, the workers' standard of living, and wages in other industries, yet the level of wages acceptable to both parties is ultimately determined by the underlying productivity of the economy. This is not to say, however, that in the short run wage advances in a particular company or industry cannot be speeded up by collective bargaining. Collective bargaining is one of the means whereby the benefits of technological advance are transmitted rapidly throughout the economy.

SUMMARY

Labor differs from the other factors of production in that it consists of the services of human beings. The terms on which labor service is sold, therefore, reflect the human being's interest in achieving satisfactory working conditions, maintaining his dignity, and having other desirable terms of employment as well as in being paid good wages.

The obvious advantage of the employer over the individual worker in bargaining over the terms of employment in the early days of the factory system led workers to combine and attempt to bargain as groups rather than as individuals. New developments always raise questions of legal status and the public welfare; the activities of labor groups were no exception. Until the 1930s there was little legislation favoring the collective-bargaining activities of labor, but there was a considerable amount of legislation protecting specific groups of laborers from the effects of unregulated bargaining. For example, many states and eventually the federal government legislated in the area of the labor of women and children. Many interesting issues of constitutional law arose in connection with this type of labor legislation which have not been examined in this chapter. As wards of the state, women and children could be protected from working long hours or in dangerous occupations while, for a long time, it was thought that such legislation could not apply to men because it would deprive them of their constitutional right to bargain to work twelve hours underground in a coal mine if they so chose. However, liberalization of court interpretations has brought about not only state but federal legislation covering hours in hazardous occupations and minimum-wage laws covering businesses in interstate commerce.

The early unions combined workers in single crafts because such groups had obvious common interests and strong bargaining positions. However, the development of modern mass-production industries brought about the formation of huge industrial unions that count as members all the workers in a broad industry. Some of the early attempts to organize workers other than on craft lines foundered on the problems of becoming embroiled in political activity. Today, since the successes of labor in obtaining favorable legislation in the 1930s, unions again tend to be active politically. However, American unions are active within the two-party system and show little interest in attempting to create a separate labor party or any other type of political organization.

The basic piece of federal labor legislation is the Wagner Act as amended by the Taft-Hartley Act. This act attempts to ban unfair labor acts on the part of both employer and union, and to protect labor's right to jobs and to collective bargaining.

Economic Terms for Review

craft unions	collective bargaining
industrial unions	strike
labor injunction	lockout
union shop	mediation
closed shop	arbitration

Questions for Review

1. How did the development of modern industry require the growth of labor unions?
2. Why has the recent growth of unions been in industrial unions?
3. What were the aims and methods of the AFL when it was founded?
4. What proportion of the labor force is unionized?
5. What was the importance of the Wagner Act?
6. What is the union argument for the closed shop?

Questions for Analysis

1. Why were the early unions mostly craft unions?
2. Why has union membership been growing more slowly than the labor force?
3. Why, would you suppose, are virtually no bank employees unionized?
4. What are the criticisms of the closed shop?
5. Why has compulsory arbitration in general not worked well?
6. What do you think has been the net effect of unions on the wage level?

Case for Decision

The Adams Connector Company has been unusually successful since John Adams began the business seven years ago. It is now a corporation employing over 100 people and making annual sales in excess of $3 million. For the last three years the company has had an agreement with the union of electrical workers.

For some months the production manager, Mr. Brown, has been secretly working on a piece of equipment that will automatically perform several operations now done by hand by skilled workmen. He has decided that the machine is now operational. Its introduction will reduce the number of workmen required in one department from 28 to 16. Mr. Adams, who handles labor relations as part of his job as president, has called in the shop steward, Bill Swingle, and the president of the local union, Fred Upshaw, to discuss with them the introduction of the machine.

Adams points out to these men that the union agreement permits the company to introduce new technological methods at its discretion. Transfers between jobs are to be based on "skill, ability, aptitude, and seniority; when skill, ability, and aptitute are roughly equivalent, seniority shall govern." When the new machine is put into use, only 16 people will be required. Normally, the 12 with the least seniority would be transferred to other departments, to the extent places could be found for them. However, it is questionable whether the 16 people with the greatest seniority will be able to handle the new machine work as well as some of the 12 with less seniority.

In Adams' opinion, he is entitled to introduce the machine and to select the 16 people to work in the department. Swingle disagrees immediately, saying that if that were the case, the seniority provisions of the agreement would be worthless and there might as well be no union to protect the interests of the workers. After some discussion, Adams and Upshaw decide to call a meeting of the 28 workers during the last thirty minutes of the workday to discuss the situation. At this meeting, the workers appear to be upset by the announcement and talk of walking out if the machine is installed. Upshaw tells them that the company has the right under the labor agreement to install the machine, that such a walkout would be contrary to the agreement, and that the national union would not support them with strike benefits. Nothing is settled at the meeting.

On the following day, Upshaw asks to meet with Adams and Brown. Adams states that he is in favor of installing the machine, selecting the 16 people wanted, and offering the other 12 their choices of other jobs—all of which would carry lower wage rates— in order of their seniority. He believes that the 16 selected would not support a walkout and that the loss of the other 12 would not be serious. Upshaw suggests that Adams install the machine and give the 16 with the greatest seniority a week to work with it. If they are unable to keep up, it will be apparent to them and they will accept transfer; if they are capable, nothing has been lost. Brown objects that the week might be costly in terms of low production and that any workers transferred would still have learning periods in their new jobs.

How would you go about installing the machine? Should its development have been kept secret? How would you have handled the development and introduction of the machine?

19
Welfare and Poverty

The existence of poverty in the midst of plenty has puzzled commentators for many decades. As far back as 1879 Henry George remarked, "This association of poverty with progress is the great enigma of our times. It is the central fact from which spring industrial, social and political difficulties that perplex the world, and with which statesmanship and philanthropy and education grapple in vain."[1] And of course Henry George was far from the first to note that the fruits of economic progress were not spread over the entire population.

THE POVERTY PROBLEM

Although many causes of poverty can be identified, their elimination is not easy. Otherwise, poverty would no doubt have disappeared long ago. From the beginning of the science, economists have been concerned with the manner in which incomes are created and allotted, but in recent years the problem has taken on much public interest and received urgent attention. The "war on poverty" has become an official program—or set of programs—of the federal government. Some types of poverty can be alleviated by improved social and political arrangements, but the creation of more adequate income by the poor themselves requires changes in the way in which the economy operates. Improved operation of the market for labor and increases in the productivity and rates of pay of many who cannot now command adequate incomes are called for.

Measurement of Poverty

In several other chapters of this book reference has been made to the very high average incomes in the United States by world standards and to the steady growth in the level of incomes, as well as to the lessening disparity between low and high incomes. One may wonder why there is a problem of poverty in the richest and most productive country in the world, where incomes have been rising for many decades. Part of the answer is simply that poverty is relative. Some people are considered poor only because there are others who are better off, and this is true even though the poor may live as well as did those not thought poor a few decades ago.

That poverty exists is indisputable. The problem does not go away merely because the poor of this generation are better off materially than were the poor of an earlier generation. But how much poverty is there?

[1] Henry George, *Progress and Poverty*, Robert Schalkenbach Foundation, New York, 1929, p. 10.

Who are the poor? How impoverished must an individual or a family be to be considered poor—and impoverished in relation to whom? These questions must be answered before those discussing poverty can know just what they are talking about. Then other questions may be raised that deal with reducing or eliminating poverty as defined by some acceptable standard.

In general, poverty might be defined along three different lines. In one way, nutritionists and others might set up some sort of minimum standards for nutrition, housing, and other necessities. Then the most economical ways of meeting these standards, through low-cost diets and the like, might be taken as the upper limit of poverty; those with incomes below this cost would be considered poor. This method has not been employed to any great degree, presumably because it assumes a knowledge of nutritional values and other standards that is not widely available, especially among those whose welfare is being measured. Poverty is relative to actual standards of living enjoyed at the moment, not to some abstract or ideal assortment of consumer goods.

A second approach is to assemble a "market basket" of goods and services thought to provide some sort of minimum acceptable standard of living by current standards. The food, clothing, housing, and other things included represent some subjective community standard of what is required for decent living. Poverty is thus not measured by what people in general consumed fifty years ago or what people today consume in Pakistan or Egypt. "A family is 'poor' if its income is insufficient to buy enough food, clothing, shelter, and health services to meet minimum requirements." [2] Obviously, the question becomes, What are the minimum standards?

Generally acceptable minimum standards rise over time as the living standards of the majority increase. Translating these minimum standards into terms of dollar income requires adjustment for changes in the price level. The Social Security Administration estimates the cost of meeting minimum standards by using as a base a calculation of the Department of Agriculture that an "economy food plan" would cost $4.90 per person per week (as of December, 1967) and that other living costs could be obtained for double that amount (in families of three or more). With other adjustments for differences in city and country living, the Social Security Administration's *poverty line* of income for an average nonfarm family of four was $3,335 for 1967 and $3,743 for 1969. The "near-poverty" income line for such families was set at about $1,000 more. In 1967 the median income for families of four was virtually $9,000—half had more and half had less—and in 1969 it was $9,433.

The Social Security Administration guidelines for nonfarm households are shown in Table 19-1. These standards are now revised annually to reflect changes in the index of consumer prices. The figures for farm households are substantially lower, especially as the size of the family increases; prior to 1968 they were 70 percent of the standards for nonfarm families and now they are 85 percent.

A third type of measurement of poverty is simply a comparison of the incomes of some lowest fraction of the population, such as a tenth or fifth, with those of other groups. If the population received equal incomes,

[2] President's Council of Economic Advisers, *Annual Report*, 1969, p. 151.

Table 19-1
Poverty and Near-Poverty Income Lines, 1967

Nonfarm Households	Poverty Income Line	Near-Poverty Income Line
1 member		
65 years and over	$1,565	$1,890
Under 65 years	1,685	2,045
2 members		
Head 65 years and over	1,970	2,655
Head under 65 years	2,185	2,945
3 members	2,600	3,425
4 members	3,335	4,435
5 members	3,930	5,080
6 members	4,410	5,700
7 members or more	5,430	6,945

Source: President's Council of Economic Advisers, *Annual Report*, 1969, p. 152.

each fifth would of course receive a fifth of the total income. By comparing the fraction of total income actually received by the lowest fifth with that of, say, the middle fifth, one obtains a measure of disparity in income. If the disparity is great, a degree of poverty is implied. We have noted in Chapter 11 that this disparity has been growing less great.

A principal difficulty with this way of defining poverty is that it provides no guidelines for improvement—how much of the total income *should* the lowest fifth or tenth receive? Indeed, some students of the poverty problem have suggested that the poor be defined as those whose incomes are less than half of the median income. If, for example, the median income were $8,000, those with incomes below $4,000 would be defined as in poverty. This approach accepts the relative nature of poverty and assumes that, as the median income rises, the poverty standard also rises. Poverty would be eliminated only when there were no incomes below this standard of half of the median. An income distribution roughly as pictured in Figure 19-1 would be implied. If $8,000 were the median income, the lowest income would be $4,000, and perhaps 30 percent of the families would have incomes between $4,000 and about $7,000. Since incomes tend to cluster around the median, perhaps 40 percent of the families would have incomes a bit below and above $8,000. The remaining 30 percent would presumably be scattered along the higher income ranges, although Figure 19-1 stops at $20,000. In actuality, of course, a very small percentage of the total receives incomes far in excess of $20,000.

Clearly, the concept of where to draw the poverty line is a changing one. Whether a tenth, a quarter, or a third of the population lives in poverty depends on the definition and where the line is drawn. As time goes on, the acceptable standard rises. It has been estimated that if the standard were $3,000 of 1954 purchasing power, well over half—59.2 percent—of families would have been classed as in poverty in the prosperous year of

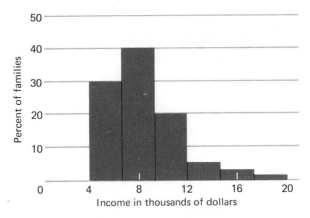

Figure 19-1. Hypothetical distribution of income.

1929. Obviously, the standard of what constituted "minimum health and decency" of the late 1960s cannot be applied to a year forty years earlier, as nowhere near a half of American families considered themselves poor in 1929 by the standards of that time.

In his Second Inaugural Address, President Franklin D. Roosevelt said that one-third of the nation was ill-fed, ill-clad, and ill-housed. Certainly there were more poor people, constituting a higher percentage of the population, in the depression year of 1936 than there had been in 1929. If the standard of 1936 were still applied today, only an extremely small percentage of families would still be considered poor.

Wherever the poverty line is drawn for the statistical purpose of estimating the size of the problem, some families will be above the line but feel that they are poor and some will be below the line but not consider themselves poor. Poverty is partly psychological. Some people feel that they are poor because they have difficulty keeping up with the Joneses. Other people live adequately in spite of low reported incomes because they are living on capital accumulated in the past. For example, a retired couple may not have much income in an accounting sense but an adequate annuity, which is mostly return of capital.

Extent of Poverty

An overall view of the extent of poverty is provided by Figure 19-2, which shows both the number of poor persons, according to the Social Security Administration standard, and the incidence of poverty, or percentage of poor in the total population. By this income standard, about 30 percent of the population were poor in 1947 and about 12 percent twenty years later. The number of poor persons declined about 20 million, including a rapid decline in the more recent years of high employment. Under the standards adopted in 1969, the number of poor persons in 1968 was estimated to be 25.4 million. Along with these declines in the number and percentage of those in poverty, the so-called *poverty gap*—the amount by which incomes of the poor were below the poverty line—also declined. This amount was about $10 billion in 1967.

But the broad statement that some 12 percent of the households can be defined as poor—about one household in eight—conceals the inci-

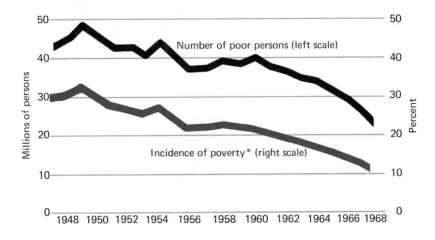

*Poor persons as percent of total noninstitutional population.

Figure 19-2. Number of poor persons and incidence of poverty, 1947–1968.
Source: President's Council of Economic Advisers, *Annual Report,* 1969, p. 154.

dence of poverty among specific groups of the population. Table 19-2
shows some characteristics of poor households and the proportion of
households with certain characteristics in the poverty classification. If
households, rather than individuals, are measured, the *incidence of
poverty* declined from 24 percent in 1959 to 16.2 percent in 1967. By
glancing down the percentage column for 1967, one can note the high
incidence of poverty among certain groups.

Older people have a high incidence of poverty, especially those unrelated individuals living together; 53.4 percent of this group had incomes
below the poverty line ($1,565 for nonfarm households and $1,095 for
farm). Such people are much more often below the poverty line than are
two-person families headed by a member over 65. Two other characteristics with high incidence of poverty are the head of the household being
female and the head of the household being nonwhite. Only 9.5 percent
of families are poor, but the percentage of nonwhite poor families is 29.9.
When the head of the family is female, the incidence of poverty goes up to
25.3 percent for white families and 54.9 percent for nonwhite families.

Characteristics of Poverty

It follows from the information in Table 19-2 that poverty is not spread
generally throughout the population but is associated with family (or individual) characteristics. Three of these characteristics brought out by the
table are that the head of the household is over 65 years of age, or is a
female, or is nonwhite. When these characteristics overlap, the incidence
of poverty becomes even more likely. That is, a household headed by a
nonwhite female over 65 is very likely to have an income below the
poverty standard.

One study of the characteristics of poor families in 1960 found that,
while one family in eight was defined as poor, a third of the families with
one of the following characteristics were poor: [3]

[3] Oscar Ornati, "Affluence and the Risk of Poverty," *Social Research,* Vol. 31, No. 3, Autumn,
1964.

Family nonwhite
Head of family female
Head of family 65 or older
Family rural
Head of family with less than eight years of education
Head of family with only part-time work experience

The incidence of poverty is much higher than one-third in families in which these characteristics are found in combination, for example in nonwhite families headed by females, older farm families, older Negro families, Negro farm families, and farm families headed by females.

Causes of Poverty

The characteristics of the poor suggest the reasons for much of the poverty that exists. But it is not logical to say that a family is poor *because* it is nonwhite, headed by a female, or headed by an older person, because many similar families are not poor. To a large extent, the incidence of poverty must be explained in terms of the way in which the individual can participate in the economy. Some people cannot earn an adequate income

Table 19-2
**Number of Poor Households
and Incidence of Poverty, 1959 and 1967**

Poor Households	1959 Millions	1959 Percentage	1967 Millions	1967 Percentage
Total	13.4	24.0	10.2	16.2
Head 65 years and over	3.9	48.6	3.8	36.3
Unrelated individuals	2.5	68.1	2.7	53.4
Families °	1.4	32.5	1.1	20.3
Head under 65 years	9.4	19.8	6.4	12.2
Unrelated individuals	2.6	36.8	2.2	27.0
White	1.9	32.9	1.6	24.4
Male	.6	24.6	.5	18.0
Female	1.3	39.1	1.1	29.0
Nonwhite	.7	54.8	.5	40.1
Male	.3	47.1	.2	29.4
Female	.4	63.5	.3	51.7
Families †	6.8	16.8	4.2	9.5
White	4.9	13.4	2.8	7.1
Male	3.8	11.4	2.0	5.4
Female	1.1	35.9	.8	25.3
Nonwhite	1.9	48.6	1.4	29.9
Male	1.3	42.1	.7	20.9
Female	.6	71.3	.7	54.9

° Two-person families only, with head 65 or older.
† Other than two-person families whose head is 65 or older.
Source: President's Council of Economic Advisers, *Annual Report*, 1969, p. 157.

because of physical or mental handicaps. Poverty among such people must be attacked through social arrangements whereby others support them, either their own families or the public. To some extent, the same is true of the aged, but here the problem is the failure of such people to have accumulated wealth in the past. If their incomes had been adequate for only a moderate standard of living and not for sufficient saving for old age, some social answer to their problems is suggested.

Many of the poor families are headed by persons who are not incapable of earning adequate incomes because of physical or mental handicaps. Nevertheless, these people are unable to share in the general output by commanding adequate incomes in the form of wages or otherwise. In other words, as real wages rise with the productivity of the economy, they do not share in the rising productivity because they are, in one way or another, outside the economy. For example, the residents of Appalachia tend to remain unemployed because the industries that once supported them—mainly coal mining—have declined in that area. Other groups have limited access to job markets: Examples are Mexican-Americans in the southwestern states and Puerto Ricans in New York City. (Puerto Ricans make up about 8 percent of the population of New York City but about a third of those on welfare.) Most of the poor families and individuals are white because most of the population is white, but the incidence of poverty is higher among nonwhite families, in which it is approximately one-third. Nearly all the poor nonwhite families are Negro, along with a small number of American Indians and Eskimos. Median income of non-whites was only 57 percent of the median income of whites in 1952, then declined relatively to the income of whites and, in recent years, moved back above the 1952 level. In other words, it reached 61 percent of the median income of whites in 1969—$5,999 as against $9,794.

Clearly, the persisting effects of racial discrimination are reflected in the distribution of incomes. Discrimination accentuates many of the char-acteristics of poverty because it affects not only hiring but the extent and quality of education and training. The obstacles in the road to profitable employment are indicated by the fact that nonwhite high school graduates have lower earnings than do white high school dropouts; in other words, the white dropouts are able to find better jobs on the average than are the nonwhite high school graduates.

The role of education in combating poverty is to make it possible for the children of the poor not to remain poor. But since poverty is relative, it is necessary for the children of the poor to become not only better educated than their parents but at least as well-educated as others their same age. The lack of a comparable education may be seen as a major cause of poverty, or of its persistence, because the children of the poor tend to stay in school less long than others and often to have inferior educational facilities. In addition, their home environments often do not contribute to their desire and ability to study or to stay in school. These children may also be handicapped in their schoolwork by less adequate health care and nutrition.

Access to jobs is limited by many characteristics of the poor. For ex-ample, the poor tend to be less mobile than others because they are limited in their choices of living locations and they are not likely to have automobiles with which to get to jobs that may not be on public transportation routes. In some cities, living areas are some distance from work areas and, in addition, the greatest growth in job openings is outside the central city.

To summarize, some poverty exists because of the inability of people who are, or can become, qualified to participate fully in the operation of the economy. "That is, in an effectively operating market economy, the fruits of increased productivity should be distributed over the whole of the economy . . . although different groups will share disproportion-ately."[4] If some groups who might be productive workers fail to share in productivity gains, the market economy is not working to reduce poverty. Specifically, there is insufficient mobility of labor for workers in disadvan-taged jobs to improve their position in large numbers. The reasons for this immobility are numerous and are usually interrelated. As for those who would be unable to participate in current production under any circumstances, they cannot look to improved operation of the economy itself for improvement; their problem is more purely a political or social problem to be attacked through such measures as social security and relief programs.

Urban Poverty

The causes of poverty are such that they lead to two distinct types of poverty — urban poverty and rural poverty. Fundamentally, both arise from lack of adequate employment opportunities, but the urban poor are more often unemployed because they are unqualified for job openings that exist while the rural poor are more often unemployed because of a lack of job openings.

Although New York City is unique because of its size and its depend-ence on white-collar, in contrast to manufacturing, employment, it illustrates many of the aspects of urban poverty. Employment within the city has grown in recent years much more slowly than in the country generally. The most rapid growth in the economy has been in the West and South. In addition, in the older sections of the country, growth has taken place in suburban areas rather than in central cities. As the sub-urban areas have grown, job holders have moved from the city to new jobs outside the city. To a large extent, they have been replaced by migrants, who frequently add to the population of poor people. The Negro population of New York City approaches 20 percent of the total, and the Puerto Rican totals about 10 percent. One in four of the Negro families is below the poverty line, and one in three of the Puerto Rican families. With the addition of poor white families, one in six families in New York is below the poverty line.

Many of the poor families receive public welfare assistance, especially aid to dependent children. Women with dependent children constitute a large fraction of the families in poverty. Only about a third of these women have husbands who live with the family. Often it appears that the husband deserts the family because his earnings, if any, do not then reduce the size of welfare payments.

Although the official unemployment rate among the poor in New York City is not high, poverty nevertheless exists because of the large number

[4] Chamber of Commerce of the United States, *The Concept of Poverty*, New York, 1965, p. 41.

of part-time workers and workers at low pay; in addition, unemployment figures do not include those who have dropped out of the labor force and no longer seek jobs. Many of the poor in the cities are ill-equipped for the types of jobs that do exist. Very few have experience or training in jobs requiring clerical or craft skills.

Rural Poverty

The existence of poverty in rural areas has, in general, except for the special problems of the residents of Appalachia and of migrant farm workers, received much less public recognition than has urban poverty. Because many of these rural families live far from population centers, they are sometimes called the invisible poor. However, a disproportionately large fraction of all families in poverty live in rural areas—nearly a half—although the rural population is only about a quarter of the total.

A special segment of the rural poor is made up of migrant farm workers, who follow a crop north as it ripens and become temporary workers to harvest it. Wages of these workers are well below even average farm wages, which in turn are well below average urban wages.

The causes of rural poverty operate in a vicious circle to perpetuate it. Because of the low incomes of much of the rural population, public services in general and education in particular are not well supported. Rural schools are frequently inferior to urban schools. In many, material related to farm life continues to be taught, in spite of dwindling employment opportunities in rural areas. The persistent migration from rural communities in the past, usually by the children of farmers, has tended to drain away the more employable and productive people, leaving behind the older and less productive. These people find it difficult to provide taxes for improved schools and other public services. When former sources of employment, such as mining and forestry, decline, a large proportion of the remaining families are left in poverty.

ANTIPOVERTY MEASURES

How to alleviate poverty has been a social and economic problem since the Industrial Revolution separated people from the land and located them in cities where they became dependent on opportunities for employment. In England, this development led to the enactment of the Poor Laws, under which local governments were charged with the support of the indigent. From the beginning, consideration of relief measures has tended to be in terms of the "deserving" poor as against those who are poor because of lack of ambition. Even in the depths of the great depression, there was much public resistance in this country to the introduction of unemployment compensation and similar measures because it was feared that some would rather get along on a small "dole" than seek employment at a somewhat higher income.

Early Measures

The American economy has always emphasized the virtues of self-reliance and independence. The English experience with the Poor Laws and the beginnings of the problem of the poor in this country led to fears that outright support of the indigent would lead to idleness. Benjamin

Franklin remarked that, "In my youth, I travelled much, and I observed in different countries, that the more public provisions were made for the poor, the less they provided for themselves, and of course became poorer. And, on the contrary, the less that was done from them, the more they did for themselves, and became richer." [5]

In fact, through the efforts of philanthropic citizens to provide means whereby the poor could increase their independence, mutual savings banks were established in this country. When De Witt Clinton was Governor of New York, he recommended to the legislature that charters be granted for savings banks and in 1818 told the legislators:

> Our statutes relating to the poor are borrowed from the English system, and the experience of that country, as well as our own, shows that pauperism increases with the augmentation of the funds applied to its relief. This evil has proceeded to such an alarming extent in the city of New York, that the burdens of heavy taxation which it has imposed, menace a diminution of the population of that city, and a depreciation of its real property. . . . Under the present system, the fruits of industry are appropriated to the wants of idleness; a laborious poor man is taxed for the support of an idle beggar; and the vice of mendicity, no longer considered degrading, infects a considerable portion of our population in large towns.[6]

One of the philanthropic groups of the day, The Society for Prevention of Pauperism, located in New York City, was told by the founders of one of the first savings banks, The Provident Institution for Savings in the Town of Boston, that:

> The greatest good is, in affording the humble journeyman, coachmen, chamber-maids, and all kinds of domestic servants, and inferior artisans, who constitute two thirds of our population, a secure disposal of their little earnings, which would otherwise be squandered, or unwisely lent to petty fraudulent dealers, on a promise of usurious interest. . . . Some examples of abjuring spiritous liquors, and laying up what was worse than wasted, have encouraged us.[7]

These quotations suggest not only the kinds of people whom the philanthropists attempted to help but also the tinge of superiority and patronage with which they regarded the "lower classes."

Until the beginnings of the present century, poverty was considered a problem primarily for private charity. Poor people were to be helped, if at all, by their wealthier neighbors. Local governments, usually the counties, provided for those who could not support themselves and had no family or private support, usually in "county homes," which the inmates helped to run by working in the fields and barns.

[5] Benjamin Franklin, "On the Price of Corn and Management of the Poor," reprinted in Charles Crome (ed.), *A Documentary History of American Thought and Society,* Allyn and Bacon, Inc., Boston, 1965.

[6] Quoted in Weldon Welfling, *Mutual Savings Banks,* Case Western Reserve University Press, Cleveland, 1968, p. 17.

[7] *Ibid.,* p. 21.

The incidence of unemployment rose so high and the resulting poverty was so widespread in the early 1930s that the federal government was drawn into the efforts to ameliorate the situation. The government adopted measures both for relief and for expanding employment. It established a Works Progress Administration, which provided many jobs on local projects, such as cleaning up beaches and improving public buildings. It also established a Public Works Administration, which administered larger projects such as dams, and a Civilian Conservation Corps, which gave many young men employment in the woods clearing trails, building campsites, and the like. Other measures were also taken, no doubt the most significant of which was the establishment of the Social Security Administration, with its pension programs for the retired and various programs of direct aid funneled through the states, such as aid for the blind and for dependent children.

Recent Measures and Proposals

It is probably accurate to say that, until the 1960s, people generally considered poverty a perennial problem – "The poor ye have always with ye." In the early 1960s, however, many social problems converged and produced pressure for direct attack on the existence of poverty by attacking the disadvantages of many of the poor. It must be realized, however, that the specific legislation of the early and mid-1960s which came to be labeled the "war on poverty" actually constitutes a relatively small part of the total measures directed against poverty. Numerous programs of government at all levels in one way or another affect the distribution of income. Even the fiscal and monetary policies that try to maintain full employment and economic growth should be included among the measures that alleviate poverty.

Policies for Full Employment

As a problem in economics, poverty was viewed by the President's Council of Economic Advisers (under Johnson) as subject to attack through four means.[8] The first means is through measures to maintain full employment and a satisfactory rate of economic growth. The second means is through measures to qualify more people for jobs and for better jobs: education, training, medical assistance, and the like. The third is through measures based on the fact that a large fraction of poor families are headed by the aged or by women who are unable to leave small children and therefore unable to participate in improved employment opportunities. For these families some other form of relief is necessary. The last means is through measures related to the fact that poverty is concentrated in certain urban and rural areas – *poverty pockets* – and that public and private investment in these areas or some means of relocating unemployed residents of these areas is needed.

Expansion of opportunities for employment greatly reduced poverty during the 1960s. In the periods of recovery and expansion after 1950, the number of persons below the poverty line declined an average of 2 million per year. But these benefits were gained mainly by households headed by men of working age, who either became employed or found

[8] President's Council of Economic Advisers, *Annual Report,* 1969, p. 155.

better jobs. Thus the number of white families headed by men under age sixty-five, defined as below the poverty line, declined from 4.7 million in 1961 to 2.8 million in 1967, but there was no change in the incidence of poverty among nonwhite families headed by females. Much of the overall improvement attributable to general prosperity has occurred among the near-poor. Some of the previously poor have become near-poor, but a larger number have improved their incomes sufficiently to reduce the total. Most of the near-poor are families of men who are employed but at very low wages.

Although the long-sustained economic expansion of the 1960s reduced the incidence of poverty considerably, this very fact makes more difficult continued improvement from this source. As improvement takes place, more of the remaining families below the poverty line are those headed by the aged or by women with dependents. Also, as the unemployment rate declines, those remaining unemployed are those most difficult to employ. Thus other measures, designed to upgrade the unemployed and to reduce discrimination, become relatively more important.

Distribution of Income

The average annual rate of growth of household income is about 3 percent. The elimination of poverty must be a slow process if it has to depend upon the incomes of the poor rising at this average rate as a result of economic growth. The President's Council estimates that if this rate of growth were shifted to 2.5 percent for the 85 percent of the population who are not poor and the one-half of 1 percent were shifted to the poor, all those below the poverty line could be brought up to it in between four and eight years. In the 1960s the share of total national income going to the poor increased substantially as unemployment fell and wages rose.

The share of income going to the poor is also increased by the operation of the tax and transfer-payment systems. The burden of taxes on the poor is heavy because of the inclusion of many state and local taxes as costs of production in prices of goods. Although the poor generally do not pay much, if any, federal income tax, they are subject to payroll taxes for social security. It is estimated that the combined burden of federal, state, and local taxes constitutes over 40 percent of the incomes below $2,000. However, transfer payments such as welfare payments and other benefits add at least 80 percent to what such incomes would be without them. In other words, transfer payments add about four-fifths as much as do other sources of income, for those with very small incomes. For all income groups above $2,000, taxes exceed transfer payments received. Social security pensions, for example, go to all those who are eligible because of past employment, regardless of current income.

Education and Training

The Congress recognized the educational disadvantages of the poor in several pieces of legislation passed during the 1960s. The Economic Opportunity Act of 1964 was a comprehensive law that established a variety of antipoverty programs. It included a Job Corps, in which disadvantaged youth would be given job training for a period of time away from home; a Neighborhood Youth Corps, designed to keep youth in school by paying them for jobs and attending training classes; an Adult Basic Education and Work Experience program, intended to upgrade basic education and skills; and Vista, a domestic program similar to the Peace Corps.

A program designed specifically for on-the-job training was set up by the Manpower Development and Training Act, which financed the training of 125,000 people in 1968. Over half of the trainees were from families below the poverty guidelines, and half were not high school graduates. The National Alliance of Businessmen sponsored a program called JOBS (job opportunities in the business sector) in which some 800 employing firms waived the usual hiring standards and incurred extra costs, reimbursed by the federal government, to train over 100,000 of the disadvantaged.

Income Maintenance

As was noted earlier, it is considered better to improve job opportunities than to increase welfare payments in the effort to reduce poverty, but it must also be recognized that over half of the poor families are headed by people who would find it difficult or impossible to benefit from the former. In the last three or four decades, the United States has developed a very large system designed to maintain incomes for a large fraction of the population, poor or not. The federal government alone, exclusive of state and local governments, private pensions, and other arrangements, transfers approximately $60 billion a year through a variety of programs. By far the largest item is now the social security benefits paid to retired people and to survivors of those who died while employed. These benefits are paid regardless of the income of the recipient, as are several other similar benefits. The President's Council's estimates of these outlays for the fiscal year 1969 are shown in Table 19-3. There are no data for several of the categories, which are accordingly left blank. The table does suggest the comprehensive nature of the arrangements for income maintenance in the face of many social risks, as well as the fact that they are not designed solely to eliminate poverty. There is no doubt, however, that without many of these programs more people would probably be below the accepted poverty line. In general, benefit programs do not lift people out of poverty unless they have other incomes — in which case they are not eligible for some of the welfare grants, such as the aid to families with dependent children.

One of the commonest criticisms of the federally assisted programs is that the states' contributions vary widely and therefore the level of welfare assistance also varies widely among the states. In four states the welfare payment for aid to families with dependent children, for example, is $40 for a family of four, while in one state it is $290 (the highest), which is just above the poverty line. This program has also been criticized for penalizing mothers who earn some income by reducing the benefits accordingly. Legislation in 1968 permitted the earning of $30 per month without reduction of benefits and beyond this amount reduction of benefits by two-thirds of additional earnings. This arrangement, of course, leaves little incentive for working. Recent proposals would liberalize this provision.

In addition to the cash-benefit programs listed in Table 19-3, the federal government has several programs through which benefits are

Table 19-3
Selected Federal Income Maintenance Programs, Fiscal Year 1969

| | *Total Outlays (Millions of Dollars)* | *Beneficiaries* | |
		Number (Thousands)	*Percentage in Households With Income Under $3,300*
Aid to families with dependent children	$ 3,206	6,146	100
Unemployment insurance:			
Federal-state unemployment compensation	2,300	5,196	20
Disability programs:			
Workmen's compensation	1,686	....	......
Veterans' compensation	2,611	2,390	24
Social security	2,691	2,278	39
Aid to the blind	92	84	100
Aid to the permanently and totally disabled	726	721	100
Assistance to those 65 years and over:			
Social security retirement and survivors' benefits	24,681	21,931	31
Old-age assistance	1,833	2,123	100
Veterans' pensions	2,127	2,252	80
Others	6,171	2,568	......
General assistance	32	700	100
Assistance in kind	10,226	....	......
Total, all programs	$58,382	....	......

Source: President's Council of Economic Advisers, *Annual Report,* 1969, p. 164.

distributed in kind. Some of these programs have developed out of programs designed for other purposes; for example, farm products purchased by the government to support crop prices may be distributed through school-lunch programs, or food stamps may be used by the poor to buy farm products in large supply. The food programs may be significant aids to welfare families as byproducts of price-support programs.

The largest program of this type is that relating to health care since the passage of the Medicare and Medicaid amendments to Social Security. Total federal outlays for health care programs were budgeted at $9 billion for fiscal 1969, nearly all of which was for these two programs. It is estimated that about a third of the Medicare beneficiaries are poor, and over four-fifths of the Medicaid beneficiaries. Another type of subsidy going largely to the poor is related to housing. A very comprehensive law, the Housing Act of 1968, includes ambitious programs for con-

struction of public housing and for *rent subsidies* (governmental contributions toward rent payments). It was designed to help finance the
construction of 75,000 housing units in fiscal 1969 and numerous units
of public and low-cost housing over succeeding years.

Many special problems make adequate housing difficult for the poor
to obtain. It is virtually impossible for housing to be constructed without
subsidy that can sell or rent at levels that can be paid by the poor or
near-poor. The average rent in public housing projects is about $50 a
month, which constitutes about a third of the income of the low-income
occupants. Costs of land and construction have risen rapidly in recent
decades, especially in cities. In some cities, such as New York, rent
controls held over from World War II discourage modernization and
investment and lead to the abandonment of properties. By United States
Census definitions, 81 percent of the housing units in New York City were
sound, with all plumbing facilities, in 1968, but 13 percent were "deteriorating" and 6 percent were "dilapidated" or lacked facilities. In poor
neighborhoods, landlords often cannot obtain rent increases to pay for
improvements because the tenants are already paying a third or more of
their incomes in rent. Rent controls often benefit the middle-income
families rather than the poor because the former usually occupy the
older buildings subject to these controls. In a recent study it was found
that 68 percent of the households in New York with incomes between
$8,000 and $15,000 were paying less than 15 percent of their incomes
in rent in controlled units, while of such households living in newer and
uncontrolled units, only 16 percent were paying as little.[9] Subsidized
housing is only about 5 percent of the total in New York City.

Retirement Payments

The Social Security System was established in 1935, considerably later
than similar programs began in some other countries. The purpose of the
program is to ensure that "covered" workers, regardless of their income
or wealth, receive a retirement income sufficient to support them. Covered
workers are those from whose wages a payroll tax is withheld by the
employer and transmitted, along with his own tax, to the government to
pay for the benefits. Coverage has been expanded constantly since the
system began and benefits have been extended. Widows and children of
covered workers are also beneficiaries. The number of recipients is now
about 22 million. The intent of the legislation is to make such benefits
a right that has been paid for during the years of employment, rather than
a benefit paid on the basis of need.

Coverage, either through the federal program or those for state and
local employees, is virtually universal. Many private pension plans supplement social security. Those regularly employed, except at the very lowest
wages, earn benefits sufficient in themselves to keep the recipients above
the poverty line when retired. At present, the minimum benefit is $55 per
month, but most covered workers qualify for more. Unfortunately, those
receiving the lowest benefits are usually those with no other income. One
of the criticized aspects of the arrangement is that recipients are penalized
if they continue to earn income above certain levels. If they earn over

[9] Chase Manhattan Bank, *Business in Brief,* April, 1969.

$2,880, their benefits are reduced dollar for dollar; earnings over $1,680 cause reductions of half a dollar for each dollar earned. These provisions are holdovers from the 1930s when it was considered desirable because of unemployment to discourage the elderly from staying in the labor market.

Proposals for Income Maintenance

Many proposals have been made from time to time that would guarantee in some fashion a minimum income for every family. Debate over the wisdom of these proposals usually centers around the problem of distinguishing between the "deserving" poor and others.[10] The costs of simply giving all poor families enough to lift them above the poverty standards are so great as to create a fear that there would be much waste if the work incentives of the poor were lessened. Some proposals therefore retain the effort to distinguish between the deserving and undeserving, but a recent one called the *negative income tax* has also received much favorable attention.

Most advanced nations, other than the United States, have adopted some form of program for outright payments to families with children. Some have adopted these programs to encourage population growth, others to alleviate poverty. In the former case, the payments tend to have little or no relationship to family income, being based on the number of children (usually the amount paid per child declining as the number increases). If such payments are ever adopted in the United States primarily as an antipoverty tool, they should of course be geared to family income. Many experts recommend this step as a means of correcting some of the defects of the current program of aid to families with dependent children, because a uniform federal system would correct the wide disparities among the states, eliminate much of the investigation and checking now done by social workers to establish eligibility, and so on. It is pointed out that moderate-income families with many children and low-income families would both benefit from such a program.

One difficulty with present programs is that they fail to cover families headed by men of working age. When such men are not covered by unemployment insurance or exhaust their benefits, welfare benefits are often not available. As noted earlier, this situation sometimes leads the head of the family to desert the family in order to make it eligible. Resistance to extending welfare benefits to able-bodied men rests on the fear of reducing work incentives, but eliminating poverty requires that the children in such families be helped to climb out of poverty.

This situation has prompted proposals whereby the government would become an "employer of last resort" in somewhat the same way as a nation's central bank serves as a lender of last resort. In other words, an unemployed person could always find employment at minimum wages on some public project or in the public service, especially fathers who have been unemployed for some period of time. Such employees would presumably have to agree to accept private employment at comparable wages, if found for them, and perhaps to accept training for private employment. The proponents of guaranteed employment note that it would guarantee the minimum wage to any man, this wage approximating

---

[10] See President's Council of Economic Advisers, *Annual Report,* 1969, pp. 170–172.

Table 19-4
Illustration of Negative Income Tax

Income Before Tax	Payment From Government	Payment to Government	Income After Tax
$ 0	$3,300	$......	$3,300
1,000	2,800	......	3,800
2,000	2,300	......	4,300
3,000	1,800	......	4,800
4,000	1,300	......	5,300
5,000	800	......	5,800
6,000	300	......	6,300
7,000	....	200	6,800

the poverty standard for families of four, and that the benefit would be earned by the recipient.

A completely different approach is involved in the proposal for a guaranteed minimum income through a negative income tax. This proposal has come from such well-known conservatives as Professor Milton Friedman of the University of Chicago.[11] The reasoning for it is that a country of the productive power and wealth of the United States can well afford to guarantee every individual and every family a minimum income for subsistence and that to do so in a straightforward manner would be cheaper in the long run than to maintain the network of public and private relief and social-work agencies now required by eligibility rules. It is reasoned that a minimum income at the poverty line is not sufficiently attractive to destroy the incentive to try to earn more in most cases and, further, that a needs or means test is no longer appropriate in the broad effort to eliminate poverty.

The problem of how to devise such a program with a minimum effect on work incentives would have to be worked out. In other words, if some minimum income like $3,300 were established, those people whose incomes were below this figure (adjusted perhaps for size of family) would receive a payment from the government instead of paying any income tax to the government. It would be desirable, of course, to encourage these recipients to earn as much as possible; hence, it would not be possible to reduce the payment dollar for dollar for any private earnings. The reduction could probably not exceed 50 percent without seriously reducing work incentives.[12] Thus benefits would in fact have to be paid to those with incomes above the minimum too, but in reduced amount. A family earning $5,000 and therefore losing benefits of half, or $2,500, would still be eligible for $800 out of the minimum guarantee of $3,300. Its income, earned plus benefit, would be $5,800. In this instance, all families with incomes under $6,600 (twice the minimum) would receive some benefit. An illustration of how the negative income tax might work is shown in Table 19-4.

[11] A similar proposal, called a guaranteed annual income, has been made by Professor James Tobin of Yale.

[12] President's Council of Economic Advisers, *Annual Report*, 1969, p. 172.

It seems likely that, because of its simplicity and straightforward approach, the negative income tax will receive considerable study. In fact, an experiment with it was being carried out in New Jersey in 1969. It has attracted much support from a variety of sources. It promises to be expensive, but it is difficult to estimate how much it would also save. To accomplish the objective, the guaranteed minimum income would have to be at or above the poverty line and, to avoid destroying work incentives, the additional payments to the near-poor and even some above that line would have to be substantial in total. The reductions in benefits related to earnings could not be great. While the plan seems revolutionary, so did social security in 1935. Social security was opposed by many who believed that if people were guaranteed a retirement income, they would make no effort to save for their old age. In fact, however, being guaranteed a minimum retirement income, people could see that additional savings would provide a more comfortable old age, and private pension plans and other forms of saving for retirement have been stimulated by the existence of social security.

Poverty Pockets

We come last to the poverty problems associated with poor areas, urban or rural. Conditions peculiar to some areas of central cities greatly intensify the incidence of poverty there. In these areas are concentrated the families whose characteristics, as we have seen earlier, are associated with poverty. Because such areas become unattractive places for new investment in business and residential structures, they deteriorate, and the deterioration becomes progressive. Property-tax rates rise because people and business firms move to the suburbs, where tax rates are lower, leaving less taxable property behind them. The central city has to reduce its services in the form of police and fire protection and education or raise its tax rates even higher. The suburbs gain taxable property in the form of business and residences and are able to provide better services at lower taxes per person; thus the migration from the central city is encouraged. Among those who are left—largely those who cannot afford to move—rates of unemployment and underemployment rise.

Consequently, one form of attack on the concentration of poverty in urban areas takes the form of efforts to rebuild and revitalize the blighted areas. Federal programs to assist slum clearance and urban redevelopment have been instituted. Without some form of federal assistance or subsidy, there is inadequate incentive for private investment in the deteriorating neighborhoods. With federal guarantees and contributions, however, funds do tend to flow into clearing old sections and rebuilding them. Under the Model Cities program, for example, local housing authorities are able to delegate to private builders the task of clearing land and building public housing, which the authorities may then purchase. Financial institutions have been willing to lend mortgage funds for such projects, which would not have been economical without the government aid. As just one example, a project in East Harlem, New York City, may be cited. This project consists of 48 units of low-income housing, authorized and purchased from private builders by the New York City Housing Authority for $935,000. Two savings banks set up a company to build the apartment house and they advanced the necessary funds, which were repaid out of permanent financing, when the project was completed, from a federal mortgage agency. A local community group was involved throughout with the planning and construction, and local residents were given preference in allocating the housing units. The project also utilized the services of a local contracting company and its local employees.

The vicious circle whereby poverty becomes more and more concentrated in urban areas unless these areas are rehabilitated is illustrated by the high costs of doing business there. It has been found that prices in the small stores that serve slum neighborhoods tend to be substantially higher than those in the main shopping areas; yet these small stores are less profitable than others. They are subject to higher costs because of small volume, slower turnover of perishables, higher insurance rates, and higher costs of granting credit.

The problem of poverty in rural areas is a paradox because, on the one hand, migration to the cities in general improves the economic condition of those who move but, on the other hand, it sometimes means that those who are left are unable to maintain enough industry and revenue to support the area. Certainly, as agriculture becomes a relatively less important segment of the economy, resources should be encouraged to flow to the growing industries. However, it is also possible to encourage economic growth in rural areas or, at least, in the smaller metropolitan areas. Several federal programs assist in area-wide planning for development in rural areas. The Department of Agriculture provides technical assistance to both public and private groups planning such development. The goal of these programs is to encourage diversification of the depressed rural economies by stimulating the construction of new industrial plants and commercial businesses near small population centers, in order to develop local markets and attract additional investment. In those areas heavily dependent on depleted natural resources—farming, mining, or forestry— decline will probably continue but can be softened by federal aid to education and programs to facilitate the movement of low-income people from poverty pockets to other sections of the country.

SUMMARY

Poverty, as defined by today's standards, exists mostly among individuals and families who are unable to profit from and share in the growth of the economy. The poverty gap—the amount by which the incomes of the poor fail to reach the poverty line—is actually a very small part of the gross national product, not much more than 1 percent. Yet eliminating this gap is a complicated problem. Although it would be within the financial power of the nation merely to tax those above the poverty line and transfer the income to those below, few would consider this a satisfactory solution. Measures to "plug in" to the economy as many as possible of those who cannot now find nonpoverty employment are the first order of business, measures which range from providing better basic education to promoting good health and nutrition to reducing discrimination. At the same time, it must be recognized that some families cannot benefit sufficiently from such measures because they are not headed by people of employable age or because the head of the family is a female with small children. Although a complicated system of income maintenance already exists, its simplification and broadening are also required before poverty can be greatly reduced.

Until recent years the popular impression was either that poverty was largely the fault of the poor themselves and that the poor were a permanent problem or, its opposite, that the growth and progress of the economy would gradually eliminate poverty (except that some people would no doubt always be poorer than others). In recent years the relationship of poverty to other social ills has been more clearly recognized, as has the fact that eliminating poverty is within the powers of the economy.

Economic Terms for Review

poverty line	poverty pockets
poverty gap	income maintenance
incidence of poverty	rent subsidies
rural poverty	negative income tax

Questions for Review

1. Where is the poverty line drawn? Would you draw it elsewhere?
2. If all incomes below $4,000 were brought up to that figure, would poverty be abolished?
3. What proportion of all families are considered poor?
4. What characteristics are most common among poor families?
5. How does social security differ from welfare?

Questions for Analysis

1. Is poverty any greater than a decade or two ago? What reasons can you think of for the increased concern about it?
2. Compare the reasons for poverty in urban and rural areas.
3. Why is less attention paid today to the distinction between the deserving and undeserving poor?
4. Do you think that the present system of welfare has encouraged migration?
5. How would a negative income tax or guaranteed annual income scheme work? Could a family pay an income tax one year and receive a negative tax the next?

Case for Decision

In the early months of the Nixon administration, a difference of opinion arose among top administration officials over how to change the existing system of welfare payments. Those with the activist view associated with Secretary Finch of the Department of Health, Education, and Welfare preferred scrapping the existing system and establishing a Family Security System (FSS). The FSS would be similar to proposals for a negative income tax. It would provide a minimum income of $1,500 for a family of four with no earnings. Any earnings, up to $3,000, would reduce this grant by half. (For a family of seven, earnings could be $4,800.)

In this view, the existing arrangements are a hodge-podge built on emergency measures taken during the great depression. The FSS would provide incentives for the 6 or 7 million "working poor" to earn incomes, while providing a basic minimum income. It was hoped that it could prevent the breakup of homes by the father's leaving in order to make his family eligible for Aid to Families of Dependent Children. It would put welfare money directly into the hands of the poor, who would be responsible for using it.

FSS payments would be higher than payments under AFDC in about a third of the states but lower than payments in a few states, such as New York and Massachusetts. The latter states could supplement the federal payments if they wished. Such states would obtain some financial relief by the federal government's paying a federal minimum of $50 for the blind, aged, and disabled. FSS would add $1.6 billion to welfare costs.

Proponents of the other view, called the conservative view and associated with Dr. Arthur Burns, the President's economic adviser, favored reforming existing plans in which administration remains with the states and the states contribute. In this view, however, a plan of revenue sharing by the federal government with the states, and federally financed programs of job training and day-care centers, would be added.

Those holding the conservative view believed that a guaranteed minimum income could reduce incentives to be self-supporting and that providing training and centers for children of working mothers would reduce the number of families on relief. Although growth of jobs would be relied on, the AFDC grants would be enlarged to a federal minimum of $40 per month and grants to the blind, aged, and disabled to $65. The national average AFDC payment was $42, but payments varied in different states from $8.50 to $65. This proposal also favored AFDC payments to families headed by unemployed males, which were ineligible in many states.

In your view, what are the pros and cons of these two proposals?

Part 7
The United States
and the World Economy

20
The World Economy

American individuals and companies transact business with others throughout the world. Essentially, there is no difference in the economic principles applicable to a transaction between a buyer in Buffalo, New York, and a seller in Niagara Falls, New York, and another transaction between the same buyer and a seller in Niagara Falls, Ontario. But there are enough differences in institutional arrangements and in popular attitudes toward foreign trade that these differences should be noted. The whole world can be viewed as a single economy, so long as trade, investment, and immigration are allowed to take place with a reasonable degree of freedom. In fact, many of the differences between domestic trade and international trade stem from the greater degree of restrictions and natural difficulties to these free movements across national boundaries.

Since everyone has a national viewpoint from which he sees the world economy, this chapter could also be titled "America in the World Economy." Most of the ensuing discussion relates to the relative importance of the United States as a world economic power and to economic problems that arise because of this country's extensive participation in the world economy.

AMERICAN FOREIGN TRADE

The sheer size of the American economy puts the United States in an almost unique position with respect to other countries. With a gross national product of over $900 billion, even if the United States imports commodities equal to only about 4 percent or 5 percent of this total, these imports represent very important export sales for industries in many other countries. American imports of commodities (exclusive of purchases of services) exceeded $36 billion in 1969, and exports were over $37 billion.

The Importance of Trade to Other Countries

Some other countries produce extensively for export and, by the same token, use the proceeds to purchase imports of raw materials and consumer goods. The importance of foreign trade to a few countries is shown in Table 20-1.

The United States is the principal customer for the exports of many countries, such as the coffee of Brazil, the bananas of the Central American Republics, and crude oil from several countries. Similarly, the United States is the principal supplier of many items for a long list of importing countries. Only a relatively small decline in American purchases of some important product can represent a serious problem for the exporting nations.

Table 20-1

Foreign Trade and Gross National Product, Selected Countries, 1967

		Percentage of GNP	
Country	GNP °	Exports	Imports
Belgium	$ 19.5	36	36
West Germany	121.0	22	19
Netherlands	22.7	42	43
Canada	57.3	23	22
Norway	8.3	42	43
South Africa	13.1	25	25
United Kingdom	108.8	18	19
United States	803.9	5	5

° In billions of United States dollars.

Source: U.S. Bureau of the Census, *Statistical Abstract of the United States*, 1969, pp. 832–835.

The importance of exports to the United States for several selected countries is summarized in Table 20-2, which compares the gross national product to such exports for eight countries in 1968. As much as 10.4 percent of Venezuela's gross national product was exported to the United States, mostly as petroleum and petroleum products, and 12.4 percent of Canada's GNP was sold to the United States. Although the relative dependence was much less for several other countires, it can be seen, for

Table 20-2

U.S. Imports from and GNP of Selected Countries, 1968

(Millions of Dollars)

Country	U.S. Imports	GNP	Percentage of Imports to GNP
Canada	$9,007	$ 72,800	12.4
Japan	4,057	141,900	2.9
Venezuela	950	9,100	10.4
Brazil	670	77,700	.9
Mexico	913	26,700	3.4
United Kingdom	2,055	86,200	2.4
Italy	1,102	74,800	1.5
West Germany	2,720	132,200	2.0

Source: U.S. Department of Commerce, "United States Foreign Trade Annual," *Overseas Business Reports*, March, 1969; *Foreign Economic Trends, passim.*

example, that a drop of 10 percent in American imports from West Germany would have reduced such export sales by nearly $300 million.

The Importance of Trade to the United States

The relatively small percentages of total output exported and of total supplies imported should not suggest that foreign trade is unimportant to the United States. In a way, the small percentages are the accidental result of the fact that the United States is a very large country, with free trade within its borders. If the states of the Union had retained sovereignty and control over trade, a great deal of the trade across state lines would be foreign trade rather than domestic. In contrast, if Europe were a single nation, much of the foreign trade of the present nations would be domestic.

In another respect, foreign trade is important to the United States. On the one hand, imports provide cheaper sources of supply than domestic production—otherwise the imports would not be purchased. Sometimes the degree of cheapness is so great that the entire supply is imported, as in the case of coffee or bananas. In other cases, some purchasers can buy more cheaply abroad, others at home. This is often because of location, those buyers located along national borders or the ocean being able to buy more cheaply abroad. As a result of these economies, consumers can obtain wanted goods more cheaply and producers can obtain raw materials more economically. On the other hand, exports constitute an important fraction of total output in many American industries, allowing American manufacturers and farmers to sell in a larger market than the domestic market alone, and providing employment to many of the labor force. A few representative figures to illustrate this situation are shown in Table 20-3. It may be observed that pulpmill products appear on both lists, exports and imports, as do other articles not listed here. It follows that market forces lead some producers to export part of their output, while some users import some of their purchases.

Since exports amount to about 5 percent of total American output, on the average exports provide roughly 5 percent of total employment; the Bureau of Labor Statistics has estimated the figure to be 4.7 percent in 1965. By broad categories, the percentage is as high as 11.5 percent in agriculture, forestry, and fisheries, 11.1 percent in mining, and 6.8 percent in all manufacturing.[1]

Although they may appear at first glance to be formidable collections of statistics, Tables 20-4 and 20-5 contain some revealing information about the nature and importance of American foreign trade. A little study of these figures illustrates several facts. The bulk of the trade with other countries is not in agricultural products, whether viewed as imports or as exports. About a sixth of the exports are agricultural and, perhaps surprisingly, only about a tenth of the imports are of this type (a more detailed breakdown of the "other" category might change these proportions somewhat). However, a large part of the nonagricultural imports are raw materials and natural resources, such as petroleum and tin. Nevertheless, a large fraction of American imports consists of manufactured goods, similar to the types commonly made also in this country, such as machin-

[1] U.S. Department of Labor, *Monthly Labor Review,* December, 1967, pp. 13–14.

Table 20-3
Exports as Percentages of Output and
Imports as Percentages of New Supply, 1966

	Exports (Millions of Dollars)	Percentage of Output
Cash grains	$3,549	29
Sulfur	79	39
Bituminous coal	458	19
Milled rice and byproducts	229	51
Construction and mining machinery	1,150	26
Aircraft	766	12
Pens and mechanical pencils	26	13
Pulpmill products	225	27

	Imports (Millions of Dollars)	Percentage of New Supply
Bananas and plantains	$ 181	100
Coffee	1,067	100
Cocoa beans	122	100
Tea	57	100
Crude rubber	181	100
Fish and shellfish	421	53
Iron ores and concentrates	462	35
Manganese ores and concentrates	78	96
Sugar and byproducts	534	20
Pulpmill products	425	33
Ceramic tile	28	16

Source: U.S. Bureau of the Census, *Statistical Abstract of the United States,* 1969, pp. 803–804.

ery and transportation equipment. These figures illustrate a commonly overlooked fact about trade, that it takes place not mainly between unlike nations but rather between advanced nations. For example, over half of American exports go to Canada and Western Europe, and many of the imports from these countries are broadly similar to the goods exported. It is true that American agricultural exports to these areas were $2,105 million in 1968 and imports from them were only $351 million. But exports of machinery were $4,824 million to these areas and imports of machinery from them were $2,248 million while exports of motor vehicles were $2,245 million and imports totaled $1,622 million. As nations develop and specialize, they find more commodities to exchange with each other.

If all the exports of all countries are added up without regard to their destinations, the important role of the United States in world trade is demonstrated. The United States is by far the largest exporter (as it is equally the largest importer) in spite of the relative unimportance of exports in gross national product. The 5 percent of gross national product exported by the United States represents 13 percent of total world exports. Although the United Kingdom exports 12 percent of its gross national product, this amount is only 8 percent of world exports and is exceeded by West Germany's share of 9 percent. Because of their small size, of course, some of the other heavily exporting nations have small shares of the total: the Netherlands, 3.5 percent; Belgium-Luxembourg, 3.2 percent; and Norway, 1 percent.

The U.S. Balance of Payments

Every transaction between a resident of the United States and a resident of another country requires that one of them pay the other, either immediately or after a credit period. The great number of transactions that occur in a given period of time gives rise to a large total of payments in each direction—from Americans and to Americans. These transactions may be classified and added together in order to summarize the financial effects of foreign trade and financial transactions, such as loans. The

Table 20-4
American Exports of Leading Commodities, by Areas, 1968
(Millions of Dollars)

	Can-ada	Ameri-can Re-publics	Western Europe	Far East	Other Areas	Total
Exports, total	$8,074	$4,704	$11,147	$6,538	$4,197	$34,660
Agricultural °	433	292	1,672	1,866	457	4,720
Grains and preparations	131	241	634	1,144	313	2,463
Fruits, nuts, vegetables	208	40	144	44	28	464
Tobacco, unmanufactured	4	5	366	106	43	524
Soybeans	77	6	433	260	34	810
Cotton	13	....	95	312	39	459
Nonagricultural °	6,140	3,476	6,579	3,177	2,722	22,094
Ores and scrap, metal	98	34	248	204	3	587
Coal, coke, and briquettes	154	40	154	172	4	524
Petroleum products	61	74	131	130	53	449
Chemicals	462	624	1,184	625	394	3,289
Machinery	2,221	1,509	2,603	1,239	1,250	8,822
Motor vehicles	2,081	429	164	109	274	3,057
Aircraft	270	219	876	212	327	1,904
Pulp, paper, and products	105	155	337	124	103	824
Metals and manufactures	564	320	714	314	204	2,116
Textile yarn, fabrics, articles	124	72	168	48	110	522
Other agricultural and non-agricultural	1,501	936	2,896	1,495	1,018	7,846

° Total of items listed only.

Source: U.S. Bureau of the Census, *Statistical Abstract of the United States*, 1969, p. 805.

Table 20-5
American Imports of Leading Commodities, by Areas, 1968
(Millions of Dollars)

	Canada	American Republics	Western Europe	Far East	Other Areas	Total
Imports, total	$9,007	$4,308	$10,142	$6,556	$3,239	$33,252
Agricultural °	77	1,663	316	339	784	3,179
Meats and preparations	48	174	186	3	335	746
Fruits, nuts, vegetables	29	327	129	135	33	653
Coffee	......	769	....	41	330	1,140
Sugar	......	393	1	160	86	640
Nonagricultural °	6,959	1,847	6,197	3,324	1,560	19,887
Alcoholic beverages	157	4	459	3	3	626
Pulp, paper, and products	1,284	3	99	19	9	1,414
Ores and scrap, metal	485	220	19	26	258	1,008
Petroleum	433	507	4	52	312	1,308
Petroleum products	19	456	94	......	468	1,037
Chemicals	292	76	523	103	141	1,135
Machinery	932	53	1,705	1,069	17	3,776
Transportation equipment	2,352	2	1,527	330	4	4,215
Iron and steel mill products	192	45	884	815	26	1,962
Nonferrous metals	629	325	484	224	150	1,812
Textile yarn, fabrics, articles	22	34	324	548	35	963
Fish	162	122	75	135	137	631
Other agricultural and nonagricultural	1,971	798	3,629	2,893	895	10,186

° Total of items listed only.

Source: U.S. Bureau of the Census, *Statistical Abstract of the United States*, 1969, p. 806.

summary takes the form of a *balance of payments* for the nation being studied. It might be noted that the balance of payments is not unique to nations or to international trade. Every individual, household, and business has a balance of payments. It is simply a list, on the one hand, of all the sources of funds such as income of various types and borrowings, and on the other hand, of all uses of funds such as expenditures and purchases of investments.

The balance of payments of the United States in 1969 is shown in Table 20-6 in abbreviated form.[2] Only the broadest categories of transactions are used. Under the credits column are those transactions that require foreigners to pay Americans, and under the debits column are all those transactions that require Americans to pay foreigners. It is clear that Americans must be paid for exports of American goods and that Americans must pay for imports of foreign goods. Besides tangible goods, services of various kinds are also bought and sold; some of these will be

[2] The deficit is the balance on liquidity basis. On the official settlements basis the deficit is smaller.

Table 20-6
U.S. Balance of Payments, 1969
(Millions of Dollars)

Credits		*Debits*	
Exports of goods and services	$55,514	Imports of goods and services	$53,564
(Balance on goods and services	1,949)		
		Remittances and pensions	1,190
(Balance on current account	759)		
		U.S. government grants and loans, net	3,828
Foreign capital flow, net	4,146	U.S. private capital flow, net	5,374
		Errors and unrecorded	2,924
Deficit	7,220		
Total	$66,880	Total	$66,880

Source: *Federal Reserve Bulletin*, July, 1970, p. A-72.

examined in a moment. In 1969 Americans sold abroad goods and services in excess of those purchased to the extent of $1,949 million. Some payments are made abroad that are not payments for goods and services but are similar to domestic transfer payments in that they merely transfer purchasing power. Some of these are remittances from immigrants to their families or similar gifts, and some are pensions; in total, such payments put over a billion dollars into the hands of those residing abroad in 1969. The remaining balance on *current account* was $759 million. The current account includes only current transactions, in contrast to capital transactions, such as loans and investments in which capital is invested in another country.

The significance of the deficit of about $7.2 billion requires comment later, but it should be noted that logic requires this deficit to be financed in some manner. The balance of payments shows that, in the aggregate, foreigners receive claims on Americans for $7.2 billion more than Americans received on foreigners.[3] To the extent that these claims were not settled in 1969, they remained outstanding and represented debts of Americans to foreigners.

An appreciable amount of the international transactions shown in the balance of payments relates to movements of funds as grants, loans, and investments. These are shown on a net basis, partly for simplicity and partly because there are few foreign governmental grants and loans to the United States. The $3.8 billion of grants and loans by the U.S. government is after repayments on prior loans by foreign governments. American investors may purchase securities and real property abroad, as they may sell such assets back to foreigners. In 1969 new purchases of securities (portfolio investments) and real property exceeded sales by the $5.4 billion shown. Similarly, foreign investors may buy American securities and

[3] The term foreigner is used for the sake of brevity. It represents persons and businesses and governments residing abroad, regardless of nationality.

Table 20-7

Exports and Imports of Goods and Services, 1969

(Millions of Dollars)

	Exports	*Imports*
Merchandise	$36,473	$35,835
Military	1,515	4,850
Transportation	3,131	3,608
Travel	2,058	3,390
Investment income	8,838	4,463
Other services	3,498	1,419
Total	$55,514	$53,564

Source: *Federal Reserve Bulletin,* July, 1970, p. A-72.

properties, as well as sell them back to Americans; the net purchases by foreigners in 1969 were $4.1 billion.

Many international transactions are estimated, with the result that the accounts do not balance until a correction is made for errors and omissions ($2.9 billion in 1969). For example, the amount spent by tourists abroad is estimated from a small sample of tourists each year. Financial transactions made this figure unusually large in 1969.

A clearer picture of the flow of payments to and from Americans is obtained by breaking down the exports and imports of goods and services. This is done in Table 20-7, which shows that roughly a third of exports and imports are not related to merchandise sales and purchases. The military exports represent receipts by the federal government for sales of military equipment; these receipts are considerably smaller than military expenditures made abroad. The exports of transportation are the sales of shipping services to foreigners and are about equal to American imports of these services. Americans spend nearly twice as much on foreign travel as foreigners spend on travel in America. These sums include expenditures for food, lodging, and other things as well as transportation. Investment income is interest, dividends, and profits from investments abroad. It may be seen that Americans collect about two times as much from investments held abroad as is paid to foreigners from investments in the United States.

One way of summarizing the American balance of payments in 1969 (which produced a larger deficit than has been typical in recent years) is to note that exports exceed imports—the *balance of trade*—and that there is also a "favorable" balance or surplus on current account. But American investments abroad and government grants and loans considerably exceed foreign investment in the United States. Consequently, on balance, foreigners have come into possession of several billion dollars, net, in 1969 and in most years since 1950.[4]

[4] In 1968 exports were $50.6 billion and imports $48.1 billion. Foreigners invested $8.7 billion in the United States, thus eliminating the deficit referred to.

INTERNATIONAL MONETARY ARRANGEMENTS

One of the complications of international economics is the fact that each country has its own currency. Arrangements have grown up whereby normally a resident of one country can easily purchase the currency of another country in which he must make payments. These arrangements constitute the markets for *foreign exchange.* In addition, the American dollar and the British pound are widely used to settle international transactions; although they are not used within a country, they may be accepted for exports and spent for imports.

International Payments

If all nations had a common currency unit, as all the 50 states use the same dollar, international finance would be somewhat simpler. This statement implies, however, that the transfer of funds from one part of the world to another would be virtually costless. Before the Federal Reserve System in this country, there was a cost to sending funds from one part of the United States to another. This cost was met by an *exchange charge,* which illustrates the present costs of exchanging one national currency for another.

Some decades ago if a businessman in St. Louis had to make a payment in New York City, he asked his local bank for a draft drawn on a New York bank. Such a draft was merely a check drawn by the St. Louis bank on its account in New York, payable to someone designated by its customer. The customer could mail this check to his creditor in New York City, who then had *local funds,* in the form of a check drawn on a New York bank. Any bank in New York City would accept the check for deposit because it would not incur any costs in collecting the funds through the New York clearinghouse. A New York bank might accept a draft drawn on a St. Louis bank only at a discount because the St. Louis bank would make a charge for sending the money called for by the check; this is why the creditor in New York demanded to be paid in New York funds. To compensate it for keeping an account in New York and for the convenience to its customer, the St. Louis bank would make a charge for the draft; it might charge the customer's account $100.50 for a draft on New York for $100. These charges have now been eliminated by the Federal Reserve System's arrangement of free transfer of funds described in Chapter 12, but such costs still exist in buying and selling foreign currencies.

The dealers in foreign exchange are primarily the international departments of large metropolitan banks. Like any dealer, a dealer in foreign exchange buys from those who wish to sell and resells to those who wish to buy. In a perfectly free market, the price would move up or down in order to balance out the amounts offered and demanded but, as we shall see, the price of foreign exchange is generally fixed by intergovernmental agreement and adjustments of supply and demand are more subtle. To understand the supply of and the demand for foreign exchange, one merely looks at the reasons for selling and for buying.

Financing Exports

The balance of payments of a nation summarizes all the transactions that require people in one nation to make payments to those in another and that give people in one nation claims to payment from others. Thus the balance of payments is a convenient summary of the demand, on the debits side of the payments table, and of the supply, on the credits side. This is so because, for example, Americans expect to get paid for all their exports and for the other items on the credit side—the securities and property they sell and for receipts of income. Since Americans expect to be paid in American dollars, foreigners must purchase this quantity of dollars from foreign exchange dealers in order to make these payments. As they do so, foreigners supply the dealers with foreign money, which the dealers can sell to Americans for the payments they must make abroad. And in turn, the dealers thus obtain dollars for further sales to foreigners, and so on.

We may use an American export as an illustration of a transaction on the credit side of the balance of payments. Suppose the export is a British import, that is, an Englishman is buying the goods. How does he, having British pounds, pay the American exporter in dollars? There are several commonly used methods. The simplest is for the Englishman to take the initiative, go to his London bank, and purchase $2,400 for (let us say) £1,000. The London bank gives him a *bank draft* for $2,400 drawn on a bank in New York, where it keeps a balance, and accepts from him—or charges his deposit account—£1,000. The English importer then mails the draft to his New York creditor, who can deposit the check at his own bank, just as if it came from an American buyer.

Another way in which the export can be handled has a different effect. The exporter may draw his draft directly on the importer if that is their arrangement.[5] The exporter then sells this *trade draft* to an American bank. The American bank buys the draft at the going rate of exchange (paying out dollars) and sends the draft to its London correspondent bank to collect from the importer. When he pays pounds, they are credited to the account of the American bank at the London bank. It can be seen that this method is essentially the same as the preceding one with this difference: In this case the American bank pays out dollars and increases its holdings of pounds abroad. In the former case a London bank reduces its holdings of dollars in the United States. Every credit transaction must have one or the other result: foreigners or their banks use up previously held dollars, making them scarcer in foreign exchange markets abroad, or Americans or their banks acquire foreign exchange, making it more plentiful in American markets.

Financing Imports

Imports are merely exports looked at from the opposite point of view. Consequently, the methods of carrying out transactions are essentially the same. Naturally, the effects on foreign exchange markets are the opposite. When an American pays for imports, one of two things happens. He buys a bank draft to send to his creditor, supplying dollars in New York and using up his bank's balance abroad. Or the exporter abroad draws a draft on the importer, which his bank collects for him, adding to its holdings of dollars while it pays him in local money. There is a supply of dollars or a demand for foreign exchange as a result of the import.

When we add together all the demands for foreign exchange represented by the debit side of the balance of payments and all the supplies

---

[5] Under other arrangements (letters of credit), the exporter may draw on a bank, with the same effects.

of foreign exchange represented by the credit side, we can see that a country with a surplus in its balance of payments tends to acquire foreign exchange. At the same time, other countries are using up previously acquired balances of its currency. When a country has a deficit over a period of years, as has the United States, it tends to run out of foreign balances and foreigners tend to accumulate dollars. How such a country restores its holdings of foreign exchange and what foreigners do with these dollars are questions to explore in a moment. First, we need a bit more information about the prices at which currencies are bought and sold — foreign exchange rates.

Foreign Exchange Rates

Like dealers in other things, foreign exchange dealers have buying and selling prices like the bid and asked prices used by dealers in securities. The exchange rate prevailing for the dollar among dealers in London on December 2, 1968, was $2.3856-$2.3858; that is, a London dealer would sell $2.3856 for 1 pound or he would buy $2.3858 for 1 pound. More specifically, he would draw a draft on New York for $2.3856 and sell it for 1 pound, or he would buy, perhaps from a British exporter, a trade draft on New York for $2.3858. The purchase would restore his New York balance, depleted by the sale, and provide a small margin of profit. Of course, actual transactions are for large quantities and the profit margin becomes adequate.

As a rule, however, exchange rates are quoted in the currency of the country in which the foreign-exchange transaction takes place. In London, dealers quote a price for the dollar and express the price in shillings and pence. Similarly, in New York, dealers quote prices for pounds, francs, and other currencies in dollars and cents. By historical accident, some currency units are worth more than $1, others less. On December 2, 1968, some of the prices at which foreign exchange was being sold in the United States were:

Canadian dollar	$ .9318
British pound	2.3848
Australian dollar	1.1130
French franc	.2019
German mark	.2506
Argentine peso	.00288
Indian rupee	.1326

The prices at which American dealers purchased these currencies on that day were slightly lower.

These prices are for *sight drafts,* which are payable as soon as received by the banks abroad on which they are drawn. When an American bank buys from an exporter a commercial time draft, drawn on a foreign importer and payable at a future date, it must discount the draft because it pays out funds immediately but will not be able to collect for, say, sixty days. Thus, a time draft has a slightly lower price, representing the discount at present rates of interest for the time period involved. On the other side of the market, dealers also sell drafts payable in the future. If an American knows that he will have to pay a debt abroad at the end of sixty days, he can avoid uncertainty about how much the foreign currency will cost by buying now such a draft payable at that time. Since the selling dealer obtains his funds now but loses his funds abroad later, he is willing to accept a price lower than that for demand drafts. On the day already mentioned, when the price of British pounds was $2.3848 for immediate delivery, the price of thirty-day futures was $2.3793 and of ninety-day futures, $2.3693.

The network of exchange rates that connects all financial centers provides a kind of international monetary system. When the system works smoothly, any currency can be used to purchase any other currency at reasonably stable exchange rates. Over the years, nations have tried various arrangements by which to provide such a smoothly operating system. Basically, there are three types of arrangements: freely fluctuating rates, rates set by the gold standard, and rates set by international agreement. Nations have generally tried to avoid the first although many students of international economics believe it would be the best arrangement. Some of the characteristics of these methods are summarized in the following sections.

Free Exchange Rates

If a nation did nothing to set the prices of other currencies in terms of its own currency, the forces of supply and demand would operate freely to set exchange rates in that country. In New York, the prices of pounds, francs, lire, and pesos would rise as the demand for them increased and fall as they became more plentiful. If a country had an overall surplus in its balance of payments, its foreign exchange dealers would find themselves accumulating balances abroad faster than they were selling them. To discourage further purchases and to stimulate sales, they would tend to lower the price or exchange rate. As in any market, the price would fall to clear the market and to eliminate the excess of supply over demand.

The surplus in the balance of payments might arise from several causes. Exports might be stimulated by a good crop year in agriculture, by growing efficiency in industry, or by opposite conditions abroad leading to increased imports in those countries. The surplus might arise because of foreign investment in the country—the equivalent of selling more securities and properties rather than merchandise exports. It might arise because of an increasing flow of investment income from foreign investments.

The freely fluctuating exchange rates would tend to restore equilibrium in the balance of payments. As exchange rates on foreign countries fell, foreign money would become cheaper and thus foreign goods would become cheaper. A bottle of French wine costing 5 francs would cost an American $1 if the exchange rate was 20 cents, but only 95 cents if the exchange rate came down to 19 cents. Thus American imports would tend to rise and create additional demands for foreign exchange. At the same time, an American product costing $1 would cost a Frenchman 5 francs if the exchange rate was 20 cents, but 5.26 francs if the rate was 19 cents. American exports would tend to decline. Other items in the balance of payments would be similarly affected. For example, stocks, bonds, and real property in the United States would also become more expensive for foreigners, and foreign investment here would be discouraged.

The arguments against adoption of freely fluctuating rates rest largely on the fear that their fluctuations would not be equilibrating, as just described, but in many circumstances destabilizing. Many transactions consist of the movement of funds from one country to another for short-term investment. If people come to expect that the value of a country's currency will decline, some wish to speculate by buying foreign currencies. They may either simply hold the foreign currency or purchase foreign short-term securities. In either event, they expect to be able later to repurchase the home currency at a lower rate. If, for example, the French franc were expected to fall from 20 cents to 19 cents, people could gain by buying $100,000 with 500,000 francs and later repurchasing 526,000 francs with the $100,000 when the rate did fall to 19 cents. But a flood of such demands for dollars might in fact force down the rate on francs much below 19 cents; as it got to 18 cents, even more speculators might be drawn into the market. The objection raised is that these gyrations of the rate could be very disruptive to normal trade in goods and services.

Something of the sort happens even in the actual situation in which currencies have *par rates of exchange* which nations have agreed to stabilize. In late 1968 fear arose that, because of concessions in wages and other costs granted following the riots in the spring, French prices would tend to rise significantly. The higher price level would reduce French exports and increase French imports, with the result that France could run out of foreign exchange and be unable to maintain the 20-cent rate. Consequently, many French people and institutions, and foreigners who had francs, began to purchase German marks, Swiss francs, and American dollars. The devaluation that they anticipated was nearly brought about by this speculative demand for foreign exchange itself, and in fact it did occur the following year.

The Gold Standard

For many years prior to World War I, exchange rates among leading nations were determined by these nations' gold standards. When two countries adopt gold standards, their currencies are automatically linked and a virtually fixed exchange rate is established. Suppose, for example, that the United States has a gold standard defining the dollar as 20 grains of gold and England has a standard defining the pound as 100 grains of gold. In terms of gold, the pound is worth five times as much as the dollar, and this rate will prevail in foreign exchange markets. It will prevail because, if the demand for pounds rises in the United States and if foreign exchange dealers tend to run out of pounds, they can replenish their pound balances by purchasing gold in the United States. They can send the gold to London and sell it for pounds. They can continue to replenish their supplies of pounds in this manner as long as the United States government is able and willing to sell gold at the mint price.

The only fluctuation possible in foreign exchange markets under the gold standard is between the *gold points* set by the cost of shipping gold. For example, if the cost of insuring, shipping, and packing 100 grains of gold (in large quantities, of course) was 2 cents, American dealers in foreign exchange could obtain a British pound by paying $5 for the gold plus 2 cents for these costs. The upper limit of the exchange rate on

London would be $5.02, the gold export point. In reverse, they could always replenish their stock of dollars in New York by buying 100 grains of gold in London for 1 pound and bringing the gold to New York, where it was worth $5. As this method would cost 2 cents, they would not accept a price below $4.98 for their pounds, and this would be the lower limit to the exchange rate, or the gold import point. Actually, the par of exchange set by the two gold standards was for many years $4.86, and market rates fluctuated between $4.84 and $4.88. Similar pars of exchange existed with most other advanced nations, as they also adopted gold standards.

Since the exchange rate is fixed under this arrangement, a disequilibrium in the balance of payments has to be corrected by other means. The gold standard tended to operate according to the following principles: A country with a deficit in its balance of payments would start to run out of reserves of foreign exchange. Bankers and dealers would restore their foreign balances by purchasing gold from the central bank and shipping it abroad. Or they might, in some instances, simply use gold the commercial banks were holding as monetary reserves. In either case, bank reserves would be reduced and banks would have to restrict loans and investments. Any tendency for the price level to rise would be slowed down, exports would become more competitive, and imports would become less attractive. In addition, the tight money would be reflected in higher interest rates, which might attract investment funds. The general deflation coming from reduced bank reserves might also lead to less full employment and reduced incomes in general, which would also tend to reduce imports.

This arrangement worked well for many years prior to World War I but later, especially in the 1930s, nations became reluctant to impose this kind of deflation to correct imbalances in international payments. With the increasing use of fiscal and monetary measures to maintain full employment and with the emphasis on full employment as a national goal, nations became more willing to adjust their exchange rates to new levels somewhat as might happen under freely fluctuating rates. That is, they more willingly accepted devaluation to a lower level, which it was expected might then be maintained without the need for deflation.

Pegged Exchange Rates

The system of international payments based on national gold standards broke down during the great depression of the 1930s. Trade was so disrupted by that depression that many countries found themselves with severe deficits as their exports declined. They ran out of reserves of foreign exchange and gold, after which they could no longer maintain stable exchange rates by supplying these in exchange for their own currencies. Some countries devalued their currencies to lower values in terms of gold and other currencies, and others permitted exchange rates to fluctuate. Indeed, some countries established new values for their currencies intentionally lower than necessary in order to give their export industries an advantage in foreign markets. This procedure was called "exporting unemployment" since it tends to restrict exports of still other countries.

Exchange-rate relationships were still further distorted during World War II. The belligerent nations, and many others, found it necessary to fix exchange rates and then to control the imports that tended to come in at those rates. The system of exchange controls, which had arisen during the 1930s, was greatly extended. Under this system, exporters and others who obtained foreign exchange were required to sell it to a government agency, which then sold it to importers and others only on the basis of priorities. Imports considered important for war or other purposes were admitted; others were limited or banned.

In order to reestablish a workable system after the war, the leading nations other than the Axis powers met in 1944 at Bretton Woods, New Hampshire, and devised the *International Monetary Fund* (IMF). The post-war system of payments is related to the operations of this international organization.

As the preceding discussion implies, if a country wishes to maintain stable exchange rates, it must have reserves in the form of foreign exchange and gold. With these reserves, it can hold down the price of foreign exchange when it would otherwise become scarce owing to a deficit in its balance of payments. The present arrangement is characterized by national holdings of such reserves and the important addition of the ability to borrow more foreign exchange from a pool held by the IMF.

The present system of payments is also characterized by the use of the dollar and the pound as international or "key" currencies. Much of the world's trade is paid for with one or the other of these currencies. A Brazilian exporter of coffee to Germany may accept in payment a draft on a New York bank. He sells this draft to the Brazilian central bank for cruzeiros, and the central bank rather than a German bank now owns the New York deposit. The Brazilian central bank may sell these dollars to a Brazilian importer of machinery from France. The French exporter sells the dollars to the Bank of France for francs. And the Bank of France may sell the dollars to a French importer of typewriters from Germany, in which case the bank deposit in New York is again owned by Germans. Only when the dollars are used to buy goods or investments in the United States does this balance become American-owned rather than a foreign balance in the United States.

Each of the central banks of the countries used in this example needs to hold reserves of dollars so that when their local demands for dollars exceed their incoming supply, they can meet the demand. Should they actually run out of dollars, they may replenish them by selling gold to the United States Treasury at the agreed-upon rate ($35 an ounce). In this respect the present system resembles the gold standard. In addition, if the imbalance is considered temporary and not caused by a *fundamental disequilibrium* such as a too-high price level, the country could borrow additional dollars up to its quota from the IMF. Or it could also borrow other currencies with which it could buy the needed dollars.

The present system is called one of adjustable pegs because the international agreements supporting the IMF allow for changes in the established exchange rates. Price levels and patterns of trade were so distorted by the war and its destruction that no one could be sure just what currencies would be worth in terms of each other. The countries participating in the IMF wanted to accomplish two things: one, to prevent countries from devaluing competitively in order to stimulate their own exports, and two, at the same time to permit such adjustments as were clearly required by the underlying values of the respective currencies. Consequently, each country agreed to an original par value, which was expressed in terms of the United States dollar and gold, and to maintain its currency within 10 percent of this value. If it found that its currency was overvalued—that it tended to buy too many imports and discourage exports—it could negotiate with the IMF (and the interested nations) a new par value.

There are 105 member nations of the IMF. Each contributed, according to a formula worked out at Bretton Woods, to a pool of dollars and gold. Each received the right to borrow freely from this pool up to a specified quota and to borrow additional sums under restrictions.[6] The IMF is thus both a pool of foreign exchange and gold and an international forum for discussion and agreement on matters of international finance. These matters include not only the proper level of a particular exchange rate but also means of reducing and eliminating exchange controls and other restrictions on international trade.

The U.S. Deficit

The IMF was established at a time when the dollar was a *scarce currency* and expected to remain one for the foreseeable future.[7] That is, great demands for imports on the part of other nations, especially in Europe where there was great wartime damage and destruction, exceeded those nations' ability to earn dollars through exports. It was expected that large grants and loans of dollars to these nations would be necessary. Some of these would come directly from the United States, but the availability of additional loans from the IMF created a further cushion. This situation did in fact exist for some years after the war. In addition to these sources of dollars, foreign nations sold gold to the United States Treasury for additional dollars.

Recovery in Europe was unexpectedly rapid. Not only were some nations able to replace American imports with domestic output but some, like Germany, were able to compete effectively in third markets against American exports. Other nations, especially Japan, became important producing and exporting nations. Nevertheless, the United States continued to have a surplus of merchandise exports over merchandise imports. Other developments, however, brought the American balance of payments into deficit. These have been briefly noted earlier: large government grants and loans, large private investments abroad, and heavy military expenditures abroad. All these expenditures placed dollars in the hands of foreigners or foreign governments. At first, foreign governments used these dollars to repay loans and to build up scarce reserves of dollars in the United States. As these reserves became more adequate, these nations used some of the dollars to purchase gold and to restore their gold reserves. In addition, they purchased large quantities of short-term securities and built up time deposits at American banks. Factors affecting the balance of payments are shown in Figure 20-1.

[6] The borrowings are actually purchases of other currencies with a nation's own currency, but since the nation is expected to buy back its own currency later, the transaction is essentially a loan.

[7] Currencies for which there is only weak demand are called *weak,* or *soft, currencies.*

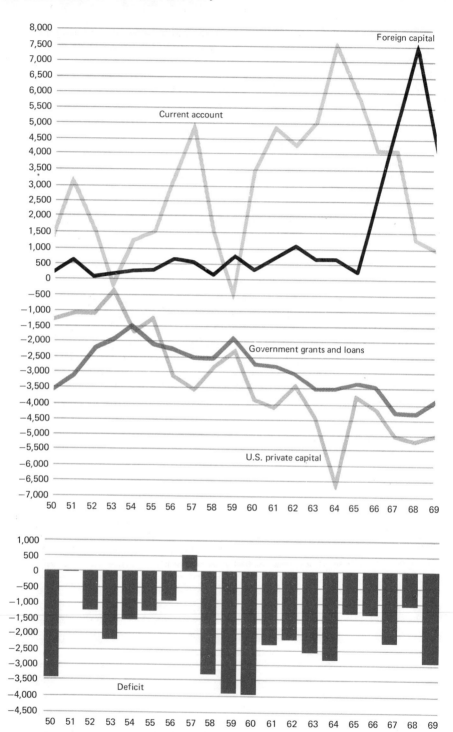

Figure 20-1. United States balance of payments, 1950–1969.   Source: *Economic Report of the President,* 1968, pp. 306–307, and 1969, pp. 324–325; *Federal Reserve Bulletin,* April, 1970, p. A-72.

The dollar balances and short-term investments held by foreign central banks are potential demands for gold from the Treasury. As a deficit nation, the United States has sold gold fairly constantly in recent years. As a result of a huge inflow in the 1930s, the gold stock was, if anything, more than adequate during and after the war. In 1950, the United States gold stock was nearly $23 billion. The reductions associated with the deficit in the balance of payments, however, brought this large sum to about $11 billion in 1970. More important, foreign-owned short-term deposits and securities continued to rise, so that they became considerably larger than the gold stock, as shown in Figure 20-2.

At times, this relationship has raised doubts as to the ability of the United States to maintain the $35 price for gold or, what amounts to the same thing, exchange rates on other currencies. Under the Johnson administration, several measures were taken to reduce the deficit. A special tax (the Interest Equalization Tax) was levied on purchases of securities abroad. American corporations and banks were asked to limit their investments abroad. American corporations operating abroad were asked to bring home a larger portion of their earnings, and they were also encouraged to borrow abroad rather than in the United States. Military expenditures were reduced by bringing home families and dependents of military people stationed abroad. The amount of foreign purchases American tourists could bring home without paying tariff duties was sharply reduced. These and similar measures have no doubt reduced the deficit to some extent, but substantial progress probably requires a reduction in military expenditures. An important factor is the ability of

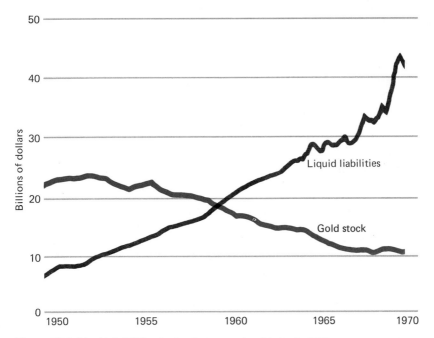

Figure 20-2. Liquid liabilities to foreigners and gold stock, 1950–1969. Source: *Economic Report of the President,* 1968, p. 312; *Federal Reserve Bulletin,* June, 1970, p. A-74; *Federal Reserve Historical Chart Book,* 1969, p. 110.

the United States to maintain price stability so that exports do not become relatively more expensive.

Since the dollar is a key currency and other nations keep a large part of their monetary reserves in the form of dollars, they are naturally concerned that the dollar not be devalued. If they strongly suspected that the United States would have to raise the price of gold and lower the international value of the dollar, they would want to use their dollars to buy gold while the $35 price was still in effect. A difficult dilemma arises in this connection. As world trade expands, each nation requires somewhat larger international reserves. The world's output of gold does not increase fast enough to supply these reserves, so more of the reserves are held in the form of dollars. Yet the more dollars foreign central banks hold, the greater they become in relation to the American gold stock, with increasing doubts that the United States could successfully "defend" the dollar if several nations decided they would rather have gold.

International Reserves

Much larger balances of foreign-owned funds exist in the world's financial centers than was true some decades ago. After World War I the practice grew up whereby central banks of some countries held their international reserves in the form of pounds or dollars in London or New York, rather than in gold. This system, called the *gold exchange standard,* permitted an economy of the existing stock of gold by concentrating it in the reserves of nations like England and the United States. International balances have been greatly increased in more recent decades by the development of international business. Many large American corporations now operate in many countries and accordingly have holdings of local moneys. At the same time, many European investors own American securities that could be sold for dollars in the United States.

When uncertainty about the stability of a currency arises, there are consequently many who may wish to profit from possible devaluation or, at least, to protect themselves against it. Speculators may wish to buy, with a weak currency, another that is not likely to be devalued. Businesses holding a weak currency try to pay their debts owed to creditors in strong-currency countries promptly, while the debtors in strong-currency countries delay paying debts in a country that may devalue, hoping to be able to buy that currency more cheaply later. During the uncertainty over the French franc in November, 1968, and the accompanying possibility that the German mark might be revalued upward, German companies delayed making payments in other countries while others hastened to pay debts expressed in German marks. Over $2.5 billion of foreign funds moved to Germany during that month, and it is estimated that over half of the movement was due to these timings of payments. Obviously, the reserves of marks held by France were seriously depleted by these purchases of marks.

The existence of fixed exchange rates, which can move up or down by only 1 percent, makes speculation more attractive. Ignoring certain costs of transactions and of borrowing money, such speculation is unusually safe. Suppose, for example, that an American company with funds in London fears that the pound will be devalued. It might buy another currency, such as dollars, either for immediate delivery or for future delivery. Suppose that when the par of exchange is $2.40 and the pound is depressed about 1 percent to $2.38, ninety-day futures are selling at about $2.36 to reflect the interest for three months. The company could sell 100,000 pounds for $236,000. If, within ninety days, the pound were devalued 10 percent to $2.16, it could buy back 100,000 pounds for $216,000. Furthermore, a speculator could arrange the same sale of pounds by "putting up" 10 percent of the value, or about $23,800, and borrowing the remainder. Thus the profit of about $20,000 would be a substantial fraction of the speculator's funds. And his risk of loss would be limited because the pound is unlikely to rise in value, since it is under pressure, and if it does, it could not go above the 1 percent premium, or about $2.42. His maximum potential loss is thus less than 3 cents per pound, or $3,000. It has been suggested that if the IMF rules were changed to permit a wider swing in market values around the par value, perhaps of 5 percent, the risks in speculation in currencies would be increased.

Because a nation gains and loses international reserves as a result of imbalances in its balance of payments, it can maintain the exchange rates fixed by IMF agreement only if it has international reserves to lose when it has a deficit or if other nations are willing to hold its currency. The volume of reserves necessary may be considerably more than would be required for ordinary movements of trade and investment because of the possibility of shifts of "hot money" when a devaluation is feared. These reserves consist of the nation's stock of monetary gold, the quota it has contributed to the IMF partly in gold and partly in its own currency, and its holdings of foreign exchange in other countries. In addition, its reserves are buttressed by its ability to borrow from the IMF. Beyond this, in recent years a network of international arrangements has grown up whereby nations agree to "swap" currencies with each other as needed. Both the Treasury and the Federal Reserve System have made such arrangements whereby additional supplies of foreign exchange can be exchanged for dollars when the former are in demand in the United States, and vice versa.

The continued growth of world trade has raised the question of whether the world's stock of gold remains adequate as the ultimate reserve in international settlements. Much of the growth of other nations' liquidity has stemmed from their acquisition of dollars, and this acquisition in turn has been possible only because the United States has had a persistent deficit in its balance of payments. If and when the deficit is eliminated, this source of additional foreign exchange holdings will be closed to other countries. If world trade continues to grow and to require larger international balances, these balances must come from increased gold production unless some substitute is devised.

As a result of these problems, the leading financial nations (called the Group of Ten) have attempted to devise some new system of international reserves they would all find acceptable. In 1968 their representatives agreed on a system of *Special Drawing Rights* (SDR's) at the IMF. Under this system, called paper gold, additional balances at the IMF would be created and the participating nations would agree to accept them from each other in settlement of payments. New SDR's would be issued annually to participating nations in proportion to their IMF quotas, and at a rate thought sufficient to supply necessary international reserves.

The participating nations' governments ratified the plan in 1969. It is expected to work something like the following: If a nation's IMF quota was 5 percent of the IMF total, it would be credited with 5 percent of a new issue of SDR's. Suppose this amount equals $100 million. If this nation wants to use these new reserves, it must exchange them for another national currency. It notifies the IMF that it wishes to use perhaps $10 million. The IMF selects one or more countries whose reserves are considered adequate for the exchange; for example, it might notify West Germany that $10 million of SDR's have been shifted to its IMF account and that it should credit the other nation with the equivalent of $10 million in marks at the German central bank. That nation could then use the marks in settlement of claims on its own currency. It would also pay interest to the IMF while its SDR's were less than the original amount, and the IMF would pass on the interest to Germany as long as it held the SDR's. When the country using its SDR's had a favorable balance of payments, other countries would return SDR's to it through the IMF.

At about the time the Group of Ten agreed to submit this plan to their governments, it was also agreed to abandon the London Gold Pool, which was an agreement whereby participating nations supplied gold as necessary to keep the market price equivalent to its official monetary values — in the case of the dollar, $35 an ounce. The leading nations agreed to cease buying and selling gold in the free market and to sell to or buy from only central banks or treasuries. Since this decision in March of 1968, there has been a "two-tier" price for gold — the official price used when official transactions take place between nations of the IMF and the free-market price. The latter remained in the neighborhood of $40 for some time but recently has been near the official price. The free market obtains new supplies from current output, mostly South African.

SUMMARY

In relation to total gross national product, American exports and imports do not appear to be highly important, but in several industries imported raw materials are much more economical than domestic ones, which may indeed not even exist. Many consumer goods are completely or largely imported, and many American industries rely on foreign markets for sales. In many other countries, foreign trade is much more important relatively, as imported goods constitute a high fraction of total expenditures.

Residents and businesses in one country have many financial transactions with those in other countries. Payments must be made either in the currency of the recipients or in a third mutually acceptable currency. Consequently, there is a system of international monetary arrangements whereby a resident of one country can purchase the currency of another country in order to make payments there or in a third country. These purchases are made through dealers, and the currency consists of bank balances. The transactions take place at prices which are called exchange rates. Various arrangements may exist whereby individual nations allow their currencies to fluctuate in price, at one extreme, or give them a fixed value in terms of gold, at the other extreme. The system now in use requires nations participating in the International Monetary Fund to peg their currencies to both gold and the United States dollar and permits them to acquire necessary reserves to defend these rates by borrowing from the IMF. In addition, there is a considerable amount of borrowing and lending of reserves between and among nations, and a recent innovation would add Special Drawing Rights to the reserves held at the IMF. In the last two decades, other nations have been able to add greatly to their holdings of the dollar, which is used as an international currency, as a result of the United States' deficit in its balance of payments.

Economic Terms for Review

balance of payments	gold points
balance of trade	pegged exchange rates
bank draft	International Monetary Fund
trade draft	international reserves
par rates of exchange	Special Drawing Rights

Questions for Review

1. If each of the states were an independent country, how would the figures for U.S. foreign trade be changed?
2. Why is foreign trade more important than is suggested by its percentage of GNP?
3. Why does the U.S. both import and export the same or similar goods?
4. How would you draw up a balance of payments for your household?
5. How does U.S. investment abroad affect the balance of payments?
6. How were exchange rates set by the gold standard?

Questions for Analysis

1. What factors account for the deficit in the U.S. balance of payments of recent years?
2. How might a country's currency become overvalued? What would happen, then, in a system of free exchange rates?
3. How is disequilibrium in a country's balance of payments corrected if exchange rates are pegged?
4. If the U.S. raised the official price of gold to $70, how would foreign trade be affected? What would other countries probably do?
5. Why were Special Drawing Rights proposed?
6. How is the dollar used as an international currency?

Case for Decision

In the first quarter of 1969, the United States incurred one of its largest balance-of-payments deficits—$1.8 billion seasonally adjusted. At the same rate, the annual figure would be $7.2 billion; the largest deficit ever incurred had been $3.9 billion, in 1960. Government estimates were that, while the deficit for the year would be large, it would not be four times that of the first quarter.

In the fourth quarter of 1967, when the deficit was nearly as large at $1.7 billion, the Johnson administration imposed restrictions on corporate investment and bank lending abroad. Around the beginning of 1969, the Nixon administration relaxed these restrictions. It was reported that the first-quarter figures led administration leaders to consider tax incentives for exports or some kind of tariff surcharges to discourage imports but that they did not favor restoring the restrictions on foreign investments.

Some felt that the situation was not as serious as it looked because, without seasonal adjustment, the deficit was $1.42 billion and this figure resulted in a gain by private foreigners of $3.12 in their holdings of dollars, while foreign central banks held $1.7 billion less. Only official holders can buy U.S. gold with their dollars. Official holdings went down during the quarter largely because the central banks paid them out to private buyers who, in turn, lent them to American banks which were short of funds.

Government reports noted "temporary developments" that worsened the balance of payments. One was a swing in corporate funds. On balance, corporations returned funds to the United States in late 1968 but invested funds abroad again in the first quarter. Another was the dock strike, which presumably reduced exports more than it did imports. (Some imports, like oil, are unloaded without the help of dock workers.)

Secretary of the Treasury Kennedy stated that the balance of payments situation was very unsatisfactory and that "more than three years of inflation and excess demand have eliminated our formerly strong trade surplus."

At roughly the same time, in England, the nationalized steel industry (British Steel Corporation) requested permission from the Prices and Incomes Board to raise prices by the dollar equivalent of about $125 million. The board cut the increase to $96 million. The corporation had estimated that the increase would have provided an after-tax profit of $24 million. The Prices and Incomes Board stated that there were other considerations than the income of the steel corporation, such as the fear that some buyers would buy foreign steel and thus worsen Britain's trade position. In addition, British auto manufacturers had argued that the requested increases would add an average of $28 to the price of a car and discourage exports; the shipbuilders had argued similarly. The Prices and Incomes Board was critical of the steel corporation for not having more specific plans and programs for reducing costs and improving efficiency.

What are the similarities between the American and British problems? What are some differences? Should the Nixon administration have relaxed the Johnson administration restrictions on foreign investment? How should the administration attack the balance of payments problem?

21

International Economics

As Adam Smith pointed out many years ago, wine could be made in Scotland if it were worthwhile to grow grapes in hothouses, but the wine would cost far more than that imported from Spain or Portugal. In the United States, much land is well adapted by its characteristics and the climate to growing wheat, as in Australia, Argentina, and Canada. In California and Florida the warm, sunny climate is favorable for growing citrus fruit; in northern Canada and in the Soviet Union cold winters are favorable for raising fur-bearing animals. Where there are deposits of iron ore and coal or where the two can be brought together at minimum cost, iron and steel tend to be produced—especially if these locations are also near markets. Obviously, minerals cannot be mined where the minerals are not in the ground. Sometimes the efficiency of a given area with respect to the production of a certain item stems from the early start of an industry there, as illustrated by the manufacture of clocks in Germany and watches in Switzerland, leading to an advantage in human skills.

INTERNATIONAL-TRADE THEORY

The efficiency with which different goods can be produced in different areas of the world depends on the resources and aptitudes with which those areas are endowed. The principle of variable proportions, noted in the discussion of wages and other incomes, is based on the fact that a given commodity can be produced with different combinations of factors of production. Farm products can be produced by intensive cultivation—using much labor and invested capital on a limited quantity of land—or by extensive cultivation. Manufactured products can be produced almost entirely by automatic machinery or with considerable use of hand labor.

Regional Specialization

As a result of geographical differences, regions tend to specialize in producing things for which they are best suited, as do human beings. Regions, however, cannot move from place to place, as labor and capital can. Instead of the factor of production land (including all its characteristics such as location and climate) moving to market, the products of a region move to where they can be sold profitably. The movement may be within a country or across national boundaries; the reasons are essentially the same. Purchasers buy from sources in other regions or nations because the goods are cheaper, and sellers sell abroad because they can sell more goods at more profitable prices. By producing goods for sale, producers are able to buy other goods which would be more costly for them to produce for themselves.

The advantages of specialization and exchange were stated by Adam Smith in a passage from *The Wealth of Nations:* [1]

> It is the maxim of every prudent master of a family, never to attempt to make at home what it will cost him more to make than to buy. The taylor does not attempt to make his own shoes, but buys them of the shoemaker. The shoemaker does not attempt to make his own clothes, but employs a taylor. The farmer attempts to make neither the one nor the other, but employs those different artificers. All of them find it for their interest to employ their whole industry in a way in which they have some advantage over their neighbours, and to purchase with a part of its produce, or what is the same thing, with the price of a part of it, whatever else they have occasion for.
>
> What is prudence in the conduct of every private family, can scarce be folly in that of a great kingdom. If a foreign country can supply us with a commodity cheaper than we ourselves can make it, better buy it of them with some part of the produce of our own industry, employed in a way in which we have some advantage.

Comparative Advantage

Adam Smith was thinking about a relatively simple situation in which one person or nation could trade with another person or nation because each could produce something more advantageously than the other. Trade would be mutually profitable because each could get something cheaper than if it were made at home. Such an advantage in trade is termed an *absolute advantage*.

Some time later David Ricardo realized that the advantage that one trader has can be relative, or comparative, rather than absolute. Since Ricardo's statement of the law of *comparative advantage*, the theory of international trade has rested largely on this law.

In effect, this principle states that if Mr. A can produce two commodities better than can Mr. B, it is still mutually profitable for them to trade unless Mr. A's advantage is equally great in both commodities. The same principle applies to regions and to nations. It is most easily illustrated by an example.

Suppose that with a given effort Mr. A can raise 80 bushels of apples or 80 bushels of potatoes while Mr. B can raise 75 bushels of apples or 40 bushels of potatoes. Suppose that the given effort is half of the man-hours they can work in a year, so that working by himself Mr. A could have 80 bushels of each while Mr. B could have 75 and 40 bushels of apples and potatoes. The situation is shown in Table 21-1, which also shows that their combined output could be 155 bushels of apples plus 120 bushels of potatoes. They could individually decide, also, to produce the two products in any other proportions that suited them better. If Mr. A wants more apples, he has to give up producing a bushel of potatoes for each additional bushel of apples, and vice versa. If Mr. B wants more apples, he has to give up about half a bushel of potatoes for each bushel of apples or, if he wants more potatoes, he has to give up nearly 2 bushels of apples in order to grow another bushel of potatoes. (He could grow another 40 bushels of potatoes at the cost of giving up 75 bushels of apples.)

[1] Adam Smith, *The Wealth of Nations,* The Modern Library, New York, 1937, p. 424.

Table 21-1
Comparative Advantage

	Mr. A	Mr. B	Total
Apples	80	75	155
Potatoes	80	40	120

If the two men decide to specialize, Mr. A could produce either 160 bushels of apples or 160 bushels of potatoes. Mr. B could produce either 150 bushels of apples or 80 bushels of potatoes. How might they specialize? If Mr. B specializes in potatoes and Mr. A in apples, total output of potatoes would be only 80 bushels, and it is now 120. Total output of apples would be 160 bushels, only slightly better than the present 155. Clearly, this specialization would cost more than it gains. But if Mr. A produces potatoes—160 bushels—Mr. B can produce 150 bushels of apples, almost as much as their combined output now. Whether this shift is worthwhile depends on whether the two men would like to have 40 more bushels of potatoes at the cost of 5 bushels of apples; and they might well do this.[2]

The advantage that Mr. B has in apple production is comparative in the sense that he is at less of a disadvantage in apple production than in potato production. The reason why Mr. A can profit from trade, even though he is better in both lines of production, is simply that by concentrating *where his advantage is greatest* he can produce potatoes which he can swap for some of Mr. B's increased output—and Mr. B can make it worthwhile for Mr. A because he can now also concentrate where he is relatively best. We can see this by examining how they might keep some of their production and swap the remainder with each other.

A gain of 40 bushels of potatoes at a cost of 5 bushels of apples should appeal to both men. How would they share the extra output gained from specialization? To Mr. A, a bushel of apples costs a bushel of potatoes. He would profit if he could get apples for less. To Mr. B, a bushel of potatoes costs nearly 2 bushels of apples. He would profit by trading, say, 1.5 bushels of apples for a bushel of potatoes. Thus Mr. A might produce 160 bushels of potatoes and trade 52 of them for 78 bushels of apples, keeping 108 bushels. He would have nearly as many apples as before and 28 'more bushels of potatoes. Mr. B would keep 72 bushels of apples, nearly as many as before, and gain 12 bushels of potatoes. With a little figuring, in fact, they can increase the total output of each product. This fact is illustrated in the appendix to this chapter.

This illustration, applicable to two men, can as well be applied to two regions or two nations. By adding some zeros to the output figures and assuming the existence of many people in Country A and Country B, we can see that the two populations can have a larger total output and can share the gains if they each specialize where they are *relatively* more efficient.

---

[2] Note that a bushel of potatoes costs Mr. A a bushel of apples and Mr. B about half a bushel of apples. Hence, a gain of 40 bushels for 5 (8 for 1) should appeal to both.

Cost Ratios

Shifting the focus of the argument to the ratios of cost rather than to the volume of output brings out this aspect of comparative advantage. All that is required for trade to be mutually beneficial is that the cost ratios between two commodities be different in two countries. It does not matter that one country may be much richer and more productive than another or that it may have an absolute advantage in both commodities. If it has a greater advantage in one commodity, trade can benefit both countries.

Benefits of Trade

The benefits of trade are illustrated by the preceding discussion. Essentially, they are no more than the obvious gains in total output that come from specialization and subsequent exchange. The gains from interregional or international trade are the same type as the gains from personal and business specialization. A lawyer has a higher standard of living if he spends his working hours earning legal fees and with this income purchases shoes, milk, housing, and other things than if he takes time from his legal practice to keep a cow, work at a cobbler's bench, repair his house, and do other work where he is at a comparative disadvantage. Similarly, he might be an excellent typist, but it pays him to devote his time to his legal cases and to hire a secretary who has a comparative advantage over the lawyer at typing—not because she is a better typist but because she is a poorer lawyer.

Trade cannot be a one-way street. Basically, a country buys its imports with its exports. There is no permanent benefit in exporting without importing, any more than there is in working for wages without ever spending the wages. Anyone so foolish—if he could survive—would in effect be giving away his labor to society because he never takes anything back. And, as we saw in Chapter 20, the operation of the foreign exchanges tends to correct such an imbalance of payments. A country that exports much and imports little acquires foreign exchange. Unless it spends this foreign exchange by investing abroad, lending abroad, or buying imports, it must continue to hold the foreign money, give it away, or purchase the international monetary metal, gold, with it. The purchase of gold is comparable to the purchase of other imports, so the principle holds.

Viewed differently, imports provide foreigners with funds with which they buy a country's exports. If foreigners cannot obtain dollars, for example, they cannot purchase American exports. They can obtain dollars only through sale of gold, borrowing (sale of securities), foreign investment by the United States (sale of property), gifts from the United States, and selling goods to the United States. It is obvious that in the long run the principal reliance has to be on the last-named.

THE PROTECTION PROBLEM

In spite of what has just been said, there has always been widespread suspicion of the economist's view of international trade and a belief that it is better to buy at home than abroad. To some extent, this belief is probably rooted in the fact that domestic output clearly provides employment and incomes and that these appear to go to foreigners when expenditure is on imports. In a short-range view, this belief is correct, but in the long run imports are the reward for exporting. Imports are other nations' exports, without which they cannot import. But the belief is also based on some obviously incorrect and naïve ideas about international trade. Some of the principal arguments are examined briefly here.

When Adam Smith noted that wine could be produced in Scotland, he also made the point that in some cases the gains from trade are so obvious that no one disputes them but, in other cases, in which the gains are less obvious, arguments against trade become more persuasive. His answer to these arguments illustrates the free-trade position:

> The natural advantages which one country has over another in producing particular commodities are sometimes so great, that it is acknowledged by all the world to be in vain to struggle against them. By means of glasses, hotbeds, and hotwalls, very good grapes can be raised in Scotland, and very good wine too can be made of them at about thirty times the expense for which at least equally good can be brought from foreign countries. Would it be a reasonable law to prohibit the importation of all foreign wines, merely to encourage the making of claret and burgundy in Scotland? But if there would be a manifest absurdity in turning towards any employment, thirty times more of the capital and industry of the country, than would be necessary to purchase from foreign countries an equal quantity of the commodities wanted, there must be an absurdity, though not altogether so glaring, yet exactly of the same kind, in turning towards any such employment a thirtieth, or even a three hundredth part more of either. Whether the advantages which one country has over another, be natural or acquired, is in this respect of no consequence. As long as the one country has those advantages, and the other wants them, it will always be more advantageous for the latter, rather to buy of the former than to make.[3]

In more modern language, we may say that if the principle of comparative advantage makes sense, restrictions on trade do not, unless they start from this principle and find circumstances in which it does not apply or in which the natural results of its operations are not wanted.

Creation of Jobs

Purchase of imports does not support employment and industry directly, but it does not follow that restriction of imports would create jobs. If imports are restricted, foreign earnings of dollars are restricted and so is foreigners' ability to buy American exports. Restriction thus has the effect of reducing employment in export industries, in which there is a comparative advantage, and shifting it to domestic industries, in which there is a comparative disadvantage. While the level of employment might remain roughly the same, output and therefore incomes earned in the domestic industries would be lower.

[3] Smith, op. cit., pp. 425–426.

Protection of High Wages

The notion that "cheap foreign goods" undermine the wage level of an importing country is prevalent but can easily be shown to be in error. High wages result from high productivity, which in turn depends on skill, capital equipment, and managerial abilities. Low wages reflect low productivity, insufficient capital, and inadequate management. Where productivity is low, wage cost per unit of output is high in spite of low wages, and where productivity is high, wage cost per unit of output is low in spite of high wages. Some commodities can be more cheaply produced abroad not because of low wages but in spite of high labor costs.

The proverbial Chinese coolie and the central European laborer in a shoe factory do not accept low wages out of their great concern for their employer's welfare but because they cannot demand a higher wage in some other employment. Their marginal output is reflected in their wage. The American worker does not receive a high wage because his employer is generous but because he can find alternative employment and his employer would rather pay the high wage than do without the labor. Wages are highest where labor is most productive and most in demand; if export industries are the most productive, they are the ones that lift the wage level. To shift resources out of these industries by reducing the level of international trade could only reduce wages. The situation is comparable to the example of the lawyer who would reduce his own earnings by producing rather than "importing" his typing services.

Different commodities have different *production functions;* that is, they require different combinations of factors of production. Some require a considerable amount of skilled manual labor. These goods tend to be cheaper in countries where skilled labor is abundant (relative to other factors of production, which have to be economized). The United States has comparative advantages in producing goods that require much capital investment and in which labor is highly productive. Gains are created by exporting machine-made goods and importing handmade goods. American agricultural products are cheap because of the productivity of vast tracts of land cultivated by a small amount of labor using a large amount of capital equipment. Even though wages are low in some other countries, they cannot produce wheat, corn, cotton, and many other products competitively.

Home Markets for Home Industries

The belief that somehow home markets should be served by home industries cannot be supported without resort to some of the other arguments listed here. On any sensible basis, it is hard to see why an American should be told by his government that he must buy his watch from an American factory, his wine from a domestic vineyard, his automobile from Detroit, or his shoes from Massachusetts if he prefers—on cost or other considerations—a Swiss watch, French wine, a German car, or English shoes. Much of this prejudice seems to stem from a confusion over the word *we*. People are heard to say, "Why should we buy goods from abroad that we can produce for ourselves?" Who are *we*? The purchasers of Swiss watches, French wine, German cars, English shoes, and South American tin and iron ore all have good and economic reasons for their purchases. Sometimes, of course, those who ask the question are producers of goods competitive with the imports.

Protection of Infant Industries

One of the most venerable arguments for limiting imports is that new domestic industries can grow up behind the protective tariff wall. This situation may exist if resources required by the *infant industry* are available but the industry cannot survive a period of competition with established industries abroad. Even so, one might ask whether the resources are not already better employed where there is a comparative advantage and whether the eventual comparative advantage to be enjoyed by the matured industry would be as great. The germ of truth in the argument is illustrated by the development of some American industries whose growth was stimulated by restriction of imports, sometimes in connection with wars. Examples are steel, chemicals, and photographic materials. Some other industries, however, even after years of some protection against competitors abroad, have not overcome their comparative disadvantage, as seems to be the case in watchmaking.

Whatever may have been the merits of the infant-industry argument in early American history or in developing nations today, it would seem to have little applicability to the United States today. In our early history, some inducements were necessary if men and capital were to move from farming to manufacturing, a change involving a whole new way of life. Today industries are well developed, and financially strong corporations need no help in introducing new products if these products promise to be profitable in the future. In fact, foreign competition can hasten the introduction of economies, just as competition from domestic rivals can.

National Security

It is sometimes argued that imports of commodities and materials necessary in time of war should be restricted so that domestic industry can be available to produce them in time of war when imports may not be available.

In recent years the steel industry has used the national-defense argument in support of its demands for protection against rising imports from abroad.[4] Imports were negligible in the early 1950s and have grown rapidly as costs have risen in the United States and other nations have increased their facilities by building modern plants; about 12 million tons of various steel products were imported in 1967. In evidence submitted to the House Ways and Means Committee in 1968, the steel industry pointed to rising imports (as well as rising domestic production), its development of military steels in the past, and to the fact that steel would become scarce in a conventional war of some duration. It quoted a Senate Staff Study to the effect that, "if the United States would rely more and more on importing steel, it would gamble with the national welfare and the national security by assuming that these imports would always be available in the future . . . we cannot allow a basic industry like the steel industry to decay." It might be noted that the "decay" of the steel industry was hardly to be expected and that any relative decline from supplying virtually 100 percent of the domestic market was related to the relative decline in the cost of foreign steel.[5]

[4] The imposition of quotas on imports of oil and refined products is based on the national-defense argument. See "Our Crazy, Costly Life with Oil Quotas," *Fortune*, June, 1969, p. 105.

[5] See The American Iron and Steel Institute, *Steel Facts*, October-November, 1968, p. 3.

While national security seems to provide a reasonable argument, it overlooks many considerations. In the first place, if the goods are non-perishable (tin, copper, and similar raw materials), they can be imported and stockpiled. Especially if the commodity is an exhaustible resource, imports should be continued rather than domestic production artificially stimulated as it is in the case of petroleum. Great domestic reserves of iron ore were exhausted by the tremendous consumption required by World War II, and steel companies have had to import a rising proportion of the total since that time.

Dependence on foreign sources is not entirely undesirable. Trade with friendly nations helps to build up their economies and make them stronger allies. Much of the foreign economic policy of the United States in recent decades has been directed towards building up the economies of the countries of the free world, partly to increase their military strength.

The argument that high-cost industries should be protected in order to be available in time of war also overlooks the fact that this availability could be obtained more cheaply. An illustration is provided by Figure 21-1. Figure 21-1A shows the supply curve of the domestic industry, and Figure 21-1B shows the supply curve of import supplies. The domestic demand is shown in Figure 21-1C, along with the resulting price P. The quantity taken is 240 units, of which the domestic industry can supply 40 units at price P and foreign supplies account for 200 units. If the total supply curve were shown in Figure 21-1C, it would show the total offered from domestic and foreign sources at each price.

Now a _tariff duty_ is levied on the commodity in order to encourage domestic production. This _protective tariff_ is a tax which is levied on imports and which makes the foreign article more expensive. At the higher price P', total consumption must decline, in this case from 240 units to 160 units (Figure 21-1C). At the higher price the domestic industry expands production to 80 units and the foreign suppliers offer only 80 units, all they can afford to sell and pay the tariff duty. Their supply curve, including the tax, is now S'_f instead of S_f because it includes the tax. It is clear that, with the decline in quantity sold, foreign supplies must be severely restricted if domestic production is to grow. Consequently the tax must be heavy and the price rise must be substantial. The extent to

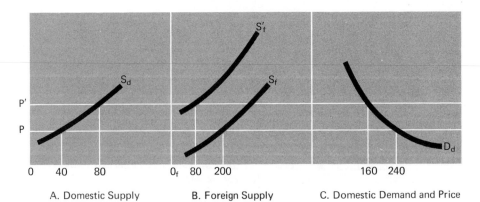

| A. Domestic Supply | B. Foreign Supply | C. Domestic Demand and Price |

Figure 21-1. Effects of a tariff.

which these influences work out depends, of course, on the elasticity of domestic demand, of foreign supply, and of domestic supply.

A much cheaper way to attain the same doubling of domestic output would be to subsidize the production of 40 units. If the price rises to P', the public pays a higher price and gets only 160 units. But the government could pay the difference between P and P' on only the additional units and the price could remain at P. The public would not buy more than 240 units at price P, so price would tend to fall. As it fell, imports would be restricted slightly, as would unsubsidized domestic production. Consequently, the government might subsidize 50 units of output and imports would be slightly less, and total consumption a little more than 240. The difference between this method and the tariff restriction is that the public continues to obtain 240 or more units, the price remains at P or a little below, and the cost of protecting the domestic industry is only the subsidy times 40 to 50 units, rather than the increase in price of the same amount as the subsidy but on all 160 units. The cost to the public in taxes would be about one-fourth as much. The general aversion and tradition against subsidizing private industry, however, militate against this method. But it should be clear that the tariff amounts to a subsidy, and a much larger one, because it is paid indirectly in the price of all units bought, not directly by the government on the marginal units.

It may also be argued, of course, that in the nuclear age "all bets are off" and arguments about sustaining wartime production may be irrelevant. If atomic war should become a reality, it may not matter whether raw materials and war supplies are available or not.

Equalizing Foreign and Domestic Costs

Another popular notion over the years has been that it would be a fair policy to tax foreign goods so as to equalize their costs with costs within the country. For reasons a bit hard to grasp, its proponents have called such a tax the *scientific tariff*. It is proposed to put the foreign and domestic producers on the same footing so that they can compete. But it is hard to see how they can compete if their costs are made the same. As soon as the foreign producers succeeded in lowering his costs, presumably the tariff would rise; as soon as the domestic producer got his costs down, the tariff should fall. The idea is based on a naïve notion of what competition is and what the basis of trade is. The only reason for trade is that costs differ; if all producers had the same costs, there would be no reason to trade.

The real effect of a law that eliminated differences in costs would be to put an end to trade. If that were the intention, it would be simpler for the Congress merely to outlaw foreign trade. Of course, this argument goes back to the one presented by Adam Smith: Where the gains from trade are obvious, there is no objection to trade. No one has been so foolish as to propose equalizing the cost of producing coffee in Brazil and in the United States by taxing the import.

Other Arguments for Restriction

Although all the arguments examined are shown to be essentially fallacious, it need not be concluded that controls over trade always cost more than they gain. The arguments examined tend to be naïve because they overlook the costs and exaggerate the gains. In other words, they ignore the principle of comparative advantage. But there may be instances in which a government recognizes the principle and the gains but does not like the results. If it takes restrictive measures with full realization of the costs in violating the principle of comparative advantage, it at least knows what it is doing.

One such situation may exist in a country which is highly concentrated in the production of only one or, at most, two commodities. Countries producing coffee, rubber, tea, tin, or oil often find one of these commodities to be a very major factor in their total economies. If they rely solely on this commodity, they increase the dangers of instability of the economy. Overproduction of coffee, either in that country or in others, can cause a severe drop in the price, in export earnings, and in the ability to import. A serious recession in industrial nations can greatly reduce shipments of tin or rubber, with even more serious consequences to the economies dependent on them. Lower incomes and unemployment are likely to ensue. In such a situation, a country is not necessarily to be criticized for encouraging the development of other industries, even though these industries admittedly do not use native resources as efficiently as do the export industries. The loss in output and efficiency may be offset by the reduction in instability.

The less developed nations of the world also believe that they are justified in protecting developing industries from foreign competition. Usually tariff protection alone will not suffice to start industrial development. Other measures are also needed. But if a nation is developing its industrial structure with the aid of government funds and loans from abroad, it may also be sensible to protect the new industries temporarily. In other words, where there is real reason to expect an infant industry to grow up, it might be wise to protect it. It must be admitted that several American industries got their initial stimulus in the period when tariff protection was general in the United States. If an industry cannot develop a comparative advantage, however, it is not an infant industry but a failure and resources are wasted if it is kept alive.

UNITED STATES TARIFF HISTORY

Industrialization in this country was greatly stimulated by the Napoleonic Wars and the War of 1812, both of which greatly reduced international trade and permitted high-cost production of previously imported goods to take place. After the War of 1812, the return of imports to market caused great distress to many small manufacturers who had begun to produce pots, pans, nails, clothing, and other articles, and so the Congress raised duties on these imports. The tariff became a sectional political issue in the United States, as the manufacturers of the Northeast wanted protection and the South wanted to be able to buy imported goods freely. Because of this sectional interest, Republican victories tended to be followed by increases in tariff duties and Democratic victories by reductions. Notable examples were the McKinley Tariff Act of 1890, considerably raising rates, and the Underwood Tariff Act of 1913, greatly lowering them. Often the lower tariff rates were designed to raise revenue rather than provide protection. A protective tariff that keeps out imports obviously raises no revenue.

Protection in the Depression

As previously noted, many countries reacted to the great depression of the early 1930s by attempting to keep out imports and stimulating exports, both to raise domestic employment. It soon became apparent that all nations could not increase exports if they were at the same time reducing imports, since the exports had to be imported somewhere. However, in 1930 the United States adopted the Smoot-Hawley Tariff, which raised American tariff rates to their highest levels in history. The reduction of imports by this country greatly increased the difficulties of other countries, which had no choice but to discriminate against American exports by raising tariffs, imposing quotas, and devaluing their currencies. The system of international payments fell into chaos, and the volume of international trade dwindled. Some nations reverted to barter, actually swapping needed commodities between government agencies in pairs of countries.

The multilateral nature of trade was suspended because of the lack of convertibility of currencies. Trade does not naturally balance between pairs of countries, any more than between pairs of people; *multilateral trade* is the rule. An individual wage earner, for example, "exports" his labor to only one or two buyers and then "imports" goods from many sellers; he does not spend all his wages on the output of his employer. In international trade, to oversimplify a bit, the United States tends to sell more to Europe than it imports, Europe sells more to South America than it imports, and South America sells more to the United States than it imports. Each roughly balances, but with the rest of the world, not with any single country.

The results of extreme protection were so obvious that the New Deal administration embarked on a reversal of international-trade policy in 1934. The Reciprocal Trade Agreements Act was passed in that year, largely through the efforts of Secretary of State Cordell Hull. That act empowered the President to negotiate tariff agreements with other countries that would mutually reduce tariffs up to 50 percent of the rates in effect in 1934.

Reciprocal Trade Agreements

Many agreements were negotiated under the Reciprocal Trade Agreements Act, which was extended or renewed eleven times until 1962. Negotiations were carried on with principal suppliers of American imports and agreements reached whereby both parties reciprocally reduced tariff barriers against imports from the other. The principle of the *unconditional most-favored* nation was then applied. Under this principle, a tariff reduction negotiated with one country is automatically extended to imports from all other countries which follow the same principle. This principle is designed to reduce or prevent discrimination in trade; without it, for example, a country might have an import duty of 10 percent of the value of a commodity coming from one country but 20 percent on the commodity shipped from other countries. Further, application of the principle greatly hastened the general reduction of tariff barriers, since new agreements did not have to be reached with other countries once agreement was reached with a principal supplier.

In subsequent extensions of the original three-year act, the President's authority to cut tariff rates was changed to 50 percent of rates existing in

1945 rather than 1934. Between 1934 and 1947, 29 agreements were negotiated. In 1947, under leadership from the United States, a *general agreement* was reached with 22 other countries. This General Agreement on Tariffs and Trade (GATT) represented a complicated negotiation wherein the 23 nations agreed simultaneously to reduce tariff barriers and to establish machinery for further reductions. The signatory nations agreed to make future reductions, to observe the unconditional most-favored-nation principle, and to avoid discrimination in trade with other nations. Under this agreement earlier reductions were made greater and extended to other commodities, so that by 1958 the average rate of import tax on dutiable imports into the United States was down to 12 percent, from 53 percent in 1930–1933.

Most of these reductions had been negotiated by 1953. An increase in protectionist sentiment during the decade of the 1950s made it more difficult to obtain extensions of the Reciprocal Trade Agreements Act, and amendments which weakened the basic principle of the act were added to it. The *escape clause* reserved to the United States the right to withdraw a tariff concession if it were found that increased imports later cause or threaten to cause "serious injury" to an industry. Under this clause several industries petitioned for relief, but advisory studies made by the United States Tariff Commission for the President found in general that these industries were in fact expanding sales in spite of increased imports, and the President refused to withdraw the tariff reductions on their commodities. The *peril-point* provision required the Tariff Commission to determine maximum reductions that could be made in tariff rates without threatening serious injury to domestic producers and below which reductions could not be negotiated.

These amendments reflect largely the protectionist sentiment that rests on the arguments for limiting trade, which have been examined. If it is agreed that trade between nations should be free, as is trade within the country, and for the same reasons, and if a tariff already in existence restricts imports and its removal would "injure" domestic producers, it follows that applying the escape clause and peril-point provision literally would prevent attainment of the objectives of the program. When the injury is recognized as the removal of an existing subsidy, it becomes clearer that the public's gain from free trade cannot be completely won without some injury of this type. It is possible to adopt other measures to ease the transition of resources from previously protected occupations, as will be noted later.

A third weakening amendment to the Trade Agreements Act was the *national security* clause. This clause provided that tariff reductions could not be negotiated which would weaken industries important to the national defense. Besides the considerations already noted with respect to the national-defense argument, it is clear that a great deal of judgment is required to determine whether an industry is important, and to what extent.

The adoption of these amendments at various times suggests that the United States has not frankly adopted a clear-cut policy of liberalizing trade between nations. The shift toward free trade following the debacle of the early 1930s was clear, but the political obstacles in the way of a clear-cut policy are very great. Liberalization of restrictions on trade has indeed been the broad goal of American trade policy since 1934, but the exceptions and loopholes have been extensive. Import quotas have been imposed on a variety of farm products, including oats, wheat, barley, rye, cotton, sugar, peanuts, and dairy products. These have been considered necessary to fit in with the programs to support domestic prices of farm products, because artificially high domestic prices attract imports, which would in turn lower domestic prices.[6] Lead, zinc, and petroleum are examples of raw materials on which import quotas are imposed. Japan has agreed to limit exports of textiles and a few other products to the United States in order to avoid limitations that were otherwise threatened. There is also a Buy American Act which requires government agencies to purchase from domestic suppliers unless a foreign price is substantially lower.

In 1962 the Reciprocal Trade Agreements Act was replaced by the Trade Expansion Act. This act was passed in response to the development of the European Economic Community, more commonly referred to as the *Common Market.*

The United States and European Regionalism

For both altruistic and selfish reasons, the United States cooperated strongly with European nations to restore their economies after World War II. For political reasons, the United States wanted strong nations in Europe to withstand the spread of communism; for economic reasons, the United States wanted strong economies abroad as markets for exports and as suppliers of imports. It was clear after the war that the European nations would need to cooperate with each other to a high degree in order to produce what each needed in reconstruction. As a result, they moved rapidly to reduce trade barriers and to restore the convertibility of their currencies. The United States helped greatly in this effort by supplying them, largely through the Marshall Plan, with needed imports paid for with American grants and loans.

Within the broader framework, Belgium, the Netherlands, and Luxembourg formed an economic union called Benelux and several nations integrated their coal and steel industries in the European Coal and Steel Community, which began in 1952. Based on these beginnings, the Common Market was established by the Treaty of Rome in 1957, by means of which six nations—the Benelux countries and West Germany, France, and Italy—agreed to make their countries just that—a common market. These nations agreed to eliminate tariff and other barriers to trade among themselves through a series of reductions, to adopt common agricultural policies, and to permit the free movement of labor and capital in the Common Market. Significantly, however, tariffs were not to be eliminated between the member nations of the Common Market and the rest of the world. The Common Market countries were to adopt uniform tariffs on imports from other countries into the Common Market.

Political considerations, largely the opposition on the part of France, made it impossible for Great Britain to be included in the Common

---

[6] Quotas are quantitative limitations on imports, rather than price limitations as exerted by tariffs. A quota may be imposed on the total amount imported, on the amount from a particular source, or the amount allowed a particular importer. In each case, some system is necessary by which to allocate the allowable volume.

Market. At the same time, the extent to which the Common Market countries appeared to be willing to transfer sovereignty to the European Economic Community and eventually to adopt some form of political union made other European countries reluctant to join. Consequently, seven countries—Great Britain, Sweden, Norway, Denmark, Portugal, Austria, and Switzerland—established a rival organization, the European Free Trade Association (EFTA). This organization is less of a union and more of a group and goes less far in anticipating a free-trade market. The members of the association agreed to eliminate trade barriers among themselves on manufactured goods only. Each may continue to pursue its own policies with respect to domestic agriculture and no formal union is anticipated. The EFTA countries eliminated tariff duties on manufactured goods in 1966 and the Common Market eliminated them in 1967.

The development of the Common Market was facilitated by the rapid economic growth of the European nations after the war. Had each been concerned with maintaining employment and thus protecting existing industry, it would probably have been impossible to cooperate in extending trade as they did. The program was begun in a spirit of attempting to liberalize all trade and the first reduction in tariffs, of 10 percent, was extended to all countries. After Great Britain's application for membership was rejected in 1962, however, the spirit changed in the direction of regionalism. In other words, the Common Market has become an entity with its own restrictions on trade from other countries into the market and with support programs for agricultural production within the Common Market.

As a result of the rise of European regionalism, President Kennedy proposed the Trade Expansion Act of 1962 as a means of establishing grounds for negotiating trade agreements with the Common Market. The act empowered the President to negotiate reductions in tariff rates in effect in 1962 by as much as 50 percent and further to eliminate all tariff duties on goods of which the Common Market and the United States together produce 80 percent of world exports. The act also provided that tariffs on some agricultural products could be eliminated, as could small ("nuisance") tariffs of 5 percent or less and duties on basic products exported by underdeveloped countries. Another change was to permit negotiation over broad categories of goods rather than on specific items. The purpose of the act, as President Kennedy said in transmitting the bill to Congress, was to give the negotiators sufficient authority to "induce the EEC to grant wider access to our goods." [7]

An important innovation in the Trade Expansion Act, and one that made it easier to gain congressional approval, was the provision for "adjustment assistance." Such assistance is in a sense a substitute for the escape clause. Assistance was provided for both companies and workers who could show that increased imports were the *major factor* leading to serious injury. In judging whether serious injury had been brought about, the existence of idle capacity, the inability to operate profitably, and unemployment were to be considered. Companies deemed to have been injured by loss of tariff protection could obtain from the government

---

[7] Another result of the possibility that American goods going into the Common Market would be subject to tariffs not applicable to goods going from one Common Market country to another was a large increase in American investment in industry within the Common Market.

technical assistance in becoming more efficient or shifting to other lines of output, financial assistance (loans or guarantees of loans) to modernize or convert to other products, and tax assistance in the form of liberalized loss carry-backs. (A loss carry-back allows a firm to deduct from one year's taxable profit part or all of a subsequent year's loss.) Workers deemed to have been injured were to become eligible for unemployment compensation, relocation allowances, and especially for retraining for new occupations. It is an interesting commentary on the often-expressed fears of liberalized trade that virtually no attempts have been made to establish cases of serious injury under this provision of the act.

The act authorized negotiations until mid-1967, but progress was unexpectedly slow. Much of the delay was caused by lack of unanimity among the EEC countries over internal agricultural and other programs, so that it was difficult to reach agreement on how much they wished to encourage or restrict such imports. As the deadline approached, however, reductions of about 75 percent on manufactured goods were agreed on and other agreements were reached to expand trade in agricultural goods and to remove nontariff barriers.

SUMMARY

Trade that takes place between political divisions of the world is essentially the same as that taking place within a nation. The differences are more of degree than of kind. Within a nation, labor tends to be more mobile because there are impediments to moving to another country in search of better employment—but such moves do take place. Similarly, most people prefer to invest their capital in their home countries—although much foreign investment takes place. Although the factors of production are less mobile between countries than within them, it is possible for goods produced in one country to be moved to another.

The combinations of the factors of production that exist in different locations lead to differences in cost of producing given goods in different places. Total output is increased if each region or nation produces those goods at which it is most proficient and trades some of its output for the output of another which is also specializing. The principle of comparative advantage points out that trade is not restricted to situations of absolute advantage. Trade need not be restricted to such exchanges as Florida oranges for Maine lobsters but can take place both between very similar and very different areas. So long as the advantage one area has in one product is greater than its advantage in another product, it profits from concentrating on the product with the greatest advantage, while another country profits from concentrating where its disadvantage is least.

In many instances a country both produces and imports a commodity, or at least similar commodities. It may even export the commodity. This is partly because costs of shipment make the delivered price sometimes lower within the country and sometimes lower in another. Generally a country does not devote a large fraction of its resources to producing an export because that industry runs into diminishing returns; however, in some instances the natural resources of a country lead it to concentrate in one or two export industries and to import a variety of goods it does not produce.

Just as a person may choose not to engage in the occupation in which he is most productive and can earn the largest income, a nation may decide to limit its participation in the gains from the principle of comparative advantage. Restriction of international trade has probably been the rule more often than the exception in world affairs. However, most of the generally held reasons for restricting trade are fallacious because they rest on misconceptions of the gains from trade. It is easier to see the gains from exporting than the gains from importing. But, fundamentally, imports are the reasons for exporting; they are what a nation buys with what it sells.

APPENDIX

In the example in the chapter, Mr. A and Mr. B could benefit by specializing, with Mr. A producing potatoes and Mr. B producing apples. Although their combined output of apples would fall slightly, their output of potatoes would rise greatly. It was noted in the chapter that with a little figuring Mr. A and Mr. B could increase their output of both potatoes and apples, should they choose to do so.

Both men need not specialize completely. We noticed in Chapter 20 that nations often produce and import the same commodity. Mr. A could specialize in potatoes, but not completely, while allowing Mr. B to specialize completely in apples. Suppose, for example, that Mr. A produces 128 bushels of potatoes, or 80 percent of his potential 160 bushels, and devotes the other one-fifth of his time to producing a fifth of his potential output of apples, or 32 bushels. Along with Mr. B's output of 150 bushels, total output of apples would be 182 bushels to go with the 128 bushels of potatoes. Thus there would be a larger output of each commodity—128 instead of 120 bushels of potatoes, and 182 instead of 150 bushels of apples.

Various other combinations could be worked out. The main point is that simply by specializing where they have comparative advantages, the two men could increase total output.

Before specialization and trade, Mr. A was producing for himself 80 bushels of potatoes; he is now producing 48 bushels more. If he can trade these 48 bushels for more than 48 bushels of apples, he will gain by having more apples than he can produce. (He is producing 32 bushels of apples and can produce 80 if he produces only 80 bushels of potatoes.)

Before trade, Mr. B was producing 75 bushels of apples and is now producing 75 more. If he can trade some of these extra 75 bushels for more than 40 bushels of potatoes, he will gain by having more potatoes than before. Let us see how they might strike a bargain. One possibility is shown in this tabulation:

Gains from Trade

	Mr. A	Mr. B	Output
Produces	32 apples and 128 potatoes	150 apples	182 bushels 128 bushels
Keeps	32 apples and 85 potatoes	85 apples	....
Trades	43 potatoes	65 apples	....
Obtains	65 apples	43 potatoes	....

This tabulation shows that if Mr. A trades away 43 bushels of potatoes, he can still keep 85 bushels, five more than he used to have. If Mr. B gives up 65 bushels of apples for these potatoes, he still has 85 bushels left, 10 more than before trade. Mr. B also gets 43 bushels of potatoes instead of the former 40. And Mr. A has more than his former 80 bushels of apples since he produces 32 bushels and obtains 65 bushels from Mr. B, for a total of 97 bushels.

The *gains from trade* are the additional outputs of the two commodities. Total output of apples is 27 bushels greater than before specialization, and total output of potatoes is 8 bushels larger. The *terms of trade* determine how the gains are shared. In this example, Mr. A has 17 more bushels of apples and Mr. B has 10 more; Mr. A has 5 more bushels of potatoes, and Mr. B has 3 more. This kind of example cannot determine exactly the terms of trade. It provides a range within which it is clear that trade is mutually beneficial. This range is set by the *cost ratios* for the two participants. For Mr. A, potatoes and apples have equal costs; he can produce either one by giving up an equal quantity of the other. For Mr. B, the cost ratio is different because potatoes cost nearly twice as much for him to produce as apples do. Therefore, if Mr. A can obtain any quantity of apples greater than 1 bushel in trade for a bushel of potatoes, he will gain. He will obtain more apples by producing potatoes and trading them. Mr. B will gain if he can obtain more than about half a bushel of potatoes for a bushel of apples. Since the cost ratios are different, any trade ratio between them is mutually profitable.

To shift to a dollars-and-cents example, suppose that in two countries prices of wheat and cloth are as tabulated below:

Cost Ratios in Two Countries

	Japan	Canada
Wheat (bushel)	¥ 3,000	C$2
Cloth (yard)	¥ 1,000	C$1

Presumably these prices reflect cost conditions in the two countries. In Japan a bushel of wheat costs three times as much as a yard of cloth, and in Canada twice as much. This tells us nothing about the absolute levels of output or income. Japan may be able to produce a great deal of both wheat and cloth per person and Canada very little, or the reverse may be true — or they may be roughly equal in total output per person. What matters is that wheat is relatively more expensive in Japan than in Canada, compared with cloth.

Japan is therefore *relatively* more efficient in producing cloth, because a unit costs only a third as much as does wheat. By the same token, Canada is relatively more efficient in producing wheat, because a unit costs only twice as much as cloth rather than three times as much. Canada's comparative advantage lies in wheat, Japan's in cloth.

In a real-world situation, Canada will sell wheat to Japan and Japan will sell cloth to Canada. If Canadians can buy cloth for less than C$1, they will gain, and if Japanese can buy wheat for less than ¥ 3,000, they will gain. The yen and the dollar will be forced by the supplies and demands in foreign exchange markets to some exchange rate that permits the underlying advantages of trade. For example, if the exchange rate becomes ¥ 1,250 = C$1, Canadians could buy ¥ 1,000 for 80 cents and thus buy a yard of cloth for less than C$1. Similarly, Japanese can buy C$2 for ¥ 2,500 and thus buy a bushel of wheat for less than ¥ 3,000. In this case the real terms of trade are 2½ yards of cloth for 1 bushel of wheat, but any terms between the two cost ratios of 3 to 1 and 2 to 1 might become the market rate.

It might be noted that these illustrations ignore costs of transportation and other costs related to trade. When these are added, the ratios between the underlying domestic costs might be altered. This fact does not disturb the underlying principle of comparative advantage, but it operates to limit the gains from trade. These illustrations also ignore the operation of diminishing returns. A nation's export industries cannot expand indefinitely without running into this principle. Whether a nation can specialize highly in a given product depends upon whether diminishing returns begin to raise marginal costs before complete specialization is reached. This is a basic reason why nations frequently both produce and import a commodity. An equilibrium is reached between the marginal costs abroad and at home; further expansion abroad would raise marginal costs above the domestic level, and further expansion at home would raise them above the foreign level.[8]

Economic Terms for Review

absolute advantage	protective tariff
comparative advantage	multilateral trade
cost ratios	reciprocal trade agreements
infant industry	Common Market
tariff duty	gains from trade

[8] This tendency was ignored in the example of Mr. A and Mr. B, when it was implied that Mr. A could increase his output of apples by 1 bushel for each bushel of potatoes given up to any extent desired. If diminishing returns is considered, the amount of one commodity given up in order to get a bushel of the other would rise after some point.

Questions for Review

1. What are some of the reasons for different costs of an item in different regions?
2. Why does Mr. B have a comparative advantage in apple production in the example in this chapter? Of what interest is this advantage to Mr. A?
3. What determines the terms of trade?
4. Do imports from low-wage countries reduce the American standard of living?
5. Should a tariff equalize foreign costs with American costs?
6. What is the unconditional most-favored-nation provision? How has it been used in postwar negotiations?
7. Why was the European Common Market formed? How did it affect American investment in Europe?

Questions for Analysis

1. The manager of a baseball team evaluates his players on a point system. He rates Smith at 90 as a third baseman and 70 as a shortstop. He rates Jones at 80 at third and 50 at short. What position should each play? Does Jones have an advantage at either position?
2. How would the allocation of resources in this country be affected by a doubling of all existing tariffs?
3. Producers of refinery products are allotted quotas of imports of crude oil. How do you think this system affects the prices of gasoline and jet fuel? exploration for oil in the United States? construction of refineries abroad?
4. Is it mutually beneficial when New Englanders buy rice from Louisiana? Is the situation different if the rice comes from Indonesia?
5. Assuming that it is public policy to encourage output of a particular industry, why is a protective tariff an inefficient means of doing so?
6. How would the imposition of an import tariff on coffee by Brazil affect the price of coffee in that country?

Case for Decision

In early 1969 two events in the state of Maine were related to United States trade policy. The U.S. Tariff Commission received a complaint from the Maine Sardine Packers Association that they were being injured by imports from Norway, Canada, South Africa, and elsewhere. Under the escape clause of the tariff laws, the commission ordered a hearing.

If granted, relief could take the form of higher tariff duties or import quotas. In no instance of complaint since 1962, however, had relief been found justified under the Trade Expansion Act of that year. Any relief granted would require the United States to negotiate reductions on other imports from affected countries.

The value of imported sardines was estimated as $16.5 million, while domestic production, mostly from Maine, was estimated as $14.0 million. The existing tariff on imported sardines ranged from

6.25 percent to 8.0 percent on sardines not packed in oil and from 10 percent to 30 percent on those packed in oil.

Another development taking place in Maine at this time consisted of efforts to establish an Atlantic World Port at Machiasport. Occidental Petroleum Corporation had proposed to build a $100 million refinery there if import quotas of sufficient crude oil could be obtained. Two distributors of refinery products joined with Occidental Petroleum in requesting import quotas. Other refining companies in the United States opposed the proposal. The refinery would have a capacity of 300,000 barrels a day, and it was planned to produce some 90,000 barrels of oil for home heating and 10,000 barrels of gasoline for the New England market. Proponents claimed that the cost of home heating would be reduced "at least 10 percent." Their proposal also included provisions for payment to the state of Maine of 15 percent of the refinery's gross profit and payments of 10 percent of the gross profit to the other five New England states.

Assuming that imports of sardines were rising, what reasons might there be? If domestic sardine packing was becoming less profitable, what reasons might exist? What is the public interest in this case? What arguments for protection might apply? How might this case apply to the problem of poverty? Why would officials of the state of Maine support both the sardine packers' complaint and the proposal for a foreign-trade zone?

The Planned Economy

The first chapters of this book pointed out that there are many different types of economic organizations or systems and that the problems of what is to be produced, what production methods are to be used, and how the national product is shared are solved in different ways. Indeed, the extent to which reliance is placed on free-market forces and private initiative in the United States is unusual. Natural as freedom of consumer choice, production for profit, competitive pricing, private property, and other characteristics of the American economy seem to Americans, these features are conspicuously absent from the economies containing most of the people of the world. If the contrasts among different forms of economic organization of society were merely expressions of preferences of different peoples, they might be objects of intellectual curiosity, as are different types of art, social customs, or other differences. But the economic organization of society is closely tied to the political organization, and in the modern world there are great rivalries between systems. The Communist system, for example, is not only a different way of organizing production and distributing the product but a great political and military rival to the Western world, which consists largely of countries relying to a much greater extent on free-market forces. For many reasons, therefore, some understanding of how other economies operate is important.

TYPES OF PLANNING

Although there are many different degrees to which countries plan their economies, principal reliance is either on free-market forces or on central-government planning and control. Reliance on free-market forces is far from complete in the United States; as we have seen, government intervenes in many markets, both directly and indirectly, with a variety of rules, regulations, guidelines, tax measures, monetary measures, and so forth. But the extent to which the government decides what will be produced is restricted mainly to what the government buys from private enterprise and to what it produces in the form of government services. In producing for government, private companies compete for resources with other producers and thereby incur costs which are covered in the prices paid. Only in time of all-out war has the government decreed that some things could not be produced at all or only in limited amounts, or set the prices that could be charged for them.

At the other extreme, as illustrated in Soviet Russia and some other Communist states, the normal situation is for a government planning bureau to determine what will be produced and to allocate the available resources to these lines of production. Consumer preference, as expressed in purchases and changes in market prices, is not the guide to whether consumer goods or capital goods are produced; rather, the government sets prices on the consumer goods it decides to produce which will match the consumer incomes it pays out in the process of production and which will just permit the consumption of this volume and this composition of goods.

Between the two extremes are many degrees of *economic freedom* and *economic planning*. Even before World Wars I and II, there was a considerable amount of public ownership of industry in Europe, especially in transportation and communication. Various nations, eager to industrialize, built railroad, canal, telegraph, and telephone systems rather than waiting for private enterprise to do so. In recent decades, socialism, in the sense of government ownership of the means of production, has been adopted to varying extents in many countries. In England, the railroads and coal companies are government-owned and operated. In the Scandinavian countries, many industries operate along government plans, even though they may be privately owned. The developing countries of the world tend to take active roles in investing government funds in new industries because they are more able to act on a large scale by raising the necessary amounts. India, for example, constructs steel mills because they are considered necessary for further development and, for the same reason, builds power plants and other basic industrial facilities. A form of voluntary planning has developed in France whereby a government agency draws up targets for production in important industries and discusses these with industrialists and unions, who can thus see their prospective markets and employment opportunities. Although voluntary, these plans are influenced by the government's ability to channel investment funds through a variety of controls over financial institutions.

Complete planning of the economy can be carried out only by some dictatorial form of government. Underlying the economic differences, this political difference is a basic contrast between free-market economies and planned or command economies. Thus economic freedoms, as assumed in the United States, are interwoven with political freedoms. The command economies, such as the Soviet Union, claim to be truly democratic, and they are in the sense in which they use the word. The Marxian Communist believes that the industrial worker in Western democracies is exploited economically and allowed to vote and exercise other political freedoms only because the system keeps in power the propertied class. That the Soviet citizen has little voice in selecting the political candidates chosen by the Communist Party and no opportunity to vote for candidates of a rival party does not bother the Marxian because he believes that, through government ownership of industry, the worker is a part of the ruling class and thus "free."

THE SOVIET ECONOMY

A study of the contrasts between the American and Soviet economic systems aids in understanding the free-market economy. Since the Russian Revolution during World War I, the Communist state has had many failures and many successes. Many things the Russians have done appear foolish by free-market standards but are not necessarily foolish by the standards and objectives of those in control. Much of the theoretical underpinning of Communist actions goes back to Karl Marx, whose theory of wages has already been discussed.

Marxian Background

It is ironic that modern Communists claim intellectual descent from Marx and that his *Das Kapital* (*Capital*) is the Communist handbook. Marx was indeed a great intellectual who, in the middle of the last century, saw that the economic system then developing was grinding the new laboring class into poverty while channeling profits into the hands of the new capitalist class. By developing and putting together theories of wages, value, and the course of history, however, Marx came to erroneous conclusions about how the system would develop in later years. Marx believed that wages tended to the subsistence level, that labor produced much more than this amount of value, that labor was therefore exploited and, further, that labor would be unable to purchase all the goods that industry tended to produce. He believed that the poor would become poorer, that recurring "crises" or depressions would force more of the bourgeoisie (property-owning class) into the ranks of the workers (proletariat) until, finally, capitalism would collapse in a final revolution, when the proletariat would seize all of industry and take over government.

After the revolution, there would be a period in which all means of production would be owned communally, output would be geared to need and, since there would no longer be any economic reasons for injustice, injustices would disappear and there would no longer be any need for government, which would "wither away."

The course of history in the century after Marx wrote took a different direction. Market forces, along with increasingly democratic participation in government, led to rising incomes for the labor factor of production as the stock of capital kept rising. One cannot claim that the capitalistic world became utopian; depressions occurred, gains in living standards were slow, and poverty persisted. But the poor became better off rather than worse, and the so-called middle class grew in numbers as more and more people were able to save and to enter business enterprises of their own. While some very large incomes continued to exist, the division of society into two groups, the rich and the poor, changed into one in which incomes were distributed less unevenly.

Marx was not only a theorist but an activist and, although he believed that the revolution was inevitable, he also believed that the proletariat could help it along. He therefore helped organize revolutionary groups or Communist Parties in several parts of Europe—the reason why he was exiled from Germany and why he did most of his writing and studying in London. His followers, convinced of the truth of Marxian economics, have never believed that the world was improving rather than getting worse. The vision of the United States and of capitalism held by the typical Communist in the Soviet Union, central Europe, or China is the vision painted by Marx over a hundred years ago.

Another ironic aspect of Communist history is that the revolution, when it actually happened, occurred in Russia. Russia was much less industrialized than the nations of Western Europe and much more agricultural.

There was as yet no large class of laborers and no concentrated group of industrial "monopolists." Russia did not fit the Marxian description of a country ready for the great revolution. But the country was exhausted by the losses in resources and manpower due to World War I. Workers revolted in the cities and demanded higher wages—their revolt was as much against the czarist government as against employers—and mutinies occurred in the army and navy. The government was overthrown and the Czar deposed when a new government of moderates assumed power in 1917. In fact, the Communists on the scene refused to participate, believing that the new government had little chance of success in any event. But the Communist leader, Lenin, and some of his associates who were exiled in Switzerland were smuggled back to Russia by the Germans. The motive of the Germans was to create further trouble in Russia that would keep the Russian war effort weak. In the end, Lenin persuaded the other Communist leaders to take the opportunity of assuming control of the country, which was accomplished rather easily because of the lack of strength of the army and the divisions among other possible governments.

The Early Communist State

As a theorist, and not expecting the revolution to occur for a long time, Marx had not concerned himself with making specific plans for it or with drawing up a blueprint of organization for the Communist state. Lenin and his associates found themselves in charge of a demoralized country; workers were in revolt against employers and government, peasants were in revolt against demands on their food supplies, the army was defeated and scattered and no longer led by officers but by elected committees, and there was mutiny in the navy. At the same time, the forces had to be rallied to keep out the soldiers from the allied nations who were attempting to stop the revolution. It is no wonder the new Communist government had its hands full.

In the first years a principal problem was to obtain sufficient agricultural products to sustain the city workers. The peasants (kulaks) resisted the heavy collections of food products forced on them because they received little in return in the form of clothing and other manufactured goods. Only by severe enforcement measures, including the death penalty, could the central government force the peasants to produce on nationalized land turned over to them and then pay the bulk of the output to the government.

In 1921 the Lenin regime retreated from its harsh stance and restored a market-price system in agriculture, whereby peasants were permitted to farm individual grants of land and sell the produce in the cities, where they could also buy goods from "capitalistic" stores. Although the peasants were taxed part of their output, a substantial portion was left for this market system of distribution, and small industries were also permitted to supply goods to the market. During the 1920s the party leaders were divided over whether to continue this form of limited state planning, where the government owned and operated the basic industries, or to return to complete control over the entire economy.

From the beginning, the *economic goal* of the state has been to industrialize rapidly—to catch up with and surpass the industrialized nations. Differences have been over the best means of doing so. In the early years, the basic problem was how to divert resources from the production of food and other consumer goods to the production or importation of capital goods. After Lenin's death and the seizure of power by Stalin, the latter returned in 1928 to the earlier policies. All efforts were turned to forcing the agricultural sector to produce as much as possible and to get as little as possible in return, so that city workers could build factories and capital goods rather than manufacture consumer goods. The peasants were forced onto collective farms, where they owned the land and output communally, and much of the output was taken as a tax or purchased at state prices, to be distributed to the cities. At the same time, a minimum of other goods was made available to the peasants. The decline in the already low standards of living among the peasants led to much resistance; many peasants slaughtered their animals rather than turn them over to collective farms. In retaliation, the government killed or exiled several million of the peasants. Although agricultural output fell at first, city workers were persuaded to continue working on minimum rations, and agricultural products were exported while the Russian people were close to starvation. But the combination of diversion of labor and imports began to build up the capital equipment of the nation. During the 1930s output rose—in some industries spectacularly—but the iron rule continued to divert virtually all surplus output to industrial development, rather than to production of consumer goods.

The Five-Year Plans

Following the shift in 1928, the economy was operated according to plans developed by a Central Planning Board (Gosplan). There have been several such plans in succession since that time. Until Stalin's death in 1953, these plans continued to squeeze as much output from the collectivized farms as possible, to hold consumer-good output low for both city and farm workers, and to divert as much of the resources as possible into the production of capital goods and military strength. By not replacing, in general, the capital inherited from the czarists in the form of housing, transportation equipment, and government buildings, the Russians could direct most production to plant and equipment.

Although the five-year plans set broad goals for the end of the period, they have been reviewed annually. The Gosplan begins by establishing production goals for major industrial products such as coal, iron and steel, cement, and electric power. These targets are sent to regional authorities, who in turn establish the inputs that will be required and send these production targets to local units. The local producing units calculate what inputs of all sorts of materials, supplies, power, and labor will be required and start the reports back to the regional boards. Here it is normally found that the required inputs exceed the production levels planned for them; thus readjustments have to be made in the quantities that can be produced, in the number and types of additional machines to be introduced, and so on. Eventually all the reports funnel back to Moscow, where final adjustments are made. All the production targets are, of course, interrelated. Some of the coal production is required for the production of iron, some of the iron and steel production is required for coal-mining machinery, both coal and machinery are required to produce electricity, and electricity is required to produce steel. The central authorities take care of inevitable imbalances partly by reserving some critical materials for later allocation and partly by leaving lower-priority producing units to scramble for themselves in finding necessary inputs.

Price and Wage Policies

The essential difference between a command economy and a market economy (from which stem many other differences in personal choices, freedoms, and civil liberties) lies in the function of prices. Prices are not abolished in a command economy, because it must use markets rather than barter. But the role of prices is entirely different. In a market economy, consumer choices affect prices so that producers respond by producing those things in greatest demand and, in the process, direct investment into appropriate capital goods. In a command economy, what to produce is decided first and then prices are set on the goods. These prices may or may not be related to the costs of production, because these costs themselves are not set in response to market forces. In other words, the prices on some consumer goods may be set much higher than the real costs in order to obtain the rationing effect of high prices, but on high-priority goods the prices may be set low.

In an accounting sense, prices generally have to cover costs so that the state farms and factories will have sufficient revenues with which to buy supplies and pay wages. But all costs may or may not be covered, according to whether the plan encourages or discourages production of a given type of goods. In the case of agriculture, the most important prices are those at which the state farms and collective farms must sell their output to government purchasing organizations.[1] As already noted, these prices are set so as to determine how much income farmers will have with which to buy manufactured goods. Until the post-Stalin years, the result was in effect that agricultural goods were simply appropriated and minimum amounts of other goods supplied in return. After paying other producing units for fertilizer, tractors, and so on, any remaining proceeds become disposable income, and this income can be manipulated as the state planners wish. Industrial prices are similarly calculated. A manufacturing plant is permitted to charge prices that, based on its planned volume, should return its expenses and perhaps a profit, which of course belongs to the state. Its expenses would include wages paid but might not include any allowance for depreciation or, before recent changes in some planning rules, any interest on funds spent for its capital goods.

At the retail level there are state stores and stores owned by consumer cooperatives. The Russian worker has freedom to spend his income as he wishes on the goods available at the prices set by government. These prices include heavy sales or turnover taxes, as a further means of reducing wage income to the level of available purchases. Because production follows the original plan rather than responding to consumer pur-

[1] State farms are large state-owned operations run much like factories, with labor being paid wages; collective farms are farms run collectively, with the farmers selling the output collectively and sharing the proceeds. In addition, it is interesting that collective farmers may farm for their own benefit individual plots of about an acre, and a surprisingly large part of total output comes to market from these plots; such sales to city buyers are permitted partly to maintain agricultural output and to provide a safety valve through which city workers can find commodities that may be in short supply at state stores. Prices on this free market fluctuate considerably with supply and demand.

chases (with some notable recent exceptions), stores may run out of some goods priced too low or accumulate goods priced too high. The consumer may find that the store has no beef or veal but that he can buy lamb or pork; there may not be a blue dress of the right size but there may be a green one, and so on. In recent years, the Russian planners have been able to permit considerably greater volume and variety of production of consumer goods, but in the early years it was considered an accomplishment if there was one kind of meat and one color of dress available.

The consumer's income, of course, depends on the wage allotted to him. There is probably as much dispersion in wage and salary payments in the Soviet Union as there is in the United States, but at lower absolute levels. In spite of Marxian ideals about people working for the good of the state, it has been necessary to employ wage incentives to accomplish the various economic plans. Occupations considered important are well-paying, by Russian standards. Scientists, professors, engineers, and others in short supply receive not only salaries several times as high as the average wage but preference in the allocation of housing, automobiles, and vacations. The overall supply of different types of labor is regulated by the state through the system of education and training. Education is highly competitive, those doing best at each level being allowed to continue to higher levels of education. Here the apparent loyalty and conviction to communism are also important, as the state is not likely to support a student who may be a "troublemaker" later. The Soviet youth's attraction for going as far as possible in education and technical training is partly due to the expectation of higher salaries and partly due to the opportunity to become a party official and attain a position of importance.

Wages are also manipulated to shift labor from occupation to occupation. A high degree of freedom of choice of jobs exists, so the state raises wages in occupations and geographical areas where labor is needed and lowers them where labor is redundant. Mobility is actually less free than it may appear, however, as the shortage of housing makes it desirable to hold on to housing even if a better job is available elsewhere. In the early days of the Communist regime, the drive to increase production was so great that virtually all available labor was pressed into service. Wages were held below the cost of living of a family so that a family needed more than a single wage earner. Women took many jobs cleaning streets, driving buses, and so on, and men were released for other work. Associated with this situation was the development of child-care centers, nursery schools, and other means of taking care of the children of working mothers.

The Role of Money

Private banking, lending, and creation of money have no role in a command economy. Banking is a state enterprise. Currency is used mainly for wage payments and flows back through consumer expenditures. Tax revenues take largely the form of sales taxes. Although Marxian theory considers interest a form of exploitation, workers are encouraged to accumulate small savings accounts in government banks and interest is paid. An important use of money income is for purchase of farm products raised on private plots, already mentioned. This market also relieves the pressure on the income of peasants who are enabled by it to obtain funds to spend in the state or cooperative stores.

The system of payments provided by the banking system automatically supplies a means of keeping watch on the state enterprises to see that they are operating according to plan and using their revenues as expected. For example, if a collective farm were to order a tractor, it would send the order first to the state bank. Here, at least in theory, the order would be checked for conformity to the plan before being sent on to the tractor factory. When accepted by the tractor factory, the state bank would pay the order by charging the account of the collective farm and adding the amount to that of the tractor factory. Thus in this system all transactions are subject to the scrutiny of the bank, much as if the Federal Reserve banks were to investigate the purpose of each check going through the System. Obviously such a close check is in fact very difficult.

Problems of Planning

In some ways planning in a command economy is not a great deal different from the corporate planning in the American market economy, and in other ways it is completely different. The fact that the job is huge does not make the difference. Total sales of some of the largest American corporations are in fact greater than the whole gross national products of several countries. Management of General Motors or of American Telephone and Telegraph involves much of the same type of decision-making at the top, passing of quotas down the line, and receiving of feedback that is basic to planning the economy in the Soviet Union, Poland, and other Communist countries. The basic difference, of course, is in the constraints on the two types of planners. The corporate planner must face the competitive market while the state planner is limited by the overall capacity of the economy.

The regional manager or plant superintendent, whether in the Soviet Union or in the United States, is judged largely on the basis of how well he carries out the plan imposed from the top. If the manager of a state factory produces the quantity assigned to him while using the inputs authorized, attaining the planned improvement in productivity, meeting the orders from other state factories or stores for his output, and producing the anticipated profit for the state, he can expect a bonus in his paycheck, promotion to a job of greater responsibility, access to better housing, and perhaps recognition in a party position in Moscow. On the other hand, if he fails, he can expect demotion, castigation in the controlled press, loss of privileges, and at certain times in the history of his system, imprisonment, exile to Siberia, or death as an enemy of the state. Thus the manager's *economic incentives,* of both the carrot and the stick variety, are very great. The difference in money and other forms of income between nearly meeting the planned targets and slightly overproducing can be very great.

Although this system tends to produce great managerial efforts to make the central plans work, it also creates many problems and difficulties. When the annual planning takes place, every manager is induced to make it appear that the potential output of his plant is less than it actually is. Knowing this, the central planners are tempted to increase all estimates of capacity, but if they do they almost certainly introduce errors and create impossible targets. The manager is also tempted to hoard and to hide materials for fear that he may be unable to buy at a later time; what he is hoarding may be badly needed by a similar plant elsewhere. A kind of black market arises in which managers try to locate needed materials and swap them for materials needed by others—what would merely take place openly in a free market. Because, at least in the past, plant costs did not include depreciation and interest, managers would attempt to show great needs for capital to be supplied by the state. But at the same time, each manager is likely to fear the effects on him of introducing new types of machinery and new methods of production. His incentive is to produce according to plan this year, not necessarily to increase output over a period of time. If output slows down while new machinery replaces old or while workers are learning new techniques, his record may suffer.

A seemingly small, but actually bothersome, difficulty arises in the way in which the production targets are stated. If the plan calls for shoes of a certain value, the manager is tempted to produce only the shoes of the highest price and perhaps, in order to maximize output, concentrate on only a few sizes regardless of consumer needs. It is difficult to build quality into the specifications; shortcuts in the manufacture of shoes or suits can increase the number produced. If the manager is to produce a given quantity of hand tools, he is tempted to produce nothing but screwdrivers unless the plan is so detailed he is told to produce given quantities of hammers, crowbars, and so on. If the specification is in terms of units, he can produce more thousands of nails by making very small ones; if the specification is in tons of nails, he does better by making very large ones. There is an old joke in Soviet Russia about the factory that one year made one huge nail and thus met its production quota. If the manager were filling competitive orders from customers, of course, these types of problems would not arise and production would follow the lines desired by buyers.

Recent Trends

Problems like those just mentioned have become more serious, oddly enough, as the Russians have succeeded in boosting output over the years. In the first few decades of the Communist state, the problem of planning was in a sense rather simple in that the objective was clearly to force the production of capital equipment and military potential at the expense of consumer goods. The planners were able to accomplish this task because they had the power of a police state to force both agricultural and industrial workers to save far more than the workers would have been willing freely to divert from consumption.

The diversion of resources by force eliminates two benefits of a system of competitive market prices. First, it substitutes for the price signals of consumer choice the choices of the planners, and second, it values both outputs and inputs arbitrarily rather than according to their relative scarcities. The goods that are produced are those which are relatively scarce in terms of the amounts desired by the planners, not in terms of what would be purchased in free markets. The inputs are those considered available in terms of the plan, and the prices at which they are used do not reflect their relative scarcity. Thus there is no automatic tendency for a particular good to be produced up to the point at which its marginal cost equals its value. Some goods may be produced in quantities at which their real costs are below this value, and the most efficient use of resources would dictate expanding the production of these goods with resources taken from the production of other goods whose marginal cost is above value.

During the Stalin regime, such considerations were given little or no attention. Steel, oil, cement, and other basic industries were to be built regardless of inefficiencies introduced into the system of pricing. No disagreement with official policy was permitted, whether in debate about economic goals and methods or in any other field of public affairs. After Stalin's death in 1953, however, a certain amount of liberalization took place under Khrushchev. It was clear to all that total output was sufficiently great that a larger fraction could take the form of consumer goods. The fear that the Russians had had of living alone in a hostile world was greatly lessened by the postwar establishment of Communist states in Poland, Hungary, Czechoslovakia, and elsewhere, as well as by the attainment of great military power. It was accordingly less easy to convince the populace that great sacrifices continued to be necessary. It was becoming more and more difficult to isolate the intellectuals, as well as ordinary people, from contacts with the Western world and knowledge of living standards and freedoms there.

Changes have therefore taken place in two opposite directions. In one, efforts have been made to "rationalize" the process of planning to take greater notice of relative scarcities and thus of real or *rational costs* of production. These efforts have necessitated attempts to bring prices more into line with these real costs, including recognition of the use of capital as a cost. They have also led to the realization that effective use of resources in production of goods of greater value necessarily suggests that profit is a measure of this effectiveness. These ideas would have been considered counterrevolutionary and held only by enemies of the state in the Stalinist era, but the problems of planning in the mid-1950s were sufficiently great that debate of these issues was permitted.

These problems also led to the second area of change, the introduction of more modern techniques of planning, both in its theoretical underpinnings and in computerization. In the early days of planning, it was not an impossible intellectual task to assemble the resources necessary to expand the basic industries and to parcel out the remainder to production considered less essential. As the types of output grew in both quantity and complexity, however, the tasks of planning grew rapidly more complex. The mere task of collecting the necessary information became much greater, and the problems of allocating resources to the production of the sophisticated types of goods required in space vehicles, complicated military equipment, and much more modern industrial equipment verged on the impossible. The rate of growth of the planning agencies was such that the entire population of the Soviet Union would be required to man these agencies alone in a few more decades.

A leading Russian theorist, Yevsei Liberman, has proposed that planning be made much less detailed at the top, with the central planners deciding mainly the amount, or proportion of gross national product, to go into investment and the broad areas into which it should be directed. Then plant managers could bid for the capital to be made available and provide plans of what and how much they would produce. Capital would be made available to those managers who could promise to use resources *profitably,* and the managers' rewards would be keyed to the rate of profit earned on the capital employed. Rewards would be geared to long-run performance rather than annual, to encourage the introduction of new methods and long-run efficiency. Some steps have been taken to permit retail stores to order goods from any factories, specifying types, sizes, and quality. Clearly, all these reforms depend upon the adoption of more market determination of prices. Otherwise, too many resources would be competed into products with artificially low prices.

Clearly, also, the Soviet planners have come to see that prices play a useful role in capitalist societies by allocating resources along the lines of their relative scarcities and values. It is conceivable that the command economies may move closer to the free-market countries in the ways in which they permit prices to be set and resources to be used. If they were to reach a situation in which they permitted virtually free consumer choice in both the selection of consumer goods and allocation of income to saving, the basic distinction in the two types of economies would be the sources of incomes. By owning all land and capital, the command economies would retain for government all rent, interest, and profit, and private income would be solely labor income of various kinds and, no doubt, transfer payments.

While such a society is as unlikely to be attained as is the pure theoretical model of either communism or purely competitive capitalism, it is interesting to compare it with the other models. In many ways the American economy, too, has been moving towards such an economy in that the relative importance of property incomes has been reduced. The largest incomes tend to consist at least partly, and often to a large extent, of property income. These incomes are those taxed most heavily by progressive income tax rates.[2] At the same time, more widespread ownership of property reduces the extent to which property income is received by only a few. Home ownership, for example, is now the general rule (except in large cities, where most people live in apartments and even in this case many apartments are cooperatively owned) whereas a few decades ago a small fraction of households owned their own homes. There are also many more owners of corporate stock and of small-business establishments. In the last century, while the population has grown seven times over, the number of businesses has grown by sixteen times and amounts to approximately 5 million units of all sizes.[3]

Soviet Economic Growth

The principal economic goal of the Soviet Union has been growth. The attainment of this goal is difficult to evaluate for several reasons. One is a problem already mentioned, the fact that growth is encouraged mainly

[2] See, however, the congressional and public discussions in recent years of the success of some large income receivers in legally avoiding income taxes. The point is not so much that some have been able to take advantage of avoidance as it is that both congressional and public opinion agree that some degree of tax should be imposed on large incomes, regardless of source.

[3] James M. Roche, "Understanding: The Key to Business-Government Cooperation," *Michigan Business Review,* March, 1969, p. 9.

in those industries considered important by the planners. Soviet output of heavy industry and of scientific instruments has increased greatly since World War II. Output of housing and automobiles has increased much less. While output can be added together in value terms, it is still questionable whether a comparison of Soviet economic growth with that of other countries is meaningful, because other countries may be more interested in growth of different industries.

A related difficulty is that of translating Soviet prices or wages into dollar or other units. Measuring Soviet wages in rubles against American wages in dollars gives an unreliable comparison of standards of living. On the one hand, the ruble probably buys more goods in the Soviet Union than is indicated by the official exchange rate; by the same token, it undoubtedly buys relatively more of some things than others and these things have different degrees of importance to Russians and Americans. For example, a ruble may buy a considerable amount of dark bread or tea but be practically useless in purchasing an automobile. On the other hand, a large part of the Soviet citizen's income is communal and, while it must be paid for in taxes or high prices, it is not an additional drain on his wage income. For example, most housing is municipally owned and rented at much less than an economic rent; similarly medical and hospital care are to a large extent publicly provided.

With due regard to the difficulties of measurement, many estimates were prepared for the Joint Economic Committee of the Congress and published in *New Directions in the Soviet Economy* in 1966. These estimates suggest that in the years 1950 to 1958 the Soviet gross national product increased at about 7 percent per year. This figure compares favorably with the rate in the United States and Great Britain, where measures to reduce inflation were slowing growth at that time. However, the rate was somewhat slower than that in West Germany and not much above that of Japan. In the period 1958 to 1965, the rate declined in the Soviet Union to about 5 percent, about one-half of 1 percent greater than in the United States but a bit lower than the rate in West Germany and France. In these years, the Japanese gross national product increased at a 12 percent annual rate.

When consideration is given to increase in population, the gross national product per person grew substantially less rapidly in the Soviet Union than in West Germany, France, and Japan in 1958 to 1965, and not much more rapidly than in Great Britain and the United States. During these years consumption per person increased about equally in the Soviet Union, the United States, and Great Britain. It should be noted here that the level of consumption is higher in the last two and hence the amount of increase represented by an equal percentage is greater. Consumption increased more rapidly in West Germany, France, and Japan.

The difficulties of measurement make a comparison of Soviet and American gross national products inexact, but a probably reasonable estimate is that the Soviet GNP is about half that of the American, and the GNP per person even less. Thus the contrasts between the two economies are great. The Soviet accomplishments in space exploration are well known. Soviet subway and bus systems are excellent in the larger cities. But accomplishments like these constitute a large fraction of the approximately $1,800 of gross national product per person, as compared with about $4,000 in the United States. Americans would find the typical Russian diet monotonous and starchy and would consider living in a single room, as many families in the Soviet Union must, and sharing common kitchen and bath facilities with other families deplorable. Only a few Soviet families, in contrast to most American, have refrigerators, vacuum cleaners, washing machines, and other appliances.

Occasionally efforts are made to compare Soviet and American standards of living by comparing the hours of work required on the average in each country to earn enough to buy certain goods. In general, an hour's labor in the United States presumably reaps about eight times as much in terms of consumer goods as in the Soviet Union for comparable work. A Soviet laborer can buy a pound of sugar with the earnings of about an hour's labor, compared with those of two or three minutes in the United States; he works over two hours to earn a dozen eggs, the American about a quarter of an hour. But these comparisons should not suggest that the Russian is poor by world standards.

Freedoms and the Economy

The way in which a society decides the ever-present economic problems—what to produce, by whom, and for whom—is interwoven with many of its other characteristics. The theoretical ideals of communism include political and personal freedoms and the absence of coercion. In practice, communism has been associated with repression and ruthless dictatorship. Whether a planned economy can grow as fast or faster than a market economy, whether it can distribute income more equitably, and other related questions may not be, therefore, the basic questions to ask in comparing the two types of economic society.

A critic of Western civilization can easily find many imperfections in the present societies that rely on market economies. It is probably a fair statement, however, that over the decades democratic societies have moved in the direction of greater economic justice, greater freedoms, greater security, and greater opportunity, along with rising standards of living. In a free society, differences in goals do arise. Some of these differences can be settled merely through the market mechanism. Those who wish to save for greater future incomes and consumption may do so, and those who want consumption now at the cost of investment and growth may spend all their incomes. Other differences have to be settled through the political process—whether overall fiscal measures should encourage investment, how much of the gross national product should be devoted to military expenditures, and so on. But underlying the process, whether economic or political, is the Western conviction that the individual is important and that dissent should be heard. And there is opposition to the majority imposing its will by force, but even more to a minority forcing its will on the majority.

The fundamental question with totally planned economies is whether it is possible for this respect for the individual and for minorities to be maintained in the political arena. If output and incomes are planned from the top, there can be no room for disagreement. As in a military campaign, all must work according to plan. It may be politically possible to merge the democratic political process with government ownership of the means of production, but one wonders how long the former would then last.

The antipathy the Western nations hold towards communism is not so much an aversion to economic planning as such, because they all participate in it through either government agencies or large corporations. Rather, the antipathy is towards a society in which political freedoms are abolished along with consumer sovereignty in the marketplace. It was an impressive lesson when the Berlin Wall was built; it was not designed to keep people out of East Berlin but to keep the East Berliners from escaping.

SUMMARY

Countries vary widely in the degree to which they rely on free-market forces to direct their economies. The Communist countries plan output and allocate incomes according to national and party objectives. In these economies consumer preference and the signals of prices and profits are relatively unimportant. The political climate of these countries is different from that of countries that rely mainly on free markets, because the economic plans must be imposed, either by force or by persuasion.

A basic economic problem faced by the command economies is that of allocating resources to different uses in some relation to the cost of these resources. Presumably, the composition of output is different from what it would be in a system of free markets; otherwise the planning would not be necessary. Consequently, the values of goods are the values assigned by the planners, and this is equally true of those goods which become costs of other goods. In reverse, the unplanned economies have a related problem, as many critics contend that the price system does not establish the most desirable set of values. The complexities of planning, along with a wider range of choices permitted by larger production, have recently led to more reliance on market prices in some of the command economies.

Even in a predominantly market economy like the United States, a great deal of economic planning takes place. The bulk of this planning is done by private industry, which plans investment programs for years ahead. The influence of government, however, is far from negligible. The economy provides what the government itself purchases, and government purchases are a substantial fraction of gross national product.

Economic Terms for Review

economic freedom	five-year plans
economic planning	economic incentives
economic goal	rational costs

Questions for Review

1. Give examples of economic planning in the United States.
2. How is reliance on free markets related to the political organization of a country?
3. How has the Marxian theory of wages been tested over the last fifty years?

4. Why is it peculiar that the Communist revolution occurred in Russia?

5. How did the Soviet planners use the peasants? Did the revolution abolish exploitation?

Questions for Analysis

1. In what forms might a Russian save? Why not in others?
2. Why is production in a planned economy likely not to reflect real costs of production?
3. Why might American or British producers object to international trade with the Soviet Union?
4. What is the role of money in the Soviet economy?
5. What are Yevsei Liberman's proposals?
6. How has the postwar economic growth in the Soviet Union compared with that in other countries?
7. Why would an underdeveloped country be tempted to copy the Soviet Union rather than the United States?
8. The only two nations to have space programs are the leading command economy and the leading free economy. How can this paradox be explained?

Case for Decision

Recently the prices of color television sets were cut in the Soviet Union by roughly one-fourth. A typical model costing 1,200 rubles (about $1,320) was reduced to 912 rubles (about $1,003). The former price is roughly the equivalent of the annual income of a typical Soviet worker. Color telecasts are received over a French system, but only for a few hours a week.

Under the five-year plan for 1966–1970, agricultural output in general was scheduled to rise about 25 percent above the targets in the 1961–1965 plan. Late in the decade it appeared that, given average weather conditions, the targets would be met. The Soviet Union appeared to be a significant exporter of sugar, cotton, and vegetable oils for the foreseeable future and ready to export grain again after being an importer following bad-weather years in 1963 and 1966. Grain exports would probably be restricted, however, because of shifts in production from food grains to feed grains for greater livestock production.

That all was not rosy, however, was indicated by a report given by First Secretary Leonid I. Breshnev. He noted that "bureaucracy" and lack of individual responsibility handicapped decision making. Productivity of Soviet farm labor was low. Many young people left rural areas for the cities. Allocations of funds for munitions limited funds for trucks, tractors, gasoline, and fertilizers. Some regional officials were caught switching funds from agriculture to industries that were behind their schedules.

Nevertheless, agricultural output had been rising and experts assigned much of the credit to a variety of incentive payments. The government purchased grain from collective farms in excess of assigned quotas at 50 percent above the quota price. For example, if a collective farm delivered 60,000 tons instead of a quota of 50,000 tons, the revenue of the farm would be 30 percent higher in total. The bonuses received by members of a collective farm are scaled to the profit of the farm. Average income on collective farms is estimated to have risen from 1966 to 1968 by 30 percent. The price received for marginal output of grain is considerably above world prices. Supplementary prices are also paid for beef and pork, and the price of milk has been raised. Such farm subsidies amounted to more than $6.5 billion in 1968.

The government has also turned from discouraging to encouraging production on small plots assigned to individual workers. It was estimated that these "private" plots amounted to 3.2 percent of total farm acreage but that they accounted for two-thirds of the output of potatoes, nearly half of the output of other vegetables, and a third of the output of milk. A Soviet economic journal stated that these plots provide people with "a businesslike grasp of their job, diligence and a feeling of responsibility, as well as other qualities needed in collective farming."

What does the relative position of TV sets as compared to agriculture say about the stage of development of the Soviet economy? Who will benefit from the reduction of prices of TV sets? Are there any similarities in government treatment of agriculture in the Soviet Union and the United States? In view of the output figures for private plots, what might happen if the Soviet planners doubled the size of each private plot? How can the Soviet government pay prices above world market prices for output and still be an exporter?

23

Economics and Social Problems

It should be clear from the preceding chapters that, in some ways, economics is a very simple subject and, in others, it is a very complicated one. It is simple in the sense that logic is simple; straight thinking simplifies problems in any field of knowledge. Economics is complex in that it deals with problems containing many variables, a number of which are unknown or only imperfectly identified. It is complex also in that, as a social science, it overlaps into other fields, such as sociology, psychology, anthropology, history, and political science. And, just as economics grew out of philosophy and was considered a branch of that study, economics has become the mother science for a variety of applied fields such as marketing, finance, agricultural economics, international economics, and so on.

APPLYING ECONOMICS

The complex problems and controversial issues in economics often result from man's inability or unwillingness to think simply and to the point. Sometimes they are not really so much problems in economics as reflections of political and social points of view. As a simple illustration, consider the question of whether an excise tax should be levied on alcoholic beverages. The difficult word in this question is *should.* The economist can analyze what the effects of a given tax will most likely be; whether the tax should be levied, then, depends upon whether society favors these effects. One simple economic result of a substantial tax on liquor is a chain of events something like this: The supply curve for the product is raised, marginal costs cannot be covered by the old price, marginal units of output are dropped, the price rises, and a new equilibrium is reached with a smaller output and a higher market price. Fewer resources are used in the distilling industry, and more resources are available for other industries. Subsequent results probably include: Government revenues from this tax rise (depending on the elasticity of demand), incomes drained off by the tax cannot be spent for other consumer products, imports of liquor may be attracted by the higher price, and many others. Should the tax be levied? About all that the economist can say, as an economist, is that it should if these results are desired but it should not if they are not desired. If you are a stockholder in a distilling company or a skilled blender of spirits, you probably have one answer; if you consider alcohol a social evil, you probably have another.

Many so-called economic problems are debated similarly at all levels of difficulty and sophistication. Whether taxes in general should be higher or lower, whether governmental expenditures should include specific projects, whether tariff protection should be increased or decreased, and many other issues arouse heated debate, not because of difficulty in the economic analysis but because of disagreement over the desirability of the expected results.

The difficulty of thinking to the point where economic problems are concerned, then, is often based on the fact that economics is one of the social sciences and thus subject to the conflict of viewpoints on social questions. The following classification is not exhaustive nor are the categories mutually exclusive, but some of the difficulties in thinking through economic problems can be illustrated under these headings: logic, personal bias, and economics as a social science.

Logic

Thinking that fails to be logical leads to erroneous conclusions in any field. In economics, the rules of logic tend to be violated in a variety of ways. A common error is to confuse the whole with the sum of its parts. It is easy to think that "what is good for General Motors is good for the country," and it is even easier to believe that what is good for one's self is good for everyone.

One example of this type of fallacious reasoning is the persistence of much public opinion against the use of fiscal policy as a tool against recession. Although leading businessmen have come to expect government to bolster inadequate aggregate demand in times of unemployment, many people still feel that "you can't spend your way into prosperity." The analogy between the individual, who cannot get rich by spending more and saving less, and the total economy is attractive but misleading. No recession was ever ended without an increase in total spending; aggregate demand, whether from consumers, business investment, or government, became adequate to take larger volumes of output off the market. Any effort to save one's way out of a depression would be self-defeating. But it would be equally fallacious to jump to the conclusion that all saving is bad and all spending (meaning consumption) is good. The individual and society both accumulate wealth by saving, but a vital difference is that, although a person can save by accumulating claims on other groups and individuals, such financial claims cancel out for society as a whole—one person's asset is another's debt. Society in the aggregate can become wealthier only by building up its stock of physical and intangible assets in the form of knowledge, skills, and talents.

Another common example of confusing the part with the whole is evident in attitudes toward protective tariffs. The employer and his employees know that they are better off if they can sell in a market protected from competition. Protection, therefore, is "good." Many other people, actually harmed by protection, agree because they tend to think that the people in this industry would be unemployed if they were not protected. Yet it is clear that if everyone had freedom from competition, everyone would also have to pay monopoly prices for what he bought and output would be restricted since it would not come from the most efficient sources.

Discussions of economic problems are full of such fallacies. Everyone knows that he would be better off with a higher income, yet it is impossible for everyone to be better off with higher monetary incomes unless there is also greater real output to be purchased. Everyone dislikes debt for himself, so he looks askance at government debt, overlooking two things: that debt is neither good nor bad in itself but its uses may be and that government debt applies to the whole society, including bondholders as well as taxpayers.

Another source of confusion lies in the problem of identifying cause and effect. Logicians recognize that one event can follow another without having been caused by it and that both events may have a common cause. People do not assume that the night causes the day or the day the night, but many people do assume that when prices and wages go up, the rising wages cause the rise in prices. Unless the monetary situation permits prices to rise, wage increases can in fact lead only to unemployment. It would behoove the economist, therefore, to consider whether the rise in wages and prices is caused by a third element.

Economics is a field in which "a little knowledge is a dangerous thing." Consider a simple problem in microeconomics, the rise in the price of a single commodity, such as bacon. Having heard of the law of supply and demand, an observer might conclude that the rise was caused by an increase in demand or a decrease in supply. Actually, an infinite number of combinations of changes might result in the higher price. The supply might be larger this year but demand larger by even more, perhaps because of a shortage of some other food. Perhaps the demand for bacon is high because of inflated incomes, which cause the demands for nearly everything to be increased. In response to the inevitable insistence that something be done about the high price, one would have to find out why the price is high. A mere introduction to economics should suggest that the reason probably is not monopolizing by farmers or by chain stores. The shoppers' strikes that appear from time to time are not likely to solve the problem either; they are not permanent changes in demand, and they do not alter the supply situation.

The misunderstandings of even the simplest economic principles are legion. A commonly heard expression is, "If the supply goes up, the demand must come down." Probably every teacher of elementary economics hears this at least once a year. The muddled reasoning may be something like this: When the supply goes up, price tends to come down; a lower price is associated with lower demand; hence, the demand must have fallen. It is hoped that no reader has this understanding of the meaning of the law of supply and demand from this text! Another favorite expression is, "You can't repeal the law of supply and demand." Perhaps this statement is true, but it does not follow that nothing can be done by using the law itself to affect a price set by supply and demand. A man may make this kind of statement to another sitting next to him in an airplane, but he would not conclude that the law of gravity had to be repealed in order for him to make the trip. Similarly, one might change the supply or demand in order to change a price.

Personal Bias

People tend to confuse the whole with the part because they view the world from their own part of it. We each have a point of view, or bias, which we tend to identify with the public interest. Since economics deals with policy problems and thereby overlaps political science, those who have economic interests to defend like to think that they are serving social interests as well. Labor unions show that higher wages are in the public interest while employer groups show that higher wages damage the public. Cement producers and automobile manufacturers identify expanded highway systems with the public interest; building contractors associate more and better housing with the public interest; college professors associate more and better education for more people with the public interest; carpenters, bricklayers, and others identify archaic building codes with the public interest.

Sometimes this identification of a policy of self-interest with the public interest has a variation in which the policy is identified with a political hero. If a President proposes a measure, some people are for it and some are against it simply because they admire that President or dislike him. This identification can even overcome a person's own self-interest, which he rationalizes away in order to defend or attack a personality.

A merchant may approve of antitrust laws for his suppliers but seek fair-trade laws to prevent his own competitors from cutting prices—and defend these laws as necessary to protect consumers. A manufacturer who would object if he could not buy materials from the cheapest source may believe that government should not allow airlines or railroads to grant his competitors reduced rates. A trucking company that buys equipment where it gets the best price may expect to move a family to a new home at a standard rate enforced by a government agency. A business executive may make a luncheon speech to fellow businessmen about the long arm of government reaching into the sacred areas of market-determined business decisions and then hurry back to his office to sign a lease for a plant built, with the aid of tax-exempt bonds, by a state that wants to attract industry; or he may write a letter to his Congressman urging legislation to reduce imports of the product he makes.

A few years ago the Congress was asked to make illegal a new product of the brewing industry—concentrated beer. This product could be used by large brewers to make bottled beer in regional plants after it was produced by and shipped from central breweries. Small brewers feared invasion of their local markets by bottling plants of large brewers, and their trade association sent a representative to convince Congressmen of the iniquity of such a situation. Even the chairman of a large brewing company admitted that the new product could "change the rules of the game and affect the welfare of every member of the brewing industry," and he thought its use should be banned except in the originating brewery. No doubt the same could have been said about the automobile—it changed the rules of the game and affected the welfare of every harness maker in the country, as kerosene changed the rules of the game for whale-oil sellers, natural gas for kerosene producers, and electricity for gas companies. One Congressman remarked, however, that he did not favor using the tax laws to prevent the production of "something the public might want." As it happened, this Congressman came from Wisconsin, a state which, until recently, attempted to minimize sales of oleomargarine, in deference to its large dairy industry, by prohibiting sales of colored oleomargarine (Wisconsin now taxes the product).

The validity of the arguments used in these examples is not the point. The point is that these arguments do not really represent economics. It may be that control of minimum rates is desirable in the case of railroads, telephone services, home delivery of milk, or service charges at banks. The users of these services and the conscientious citizen in general, however, may logically ask himself whether the criteria for these decisions are economic, social, business, political, or some other kind.

Economics as a Social Science

Reasoning in economics is sometimes complicated by the fact that economics is one of the social sciences—a study of society. Not only does its subject matter become involved with other types of social problems, but the solutions to these problems are seldom reached on grounds of economic analysis alone. Good economics might dictate a tax increase; yet the President or the Congress might fear the loss of public support. Good economics might dictate a tax cut; yet the President or Congress might fear the charge of fiscal irresponsibility.

Rather than talk about good economics or bad economics, it might be better to speak of good economists and bad economists. How can they be distinguished? By the same methods used to distinguish good medical diagnosticians, baseball managers, philosophers, and musicians. Unfortunately, the only persons qualified to judge are those who are already experts in the field. But fortunately, except in matters in which taste is important, such as art and music, the experts have, consciously or unconsciously, set standards by which to judge their colleagues' competence. In the natural and social sciences these standards are something like this: (1) Is the problem he attacks identified and segregated? (2) Are his conclusions based on logical thinking? (3) Are all the available facts considered? (4) Are there alternative solutions that he may have overlooked? (5) If inconsistent with generally held expert opinion, can his conclusion be fitted into a logical framework of theory?

Economics makes progress, as do all the sciences. New insights and new hypotheses are sometimes at first considered unworthy of further attention because they are inconsistent with generally held notions. But if they are actually valid, a free marketplace of ideas tends to provide other venturesome souls who examine the ideas further and, if the ideas prevail, they are accepted more and more widely. A well-known example is the contribution to economic thought of John Maynard Keynes in the 1930s. Some of his proposals for fiscal policy were considered close to nonsense at the time, but they have since become basic principles. On the other hand, some of his suggestions have been tested and found to be inexact, and thus adopted only after modification, while others have been recognized as really restatements of old truths.

Economics, being a social science, is subject to a difficulty not present in the natural sciences. One aspect of the difficulty is that everyone knows some economics, whether he is aware of it or not. The economist, by and large, uses the vocabulary of the man on the street. The economist studies prices, wages, interest rates, costs, production, and so on. Everyone knows something about these things. But what he knows or thinks he knows may be at variance with what the economist knows, for reasons already mentioned. Another aspect of the difficulty is that economics comes to be part of the general knowledge of society, but the ideas developed by the leading economists require a period of time to become accepted. By the time they are widely known and accepted, they may no longer be applicable because conditions have changed, yet they are now part of the "folklore." At one time an automatic gold standard was probably the best monetary system yet devised; it was supported by economic analysis and eventually was widely accepted as a good institution. Although in the succeeding generations payments arrangements and economic policies have changed considerably, it is probably still widely thought that a country that does not have an automatic gold standard is in some sense unsound.

One reason for the persistence of old ideas is the confusion of means and ends. The gold standard of a hundred years ago was probably the best available means of attaining such ends as greater stability of the price level and encouragement of international trade and investment. (Incidentally, the tendency of man to be inconsistent is also illustrated in the adoption of the gold standard by countries which, at the same time, were levying tariffs to reduce international trade.) At present, only a small minority of professional economists would argue that an automatic gold standard is now a superior means of attaining these ends. Yet the belief that the gold standard is a good thing is deeply imbedded in popular thought, and it is considered a desirable end in itself.

Discoveries made in the natural sciences such as biology and chemistry may at times completely upset older theories, but the public generally has little knowledge of these developments. More important, if people do know of the changes, they know that they can only gain from them. They have no vested interests in the old ideas. But in economic matters the public does have firm beliefs and, when economists find that old ideas are no longer applicable to new situations, there is resistance to acceptance of the new. It may not be of concern to the academic economist whether the public thinks he is right or wrong, but it is important to society in general if, in reflection of the public attitude, policies that would improve the economic lot of society are rejected or delayed.

ECONOMIC AND SOCIAL GOALS

Like other areas of knowledge, economics can be used by individuals and by societies in their pursuit of certain goals. The goals in which the individual is interested are partly those affecting himself and his family and partly those affecting other groups with which he identifies, including finally the nation or the world.

Most of a person's economic goals can probably be reduced to, or associated with, the single aim of adequate income. What is adequate, of course, depends upon many factors. The poverty level as defined in the United States is a much larger income than is available to most of the world's population. By and large, however, it is probably fair to say that if asked for their concept of an adequate income, most people would think of one somewhat larger than their own! Consequently, a common goal of practically everyone, and thus of society generally, is a rising income.

But a rising income is not the sole goal of most people. Incomes are meaningful only in terms of prices, and wildly fluctuating price levels are disrupting not only to the economy but to people. Consequently, there is a general consensus that a highly stable price level is also desirable.

For the individual, one of the great risks of economic life is the possibility of unemployment. While greatly reduced and widely covered by compensation today, this risk still exists. Widespread unemployment affects not only the unemployed but nearly everyone else, to some degree, in taxes, reduced profits, depressed investments, or otherwise. Maximum employment is therefore another generally accepted goal, as expressed in the Employment Act of 1946.

We could arrive at a very lengthy list of economic goals simply by thinking of current economic problems and listing the desired solutions. By doing so, we would illustrate that, at this level of discussion, there are perhaps no purely economic problems; they all have social dimensions. For example, it is generally agreed that the economic system should provide an "equitable" distribution of individual incomes—who is in favor of an inequitable system? But who can agree on what is equitable? If there were a purely competitive economy in which everyone started out with equality of opportunity, there would probably be a high degree of agreement that people should receive what they earn—incomes proportionate to their contribution to the total. In the real world, however, value judgments must be made, and these judgments may alter considerably our concept of equitable distribution of income. The extent of education of the poor and how education affects income, the extent to which income can depend upon inherited wealth, the relative tax contributions of persons with different incomes, and a host of other factors must be considered.

In thinking of the goals to which economics can contribute, we may tend to take certain political and social values for granted. It might be possible, and at some stages of economic development highly likely, for total output and incomes to be increased by much more government control of the economy. Government can force savings in the form of taxes and spend the revenues for construction of factories, power plants, and railroads. By a process of examinations and aptitude tests, people can be selected for training to be managers, physicians, engineers, or scientists. But American traditions and social values do not accept these methods of attaining economic growth, price-level stability, and maximum employment.

The present is a period of much questioning of social values and social institutions, including the operation of the economic system. There is a real danger that criticism of the admitted ills of the present social system can become all-inclusive and attack institutions which can serve well in the process of improvement. Obviously, racial injustice, poverty, and war are all aspects of society that should be reduced and, ideally, eliminated. But merely saying so does not make the task of doing so easy. Today, war is synonymous with an unpopular conflict in Southeast Asia, but to the older generation it is also synonymous with the conflict in which the threat of Nazi domination of Europe and perhaps of the world was prevented. Today, poverty is an anachronism in the world's richest nation; yet to those who remember the 1930s, poverty is also the condition in which a large fraction of the population was plunged and out of which these people worked in their own lifetimes.

Progress and change have their costs as well as their benefits. They must be sought, but the costs must also be weighed. On this point, economics can perhaps be most useful in the modern drive for reform. Improvement at any cost can turn out to be wasteful and, unfortunately, improvement often seems to lead to new problems. Certainly, reformers were right when, half a century ago, they worked to eliminate child labor. But in their old age, many of these same people, still interested in social problems, were working to curb juvenile delinquency. Affluence does not eliminate social problems; it seems merely to change their nature. At least, new problems arise about as fast as old ones are solved. This is not to say, by any means, that juvenile delinquency is a necessary result or cost of the abolition of child labor. It does suggest, however, that eliminating one problem may not be sufficient unless steps are taken at the same time to prevent another.

As measures are suggested and promoted to reduce further these social problems, some sort of cost-benefit analysis needs to be used in thinking about them — something akin to the economist's device of using marginal cost and marginal revenue. Measures, for example, to reduce poverty can be justified up to the point where they do more harm than good. The problem facing the citizen in a democracy is to measure the harm and the good. The solution to this problem cannot be supplied by a market in dollars and cents alone but by a market in which ideas can compete freely with each other and in which the proponents of any idea can be heard if they can justify the hearing.

Index